The best basis for user-centered interaction design, both as a primer for students as an introduction to the field, and as a resource for researchers and practitioners to fall back on. It should be labelled 'start here'.

Prof. Pieter Jan Strappers, ID-StudioLab, Delft University of Technology

The first edition of *Interaction Design* has been my textbook of choice for general HCI courses at both undergraduate and masters level for several years. It is authoritative while also being eminently readable and thought-provoking for students. It achieves a good balance between the human, computing and design aspects of the subject. The second edition strengthens the treatment of data gathering and analysis and approaches to evaluation, and introduces a welcome focus on affective aspects of interaction, reflecting recent research developments in the discipline. I am looking forward to working with this new edition.

Prof. Ann Blandford, Director of UCL Interaction Centre and Professor of Human-Computer Interaction, University College London

In the field of interaction design one book stands out, a book that has established itself at the core of the discipline. With this new edition, the authors have successfully strengthened that position. The new structure and timely content make the book highly relevant and much needed. Anyone who wants to learn about the fundamentals of interaction design should read this book.

Dr. Erik Stolterman, Director, Human-Computer Interaction Design, Indiana University

This new edition of *Interaction Design* is welcome and timely support for those of us teaching and researching in the field. It fills in the gaps that were emerging in the first edition, as new innovative technologies become available and older ones change so much. I value this text for the way it is so grounded in real examples and actual human practices, and for its strong design focus. It is a most useful and usable book.

Dr. Toni Robertson, Interaction Design and Work Practice Lab, University of Technology, Sydney

This book is one of those rare finds—it fills several niche markets brilliantly. Where other texts on HCI aim either at the high postgraduate or lower undergraduate level, this nicely fills the gap between—either as a very accessible teaching text for mid-level students in both computing or information science, or for practitioners who wish to broaden their skills to include interaction design. It is also a very handy book to give to your computing colleagues to read when they want to know why you find your field so exciting—I have seen many getting hooked on HCI by the first edition of the text and I can only see many more going the same way with the new improved second edition.

iversity of South Africa

INTERACTION DESIGN

INTERACTION DESIGN

beyond human-computer interaction

Second edition

SHARP • ROGERS • PREECE

John Wiley & Sons, Ltd

Telephone (+44) 1243 779777

Email (for orders and customer service enquiries): cs-books@wiley.co.uk
Visit our Home Page on www.wiley.com

Other Wiley Editorial Offices

John Wiley & Sons Inc., 111 River Street, Hoboken, NJ 07030, USA

Jossey-Bass, 989 Market Street, San Francisco, CA 94103-1741, USA

Wiley-VCH Verlag GmbH, Boschstr. 12, D-69469 Weinheim, Germany

John Wiley & Sons Australia Ltd, 42 McDougall Street, Milton, Queensland 4064, Australia

John Wiley & Sons (Asia) Pte Ltd, 2 Clementi Loop #02-01, Jin Xing Distripark, Singapore 129809

John Wiley & Sons Canada Ltd, 6045 Freemont Blvd, Mississauga, ONT, L5R 4J3, Canada

Wiley also publishes its books in a variety of electronic formats. Some content that appears in print may not be available in electronic books.

Library of Congress Cataloging-in-Publication Data:

Sharp, Helen.
Interaction design : beyond human-computer interaction / Helen Sharp, Yvonne Rogers and Jenny Preece.—2nd ed.
p. cm.
Includes bibliographical references and index.
ISBN 978-0-470-01866-8 (pbk. : alk. paper)
1. Human-computer interaction. I. Rogers, Yvonne. II. Preece, Jennifer. III. Title.
QA76.9.H85P72 2006
004'.019—dc22

2006030649

British Library Cataloguing in Publication Data

A catalogue record for this book is available from the British Library

ISBN 978-0-470-01866-8 (PB)

Typeset in 10/14 Bembo by Laserwords Private Limited, Chennai, India
Printed and bound by Graphos SA, Barcelona, Spain
This book is printed on acid-free paper responsibly manufactured from sustainable forestry in which at least two trees are planted for each one used for paper production.

Contents

Foreword

My bookshelf is full of HCI texts. Some are great, some not so great. This is one of the greats. That's why I've been using the first edition for my Georgia Tech College of Computing undergraduate HCI class for the past four years and will move on to using this second edition as soon as it is 'hot off the press'.

I like this text because it emphasizes the *process* of user interface design rather than the artifacts and technology of UI design. It is *process* that I believe is the most important part of UI design, and the hardest for technology-oriented students to appreciate.

Importantly, the process discussion does not just say 'first do this, then do that, next do such and such.' Yes, the text of necessity *prescribes*, but more importantly, it also *describes*, with lots of examples and for-instances to help the reader fully understand and appreciate the prescription.

The prescription is right on, and can be boiled down to Hansen's classic admonition 'know thy user' (Hansen 1971)[1] followed by 'consider alternatives,' 'prototype early, prototype often' and 'test early, test often'—or, as some would say, 'fail early, fail often', since there will surely be some failures in the testing.

When I first started teaching a full semester-long HCI course to computer science students about thirty years ago, I spent much more time than now on details of interaction devices and interaction techniques and software structures. That was at a time when GUIs were just becoming popular, and students had limited experience and exposure to their concepts, capabilities, and underlying software architectures. While I did preach 'know thy

[1]Hansen, W., 'User Engineering Principles for Interactive Systems,' Proceedings 1971 Fall Joint Computer Conference, pp. 523–532.

user,' task analysis etc., I did not spend enough time helping students really understand how to do it, so their projects were often too technology-centric rather than user-centric.

Over time, my teaching shifted more and more away from technology and more and more toward process. This is much easier than thirty years ago, because unlike then, today virtually every student has experience not just with GUIs but with lots of off-the-desktop UIs: cell phones, PDAs, VCRs and DVDs, phone-based voice response systems, home appliances, car navigation systems, and many more. So students are generally familiar with what is possible in the UI. Chapter 6 of the book gives a nice overview of contemporary trends in UI design (as well as a bit of history) without getting into unnecessary details of how the technology works. On the other hand, students, both then and now, are mostly clueless when it comes to being able to design a good UI.

Most teachers have discovered, as have I, that the best way to teach the UI design process and design itself is to have students working in teams actually go through the design process from start to finish. If the teams can be interdisciplinary (such as from computing, psychology, design, architecture, engineering, media studies), then they can learn a lot from one another—so much the better. In the course my Georgia Tech colleagues and I teach, the teams do a four-phase project, of 1) task analysis and user definition, 2) sketch out three alternative designs, 3) based on feedback from the class, the TA, and the instructor, select and prototype one design, and 4) define and carry out usability tests on the prototype. Students invariably (some sooner than others) get past the stage of blaming dumb users instead of acknowledging flaws in their design, and go on to develop an appreciation for the complexity of design decision-making. They learn that users are not like themselves, and that not all users are alike. Most are humbled by the experience.

This text is wonderfully suited for use with such a project-oriented course! But that's not the only reason I like the text.

The Chapter 2 discussion of understanding the design space, conceptualizing the design space, and accompanying theories, models and frameworks is tremendously important for students to 'get' early on in their studies. The basic goal is to start thinking about big-picture concepts and ideas in the problem space—to develop what I have called for many years the Conceptual Design. This necessarily is the starting point for actually doing a design. Students generally have trouble appreciating the importance of thinking through different conceptual design approaches before getting into the specifics of screen designs, menu structures, etc. Understanding that there might be several conceptual designs does not come easily.

The Chapter 4 discussion of design for collaboration and communication introduces students to a set of concerns that are crucial to one of the fastest-growing and probably the most prevalent uses of computers—to communicate with others. This goes way beyond the usual UI design guidelines and is important background for designers of such systems.

Similarly, Chapter 5 on affective aspects addresses a set of UI design concerns in a way that, to my knowledge, are not discussed in any other general UI design text. Recognizing the emotions that users might feel while using an interface—frustration, anger, happiness, satisfaction, etc.—and then understanding how to create positive feelings and avoid negative feelings—is a fruitful way to bring to the table not just the usual user interface guidelines but an important way of thinking about UI design.

A nice reorganization from the first edition is that all of the data collection and analysis material is now concentrated in Chapters 7 and 8. Previously, it was spread across four chapters on requirements gathering and evaluation—between which there is much commonality of methods, just a difference in how the results are used.

Three very nice features of the first edition are carried over to this version: the use of 'Boxes' to provide real-life examples of ideas presented in the text; 'Activities' that suggest things for the reader to do—often fun things, like watching a TV show with the sound off to better appreciate the role of gestures in communications; and interviews with HCI researchers and practitioners.

Remember to look at the book's website, which has even more case studies than in the past.

This text is not just for classroom use; the practitioner of UI design who is working from experience without formal instruction will surely find this book very helpful and useful.

A well-known HCI mantra is '*users* perform *tasks* using *computers*.' This implies that the user interface designer needs to know about users, tasks, and computers. The major strength of this book is teaching how to learn about users and the tasks they perform and then to apply that knowledge in creating, evaluating, and refining designs that do indeed allow users to perform their tasks. That's the process to which I referred earlier. And the book is grounded in a host of examples that make the process come alive!

I recommend this text to my fellow HCI teachers. It's a gem.

Jim Foley
GVU Center and College of Computing
Georgia Tech
Atlanta, GA

Foreword to the first edition

As predicted by many visionaries, devices everywhere are getting 'smarter'. My camera has a multi-modal hierarchical menu and form interface. Even my toaster has a microprocessor. Computing is not just for computers anymore. So when the authors wrote the subtitle 'beyond human-computer interaction', they wanted to convey that the book generalizes the human side to people, both individuals and groups, and the computer side to desktop computers, handheld computers, phones, cameras ... maybe even toasters.

My own interest in this book is motivated by having been a software developer for 20 years, during which time I was a professor and consultant for 12. Would the book serve as a textbook for students? Would it help bring software development practice into a new age of human-centered interaction design?

A textbook for students . . .

More than anything, I think students need to be motivated, inspired, challenged, and I think this book, particularly Chapters 1–5[2], will do that. Many students will not have the motivating experience of seeing projects and products fail because of a lack of attention, understanding, and *zeal* for the user, but as I read the opening chapters, I imagined students thinking, 'This is what I've been looking for!' The interviews will provide students with the wisdom of well-chosen experts: what's important, what worked (or didn't), and why. I see students making career choices based on this motivating material.

The rest of the book covers the art and some of the science of interaction design, the basic knowledge needed by practitioners and future innovators. Chapters 6–9 give a current view of analysis, design, and prototyping, and the book's website should add motivating examples. Chapters 10–14 cover evaluation in enough depth to facilitate understanding, not just rote application. Chapter 15 brings it all together, adding more depth. For each topic, there are ample pointers to further reading, which is important because interaction design is not a one-book discipline.

Finally, the book itself is pedagogically well designed. Each chapter describes its aims, contains examples and subtopics, and ends with key points, assignments, and an annotated bibliography for more detail.

A guide for development teams . . .

When I lead or consult on software projects, I face the same problem over and over: many people in marketing and software development—these are the people who have the most input into design, but it applies to any members of multidisciplinary teams—have little knowledge or experience building systems with a user-centered focus. A user-centered focus requires close work with users (not just customer–buyers), from analysis through design, evaluation, and maintenance. A lack of user-centered focus results in products and services that often do not meet the needs of their intended users. Don Norman's design books have convinced many that these problems are not unique to software, so this book's focus on interaction design feels right.

To help software teams adopt a user-centered focus, I've searched for books with end-to-end coverage from analysis, to design, to implementation (possibly of prototypes), to evaluation (with iteration). Some books have tried to please all audiences and have

[2]Chapter numbers refer to the first edition.

become encyclopedias of user interface development, covering topics worth knowing, but not in enough detail for readers to understand them. Some books have tried to cover theory in depth and tried to appeal to developers who have little interest in theory. Whatever the reasons for these choices, the results have been lacking. This book has chosen fewer topics and covered them in more depth; enough depth, I think, to put the ideas into practice. I think the material is presented in a way that is understandable by a wide audience, which is important in order for the book to be useful to whole multidisciplinary teams.

A recommended book . . .

I've been waiting for this book for many years. I think it's been worth the wait.

As the director of the HCI Bibliography project (www.hcibib.org), a free-access HCI portal receiving a half-million hits per year, I receive many requests for suggestions for books, particularly from students and software development managers. To answer that question, I maintain a list of recommended readings in ten categories (with 20 000 hits per year). Until now, it's been hard to recommend just one book from that list. I point people to some books for motivation, other books for process, and books for specific topics (e.g. task analysis, ergonomics, usability testing). This book fits well into half the categories in my list and makes it easier to recommend one book to get started and to have on hand for development.

I welcome the commitment of the authors to building a website for the book. It's a practice that has been adopted by other books in the field to offer additional information and keep the book current. The site also presents interactive content to aid in tasks like conducting surveys and heuristic evaluations. I look forward to seeing the book's site present new materials, but as director of www.hcibib.org, I hope they use links to, instead of re-inventing, existing resources.

Gary Perlman
Columbus, Ohio

Preface

Welcome to the second edition of *Interaction Design: Beyond Human-Computer Interaction*, and our interactive website at `www.id-book.com`. Building on the success of the first edition, we have updated, clarified and streamlined the book to provide an accessible introduction to the multi-disciplinary field of Interaction Design.

This textbook is for undergraduate and masters students from a range of backgrounds studying classes in human-computer interaction, interaction design, web design, software engineering, information systems and information studies. A broad range of professionals and technology users will also find this book useful, as will graduate students who are moving into this area from related disciplines.

Our book is called *Interaction Design: Beyond Human-Computer Interaction* because interaction design is concerned with a broader scope of issues, topics, and paradigms than has traditionally been within the scope of human-computer interaction (HCI). To be successful, interaction designers need a mixed set of skills from psychology, human-computer interaction, web design, computer science, information systems, marketing, entertainment, sociology and business. We define interaction design as:

> ***Designing interactive products to support the way people communicate and interact in their everyday and working lives.***

Interaction design relies on an understanding of the capabilities and desires of people and on the kinds of technology available to interaction designers, as well as a knowledge of how to identify requirements and evolve them into a suitable design. Our textbook provides an introduction to all of these areas, teaching practical techniques to support development as well as discussing possible technologies and design alternatives.

The number of different types of interface available to today's interaction designers has increased steadily over the last 5 years, so our text likewise has been expanded to cover this variety. For example, we discuss and provide examples of robotic, wearable, shareable, mixed reality and multi-model interfaces as well as more traditional desktop, multimedia and web interfaces. To bring the book right up-to-date, we have also included examples from contemporary research.

The book has 15 chapters and includes discussion of the wide range of interfaces that are now available, how cognitive, social, and affective issues apply to interaction design, and how to gather, analyse and present data for interaction design. A central theme is that design and evaluation are interleaving, highly iterative processes, with some roots in theory but which rely strongly on good practice to create usable products. The book has a 'hands-on' orientation and explains how to carry out a variety of techniques. It also has a strong pedagogical design and includes many activities (with detailed comments), assignments, and the special pedagogic features discussed below.

The style of writing is intended to be accessible to students, as well as professionals and general readers. It is largely conversational in nature and includes anecdotes, cartoons, and case studies. Many of the examples are intended to relate to readers' own experiences. The book and the associated website are also intended to encourage readers to be active when reading and to think about seminal issues. For example, one feature we have included in the book is the 'dilemma', where a controversial topic is aired. The aim is for readers to understand that much of interaction design needs consideration of the issues, and that they need to learn to weigh up the pros and cons and be prepared to make trade-offs. We particularly want readers to realize that there is rarely a right or wrong answer, although there is a world of difference between a good design and a poor design.

This book is accompanied by a website at `www.id-book.com`, which provides a variety of resources and interactivities, including extensive case study material that presents more in-depth coverage of the design process. The website offers a place where readers can learn how to design websites and other kinds of multimedia interfaces. Rather than just provide a list of guidelines and design principles, we have developed various interactivities, including online tutorials and step-by-step exercises, intended to support learning by doing. There are also PowerPoint slides for instructors, which can be downloaded and adapted for specific classes.

Changes from the first edition

The new edition has been produced in full colour, providing an added dimension to the overall structure, layout and illustrations. Interaction design is moving very quickly, with new developments coming thick and fast. We have included many new images to illustrate these. To reflect the dynamic nature of the field, the second edition has been substantially updated throughout with many new examples that cover the recent advances. In addition, we have included several case studies which discuss different aspects of interaction design. These case studies are summarized in this book, and expanded upon on the book website. In the future we may add other case studies that are not previewed in the book so readers are encouraged to check the website from time to time.

As well as updating the material, we have restructured the chapters and their contents. Older material that is no longer mainstream has been removed to make way for the newer material, and other material has been repositioned. The most significant changes include the addition of one new chapter, Chapter 6 *Interfaces and Interactions*, which has been included in response to reader feedback. This covers the wide range of modern interfaces available to the interaction designer, but also describes earlier developments, thus providing context for the later technologies. It highlights both practical issues and research directions for each interface type. The old Chapter 15 on case studies has been removed (although this whole chapter is still downloadable from the website), as we have considerably enhanced the provision of case studies throughout the book and on the book website (see below).

Also in response to reader feedback, the material on data gathering and analysis has been streamlined and brought together in Chapters 7 and 8. The material on data analysis has been extended, and we now also cover data interpretation and presentation. This streamlining has allowed us to expand the evaluation chapters with additional examples.

Special features

We use both the textbook and the web to teach about interaction design. To promote good pedagogical practice, we include the following features:

Chapter design

Each chapter is designed to motivate and support learning:

- *Aims* are provided so that readers develop an accurate model of what to expect in the chapter.
- *Key points* at the end of the chapter summarize what is important.
- *Activities* are included throughout the book and are considered an essential ingredient for learning. They encourage readers to extend and apply their knowledge. Comments are offered directly after the activities, because pedagogic research suggests that turning to the back of the text annoys readers and discourages learning.
- An *assignment* is provided at the end of each chapter. This can be set as a group or individual project. The aim is for students to put into practice and consolidate knowledge and skills either from the chapter that they have just studied or from several chapters. Some of the assignments build on each other and involve developing and evaluating designs or actual products. Hints and guidance are provided on the website.
- *Boxes* provide additional and highlighted information for readers to reflect upon in more depth.
- *Dilemmas* offer honest and thought-provoking coverage of controversial or problematic issues.
- *Case studies* illustrating the application of interaction design techniques have been included throughout. Overviews of the case studies are included in the book, with full length versions on the `www.id-book.com` website.
- *Further reading* suggestions are provided at the end of each chapter. These refer to seminal work in the field, interesting additional material, or work that has been heavily drawn upon in the text.
- *Interviews* with nine practitioners and visionaries in the field enable readers to gain a personal perspective of the interviewees' work, their philosophies, their ideas about what is important, and their contributions to the field.
- *Cartoons* are included to make the book enjoyable.

`www.id-book.com` website

The aim of the website is to provide you with an opportunity to learn about interaction design in ways that go 'beyond the book'. Additional in-depth material, hands-on interactivities, and material to support students' learning from the text are provided. Specific features include:

- Hands-on interactivities, including designing a questionnaire, customizing a set of heuristics, doing a usability analysis on 'real' data, and interactive tools to support physical design.
- Expanded case studies. The text includes brief overviews of case studies and full versions are available from the website.
- Hints and guidance on the assignments outlined in the book.
- Suggestions for additional material to be used in seminars, lab classes, and lectures.
- OHP slides to support the 15 chapters of the book.

Readership

This book will be useful to a wide range of readers with different needs and aspirations.

Students from Computer Science, Software Engineering, Information Systems, Information Studies, Psychology, Sociology, and related disciplines studying courses in Interaction Design and Human-Computer Interaction will learn the knowledge, skills, and techniques for designing and evaluating state-of-the-art products and websites, as well as traditional computer systems.

Web and *interaction designers*, and *usability professionals* will find plenty to satisfy their need for immediate answers to problems as well as for building skills to satisfy the demands of today's fast moving technical market.

Users who want to understand why certain products can be used with ease while others are unpredictable and frustrating will take pleasure in discovering that there is a discipline with practices that produce usable systems.

Researchers and *developers* who are interested in exploiting the potential of web, wireless, and collaborative technologies will find that, as well as offering guidance, techniques, and much food for thought, a special effort has been made to include examples of state-of-the-art systems.

In the next section we recommend various routes through the text for different kinds of readers.

How to use this book

Interaction Design is not a linear design process but is essentially iterative and some readers and experienced instructors will want to find their own way through the chapters. Others, and particularly those with less experience, may prefer to work through chapter by chapter. Readers will also have different needs. For example, students of Psychology will come with different background knowledge and needs from those of Computer Science. Similarly, professionals wanting to learn the fundamentals in a one-week course have different needs. This book and the website are designed to be used in various ways. The following suggestions are provided to help you decide which way is best for you.

From beginning to end

There are 15 chapters, which progress through the interaction design process from background information to evaluation, so if students study one chapter per week during a fifteen-week semester course then this will represent a coherent thread through the field of interaction design. However, some of the chapters contain more material than could be covered in this way, and we recommend that you consider in advance which aspects of each chapter to study. In particular, Chapter 6 is not designed to be read from beginning to end, but should be treated more as a historical overview of three decades of interface development that can be read as three sections (one per decade) or dipped into when learning about a particular type of interface. Also, Chapter 8 on data analysis contains examples of theoretical frameworks for analysing qualitative data which will require more time and effort to study than the simpler analysis techniques introduced earlier. These could be skipped over in a sequential reading of the text, but particularly pertinent ones might form the basis of a discussion in a more advanced class on interaction design.

Getting a quick overview

For those who want to get a quick overview or just the essence of the book, we suggest you read Chapters 1, 9, and 12. Chapter 1 provides an introduction to interaction design and is essential for anyone using this book. Chapter 9 discusses the process of interaction design. Chapter 12 provides an introduction to the issues involved in evaluation. *These chapters are recommended for everyone.*

Suggestions for computer science students

As well as studying Chapters 1, 9 and 12, Chapters 10 and 11 contain the material that will feel most familiar to any students who have been introduced to software development. In addition, Chapter 9 discusses lifecycle models in software engineering and HCI and how they are related. These chapters cover the process of interaction design and the activities it involves, including establishing requirements, conceptual design, and physical design.

Suggestions for information systems and information studies students

Information systems students will benefit from reading the whole text, but instructors may want to find additional examples of their own to illustrate how issues apply to business applications. Similarly, information studies instructors may add examples from digital libraries and other applications that provide information resources. Some students may be tempted to skip Chapters 3–5 but we recommend that they read these chapters since they provide important foundational material. This book does not cover how to develop business cases or marketing.

Suggestions for psychology and cognitive science students

Chapters 3–5 cover how theory and research findings have been applied to interaction design. They discuss the relevant issues and provide a wide range of studies and systems that have been informed by cognitive, social, and affective issues. Chapters 1 and 2 also cover important conceptual knowledge, necessary for a good grounding in interaction design. Chapter 6 discusses the wide range of interfaces available and the practical and research issues related to each, showing how theoretical ideas may be translated into more concrete practical guidance.

Practitioner and short course route

Many people want the equivalent of a short intensive 2–5 day course. The best route for them is to read Chapters 1, 9, and 12 and dip into the rest of the book for reference. For those who want practical development skills, we recommend Chapter 11. Chapter 6 provides an extensive overview of interfaces that can be dipped into.

Web designer route

Web designers who have a background in technology and want to learn how to design usable and effective websites are advised to read Chapters 1, 10, 11, 12, 13, 14, and 15, and relevant sections in Chapter 6. These chapters cover key issues that are important when designing and evaluating the usability of websites. A worked assignment runs through these chapters.

Usability professionals' route

Usability professionals who want to extend their knowledge of evaluation techniques and read about the social and psychological issues that underpin design of web, wireless, and collaborative systems are advised to read Chapter 1 for an overview, then select from Chapters 12–15 on evaluation. Chapters 3, 4, and 5 provide discussion of seminal user issues (cognitive, social, and affective aspects). There is new material throughout the rest of the book, which will also be of interest for dipping into as needed. This group may also be particularly interested in Chapter 11 which provides practical design examples, and the case studies which are spread throughout the book.

Plan your own path

For people who do not want to follow the 'beginning-to-end' approach or the suggestions above, there are many ways to use the text. Chapters 1, 9 and 12 provide a good overview of the topic. Chapter 1 is an introduction to key issues in the discipline and Chapters 9 and 12 offer introductions to design and evaluation. Chapters 2–5 cover human issues while Chapter 6 provides a comprehensive view of the various interfaces available and can be used flexibly to focus on interfaces that are particularly pertinent to your own goals. Chapters 7 and 8 look at data gathering, analysis, interpretation and presentation. Requirements and evaluation activities rely on the material in these chapters, so if you want to cover practical activities, then some study of these chapters will be needed although it is not necessary to study every element in depth. Practical techniques for establishing requirements are in Chapter 10 and techniques for prototyping and design are in Chapter 11. Chapters 12–15 cover the various approaches to evaluation—you may choose to look at usability testing and field studies (Chapter 14) or analytical evaluation (Chapter 15) or both chapters. Case studies are included throughout the book, but you could focus on one or two of them in depth, using the material on the website as a basis to expand areas particularly of interest. Another approach is to start with one or two of the evaluation chapters after first reading Chapters 1, 9, 12, then move into the design section, drawing on Chapters 2–6 as necessary.

Acknowledgements

Many people have helped to make the second edition a reality. We have benefited from the advice and support of our many professional colleagues across the world, our students, friends, and families, and we thank you all. We also warmly thank the following people for reviewing the manuscript and making many helpful suggestions for improvements: Alia I. Abdelmoty, Lynne Baillie, Alan Blackwell, Nick Bryan-Kinns, Sandra Cairncross, Deryn Graham, John Halloran, Paul Irvine, Chris Johnson, Ian Mackie, Michael Mahemoff, Alan Newell, Janet Read, Shamus Smith, James Tam and George Weir. Yvonne would like to thank her colleagues at Indiana University for providing constructive feedback on earlier drafts, in particular, Jeff Bardzell, Eli Blevis, Kay Connelly, Blaise Cronin, Dennis Groth, Youn-Kyung Lim and Alice Robbin. She also thanks her students for their continuous supply of interesting articles and websites, keeping her up-to-date with the very latest developments, especially Richie Hazlewood, Justin Donaldson and Tyler Waite. Helen would like to thank Judith Segal, Debbie Stone and Mark Woodroffe for helping to shape her ideas about Interaction Design, and Lynne Coventry, Daisy Mwanza, Debra Haley, Luis Palacios, Josie Taylor, and Giasemi Vavoula, for help with writing the case studies. Jenny would like to thank the members of the Human-Computer Interaction Laboratory at the University of Maryland, who help to keep her updated through their discussions and seminars, especially Ben Bederson, Allison Druin, and Ben Shneiderman. She would also like to thank her colleagues in the International Children's Digital Library Community Project, particularly Jade Burro, Allison Druin, Anita Komlodi and Weimin Hou.

We are particularly grateful to Sara Bly, Karen Holtzblatt, Jakob Nielsen, Abigail Sellen, Suzanne Robertson, Gitta Salomon, Ben Shneiderman, Gillian Crampton Smith, and Terry Winograd for generously contributing in-depth interviews.

The following people generously developed additional case studies: Sylvie Charland, Heather Collins, Matt Davies, Simone Diniz Junqueira Barbosa, Vanessa Evers, John Halloran, Hans Hillen, Assadour Kirijian, Aaron Loehrlein, Matthew Myers, Raquel Oliveira Prates and Clarisse S. de Souza. We thank Jonathan Lazar for generously helping us to identify some of the case studies and for commenting on drafts.

A special 'thank you' goes to our webmaster for the last 5 years, Harry Brignull, who has been helpful, knowledgeable, available and supportive throughout the development and maintenance of the www.id-book.com website. He also supplied various interactive materials.

We are grateful to our editors at Wiley: David Barnard, Deborah Egleton and Jonathan Shipley. Thanks also to Claire Jardine for her work on copyright clearance.

About the authors

The authors are all senior academics with a background in teaching, researching, and consulting in Australia, Brazil, Canada, Europe, Mexico, UK, and the USA. Having worked together on two other successful textbooks, they bring considerable experience in curriculum development, using a variety of media for distance learning as well as face-to-face teaching. They have considerable knowledge of creating learning texts and websites that motivate and support learning for a range of students.

All three authors are specialists in interaction design and human-computer interaction (HCI). In addition, they bring skills from other disciplines. Yvonne Rogers is a cognitive scientist, Helen Sharp is a software engineer, and Jenny Preece works in information systems and information studies. Their complementary knowledge and skills enable them to cover the breadth of concepts in interaction design and HCI to produce an interdisciplinary text and website. They have collaborated closely, supporting and commenting upon each other's work, to produce a high degree of integration of ideas with one voice. They have shared everything from initial concepts, through writing, design and production.

Yvonne Rogers has just returned to the UK to take up a chair in Human-Computer Interaction at the Open University. From 2003–2006, she was a professor of Informatics and Information Science at Indiana University. Before that, she was a Professor of Computer Science and Artificial Intelligence at the former School of Cognitive and Computing Sciences (now the Department of Informatics) at Sussex University, UK, where in 1997 she co-founded with the late Mike Scaife the Interact Lab, an interdisciplinary research center that was concerned with the possible interactions between people, technologies, and representations. She has also worked as a senior researcher at Alcatel Telecommunications company and has been a visiting professor at Stanford University, Apple Computer Inc., and the University of Queensland.

Yvonne is well-known for her work in human-computer interaction, interaction design, computer-supported cooperative work, UbiComp and interactive learning environments. Her research focuses on augmenting and extending everyday, learning, and work activities with interactive technologies that move beyond the desktop. This involves designing user experiences through appropriating and assembling a diversity of pervasive technologies. A main focus is not the technology *per se* but the design and integration of the digital representations that are presented via them to support social and cognitive activities in ways that extend our current capabilities. Yvonne was one of the founding Principal Investigators of the six-year UK Equator interdisciplinary research collaboration (2000–2006). Many of the innovative projects are reported in this textbook, including the research she led on the design of pervasive and mobile technologies for enhancing and provoking the way children learn, understand, and play.

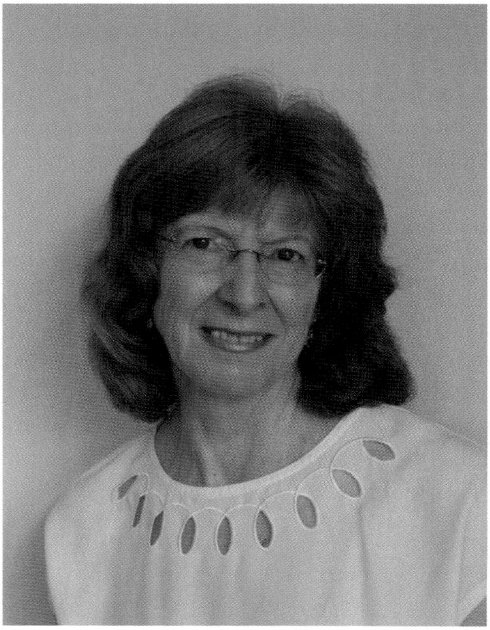

Jenny Preece is Professor and Dean of the College of Information Studies at the University of Maryland. Prior to joining the University of Maryland in 2005 Jenny was Professor and Department Chair of Information Systems at University of Maryland Baltimore County (UMBC). Before coming to the USA in 1996 Jenny was a Research Professor at South Bank University, London, for two years where she created and directed an interdisciplinary center for People and Systems Interaction. In the mid-1980s, Jenny joined the Open University (OU) where she was an Associate Professor. At the OU she worked on a variety of projects in computer-based education, human-computer interaction and computer education. Jenny and Yvonne, with a team of academics from the UK and Holland, developed the first Masters distance learning course on human-computer interaction, which was regularly studied by around 1000 students. This experience provided the foundation for authoring one of the first major texts in HCI—*Human Computer Interaction* (1994), Preece, J., Rogers, Y., Sharp, H., Benyon, D., Holland, S., Carey, T—and initiated the successful authoring partnership between Helen, Yvonne and Jenny.

Jenny's teaching and research interests include: online communities of interest, communities of practice, social computing, and human-computer interaction. She was one of the first researchers to point out the importance of online communities for providing social and emotional support to their members as well as for obtaining and exchanging information, particularly in patient support communities. She has also researched the differences in participants' behavior in different types of online communities including the reasons why people do or do not participate. Jenny has written extensively on these topics and her work includes a book entitled *Online Communities: Designing Usability, Supporting Sociability* (Preece, 2000).

Helen Sharp is Associate Professor at the Open University and a Senior Visiting Fellow at the Centre for HCI Design at City University London. Although Helen first joined her current department about 20 years ago, she has held permanent and visiting positions at other institutions during that time, including City University London, University College London, Middlesex University, and various publishing companies.

Helen was originally trained as a software engineer and she developed and maintained a variety of software applications for several years, watching the frustration of the systems' users and the clever 'work-arounds' they developed when the delivered systems did not support them in their jobs. It was this experience that inspired her to investigate HCI, user-centred design and the other related disciplines that now underpin the field of interaction design. Her research interests focus on the intersection between interaction design and software engineering: in particular, how to ensure that the needs of the user are incorporated into the design of interactive products.

1

1.1 Introduction

How many interactive products are there in everyday use? Think for a minute about what you use in a typical day: cell (mobile) phone, computer, personal organizer, remote control, coffee machine, ATM, ticket machine, library information system, the web, photocopier, watch, printer, stereo, DVD player, calculator, video game . . . the list is endless. Now think for a minute about how usable they are. How many are actually easy, effortless, and enjoyable to use? All of them, several, or just one or two? This list is probably considerably shorter. Why is this so?

Think about when some device caused you considerable grief—how much time did you waste trying to get it to work? Two well-known interactive devices that cause numerous people immense grief are the photocopier that doesn't copy the way they want and the VCR or DVD that records a different program from the one they thought they had set or none at all. Why do you think these things happen time and time again? Moreover, can anything be done about it?

Many products that require users to interact with them to carry out their tasks, e.g. buying a ticket online from the web, photocopying an article, setting the alarm on a digital clock, have not necessarily been designed with the users in mind. Typically, they have been engineered as systems to perform set functions. While they may work effectively from an engineering perspective, it is often at the expense of how the system will be used by real people. A main aim of interaction design is to redress this concern by bringing usability into the design process. In essence, it is about developing interactive products[1] that are easy, effective, and enjoyable to use—from the users' perspective.

In this chapter we begin by examining what interaction design is. We look at the difference between good and poor design, highlighting how products can differ radically in how usable they are. We then describe what and who is involved in the process of interaction design. The user experience, which has become a central concern of interaction design, is then introduced. Finally, we outline how to characterize the user experience in terms of usability, user experience goals, and design principles. An assignment is presented at the end of the chapter in which you have the opportunity to put into practice what you have read by evaluating the design of an interactive product.

The main aims of this chapter are to:

- **Explain the difference between good and poor interaction design.**
- **Describe what interaction design is and how it relates to human–computer interaction and other fields.**
- **Explain what is meant by the user experience and usability.**

[1] We use the term *interactive products* generically to refer to all classes of interactive systems, technologies, environments, tools, applications, services, and devices.

1

What is interaction design?

- **Describe what and who is involved in the process of interaction design.**
- **Outline the different forms of guidance used in interaction design.**
- **Enable you to evaluate an interactive product and explain what is good and bad about it in terms of the goals and core principles of interaction design.**

1.2 Good and poor design

A central concern of interaction design is to develop interactive products that are usable. By this is generally meant easy to learn, effective to use, and providing an enjoyable user experience. A good place to start thinking about how to design usable interactive products is to compare examples of well and poorly designed ones. Through identifying the specific weaknesses and strengths of different interactive systems, we can begin to understand what it means for something to be usable or not. Here, we describe two examples of poorly designed products—a voice mail system used in hotels and the ubiquitous remote control device—and contrast these with two well-designed examples of products that perform the same function.

(i) Voice mail system

Imagine the following scenario. You're staying at a hotel for a week while on a business trip. You discover you have left your cell phone at home so you have to rely on the hotel's facilities. The hotel has a voice mail system for each room. To find out if you have a message, you pick up the handset and listen to the tone. If it goes 'beep beep beep' there is a message. To find out how to access the message you have to read a set of instructions next to the phone.

You read and follow the first step:

"1. Touch 41."

The system responds, "You have reached the Sunny Hotel voice message center. Please enter the room number for which you would like to leave a message."

You wait to hear how to listen to a recorded message. But there are no further instructions from the phone. You look down at the instruction sheet again and read:

"2. Touch★, your room number, and #."

You do so and the system replies, "You have reached the mailbox for room 106. To leave a message type in your password."

You type in the room number again and the system replies, "Please enter room number again and then your password."

You don't know what your password is. You thought it was the same as your room number. But clearly not. At this point you give up and call reception for help. The person at the desk explains the correct procedure for recording and listening to messages. This involves typing in, at the appropriate times, the room number and the extension number of the phone (the latter is your password, which is different from the room number). Moreover, it takes six steps to access a message and five steps to leave a message. You go out and buy a new cell phone.

What is problematic with this voice mail system?

- It is infuriating.
- It is confusing.
- It is inefficient, requiring you to carry out a number of steps for basic tasks.
- It is difficult to use.
- It has no means of letting you know at a glance whether any messages have been left or how many there are. You have to pick up the handset to find out and then go through a series of steps to listen to them.
- It is not obvious what to do: the instructions are provided partially by the system and partially by a card beside the phone.

Now consider the following phone answering machine. Figure 1.1 shows two small sketches of an answering machine phone. Incoming messages are represented using physical marbles. The number of marbles that have moved into the pinball-like chute indicates the number of messages. Dropping one of these marbles into a slot in the machine causes the recorded message to play. Dropping the same marble into another slot on the phone dials the caller who left the message.

How does the 'marble' answering machine differ from the voice mail system?

- It uses familiar physical objects that indicate visually at a glance how many messages have been left.
- It is aesthetically pleasing and enjoyable to use.
- It only requires one-step actions to perform core tasks.
- It is a simple but elegant design.
- It offers less functionality and allows anyone to listen to any of the messages.

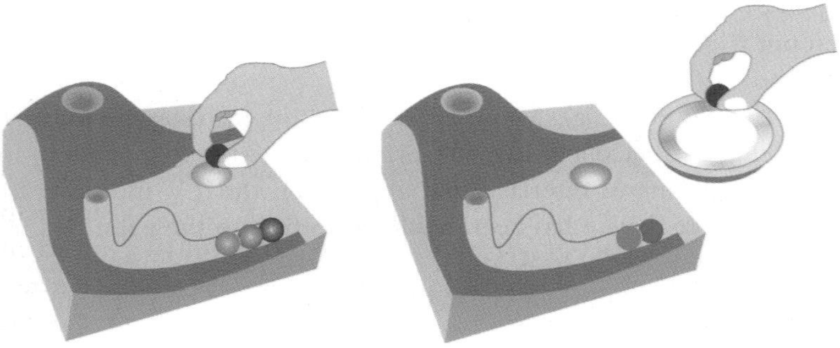

Figure 1.1 *The marble answering machine (Bishop, cited by Crampton Smith, 1995)*

The marble answering machine was designed by Durrell Bishop while a student at the Royal College of Art in London (described by Crampton Smith, 1995). One of his goals was to design a messaging system that represented its basic functionality in terms of the behavior of everyday objects. To do this, he capitalized on people's everyday knowledge of how the physical world works. In particular, he made use of the ubiquitous everyday action of picking up a physical object and putting it down in another place. This is an example of an interactive product designed with the users in mind. The focus is on providing them with an enjoyable experience but one that also makes efficient the activity of receiving messages. However, it is important to note that although the marble answering machine is a very elegant and usable design, it would not be practical in a hotel setting. One of the main reasons is that it is not robust enough to be used in public places, for example, the marbles could easily get lost or be taken as souvenirs. Also, the need to identify the user before allowing the messages to be played is essential in a hotel setting. When considering the usability of a design, therefore, it is important to take into account *where* it is going to be used and *who* is going to use it. The marble answering machine would be more suited in a home setting—provided there were no children who might be tempted to play with the marbles!

(ii) Remote control device

Every home entertainment system, be it the TV, cable, music system, DVD player, VCR, etc., comes with its own remote control device. Each one is different in terms of how it looks and works. Many have been designed with a dizzying array of small, multicolored and double-labeled buttons (one on the button and one above or below it), that often seem arbitrarily positioned in relation to one another. Many viewers, especially when sitting in their living room, find it difficult to locate the right ones even for the simplest of tasks, like pausing or finding the main menu. It can be especially frustrating for those who need to put their reading glasses on each time to read the buttons. The remote control device appears like it has been put together very much as an afterthought.

In contrast, the TiVo remote control, designed as part of a digital video recorder, is in a class of its own (see Figure 1.2a). Much effort and thought has gone into its design. The buttons are large, clearly labeled and logically arranged, making them easy to locate and use in conjunction with the menu interface that appears on the TV monitor. In terms of its physical form, the remote device has been designed to fit into the palm of a hand, having a peanut shape. It also has a playful look and feel about it; colorful buttons and cartoon icons have been used that are very distinctive, making it easy to identify them in the dark and without having to put reading glasses on.

How was it possible to create such a usable and appealing remote device where so many others have failed? The answer is simple; TiVo took the time and effort to follow

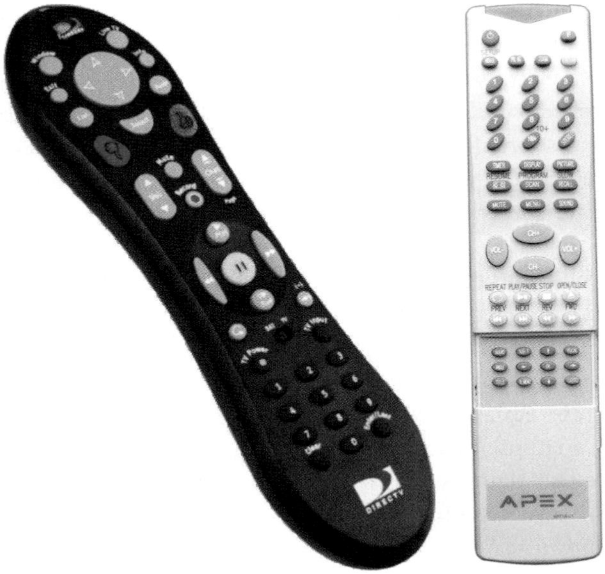

(a) (b)

Figure 1.2 *Two contrasting remote control devices: (a) the TiVo remote. TiVo Inc.; (b) a standard remote. How do they differ in their design and use?*

a user-centered design process. Specifically, TiVo's director of product design at the time involved potential users in the design process, getting their feedback on everything from the feel of the device in the hand to where best to place the batteries—making them easy to replace but not to fall out. He and his design team also resisted the trap of 'buttonitis'—which so many other remote controls have fallen victim to—where buttons breed like rabbits, one for every new function. They did this by restricting the number of *control* buttons embedded in the device to the essential ones. Other functions were then represented as part of the menu options and dialog boxes displayed on the TV monitor, that could then be selected via the core set of physical control buttons. The result was a highly usable and pleasurable device, that has received much praise and numerous design awards.

1.2.1 What to design

Designing usable interactive products requires considering who is going to be using them, how they are going to be used, and where they are going to be used. Another key concern is understanding the kind of *activities* people are doing when *interacting* with the products. The appropriateness of different kinds of interfaces and arrangements of input and output devices depends on what kinds of activities need to be supported. For example, if the activity to be supported is to let people communicate with each other at a distance, then a system that allows easy input of messages (spoken or written) that can be readily accessed by the intended recipient is essential. In addition, an interface that allows the users to interact with the messages, e.g. edit, annotate, store, would be very useful.

The range of activities that can be supported is diverse. Just think for a minute what you can currently do using computer-based systems: send messages, gather information, write essays, control power plants, program, draw, plan, calculate, play games—to name but a few. Now think about the types of interfaces and interactive devices that are available. They, too, are equally diverse: multimedia applications, virtual reality environments, speech-based systems, handheld devices, and large interactive displays—to name but a few. There are also many ways of designing how users can interact with a system, e.g. via the use of menus, commands, forms, icons, touchscreens, sensors, etc. Furthermore, a range of innovative everyday artifacts are being created, using novel materials, such as interactive toys, smart mirrors, and wearables (see Figure 1.3). The interfaces for everyday consumer items, like cameras, microwave ovens, and washing machines, that used to be physical and the realm of *product* design, are now increasingly digitally based, requiring *interaction* design. What this all amounts to is a multitude of choices and decisions that interaction designers have to make for an ever-increasing range of products.

A key question for interaction design is: how do you optimize the users' interactions with a system, environment, or product, so that they support and extend the users' activities in effective, useful, and usable ways? One could use intuition and hope for the best. Alternatively, one can be more principled in deciding which choices to make by basing them on an understanding of the users. This involves:

- Taking into account what people are good and bad at.
- Considering what might help people with the way they currently do things.
- Thinking through what might provide quality user experiences.
- Listening to what people want and getting them involved in the design.
- Using 'tried and tested' user-based techniques during the design process.

The aim of this book is to cover these aspects with the goal of teaching you how to carry out interaction design. In particular, it focuses on how to identify users' needs and the context of their activities, and from this understanding, move to designing usable, useful, and pleasurable interactive products.

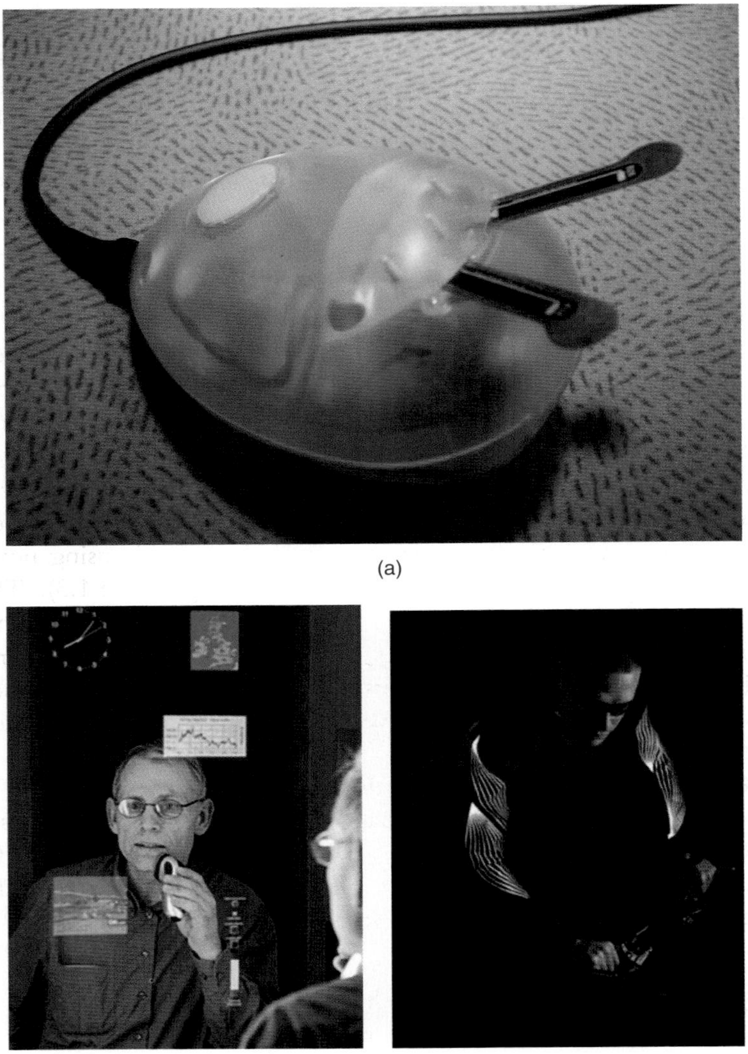

(a) (b) (c)

__Figure 1.3__ Novel forms of interactive products. (a) An interactive music toy (Beatbug) developed by Tod Machover to allow the creation, manipulation, and sharing of rhythm. When the beatbugs are connected via a network, groups of children holding one can share and develop collaborative rhythms of music. (b) An example of ambient intelligence: Philips bathroom mirror that displays the time, weather, and other personal information, including heart rate and weight. (c) A wearable concept: the 'illum' commuting jacket that lights up at night using electroluminescent muscle-fiber graphics

Activity 1.1

How does making a phone call differ when using:

- a public phone box
- a cell phone?

How have these devices been designed to take into account 1. the kind of users, 2. the type of activity being supported, and 3. the context of use?

Comment

1. Public phones are designed to be used by the general public. Many have Braille embossed on the keys and speaker volume control to enable people who are blind and hard of hearing to use them.
   Cell phones are intended for all user groups, although they can be difficult to use for people who are blind or have limited manual dexterity.
2. Most phone boxes are designed with a simple mode of interaction: insert card or money and key in the phone number. If engaged or unable to connect, the money or card is returned when the receiver is replaced. There is also the option of allowing the caller to make a follow-on call by pressing a button rather than collecting the money and reinserting it again.
   Cell phones have a more complex mode of interaction. More functionality is provided, including contact book, saved messages, schedules, customized settings, voice mail, and security settings. In addition, most cell phones now include a whole host of other non-phone-based functions, including games, digital camera, calculator, and clock.
3. Phone boxes are intended to be used in public places, say on a street corner or in an airport, and so have been designed to give the user a degree of privacy and noise protection through the use of hoods and booths.
   Cell phones have been designed to be used anywhere and can be set to alert the user to a call waiting in different ways. These include silent vibrate mode for use in meetings and loud customized ring tones for everyday and outdoor use.

1.3 What is interaction design?

By interaction design, we mean

> ***designing interactive products to support the way people communicate and interact in their everyday and working lives.***

Put another way, it is about creating user experiences that enhance and augment the way people work, communicate, and interact. More generally, Winograd (1997, p. 160) describes it as "designing spaces for human communication and interaction." Thackara views it as "the why as well as the how of our daily interactions using computers" (2001, p. 50).

A number of terms have been used to emphasize different aspects of what is being designed, including user interface design, software design, user-centered design, product design, web design, experience design, and interactive system design. Interaction design is increasingly being accepted as the umbrella term, covering all of these aspects. Indeed, many practitioners and designers, who ten years ago would have described what they were doing as interface design or interactive system design, now promote what they are doing as interaction design.

The focus of interaction design is very much concerned with practice, i.e. how to design user experiences. It is not wedded to a particular way of doing design, but is more eclectic, promoting the use of a range of methods, techniques, and frameworks. Some interaction designers have since begun to put forward their own perspective, for example, Cooper and Reiman (2003) present their take on interaction design as 'goal-directed' and Lowgren and Stolterman (2004) as 'thoughtful.'

How does interaction design differ from other approaches to the design of computer-based systems, such as software engineering? A simple analogy to another profession, concerned with creating buildings, may clarify this difference. In his account of interaction design, Terry Winograd asks how architects and civil engineers differ when faced with the problem of building a house. Architects are concerned with the people and their interactions with each other and with the house being built. For example, is there the right mix of family and private spaces? Are the spaces for cooking and eating in close proximity? Will people live in the space being designed in the way it was intended to be used? In contrast, engineers are interested in issues to do with realizing the project. These include practical concerns like cost, durability, structural aspects, environmental aspects, fire regulations, and construction methods. Just as there is a difference between designing and building a house, so too is there a distinction between designing an interactive product and engineering the software for it.

1.3.1 The components of interaction design

We view interaction design as fundamental to all disciplines, fields, and approaches that are concerned with researching and designing computer-based systems for people (see Figure 1.4). Why are there so many and what do they all do? Furthermore, how do the various disciplines, fields, and design approaches differ from one another?

We have already described the distinction between interaction design and software engineering. The differences between interaction design and the other approaches referred

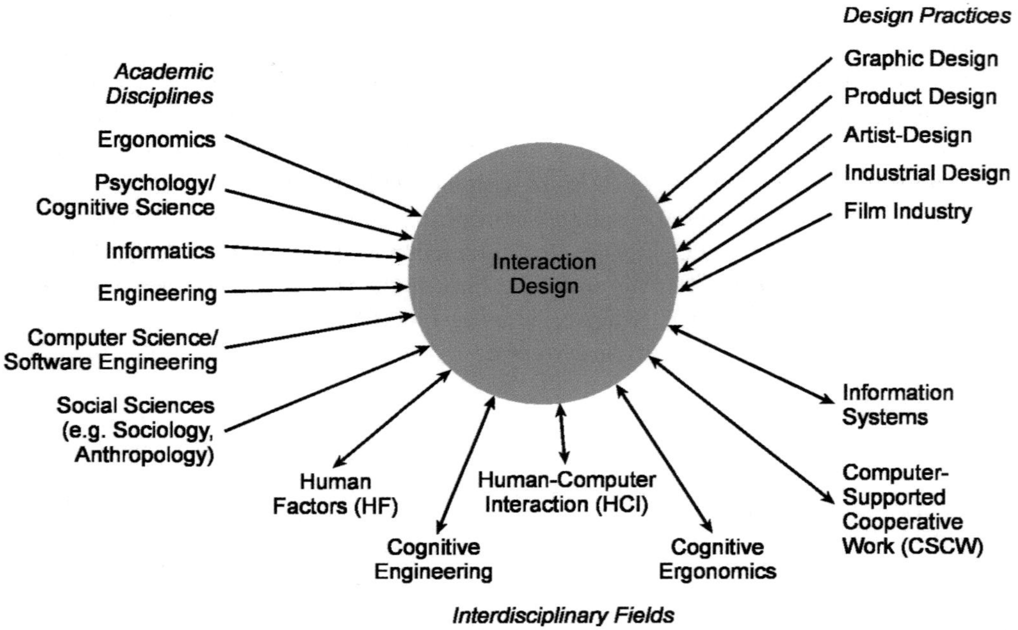

Figure 1.4 *Relationship among contributing academic disciplines, design practices, and interdisciplinary fields concerned with interaction design*

to in the figure is largely down to which methods, philosophies, and lenses they use to study, analyse, and design computers. Another way they vary is in terms of the scope and problems they address. For example, Information Systems is concerned with the application of computing technology in domains like business, health, and education, whereas Computer-Supported Cooperative Work (CSCW) is concerned with the need also to support multiple people working together using computer systems (Greif, 1988).

Box 1.1
Is Interaction Design beyond HCI?

We see the main difference between Interaction Design (ID) and Human–Computer Interaction (HCI) as one of scope. ID has cast its net much wider, being concerned with the theory, research, and practice of designing user experiences for all manner of technologies, systems, and products, whereas HCI has traditionally had a

narrower focus, being "concerned with the design, evaluation, and implementation of interactive computing systems for human use and with the study of major phenomena surrounding them" (ACM SIGCHI, 1992, p. 6). That is one of the reasons why we chose to call our book *Interaction Design: Beyond Human–Computer Interaction*, to reflect the wider scope.

***What about Human Factors and Ergonomics?* We see Ergonomics and Human Factors as having closely overlapping goals with HCI, being concerned with understanding the interactions among humans and other aspects of a system in order to optimize human well-being and overall system performance (Human Factors Society, 2005).** ■

1.3.2 Who is involved in interaction design?

From Figure 1.4 it can also be seen that many people are involved, ranging from social scientists to film-makers. This is not surprising given that technology has become such a pervasive part of our lives. But it can all seem rather bewildering to the onlooker. How do the assortment of players work together?

Designers need to know many different things about users, technologies, and interactions between them in order to create effective user experiences. At the very least, they need to understand how people act and react to events and how they communicate and interact with each other. To be able to create engaging user experiences they also need to understand how emotions work, what is meant by aesthetics, desirability, and the role of narrative in human experience. Developers also need to understand the business side, the technical side, the manufacturing side, and the marketing side. Clearly, it is difficult for one person to be well versed in all of these diverse areas and also know how to apply the different forms of knowledge to the process of interaction design. Most interaction design is done by multidisciplinary teams, where the skill sets of engineers, designers, programmers, psychologists, anthropologists, sociologists, artists, toy makers, and others are drawn upon. It is rarely the case, however, that a design team would have all of these professionals working together. Who to include in a team will depend on a number of factors, including a company's design philosophy, its size, purpose, and product line.

One of the benefits of bringing together people with different backgrounds and training is the potential of many more ideas being generated, new methods developed, and more creative and original designs being produced. However, the down side is the costs involved. The more people there are with different backgrounds in a design team, the more difficult it can be to communicate and progress forward the designs being generated. Why? People with different backgrounds have different perspectives and ways of seeing and talking about the world (see Figure 1.5). What one person values as important others may not even see (Kim, 1990). Similarly, a computer scientist's understanding of the term 'representation' is often very different from a graphic designer's or a psychologist's.

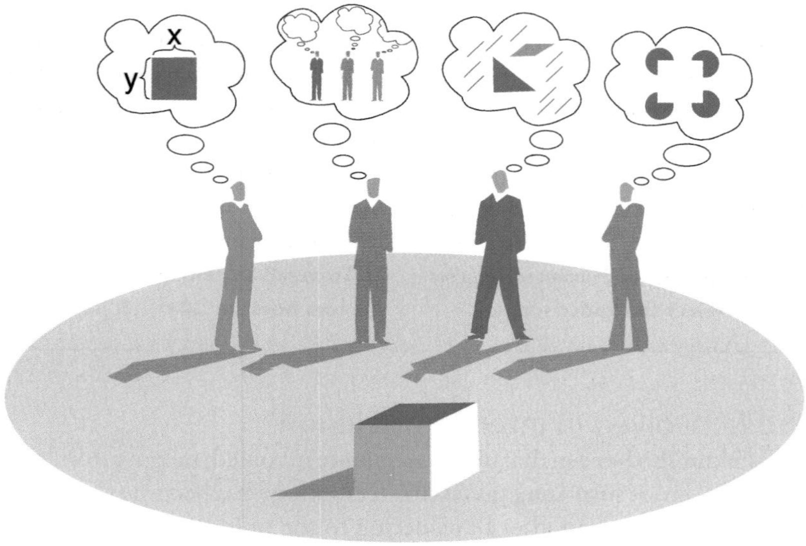

***Figure 1.5** Four different team members looking at the same square, but each seeing it quite differently*

What this means in practice is that confusion, misunderstanding, and communication breakdowns can surface in a team. The various team members may have different ways of talking about design and may use the same terms to mean quite different things. Other problems can arise when a group of people is 'thrown' together who have not worked as a team. For example, the Philips Vision of the Future Project found that its multidisciplinary teams—who were responsible for developing ideas and products for the future—experienced a number of difficulties, namely, that project team members did not always have a clear idea of who needed what information, when, and in what form (Lambourne *et al.*, 1997).

Activity 1.2

In practice, the makeup of a given design team depends on the kind of interactive product being built. Who do you think should be involved in developing:

1. **A public kiosk providing information about the exhibits available in a science museum?**
2. **An interactive educational website to accompany a TV series?**

Comment

Each team will need a number of different people with different skill sets. For example, the first interactive product would need:

1. **Graphic and interaction designers, museum curators, educational advisors, software engineers, software designers, usability engineers, ergonomists.**

The second project would need:

2. **TV producers, graphic and interaction designers, teachers, video experts, software engineers, software designers, usability engineers.**

In addition, as both systems are being developed for use by the general public, representative users, such as school children and parents, should be involved.

In practice, design teams often end up being quite large, especially if they are working on a big project to meet a fixed deadline. For example, it is common to find teams of 15 people or more working on a website project for an extensive period of time, like six months. This means that a number of people from each area of expertise are likely to be working as part of the project team.

1.3.3 Interaction design consultants

Interaction design is now widespread in product development. In particular, website consultants, global corporations, and the computing industries have all realized its pivotal role in successful interactive products. The presence or absence of good interaction design can make or break a company. To get noticed in the highly competitive field of web products requires standing out. Being able to say that your product is easy, effective, and engaging to use is seen as central to this. Marketing departments are also realizing how branding, the number of hits, customer return rate, and customer satisfaction are greatly affected by the usability of a website.

In response to the growing demand for interaction design a number of consultancies have established themselves. These include the NielsenNorman Group, Cooper, Swim and IDEO. Swim was set up in the mid-1990s by Gitta Salomon as a small company to assist clients with the design of interactive products (see the interview with her at the end of this chapter). She points out how often companies realize the importance of interaction design but don't know how to do it themselves. So they get in touch with companies, like Swim, with their partially developed products and ask them for help. This can come in the form of an expert 'crit' in which a detailed review of the usability and design of the product is given (for more on expert evaluation, see Chapter 15). More extensively, it can involve helping clients create their products.

IDEO is a much larger enterprise, with several branches worldwide and over 25 years of experience in the area. They design products, services, and environments for other companies, pioneering new user experiences (Spreenberg *et al.*, 1995). They have developed thousands of products for numerous clients, each time following their particular brand of interaction design (see Figure 1.6). Some of their most famous designs include the first mouse used by Apple, the Palm V and mMode, the integrated service platform for AT&T cell phones. They were also involved in the design of the TiVo system.

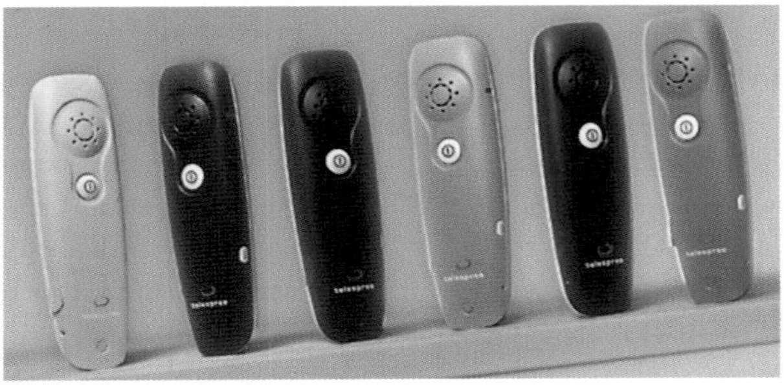

Figure 1.6 *An innovative product developed by IDEO: wireless cell phones for Telespree. The phones were designed to be inexpensive, playful, and very simple to use, employing voice recognition for driving the interaction and only one button for turning them on and off*

Box 1.2
What's in a name? From interface designers to user experience architects

Fifteen years ago, when a company wanted to develop an interface for an interactive product it advertised for interface designers. Such professionals were primarily involved in the design and evaluation of widgets for desktop applications. Now that the potential range of interactive products has greatly diversified, coupled with the growing realization of the importance of getting the interface right, a number of other job descriptions have begun to emerge. These include:

- **Interactive/interaction designers (people involved in the design of all the interactive aspects of a product).**
- **Usability engineers (people who focus on evaluating products, using usability methods and principles).**
- **Web designers (people who develop and create the visual design of websites, such as layouts).**
- **UI designers (people experienced in user-centered design methodologies).**
- **UI design engineers (people who develop and model the end user experience, using task, workflow analytic methods, and low and high-level prototyping tools).**
- **Information architects (people who come up with ideas of how to plan and**

structure interactive products, especially websites).

- **User experience (UX) designers/architects/researchers (people who do all the above but who may also carry out ethnographic field studies to research into users' needs and convert them into actionable results).** ■

1.4 The user experience

A concept that has become central to interaction design is the *user experience*. By this it is meant how a product behaves and is used by people in the real world. As stressed by Jesse Garrett (2003, p. 10), "every product that is used by someone has a user experience: newspapers, ketchup bottles, reclining armchairs, cardigan sweaters." More specifically, it is about how people feel about a product and their pleasure and satisfaction when using it, looking at it, holding it, and opening or closing it. It includes their overall impression of how good it is to use right down to the sensual effect small details have on them, such as how smoothly a switch rotates or the sound of a click and the touch of a button when pressing it.

"How many times have I warned you? Never stick your tongue on a frozen computer screen!"

It is important to point out that one cannot design a user experience, only design *for* a user experience. In particular, one cannot design a sensual experience, but only create the design features that can evoke it. For example, the outside case of a cell phone can be designed to be smooth, silky, and fit in the palm of a hand that when held, touched, looked at, and interacted with can provoke a sensual and satisfying user experience. Conversely, if it is designed to be heavy and awkward to hold, it is much more likely to end up providing a poor user experience, that is uncomfortable and unpleasant.

Activity 1.3
The iPod phenomenon

Apple Computer's first (and subsequent) generation of iPods were a phenomenonal success. How do you think this happened?

Comment

Apple realized early on that successful interaction design involves creating interactive products that have a *quality user experience*. The sleek appearance of the iPod music player, its simplicity of use, its elegance in style, its distinct plain white color, a novel interaction style that many people discovered was a sheer pleasure to learn and use, the catchy naming of its product and content (iTunes, iPod), among many other design features, led to it becoming one of the greatest of its kind and a must-have fashion item for teenagers, students, and others alike. While there were many competing MP3 players on the market at the time, some with more powerful functionality, other with bigger screens, more memory, cheaper, easier to use, etc., the quality of the overall user experience paled in comparison with that provided by the iPod.

There are many aspects of the user experience that can be considered and ways of taking them into account when designing interactive products. Of central importance is the usability, the functionality, the aesthetics, the content, the look and feel, and the sensual and emotional appeal. In addition, Jack Carroll (2004) stresses other wide-reaching aspects including fun, health, social capital (the social resources that develop and are maintained through social networks, shared values, goals, and norms), and cultural identity, e.g. age, ethnicity, race, disability, family status, occupation, education. At a more subjective level, John McCarthy and Peter Wright (2004) discuss the importance of people's expectations and the way they make sense of their experiences when using technology (see Chapter 5 for more on this).

How realistic is it for interaction designers to take all of these factors (and potentially many others) into account and, moreover, be able to translate and combine them to produce quality user experiences? Put frankly, there is no magic formula to help them. As of yet, there is not a unifying theory or framework that can be readily applied by interaction designers. Many of the aspects mentioned are only beginning to be understood. New conceptual frameworks that try to combine them are just emerging. What is established in the field of interaction design, however, are tried and tested design methods, a lot of prescriptive advice, and many relevant research findings. Here, we begin by examining these by outlining the core processes and goals of interaction design.

Figure 1.7 *An advert for Apple's iPod on its online store site*

1.5 The process of interaction design

The process of interaction design involves four basic activities:

1. Identifying needs and establishing requirements for the user experience.
2. Developing alternative designs that meet those requirements.
3. Building interactive versions of the designs so that they can be communicated and assessed.
4. Evaluating what is being built throughout the process and the user experience it offers.

These activities are intended to inform one another and to be repeated. For example, measuring the usability of what has been built in terms of whether it is easy to use provides feedback that certain changes must be made or that certain requirements have not yet been met. Eliciting responses from potential users about what they think and feel about what has been designed, in terms of its appeal, touch, engagement, usefulness, etc., can help explicate the nature of the user experience that the product evokes.

Evaluating what has been built is very much at the heart of interaction design. Its focus is on ensuring that the product is usable. It is usually addressed through a user-centered approach to design, which, as the name suggests, seeks to involve users throughout the design process. There are many different ways of achieving this: for example, through observing users, talking to them, interviewing them, testing them using performance tasks, modeling their performance, asking them to fill in questionnaires, and even asking them to become co-designers. The findings from the different ways of engaging and eliciting knowledge from users are then interpreted with respect to ongoing design activities (we give more detail about all these aspects of evaluation in Chapters 12–15).

Equally important as involving users when evaluating an interactive product is understanding what people do. Chapters 3, 4, and 5 explain in detail how people act and interact with one another, with information, and with various technologies, together with describing their abilities, emotions, needs, desires, and what causes them to get annoyed, frustrated, lose patience, and get bored. Such knowledge can greatly help designers determine which solutions to choose from the many design alternatives available, and how to develop and test these further. Chapter 10 describes how an understanding of people and what they do can be translated to requirements, while Chapters 9 and 11 discuss how to involve users effectively in the design process.

A main reason for having a better understanding of people in the contexts in which they live, work, and learn is that it can help designers understand how to design interactive products that will fit those niches. A collaborative planning tool intended to be used by teams of scientists for a space mission working in different parts of the world will have quite different needs from one targeted at customer and sales agents to be used in a furniture store to draw up kitchen layout plans. Understanding the differences between people can also help designers appreciate that one size does not fit all; what works for one user group may be totally inappropriate for another. For example, children have different expectations about how they want to learn or play from adults. They may find having interactive quizzes and cartoon characters helping them along to be highly motivating, whereas most adults find them annoying. Conversely, adults often like talking-heads discussions about topics, but children find them boring. Just as everyday objects like clothes, food, and games are designed differently for children, teenagers, and adults, so, too, must interactive products be designed for different kinds of user.

Learning more about people and what they do can also reveal incorrect assumptions that designers may have about particular user groups and what they need. For example, it is often assumed that because of ailing vision and dexterity, old people want things to be big—be it text or graphical elements appearing on a screen or the physical controls, like dials and switches, used to control devices. This may be true for some old people but studies have also shown that many people in their 70s, 80s, and older are perfectly capable of interacting with standard-sized information and even small-size interfaces, e.g. PDAs, just as well as those in their teens and 20s can even though, initially, some might think they will find it difficult (Siek *et al.*, 2005). It is increasingly the case that as people get older they do not like to consider themselves as lacking in cognitive and manual skills. Being aware of people's sensitivities is as important as knowing how to design for their capabilities.

Being aware of cultural differences is also an important concern for interaction design, particularly for products intended for a diverse range of user groups from different countries. An example of a cultural difference is the dates and times used in different countries. In the USA, for example, the date is written as month, day, year, e.g. 05/21/06, whereas in other countries it is written in the sequence of day, month, year, e.g. 21/05/06. This can cause problems to designers when deciding on the format of online forms, especially if intended for global use. It is also a concern for products that have time as a function, e.g. operating systems, digital clocks, car dashboards. Which cultural group do they give preference to? How do they alert users to the format that is set as default? This raises the question of how easily an interface designed for one user group can be used and accepted by another (Callahan, 2005). Moreover, why is it that certain products, like the iPod, are universally accepted by people from all parts of the world whereas websites are designed differently and reacted to differently by people from different cultures?

As well as there being standard differences in the way cultures communicate and represent information, designers from different cultures (that can be cross- or within-country) will often use different form factors, images, and graphical elements when creating products and dialog features for an interface. This can take the form of contrasting designs, where different colors, types of images, and structuring of information are used to appeal to people in different countries (see Figure 1.8).

***Figure 1.8** Anna the online sales agent, designed to be subtley different for UK and US customers. What are the differences and which is which? What should Anna's appearance be like for other countries, like India, South Africa, or China?*

1.6 Interaction design and the user experience

Part of the process of understanding users is to be clear about the primary objective of developing an interactive product for them. Is it to design an efficient system that will allow them to be highly productive in their work, or is it to design a learning tool that will be challenging and motivating, or is it something else? To help identify the objectives we suggest classifying them in terms of usability and user experience goals. Usability goals are viewed as being concerned with meeting specific usability criteria, e.g. efficiency, whereas user experience goals are largely concerned with explicating the nature of the user experience, e.g. to be aesthetically pleasing. It is important to note, however, that the distinction between the two types of goal is not clear-cut, since usability is fundamental to the quality of the user experience and, conversely, aspects of the user experience, such as how it feels and looks, are inextricably linked with how usable the product is. We distinguish between them here to help clarify their roles but stress the importance of considering them together when designing for a user experience.

1.6.1 Usability goals

Usability is generally regarded as ensuring that interactive products are easy to learn, effective to use, and enjoyable from the user's perspective. It involves optimizing the interactions people have with interactive products to enable them to carry out their activities at work, school, and in their everyday life. More specifically, usability is broken down into the following goals:

- effective to use (effectiveness)
- efficient to use (efficiency)
- safe to use (safety)
- having good utility (utility)
- easy to learn (learnability)
- easy to remember how to use (memorability).

Usability goals are typically operationalized as questions. The purpose is to provide the interaction designer with a concrete means of assessing various aspects of an interactive product and the user experience. Through answering the questions designers can be alerted very early on in the design process to potential design problems and conflicts that they might not have considered. However, simply asking "is the system easy to learn?" is not going to be very helpful. Asking about the usability of a product in a more detailed way, for example, "how long will it take a user to figure out how to use the most basic functions for the new web browser; how much can they capitalize on from their prior experience, and how long would it take a user to learn the whole set of functions?" will elicit far more information. Below we give a description of each goal and a question for each one.

Effectiveness is a very general goal and refers to how good a product is at doing what it is supposed to do.

Question: Is the product capable of allowing people to learn, carry out their work efficiently, access the information they need, or buy the goods they want?

Efficiency refers to the way a product supports users in carrying out their tasks. The marble answering machine described at the beginning of this chapter was considered efficient in that it let the user carry out common tasks, e.g. listening to messages, through a minimal number of steps. In contrast, the voice mail system was considered inefficient because it required the user to carry out many steps and learn an arbitrary set of sequences for the same common task. This implies that an efficient way of supporting common tasks is to let the user use single button or key presses. An example of where this kind of efficiency mechanism has been employed effectively is in online shopping. Once users have entered all the necessary personal details in an online form to make a purchase, they can let the website save all their personal details. Then, if they want to make another purchase at that site, they don't have to re-enter all their personal details again. A highly successful mechanism patented by `Amazon.com` is the one-click option, which requires users only to click a single button when they want to make another purchase.

Question: Once users have learned how to use a product to carry out their tasks, can they sustain a high level of productivity?

Safety involves protecting the user from dangerous conditions and undesirable situations. In relation to the first ergonomic aspect, it refers to the external conditions where people work. For example, where there are hazardous conditions—like X-ray machines or chemical plants—operators should be able to interact with and control computer-based systems remotely. The second aspect refers to helping any kind of user in any kind of situation avoid the dangers of carrying out unwanted actions accidentally. It also refers to the perceived fears users might have of the consequences of making errors and how this affects their behavior. To make interactive products safer in this sense involves (i) preventing the user from making serious errors by reducing the risk of wrong keys/buttons being mistakenly activated (an example is *not* placing the quit or delete-file command right next to the save command on a menu) and (ii) providing users with various means of recovery should they make errors. Safe interactive systems should engender confidence and allow the user the opportunity to explore the interface to try out new operations (see Figure 1.9a). Other safety mechanisms include undo facilities and confirmatory dialog boxes that give users another chance to consider their intentions (a well-known example is the appearance of a dialog box, after issuing the command to delete everything in the trashcan, saying: "Are you sure you want to remove all the items in the Trash permanently?" See Figure 1.9b).

Question: What is the range of errors that are possible using the product and what measures are there to permit users to recover easily from them?

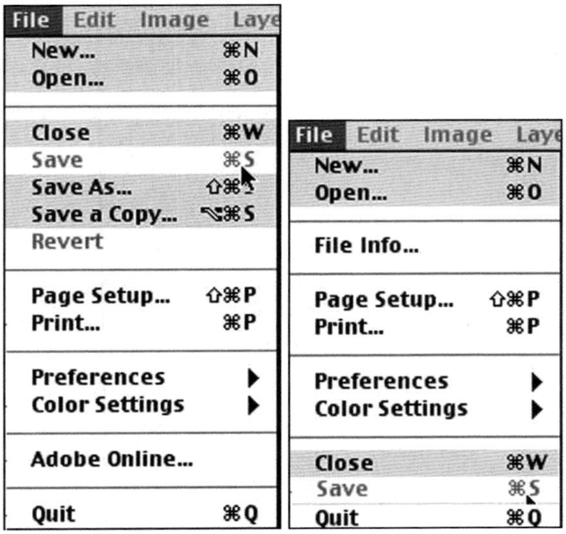

(a)

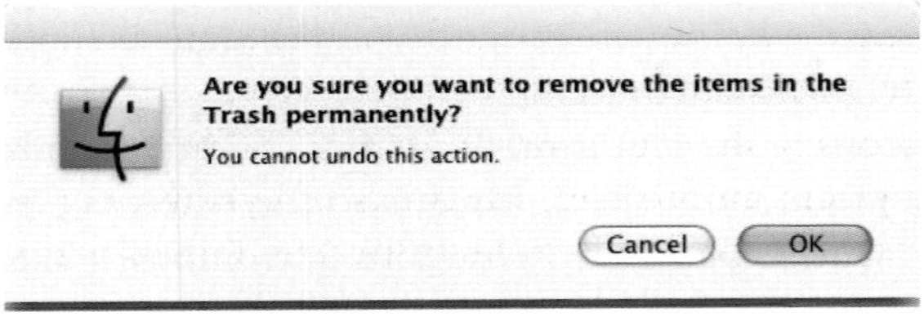

(b)

Figure 1.9 *(a) A safe and unsafe menu. Which is which and why? (b) A warning dialog box for Mac OS X*

Utility refers to the extent to which the product provides the right kind of functionality so that users can do what they need or want to do. An example of a product with high utility is an accounting software package that provides a powerful computational tool that accountants can use to work out tax returns. An example of a product with low utility is a software drawing tool that does not allow users to draw freehand but forces them to use a mouse to create their drawings, using only polygon shapes.

Question: Does the product provide an appropriate set of functions that will enable users to carry out all their tasks in the way they want to do them?

Learnability refers to how easy a system is to learn to use. It is well known that people don't like spending a long time learning how to use a system. They want to get started straight away and become competent at carrying out tasks without too much effort. This is especially so for interactive products intended for everyday use, e.g. DVD players, email, and those used only infrequently, e.g. videoconferencing. To a certain extent, people are prepared to spend longer learning more complex systems that provide a wider range of functionality, e.g. web authoring tools, word processors. In these situations, CD-ROM and online tutorials can help by providing interactive step-by-step material with hands-on exercises. However, many people find these difficult to relate to the tasks they want to accomplish. A key concern is determining how much time users are prepared to spend learning a product. It seems a waste if a product provides a range of functionality which the majority of users are unable or not prepared to spend time learning how to use.

Question: Is it possible for the user to work out how to use the product by exploring the interface and trying out certain actions? How hard will it be to learn the whole set of functions in this way?

Memorability refers to how easy a product is to remember how to use, once learned. This is especially important for interactive products that are used infrequently. If users haven't used an operation for a few months or longer, they should be able to remember or at least rapidly be reminded how to use it. Users shouldn't have to keep relearning how to carry out tasks. Unfortunately, this tends to happen when the operations required to be learned are obscure, illogical, or poorly sequenced. Users need to be helped to remember how to do tasks. There are many ways of designing the interaction to support this. For example, users can be helped to remember the sequence of operations at different stages of a task through meaningful icons, command names, and menu options. Also, structuring options and icons so they are placed in relevant categories of options, e.g. placing all the drawing tools in the same place on the screen, can help the user remember where to look to find a particular tool at a given stage of a task.

Question: What kinds of interface support have been provided to help users remember how to carry out tasks, especially for products and operations they use infrequently?

Box 1.3
Passworditus

We are now being asked to create and remember increasing numbers of passwords. We need them to enable us to log onto the various computers we use at work and home, and again to gain access to our email accounts, online accounts, web accounts, bank accounts, etc. Registration for the majority of online services also requires that we create new usernames and passwords.

This constant need for security, however, ends up giving most users a case of *passworditus*. Media people and other intensive online users suffer particularly. They are likely to have large numbers of accounts for different services.

For example, Bill Thompson (2004), a commentator for the BBC World Service program, admitted to having 30 separate accounts, not to mention his Windows laptop demanding he change his password every three months. How does he (and we) cope with this cognitive demand, especially for services used infrequently? The answer: with much frustration, often adopting workarounds that are none too healthy.

To begin, most of us create a password based on the name of our partners, children, pets or favorite cartoon character. Although, according to Yahoo! (2004), the most common password is still 'password,' followed closely by 'God,' 'sex,' 'money,' and 'love.' When we're asked to create new passwords most of will use the same one—despite knowing it is not a very good idea. The more conscientious among us are likely to forget many of them, or muddle them up, especially if we use them infrequently. To add to our misery, many online sites have become wise to our fondness for pet names (which can be more easily descrambled), and now require us to create and memorize passwords that comprise a mix of upper and lower case alphabetic and numeric characters that are greater than eight characters, and that do not sound like words or names—all of which makes it much harder for us to remember them. To their credit, many service providers try to help the hapless and frustrated user log on to their service again by providing a 'forgotten your password?' option at the login dialog box. But relying on passwords being sent via email each time is time-consuming and tedious. Will it ever be possible for someone to invent a single login/password configuration that will be robust enough not to be broken into and yet easy enough to remember? ■

Activity 1.4

How long do you think it *should* take to learn how to use the following interactive products and how long does it *actually* take most people to learn them? How memorable are they?

1. Using a DVD or VCR to play a movie.
2. Using a DVD or VCR recorder to record two TV programs.
3. Using an authoring tool to create a website.

Comment

1. To play a DVD or video should be as simple as turning the radio on, should take less than 30 seconds to work out, and then should be straightforward to do subsequently. Most people are able to fathom how to play a DVD or video. However, many TV systems require the user to switch to the DVD or video channel using one or two remote

control devices. Other settings may also need to be configured before the DVD/video will play, like typing in a code for adult restricted movies. Most people are able to remember how to play a movie once they have used a particular product.

2. **Recording is a more complex operation and should take a couple of minutes to learn how to do and to check that the programming is correct. VCR players are renowned for their notorious interfaces, resulting in few people remembering how to pre-record programs. DVD recorders generally have been designed with better interfaces that provide viewers with more interactive feedback and cues, using menus and dialog boxes that appear on the TV itself. An example of a well-designed interface is TiVo, where viewers need only to remember the first letter or two of a program they want to watch and then select from a scrolling menu on the TV screen.**
3. **A well-designed authoring tool should let the user create a basic page in about 20 minutes. Learning the full range of operations and possibilities is likely to take much longer, possibly a few days. In reality, there are some good authoring tools that allow the user to get started straight away, providing templates that they can adapt. Most users will extend their repertoire, taking another hour or so to learn more functions. However, very few people actually learn to use the full range of functions provided by the authoring tool. Users will tend to remember frequently used operations, e.g. cut and paste or inserting images, especially if they are consistent with the way they are carried out in other software applications. However, less frequently used operations may need to be relearned, e.g. formatting tables.**

As well as couching usability goals in terms of specific questions, they are turned into *usability criteria*. These are specific objectives that enable the usability of a product to be assessed in terms of how it can improve (or not) a user's performance. Examples of commonly used usability criteria are time to complete a task (efficiency), time to learn a task (learnability), and the number of errors made when carrying out a given task over time (memorability). These can provide quantitative indicators of the extent to which productivity has increased, or how work, training, or learning have been improved. They are also useful for measuring the extent to which personal, public, and home-based products support leisure and information-gathering activities. However, they do not address the overall quality of the user experience, which is where user experience goals come into play.

1.6.2 User experience goals

There are a number of user experience goals that are beginning to be articulated in interaction design. They include both positive and negative ones, for example:

- satisfying
- enjoyable
- engaging
- pleasurable
- exciting
- entertaining
- helpful
- motivating
- aesthetically pleasing
- supportive of creativity
- cognitively stimulating
- rewarding
- fun
- provocative
- surprising
- emotionally fulfilling
- challenging
- enhancing sociability
- boring
- frustrating
- annoying
- cutesy

Many of these are subjective qualities and concerned with how a system *feels* to a user. They differ from the more objective usability goals in that they are concerned with how users experience an interactive product from their perspective, rather than assessing how useful or productive a system is from its own perspective. Whereas the terms used to describe usability goals comprise a small distinct set, many more terms are used to describe the multifaceted nature of the user experience. They also overlap with what they are referring to. In so doing, they offer subtely different ways of expressing the way an experience varies for the same activity over time, technology, and place. For example, we may describe listening to music in the shower as highly pleasurable, while consider it more apt to describe listening to music in the car as enjoyable. Similarly, listening to music on a high-end powerful music system may invoke in us exciting and emotionally fulfilling feelings, while listening to it on an MP3 player may be enjoyable when on the move. The process of selecting terms that best convey a user's feelings, state of being, emotions, sensations, etc., when using or interacting with a product at a given time and place, can help designers understand the multifaceted and changing nature of the user experience. Similar to usability goals, user experience concepts are most useful when turned into specific questions. For example, when considering how engaging an interactive virtual agent is for an online store, one can ask:

How long do users interact with the virtual sales agent? Do they suspend their disbelief when typing in questions?

To consider the effect of its appeal one can ask:

What is the user's immediate response to the agent's appearance? Is it one of mockery, dismay, or enjoyment? Do they smile, laugh, or scoff?

The concepts can be further defined in terms of elements that contribute to making a user experience pleasurable, fun, exciting, etc. They include attention, pace, play, interactivity, conscious and unconscious control, style of narrative, and flow. In particular, the concept of flow (Csikszentmihalyi, 1997) is becoming popular in interaction design for informing the design of user experiences for websites, video games, and other interactive products. It refers to a state of intense emotional involvement that comes from being completely involved in an activity, like playing music, and where time flies. Instead of designing web interfaces to cater for visitors who know what they want, they can be designed to induce a state of flow, leading the visitor to some unexpected place, where they become completely absorbed. In an interview with *Wired* magazine, Csikszentmihalyi (1996) uses the analogy of a gourmet meal to describe how a user experience can be designed to be engrossing, "starting off with the appetizers, moving on to the salads and entrées, and building toward dessert and not knowing what will follow."

How do concepts of the user experience fare in relation to usability? Until recently, traditional HCI has championed the usability of a system in terms of efficiency, utility, etc., while overlooking the role played by other aspects of the user experience, such as aesthetics, etc. However, a sea change has happened in HCI in the last few years, and those involved in shaping the field have begun in earnest to take on board other aspects of the user experience (see Blythe *et al.*, 2003; Wilson, 2005). Even Don Norman (2004), a staunch advocate of usability, changed his way of thinking about interaction design when discovering there was a positive correlation between usability and aesthetics. He first read about this from the findings of two studies conducted independently by Japanese and Israeli researchers in the late 1990s: they both found that attractive interfaces for functionally equivalent ATM machines were perceived to be easier to use than unattractive ones (see Figure 1.10).

Those working in the computer games industry have acknowledged for a long time that there is an important relationship between pleasure and usability. Counter-intuitively, they also realized it can work in a negative direction. Many gamers enjoy and find most challenging non-easy video games, which contravene usability goals (Frohlich and Murphy, 1999). Banging a plastic hammer to hit a virtual nail represented on the computer screen, compared with using a more efficient way to do the same thing, e.g. selecting an option using command keys, may require more effort and be more error-prone but can result in a much more enjoyable and fun experience.

Not all usability and user experience goals will be relevant to the design and evaluation of an interactive product being developed. Some combinations will also be incompatible. For example, it may not be possible or desirable to design a process control system that is both safe and fun. Recognizing and understanding the nature of the relationship between usability and other user experience goals is central to interaction design. It enables designers to become aware of the consequences of pursuing different combinations when designing products and highlight potential trade-offs and conflicts. As suggested by Jack Carroll (2004), articulating the interactions of the various components of the user's experience can lead to a deeper and more significant interpretation of the role of each component.

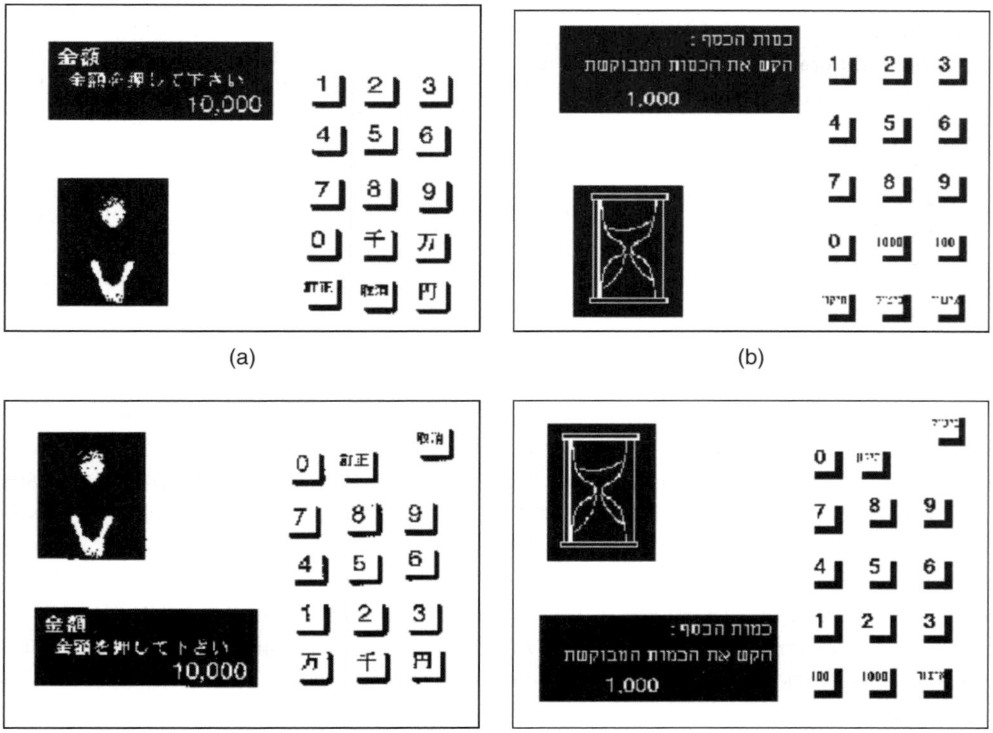

(a) (b) (c) (d)

Figure 1.10 Are attractive interfaces more or less usable? An original Japanese interface, rated (a) high and (c) low on apparent usability and aesthetics ***(Kurosu and Kashimura, 1995)*** *and the equivalent Israeli interface rated (b) high and (d) low on apparent usability and aesthetics* ***(Tractinsky, N. 1997)***

Activity 1.5

Study the four screens in Figure 1.10 for the two different ATM designs. The screens in Figure 1.10 (a) and (c) were developed by Japanese researchers and the screens in Figure 1.10 (b) and (c) were developed by Israelis. Compare these pairs of screen to identify how they differ and suggest why screens (a) and (b) were rated high on usability while (c) and (d) were rated low.

Comment

Aesthetic differences can be subtle, especially concerning page layout. The differences here are:

1. **In (a) and (b) the keypad runs from 1 to 9 top to bottom, while in (c) and (d) it runs from 1 to 9 from bottom to top.**
2. **The positioning of the amount of money is placed in the top left hand corner in (a) and (b) making it prominent and easy to find. In (c) and (d) the amount is in the bottom left hand corner.**
3. **The keypad in (a) and (b) is symmetrical, while asymmetrical in (c) and (d).**

1.6.3 Design principles

Design principles are used by interaction designers to aid their thinking when designing for the user experience. These are generalizable abstractions intended to orient designers towards thinking about different aspects of their designs. A well-known example is feedback: products should be designed to provide adequate feedback to the users to ensure they know what to do next in their tasks. Design principles are derived from a mix of theory-based knowledge, experience, and common sense. They tend to be written in a prescriptive manner, suggesting to designers what to provide and what to avoid at the interface—if you like, the dos and don'ts of interaction design. More specifically, they are intended to help designers explain and improve their designs (Thimbleby, 1990). However, they are not intended to specify how to design an actual interface, e.g. telling the designer how to design a particular icon or how to structure a web portal, but act more like triggers to designers, ensuring that they have provided certain features at an interface.

A number of design principles have been promoted. The best known are concerned with how to determine what users should see and do when carrying out their tasks using an interactive product. Here we briefly describe the most common ones: visibility, feedback, constraints, consistency, and affordances. Each of these has been written about extensively by Don Norman (1988) in his bestseller *The Design of Everyday Things*.

Visibility. The importance of visibility is exemplified by our contrasting examples at the beginning of the chapter. The voice mail system made the presence and number of waiting messages invisible, while the answer machine made both aspects highly visible. The more visible functions are, the more likely users will be able to know what to do next. Norman (1988) describes the controls of a car to emphasize this point. The controls for different operations are clearly visible, e.g. indicators, headlights, horn, hazard warning lights, indicating what can be done. The relationship between the way the controls have been positioned in the car and what they do makes it easy for the driver to find the appropriate control for the task at hand.

In contrast, when functions are 'out of sight,' it makes them more difficult to find and know how to use. For example, devices and environments that have become automated through the use of sensor-technology (usually for hygiene and energy-saving reasons)—like faucets, elevators, and lights—can sometimes be more difficult for people to know how to control, especially how to activate or deactivate them. This can result in users getting caught out and frustrated (see Figure 1.11). Highly visible controlling devices, like knobs, buttons, and switches, which are intuitive to use, have been replaced by invisible and ambiguous 'activating zones' where people have to guess where to move their hands, bodies, or feet on, into, or in front of to make them work.

Feedback. Related to the concept of visibility is feedback. This is best illustrated by an analogy to what everyday life would be like without it. Imagine trying to play a guitar, slice bread using a knife, or write using a pen if none of the actions produced any effect for several seconds. There would be an unbearable delay before the music was produced,

Figure 1.11 *A sign in the restrooms at Cincinnati airport. Because it is not visible to the user as to what to do to turn the faucet on and off, a sign has been added to explain what is normally an everyday and well-learned activity. It does not explain, however, what to do if you are wearing black clothing*

the bread was cut, or the words appeared on the paper, making it almost impossible for the person to continue with the next strum, saw, or stroke.

Feedback is about sending back information about what action has been done and what has been accomplished, allowing the person to continue with the activity. Various kinds of feedback are available for interaction design—audio, tactile, verbal, visual, and combinations of these. Deciding which combinations are appropriate for different kinds of activities and interactivities is central. Using feedback in the right way can also provide the necessary visibility for user interaction.

Constraints. The design concept of constraining refers to determining ways of restricting the kinds of user interaction that can take place at a given moment. There are various ways this can be achieved. A common design practice in graphical user interfaces is to deactivate certain menu options by shading them, thereby restricting the user to only actions permissible at that stage of the activity (see Figure 1.12). One of the advantages of this form of constraining is that it prevents the user from selecting incorrect options and thereby reduces the chance of making a mistake. The use of different kinds of graphical representations can also constrain a person's interpretation of a problem or information space. For example, flow chart diagrams show which objects are related to which, thereby constraining the way the information can be perceived. The physical design of a device can

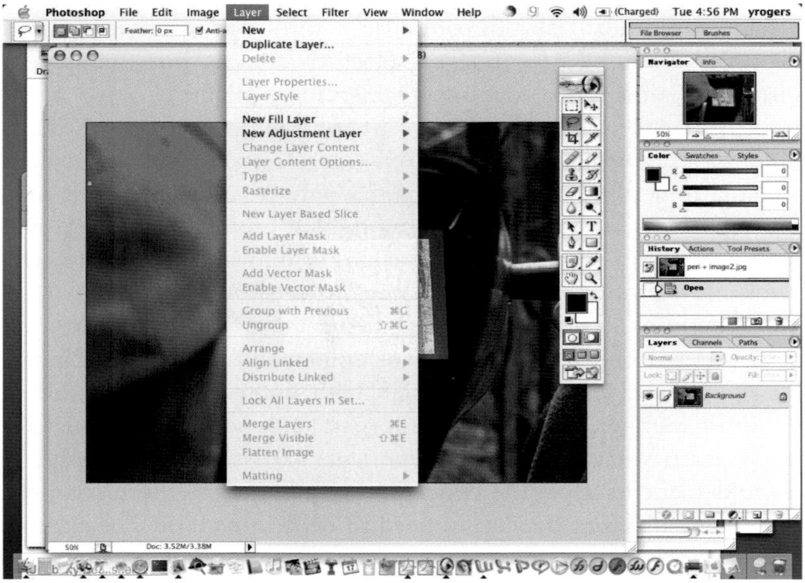

Figure 1.12 *A menu showing restricted availability of options as an example of logical constraining. Shaded area indicates deactivated options*

also constrain how it is used, for example, the external slots in a computer or PDA have been designed to only allow a cable or card to be inserted in a certain way. Sometimes, however, the physical constraint is ambiguous, as shown in Figure 1.13.

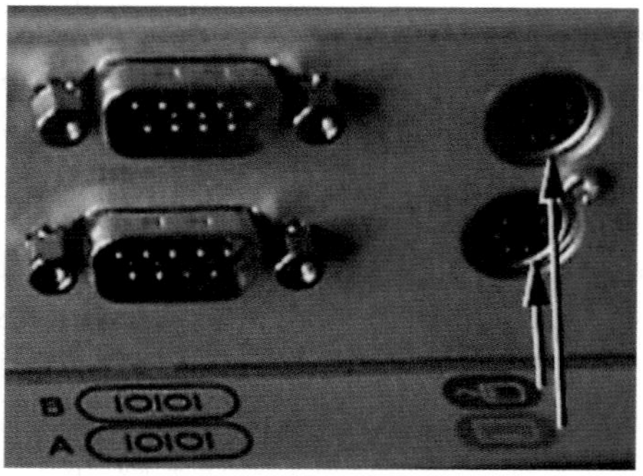

Figure 1.13 *Where do you plug in the mouse and keyboard? This figure shows part of the back of a computer. There are two sets of connectors; the two on the right are for a mouse and a keyboard. They look identical and are physically constrained in the same way. How do you know which is which? Do the labels help?*

Consistency. This refers to designing interfaces to have similar operations and use similar elements for achieving similar tasks. In particular, a consistent interface is one that follows rules, such as using the same operation to select all objects. For example, a consistent operation is using the same input action to highlight any graphical object at the interface, such as always clicking the left mouse button. Inconsistent interfaces, on the other hand, allow exceptions to a rule. An example of this is where certain graphical objects, e.g. email messages presented in a table, can be highlighted only by using the right mouse button, while all other operations are highlighted using the left button. A problem with this kind of inconsistency is that it is quite arbitrary, making it difficult for users to remember and making the users more prone to mistakes.

One of the benefits of consistent interfaces, therefore, is that they are easier to learn and use. Users have to learn only a single mode of operation that is applicable to all objects. This principle works well for simple interfaces with limited operations, like a mini CD player with a small number of operations mapped onto separate buttons. Here, all the user has to do is learn what each button represents and select accordingly. However, it can be more problematic to apply the concept of consistency to more complex interfaces, especially when many different operations need to be designed for. For example, consider how to design an interface for an application that offers hundreds of operations, e.g. a word-processing application. There is simply not enough space for a thousand buttons, each of which maps onto an individual operation. Even if there were, it would be extremely difficult and time-consuming for the user to search through them all to find the desired operation. A much more effective design solution is to create categories of commands that can be mapped into subsets of operations.

Affordance is a term used to refer to an attribute of an object that allows people to know how to use it. For example, a mouse button invites pushing (in so doing activating clicking) by the way it is physically constrained in its plastic shell. At a very simple level, to afford means "to give a clue" (Norman, 1988). When the affordances of a physical object are perceptually obvious it is easy to know how to interact with it. For example, a door handle affords pulling, a cup handle affords grasping, and a mouse button affords pushing. Norman introduced this concept in the late 1980s in his discussion of the design of everyday objects. Since then, it has been much popularized, being used to describe how interface objects should be designed so that they make obvious what can be done to them. For example, graphical elements like buttons, icons, links, and scrollbars are talked about with respect to how to make it appear obvious how they should be used: icons should be designed to afford clicking, scrollbars to afford moving up and down, buttons to afford pushing.

Unfortunately, the term 'affordance' has become rather a catch-all phrase, losing much of its potency as a design principle. Norman (1999), who was largely responsible for originally promoting the concept in his book *The Design of Everyday Things* (1988), despairs at the way it has come to be used in common parlance:

> ***"I put an affordance there," a participant would say, "I wonder if the object affords clicking . . ." affordances this, affordances that. And no data, just opinion. Yikes! What had I unleashed upon the world? Norman's (1999) reaction to a CHI-Web discussion.***

He has since tried to clarify his argument about the utility of the concept by saying there are two kinds of affordance: perceived and real. Physical objects are said to have real affordances, like grasping, that are perceptually obvious and do not have to be learned. In contrast, user interfaces that are screen-based are virtual and do not have these kinds of real affordances. Using this distinction, he argues that it does not make sense to try to design for real affordances at the interface—except when designing physical devices, like control consoles, where affordances like pulling and pressing are helpful in guiding the user to know what to do. Alternatively, screen-based interfaces are better conceptualized as *perceived* affordances, which are essentially learned conventions. In conclusion, Norman argues that other design concepts, like feedback and constraints, are more useful for helping designers develop graphical user interfaces.

There are also numerous websites and guidebooks that provide more exhaustive sets of design principles that we have just touched upon here, with specific examples for designing the web, GUIs, and more generally interaction design. Two of the most well-known websites that provide design principles with examples to illustrate how to use them are Tog's First Principles of Interaction Design (`asktog.com`) and Jakob Nielsen's `useit.com` site.

Applying design principles in practice

One of the problems of applying more than one of the design principles in interaction design is that trade-offs can arise between them. For example, the more you try to constrain an interface, the less visible information becomes. The same can also happen when trying to apply a single design principle. For example, the more an interface is designed to 'afford' through trying to resemble the way physical objects look, the more it can become cluttered and difficult to use. Consistency can be a problematic design principle; trying to design an interface to be consistent with something can make it inconsistent with something else. Furthermore, sometimes inconsistent interfaces are actually easier to use than consistent interfaces. Grudin (1989) illustrates the consistency dilemma with an analogy to where knives are stored in a house. Knives come in a variety of forms, e.g. butter knives, steak knives, table knives, fish knives. An easy place to put them all and subsequently locate them is in the top drawer by the sink. This makes it easy for everyone to find them and follows a simple consistent rule. But what about the knives that don't fit or are too sharp to put in the drawer, like carving knives and bread knives? They are placed in a wooden block. And what about the best knives kept only for special occasions? They are placed in the cabinet in the other room for safekeeping. And what about other knives like putty knives and paint-scraping knives used in home projects (kept in the garage) and jack knives (kept in one's pockets or backpack)? Very quickly the consistency rule begins to break down.

Grudin notes how in extending the number of places where knives are kept inconsistency is introduced, which in turn increases the time needed *to learn* where they are all stored. However, the placement of the knives in different places often makes it *easier* to find them because they are at hand for the context in which they are used and also next to the other objects used for a specific task, e.g. all the home project tools are stored together in a box in the garage. The same is true when designing interfaces: introducing inconsistency can make it more difficult to learn an interface but in the long run can make it easier to use.

Activity 1.6

One of the main design principles which Nielsen has proselytized, especially for website design, is simplicity. He proposes that designers go through all of their design elements and remove them one by one. If a design works just as well without an element, then remove it. Do you think this is a good design principle? If you have your own website, try doing this and seeing what happens. At what point does the interaction break down?

Comment

Simplicity is certainly an important design principle. Many designers try to cram too much into a screenful of

space, making it unwieldy for people to find what they are interested in. Removing design elements to see what can be discarded without affecting the overall function of the website can be a salutary lesson. Unnecessary icons, buttons, boxes, lines, graphics, shading, and text can be stripped, leaving a cleaner, crisper, and easier-to-navigate website. However, graphics, shading, coloring, and formatting can make a site aesthetically pleasing and enjoyable to use. Plain vanilla sites with just lists of text and a few hyperlinks may not be as appealing and may put certain visitors off returning. Good interaction design involves getting the balance between aesthetic appeal and the right amount and kind of information per page.

Box 1.4
Usable usability: which terms do I use?

The various terms proposed for describing the different aspects of usability can be confusing. They are often used interchangeably and in different combinations. Some people talk about usability design principles, others usability heuristics, and others design concepts. The key is understanding how to use the different levels of guidance. 'Guidelines' is the most general term used to refer to *all forms* of guidance. 'Goals' refer to the high-level usability aims of the system, e.g. it should be efficient to use. 'Principles' refer to general guidance intended to inform the design and evaluation of a system. 'Rules' are low-level guidance that refer to a particular prescription that must be followed. 'Heuristics' is a general term used to refer to design and usability principles when applied to a particular design problem.

Concept	*Level of guidance*	*Also sometimes called*	*How to use*
Usability goals	General		Setting up usability criteria for assessing the acceptability of a system, e.g. "How long does it take to perform a task?".
User experience goals	General	Pleasure factors	Identifying the important aspects of the user experience, e.g. "How can you make the interactive product fun and enjoyable?".

Design principles	General	Heuristics when used in practice Design concepts	As reminders of what to provide and what to avoid when designing an interface, e.g. "What kind of feedback are you going to provide at the interface?".
Usability principles	Specific	Heuristics when used in practice	Assessing the acceptability of interfaces, used during heuristic evaluation, e.g. "Does the system provide clearly marked exits?".
Rules	Specific		To determine if an interface adheres to a specific rule when being designed and evaluated, e.g. "Always provide a backwards and forwards navigation button on a web browser".

Dilemma
Device clutter: convergence or specialization?

Look around your living room and you are likely to see a range of home entertainment systems, each with its own remote control. One for the TV, one for the DVD player, one for the CD player, one for the sound system, one for the robot toy, and so on. According to a survey carried out by Intel at the end of 2004, over 50% of British households owned five or more remote controls and 25% had more than seven. For many of us, it can be frustrating to learn how to use them all and then remember how to use them. Often there is a lack of consistency between the remote controls—the ways of operating them can be quite different, even for the most basic of functions, e.g. switching on and off, stopping, rewinding, or increasing volume. The same holds true for our ever-increasing collection of personal devices, where even the most basic controls on PDAs, MP3s, cell phones, digital cameras, etc., can be inconsistent.

How can we reduce the usability problems that come with device clutter? One approach is convergence. By this is meant designing a single control, hand-held, or PC that does everything. Already we are seeing a new generation of cell phones that has moved towards a model of multifunction convergence; as well as enabling phone calls and texting, cell

phones now offer an increasing number of other functions, including taking and sending pictures, video streaming, live multiplayer games, huge memory storage, and a personal music system. Likewise, several companies have begun developing a single powerful PC targetted for the living room, which combines the functionality of all manner of devices and systems all in one box.

But is it possible to design a usable, all-in-one interface, for controlling a multifunction single device/PC? In particular, can an interface be designed that is easy to understand by users, especially those who are not technology savvy, which enables them to seamlessly and effortlessly switch between quite different activities, such as listening to music, making a call, taking a picture, and watching streaming video? Compromises can result when one device is asked to do the work of many. In particular, the complexity required can often result in a confusing interface. The result can be an overbloated and overspecified device that is impossible to use. In contrast, specialization may be a better solution where the form, factor, look and feel, and features of a single device are designed for a specific task. The major benefit of doing so is that the device is designed to fit the task and person using it.

James Landay (2005), a director of Intel research, however, thinks that just like the GUI desktop interface made it possible for a wide range of users to easily carry out multiple tasks on a PC so, too, will a ubiquitous and easy-to-use interface for multifunction home and personal devices be able to achieve this. What do you think? ■

Assignment

This assignment is intended for you to put into practice what you have read about in this chapter. Specifically, the objective is to enable you to define usability and user experience goals and to transform these and other design principles into specific questions to help evaluate an interactive product.

Find an everyday handheld device, e.g. remote control, digital camera, cell phone and examine how it has been designed, paying particular attention to how the user is meant to interact with it.

(a) From your first impressions, write down what first comes to mind as to what is good and bad about the way the device works.

(b) Give a description of the user experience resulting from interacting with it.

(c) Based on your reading of this chapter and any other material you have come across, compile a set of usability and user experience goals that you think will be most relevant in evaluating the device. Decide which are the most important ones and explain why.

(d) Translate each of your set of usability and user experience goals into two or three specific questions. Then use them to assess how well your device fares.

(e) Repeat (c) and (d) using the design principles outlined in the chapter.
(f) Finally, discuss possible improvements to the interface based on the answers obtained for (d) and (e).

Summary

In this chapter we have looked at what interaction design is and why it is growing in importance. To begin, a number of good and bad designs were presented to illustrate how interaction design can make a difference. We described who and what is involved in interaction design, and the core set of design processes that need to be followed. We explained in detail what usability and user experience are and how they have been characterized, and how to operationalize them in order to assess the quality of a user experience resulting from interacting with an interactive product. The increasing emphasis on designing for the user experience and not just usable products was stressed. A number of core design principles were also introduced that provide guidance for helping inform the interaction design process.

Key points

- Interaction design is concerned with designing interactive products to support the way people communicate and interact in their everyday and working lives.
- Interaction design is multidisciplinary, involving many inputs from wide-ranging disciplines and fields.
- Central to interaction design is determining how to create quality user experiences.
- Optimizing the interaction between users and interactive products requires taking into account a number of interdependent factors, including context of use, types of activity, cultural differences, and user groups.
- Identifying and specifying relevant usability and user experience goals can help lead to the design of good interactive products.
- Design principles, like feedback and simplicity, are useful heuristics for analyzing and evaluating aspects of an interactive product.

Further Reading

Here we recommend a few seminal readings on interaction design and the user experience. A more comprehensive list of useful books, articles, websites, videos, and other material can be found at our website.

COOPER, A. and REIMAN, R. (2003) *About Face 2.0: The essentials of interaction design.* John Wiley. This is a second edition of '*About Face*' and provides an updated overview of what is involved in interaction design, written in a very personable style that appeals to practitioners and students alike. It focuses primarily on designing for desktop platforms but also includes chapters on the web and device platforms.

GARRETT, J.J. (2003) *The Elements of User Experience: User Centered Design for the Web*. Easy Riders. This is a coffee-table introductory book to interaction design that focuses on how to ask the right questions when designing for a user experience. It emphasizes the importance of understanding how products work on the outside, i.e. when a person comes into contact with them and tries to work with them. It also takes into account a business perspective.

GRUDIN, J. (1990) The computer reaches out: the historical continuity of interface design. In *CHI '90 Proceedings*, pp. 261–268. This is an overview of how the interface has developed during the 30 years leading to the 1990s. Although somewhat dated, it is a classic of its time.

LIDWELL, W., HOLDEN, K. and BUTLER, J. (2003) *Universal Principles of Design*. Rockport Publishers, Inc. This book presents over 100 design principles that include consistency, accessibility, and visibility but also some lesser known ones, such as constancy, chunking, and symmetry. They are alphabetically ordered (for easy reference) with a diversity of examples to illustrate how they work and can be used.

NORMAN, D. (1988) *The Design of Everyday Things*. Doubleday (especially Chapter 1). Norman's writing is accessible and enjoyable to read. He writes extensively about the design and usability of everyday objects like doors, faucets, and fridges. These examples provide much food for thought in relation to designing interfaces.

NORMAN, D. (1999) *ACM Interactions Magazine*, May/June, 38–42. Affordances, conventions, and design. This is a short and thought-provoking critique of design principles.

WINOGRAD, T. (1997) From computing machinery to interaction design. In P. Denning and R. Metcalfe (eds) *Beyond Calculation: The Next Fifty Years of Computing*. Springer-Verlag, pp. 149–162. Terry Winograd provides an overview of how interaction design has emerged as a new area, explaining how it does not fit into any existing design or computing fields. He describes the new demands and challenges facing the profession.

INTERVIEW with Gitta Salomon

Gitta Salomon is a consultant interaction designer. She founded Swim Interaction Design Studio (`swimstudio.com`) in 1996 as a consultancy company to assist clients with the design of interactive products. Recently, many of her clients have included start-up companies, developing web-based and other products, who realize the importance of interaction design in ensuring their products are successful but don't know how to do this. Often they get in touch with Swim with partially developed products and ask for help with their interaction design. Swim has consulted for a range of clients, including Apple Computer, Nike, IBM, DoubleClick, Webex, and Gap, Inc.

YR: What is your approach to interaction design?
GS: I've devised my own definition: interaction design is the design of products that reveal themselves over time. Users don't necessarily see all the functionality in interactive products when they first look at them. For example, the first screen you see on a cell phone doesn't show you everything you can do with it. As you use it, additional functionality is revealed to you. Same thing with a web-based application or a Window's application—as you use them you find yourself in different states and suddenly you can do different things. This idea of revealing over time is possible because there is a microprocessor behind the product and usually there is also a dynamic display. I believe this definition characterizes the kind of products we work on—which is a very wide range, not just web products.

YR: How would you say interaction design has changed in the years since you started Swim?
GS: I don't think what we do has changed fundamentally, but the time frame for product development is much shorter. And seemingly more people think they want interaction design assistance. That has definitely changed. There are more people who don't necessarily know what interaction design is, but they are calling us and saying "we need it." All of a sudden there is a great deal of focus and money on all of these products that are virtual and computationally based, which require a different type of design thinking.

YR: So what were the kinds of projects you were working on when you first started Swim?

GS: They were less web-centric. There was more software application design and a few hardware/software type things. Between 2001 and 2004, the focus shifted to almost exclusively web-based applications. However, these are quite similar to software applications—they just have different implementation constraints. More recently, the hardware/software products are starting to pick up again—it does seem that information appliances are going to take off. The nature of the problems we solve hasn't changed much; it's the platform and associated constraints that change.

YR: What would you say are the biggest challenges facing yourself and other consultants doing interaction design these days?

GS: One of the biggest challenges is remembering that half of what we do is the design work and the other half is the communication of that design work. The clients almost never bridge the gap for us: we need to bridge it. We always have to figure out how to deliver the work so it is going to have impact. We are the ones who need to ensure that the client is going to understand the deliverable and know what to do with it. That part of the work is oftentimes the most difficult. It means we've got to figure out what is going on internally with the client and decide how what we deliver will be effective. In some cases you just start seeing there is no place to engage with the client. And I think that is a very difficult problem. Most people right now don't have a product development process. They are just going for it. And we have to figure out how to fit into what is best described as a moving train.

YR: And what do you use when you try to communicate with them? Is it a combination of talking, meetings, and reports?

GS: We do a number of different things. Usually we will give them a written document, such as a report or a critique of their product. Sometimes we will give them interactive prototypes in Director, Flash, or HTML, things that simulate what the product experience would feel like. In the written materials, I often name the things that we all need to be talking about. Then at least we all have a common terminology to discuss things. It is a measure of our success if they start using the words that we gave them, because we truly have influenced their thinking. A lot of times we'll give them a diagram of what their system is like, because nobody has ever visualized it. We serve as the visualizers, taking a random assortment of vaguely defined concepts and giving some shape to them. We'll make an artifact, which allows them to say "Yes, it is like that" or "No, it's not like that, it's like this . . . ." Without something to point to they couldn't even say to each other "No, that is not what I mean" because they didn't know if they were talking about the same thing. Many times we'll use schematic diagrams to represent system behavior. Once they have these diagrams then they can say "Oh no, we need all this other stuff in there, we forgot to tell you." It seems that nobody is writing complete lists of functionality, requirements, specifications, or complete documentation anymore. This means the product ideas stay in somebody's head until we make them tangible through visualization.

YR: So this communication process is just as important as the ideas?
GS: I think it is, a lot of times.

YR: So, how do you start with a client?
GS: For clients who already have something built, I find that usually the best way for us to get started is to begin with the client doing a comprehensive demo of their product for us. We will usually spend a whole day collecting information. Besides the demo, they tell us about their target market, competitors, and a whole range of things. Over a longer period of time, we use the product and observe other people using it to get a much broader picture. Because the client's own vision of their product is so narrow, we have to step back from what they initially tell us.

YR: So do you write notes, and then try and put it together afterwards, or—what?
GS: We use all kinds of things. We use notes and video, and we sit around with tracing paper and marker pens. When reviewing the materials, I often try and bring them together in some sort of thematic way. It's often mind-boggling to bring a software product that's been thrown together into any kind of coherent framework. It's easy to write a shopping list of observations, but we want to assemble a larger structure and framework and that takes time to construct. We need to reflect and stew on what was done and what, maybe, should have been done. We need to highlight the issues and put them into some kind of larger order. If you always operate at a low level of detail, like worrying and critiquing the size of a button, you end up solving only local issues. You never really get to the big interaction design problems of the product, the ones that should be solved first.

YR: If you're given a prototype or product to evaluate and you discover that it is really bad, what do you do?
GS: Well, I almost never have the guts to go in and say something is fundamentally flawed. And that's perhaps not the best strategy anyway, because it's your word against theirs. Instead, I think it is always about making the case for why something is wrong or flawed. Sometimes I think we are like lawyers. We have to assemble the case for what's wrong with the product. We have to make a convincing argument, one that allows the client to get past their biases and grasp where and why things have gone wrong. ■

2

2.1 Introduction

Imagine you have been asked to design an application to let people organize, store, and retrieve their assortment of files, e.g. email, photos, movies, MP3, chats, documents, in a fast, efficient, and enjoyable way. What would you do? How would you start? Would you begin by sketching out how the interface might look, work out how the system architecture should be structured, or simply start coding? Or, would you start by asking users about their current experiences of saving files and look at existing tools, e.g. Google desktop search, and, based on this, begin thinking about why and how you were going to design the application?

Interaction designers would begin by doing the latter. It is important to realize that having a clear understanding of why and how you are going to design something, before writing any code, can save enormous amounts of time, effort, and money later on in the design process. Ill thought out ideas, incompatible and unusable designs can be refined while it is relatively easy and painless to do so. Once ideas are committed to code they become much harder to throw away. Such preliminary thinking through of ideas about the user experience and what kinds of designs might be appropriate is, however, a skill that needs to be learned. It is not something that can be done overnight by following a checklist, but requires practice in learning to identify, understand, and examine the issues—just like learning to write an essay or to program. In this chapter we describe the steps involved. In particular, we focus on what it takes to understand and conceptualize interaction.

The main aims of this chapter are to:

- **Explain what is meant by the problem space.**
- **Explain how to conceptualize interaction.**
- **Describe what a conceptual model is and how to begin to formulate one.**
- **Discuss the pros and cons of using interface metaphors as part of a conceptual model.**
- **Outline the core interaction types for informing the development of a conceptual model.**
- **Introduce theories, models, and frameworks as a way of informing interaction design.**

2

Understanding and conceptualizing interaction

2.2 Understanding the problem space

In the process of creating an interactive product, it can be tempting to begin at the 'nuts and bolts' level of design. By this, we mean working out how to design the physical interface and what technologies and interaction styles to use, e.g. whether to use touchscreen, speech, graphical user interface, sensor interface, etc. A problem with trying to solve a design problem beginning at this level is that usability and user experience goals can be overlooked. For example, consider the problem of providing drivers with better navigation and traffic information. How might you achieve this? One could tackle the problem by thinking straight away about a good technology or a particular kind of interface to use. For example, one might think that augmented reality, where images are superimposed on objects in the real world (see Figure 2.1a), would be appropriate, since it can be useful for integrating additional information with an ongoing activity, e.g. overlaying X-rays on a patient during an operation. In the context of driving, it could be effective for displaying information to drivers who need to find out where they are going and what to do at certain points during their journey. In particular, images of places and directions to follow could be projected inside the car, on the dashboard or rear-view mirror or windshield (see Figure 2.1b). However, there is a problem with this proposal: it is likely to be unsafe. It could easily distract drivers, encouraging them to switch their attention from the road to the images being projected.

While it is certainly necessary at some point to decide how to design the physical aspects, it is better to make these kinds of decisions *after* articulating the nature of the problem space. By this, we mean understanding and conceptualizing what is currently the user experience/product and how this is going to be improved or changed. This requires a design team thinking through how their ideas will support or extend the way people communicate and interact in their everyday activities. In the above example, it involves finding out what is problematic with existing forms of navigating while driving, e.g. trying to read maps while moving the steering wheel or looking at a small navigation display mounted on the dashboard when approaching a roundabout, and how to ensure that drivers can continue to drive safely without being distracted.

As emphasized in Chapter 1, identifying usability and user experience goals is a prerequisite to understanding the problem space. Another important consideration is to make explicit underlying assumptions and claims. By an assumption is meant taking something for granted, e.g. people will want to watch movies on their cell phones. By a claim is meant stating something to be true when it is still open to question, e.g. a multimodal style of interaction for controlling a car navigation system—one that involves speaking while driving—is perfectly safe. Writing down your assumptions and claims and then trying to defend and support them can highlight those that are vague or wanting. In so doing, poorly constructed design ideas can be reformulated. In many projects, this process

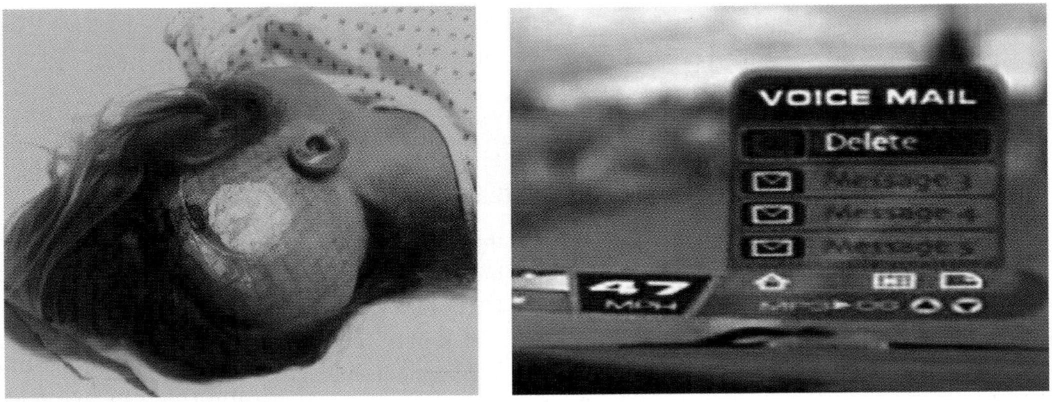

(a) (b)

Figure 2.1 *(a) Overlaying X-rays on a patient during an operation. (b) A screen shot taken from HP's vision of the future, CoolTown. In this hypothetical scenario, digital information about the car's state and the driver's navigation plans is projected onto the windshield. A multimodal voice browsing interface is proposed that allows the driver to control interactions with the vehicle when driving. How safe do you think this would be?*

involves identifying human activities and interactivities that are problematic and working out how they might be improved through being supported with a different set of operations. In others, it can be more speculative, requiring thinking through what to design for an engaging user experience.

The process of articulating the problem space is typically done as a team effort. Invariably, team members will have differing perspectives on the problem space. For example, a project manager is likely to be concerned about a proposed solution in terms of budgets, timelines, and staffing costs, whereas a software engineer will be thinking about breaking it down into specific technical concepts. It is important that the implications of pursuing each perspective are considered in relation to one another. While being time-consuming and sometimes resulting in disagreements among the team, the benefits of this process can far outweigh the associated costs. There is much less chance of incorrect assumptions and unsupported claims creeping into a design solution that turn out to be unusable or unwanted. Furthermore, spending time enumerating and reflecting upon ideas during the early stages of the design process enables more options and possibilities to be considered. Box 2.1 presents a hypothetical scenario of a team working through their assumptions and claims, showing how, in so doing, problems are explicated and explored, leading to a specific avenue of investigation agreed on by the team.

Box 2.1

A hypothetical scenario showing the assumptions and claims (*italicized*) made by different members of a design team and how they are resolved

A large software company has decided it needs to develop an upgrade of its web browser because its marketing team has discovered that many of its customers have switched over to using another browser. They *assume* something is wrong with theirs and that their rivals have a better product. But they don't know what the problem is with theirs. The design team put in charge of this project *assume* they need to improve the usability of a number of the browser's functions. They *claim* that this will win back users by making features of the interface simpler, more attractive, and more flexible to use.

The user experience researchers on the design team conduct an initial user study investigating how people use their company's web browser. They also look at other web browsers on the market and compare their functionality and usability. They observe and talk to many different users. They discover several things about the usability of their web browser, some of which they were not expecting. One revelation is that many of their customers have never actually used the bookmarking feature. They present their findings to the rest of the team and have a long discussion about why each of them thinks the bookmarking function is not being used. One member points out that the web browser's function for organizing URLs requires dragging individual URLs into a hierarchical folder. She *claims* that this is very time-consuming, fiddly, and error-prone, and *assumes* this is the reason why many users do not use it. Another member backs her up, saying how awkward it is to use this method when wanting to move large numbers of URLs between folders. One of the user experience engineers agrees, noting how several of the users he talked to mentioned how difficult they found it when trying to move a number of web addresses between folders and how they often ended up accidentally putting URLs into the wrong folders.

A software engineer reflects on what has been said, and makes the *claim* that the bookmark function is no longer needed since he *assumes* that most people do what he does, which is to revisit a website by scanning through their history list of previously visited sites. Another member of the team disagrees with him, *claiming* that many users do not like to leave a trail of all the sites they have ever visited for anyone else to see and would prefer to be able to save only URLs they want to revisit. The bookmark function provides them with this option.

After much discussion on the pros and cons of bookmarking versus history lists, the team decides to investigate further how to support effectively the saving, ordering, and retrieving of web pages in a web browser. All agree that the format of the existing web browser's hierarchical structure is too rigid and that one of their priorities is to see how they can create a simpler set of operations. ■

Consider another actual example. Smartphones (also called 3G handsets in Europe) came into being in 2002, with Orange's SPV (stands for Sound, Pictures, Video) being the first on the market. There was much hype about the amazing set of features they were offering, including full color web browsing, streaming video, predictive text, playing music in MP3 format, and multiplayer video games. An assumption that many of the phone companies made in developing the new generation of phone services was that customers would want to use their cell phone to make video calls, download songs and movies, watch sports highlights, browse the web, etc.—all while on the move. To what extent do you think this assumption is correct?

The problem space identified by the cell phone companies was very open-ended. Unlike the hypothetical scenario presented in Box 2.1 for the web browser, there was no specific problem that needed to be addressed. Alternatively, the phone companies sought to provide a whole suite of new functions that would create a quite different user experience from what was offered by the previous generation of cell phones. A *claim* made by the companies was that people would be prepared to pay a higher premium for this more extensive range of services. An *assumption* was that users would be happy doing all the things they can currently do on a PC, but using a much smaller handheld device, because they can do them while on the move. A further *claim* was that the Smartphone would become the next must-have fashion item that many users would want to own.

For one user group, known in the advertising business as YAFs (Young Active Fun), these assumptions and claims are proving to be true. Many young people enjoy playing multiplayer games on their cell phones, taking and sending pictures, downloading and listening to music, etc., and showing off their phones to one another. For example, in India, 'gaming on the move' has become one of the fastest-growing cell phone activities among the tech-savvy young. Analysts have predicted that over 220 million people in India will be playing games on their cell phones by 2009 (BBC Worldnews, 2004). For other user groups, however, such claims and assumptions are proving incorrect. A large number of users have discovered that carrying out multimedia-based activities using a cell phone is too expensive, too cumbersome, or too impoverished compared with what they can do when using much faster PCs and much larger and higher-resolution displays. In another survey conducted by Continental Research, 36% of British phone users having multimedia capabilities were found to have never sent a multimedia message.

As well as the reasons stated above it was discovered that many phone users simply did not know how to use the array of functions and shied away from learning how (Ward, 2004).

Explicating people's assumptions and claims about why they think something might be a good idea (or not) enables the design team as a whole to view multiple perspectives on the problem space and in so doing reveal conflicting and problematic ones. The following framework is intended to provide a set of core questions to aid design teams in this process:

- Are there problems with an existing product or user experience? If so, what are they?
- Why do you think there are problems?
- How do you think your proposed design ideas might overcome these?
- If you have not identified any problems and instead are designing for a new user experience how do you think your proposed design ideas support, change, or extend current ways of doing things?

Activity 2.1

Use the framework to explicate the main assumptions and claims behind the design of an online photo sharing and management application.

Comment

The sharing of digital images on the web, so that potentially anyone can view them and add comments, is a new experience that is capitalizing on the hugely successful phenomenon of blogging. While there were already a number of applications available on the web that enabled people to place their photo collections on a shared server, they have been primarily designed as personal spaces for individuals, family, and friends. In contrast, Flickr was one of the first blog-based photo-sharing services. An assumption was that just as people like to blog, i.e. share their experiences via text-based entries on the web and invite comments from anyone in the world, so too would people want to share with the rest of the world their photo collections and get comments back on them. In this way the company was extending the user experience of blogging into the realm of image sharing. A claim from Flickr's website (2005) was that it "is almost certainly the best online photo management and sharing application in the world" because it provides many easy-to-use functions for uploading, storing, classifying, and viewing people's photos. One innovative function that was designed was the ability to tag/annotate parts of a photo, e.g. someone in a crowd, with personal commentary, e.g. "that's me".

2.3 Conceptualizing the design space

Having a good understanding of the problem space greatly helps design teams progress to the next phase of the design process, which is to *conceptualize* the design space. Primarily this involves describing what the system is going to be to the users, through developing a *conceptual model*—we explain how to do this in the next section. The design space can also be conceptualized in other ways, including exploring the nature of the interaction that underlies user activities (see Section 2.3.4) and through the lenses of different theories, models, and frameworks (see Section 2.4). A benefit of conceptualizing the design space using one or more of these is that it can inform and systematically structure a design solution.

2.3.1 Conceptual models

> ***A conceptual model is a high-level description of how a system is organized and operates.* (Johnson and Henderson, 2002, p. 26)**

Many people have difficulty understanding what a conceptual model is, and yet it is one of the most fundamental parts of interaction design, as noted by David Liddle (1996), a renowned interaction designer:

> ***The most important thing to design is the user's conceptual model. Everything else should be subordinated to making that model clear, obvious, and substantial. That is almost exactly the opposite of how most software is designed.* (Liddle, 1996, p. 17)**

So what exactly is a conceptual model? How do design teams develop one and how do they know when they have a good one? Here, we begin to address these questions by drawing on Johnson and Henderson's (2002) account of conceptual models.

They define a conceptual model as an abstraction that outlines what people can do with a product and what concepts are needed to understand how to interact with it. It is important to stress that it is *not* a description of the user interface but a structure outlining the concepts and the relationships between them that will form the basis of the product or system. In so doing, it enables "designers to straighten out their thinking before they start laying out their widgets" (p. 28). In a nutshell, a conceptual model provides a working strategy; a framework of general concepts and their interrelations. Johnson and Henderson (2002) propose that a conceptual model should comprise the following components:

- The major metaphors and analogies that are used to convey to the user how to understand what a product is for and how to use it for an activity.
- The concepts that users are exposed to through the product, including the task–domain objects they create and manipulate, their attributes, and the operations that can be performed on them.

- The relationships between those concepts, e.g. whether one object contains another, the relative importance of actions to others, and whether an object is part of another.
- The mappings between the concepts and the user experience the product is designed to support or invoke.

How the various metaphors, concepts, and their relationships are organized determines how the users will subsequently think of a product and the operations they can carry out on it. To show how each of the components can be operationalized for a specific design problem, we revisit our hypothetical scenario of the design team responsible for upgrading the company's web browser. We outline below an initial description of part of the conceptual model for the upgrade (*Note*: It would need to include more components for describing all of the functions of a web browser).

(i) The major metaphors and analogies

The main metaphor is browsing, the idea of following links in a page through exploring what is there. It draws on the analogy of window shopping (Glossary, 2005). Another metaphor is bookmarking. Web pages are ordered as a chronological list of sites visited over time and labeled as bookmarks that are selected by the reader, similar to the way bits of card, post-its, etc. are used to mark a place to return to in a physical book.

(ii) The concepts

These include web pages (URLs), dynamic and static web pages, links, lists, folders of URLs, obsolete URLs, saving a URL, revisiting a URL, organizing saved URLs, updating URLs, sending a URL, listing saved URLs, deleting saved URLs, reorganizing URLs.

(iii) The relationships between concepts

These include one object contains another, e.g. a folder contains a collection of related URLs, the relative importance of actions to others, e.g. the ability to add a URL to a list of saved websites the browser is currently pointing to is more important than the ability to move the position of saved URLs around the list, and an object is a specialization of another, e.g. a dynamic web page is a special kind of web page.

(iv) The mappings

A saved URL corresponds to a web page on the Internet. When the user clicks on the URL, their web browser points to the web page and it appears on their screen.

By exploring the relationships between the various components of the conceptual model, the design team can debate the merits of providing different methods and how they support the main concepts, e.g. saving, revisiting, categorizing, reorganizing, and their mapping to the task domain. They can also begin discussing whether a new metaphor may be preferable that combines the activities of browsing and searching. In turn, this can lead the design team to articulate the importance of containership as a relationship. For example, what is the best way to sort and revisit saved objects and how many and what types of containers, e.g. folders, bars, are most fitting for the task domain? The same enumeration of concepts can be repeated for other functions of the web browser—both current and new. In so doing, the design team can begin to systematically work out what will be the most simple, effective, and memorable way of supporting users while browsing the Internet.

Developing a conceptual model can at first seem daunting, especially for those not trained or versed in thinking at an abstract level. It can be much easier to talk about a design idea in concrete terms, such as deciding upon the look and feel of a proposed system, the layout of menu options and other graphical elements, and where information will appear on a screen. But as stressed throughout this chapter, these types of decisions should not be made until the foundations of the system have been worked out—just as architects and interior designers would not think about which color curtains to have before they have decided upon where the windows will be placed in a plan for a new building.

The benefits of conceptualizing a design in general terms early on in the design process encourages design teams:

- To orient themselves towards asking specific kinds of questions about how the conceptual model will be understood by the targeted users.
- Not to become narrowly focused early on.
- To establish a set of common terms they all understand and agree upon, reducing the chance of misunderstandings and confusion arising later on.

Once formulated and agreed upon, a conceptual model becomes a shared blueprint. This can be represented as a textual description and/or in a diagrammatic form, depending on the preferred *linga franca* used by the design team. As you will see later in Chapter 11, the conceptual model is used by the design team as the basis from which to develop more detailed and concrete aspects of the design.

In the next section we describe two interactive products that have become classics in their time. Both were based on very clear and simple conceptual models. It is important to note that they were developed before Johnson and Henderson's (2002) framework was published, but that there are similarities between the way they have been characterized in the literature. In particular, they both emphasize the use of analogy with the physical world and identify core concepts that made them successful products (Winograd, 1996; Smith *et al.*, 1982). Where they differ is in emphasizing the extra value of taking a physical artifact and making it into an interactive digital entity.

2.3.2 Examples of best practice

The spreadsheet—VisiCalc (Bricklin and Frankston)

An example of a good conceptual model that has stood the test of time is that which underlies the ubiquitous spreadsheet, originally conceived by Dan Bricklin and Bob Frankston and implemented as a software tool called VisiCalc (`www.bricklin.com`). The main reason why this conceptual model has been so successful is that it was simple, clear, and obvious to the users how to use the application and what it could do for them. As Frankston notes, somewhat modestly, in an email to a colleague: "it is just a tool to allow others to work out their ideas and reduce the tedium of repeating the same calculations."

Bricklin and Frankston understood the kind of tool that would be useful to both professionals, e.g. accountants, and lay persons. They also emphasized the need to design it to be intuitive and, importantly, leverage off existing practice. They worked out a set of concepts that were operationalized in terms of the task domain in a way that substantially extended the range of computations accountants could do. These were developed into very effective, usable, and powerful operations.

The conceptual model was based on an analogy of the paper-based ledger sheet that was used in accounting practice at the time (Winograd, 1996). Bricklin and Frankston also conceptualized problematic aspects of the task domain that could substantially be improved upon through using a computer-based tool. For example, they observed that a core financial activity is forecasting. This requires projecting financial results based on assumptions about a company, such as projected and actual sales, investments, infrastructure, and costs. The amount of profit or loss is calculated for different projections. A company may want to determine how much loss it will incur before it achieves break-even, based on different amounts of investment, for different periods of time. Financial analysts need to see a spread of projections for different time periods. Doing this kind of multiple projecting by hand requires much effort and is subject to human error. Using a calculator can reduce the computational load of doing numerous sums but there is still much key pressing and writing down of partial results to be done—again making the process protracted and prone to errors.

Bricklin and Frankston exploited the interactivity provided by microcomputers and developed an application that was capable of *interactive* financial modeling. Key goals of their conceptual model were: (i) to create a spreadsheet that was *analogous* to a ledger sheet in the way it looked, with columns and rows, that allowed people to capitalize on their familiarity with how to use this kind of representation; (ii) to make the spreadsheet interactive, by allowing the user to input and change data in any of the cells in the columns or rows; and (iii) to have the computer perform a range of different calculations and recalculations in response to user input. For example, the last column could be programmed to display the sum of all the cells in the columns preceding it. With the computer doing all the calculations, together with an easy-to-learn-and-use

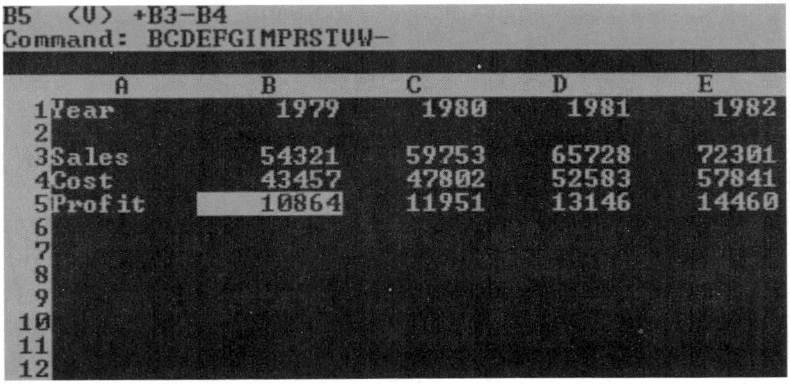
B5 (V) +B3-B4
Command: BCDEFGIMPRSTVW-
A B C D E
1 Year 1979 1980 1981 1982
2
3 Sales 54321 59753 65728 72301
4 Cost 43457 47802 52583 57841
5 Profit 10864 11951 13146 14460
6
7
8
9
10
11
12

Figure 2.2 *A screenshot of the original VisiCalc interface. At the top left-hand corner is where the user typed in operations to be performed (in this case subtracting row 4 from row 3 to work out the profit). The main area has columns labeled A, B, C, etc. across the top and rows 1, 2, 3, etc. down the side. The cursor highlights a cell which displays the calculated results*

interface, users were provided with an *easy-to-understand* tool, based on a simple conceptual model (see Figure 2.2). Moreover, it gave them a new way of effortlessly working out any number of forecasts—*greatly extending* what they could do before with existing technology.

The simplicity of this conceptual model is clear and it is not surprising that it received much critical acclaim. For various business reasons, however, VisiCalc did not become a successful commercial product. But many of the basic concepts and the metaphor that were inherent in its conceptual model became widely adopted by other software companies. Most notable, as acknowledged by Bricklin and Frankston on their website, is Microsoft's Excel 97 spreadsheet which has many similarities to VisiCalc—even 18 years after its inception (see Figure 2.3).

The Star interface (based on Miller and Johnson, 1996 and Smith et al., 1982)

Another classic of its time was the 8010 'Star' system, developed by Xerox in 1981, that revolutionized the way interfaces were designed for personal computing. Like VisiCalc, it received great acclaim but was not commercially successful, and lo and behold many aspects of its conceptual model were borrowed and adapted by other companies, such as Apple and Microsoft, that later appeared in their very successful Mac and Windows products.

Star was designed as an office system, targeted at workers not interested in computing *per se*. An important consideration was to make the computer as 'invisible' to the users

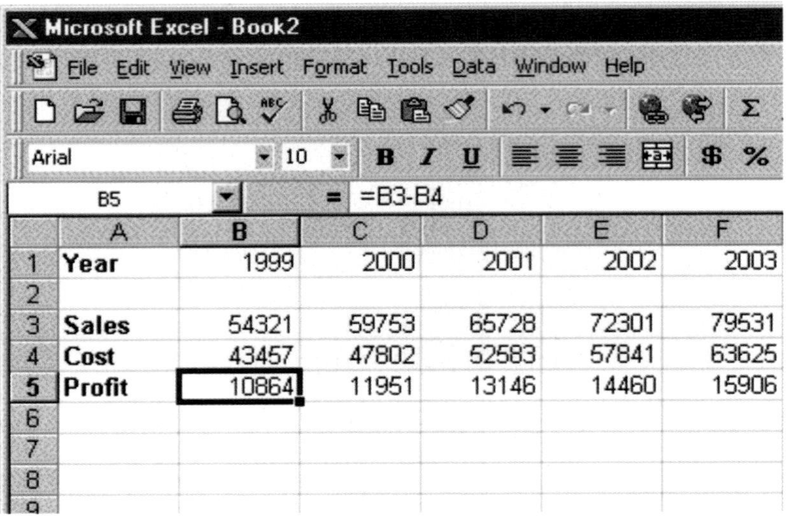

Figure 2.3 *A screenshot of Microsoft's 97 Excel spreadsheet. Note the way the columns and rows are organized and the space at the top for typing in operations are the same as they were in VisiCalc*

as possible and to design applications that were suitable for them. The Star developers spent several person-years at the beginning of the project working out an appropriate conceptual model for such an office system. In the end they selected a conceptual model based on an analogy to a physical office. They wanted office workers to imagine the computer to be like an office environment, by acting on electronic counterparts of physical objects in the real world. Their assumption was that this would simplify and clarify the electronic world, making it seem more familiar, less alien, and easier to learn (see Figure 2.4).

The Star was based on a conceptual model that included the familiar knowledge of an office. Paper, folders, filing cabinets, and mailboxes were represented as icons on the screen and were designed to possess some of the properties of their physical counterparts. Dragging a document icon across the desktop screen was seen as equivalent to picking up a piece of paper in the physical world and moving it (but this of course is a very different action). Similarly, dragging an electronic document onto an electronic folder was seen as being analogous to placing a physical document into a physical cabinet. In addition, new concepts that were incorporated as part of the desktop metaphor were operations that could not be performed in the physical world. For example, electronic files could be placed onto an icon of a printer on the desktop, resulting in the computer printing them out.

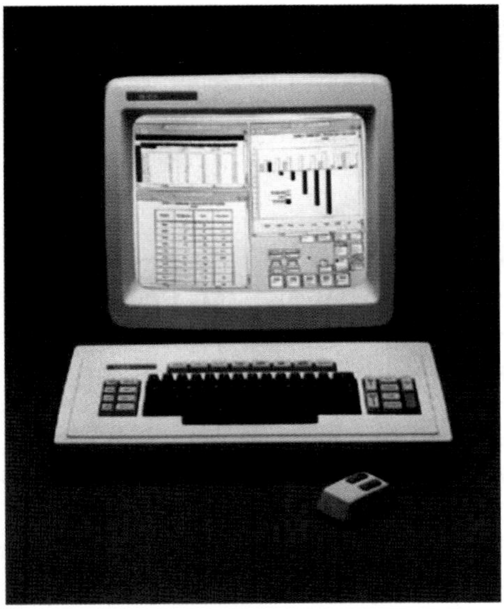

(a)

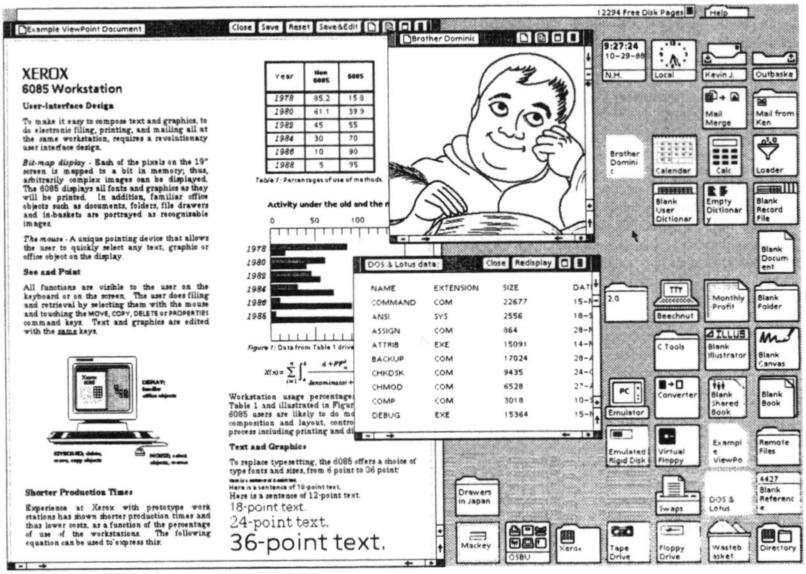

(b)

Figure 2.4 *(a) The Xerox Star computer and (b) GUI interface*

Dilemma

Over-specified applications: a question of more choice or more confusion?

The best conceptual models are those that appear simple and clear to their users and are task-oriented. However, all too often applications can end up being based on overly complex conceptual models, especially if they are the result of a series of upgrades, where more and more functions and ways of doing something are added to the original conceptual model. Whereas in the first version of the software there may have been one way of doing something, later versions are often designed to allow several ways of performing the same operation. For example, some operating and wordprocessing systems now make it possible for the user to carry out the same activity in a number of different ways, e.g. to delete a file the user can issue a command like CtrlD, speak to the computer by saying "delete file," or drag an icon of the file to the recycle bin. Users have to learn each of the different styles to decide which they prefer. Many users prefer to stick to the methods they have always used and trusted and, not surprisingly, become annoyed when they find a simple way of doing something has been changed, albeit more flexibly, now allowing them to do it in three or more different ways. Is providing multiple ways of carrying out the same operation desirable? What do you think? ■

2.3.3 Interface metaphors and analogies

An interface metaphor is considered to be a central component of a conceptual model. It provides a structure that is similar in some way to *aspects* of a familiar entity (or entities) but that also has its own behaviors and properties. Consider the term search engine. It has been designed to invite comparison with a common object—a mechanical engine with several parts working—together with an everyday action—searching by looking through numerous files in many different places to extract relevant information. The functions supported by a search engine also include other features besides those belonging to an engine that searches, such as listing and prioritizing the results of a search. It also does these actions in quite different ways from how a mechanical engine works or how a human being might search a library for books on a given topic. The similarities implied by the use of the term 'search engine,' therefore, are at a general level. They are meant to conjure up the essence of the process of finding relevant information, enabling the user to link these to less familiar aspects of the functionality provided.

Box 2.2
Why are metaphors so popular?

People frequently use metaphors and analogies (here we use the terms interchangeably) as a source of inspiration to understand and explain to others what they are doing or trying to do, in terms that are familiar to them. They are an integral part of human language (Lakoff and Johnson, 1980). Metaphors are commonly used to explain something that is unfamiliar or hard to grasp by way of comparison with something that is familiar and easy to grasp. For example, they are commonly employed in education, where teachers use them to introduce something new to students by comparing the new material with something they already understand. An example is the comparison of human evolution with a game. We are all familiar with the properties of a game: there are rules, each player has a goal to win (or lose), there are heuristics to deal with situations where there are no rules, there is the propensity to cheat when the other players are not looking, and so on. By conjuring up these properties, the analogy helps us begin to understand the more difficult concept of evolution—how it happens, what rules govern it, who cheats, and so on.

It is not surprising, therefore, to see how widely metaphors and analogies have been applied in interaction design. Both have been used, in overlapping ways, to conceptualize abstract, hard to imagine, and difficult to articulate computer-based concepts and interactions in more concrete and familiar terms and as graphical visualizations at the interface. This use includes:

- As a way of conceptualizing a particular interaction style, e.g. using the system as a tool.
- As part of the conceptual model instantiated at the interface, e.g. the desktop metaphor.
- As a way of describing computers, e.g. the Internet highway.
- As names for describing specific operations, e.g. 'cut' and 'paste' commands for deleting and copying objects (analogy taken from the media industry).
- As part of the training material aimed at helping learning, e.g. comparing a wordprocessor with a typewriter.

In many instances, it is hard *not* to use metaphorical terms, as they have become so ingrained in the language we use to express ourselves. This is increasingly the case when talking about computers. Just ask yourself or someone else to describe how the Internet works. Then try doing it without using a single metaphor. ■

Activity 2.2

Interface metaphors are often composites, i.e. they combine quite different pieces of familiar knowledge with the system functionality. We already mentioned the search engine as one such example. Can you think of any others?

Comment

Some other examples include:

Scrollbar—combines the concept of a scroll with a bar, as in bar chart.

Toolbar—combines the idea of a set of tools with a bar.

Web Portal—a gateway to a particular collection of pages of networked information.

Benefits of interface metaphors

Interface metaphors have proven to be highly successful, providing users with a familiar orienting device and helping them understand and learn how to use a system. People find it easier to learn and talk about what they are doing at the computer interface in terms familiar to them—whether they are computer-phobic or highly experienced programmers. Metaphorically-based commands used in Unix, like 'lint' and 'pipe,' have very concrete meanings in everyday language that, when used in the context of the Unix operating system, metaphorically represent some aspect of the operations they refer to. Although their meaning may appear obscure, especially to the novice, they make sense when understood in the context of programming. For example, Unix allows the programmer to send the output of one program to another by using the pipe | symbol. Once explained, it is easy to imagine the output from one container going to another via a pipe.

Activity 2.3

Suggest two computing metaphors that have become common parlance whose original source of reference is (or always was) obscure?

Comment

Two are:

Java—The programming language Java originally was called Oak, but that name had already been taken. It is not clear how the developers moved from Oak to Java. Java is a name commonly associated with coffee. Other Java-based metaphors that have been spawned include Java beans

(a reusable software component) and the steaming coffee-cup logo.

Bluetooth—Bluetooth is used in a computing context to describe the wireless technology that is able to unite technology, communication, and consumer electronics. The name is taken from King Harald Blue Tooth, who was a 10th century legendary Viking king responsible for uniting Scandinavia and thus getting people to talk to each other.

Opposition to using interface metaphors

A mistake sometimes made by designers is to try to design an interface metaphor to look and behave literally like the physical entity it is being compared with. This misses the point about the benefit of developing interface metaphors. As stressed earlier, they are meant to be used to map familiar to unfamiliar knowledge, enabling users to understand and learn about the new domain. Designing interface metaphors only as literal models of the thing being compared with has understandably led to heavy criticism. One of the most outspoken critics is Ted Nelson (1990), who considers metaphorical interfaces as "using old half-ideas as crutches" (p. 237). Other objections to the use of metaphors in interaction design include:

Breaks the rules. Several commentators have criticized the use of interface metaphors because of the cultural and logical contradictions involved in accommodating the metaphor when instantiated as a GUI. A pet hate is the recycle bin (trashcan) that used to sit on the desktop. Logically and culturally (i.e. in the real world), it should be placed under the desk. If this same rule was followed in the virtual desktop, users would not be able to see the bin because it would be occluded by the desktop surface. A counter-argument to this objection is that it does not matter whether rules are contravened. Once people understand why the bin is on the desktop, they readily accept that the real-world rule had to be broken. Moreover, the unexpected juxtaposition of the bin on the desktop can draw to the user's attention the additional functionality that it provides. The trashcan now appears in the toolbar of the Mac operating systems—but the same logic applies—is a trashcan a tool? Moreover, does it matter?

Too constraining. Another argument against interface metaphors is that they are too constraining, restricting the kinds of computational tasks that would be useful at the interface. An example is trying to open a file that is embedded in several hundreds of files in a directory. Having to scan through hundreds of icons on a desktop or scroll through a list of files seems a very inefficient way of doing this. A better way is to allow users to instruct the computer to open the desired file by typing in its name (assuming they can remember the name of the file).

Conflicts with design principles. By trying to design the interface metaphor to fit in with the constraints of the physical world, designers are forced into making bad design solutions that conflict with basic design principles. Ted Nelson used the trashcan as an example of such violation: "a hideous failure of consistency is the garbage can on the Macintosh, which means either 'destroy this' or 'eject it for safekeeping'' ' (Nelson, 1990). The trashcan has now been designed to transform into an abstract 'eject' icon on the Mac when an icon of an external drive, disk, or memory stick is selected from the desktop and moved towards it, thereby reducing the ambiguity associated with the original metaphor.

Not being able to understand the system functionality beyond the metaphor. It has been argued that users may get fixed in their understanding of the system based on the interface metaphor. In so doing, they may find it difficult to see what else can be done with the system beyond the actions suggested by the interface metaphor. Nelson (1990) also argues that the similarity of interface metaphors to any real objects in the world is so tenuous that it hinders more than it helps. We would argue the opposite: because the link is tenuous and there are only a certain number of similarities, it enables the user to see both the dissimilarities and how the metaphor has been extended.

Overly literal translation of existing bad designs. Sometimes designers fall into the trap of trying to create a virtual object to resemble a familiar physical object that is itself badly designed. A well-known example is the virtual calculator, which is designed to look and behave like a physical calculator. The interface of many physical calculators, however, has been poorly designed in the first place, based on poor conceptual models, with excessive use of modes, poor labeling of functions, and difficult-to-manipulate key sequences (Mullet and Sano, 1995). The design of the calculator in Figure 2.5(a) has even gone as far as replicating functions needing shift keys, e.g. deg, oct, and hex, which could have been redesigned as dedicated software buttons. Trying to use a virtual calculator that has been designed to emulate a poorly designed physical calculator is much harder than using the physical device itself. A better approach would have been for the designers to think about how to use the computational power of the computer to support the kinds of tasks people need to do when performing calculations (cf. the spreadsheet design). The calculator in Figure 2.5(b) has been designed to do this to some extent, by moving the buttons closer to each other (minimizing the amount of mousing) and providing flexible display modes with one-to-one mappings with different functions.

Limits the designer's imagination in conjuring up new paradigms and models. Designers may fixate on 'tired' ideas, based on well-known technologies, that they know people are very familiar with. Nelson points out that one of the dangers of always looking backwards is that it prevents the designer from thinking of new functionality to provide. For example, Gentner and Nielsen (1996) discuss how they used a book metaphor for designing the user interface to Sun Microsystems' online documentation. In hindsight they realized how it had blinkered them in organizing the online material, preventing them from introducing desirable functions such as the ability to reorder chapters according to their relevance scores after being searched.

Clearly, there are pitfalls in using interface metaphors in interaction design. Indeed, this approach has led to some badly designed conceptual models, that have resulted in confusion and frustration. However, this does not have to be the case. Provided designers are aware of the

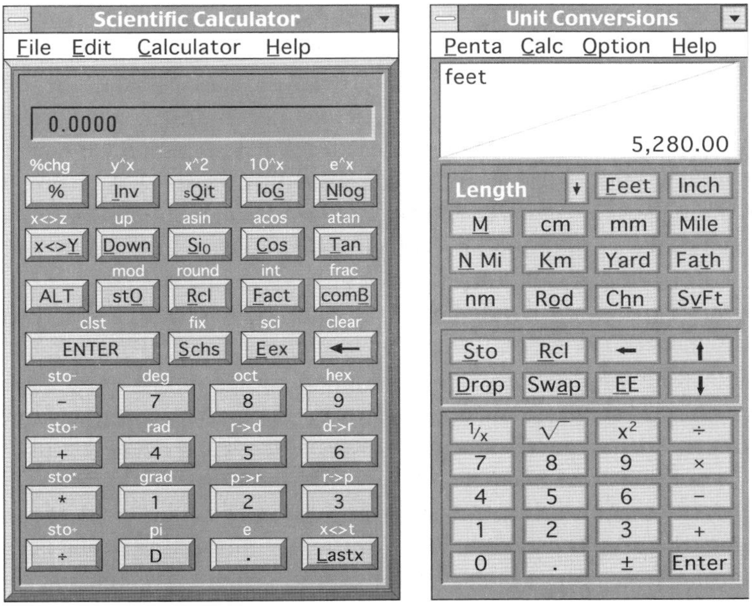

(a) (b)

Figure 2.5 *Two virtual calculators where (a) has been designed too literally and (b) more appropriately for a computer screen*

dangers and try to develop interface metaphors that effectively combine familiar knowledge with new functionality in a meaningful way, then many of the above problems can be avoided.

Activity 2.4

Examine a web browser you use and describe the metaphors that have been incorporated into its design.

Comment

Many aspects of a web browser are based on metaphors, including:

- **a range of toolbars, such as a button bar, navigation bar, favorite bar, history bar**
- **tabs, menus, organizers**
- **search engines, guides**
- **bookmarks, favorites**
- **icons for familiar objects like stop lights, home.**

2.3.4 Interaction types

Another way of conceptualizing the design space is in terms of the user's interactions with a system or product. This can help designers formulate a conceptual model by determining what kinds of interaction to use, and why, before committing to a particular interface. There are a number of possible interfaces available for designers to implement, including speech-based, GUI, multimedia, tangible, and wearables. Note that we are distinguishing here between interface types, which will be discussed in Chapter 6, and interaction types, which we discuss in this section. While cost and other product constraints will often dictate which of these can be used for a given application, considering the interaction type that will best support a user experience can highlight the trade-offs, dilemmas, and pros and cons of using a particular interface type.

Consider the following problem description: a company has been asked to design a computer-based system that will encourage autistic children to communicate and express themselves better. What type of interaction would be appropriate to use at the interface for this particular user group? It is known that autistic children find it difficult to express what they are feeling or thinking through talking and are more expressive when using their bodies and limbs. Clearly an interaction style based on talking would not be effective but one that involves the children interacting with a system by moving in a physical and/or digital space would seem a more promising starting point.

We suggest four fundamental types of interaction someone can have with a product/system. These are not meant to be mutually exclusive, e.g. someone can interact with a system based on different kinds of activities, nor are they meant to be definitive. They are:

1. *Instructing*—where users issue instructions to a system. This can be done in a number of ways, including: typing in commands, selecting options from menus in a windows environment or on a touch screen, speaking aloud commands, pressing buttons, or using a combination of function keys.
2. *Conversing*—where users have a dialog with a system. Users can speak via an interface or type in questions to which the system replies via text or speech output.
3. *Manipulating*—where users interact with objects in a virtual or physical space by manipulating them, e.g. opening, holding, closing, placing. Users can hone in on their familiar knowledge of how to interact with objects.
4. *Exploring*—where users move through a virtual environment or a physical space. Virtual environments include 3D worlds and virtual reality systems. They enable users to hone in on their familiar knowledge of physically moving around. Physical spaces that use sensor-based technologies include smart rooms and ambient environments, also enabling people to capitalize on familiarity.

Instructing

This type of interaction describes how users carry out their tasks by telling the system what to do. Examples include giving instructions to a system to perform operations such as tell the time, print a file, and remind the user of an appointment. A diverse range of products has been designed based on this model, including VCRs, hi-fi systems, alarm clocks, and computers. The way in which the user issues instructions can vary from pressing buttons to typing in strings of characters. Many activities are readily supported by giving instructions.

Operating systems like Unix and Linux have been designed primarily as command-based systems, where users issue instructions at the prompt as a command or set of commands. In Windows and other GUI-based systems, control keys or the selection of menu options via a mouse are used. Typically, a wide range of functions are provided from which users have to select when they want to do something to the object on which they are working. For example, a user writing a report using a wordprocessor will want to format the document, count the number of words typed, and check the spelling. The user instructs the system to do these operations by issuing appropriate commands. Typically, commands are carried out in a sequence, with the system responding appropriately (or not) as instructed.

One of the main benefits of designing an interaction based on issuing instructions is that the interaction is quick and efficient. It is particularly fitting where there is a need to frequently repeat actions performed on multiple objects. Examples include the repetitive actions of saving, deleting, and organizing files.

Activity 2.5

There are many different kinds of vending machines in the world. Each offers a range of goods, requiring the user initially to part with some money. Figure 2.6 shows photos of two different vending machines, one that provides soft drinks and the other a range of snacks. Both use an instructional mode of interaction. However, the way they do so is quite different.

What instructions must be issued to obtain a can of coke from the first machine and a bar of chocolate from the second? Why has it been necessary to design a more complex mode of interaction for the second vending machine? What problems can arise with this mode of interaction?

Comment

The first vending machine has been designed using simple instructions. There are a small number of drinks to choose from and each is represented by a large button displaying the label of each drink. The user simply has to press one button and this should have the effect of returning the selected drink. The second

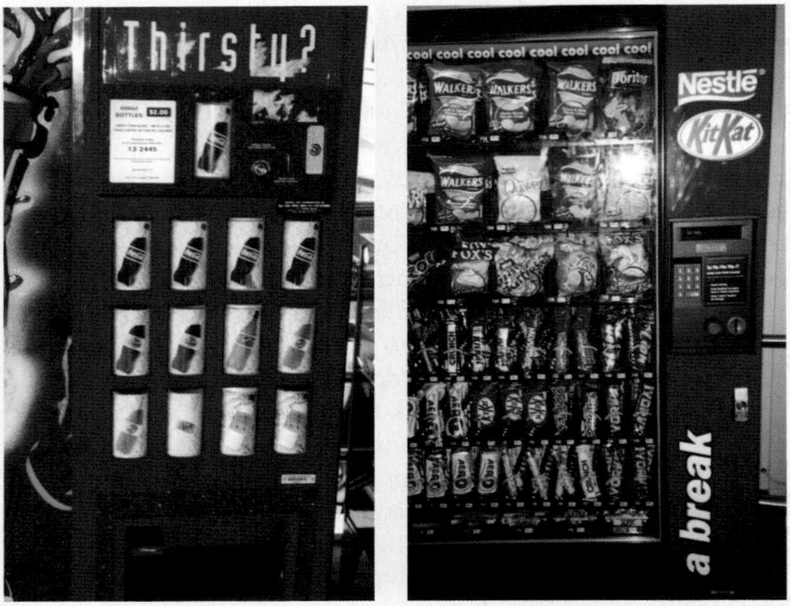

Figure 2.6 *Two different types of vending machine*

machine is more complex, offering a wider range of snacks. The trade-off for providing more choices, however, is that the user can no longer instruct the machine by using a simple one-press action but is required to use a more complex process, involving: (i) reading off the code, e.g. C12, under the item chosen; then (ii) keying this into the number pad adjacent to the displayed items; and (iii) checking the price of the selected option and ensuring that the amount of money inserted is the same or greater (depending on whether or not the machine provides change). Problems that can arise from this type of interaction are the customer misreading the code and/or miskeying in the code, resulting in the machine not issuing the snack or providing the wrong item.

A better way of designing an interface for a large number of choices of variable cost might be to continue to use direct mapping, but use buttons that show miniature versions of the snacks placed in a large matrix (rather than showing actual versions). This would use the available space at the front of the vending machine more economically. The customer would need only to press the button of the object chosen and put in the correct amount of money. There is less chance of error resulting from pressing the wrong code or keys. The trade-off for the vending company, however, is that the machine is less flexible in terms of which snacks it can sell. If a new product line comes out they will also need to replace part of the physical interface to the machine—which would be costly.

Activity 2.6

Another ubiquitous vending machine is the ticket machine. Typically, a number of instructions have to be given in a sequence when using one of these. Consider ticket machines designed to issue train tickets at railway stations—how often have you (or the person in front of you) struggled to work out how to purchase a ticket and made a mistake? How many instructions have to be given? What order are they given in? Is it logical or arbitrary? Could the interaction have been designed any differently to make it more obvious to people how to issue instructions to the machine to get the desired train ticket?

Comment

Ticketing machines vary enormously from country to country and from application to application. They are often not standardized. Therefore, a person's knowledge of the Eurostar ticketing machine in London will not be useful when buying a ticket for the Sydney Monorail or cinema tickets for the Odeon. Sometimes the interaction has been designed where the user has to specify the type of ticket first, e.g. adult, child, the kind of ticket, e.g. single, return, special saver, then the destination, and finally to insert their money. Others require that the user insert a credit card first, before selecting the destination and the type of ticket.

Conversing

This form of interaction is based on the idea of a person having a conversation with a system, where the system acts as a dialog partner. In particular, the system is designed to respond in a way another human being might when having a conversation. It differs from the activity of instructing insofar as it encompasses a two-way communication process with the system acting like a partner rather than a machine that obeys orders. It has been most commonly used for applications where the user needs to find out specific kinds of information or wants to discuss issues. Examples include advisory systems, help facilities, and search engines.

The kinds of conversation that are currently supported range from simple voice-recognition, menu-driven systems that are interacted with via phones to more complex natural language-based systems that involve the system parsing and responding to queries typed in by the user. Examples of the former include banking, ticket booking, and train-time inquiries, where the user talks to the system in single-word phrases and numbers e.g. yes, no, three, in response to prompts from the system. Examples of the latter include search engines and help systems, where the user types in a specific query e.g. "how do I change the margin widths?", to which the system responds by giving various answers.

A main benefit of developing a conceptual model that uses a conversational style of interaction is that it allows people, especially novices, to interact with a system in a way that is familiar to them. For example, the search engine 'Ask Jeeves for Kids!' allows children to ask a question in a way they would when asking their teachers or parents—rather than making them reformulate their question in terms of keywords and Boolean logic. Similarly, the generation of virtual representatives that have been incorporated into online store websites offer customers quick and direct answers to their product-related queries. An example is Anna, whose appearance was commented upon in the last chapter. She is a semi-cartoon character fronting the Swedish furniture store Ikea's Help center (`www.ikea.com`) by directing the user to a part of the store's website in response to his or her questions typed in at the dialog box (see Figure 2.7). For example, when a user types in "do you have any kitchen chairs?" Anna replies "please have a look at the chairs" and a page of chairs is automatically displayed. The system matches keywords in the queries to a database of suitable web pages or answers.

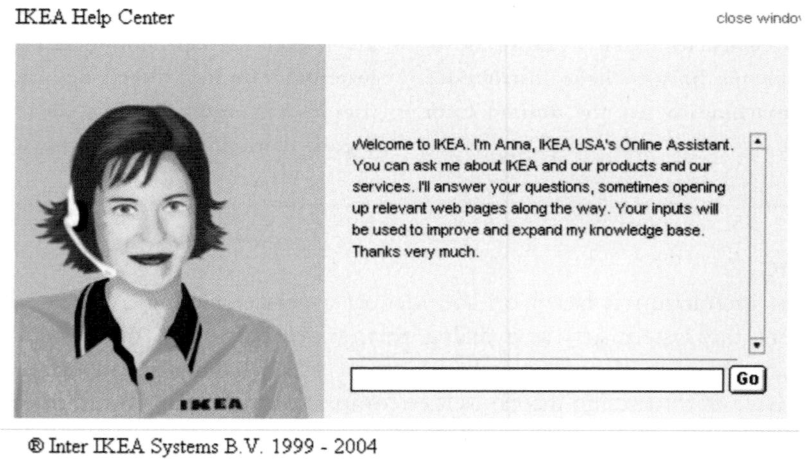

Figure 2.7 *An example of an online agent, Anna, designed by Verity for Ikea furniture store*

A disadvantage of this approach is the potential misunderstandings that can arise when the system is unable to answer the user's question in the way the user expects. This tends to happen when more complex questions are asked that cannot rely on single keyword matching. For example, a child might type in a seemingly simple question to Ask Jeeves for Kids, like "How many legs does a centipede have?" to which Jeeves replies with the following:

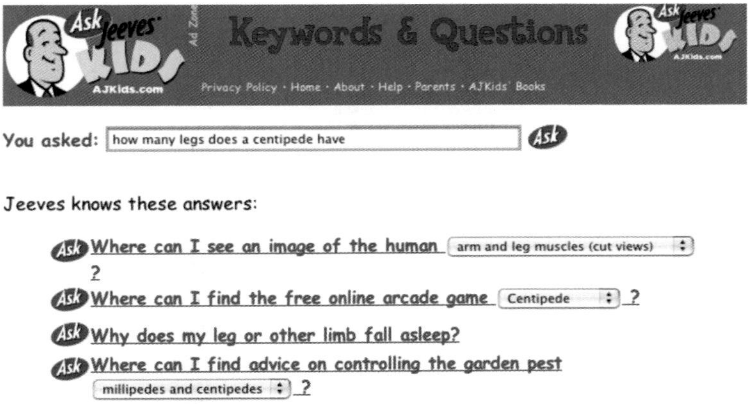

Ask Jeeves for kids

While these are potentially interesting links, it is unlikely that the original question will be answered by following any of them.

Another problem that can arise from using a conversational-based interaction type is that certain kinds of tasks are transformed into cumbersome and one-sided interactions. This is especially true for automated phone-based systems that use auditory menus to advance the interaction. Users have to listen to a voice providing several options, then make a selection, and repeat through further layers of menus before accomplishing their goal, e.g. reaching a real human, paying a bill. Here is the beginning of a dialog between a user who wants to find out about car insurance and an insurance company's reception system:

<user dials an insurance company>

"Welcome to St. Paul's Insurance Company. Press 1 if new customer, 2 if you are an existing customer"

<user presses 1>

"Thank you for calling St. Paul's Insurance Company. If you require house insurance press 1, car insurance press 2, travel insurance press 3, health insurance press 4, other press 5"

<user presses 2>

"You have reached the car insurance division. If you require information about fully comprehensive insurance press 1, 3rd-party insurance press 2 . . . "

"If you'd like to press 1, press 3. If you'd like to press 3, press 8. If you'd like to press 8, press 5..."

Manipulating

This form of interaction involves manipulating objects and capitalizes on users' knowledge of how they do so in the physical world. For example, virtual objects can be manipulated by moving, selecting, opening, and closing. Extensions to these actions include zooming in and out, stretching, and shrinking—actions that are not possible with objects in the real world. Physical toys and robots have also been embedded with computation and capability that enables them to act and react in programmable ways depending on whether they are squeezed, touched, sensed, or moved. Tagged physical objects, e.g. balls, bricks, blocks, that are manipulated in a physical world, e.g. placed on a surface, can result in other physical and digital events occurring, such as a lever moving or a sound, comment, or animation being played. For example, the Chromarium color cubes were designed to enable children to mix colors (a very familiar physical activity) using a novel form of physical–digital interaction (Rogers *et al.*, 2002a). The two colored cubes have hidden RFID tags[1] embedded in them; when they are placed next to a RFID reader (in this case a covered plinth on the table), a computer detects which colors are face up. In Figure 2.8 the faces showing are red and yellow. Their digital counterparts are depicted on the large vertical screen on the wall, together with an animation of the resulting color when the two colors are mixed—in this case it is orange.

What might be the advantages of using a physical–digital form of manipulation? One of the main benefits, when used in this context, is to encourage creativity and playfulness. In a study exploring color mixing, it was found that young children (aged 4–6 years) were far

[1]RFID stands for Radio Frequency Identification and is a method of remotely storing and retrieving data using tags that come in the form of stickers, disks, cards, etc., which can receive and respond to queries sent wirelessly from an RFID transceiver.

Figure 2.8 *The Chromarium color cubes. Turning the two physical cubes on the table results in digital counterpart colors being mixed on the display, depending on which surface of the cubes are face up on the table*

more creative, collaborative, and reflective when mixing colors with the physical–digital cubes compared with mixing digital colored disks as part of software applications (Rogers *et al.*, 2002a). In particular, they explored many more combinations and tried to see if they could change the density of the colors being mixed, for example, by placing the cubes on top of each other and pressing them hard on the table.

The MIT Media Lab has also developed a new generation of digital manipulatives—computationally-enhanced physical artifacts (see Figure 2.9). One form of manipulative—the Cricket—comprises a tiny microchip processor, that is capable of two-way infrared communication and controlling motors and sensors (Resnick *et al.*, 1998). Crickets can be programmed and combined with physical artifacts, sensors, and motors to enable students to explore programming concepts in novel physical ways.

A framework that has been highly influential in informing the design of software applications is *direct manipulation* (Shneiderman, 1983). It proposes that digital objects be designed at the interface that can be interacted with in ways that are analogous to how physical objects in the physical world are manipulated. In so doing, direct manipulation interfaces are assumed to enable users to feel that they are directly controlling the digital objects represented by the computer. To enable this to happen, Shneiderman (1983) has outlined three core principles that need to be followed. These are:

- continuous representation of the objects and actions of interest;
- rapid reversible incremental actions with immediate feedback about the object of interest;
- physical actions and button pressing instead of issuing commands with complex syntax.

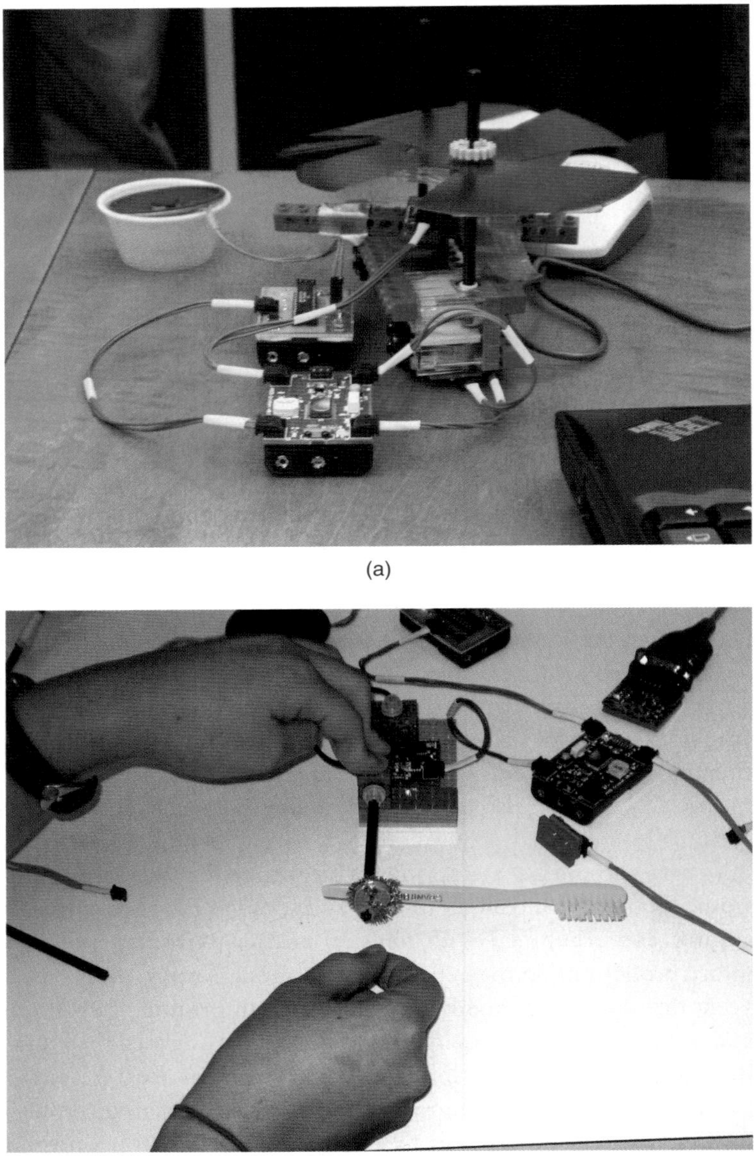

(a)

(b)

Figure 2.9 *(a) Two Cricket components, roughly the size of a matchbox car. (b) Crickets can be programmed and combined with physical artifacts, sensors, and motors to create novel working physical models*

According to these principles, an object on the screen remains visible while a user performs physical actions on it and any actions performed on it are immediately visible. For example, a user can move a file by dragging an icon that represents it from one part of the desktop to another. Shneiderman points out that there are many benefits of direct manipulation. These include:

- helping beginners learn basic functionality rapidly;
- enabling experienced users to work rapidly on a wide range of tasks;
- allowing infrequent users to remember how to carry out operations over time;
- preventing the need for error messages, except very rarely;
- showing users immediately how their actions are furthering their goals;
- reducing users' experiences of anxiety;
- helping users gain confidence and mastery and feel in control.

Apple Computer Inc. was one of the first computer companies to design an operating environment that used direct manipulation as its central mode of interaction. The highly successful Macintosh desktop demonstrates the main principles of direct manipulation (see Figure 2.10). One of their assumptions was that people expect their physical actions to have physical results, so when a drawing tool is used, a corresponding line should appear and when a file is placed in the trashcan, a corresponding sound or visual cue showing it has been successfully thrown away is used (Apple Computer Inc., 1987). A number of visual and auditory cues was used to provide such feedback, including various animations and sounds, e.g. shrinking and expanding icons accompanied with '*shhhlicc*' and '*crouik*' sounds to represent opening and closing of files). Much of the interaction design was geared towards providing clues to the user to know what to do, to feel comfortable, and to enjoy exploring the interface. More recent Mac interfaces follow the same principles, but have become more colorful, use more animation, and provide more detailed icons that have a 3D perspective.

Many applications have been developed based on some form of direct manipulation, e.g. wordprocessing packages, video games, learning tools, and image editing tools. However, while direct manipulation interfaces provide a very versatile mode of interaction they do have their drawbacks. In particular, not all tasks can be described by objects and not all actions can be undertaken directly. Some tasks are also better achieved through issuing commands. For example, consider how you edit an essay using a wordprocessor. Suppose you had referenced work by Ben Shneiderman but had spelled his name as Schneiderman, with an extra 'c' throughout the essay. How would you correct this error using a direct manipulation interface? You would need to read through your essay and manually select the 'c' in every 'Schneiderman,' highlighting and then deleting it. This would be very tedious and it would be easy to miss one or two. By contrast, this operation is relatively effortless and also likely to be more accurate when using a command-based interaction. All you

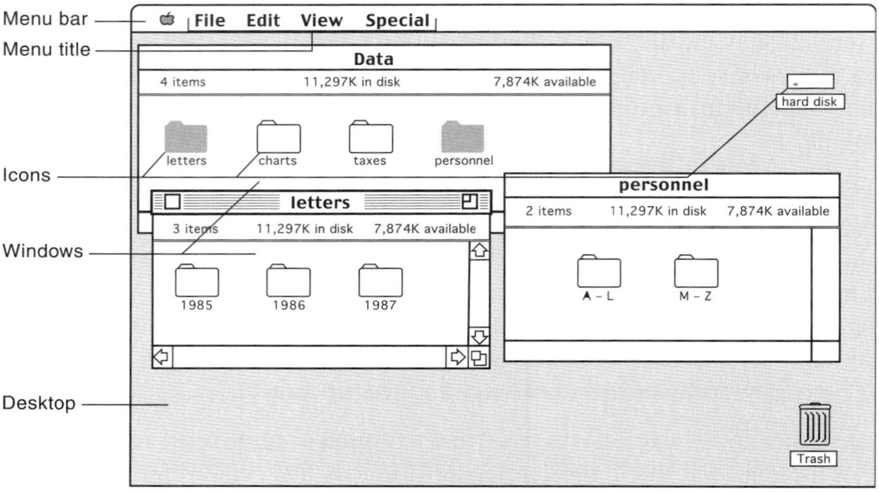

(a)

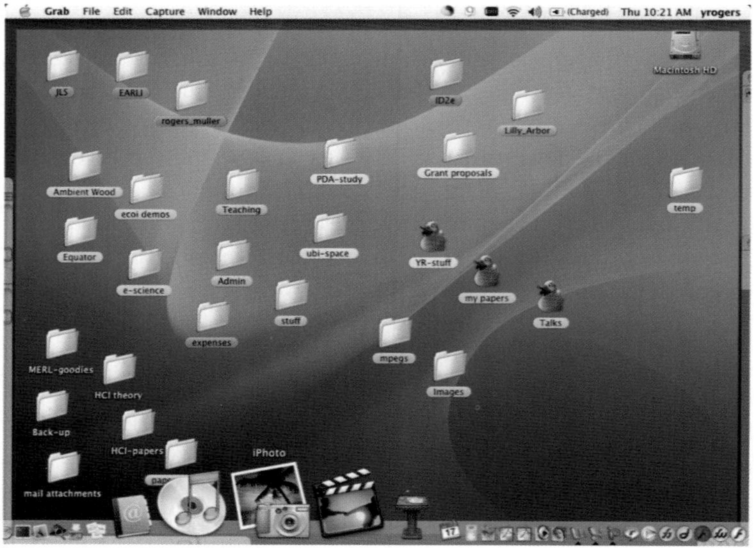

(b)

Figure 2.10 *Two screen shots of (a) an original (1987) and (b) more recent (2005) Mac desktop interface. What are the main differences?*

need to do is instruct the wordprocessor to *find* every 'Schneiderman' and *replace* it with 'Shneiderman.' This can be done through selecting a menu option or using a combination of command keys and then typing the changes required into the dialog box that pops up.

Exploring

This mode of interaction involves users moving through virtual or physical environments. For example, users can explore aspects of a virtual 3D environment, e.g. the interior of a building. Physical environments can also be embedded with sensing technologies that, when they detect the presence of someone or certain body movements, respond by triggering certain digital or physical events to occur. Similar to direct manipulation and direct manipulatives, the fundamental idea is to enable people to explore and interact with an environment, be it physical or digital, by exploiting their knowledge of how they move and navigate through existing spaces.

Many 3D virtual environments have been built that include virtual worlds designed for people to move between various rooms and buildings to learn, e.g. virtual universities, and fantasy worlds where people wander around different parts to socialize, e.g. virtual parties. A number of virtual landscapes depicting cities, parks, buildings, rooms, and datasets have also been built, both realistic and abstract, that enable users to fly over them and zoom in and out of different parts. For example, a team of computer scientists at University College London has built a number of city-scale environments, including the City of London (see Figure 2.11), that can be explored on a desktop machine or using a specially built CAVE system. A CAVE (Computer Automatic Virtual Environment) is designed to provide a sense of immersion through providing 3D video images and audio. When inside a CAVE, the user is presented with high-resolution stereo images projected in real time on its walls and the floor. When viewed through shutter glasses, the left/right stereo images are presented separately to the left and right eyes, respectively, producing the illusion of 3D objects appearing both within and beyond the walls of the CAVE. The images are presented with reference to the user's viewpoint, which is continuously updated. The user navigates through a virtual environment by moving his body, arms, and head in the CAVE.

Other virtual environments that have been built include worlds that are larger than life, enabling users to move around them, experiencing things that are normally impossible or invisible to the eye (Figure 2.12a); highly realistic representations of architectural designs, allowing clients and customers to imagine how they will use and move through planned buildings and public spaces (Figure 2.12b) and visualizations of complex datasets that scientists can virtually climb inside and experience (Figure 2.13).

A number of physical environments have been developed in which are embedded sensor technologies and other location-detection technologies. They are often called context-aware environments: the location and/or presence of people in the vicinity of a sensing device is detected and based on this, the environment decides which digital information to provide

Figure 2.11 *An example of a 3D virtual city*

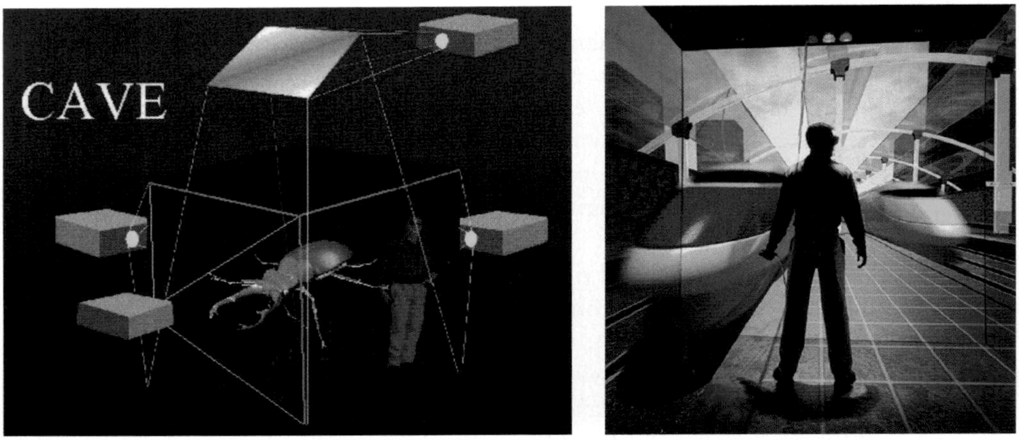

(a) (b)

Figure 2.12 *A CAVE that enables the user to stand near a 10-meter insect like a grasshopper, be swallowed and end up in its abdomen, and a life-like simulation of a newly designed train station that enables users to imagine what it would be like to walk through it*

Figure 2.13 NCSA's CAVE being used by a scientist to move through 3D visualizations of their datasets

on a device, e.g. a PDA, or which action to perform, e.g. changing lights in a room, that is considered relevant or useful to the person at a particular time and place. For example, a number of electronic tourist guides have been developed that run on mobile devices, e.g. PDAs and cell phones equipped with GPS, that provide information about restaurants, historical buildings, and other places of interest as the tourist wanders near them in an unfamiliar city (Cheverst *et al.*, 2000). Physically embedded environments have also been designed to extend how children learn. For example, the Ambient Wood project was designed as an outdoor learning experience where a physical woodland was wired to present various forms of digital information to children, as they moved around it (Rogers *et al.*, 2005). Depending on which part of the woodland they passed by, e.g. a particular kind of tree, a bush, a hole, an image would occasionally pop up on a PDA they were carrying, or a sound was played via hidden speakers or heard through a special handheld audio device—the ambient horn (see Figure 2.14). The idea was to provide contextually-relevant digital information that would enhance the 'usual' physical experience available to children when exploring an outdoor world.

Another example of a context-aware physical environment is the smart home. This is a real house embedded with a complex network of sensors and audio/video recording devices, with the purpose of detecting and identifying various environmental parameters, e.g. temperature, human presence, and aspects of the occupant's behavior, e.g. the occupant's routines and deviations. The idea behind the design of smart homes is that through using the

(a)

(b)

Figure 2.14 *The Ambient Wood. Children (a) listening to ambient sounds and (b) viewing images that popped up as they walked past certain locations in the wired wood*

various data collected and/or monitored, contextually relevant forms of digital information can be provided to the occupants or others, e.g. caregivers, family members, at appropriate times in different parts of the house or other places. A few, much publicized, smart homes were built based on this philosophy, including the 'Aware Home' in the USA (Abowd *et al.*, 2000), the 'Ubiquitous Home' in Japan (Yamazake, 2005), and the 'Orange-at-Home' in the UK (Harper, 2003). Living experiments were subsequently conducted to see how real families would respond and adapt to such a set-up, over a period of several months.

Activity 2.7

Online and video games often involve players moving through a virtual environment, e.g. chasing someone, running from someone, driving a vehicle through hazardous terrain, and manipulating objects, e.g. using swords, holding steering wheels, opening doors. Rich and highly realistic graphical interfaces are used, where gamers are represented graphically on screen as 3D realistic avatars that are moved and controlled via a joystick and/or pushing buttons on a console. In the early days of gaming, however, games developers were largely restricted to instruction-based types of interaction. For example, the ZORK game introduced in the early 1980s (Figure 2.15) required the players to move around the virtual environment by typing in text commands. To what extent do you think this affects the gaming experience? Do you think the early text-based games were as engaging and exciting as modern-day ones (see Figure 2.16)?

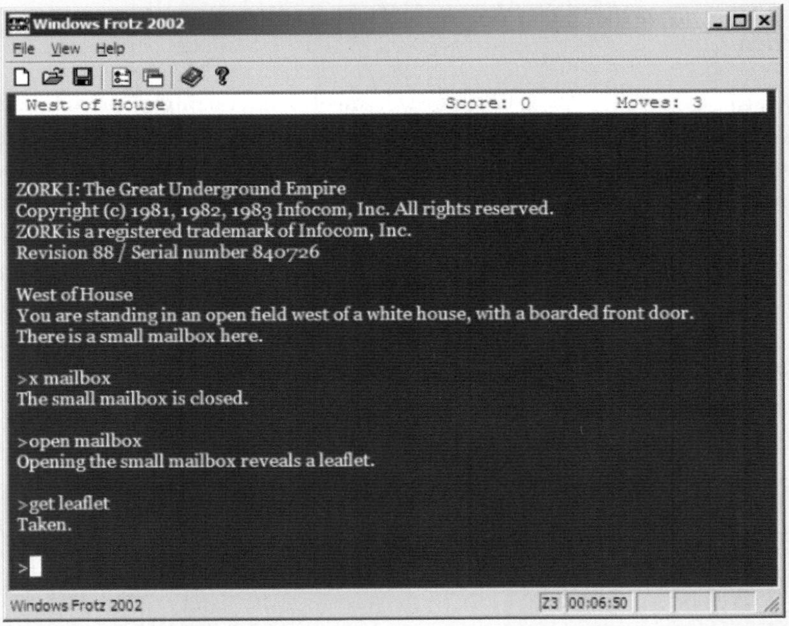

Figure 2.15 *A game using a text-based instruction mode of interaction*

Figure 2.16 *A 3D virtual game (Voodoo Island), involving an avatar-based mode of interaction*

Comment

The early text-based games required the user to imagine aspects of the game and to remember a large number of text commands to enable them to move around and progress with the game. In this respect, the user experience can be viewed as less gripping and involve more mental effort than more recent video games. Drama and tension are added when games involve interacting with rich and realistic graphics, listening to accompanying stereo sounds, and seeing flashing text cues. Perhaps the main difference between the two gaming experiences is similar to that between reading a book on the sofa and watching a 3D movie in an IMAX theatre; both can be very engaging but in quite different ways.

Box 2.3
Which is best—agent, context-aware, direct manipulation, or command-based interactions?

A big debate in interaction design is concerned with how and who controls an interface. The different forms of interaction available vary in terms of how much control a user has and how much the computer has. At one end of the spectrum are (i) command-based and (ii) direct manipulation interfaces where the user is primarily in control of the interaction. At the other end are (i) agents, e.g. guides, wizards, companions, assistants, and (ii) context-aware environments where the system is largely in control, deciding what to do and making suggestions to the user.

Advocates of the agent approach, e.g. Nicholas Negroponte claim it can be much more versatile than direct manipulation or command-based interfaces, allowing users to do what they want to do through delegating the boring and time-consuming tasks to an agent. Negroponte uses the analogy of a well-trained English butler who answers the phone, tends to a person's needs, fends off callers, and tells 'white lies' if necessary on his master's behalf. Similarly, a *digital* butler is designed to read a user's email and flag the important ones, scout the web and newsgroups for interesting information, screen unwanted electronic intrusions, and so on. This approach assumes that people like to delegate work to others rather than directly interact with computers themselves.

Proponents of the context-aware approach argue that enabling the environment to monitor, recognize, and detect deviations in a person's behavior enables timely information to be provided that can be helpful and even critical at times, e.g. Abowd and Mynatt (2000). For example, elderly people's movements can be detected in the home and emergency or care services alerted if something untoward happens to them that might otherwise go unnoticed, e.g. they fall over and break a leg and are unable to get to a telephone.

The problem with delegating tasks to agents or leaving it to the environment to determine how to respond in a certain way is that it is very difficult to accurately predict all the things users want done, what is really happening to them, or the type of information they might want or find useful at a particular time. If the agents do the tasks incorrectly or the environment provides inappropriate information, frustration and anger will ensue. For example, a person may choose to take a rest in an unexpected area (on the carpet), which could be detected as a fall. Moreover, many users do not want to be constantly monitored, as it violates their sense of privacy, nor do they like to be told what to do by a computer system. Imagine your car deciding you should be driving more slowly because it is raining.

Advocates of the direct manipulation approach, e.g. Ben Shneiderman, suggest that it is preferable because it allows users to enjoy mastery and being in control. People like to know what is going on, be involved in the action, and have a sense of power over the computer—all of which direct manipulation interfaces support.

Advocates of the command-based approach go one step further, arguing that many tasks are best carried

out at an abstract level, where the user is completely in control. Issuing abstract commands based on a carefully designed set of syntax and semantics is often a very efficient and elegant way of performing many operations. This is especially the case for repetitive operations, where the same action needs to be performed on multiple objects. Examples include sorting out files, deleting accumulated email messages, opening and closing files, and installing applications comprising multiple files—which when done by direct manipulation or through delegation can be inefficient or ambiguous.

To what extent do you need to be in control in your everyday and working life? Are you happy to let the computer monitor and decide what you need or do you prefer to tell the computer what you want doing? ■

Other Ways of Conceptualizing Activities

Besides the four core activities of instructing, conversing, manipulating, and exploring, there are many other ways of describing the specific domain and context-based activities users engage in, such as learning, working, socializing, browsing, writing, problem-solving, decision-making, and information-searching—to name but a few. We suggest that when considering how to design for these, it is useful to think about them in terms of the core interaction types, and in so doing, tease out the dilemmas and issues that might arise when using a particular interface.

Another way of classifying activity types is in terms of the context in which they are conducted. McCullough (2004) suggests 30 different kinds of situated activities, organized by: work, e.g. presenting to groups, documenting, home, e.g. recharging oneself, resting, in town, e.g. eating, drinking, and talking, and on the road, e.g. walking, driving. The purpose of his framework is to help designers be less ad hoc and more systematic when thinking about the usability of technology-modified places in the environment. Similarly, our set of core interaction types is intended to help designers evaluate the user activities involved in a user experience, and to contemplate the pros and cons of using different interface types to support them. Specific design and research concerns are outlined in Chapter 6 when considering *interaction* types in relation to *interface* types.

Box 2.4
From controlling to coupling: A new way of conceptualizing interactions

The quest to develop new interaction techniques that go beyond the WIMP interface requires different conceptualizing for the nature of the interaction between

person and environment. Rather than considering how to design a dialog for a user and a system, new frameworks are needed that can inform how to design a particular kind of interface and interaction style. For example, a different way of thinking is needed about what people can or might do in the physical world (and how they might react) when provided with contextually-relevant digital information at certain times, as a result of having their 'presence,' 'states,' and 'levels' being detected, e.g. emotional state, state of learning, information needs, when using sensing and tracking technologies. Instead of the user controlling an input device to interact with a computer, the ubiquitous environment has to detect the location of someone and determine what information, e.g. a sound, a message, an image, to present via a personal display, e.g. cell phone, PDA, or public display, e.g. a wall display, speakers.

One way of describing these different forms of interactions is in terms of the *coupling* between an action and an effect. Couplings can be viewed as tight or loose. A tight coupling is where an action, e.g. an arm gesture, causes an effect that is obvious and immediate to a person or persons present, e.g. a light switches on. A loose coupling is where the relationship between an action and effect is not obvious or immediate, e.g. a person walking past a hidden sensor in the environment may trigger a message to appear on someone else's cell phone. Neither person may perceive or understand how the event was caused. The decision of how tight to design the coupling will depend on the nature of the user experience. Loose couplings involving ambiguity are a powerful tactic to use when developing interactive games (Rogers and Muller, 2005). Tight couplings are considered necessary where feedback needs to be visible and immediate, such as being able to turn on the lights or taps and get instant light or water (see Chapter 1).

The notion of coupling is very different from the conceptualization of a user having a dialog with a system or directly manipulating an interface, where the user is very much in control of the interaction, with the system *responding* to the user's requests. A coupling may involve a one-off action–effect, e.g. switching on the light, or a series of interactions, e.g. interacting with a virtual character to find out more about its likes/dislikes. Accordingly, feedback may be designed to be immediate or delayed.

This different perspective on user interaction requires thinking differently about how to design for user experiences. New frameworks have begun to appear to provide guidance. For example, Benford *et al.*'s (2005) framework describes how to analyze the movements of sensing-based interfaces in terms of whether they are to be expected, sensed, and desired by the users while Bellotti *et al.*'s (2002) framework poses questions to designers as to how to compensate for the lack of GUI features in sensor-based interactions, e.g. obvious feedback and user control. ■

2.4 Theories, models, and frameworks

Other sources of inspiration and knowledge that are used to inform design and guide research are theories, models, and frameworks (Carroll, 2003). A theory is a well-substantiated explanation of some aspect of a phenomenon, for example, the theory of information processing that explains how the mind, or some aspect of it, is assumed to work. A model is a simplification of some aspect of human–computer interaction intended to make it easier for designers to predict and evaluate alternative designs. A framework is a set of interrelated concepts and/or a set of specific questions that is intended to inform a particular domain area, e.g. collaborative learning, online communities, or an analytic method, e.g. ethnographic studies.

Theories. Over the last 30 years, numerous theories have been imported into human–computer interaction, providing a means of analyzing and predicting the performance of users carrying out tasks for specific kinds of computer interfaces and systems. These have been primarily cognitive, social, and organizational in origin. For example, cognitive theories about human memory were used in the 1980s to determine what were the best ways of representing operations, given people's memory limitations. One of the main benefits of applying such theories in interaction design is to help identify factors, e.g. cognitive, social, and affective, relevant to the design and evaluation of interactive products. Some of the most influential theories in HCI, e.g. Fitt's Law, and others that are making their mark, e.g. distributed cognition, will be covered in later chapters.

Models. Models are typically abstracted from a theory coming from a contributing discipline, e.g. psychology, that can be directly applied to interaction design. For example, Norman (1988) developed a number of models of user interaction based on theories of cognitive processing arising out of cognitive science, that were intended to explain the way users interacted with interactive technologies. These include his cyclical seven stages of action model (see Chapter 3)—that describes how users move from their plans to executing physical actions they need to perform to achieve them, to evaluating the outcome of their actions with respect to their goals. Another highly influential model based on cognitive theory that made its mark in the 1980s was Card, Moran, and Newell's keystroke model (see Chapters 3 and 15). This was used by a number of researchers and designers as a predictive way of analyzing user performance for different interfaces to determine which would be the most effective. More recent models developed in interaction design are user models, that predict what information users want in their interactions, and models that characterize core components of the user experience, such as Norman's (2004) model of emotional design (Chapter 5).

Frameworks. A number of frameworks have been introduced in interaction design to help designers constrain and scope the user experience for which they are designing. In contrast to a model—which is a simplification of a phenomenon—a framework offers advice to designers as to what to design or look for. This can come in a variety of forms, including steps, questions, concepts, challenges, principles, and dimensions. Frameworks, like models, have traditionally been based on theories of human behavior, but they are increasingly being developed from the experiences of actual design practice and the findings arising from user studies.

There are many frameworks that have been published in the HCI/interaction design literatures, covering different aspects of the user experience and a diversity of application areas. For example, there are frameworks for helping designers think about how to conceptualize learning, working, socializing, fun, emotion, etc., and others that focus on how to design particular kinds of technologies to evoke certain responses, e.g. persuasive technologies and pleasurable products (see Chapter 5). A classic early example of a conceptual framework that has been highly influential in human–computer interaction is Norman's (1988) explication of the relationship between the design of a conceptual model and a user's understanding of it (see Figure 2.17). The framework depicts three interacting components: the designer, the user, and the system. Behind each of these are:

- The designer's model—the model the designer has of how the system should work.
- The system image—how the system actually works is portrayed to the user through the interface, manuals, help facilities, etc.
- The user's model—how the user understands how the system works.

The framework is simple but highly effective: it provides a powerful visualization, making explicit the relationship between how a system *should* function, how it is *presented* to the users, and how it is *understood* by the users. In an ideal world, users should be able to carry out their tasks in the way intended by the designer by interacting with the system image which makes it obvious what to do. If the system image does not make the designer's model clear to the users, it is likely that they will end up with an incorrect understanding of the system, which in turn will increase the chances of their using the system ineffectively

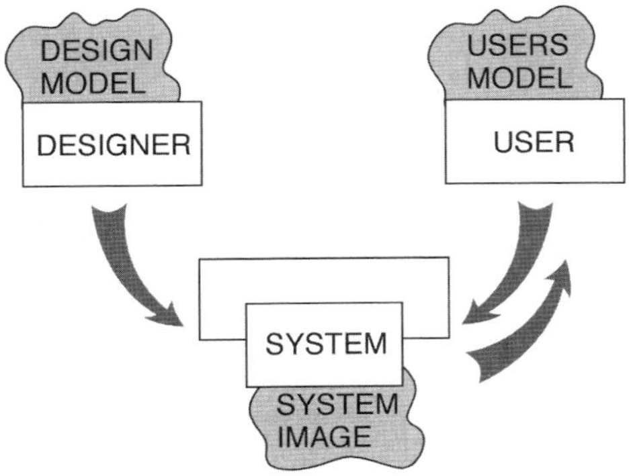

Figure 2.17 *The designer's model, the user's model and the system image (Norman, 1988)*

and making errors. This has been found to happen often in the real world. By drawing attention to this potential discrepancy, designers can be made aware of the importance of trying to bridge the gap more effectively.

Theories, models, and frameworks are not mutually exclusive but overlap in their way of conceptualizing the problem and design space, varying in their level of rigor, abstraction, and purpose. Theories tend to be comprehensive, *explaining* human–computer interactions; models tend to *simplify* some aspect of human–computer interaction, providing a basis for designing and evaluating systems; frameworks tend to be *prescriptive*, providing designers with concepts, questions, and principles to consider when designing for a user experience.

Assignment

The aim of this assignment is for you to think about the appropriateness of different kinds of conceptual models that have been designed for similar physical and digital information artifacts.

(a) Compare the ways the following information artifacts are organized:

- a personal pocket-sized calendar/diary (one week to a page);
- a wall calendar (one month to a page, usually with a picture/photo);
- a wall planner (displaying the whole year).

What are the main concepts and metaphors that have been used for each (think about the way time is conceptualized for each of them)?

(b) Using Johnson and Henderson's (2002) framework, describe the conceptual models that underlie the design of:

- an electronic *personal* calendar found on a personal organizer or handheld computer;
- a *shared* calendar found on the web.

How do they differ and what are the main benefits compared with the equivalent physical artifacts? What new functionality has been provided? What interface metaphors have been used? Do you think new users will have problems understanding how these kinds of interactive calendars work? What aspects of the conceptual model might be confusing?

Summary

This chapter has explained the importance of understanding and conceptualizing a design space before trying to build anything. It has stressed throughout the need to be explicit about the claims and assumptions behind design decisions that are suggested. It described an approach to formulating a conceptual model and then provided two classic examples of very well designed conceptual models. It also discussed the pros and cons of using interface metaphors as part of the conceptual model. Finally, it considered other ways of conceptualizing interaction, in terms of interaction types, theories, models, and frameworks.

Key points

- It is important to have a good understanding of the problem space, specifying what it is you are doing, why, and how it will support users in the way intended.
- A fundamental aspect of interaction design is to develop a conceptual model.
- A conceptual model is a high-level description of a product in terms of what users can do with it and the concepts they need to understand how to interact with it.
- Decisions about conceptual design should be made before commencing any physical design, e.g. choosing menus, icons, dialog boxes.
- Interface metaphors are commonly used as part of a conceptual model.
- Interaction types, e.g. conversing, instructing, provide a way of thinking about how best to support the activities users will be doing when using a product or service.
- Theories, models, and frameworks provide another way of framing and informing design and research.

Further Reading

JOHNSON, J. and HENDERSON, A. (2002) Conceptual Models: Begin by Designing What to Design. *Interactions*, January/February 2002, ACM Press, pp. 25–32. This paper explains what a conceptual model is and shows how to construct one and why it is necessary to do so. It is very cogently argued and shows how and where this design activity can be integrated into interaction design.

MCCULLOUGH, M. (2004) *Digital Ground: Architecture, Pervasive Computing and Environmental Knowing*. MIT Press. This book presents many new ideas, concepts, and frameworks for designing pervasive technologies. In particular, it discusses in depth the many new challenges confronting interaction designers and architects when working out how to embed information technology into the ambient social complexities of the physical world.

LAUREL, B. (ed.) (1990) *The Art of Human Computer Design* has a number of papers on conceptual models and interface metaphors. Two that are definitely worth reading are: Tom Erickson, "Working with interface metaphors" (pp. 65–74), which is a practical hands-on guide to designing interface metaphors (covered later in this book), and Ted Nelson's polemic, "The right way to think about software design" (pp. 229–234), which is a scathing attack on the use of interface metaphors.

JOHNSON, M. and LAKOFF, G. (1980) *Metaphors We Live By*. The University of Chicago Press. Those wanting to find out more about how metaphors are used in everyday conversations should take a look at this text.

There are many good articles on the topic of interface agents. A classic is:

LANIER, J. (1995) Agents of alienation. *ACM Interactions*, **2**(3), 66–72. *The Art of Human Computer Design* also provides several thought-provoking articles, including one called "Interface agents: metaphors with character" by Brenda Laurel (pp. 355–366) and another called "Guides: characterizing the interface" by Tim Oren *et al.* (pp. 367–382).

BANNON, L. (1977) Problems in human–machine interaction and communication. *Proc HCI'97*, San Francisco. Bannon presents a critical review of the agent approach to interface design.

MIT'S MEDIA LAB (`www.media.mit.edu`) is a good place to find out what are the latest research paradigms and technological innovations.

INTERVIEW with Terry Winograd

Terry Winograd is a Professor of Computer Science at Stanford University and one of the founding faculty of a new Interdisciplinary Design Program at Stanford, known as the 'd.school.' He has done extensive research and writing on the design of human–computer interaction. His early research on natural language understanding by computers, was a milestone in artificial intelligence, and he has written two books and numerous articles on that topic. His book, *Bringing Design to Software*, brings together the perspectives of a number of leading researchers and designers.

YR: Tell me about your background and how you moved into interaction design.

TW: I got into interaction design through a couple of intermediate steps. I started out doing research in artificial intelligence. I became interested in how people interact with computers, in particular, when using ordinary language. It became clear after years of working on that, however, that the computer was a long way off from matching human abilities. Moreover, using natural language with a computer when it doesn't really understand you can be very frustrating and in fact a very bad way to interact with it. So, rather than trying to get the computer to imitate a person, I became interested in other ways of taking advantage of what computers can do well and what people can do well. That led me into the general field of HCI. As I began to look at what was going on in that field and to study it, it became clear that it was not the same as other areas of computer science. The key issues were about how the technology fits with what people could do and what they wanted to do. In contrast, most of computer science is really dominated by how the mechanisms operate.

I was very attracted to thinking more in the style of design disciplines, such as product design, urban design, architecture, and so on. I realized that there was an approach that you might call a design way, that puts the technical aspects into the background with respect to understanding the interaction. Through looking at these design disciplines, I realized that there was something unique about interaction design, which is that it has a dialogic temporal element. By this I mean a human dialog: not in the sense of using ordinary language, but in the sense of thinking about the sequence and the flow of interaction.

So I think of interaction design as being about designing a space for people, where that space has to have a temporal flow. It has to have a dialog with the person.

YR: Could you tell me a bit more about what you think is involved in interaction design?
TW: One of the biggest influences is product design. I think that interaction design overlaps with it, because they both take a very strong user-oriented view. Both are concerned with finding a user group, understanding their needs, then using that understanding to come up with new ideas. They may be ones that the users don't even realize when you begin. It is then a matter of trying to translate who it is, what they are doing, and why they are doing it into possible innovations. In the case of product design it is products. In the case of interaction design it is the way that a system interacts with the person.

YR: What do you think are important inputs into the design process?
TW: One of the characteristics of design fields as opposed to traditional engineering fields is that there is much more dependence on case studies and examples than on formulas. Whereas an engineer knows how to calculate something, an architect or a designer is working in a tradition where there is a history over time of other things people have done. People have said that the secret of great design is to know what to steal and to know when some element or some way of doing things that worked before will be appropriate to your setting and then adapt it. Generally you can't apply it directly, but I think a big part of doing good design is experience and exposure. You have to have seen a lot of things in practice and understood what is good and bad about them, to then use these to inform your design.

YR: How do you see the relationship between studying interaction design and the practice of it? Is there a good dialog between research and practice?
TW: Academic study of interaction design is a tricky area because so much of it depends on a kind of tacit knowledge that comes through experience and exposure. It is not the kind of thing you can set down easily as, say, you can scientific formulas. A lot of design research tends to be methodological. It is not about the design *per se* but is more about how you go about doing design, in particular, knowing what are the appropriate steps to take and how you put them together.

YR: How do you see the field of interaction design taking on board the current explosion in new technologies—for example mobile, ubiquitous, infrared, and so on? Is it different, say, from 20 years ago when it was just about designing software applications to sit on the desktop?
TW: I think a real change in people's thinking has been to move from interface design to interaction design. This has been pushed by the fact that we do have all kinds of devices nowadays. Interface design used to mean graphical interfaces, which meant designing menus and other widgets. But now when you're talking about handheld devices, gesture interfaces, telephone interfaces and so on, it is clear that you can't focus just on the

widgets. The widgets may be part of any one of these devices but the design thinking as a whole has to focus on the interaction.

YR: What advice would you give to a student coming into the field on what they should be learning and looking for?
TW: I think a student who wants to learn this field should think of it as a kind of dual process, that is what Donald Schön calls "reflection in action," needing both the action and the reflection. It is important to have experience with trying to build things. That experience can be from outside work, projects, and courses where you are actually engaged in making something work. At the same time you need to be able to step back and look at it not as "What do I need to do next?" but from the perspective of what you are doing and how that fits into the larger picture. The courses we are developing for the d.school are all built around this approach. Students work on interdisciplinary projects that are unique to each course, but in all of them we maintain a central focus on being user-centered, developing ideas through iterative prototyping, and being mindful of the design process while engaging in it.

YR: Are there any classic case studies that stand out as good exemplars of interaction design?
TW: I still use the Xerox Star as an exemplar because so much of what we use today was there. When you go back to look at the Star, it seems very ordinary until you see it in the context of when it was first created. I also think some exemplars that are very interesting are ones that weren't commercial successes. For example, I use the PenPoint system that was developed for pen computers by Go. Again, they were thinking fresh. They set out to do something different and they were much more conscious of the design issues than somebody who was simply adapting the next version of something that already existed. PalmPilot is another good example, because they looked at the problem in a different way to make something work. Another interesting exemplar, which other people may not agree with, is Microsoft Bob—not because it was a successful program—because it wasn't—but because it was a first exploration of a certain style of interaction, using animated agents. You can see very clearly from these exemplars what design trade-offs the designers were making and why, and then you can look at the consequences.

YR: Finally, what are the biggest challenges facing people working in this area?
TW: I think one of the biggest challenges is what Pelle Ehn calls the dialectic between tradition and transcendence. That is, people work and live in certain ways already, and they understand how to adapt that within a small range, but they don't have an understanding or a feel for what it would mean to make a radical change, for example, to change their way of doing business on the Internet before it was around, or to change their way of writing from pen and paper when word processors weren't around. The designer needs to envision things that fill real needs for users, but which the users can't yet envision. ■

3

3.1 Introduction

Imagine trying to drive a car by using just a computer keyboard. The four arrow keys are used for steering, the space bar for braking, and the return key for accelerating. To indicate left you need to press the F1 key and to indicate right the F2 key. To sound your horn you need to press the F3 key. To switch the headlights on you need to use the F4 key, and to switch the windscreen wipers on the F5 key. Now imagine as you are driving along a road a ball is suddenly kicked in front of you. What would you do? Bash the arrow keys and the space bar madly while pressing the F3 key? How would you rate your chances of missing the ball?

Most of us would balk at the very idea of driving a car this way. Many early video games, however, were designed along these lines: the user had to press an arbitrary combination of function keys to drive or navigate through the game. There was little, if any, consideration of the user's capabilities. While some users regarded mastering an arbitrary set of keyboard controls as a challenge, many users found them very limiting, frustrating, and difficult to use. More recently, computer consoles have been designed with the user's capabilities and the demands of the activity in mind. Much better ways of controlling and interacting, such as through using joysticks and steering wheels, are provided that map much better onto the physical and cognitive aspects of driving and navigating.

In this chapter we examine some of the core cognitive aspects of interaction design. Specifically, we consider what humans are good and bad at and show how this knowledge can be used to *inform* the design of technologies that both *extend* human capabilities and *compensate* for their weaknesses. We also look at some of the influential cognitive-based conceptual frameworks that have been developed for explaining the way humans interact with computers. (Other ways of conceptualizing human behavior that focus on the social and affective aspects of interaction design are presented in the following two chapters.)

The main aims of this chapter are to:

- **Explain what cognition is and why it is important for interaction design.**
- **Describe the main ways cognition has been applied to interaction design.**
- **Provide a number of examples in which cognitive research has led to the design of more effective interactive products.**
- **Explain what mental models are.**
- **Give examples of conceptual frameworks that are useful for interaction design.**
- **Enable you to try to elicit a mental model and be able to understand what it means.**

3

Understanding users

3.2 What is cognition?

Cognition is what goes on in our heads when we carry out our everyday activities. It involves cognitive processes, like thinking, remembering, learning, daydreaming, decision-making, seeing, reading, writing, and talking. As Figure 3.1 indicates, there are many different kinds of cognition. Norman (1993) distinguishes between two general modes: experiential and reflective cognition. The former is a state of mind in which we perceive, act, and react to events around us effectively and effortlessly. It requires reaching a certain level of expertise and engagement. Examples include driving a car, reading a book, having a conversation, and playing a video game. In contrast, reflective cognition involves thinking, comparing, and decision-making. This kind of cognition is what leads to new ideas and creativity. Examples include designing, learning, and writing a book. Norman points out that both modes are essential for everyday life, but that each requires different kinds of technological support.

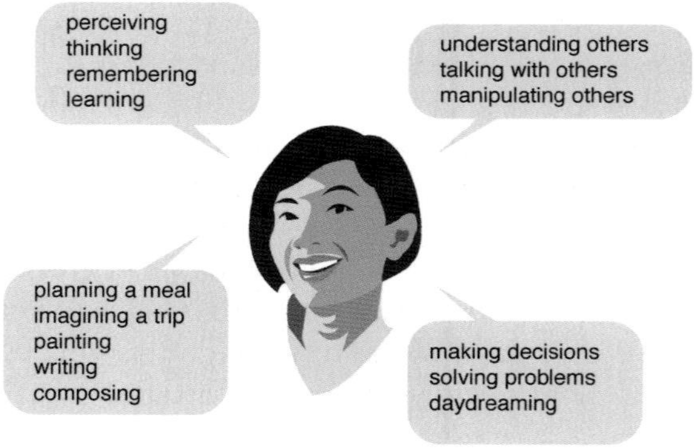

Figure 3.1 *What goes on in the mind?*

Cognition has also been described in terms of specific kinds of processes. These include:

- attention
- perception and recognition
- memory
- learning
- reading, speaking, and listening
- problem-solving, planning, reasoning, decision-making.

It is important to note that many of these cognitive processes are interdependent: several may be involved for a given activity. It is rare for one to occur in isolation. For example, when you try to learn material for an exam, you need to attend to the material, perceive and recognize it, read it, think about it, and try to remember it. Below we describe the various kinds in more detail, followed by a summary box highlighting core design implications for each. Most relevant (and most thoroughly researched) for interaction design is memory, which we describe in greatest detail.

Attention is the process of selecting things to concentrate on, at a point in time, from the range of possibilities available. Attention involves our auditory and/or visual senses. An example of auditory attention is waiting in the dentist's waiting room for our name to be called out to know when it is our time to go in. An example of visual attention is scanning the football results in a newspaper to attend to information about how our team has done. Attention allows us to focus on information that is relevant to what we are doing. The extent to which this process is easy or difficult depends on (i) whether we have clear goals and (ii) whether the information we need is salient in the environment.

(i) *Our goals*. If we know exactly what we want to find out we try to match this with the information that is available. For example, if we have just landed at an airport after a long flight and want to find out who had won the World Cup, we might scan the headlines at the newspaper stand, check the web, call a friend, or ask someone in the street. When we are not sure exactly what we are looking for we may browse through information, allowing it to guide our attention to interesting or salient items. For example, when we go to a restaurant we may have the general goal of eating a meal but only a vague idea of what we want to eat. We peruse the menu to find things that whet our appetite, letting our attention be drawn to the imaginative descriptions of various dishes. After scanning through the possibilities and imagining what each dish might be like (plus taking into account other factors, such as cost, who we are with, what the specials are, what the waiter recommends, whether we want a two- or three-course meal, and so on), we may then make a decision.

(ii) *Information presentation*. The way information is displayed can also greatly influence how easy or difficult it is to attend to appropriate pieces of information. Look at Figure 3.2 and try the activity (based on Tullis, 1987). Here, the information-searching tasks are very precise, requiring specific answers. The information density is identical in both displays. However, it is much harder to find the information in the bottom screen than in the top screen. The reason for this is that the information is very poorly structured in the bottom, making it difficult to find the information. In the top, the information has been ordered into meaningful categories with blank spacing between them making it easier to select the necessary information.

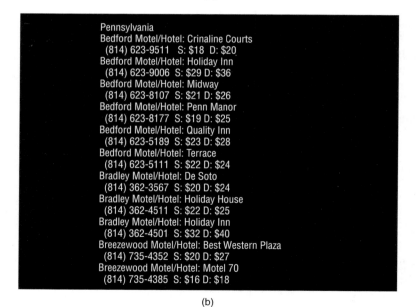

South Carolina

City	Motel/Hotel	Area code	Phone	Rates Single	Double
Charleston	Best Western	803	747-0961	$26	$30
Charleston	Days Inn	803	881-1000	$18	$24
Charleston	Holiday Inn N	803	744-1621	$36	$46
Charleston	Holiday Inn SW	803	556-7100	$33	$47
Charleston	Howard Johnsons	803	524-4148	$31	$36
Charleston	Ramada Inn	803	774-8281	$33	$40
Charleston	Sheraton Inn	803	744-2401	$34	$42
Columbia	Best Western	803	796-9400	$29	$34
Columbia	Carolina Inn	803	799-8200	$42	$48
Columbia	Days Inn	803	736-0000	$23	$27
Columbia	Holiday Inn NW	803	794-9440	$32	$39
Columbia	Howard Johnsons	803	772-7200	$25	$27
Columbia	Quality Inn	803	772-0270	$34	$41
Columbia	Ramada Inn	803	796-2700	$36	$44
Columbia	Vagabond Inn	803	796-6240	$27	$30

(a)

Pennsylvania
Bedford Motel/Hotel: Crinaline Courts
(814) 623-9511 S: $18 D: $20
Bedford Motel/Hotel: Holiday Inn
(814) 623-9006 S: $29 D: $36
Bedford Motel/Hotel: Midway
(814) 623-8107 S: $21 D: $26
Bedford Motel/Hotel: Penn Manor
(814) 623-8177 S: $19 D: $25
Bedford Motel/Hotel: Quality Inn
(814) 623-5189 S: $23 D: $28
Bedford Motel/Hotel: Terrace
(814) 623-5111 S: $22 D: $24
Bradley Motel/Hotel: De Soto
(814) 362-3567 S: $20 D: $24
Bradley Motel/Hotel: Holiday House
(814) 362-4511 S: $22 D: $25
Bradley Motel/Hotel: Holiday Inn
(814) 362-4501 S: $32 D: $40
Breezewood Motel/Hotel: Best Western Plaza
(814) 735-4352 S: $20 D: $27
Breezewood Motel/Hotel: Motel 70
(814) 735-4385 S: $16 D: $18

(b)

Figure 3.2 *Two different ways of structuring the same information at the interface: one makes it much easier to find information than the other*

Activity 3.1

Look at the top screen of Figure 3.2 and: (i) find the price for a double room at the Quality Inn in Columbia; (ii) find the phone number of the Days Inn in Charleston. Then look at the bottom screen in Figure 3.2 and: (i) find the price of a double room at the Holiday Inn in Bradley; (ii) find the phone number of the Quality Inn in Bedford. Which took longer to do?

In an early study Tullis found that the two screens produced quite different results: it took an average of 3.2 seconds to search the top screen and 5.5 seconds to find the same kind of information in the bottom screen. Why is this so, considering that both displays have the same density of information (31%)? The primary reason is the way the characters are grouped in the display. In the top screen they are grouped into vertical categories of information, e.g. place, kind of accommodation, phone number, and rates, that have columns of space between them. In the bottom screen the information is bunched up together, making it much harder to search through.

Box 3.1
Sliced attention

Many of us now spend a large proportion of our time staring at a computer screen. While focusing on one task at the screen we switch constantly between others, for example, every 5–10 minutes while writing this chapter I check my email, breaking off sometimes in mid-sentence to see who has sent me a message and then finding myself diverted to looking at the latest news item or website recommended to me by a colleague. Like nearly everyone else, I am addicted; I can't stop myself from looking.

I have watched others engaged in 'multi-apping' to the point of awe. For example, while attending a talk at a conference I watched a student volunteer in front of me deftly switch between four ongoing instant message chats (one at the conference, one at school, one with friends, one at her part-time job), read, answer, delete, and place all new messages in various folders of her two email accounts, check and scan through a large list of blogs and news feeds—while appearing to listen to the talk, take some notes, google the speaker's background, and open up his publications. When she had a spare moment she played a game of patience. I must say, I felt quite exhausted just watching her for 10 minutes. It was as if she was capable of living in multiple worlds all at the same time while not letting a moment go to waste. But how much did she take in of the talk?

Moreover, is it possible to pay attention to and not get distracted from the main ongoing activity in our work, e.g. writing an essay, listening to a lecture, when simultaneously engaged in numerous 'back channel', screen-based activities? Surely there must be some detrimental effects? As noted by Katie Hafner (2005), a technology reporter, "distracting oneself used to consist of sharpening a half-dozen pencils or lighting a cigarette. Today, there is a universe of diversions to buy, hear, watch and forward, which makes focussing on a task all the more challenging."

DESIGN IMPLICATIONS
Attention

- Make information salient when it needs attending to at a given stage of a task.
- Use techniques like animated graphics, color, underlining, ordering of items, sequencing of different information, and spacing of items to achieve this.
- Avoid cluttering the interface with too much information. This especially applies to the use of color, sound, and graphics: there is a temptation to use lots of them, resulting in a mishmash of media that is distracting and annoying rather than helping the user attend to relevant information.
- Search engines and form fill-ins that are simple are much easier to use, like the Google search engine (see Figure 3.3). The main reason is that users can more quickly find where on the screen to type in their search.

Figure 3.3 The Google search engine

Perception refers to how information is acquired from the environment, via the different sense organs, e.g. eyes, ears, fingers, and transformed into experiences of objects, events, sounds, and tastes (Roth, 1986). It is complex, involving other cognitive processes such as memory, attention, and language. Vision is the most dominant sense for sighted individuals, followed by hearing and touch. With respect to interaction design it is important to present information in a way that can be readily perceived in the manner intended.

As was demonstrated in Activity 3.1, grouping items together and leaving spaces between them can aid attention. In addition, many web designers recommend using blank space (more commonly known as white space) when grouping objects together on a screen as it helps users to perceive and locate items more easily and quickly. However, some researchers suggest that too much white space can be detrimental, making it sometimes harder to find information (Spool *et al.*, 1997). In a study comparing web pages displaying the same amount of information, but which were structured using different graphical methods, it was found that people took less time to locate items for information that was grouped using a border than when using color contrast (Weller, 2004; see Figure 3.4). The findings suggest that using contrasting color is not a good way to group information on a screen and that using borders is more effective (Galitz, 1997).

Combinations of different media need also to be designed to allow users to recognize the composite information represented in them in the way intended. The use of sound and animation together needs to be coordinated so they happen in a logical sequence. An example of this is the design of lip-synch applications, where the animation of an avatar's or agent's face to make it appear to be talking must be carefully synchronized with the speech that is emitted. A slight delay between the two can make it difficult and disturbing to perceive what is happening—as sometimes happens when film dubbing gets out of synch. A general design principle is that information needs to be represented in an appropriate form to facilitate the perception and recognition of its underlying meaning.

DESIGN IMPLICATIONS
Perception

Representations of information need to be designed to be perceptible and recognizable across different media:

- Icons and other graphical representations should enable users to readily distinguish their meaning.
- Bordering and spacing are effective visual ways of grouping information that makes it easier to perceive and locate items.

Black Hills Forest Cheyenne River Social Science South San Jose Badlands Park Juvenile Justice	Peters Landing Public Health San Bernardino Moreno Valley Altamonte Springs Peach Tree City	Jefferson Farms Psychophysics Political Science Game Schedule South Addision Cherry Hills Village	Devlin Hall Positions Hubard Hall Fernadino Beach Council Bluffs Classical Lit
Results and Stats Thousand Oaks Promotions North Palermo Credit Union Wilner Hall	Highland Park Machesney Park Vallecito Mts. Rock Falls Freeport Slaughter Beach	Creative Writing Lake Havasu City Engineering Bldg Sports Studies Lakewood Village Rock Island	Sociology Greek Wallace Hall Concert Tickets Public Radio FM Children's Museum
Performing Arts Italian Coaches Mckees Rocks Glenwood Springs Urban Affairs	Rocky Mountains Latin Pleasant Hills Observatory Public Affairs Heskett Center	Deerfield Beach Arlington Hill Preview Game Richland Hills Experts Guids Neff Hall	Writing Center Theater Auditions Delaware City Scholarships Hendricksville Knights Landing
McLeansboro Experimental Links Graduation Emory Lindquist Clinton Hall San Luis Obispo	Brunswick East Millinocket Women's Studies Vacant News Theatre Candlewood Isle	Grand Wash Cliffs Indian Well Valley Online Courses Lindquist Hall Fisk Hall Los Padres Forest	Modern Literature Studio Arts Hugher Complex Cumberland Flats Central Village Hoffman Estates

Webmaster Russian Athletics Go Shockers Degree Options Newsletter	Curriculum Emergency (EMS) Statistics Award Documents Language Center Future Shockers	Student Life Accountancy Mc Knight Center Council of Women Commute Small Business	Dance Gerontloge Marketing College Bylaws Why Wichita? Tickets
Gelogy Manufacturing Management UCATS Alumni News Saso	Intercollegiate Bowling Wichita Gateway Transfer Day Job Openings Live Radio	Thinker & Movers Alumni Foundations Corbin Center Jardine Hall Hugo Wall School	Career Services Doers & Shockers Core Values Grace Wilkie Hall Strategic Plan Medical Tech
Educational Map Physical Plant Graphic Design Non Credit Class Media Relations Advertising	Beta Alpha Psi Liberal Arts Counseling Biological Science Duerksen Fine Art EMT Program	Staff Aerospace Choral Dept. Alberg Hall French Spanish	Softball, Men's McKinley Hall Email Dental Hygiene Tenure Personnel Policies
English Graduate Complex Music Education Advising Center Medical School Levitt Arena	Religion Art Composition Physics Entrepreneurship Koch Arena Roster	Parents Wrestling Philosopy Wichita Lyceum Fairmount Center Women's Museum	Instrmental Nrsing Opera Sports History Athletic Dept. Health Plan

Figure 3.4 *Two ways of structuring information on a web page. It takes more time for people to find a named item in the top one than in the bottom one, suggesting that using bordering as a grouping method helps searching while using contrasting color hinders it*

- Sounds should be audible and distinguishable so users understand what they represent.
- Speech output should enable users to distinguish between the set of spoken words and also be able to understand their meaning.
- Text should be legible and distinguishable from the background, e.g. it is OK to use yellow text on a black or blue background but not on a white or green background.
- Tactile feedback used in virtual environments should allow users to recognize the meaning of the various touch sensations being emulated. The feedback should be distinguishable so that, for example, the sensation of squeezing is represented in a tactile form that is different from the sensation of pushing.

Memory involves recalling various kinds of knowledge that allow us to act appropriately. It is very versatile, enabling us to do many things. For example, it allows us to recognize someone's face, remember someone's name, recall when we last met them, and know what we said to them last. Simply, without memory we would not be able to function.

It is not possible for us to remember everything that we see, hear, taste, smell, or touch, nor would we want to, as our brains would get completely overloaded. A filtering process is used to decide what information gets further processed and memorized. This filtering process, however, is not without its problems. Often we forget things we would dearly love to remember and conversely remember things we would love to forget. For example, we may find it difficult to remember everyday things like people's names and phone numbers, or scientific knowledge such as mathematical formulae. On the other hand, we may effortlessly remember trivia or tunes that cycle endlessly through our heads.

How does this filtering process work? Initially, encoding takes place determining which information is attended to in the environment and how it is interpreted. The extent to which it takes place affects our ability to recall that information later. The more attention that is paid to something and the more it is processed in terms of thinking about it and comparing it with other knowledge, the more likely it is to be remembered. For example, when learning about a topic it is much better to reflect upon it, carry out exercises, have discussions with others about it, and write notes than just passively read a book or watch a video about it. Thus, how information is interpreted when it is encountered greatly affects how it is represented in memory and how easy it is to retrieve subsequently.

Another factor that affects the extent to which information can be subsequently retrieved is the context in which it is encoded. One outcome is that sometimes it can be difficult for people to recall information that was encoded in a different context from the one they currently are in. Consider the following scenario:

> ***You are on a train and someone comes up to you and says hello. You don't recognize him for a few moments but then realize it is one of your neighbors. You are only used to seeing your neighbor in the hallway of your apartment block and seeing him out of context makes him difficult to recognize initially.***

Another well-known memory phenomenon is that people are much better at recognizing things than recalling things. Furthermore, certain kinds of information are easier to recognize than others. In particular, people are very good at recognizing thousands of pictures even if they have only seen them briefly before.

Activity 3.2

Try to remember the dates of all the members of your family's and your closest friends' birthdays. How many can you remember? Then try to describe what is on the cover of the last CD/DVD you bought. Which is easiest and why?

Comment

It is likely that you remembered much better what was on the CD/DVD cover (the image, the colors, the title) than the birthdays of your family and friends. People are very good at remembering visual cues about things, for example the color of items, the location of objects (a book being on the top shelf), and marks on an object, e.g. a scratch on a watch, a chip on a cup. In contrast, people find other kinds of information persistently difficult to learn and remember, especially arbitrary material like birthdays and phone numbers.

Instead of requiring users to recall from memory a command name from a possible set of hundreds or even thousands, GUIs provide visually-based options that users can browse through until they recognize the operation they want to perform. Likewise, web browsers provide facilities for displaying lists of URLs that have been visited. This means that users need only recognize a name of a site when scanning through a list of URLs.

Activity 3.3

What strategies do you use to help you remember things?

Comment

People often write down what they need to remember on a piece of paper. They also ask others to remind them. Another approach is to use various mental strategies, like mnemonics. A mnemonic involves taking the first letters of a set of words in a phrase or set of concepts and using them to make a more memorable phrase, often using bizarre and idiosyncratic connections. For example, some people have problems working out where east is in relation to west and vice versa, i.e. is it to the left or right. A mnemonic to help figure this out is to take the first letters of the four main points of the compass and then use them in the phrase 'Never Eat Shredded Wheat,' mentally recited in a clockwise sequence.

Personal information management (PIM) has become a growing concern for many people. The number of documents created, images, music files, and videoclips downloaded, emails and attachments saved, URLs bookmarked, and so on increases every day. A major problem is deciding where and how to save them, e.g. in hierarchical or flat folders, and then remembering what they were called and where to find them again. Naming is the most common means of encoding them, but trying to remember a name of a file you created some time back can be very difficult, especially if you have tens of thousands of named files. How might such a process be facilitated, taking into account people's memory abilities?

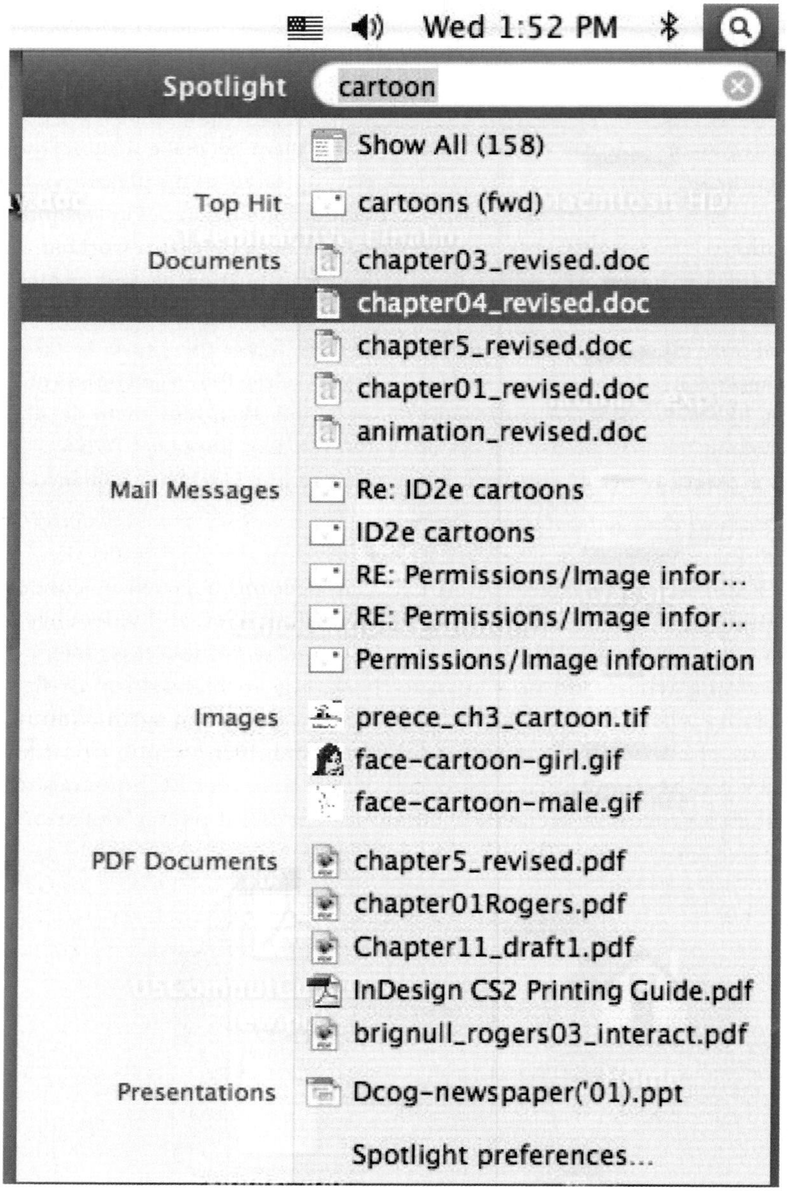

Figure 3.5 *Apple Computer's Spotlight search tool*

Mark Lansdale and Ernest Edmonds (1992) suggest that it is profitable to view this kind of remembering as involving two memory processes: recall-directed, followed by recognition-based scanning. The first refers to using memorized information about the required file to get as close to it as possible. The more exact this is the more success the user will have in tracking down the desired file. The second happens when recall has failed to produce what a user wants and so requires reading through a list. To illustrate the difference between these two processes, consider the following scenario: a user is trying to access a couple of websites she visited the week before that compared the selling price of cars offered by different dealers. The user is able to recall the name of one website, 'autobargains.com.' She types this in and the website appears. This is an example of successful recall-directed memory. However, the user is unable to remember the name of the second one. She vaguely remembers it was something like 'alwaysthecheapest.com,' but typing this in proves unsuccessful. Instead, she switches to scanning her history list and selects the folder labeled more than six days ago. She notices two or three URLs that could be the one desired at the top of the list, and on the second attempt she finds the website she is looking for. In this situation, the user initially tries recall-directed memory and when this fails, adopts the second strategy of recognition-based scanning—which takes longer but eventually results in success.

File management systems should be designed to optimize both kinds of memory processes. In particular, systems should be developed that let people use whatever memory they have to limit the area being searched and then represent the information in this area of the interface so as to maximally assist them in finding what they need. The system should provide the user with a number of ways of encoding documents mnemonically, including time stamping, categorizing, flagging, and attribution, e.g. color, text, icon, sound, or image. Powerful search engines have gone a long way towards helping people track down the files they want. For example, various search and find tools, such as Apple's Spotlight, enable the user to type a full or partial name or even the first letter of a file that it then searches for in the entire system, including emails, contacts, images, calendars, and applications. Figure 3.5 shows part of a list of 158 files that Spotlight matched to the user's phrase 'cartoon', prioritized in terms of what the user may be looking for, such as chapters and images.

Box 3.2
The problem with the magical number 7 plus or minus 2

Perhaps the best known finding in psychology (certainly the one that nearly all students remember many years after they have finished their studies) is George Miller's (1956) theory that 7±2 chunks of information can be held in short-term memory at any one time. By short-term memory he meant a memory store

in which information was assumed to be processed when first perceived. By chunks he meant a range of items like numbers, letters, or words. According to Miller's theory, therefore, people's immediate memory capacity is very limited. They are able to remember only a few words or numbers that they have heard or seen. If you are not familiar with this phenomenon, try out the following exercise: read the first list below (or get someone to read it to you), cover it up, and then try to recall as many of the items as possible. Repeat this for the other lists.

- 3, 12, 6, 20, 9, 4, 0, 1, 19, 8, 97, 13, 84
- cat, house, paper, laugh, people, red, yes, number, shadow, broom, rain, plant, lamp, chocolate, radio, one, coin, jet
- t, k, s, y, r, q, x, p, a, z, l, b, m, e

How many did you correctly remember for each list? Between 5 and 9, as suggested by Miller's theory?

Chunks can also be combined items that are meaningful. For example, it is possible to remember the same number of two-word phrases like hot chocolate, banana split, cream cracker, rock music, cheddar cheese, leather belt, laser printer, tree fern, fluffy duckling, cold rain. When these are all muddled up, e.g. split belt, fern crackers, banana laser, printer cream, cheddar tree, rain duckling, hot rock, however, it is much harder to remember as many chunks. This is mainly because the first set contains all meaningful two-word phrases that have been heard before and require less time to be processed in short-term memory, whereas the second set are completely novel phrases that don't exist in the real world. You need to spend time linking the two parts of the phrase together while trying to memorize them. This takes more time and effort to achieve. Of course it is possible to do if you have time to spend rehearsing them, but if you are asked to do it having heard them only once in quick succession, it is most likely you will remember only a few.

You may be thinking by now, "OK, this is interesting, but what has it got to do with interaction design?" Well, not only does this 50-year-old theory have a special place in psychology, it has also made a big impression in HCI. Unfortunately, however, for the wrong reasons. Many designers have heard or read about this phenomenon and think, ah, here is a bit of psychology I can usefully apply to interface design. Would you agree with them? If so, how might people's ability to only remember 7±2 chunks that they have just read or heard be usefully applied to interaction design?

According to a survey by Bob Bailey (2000), several designers have been led to believe the following guidelines and have even created interfaces based on them:

- Have only seven options on a menu.
- Display only seven icons on a menu bar.
- Never have more than seven bullets in a list.
- Place only seven tabs at the top of a website page.

> - **Place only seven items on a pull-down menu.**
>
> **All of these are wrong. Why? The simple reason is that these are all items that can be scanned and rescanned visually and hence do *not* have to be recalled from short-term memory. They don't just flash up on the screen and disappear, requiring the user to remember them before deciding which one to select. If you were asked to find an item of food most people crave in the set of single words listed above, would you have any problem? No, you would just scan the list until you recognized the one (chocolate) that matched the task and then select it—just as people do when interacting with menus, lists, and tabs—regardless of whether they comprise three or 30 items. What the users are required to do here is not remember as many items as possible, having only heard or seen them once in a sequence, but instead *scan* through a set of items until they *recognize* the one they want. Quite a different task. Furthermore, there is much more useful psychological research that can be profitably applied to interaction design.** ■

Memory load. Phone banking has become increasingly popular in the last few years. It allows customers to carry out financial transactions, such as paying bills and checking the balance of their accounts, at their convenience. One of the problems confronting banks that provide this facility, however, is how to manage security concerns. Anyone can phone up a bank and pretend to be someone else. How do the banks prevent fraudulent transactions?

One solution has been to develop rigorous security measures whereby customers must provide various pieces of information before gaining access to their accounts. Typically, these include providing the answers to a combination of the following:

- their zip code or post code
- their mother's maiden name
- their birthplace
- the last school they attended
- the first school they attended
- a password of between 5 and 10 letters
- a *memorable* address (not their home)
- a *memorable* date (not their birthday).

Many of these are relatively easy to remember and recall as they are very familiar. But consider the last two. How easy is it for someone to come up with such *memorable* information and then be able to recall it readily? Perhaps the customer can give the address and birthday of another member of their family as a memorable address and date. But what about the request for a password? Suppose a customer selects the word 'interaction' as a password—fairly easy to remember. The problem is that the bank operators do not ask for the full password, because of the danger that someone in the vicinity might overhear and write it down. Instead they are instructed to ask the customer to provide specific letters from it, like the seventh followed by the fifth. However, such information does not spring readily to mind. Instead, it requires mentally counting each letter of the password until the desired one is reached. How long does it take you to determine the seventh letter of the password 'interaction'? How did you do it?

To make things harder, banks also randomize the questions they ask. Again, this is to prevent someone who might be overhearing from memorizing the sequence of information. However, it also means that the customers themselves cannot learn the sequence of information required, meaning they have to generate different information every time they call up the bank.

This requirement to remember and recall such information puts a big memory load on customers. Some people find such a procedure quite nerve-wracking and are prone to forget certain pieces of information. As a coping strategy they write down their details on a sheet of paper. Having such an external representation at hand makes it much easier for them to read off the necessary information rather than having to recall it from memory. However, it also makes them vulnerable to the very fraud the banks were trying to prevent, should anyone else get hold of that piece of paper!

Activity 3.4

How else might banks solve the problem of providing a secure system while making the memory load relatively easy for people wanting to use phone banking? How does phone banking compare with online banking?

Comment

An alternative approach is to provide the customers with a PIN and ask them to key this in on their phone keypad, followed by asking one or two questions like their zip or post code, as a backup. Online banking has similar security risks to phone banking, and hence this requires a number of security measures to be enforced. These include that the user sets up a nickname and a password. For example, some banks require typing in three randomly selected letters from a password each time the user logs on. This is harder to do online than when asked over the phone, mainly because it interferes with the normally highly automated process of typing in a password. You really have to think about what letters and numbers are in your password; for example, has it got two letter f's after the number 6, or just one?

Researchers have also investigated whether images could be used instead of alphanumerics for passwords. The idea is based on the principle that recognition is better than recall: users should be able to remember their passwords more accurately if they are required to recognize a set of images from a display that make up their password than if they have to recall a sequence of alphanumerics. To this end, the graphical authentication approach has been developed which asks people to select a series of images from different matrices of options. The images can be faces, cartoons, or photos of scenes or objects, e.g. sunset, dog or even abstract images. To enable the process to be secure, however, requires people selecting a sequence of four to eight images and subsequently being able to recognize each item in the correct sequence. In other words, both recall (of the sequence) and recognition are involved. Studies have shown that while the graphical approach appears an attractive alternative it has yet to demonstrate convincingly an advantage over the use of alphanumerics. Moreover, it takes much longer to create and subsequently select a sequence of images each time a person logs on than typing in a set of letters and numbers at a keyboard (De Angeli *et al.*, 2005).

Box 3.3
Using UbiComp technology as a memory aid for cooking

People suffering from memory impairments can find it difficult to complete common household tasks, like cooking and washing up, where they may forget a step or where they were. These can be exacerbated if the person gets disrupted, e.g. the phone rings, and where they may end up not adding an ingredient or adding the washing up liquid twice. A prototype system called Cook's Collage was designed to provide surrogate memory support for general cooking tasks (Tran *et al.*, 2005). Cameras were mounted underneath cabinets to capture still images of a cooking activity. These were then displayed as a series of images, in the form of a cartoon strip, on a flat-panel display mounted on an eye-level kitchen cabinet (see Figure 3.6). Preliminary evaluation of the prototype, being used by old people while cooking, showed them using it mainly as an *aide-memoire*, checking to see whether they had added certain ingredients after being distracted from the cooking task at hand.

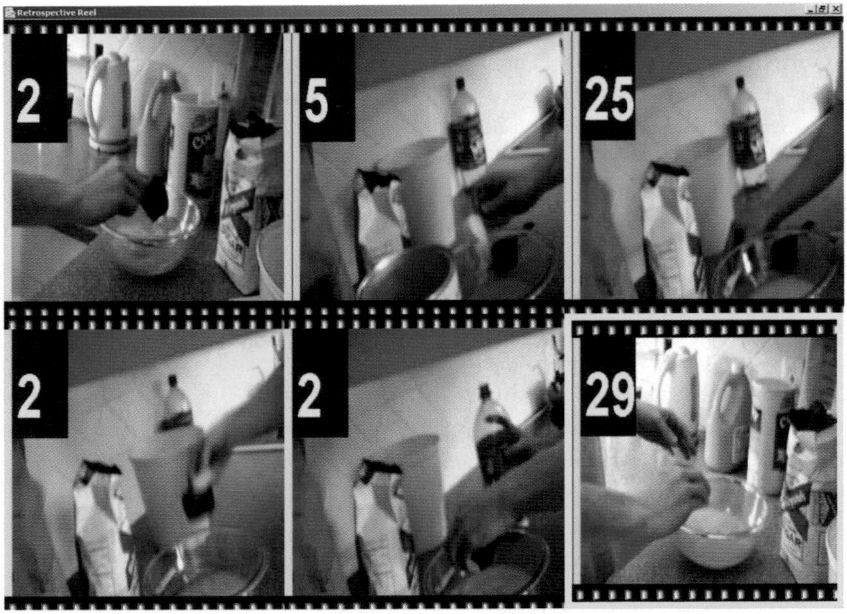

Figure 3.6 A screenshot of Cook's Collage showing images of a recent cooking activity. The strip is designed to be read backwards, starting with the highlighted image. This shows to the cook that he previously added the 29th scoop (!) of sugar and in the previous image two scoops of soda water

DESIGN IMPLICATIONS
Memory

- Do not overload users' memories with complicated procedures for carrying out tasks.
- Design interfaces that promote *recognition* rather than *recall* by using menus, icons, and consistently placed objects.
- Provide users with a variety of ways of encoding digital information, e.g. files, emails, images, to help them remember where they have stored them, through the use of categories, color, flagging, time stamping, icons, etc.

Learning can be considered in terms of (i) how to use a computer-based application or (ii) using a computer-based application to understand a given topic. Jack Carroll (1990) and his colleagues have written extensively about how to design interfaces to help learners develop computer-based skills. A main observation is that people find it very hard to learn by following a set of instructions in a manual. Instead, they much prefer to 'learn through doing.' GUIs and direct manipulation interfaces are good environments for supporting this kind of active learning by supporting exploratory interaction and, importantly, allowing users to 'undo' their actions, i.e. return to a previous state if they make a mistake by clicking on the wrong option. Carroll has also suggested that another way of helping learners is by using a 'training-wheels' approach. This involves restricting the possible functions that can be carried out by a novice to the basics and then extending these as the novice becomes more experienced. The underlying rationale is to make initial learning more tractable, helping the learner focus on simple operations before moving on to more complex ones.

There have been numerous attempts to harness the capabilities of different technologies to help learners understand topics. One of the main benefits of interactive technologies, such as web-based, multimedia, and virtual reality, is that they provide alternative ways of representing and interacting with information that are not possible with traditional technologies, e.g. books, video. In so doing, they have the potential of offering learners the ability to explore ideas and concepts in different ways. For example, interactive multimedia has been designed to help children learn abstract concepts, e.g. mathematical formulae, notations, laws of physics, that they find difficult to grasp when represented in other media. Different representations of the same process, e.g. a graph, a formula, a sound, a simulation, are displayed and interacted with in ways that make their relationship with each other more explicit to the learner.

One form of interactivity that has been found to be highly effective is 'dynalinking' (Rogers and Scaife, 1998). Abstract representations, such as diagrams, are linked together with a more concrete illustration of what they stand for, such as simulation. Changes in one are matched by changes in the other, enabling a better understanding of what the abstraction means. An example where it has been used is in the design of Pondworld, aimed at helping students learn ecological concepts, e.g. food webs. A concrete simulation showed various organisms swimming and moving around and occasionally an event where one would eat another, e.g. a snail eating the weed. This was annotated and accompanied by various eating sounds, e.g. chomping to attract the children's attention. The children could also interact with the simulation. When an organism was clicked on, it would say what it was and what it ate, e.g. "I'm a weed. I make my own food". The concrete simulation was dynalinked with other abstract representations of the pond ecosystem. One of these was an abstract food web diagram (see Figure 3.7). The children were encouraged to interact with the interlinked diagrams in various ways and to observe what happened in the concrete simulation when something was changed in the diagram and vice versa. The evaluation study showed that children understood much better the purpose of the diagrams and improved significantly in their ability to reason about the ecosystem (Rogers *et al.*, 2003).

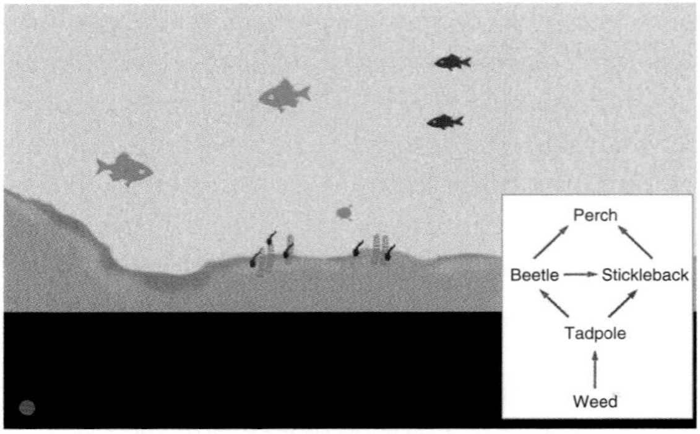

Figure 3.7 *Dynalinking used in the Pondworld software*

Dynalinking has been used in other domains to explicitly show relationships among multiple dimensions where the information to be understood or learned is complex (Sutcliffe, 2002). For example, it can be useful for domains like economic forecasting, molecular modeling, and statistical analyses.

Dilemma
Evolutionary versus revolutionary upgrading

A constant dilemma facing designers involved in upgrading software is where and how to place new functions. Decisions have to be made on how to incorporate them with the existing interface design. Do they try to keep the same structure and add more buttons/menu options, or do they design a new model of interaction that is better suited to organizing and categorizing the increased set of functions? If the former strategy is followed, users do not have to learn a new conceptual model every time they upgrade a piece of software. The down side of trying to keep the same interface structure, however, is that it can easily get overloaded.

A problem when upgrading software, therefore, is working out how to redesign the interaction so that the amount of relearning, relative to the gains from the new functionality, is acceptable by users. ■

DESIGN IMPLICATIONS
Learning

- Design interfaces that encourage exploration.
- Design interfaces that constrain and guide users to select appropriate actions when initially learning.
- Dynamically link concrete representations and abstract concepts to facilitate the learning of complex material.

Reading, speaking, and listening are three forms of language processing that have similar and different properties. One similarity is that the meaning of sentences or phrases is the same regardless of the mode in which it is conveyed. For example, the sentence "Computers are a wonderful invention" essentially has the same meaning whether one reads it, speaks it, or hears it. However, the ease with which people can read, listen, or speak differs depending on the person, task, and context. For example, many people find listening much easier than reading. Specific differences between the three modes include:

- Written language is permanent while listening is transient. It is possible to reread information if not understood the first time round. This is not possible with spoken information that is being broadcast.
- Reading can be quicker than speaking or listening, as written text can be rapidly scanned in ways not possible when listening to serially presented spoken words.
- Listening requires less cognitive effort than reading or speaking. Children, especially, often prefer to listen to narratives provided in multimedia or web-based learning material than to read the equivalent text online.
- Written language tends to be grammatical while spoken language is often ungrammatical. For example, people often start a sentence and stop in mid-sentence, letting someone else start
speaking.
- There are marked differences between people in their ability to use language. Some people prefer reading to listening, while others prefer listening. Likewise, some people prefer speaking to writing and vice versa.
- Dyslexics have difficulties understanding and recognizing written words, making it hard for them to write grammatical sentences and spell correctly.
- People who have hearing or sight problems are restricted in the way they can process language.

Many applications have been developed either to capitalize on people's reading, writing, and listening skills, or to support or replace them where they lack or have difficulty with them. These include:

- Interactive books and web-based material that help people to read or learn foreign languages.
- Speech-recognition systems that allow users to provide instructions via spoken commands, e.g. wordprocessing dictation, home control devices that respond to vocalized requests.
- Speech-output systems that use artificially generated speech, e.g. written-text-to-speech systems for the blind.
- Natural-language systems that enable users to type in questions and give text-based responses, e.g. the Ask search engine.
- Cognitive aids that help people who find it difficult to read, write, and speak. A number of special interfaces have been developed for people who have problems with reading, writing, and speaking, e.g. see Edwards (1992).
- Customized input and output devices that allow people with various disabilities to have access to the web and use wordprocessors and other software packages.
- Interaction techniques that allow blind people to read graphs and other visuals on the web through the use of auditory navigation and tactile diagrams (Petrie *et al.*, 2002).

DESIGN IMPLICATIONS
Reading, speaking, and listening

- Keep the length of speech-based menus and instructions to a minimum. Research has shown that people find it hard to follow spoken menus with more than three or four options. Likewise, they are bad at remembering sets of instructions and directions that have more than a few parts.
- Accentuate the intonation of artificially generated speech voices, as they are harder to understand than human voices.
- Provide opportunities for making text large on a screen, without affecting the formatting, for people who find it hard to read small text.

Problem-solving, planning, reasoning, and decision-making are all processes involving reflective cognition. They include thinking about what to do, what the options are, and what the consequences might be of carrying out a given action. They often involve conscious processes (being aware of what one is thinking about), discussion with others (or oneself), and the use of various kinds of artifacts, e.g. maps, books, pen and paper. For example, when planning the best route to get somewhere, say a foreign city, we may ask others, use a map, get instructions from the web, or a combination of these. Reasoning also involves working through different scenarios and deciding which is the best option or solution to a given problem. In the route-planning activity we may be aware of alternative routes and reason through the advantages and disadvantages of each route before deciding on the best one. Many a family argument has come about because one member thinks he or she knows the best route while another thinks otherwise.

Comparing different sources of information is also common practice when seeking information on the web. For example, just as people will phone around for a range of quotes, so too will they use 'comparison' search engines, e.g. cheapflights.com, that list products in terms of their prices available on other sites.

The extent to which people engage in reflective cognition depends on their level of experience with a domain, application, or skill. Novices tend to have limited knowledge and will often make assumptions about what to do using other knowledge about similar situations. They tend to act by trial and error, exploring and experimenting with ways of doing things. As a result they may start off being slow, making errors, and generally being inefficient. They may also act irrationally, following their superstitions and not thinking ahead to the consequences of their actions. In contrast, experts have much more knowledge and experience and are able to select optimal strategies for carrying out their tasks. They are likely to be able to think ahead more, considering what the consequences might be of opting for a particular move or solution (as do expert chess players).

Box 3.4
Wanted: an interface that the police can use

In 2004 the San Jose police department installed a new mobile dispatch system in every police car that used a windows-based touch-screen computer. But the system was found to be too complex and difficult to use (Hafner, 2004). Part of the problem was that routine tasks, e.g. calling for assistance, that should have been straightforward to do were transformed into overly complicated tasks, requiring long sequences. The system was designed to aid police in rapid decision-making when driving their cars, but the interface was found to be too cluttered and behaved too much like a Windows computer. As one police officer said: "do you think if you're hunkered down and someone's shooting at you in your car, you're going to be able to sit there and look for Control or Alt or Function? No you are going to look for the red button." After consultation with police officers the interface was designed to be much simpler and with fewer steps required for critical actions.

DESIGN IMPLICATIONS
Problem-solving, planning, reasoning, and decision-making

- Provide additional hidden information that is easy to access for users who wish to understand more about how to carry out an activity more effectively, e.g. web searching.
- Use simple and memorable functions at the interface for computational aids intended to support rapid decision-making and planning that takes place while on the move.

3.3 Cognitive frameworks

A number of conceptual frameworks have been developed to explain and predict user behavior based on theories of cognition. In this section, we outline the influential ones that have been developed for interaction design, which are:

- mental models
- theory of action
- information processing
- external cognition
- distributed cognition.

3.3.1 Mental models

In Chapter 2 we pointed out that a successful system is one based on a conceptual model that enables users to readily learn a system and use it effectively. People primarily develop knowledge of how to interact with a system and, to a lesser extent, how that system works. These two kinds of knowledge are often referred to as a user's mental model.

It is assumed that mental models are used by people to reason about a system, and in particular, to try to fathom out what to do when something unexpected happens with the system or when encountering unfamiliar systems. The more someone learns about a system and how it functions, the more their mental model develops. For example, TV engineers have a 'deep' mental model of how TVs work that allows them to work out how to fix them. In contrast, an average citizen is likely to have a reasonably good mental model of how to operate a TV but a 'shallow' mental model of how it works. Within cognitive psychology, mental models have been postulated as internal constructions of some aspect of the external world that are manipulated, enabling predictions and inferences to be made (Craik, 1943). This process is thought to involve the 'fleshing out' and the 'running' of a mental model (Johnson-Laird, 1983). This can involve both unconscious and conscious mental processes, where images and analogies are activated.

Activity 3.5

To illustrate how we use mental models in our everyday reasoning, imagine the following two scenarios:

1. **You arrive home from a holiday on a cold winter's night to a cold house. You have a small baby and you need to get the house warm as quickly as possible. Your house is centrally heated. Do you set the thermostat as high as possible or turn it to the desired temperature, e.g. 70°F?**
2. **You arrive home from being out all night starving hungry. You look in the fridge and find all that is left is an uncooked pizza. The instructions on the packet say heat the oven to 375°F and then place the pizza in the oven for 20 minutes. Your oven is electric. How do you heat it up? Do you turn it to the specified temperature or higher?**

Comment

Most people when asked the first question imagine the scenario in terms of what they would do in their own house and choose the first option. A typical explanation is that setting the temperature to be as high as possible increases the rate at which the room warms up. While many people may believe this, it is incorrect. Thermostats work by switching on the heat and keeping it going at a constant speed until the desired temperature set is reached, at which point they cut out. They cannot control the rate at which heat is given out from a heating system. Left at a given setting, thermostats will turn the heat on and off as necessary to maintain the desired temperature.

When asked the second question, most people say they would turn the oven to the specified temperature and put the pizza in when they think it is at the desired temperature. Some people answer that they would turn the oven to a higher temperature in order to warm it up more quickly. Electric ovens work on the same principle as central heating, and so turning the heat up higher will not warm it up any quicker. There is also the problem of the pizza burning if the oven is too hot!

Why do people use erroneous mental models? It seems that in the above scenarios, they are running a mental model based on a general valve theory of the way something works (Kempton, 1986). This assumes the underlying principle of 'more is more:' the more you turn or push something the more it causes the desired effect. This principle holds for a range of physical devices, such as faucets and radio controls, where the more you turn them the more water or volume is given. However, it does not hold for thermostats, which instead function based on the principle of an on–off switch. What seems to happen is that in everyday life people develop a core set of abstractions about how things work, and apply these to a range of devices, irrespective of whether they are appropriate.

Using incorrect mental models to guide behavior is surprisingly common. Just watch people at a pedestrian crossing or waiting for an elevator. How many times do they press the button? A lot of people will press it at least twice. When asked why a common reason given is that they think it will make the lights change faster or ensure the elevator arrives. This seems to be another example of following the 'more is more' philosophy: it is believed that the more times you press the button the more likely it is to result in the desired effect.

Many people's understanding of how computer-based technologies and services, e.g. the Internet, wireless networking, broadband, search engines, viruses, work is poor. Their mental models are often incomplete, easily confusable, based on inappropriate analogies, and superstition (Norman, 1983). As a consequence, they find it difficult to identify, describe, or solve a problem, and lack the words or concepts to explain what is happening.

If people could develop better mental models of interactive systems they would be in a better position to know how to carry out their tasks efficiently, and know what to do if a system started malfunctioning. Ideally, they should be able to develop a mental model that matches the conceptual model. But to what extent is this realistic given that most people are resistant to spending much time learning about how things work, especially if it involves reading manuals or other documentation? Alternatively, if interactive technologies could be designed to be more *transparent*, then it might be easier to understand them in terms of how they work and what to do when they don't. Transparency involves including:

- useful feedback in response to user input
- easy-to-understand and intuitive ways of interacting with the system.

In addition, it requires providing the right kind and level of information, in the form of:

- clear and easy-to-follow instructions
- appropriate online help and tutorials
- context-sensitive guidance for users, set at their level of experience, explaining how to proceed when they are not sure what to do at a given stage of a task.

Dilemma
How much transparency?

How much and what kind of transparency do you think a designer should provide in an interactive product? This is not a straightforward question to answer and depends a lot on the requirements of the targeted user groups. Some users simply want to get on with their tasks and don't want to have to learn about how the thing they are using works. In this situation, the system should be designed to make it obvious what to do and how to use it. For example, most cell phone users want a simple 'plug-and-play' type interface, where it is straightforward to carry out functions like saving an address, text messaging, and making a call. Functions that are difficult to learn can be off-putting. Users simply won't bother to make the extra effort, meaning that many of the functions provided are never used. Other users like to understand how the device they are using works in order to make informed decisions about how to carry out their tasks, especially if there are numerous ways of doing something. Some search engines have been designed with this in mind: they provide background information on how they work and how to improve one's searching techniques (see Figure 3.8).

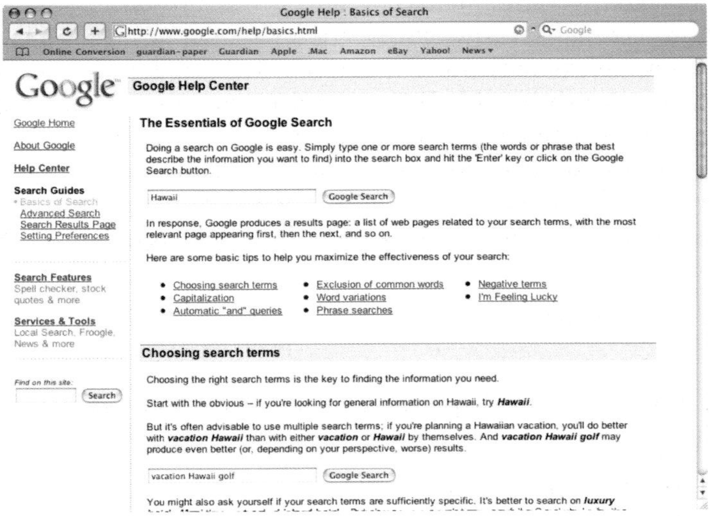

Figure 3.8 *The Google help center which provides extensive information about how to make your searching strategy more effective*

3.3.2 Theory of action

Another way of conceptualizing how users interact with interactive products is in terms of their goals and what they need to do to achieve them. Norman's (1986) theory of action specifies what users do at the interface in terms of seven stages of an activity:

- Establish a goal.
- Form an intention.
- Specify an action sequence.
- Execute an action.
- Perceive the system state.
- Interpret the state.
- Evaluate the system state with respect to the goals and intentions.

The theory proposes that the stages take place sequentially. To illustrate how these are cycled through, consider the task of finding out about the latest news for the day. First, the user sets a goal to find out about the latest news via a news website. Next, it involves forming an intention, e.g. check out the BBC website, then specifying what to do, e.g. move cursor to link on browser), followed by executing that action sequence, e.g. move mouse, click on mouse button. To assess the outcome of the action and whether it meets the user's goal involves perceiving what has happened at the interface, e.g. seeing a new page pop up on the screen, interpreting it, e.g. reading that it is the BBC newsite, and then evaluating it with respect to the goal, e.g. now able to read the latest news.

In reality, however, human activity does not proceed in such an orderly and sequential manner. It is more often the case that some stages are missed, others repeated, while others appear out of order. Furthermore, many users do not have a clear goal in mind but react to what appears on the screen, such as when they are browsing the web or revisiting emails. It must be stressed, therefore, that the theory is only meant as an *approximation* of what happens and has been deliberately simplified. It is intended to help designers and researchers think about how best to design interfaces to enable users to monitor their actions with respect to their goals in terms of the various stages of action.

At a general level, it suggests the importance of providing feedback about the system state so that users can check to see whether their goals and intentions have been met. An example is the use of visual reminders, which can be designed to support the different stages of action. Dialog boxes can trigger the generation of intentions by reminding users of what is possible. Menus can aid the stages of intention formation and action specification through allowing users to browse, scan, and point at an option. Feedback, such as the different cursor icons used at an interface, inform users that an operation is currently being executed.

It is important to note that while interaction styles can be specifically geared towards certain action stages, they may do so at the expense of others. For example, while menus are good at helping users form intentions, they can also distract them by providing a range of choices that can lead them astray from their initial intentions. How many times have you changed your mind about what you planned to do based on what catches your eye when browsing a set of menu options or hyperlinks on a website? And, how often have you been tempted to add features like sounds, animations, colors, and fancy backgrounds to a Powerpoint presentation because you happen upon them in the menu options—even though they were not part of your original intention to create a set of slides for a talk? Such reaction-based actions are common, especially for GUI-based interfaces.

Related to the theory of action is the gulf of execution and the gulf of evaluation (Norman, 1986; Hutchins *et al.*, 1986). The 'gulfs' explicate the gaps that exist between the user and the interface and point to how to design the latter to enable the user to cope with them. The first one—the gulf of execution—describes the distance from the user to the physical system while the second one—the gulf of evaluation—is the distance from the physical system to the user (see Figure 3.9). Norman and his colleagues suggest that designers and users need to concern themselves with how to bridge the gulfs in order to reduce the cognitive effort required to perform a task. This can be achieved, on the one hand, by designing usable interfaces that match the psychological characteristics of the user, e.g. taking into account their memory limitations, and, on the other hand, by the user learning to create goals, plans, and action sequences that fit with how the interface works.

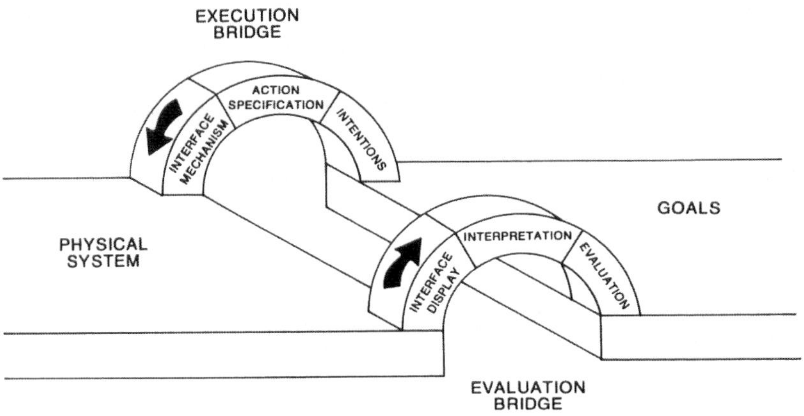

Figure 3.9 *Bridging the gulfs of execution and evaluation*

Over the last two decades, the gulfs have had considerable impact on how researchers conceptualize and design new interfaces and tools. Lieberman and Fry (1995) used the concepts to directly inform the design of a debugging environment, called ZStep 94, intended to help programmers overcome the gulfs of execution and evaluation when translating their intentions of how a program should be written with their actual coding. Instead of having to imagine how a piece of code will work over time, graphical tools were provided at the interface that dynamically visualized the process for the programmer (see Figure 3.10). In so doing, the gulf of execution is reduced, requiring much less cognitive effort by the programmer. Nowadays, such debugging tools are commonplace.

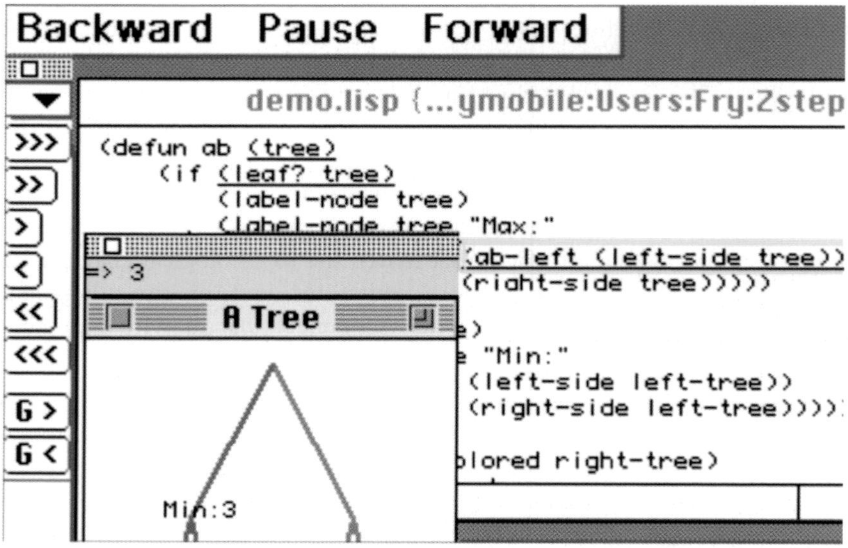

Figure 3.10 *ZStep 94: an early debugging tool that visualized code over time, inspired by the concepts of the gulf of execution and evaluation (Lieberman and Fry, 1995)*

New conceptual frameworks have also been spawned. Quintana *et al.* (2000) have used the gulfs as the basis of their learner-centered design (LCD) approach, that has been influential in informing the design of educational applications. They stress the need to bridge the 'gulf of expertise' between a learner and the domain they are learning about. Bellotti *et al.* (2002) have also used it as the basis of their 'making sense' framework that addresses the new challenges facing designers when developing ubiquitous computing systems.

3.3.3 Information processing

Another approach to conceptualizing how the mind works has been to use metaphors and analogies. A number of comparisons have been made, including conceptualizing the mind as a reservoir, a telephone network, and a digital computer. One prevalent metaphor from cognitive psychology is the idea that the mind is an information processor. Information is thought to enter and exit the mind through a series of ordered processing stages (see Figure 3.11). Within these stages, various processes are assumed to act upon mental representations. Processes include comparing and matching. Mental representations are assumed to comprise images, mental models, rules, and other forms of knowledge.

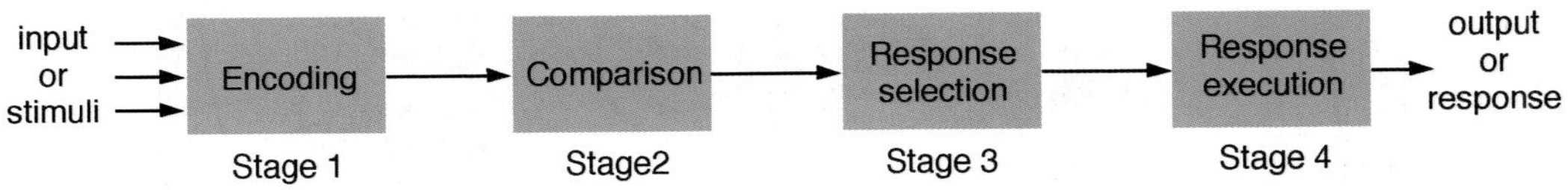

Figure 3.11 *Human information processing model*

The information processing model provides a basis from which to make predictions about human performance. Hypotheses can be made about how long someone will take to perceive and respond to a stimulus (also known as reaction time) and what bottlenecks occur if a person is overloaded with too much information. A classic approach is the human processor model, which models the cognitive processes of a user interacting with a computer (Card *et al.*, 1983). Based on the information processing model, cognition is conceptualized as a series of processing stages, where perceptual, cognitive, and motor processors are organized in relation to one another (see Figure 3.12). The model predicts which cognitive processes are involved when a user interacts with a computer, enabling calculations to be made of how long a user will take to carry out various tasks. This can be useful when comparing different interfaces. For example, it has been used to compare how well different wordprocessors support a range of editing tasks (see section 15.4).

The information processing approach is based on modeling mental activities that happen *exclusively* inside the head. However, most cognitive activities involve people interacting with external kinds of representations, like books, documents, and computers—not to mention one another. For example, when we go home from wherever we have been we do not need to remember the details of the route because we rely on cues in the environment, e.g. we know to turn left at the red house, right when the road comes to a T-junction, and so on. Similarly, when we are at home we do not have to remember where everything is because information is 'out there.' We decide what to eat and drink by scanning the items in the fridge, find out whether any messages have been left by glancing at the

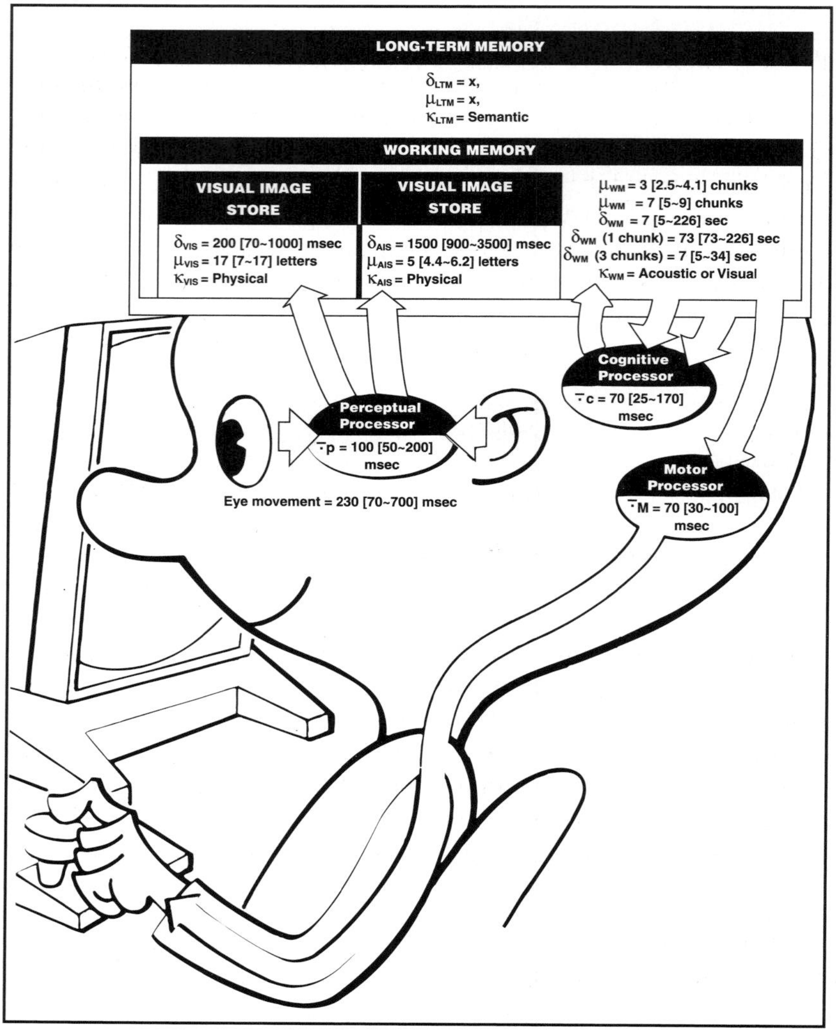

Figure 3.12 *The human processor model*

answering machine to see if there is a flashing light, and so on. To what extent, therefore, can we say that information processing models are truly representative of everyday cognitive activities? Moreover, do they adequately account for how people interact with computers and other devices?

Several researchers have argued that existing information processing approaches are too impoverished:

> ***The traditional approach to the study of cognition is to look at the pure intellect, isolated from distractions and from artificial aids. Experiments are performed in closed, isolated rooms, with a minimum of distracting lights or sounds, no other people to assist with the task, and no aids to memory or thought. The tasks are arbitrary ones, invented by the researcher. Model builders build simulations and descriptions of these isolated situations. The theoretical analyses are self-contained little structures, isolated from the world, isolated from any other knowledge or abilities of the person. (Norman, 1990, p. 5)***

Instead, there has been an increasing trend to study cognitive activities in the context in which they occur, analyzing cognition as it happens "in the wild" (Hutchins, 1995). A central goal has been to look at how structures in the environment can both aid human cognition and reduce cognitive load. Two approaches that have adopted this approach are 'external' and 'distributed' cognition, which we now turn our attention to.

3.3.4 External cognition

People interact with or create information through using a variety of external representations, e.g. books, multimedia, newspapers, web pages, maps, diagrams, notes, drawings, and so on. Furthermore, an impressive range of tools have been developed throughout history to aid cognition, including pens, calculators, and computer-based technologies. The *combination* of external representations and physical tools has greatly extended and supported people's ability to carry out cognitive activities (Norman, 1993). Indeed, they are such an integral part that it is difficult to imagine how we would go about much of our everyday life without them.

External cognition is concerned with explaining the cognitive processes involved when we interact with different external representations (Scaife and Rogers, 1996). A main goal is to explicate the cognitive benefits of using different representations for different cognitive activities and the processes involved. The main ones include:

1. Externalizing to reduce memory load.
2. Computational offloading.
3. Annotating and cognitive tracing.

1. Externalizing to reduce memory load

A number of strategies have been developed for transforming knowledge into external representations to reduce memory load. One such strategy is externalizing things we find difficult to remember, such as birthdays, appointments, and addresses. Diaries, personal reminders, and calendars are examples of cognitive artifacts that are commonly used for this purpose, acting as external reminders of what we need to do at a given time, e.g. buy a card for a relative's birthday.

Other kinds of external representations that people frequently employ are notes, like post-it notes, shopping lists, and to-do lists. Where these are placed in the environment can also be crucial. For example, people often place post-it notes in prominent positions, such as on walls, on the side of computer monitors, by the front door, and sometimes even on their hands, in a deliberate attempt to ensure they do remind them of what needs to be done or remembered. People also place things in piles in their offices and by the front door, indicating what needs to be done urgently and what can wait for a while.

Externalizing, therefore, can help reduce people's memory burden by:

- reminding them to do something, e.g. get something for their mother's birthday
- reminding them of what to do, e.g. buy a card
- reminding them of when to do something, e.g. send it by a certain date.

A number of computer-based applications have been developed to reduce the burden on people to remember things, including web-based to-do list services, e.g. Ta-da™, email, and text messaging for meetings, birthdays, etc. Specialized prosthetic devices have also been designed for people with memory problems, such as the memory aid for cooking depicted in Box 3.3.

2. Computational offloading

Computational offloading occurs when we use a tool or device in conjunction with an external representation to help us carry out a computation. An example is using pen and paper to solve a math problem.

Activity 3.6

1. Multiply 2 by 3 in your head. Easy. Now try multiplying 234 by 456 in your head. Not as easy. Try doing the sum using a pen and paper. Then try again with a calculator. Why is it easier to do the calculation with pen and paper and even easier with a calculator?

2. Try doing the same two sums using Roman numerals.

Comment

1. Carrying out the sum using pen and paper is easier than doing it in your head because you 'offload' some of the computation by writing down partial results and using them to continue with the calculation. Doing the same sum with a calculator is even easier, because it requires only eight simple key presses. Even more of the computation has been offloaded onto the tool. You need only follow a simple internalized procedure (key in first number, then the multiplier sign, then next number, and finally the equals

sign) and then read off the result from the external display.

2. Using Roman numerals to do the same sum is much harder: 2 by 3 becomes II × III, and 234 by 456 becomes CCXXXIIII × CCC-CXXXXXVI. The first calculation may be possible to do in your head or on a bit of paper, but the second is incredibly difficult to do in your head or even on a piece of paper (unless you are an expert in using Roman numerals or you 'cheat' and transform it into Arabic numerals). Calculators do not have Roman numerals so it would be impossible to do on a calculator.

Hence, it is much harder to perform the calculations using Roman numerals than algebraic numerals—even though the problem is equivalent in both conditions. The reason for this is that the two kinds of *representation* transform the task into one that is easy and one that is more difficult, respectively. The kind of tool used also can change the nature of the task to being more or less easy.

3. Annotating and cognitive tracing

Another way in which we externalize our cognition is by modifying representations to reflect changes that are taking place that we wish to mark. For example, people often cross things off in a to-do list to show that they have been completed. They may also reorder objects in the environment by creating different piles as the nature of the work to be done changes. These two kinds of modification are called annotating and cognitive tracing:

- *Annotating* involves modifying external representations, such as crossing off or underlining items.
- *Cognitive tracing* involves externally manipulating items into different orders or structures.

Annotating is often used when people go shopping. People usually begin their shopping by planning what they are going to buy. This often involves looking in their cupboards and fridge to see what needs stocking up. However, many people are aware that they won't remember all this in their heads and so often externalize it as a written shopping list. The act of writing may also remind them of other items that they need to buy, which they may not have noticed when looking through the cupboards. When they actually go shopping at the store, they may cross off items on the shopping list as they are placed in the shopping basket or cart. This provides them with an annotated externalization, allowing them to see at a glance what items are still left on the list that need to be bought. Some displays, e.g. tablet PCs, large interactive displays, and PDAs, enable users to physically annotate documents, such as circling data or writing notes, using styluses or their fingertips (see Chapter 6). The annotations can be stored with the document, enabling the users to revisit their's or other's externalizations at a later date.

Cognitive tracing is useful in situations where the current state of play is in a state of flux and the person is trying to optimize their position. This typically happens when playing games, such as:

- In a card game the continued rearrangement of a hand of cards into suits, ascending order, or same numbers to help determine what cards to keep and which to play, as the game progresses and tactics change.
- In Scrabble, where shuffling around letters in the tray helps a person work out the best word given the set of letters (Maglio *et al.*, 1999).

It has also been used as an interactive function, for example, letting students know what they have studied in an online e-learning package. An interactive diagram can be used to highlight all the nodes visited, exercises completed, and units still to study.

A general cognitive principle for interaction design based on the external cognition approach is to provide external representations at an interface that reduce memory load and facilitate computational offloading. Different kinds of information visualizations can be developed that reduce the amount of effort required to make inferences about a given topic, e.g. financial forecasting, identifying programming bugs. In so doing, they can extend or amplify cognition, allowing people to perceive and do activities that they couldn't do otherwise. For example, information visualizations (see Chapter 6) represent masses of data in a visual form that can make it easier to make cross-comparisons across dimensions. GUIs are also able to reduce memory load significantly through providing external representations, e.g. Wizards, dialog boxes, that guide users through their interactions.

Box 3.5
Context-sensitive information: shopping reminders on the move

Wireless communication systems that use GPS technology can provide people on the move with context-sensitive information. Information such as reminders and to-do lists can be triggered and played via a handheld device e.g. cell phone, or other technology e.g. car audio system, whenever it is deemed appropriate, relative to a person's location or specific time. An early prototype, called comMotion (Marmasse and Schmandt, 2000), used a speech-output system to inform people of the groceries they needed to buy, such as milk, whenever they drove or cycled past a store that sold them (see Figure 3.13).

How useful is this kind of externalization? Are people really that bad at remembering things? In what ways is it an improvement over other reminder techniques, such as shopping lists written on paper or lists stored on handheld devices, e.g. cell phones? Certainly, it is

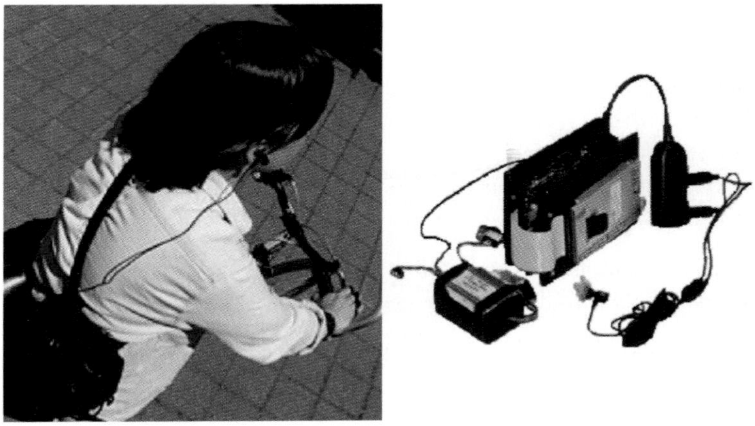

Figure 3.13 ComMotion: a context-aware reminder system

more difficult to look at a hand-written list while on the move compared with listening to a verbal reminder. But is this kind of external aid useful or desirable?

For people who suffer from various memory disorders e.g. Alzheimers, there is clearly much potential for such context-aware reminder systems being able to assist them in their daily lives. But for others, it may result in them depending more and more on spoken or visual reminders, popping up all the time to tell them what they should be doing, when, and where. They may well be reminded to buy the milk but at what price? Losing their own ability to remember?

3.3.5 Distributed cognition

The distributed cognition approach studies the nature of cognitive phenomena across individuals, artifacts, and internal and external representations (Hutchins, 1995). Typically, it involves describing a 'cognitive system,' which entails interactions among people, the artifacts they use, and the environment they are working in (see Figure 3.14). It differs from the external cognition approach in that it provides a more extensive account of the cognitive system.

An example of a cognitive system is an airline cockpit, where a top-level goal is to fly the plane. This involves:

- the pilot, co-pilot, and air traffic controller *interacting* with one another
- the pilot and co-pilot *interacting* with the instruments in the cockpit

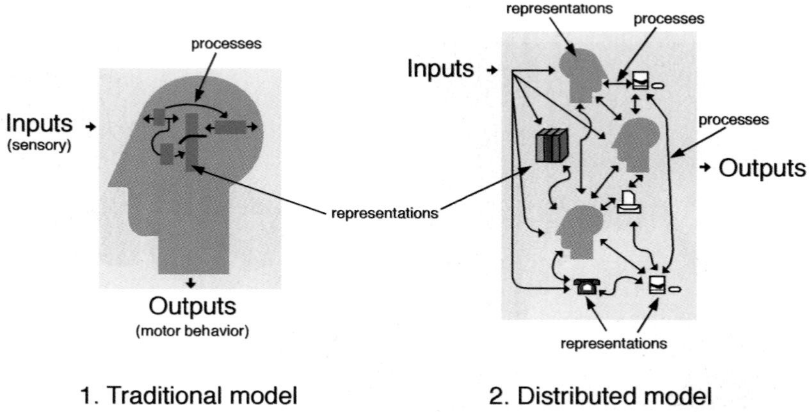

Figure 3.14 *Comparison of traditional and distributed cognition approaches*

- the pilot and co-pilot *interacting* with the environment in which the plane is flying, e.g. sky, runway.

A primary objective of the distributed cognition approach is to describe these interactions in terms of how information is propagated through different media. By this is meant how information is represented and re-represented as it moves across individuals and through the array of artifacts that are used, e.g. maps, instrument readings, scribbles, spoken word, during activities. These transformations of information are referred to as changes in *representational state*.

This way of describing and analyzing a cognitive activity contrasts with other cognitive approaches, e.g. the information processing model, in that it focuses not on what is happening inside the head of *an* individual, but on what is happening across a system of individuals and artifacts. For example, in the cognitive system of the cockpit, a number of people and artifacts are involved in the activity of 'flying to a higher altitude.' The air traffic controller initially tells the co-pilot when it is safe to fly to a higher altitude. The co-pilot then alerts the pilot, who is flying the plane, by moving a knob on the instrument panel in front of them, indicating that it is now safe to fly (see Figure 3.15). Hence, the information concerning this activity is transformed through different media (over the radio, through the co-pilot, and via a change in the position of an instrument).

A distributed cognition analysis typically involves examining:

- The distributed problem-solving that takes place (including the way people work together to solve a problem).
- The role of verbal and non-verbal behavior (including what is said, what is implied by glances, winks, etc. and what is not said).
- The various coordinating mechanisms that are used, e.g. rules, procedures.

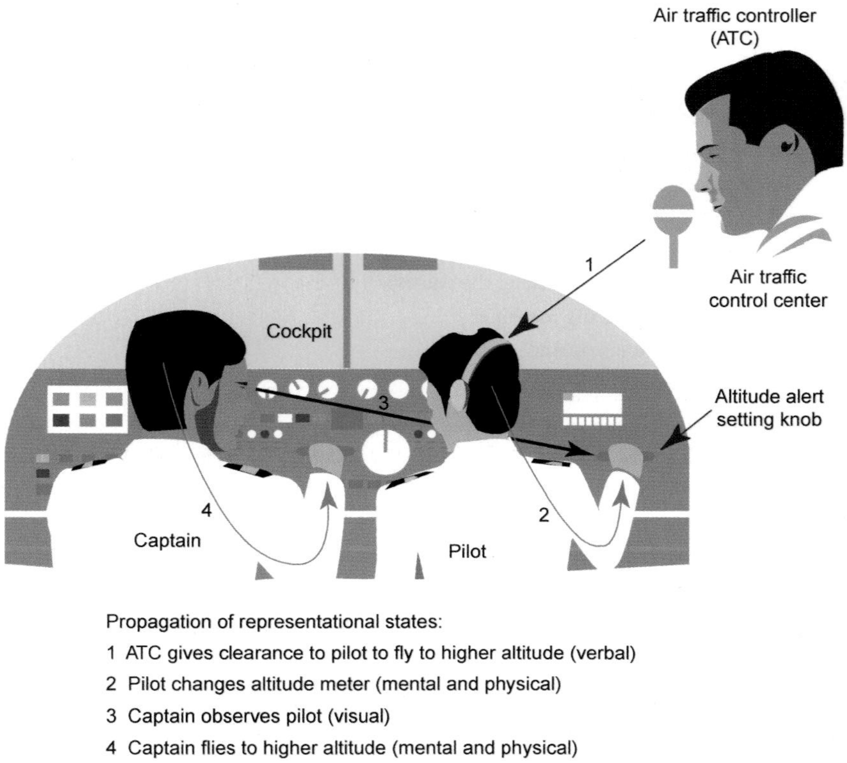
Air traffic controller
(ATC)
Air traffic
control center
Altitude alert
setting knob
Cockpit
Captain
Pilot
1
2
3
4
Propagation of representational states:
1 ATC gives clearance to pilot to fly to higher altitude (verbal)
2 Pilot changes altitude meter (mental and physical)
3 Captain observes pilot (visual)
4 Captain flies to higher altitude (mental and physical)

Figure 3.15 *A cognitive system in which information is propagated through different media*

- The various ways communication takes place as the collaborative activity progresses.
- How knowledge is shared and accessed.

Chapter 8 describes in more detail how to conduct a distributed cognition analysis.

Assignment

The aim of this assignment is for you to elicit mental models from people. In particular, the goal is for you to understand the nature of people's knowledge about an interactive product in terms of how to use it and how it works.

(a) First, elicit your own mental model. Write down how you think a cash machine (ATM) works. Then answer the following questions (abbreviated from Payne, 1991):

- How much money are you allowed to take out?

- If you took this out and then went to another machine and tried to withdraw the same amount, what would happen?
- What is on your card?
- How is the information used?
- What happens if you enter the wrong number?
- Why are there pauses between the steps of a transaction?
- How long are they?
- What happens if you type ahead during the pauses?
- What happens to the card in the machine?
- Why does it stay inside the machine?
- Do you count the money? Why?

Next, ask two other people the same set of questions.

(b) Now analyze your answers. Do you get the same or different explanations? What do the findings indicate? How accurate are people's mental models of the way ATMs work? How transparent are the ATM systems they are talking about?

(c) Next, try to interpret your findings with respect to the design of the system. Are any interface features revealed as being particularly problematic? What design recommendations do these suggest?

(d) Finally, how might you design a better conceptual model that would allow users to develop a better mental model of ATMs (assuming this is a desirable goal)?

This exercise is based on an extensive study carried out by Steve Payne on people's mental models of ATMs. He found that people do have mental models of ATMs, frequently resorting to analogies to explain how they work. Moreover, he found that people's explanations were highly variable and based on ad hoc reasoning.

Summary

This chapter has explained the importance of understanding users, especially their cognitive aspects. It has described relevant findings and theories about how people carry out their everyday activities and how to learn from these when designing interactive products. It has provided illustrations of what happens when you design systems with the user in mind and what happens when you don't. It has also presented a number of conceptual frameworks that allow ideas about cognition to be generalized across different situations.

Key Points

- Cognition comprises many processes, including thinking, attention, learning, memory, perception, decision-making, planning, reading, speaking, and listening.

- The way an interface is designed can greatly affect how well people can perceive, attend, learn, and remember how to carry out their tasks.
- The main benefits of conceptual frameworks and cognitive theories are that they can explain user interaction and predict user performance.

Further Reading

JACKO, J. and SEARS, A. (eds) (2003) *The Human–Computer Interaction Handbook: Fundamentals, Evolving Technologies and Emerging Applications*. Lawrence Erlbaum Associates. Section II introduced by Mary Czerwinski provides some good overview chapters on human aspects of HCI, including Perceptual-Motor Interaction (Romeo Chua, Daniel J. Weeks and David Goodman), Human Information Processing (Robert W. Proctor and Kim-Phuong L. Vu), and Mental Models (Gerrit C. van der Veer and Maria del Carmen Puerta Melguizo).

RASKIN, J. (2000) *The Humane Interface*. Addison-Wesley. This thought-provoking book by the late Jef Raskin re-examines the cognitive foundations of interaction design, explicating why interfaces fail or succeed. It is written in a personable and witty style with many insightful anecdotes.

MULLET, K. and SANO, D. (1995) *Designing Visual Interfaces*. SunSoft Press. This is an excellent book on the dos and don'ts of interactive graphical design. It includes many concrete examples that have followed (or not) design principles based on cognitive issues.

CARROLL, J. (ed.) (1991) *Designing Interaction*. Cambridge University Press. This edited volume provides a good collection of papers on cognitive aspects of interaction design.

NORMAN, D. (1988) *The Psychology of Everyday Things*. Basic Books.

NORMAN, D. (1993) *Things that Make Us Smart*. Addison-Wesley. These two early books by Don Norman provide many key findings and observations about people's behavior and their use of artifacts. They are written in a stimulating and thought-provoking way, using many examples from everyday life to illustrate conceptual issues. He also presents a number of psychological theories, including external cognition, in an easily digestible form.

ROGERS, Y., RUTHERFORD, A. and BIBBY, P. (eds) (1992) *Models in the Mind*. Academic Press. This volume provides a good collection of papers on eliciting, interpreting, and theorizing about mental models in HCI and other domains.

4

4.1 Introduction

Imagine going to school or work each day and sitting in a room alone with no distractions. At first, it might seem blissful. You'd be able to get on with your work. But what if you discovered you had no access to email, phones, the Internet, and other people? On top of that there is nowhere to get coffee. How long would you last? Probably not very long. Humans are inherently social: they live together, work together, learn together, play together, interact and talk with each other, and socialize. It seems only natural, therefore, to develop interactive systems that support and extend these different kinds of sociality.

There are many kinds of sociality and many ways of studying it. In this chapter our focus is on how people communicate and collaborate in their working and everyday lives. We examine how collaborative technologies (also called groupware) have been designed to support and extend communication and collaboration. We also look at the social factors that influence the success or failure of user adoption of such technologies. Finally, we describe the social phenomena that have emerged as a result of the use and appropriation of a diversity of web services, devices, and technologies, including the sharing of photos, the development of virtual friends, and the creation of different forms of social networks.

The main aims of this chapter are to:

- **Explain what is meant by communication and collaboration.**
- **Describe the social mechanisms that are used by people to communicate and collaborate.**
- **Outline the range of collaborative systems that have been developed to support this kind of social behavior.**
- **Describe some of the new forms of social behavior that have emerged as a result of the proliferation of mobile devices, web-based services, and applications.**

4

Designing for collaboration and communication

4.2 Social mechanisms in communication and collaboration

A fundamental aspect of everyday life is being social—talking to one other. We continuously update each other about news, changes, and developments on a given project, activity, person, or event. For example, friends and families keep each other posted on what's happening at work, school, at the pub, at the club, next door, in soap operas, and in the news. Similarly, people who work together keep each other informed about their social lives and everyday happenings—as well as what is happening at work, for instance when a project is about to be completed, plans for a new project, problems with meeting deadlines, rumors about closures, and so on.

The kinds of information that are circulated in different social circles are diverse, varying among social groups and across cultures. The frequency with which it is disseminated is also highly variable. It can happen continuously throughout the day, once a day, weekly, or infrequently. The means by which communication happens are also flexible—it can take place via face-to-face conversations, telephone, videophone, instant messaging, texting, email, fax, and letters. Non-verbal communication also plays an important role in augmenting face-to-face conversation, involving the use of facial expressions, back channeling ('aha' and 'umm'), voice intonation, gesturing, and other kinds of body language.

Underlying the various forms of communication are mechanisms and practices that have evolved to enable us to maintain social order. Rules, procedures, and conventions have been established whose function it is to let people know how they should behave in social groups. Below we describe three core forms of social mechanisms that are used, and then show how technological systems have been and can be designed to support these:

- The use of conversational mechanisms to facilitate the flow of talk and help overcome conversational breakdowns.
- The use of coordination mechanisms to allow people to work and interact together.
- The use of awareness mechanisms to find out what is happening, what others are doing, and, conversely, to let others know what is happening.

4.2.1 Conversational mechanisms

Talking is something that is effortless and comes naturally to most people. And yet holding a conversation is a highly skilled collaborative achievement, having many of the qualities of a musical ensemble. Below we examine what makes up a conversation. We begin by examining what happens at the beginning:

A: Hi there.

B: Hi!

C: Hi.

A: All right?

C: Good. How's it going?

A: Fine, how are you?

C: Good.

B: OK. How's life treating you?

Such mutual greetings are typical. A dialog may then ensue in which the participants take turns asking questions, giving replies, and making statements. Then when one or more of the participants wants to draw the conversation to a close, they do so by using either implicit or explicit cues. An example of an implicit cue is when a participant looks at his watch, signaling indirectly to the other participants that he wants the conversation to draw to a close. The other participants may choose to acknowledge this cue or carry on and ignore it. Either way, the first participant may then offer an explicit signal, by saying, "Well, I must be off now. Got work to do," or, "Oh dear, look at the time. Must dash. Have to meet someone." Following the acknowledgment by the other participants of such implicit and explicit signals, the conversation draws to a close, with a farewell ritual. The different participants take turns saying, "Bye," "Bye then," "See you," repeating themselves several times, until they finally separate.

Activity 4.1

How do you start and end a conversation when using (i) the phone and (ii) instant messaging (IM)?

Comment

The person answering the call will initiate the conversation by saying "hello" or more formally, the name of their company/department (and sometimes the phone number being called). If the phone has caller ID it can let the person answering the call know who he is talking to, which can enable him to be more personal, e.g. "Hello John, how are you doing?". Phone conversations usually start with a mutual greeting and end with a farewell one. In contrast, conversations that take place using IM have started to evolve new conventions. According to a Korean colleague—who is an avid user of IM—the older generation still tends to use opening and ending greetings when joining and leaving an IM, while the younger generation of users generally does without them, simply starting their message with what they want to talk about, and then stopping when they have got an answer, as if in the middle of a conversation. For example, an IM user might begin by typing "did you see the movie, Batman?," which is followed by a short conversation with someone on line, for example, "Yes" "How is it?" "It was just so so . . . " and then abruptly leave. Shorthand

abbreviations are sometimes used among friends, like 'l8tr' (later), 'bb' (bye bye), 'cu' (see you), and 'ttyl' (talk to you later). Emoticons are also used among close friends and family when signing off, such as.

Such conversational mechanisms enable people to coordinate their 'talk' with one another, allowing them to know how to start and stop. Throughout a conversation further 'turn-taking' rules are followed, enabling people to know when to listen, when it is their cue to speak, and when it is time for them to stop again to allow the others to speak. Sacks *et al.* (1978)—who are famous for their work on conversation analysis—describe these in terms of three basic rules:

- Rule 1: the current speaker chooses the next speaker by asking an opinion, question, or request.
- Rule 2: another person decides to start speaking.
- Rule 3: the current speaker continues talking.

The rules are assumed to be applied in the above order, so that whenever there is an opportunity for a change of speaker to occur, e.g. someone comes to the end of a sentence, rule 1 is applied. If the listener to whom the question or opinion is addressed does not accept the offer to take the floor, the second rule is applied, and someone else taking part in the conversation may take up the opportunity and offer a view on the matter. If this does not happen then the third rule is applied and the current speaker continues talking. The rules are cycled through recursively until someone speaks again.

To facilitate rule following, people use various ways of indicating how long they are going to talk and on what topic. For example, a speaker might say right at the beginning of their turn in the conversation that he has three things to say. A speaker may also explicitly request a change in speaker by saying, "OK, that's all I want to say on that matter. So, what do you think?" to a listener. More subtle cues to let others know that their turn in the conversation is coming to an end include the lowering or raising of the voice to indicate the end of a question or the use of phrases like, "You know what I mean?" or simply, "OK?" Back channeling (uhhuh, mmm), body orientation, e.g. moving away from or closer to someone, gaze (staring straight at someone or glancing away), and gesture, e.g. raising of arms, are also used in different combinations when talking, to signal to others when someone wants to hand over or take up a turn in the conversation.

Another way in which conversations are coordinated and given coherence is through the use of adjacency pairs (Shegloff and Sacks, 1973). Utterances are assumed to come in pairs in which the first part sets up an expectation of what is to come next and directs the way in which what does come next is heard. For example, A may ask a question to which B responds appropriately:

A: So shall we meet at 8:00?

B: Um, can we make it a bit later, say 8:30?

Sometimes adjacency pairs get embedded in each other, so it may take some time for a person to get a reply to their initial request or statement:

A: So shall we meet at 8:00?

B: Wow, look at him.

A: Yes, what a funny hairdo!

B: Um, can we make it a bit later, say 8:30?

For the most part people are not aware of following conversational mechanisms, and would be hard pressed to articulate how they can carry on a conversation. Furthermore, people don't necessarily abide by the rules all the time. They may interrupt each other or talk over each other, even when the current speaker has clearly indicated a desire to hold the floor for the next two minutes to finish an argument. Alternatively, a listener may not take up a cue from a speaker to answer a question or take over the conversation, but instead continue to say nothing even though the speaker may be making it glaringly obvious it is the listener's turn to say something. Often times a teacher will try to hand over the conversation to a student in a seminar, by staring at her and asking a specific question, only to see the student look at the floor and say nothing. The outcome is an embarrassing silence, followed by either the teacher or another student picking up the conversation again.

Other kinds of breakdowns in conversation arise when someone says something that is ambiguous and the interlocutor misinterprets it to mean something else. In such situations the participants will collaborate to overcome the misunderstanding by using repair mechanisms. Consider the following snippet of conversation between two people:

A: Can you tell me the way to get to the Multiplex Ranger cinema?

B: Yes, you go down here for two blocks and then take a right (pointing to the right), go on till you get to the lights and then it is on the left.

A: Oh, so I go along here for a couple of blocks and then take a right and the cinema is at the lights (pointing ahead of him)?

B: No, you go on *this* street for a couple of blocks (gesturing more vigorously than before to the street to the right of him while emphasizing the word 'this').

A: Ahhhh! I thought you meant *that* one: so it's *this* one (pointing in the same direction as the other person).

C: Uh-hum, yes that's right, *this* one.

Detecting breakdowns in conversation requires the speaker and listener to be attending to what the other says (or does not say). Once they have understood the nature of the failure, they can then go about repairing it. As shown in the above example, when the listener misunderstands what has been communicated, the speaker repeats what she said earlier, using a stronger voice intonation and more exaggerated gestures. This allows the speaker to repair the mistake and be more explicit to the listener, allowing her to understand and follow better what they are saying. Listeners may also signal when they don't understand something or want further clarification by using various tokens, like "Huh?" or "What?" (Schegloff, 1981), together with giving a puzzled look (usually frowning). This is especially the case when the speaker says something that is vague. For example, they might say "I want it" to their partner, without saying what *it* is they want. The partner may reply using a token or, alternatively, explicitly ask, "What do you mean by *it*?"

Taking turns also provides opportunities for the listener to initiate repair or request clarification, or for the speaker to detect that there is a problem and to initiate repair. The listener will usually wait for the next turn in the conversation before interrupting the speaker, to give the speaker the chance to clarify what is being said by completing the utterance (Suchman, 1987).

Activity 4.2

How do people repair breakdowns in conversations when using the phone or email?

Comment

In these settings people cannot see each other and so have to rely on other means of repairing their conversations. Furthermore, there are more opportunities for breakdowns to occur and fewer mechanisms available for repair. When a breakdown occurs over the phone, people will often shout louder, repeating what they said several times, and use stronger intonation. When a breakdown occurs via email, people may literally spell out what they meant, making things much more explicit in a subsequent email, using capitals, emoticons, exclamations, bold, highlighting, etc. If the message is beyond repair they may resort to another mode of communication that allows greater flexibility of expression, either telephoning or speaking to the recipient face-to-face.

Kinds of conversations

Conversations can take a variety of forms, such as an argument, a discussion, a debate, a chat, a *tête-à-tête*, or giving someone a 'telling off.' A well-known distinction in conversation types is between formal and informal communication. Formal communication involves assigning certain roles to people and prescribing *a priori* the types of turns that people are allowed to take in a conversation. For example, at a board meeting, it is decided who is allowed to speak, who speaks when, who manages the turn-taking, and what the participants are allowed to talk about.

In contrast, informal communication is the chat that goes on when people socialize. It also commonly happens when people bump into each other and talk briefly. This can occur in corridors, at the coffee machine, when waiting in line, and walking down the street. Informal conversations include talking about impersonal things such as the weather (a favorite) and the cost of living, or more personal things like how someone is getting on with a new roommate. It also provides an opportunity to pass on gossip, such as who is going out to dinner with whom. In office settings, such chance conversations have been found to serve a number of functions, including coordinating group work, transmitting knowledge about office culture, establishing trust, and general team-building (Kraut *et al.*, 1990). It is also the case that people who are in physical proximity, such as those whose offices or desks are close to one another, engage much more frequently in these kinds of informal chats than those who are in distant corridors or buildings. Most companies and organizations are well aware of this and often try to design their office space so that people who need to work closely together are placed close to one another in the same physical space.

4.2.2 Designing collaborative technologies to support conversation

As we have seen, 'talk' and the way it is managed is integral to coordinating social activities. One of the challenges confronting designers is to consider how the different kinds of communication can be facilitated and supported in settings where there may be obstacles preventing it from happening 'naturally.' A central concern has been to develop systems that allow people to communicate with each other when they are in *physically different locations* and thus not able to communicate in the usual face-to-face manner. In particular, a key issue has been to determine how to allow people to carry on communicating as if they were in the same place, even though they are geographically separated—sometimes many thousands of miles apart. Another challenge has been to design collaborative technologies to help co-located groups communicate and work together more effectively, especially when creating and sharing content.

Box 4.1
The Coordinator: making explicit what is normally implicit in conversations

One of the earliest collaborative systems that was developed, based on a theory of conversational mechanisms, was the Coordinator system (Winograd and Flores, 1986). It was developed to help people work more effectively through improving

the way they communicate with one another. An assumption was that communication could be improved if people could distinguish among the kinds of commitments they make in conversation that are normally implicit. The rationale behind the Coordinator system was to enable users to develop a better awareness of the value of using such 'speech acts.'

Speech act theory is concerned with the functions utterances have in conversations (Austin, 1962; Searle, 1969). A common function is a request that is asked indirectly (known as an indirect speech act). For example, when someone says, "It's hot in here" they may really be asking if it would be OK to open the window because they need some fresh air. Speech acts range from formalized statements, e.g. "I hereby declare you man and wife", to everyday utterances, e.g. "how about dinner?". Each utterance varies in its force. For example, a command to do something has quite a different force from a polite comment about the state of affairs.

The Coordinator system was targeted at a variety of work settings, including sales, finance, general management, and planning. Emails could be sent between people in the form of explicit speech acts. For example, when sending someone a request, say "Could you get the report to me," the sender could also select the menu option 'request.' This would be placed in the subject header of the message, thereby explicitly specifying the nature of the speech act. Other speech-act options included offer, promise, inform, and question. The system also asked the user to fill in the dates by which the request should be completed. The user receiving such a message had the option of responding with another labeled speech act. These included:

- acknowledge
- promise
- counter-offer
- decline
- free form.

Thus, the Coordinator was designed to provide a conversational structure, allowing users to make clear the status of their work and, likewise, to be clear about the status of others' work in terms of various commitments.

The Coordinator and its successors have been found to be most successful in organizations that are hierarchical and need a highly structured system for the management of orders, such as large manufacturing divisions of companies, and where previous support has been mainly in the form of a hodgepodge of paper forms and inflexible task-specific data processing applications (Winograd, 1994). It has received less favorable responses in other kinds of organizations, where many of the people who tried using it in their work either abandoned it or resorted to using only the free-form message facility, which had no explicit demands associated with it. The reason for its failure in these settings was that the system asked too much of people to change the ways they

communicated and worked. Requiring them to specify *explicitly* the nature of their implicit speech acts was found to be artificial and awkward. While some people may be very blatant about what they want doing, when they want it done by, and what they are prepared to do, most people tend to use more subtle and indirect forms of communication to advance their collaborations with others. ■

Communicating in physically different locations. Email, videoconferencing, videophones, computer conferencing, chatrooms, and instant messaging are well-known examples of some of the collaborative technologies that have been developed to support people communicating at a distance. In addition, online MUDs (multi-user role-playing environments) and MOOs (text-based environments that grew out of MUDs, enabling users to construct their own worlds using objects) were originally created to enable people to communicate exclusively using text (see Figure 4.1). The idea was that anyone anywhere who joined the MUD or MOO could take part in a text-based collaborative activity, e.g. playing a game, holding a seminar, or creating a world, by typing their moves and conversations at the prompt. More recently, 3D virtual worlds (also called collaborative virtual environments) have been bolted onto the front end of the text spaces. Instead of typing what they are doing and where they are in a game, narrative, or virtual seminar, players enter and move around virtual rooms and other spaces in the guise of avatars (see Figure 4.1). Advocates of the text-based approach, however, have argued that much is lost with having a graphical representation of the world, since participants no longer have to use their imagination to interpret the text:

> ***. . . the sensorial parsimony of plain text tends to entice users into engaging their imaginations to fill in missing details while, comparatively speaking, the richness of stimuli in fancy virtual realities has an opposite tendency, pushing users' imaginations into a more passive role.*** **(Curtis, 1992)**

Activity 4.3

Look at the two screen shots in Figure 4.1. How does the text-based conversation in the MUD ZORKI differ from that taking place in the 3D graphical world 'theU?'

Comment

The conversation taking place in ZORKI is command-based. The user types in an action she wants to carry out in the

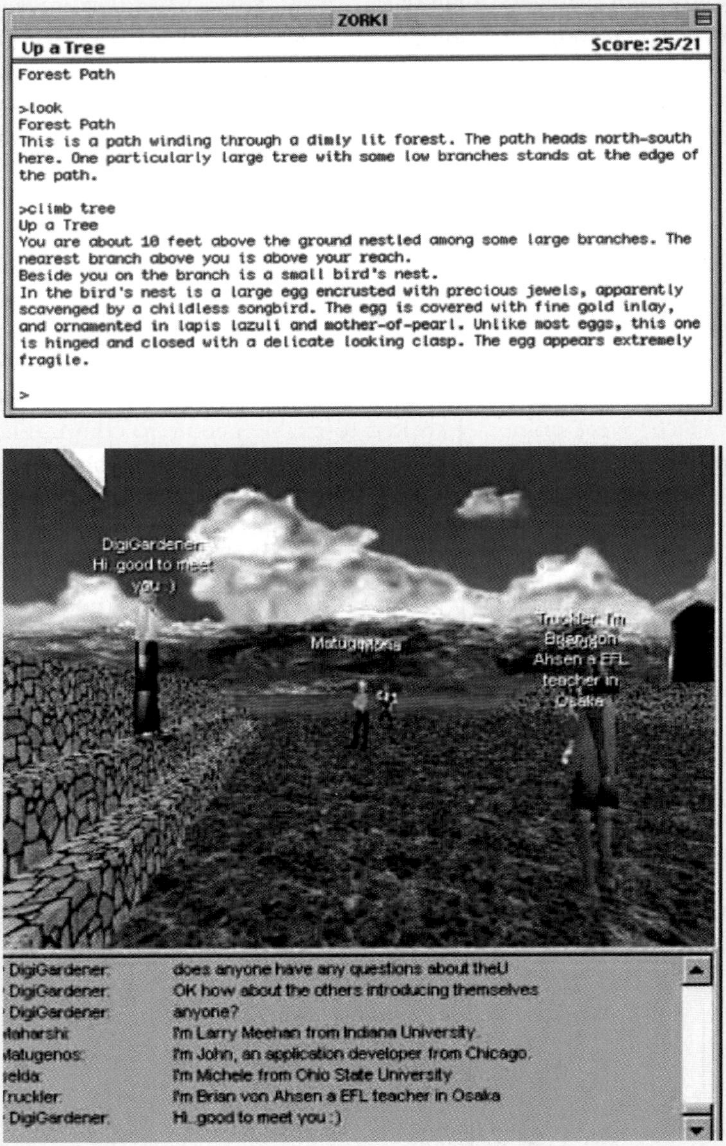

Figure 4.1 *A sample of a text-based conversation from an early MUD, called ZORKI, and a conversation held at the virtual 'theU'*

imaginary world and the MUD responds by describing the outcome of her action and what other options are available. It requires much imagination on the part of the players to work out what they are doing, where they are, and where they can go. In contrast, the 3D graphical world visually depicts where the players are and what they look like. Much less cognitive effort is involved in working out what is going on. The conversation is also more colloquial, resembling one that takes place in everyday life rather than in a fictional world.

Media spaces were also experimented with in the late 1980s and 1990s, combining audio, video, and computer systems to "extend the world of desks, chairs, walls and ceilings" (Harrison *et al.*, 1997). The idea behind their design was that people distributed over space and time would be able to communicate and interact with one another as if they were physically present. An early example was the Xerox Media Space that was designed to support the informal types of communication that occur in hallways and at water coolers, providing opportunities for people in the company, located in different offices, to engage in social chat while at their desks (Mackay, 1999). Other examples included Hydra (see Figure 4.2), Cruiser, and the VideoWindow system (see Box 4.2).

***Figure 4.2** The Hydra system: Each 'hydra' unit consists of a camera, monitor, and speaker and is meant to act as a surrogate for a person in a different space. The design is intended to preserve the personal space that people have in face-to-face meetings, simulating where they would sit in the physical space if they were physically present (Sellen et al., 1992)*

Box 4.2

A number of researchers have tried to capitalize on the social phenomenon of informal communication and the important role it plays at work. In particular, they have been interested in finding ways of using audio–video links to *mimic* physical settings that are conducive to informal communication for people who are geographically separated. One of the first systems to be built, at Bellcore in 1989, was the *VideoWindow System* (see Figure 4.3). The goal was to design a shared space that would allow people in different locations to carry on a conversation as they would do if sitting in the same room drinking coffee together. Two lounge areas that were 50 miles apart were connected with high-bandwidth video channels and full-duplex four-channel audio. Connecting them was a 3 foot × 8 foot 'picture-window' onto which video images were projected. The large size was meant to allow viewers to see a room of people roughly the same size as themselves. The system was designed to be active 24 hours a day, so that anyone entering one room could speak to whoever happened to be in the other room.

A study by Kraut *et al.* (1990) of how effective the system was showed that, in general, many of the interactions that took place between the remote conversants were indeed indistinguishable from similar face-to-face interactions—with the exception that they spoke a bit louder and constantly talked about the video system. However, they also

Figure 4.3 *Diagram of VideoWindow system in use*

found that people who were in the same room tended to talk more with each other than with those in the video-linked room. Various usability problems were identified as contributing to this reluctance to talk with video images of other people. One of these was the tendency for people to move closer to the picture window to strike up a conversation with someone (which is what one would normally do in a face-to-face setting); this had the opposite effect to what the person intended, as it moved his or her head out of the picture and also out of microphone range, meaning he or she could not be seen or heard. Thus, rather than getting nearer to the other person, this behavior had the counter-intuitive effect of removing him or her from the 'picture.' Moreover, there was no way for participants to know whether they were being seen and heard by the others in the other room. This inability to monitor how others are or are not 'receiving' you caused numerous problems. Another problem was that the system allowed only public conversations, meaning that they could be heard by everyone in the rooms. Such public broadcasting contrasts with how people normally engage in informal face-to-face conversations, where they will often whisper and conspire with each other when a topic becomes more private or secret. Such private conversations clearly could not be supported by the VideoWindow system.

Another early system, Cruiser, was designed to support informal communication by placing separate audio and video equipment on the desktop of each person who was connected to the system (Fish, 1989). This set-up differed from the VideoWindow system in that it enabled both public and private interactions to take place. It also provided additional functionality that allowed people to initiate conversations by typing in a cruise command followed by a question like, "I'm bored. Anyone want a chat?" or "Can someone help me?"—the aim here being explicitly to encourage people to engage in the kind of talk that they normally do when they bump into each other, but this time over the computer network. A further conversation mechanism built into Cruiser was a 'glance' feature that allowed users to check whether the person they wanted to talk to was in fact available before trying to initiate a conversation.

Many commercial systems are now commonly used to support multiple connections among sites, using a combination of desktop and audio–video links. These can be very useful for virtual teams and centers that have multiple groups working at a number of different sites. High Definition TV has also improved the resolution and quality of images that can make people seem more present. ■

Activity 4.4

Do you think it is better to develop technologies that will allow people to talk at a distance as if they were face-to-face or to develop technologies that will support new ways of conversing?

Comment

On the one hand, it seems a good idea to develop technologies supporting people communicating at a distance that emulate the way they hold conversations in face-to-face situations. After all, this means of communicating is so well established and second nature to people. Phones and videoconferencing have been developed essentially to support face-to-face conversations. It is important to note, however, that conversations held in this way are not the same as when face-to-face. People have adapted the way they hold conversations to fit in with the constraints of the respective technologies. As mentioned earlier, they tend to shout more when misunderstood over the phone. They also tend to speak more loudly when talking on the phone, since they can't monitor how well the person can hear them at the other end of the phone. Likewise, people tend to project themselves more when taking part in a videoconference. They also take longer conversational turns and interrupt each other less (O'Connaill *et al.*, 1993), while turn-taking appears to be much more explicit and greetings and farewells more ritualized.

On the other hand, it is interesting to look at how the new communication technologies have been extending the way people talk and socialize. SMS texting and instant messaging enable quite different ways of holding a conversation at a distance. Texting enables people to hold fragmentary conversations over long periods, commenting on what each is doing or thinking, allowing the other to keep posted on current developments. The conversation typically comprises short phrases that are typed in or selected from a menu of pre-stored phrases. These kinds of 'streamlined' conversations are coordinated simply by taking turns sending and receiving messages. Online chatting and instant messaging have also resulted in new genres of conversation that compensate for the constraints of the medium, where shorthand and abbreviations are frequently used, e.g. the use of expressions like 'LOL'—laugh out loud—in response to someone typing in something funny that has happened to them. They also allow hundreds and even thousands of people to take part in the same conversations, which is not possible in face-to-face settings.

Figure 4.4 *The Dynamo system in use at a sixth form college in the UK. The student with the spikey blond hair is showing various media he has created to the girl sitting next to him. Others sitting around the display are drawn into his show and subsequently hold a conversation about it (Brignull et al., 2004)*

Communicating in co-located settings. A number of shareable interfaces (see Chapter 6) have been developed to facilitate communication and collaboration among co-located groups, including smartboards, tabletops, and various forms of public displays. One approach has been to situate interactive shared displays in public spaces, e.g. hallways, reception areas, that are intended to encourage people to meet and socialize through posting messages or adding opinions. For example, the Notification Collage system (Greenberg and Rounding, 2001) and the Plasma Posters (Churchill *et al.*, 2003) were originally designed to enable people to send notes, news items, and other materials from the PCs in their offices to a large public display. In contrast, the Dynamo system was designed to enable social groups to readily share and exchange a variety of media on a large shared display by hooking up their memory sticks, laptops, cameras, and other devices, in the vicinity of the display (Izadi *et al.*, 2003). A study of its deployment in a sixth form common room in the UK showed how students often used it as a conversational prop while displaying and manipulating media on the shared display, which in turn led to impromptu conversations between those sitting in the room (Brignull *et al.*, 2004).

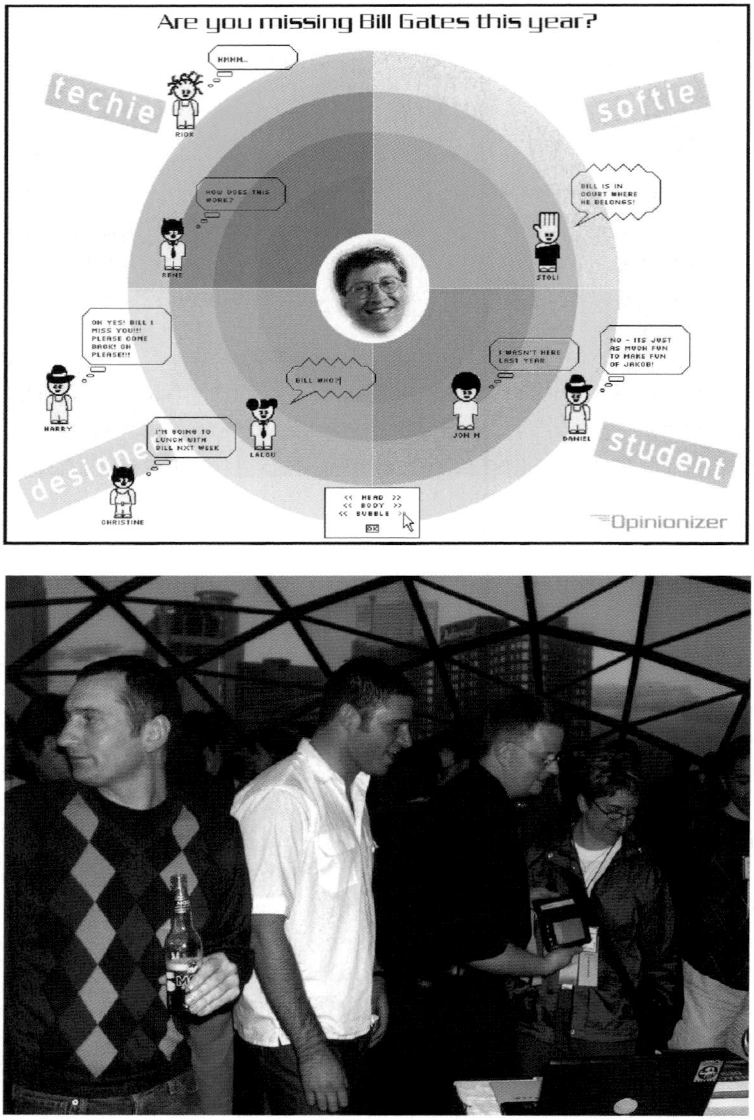

Figure 4.5 *The Opinionizer interface and a photo of it being used at a book launch party*

Box 4.3
Can technologies be designed to help people break the ice and socialize?

Have you ever found yourself at a party, wedding, conference, or other social gathering, standing awkwardly by yourself, not knowing who to talk to or what to talk about? Social embarrassment and self-consciousness affect most of us at such moments and is most acute when one is a newcomer and by oneself, such as a first-time attendee at a conference. How can we help make conversation initiation easier and less awkward among people who do not know each other?

A number of mechanisms have been employed by organizers of social events, such as asking old-timers to act as mentors and the holding of various kinds of ice-breaking activities. Badge-wearing, the plying of alcohol and food, and introductions by others are also common ploys. While many of these methods can help, engaging in ice-breaking activities requires people to act in a way that is different to the way they normally socialize and which they may find equally uncomfortable or painful to do. They often require people to agree to join in a collaborative game, which they can find embarrassing. This can be exacerbated by the fact that once people have agreed to take part it is difficult for them to drop out, because of the perceived consequences it will have on the others and themselves, e.g. seen by the others as a spoilsport or party-pooper. Having had one such embarrassing experience, most people will shy away from any further kinds of ice-breaking activities.

How might less intrusive mechanisms be developed using collaborative technologies? One line of research has investigated how computer-based, matchmaking techniques can be used based on algorithms that determine which preferences and views shared among people would make them suitable conversational partners. The profiles of like-minded people are revealed to one other when in close proximity via LCD name tags that light up (Borovoy *et al.*, 1998) or as icons that appear on a person's cell phone display (Burak and Sharon, 2004). While such explicit revelations of what is normally hidden and discreet can be entertaining for some, for others it can feel invasive and an unnatural way of meeting someone.

An alternative approach is to design a physical space where people can enter and exit a conversation with a stranger in more subtle ways, i.e. one where people do not feel threatened or embarrassed, and which does not require a high level of commitment. The Opinionizer system was designed along these lines, with the aim of encouraging people in an informal gathering to share their opinions visually

and anonymously (Brignull and Rogers, 2003). The collective creation of opinions via a public display was intended to provide a talking point to others standing beside it, and to comment on to their neighbor. Users submit their opinions by typing them in at a public keyboard. To add 'color' and 'personality' to their opinions, a selection of small cartoon avatars and speech bubbles were available. The screen was also divided into four labeled quadrants representing different backgrounds, e.g. 'techie,' 'softie,' 'designer,' or 'student', to provide a further talking point.

When the Opinionizer was placed in various social gatherings, a 'honey-pot' effect was observed: as the number of people in the immediate vicinity of the Opinionizer increased, a sociable 'buzz' was created in the area. By standing in this space and showing an interest, e.g. visibly facing the screen or reading the text, people gave off a tacit signal to others that they were open to discussion and interested in meeting new people. ■

Computer-mediated communication. Collaborative technologies have been designed to support different kinds of communication, from informal to formal and from one-to-one to many-to-many conversations. Collectively, such technologies are often referred to as computer-mediated communication (CMC). The range of systems that support computer-mediated communication is quite diverse. A summary of the different types is shown in Table 4.1, highlighting how they support, extend, and differ from face-to-face communication. A conventionally accepted classification system of CMC is to categorize them in terms of either synchronous or asynchronous communication. We have also included a third category: systems that support CMC in combination with other

(i) Synchronous communication

Where conversations in real time are supported by letting people talk with each other either using their voices or through typing. Both modes seek to support non-verbal communication to varying degrees.

Examples

- **Talking with voice: videophones, videoconferencing (desktop or wall), media spaces, Voice Over IP (VOIP).**
- **Talking via typing: text messaging (typing in messages using cell phones), instant messaging (real-time interaction via PCs), chatrooms, MUDs, virtual worlds.**

Table 4.1 *Classification of computer-mediated communication (CMC) into three types: (i) synchronous communication, (ii) asynchronous communication, and (iii) CMC combined with other activity*

New kinds of functionality

- Virtual worlds allow communication to take place via a combination of graphical representations of self (in the form of an avatar) with a separate chatbox or overlaying speech bubbles.
- Virtual worlds allow people to represent themselves as virtual characters, taking on new personas, e.g. opposite gender, and expressing themselves in ways not possible in face-to-face settings.
- Virtual worlds, MUDs, and chatrooms have enabled new forms of conversation mechanisms, such as multi-turn-taking, where a number of people can contribute and keep track of a multi-streaming text-based conversation.
- Instant messaging allows users to multi-task by holding numerous conversations at once.

Benefits

- Not having to physically face people may increase shy people's confidence and self-esteem to converse more in 'virtual' public.
- It allows people to keep abreast of the goings-on in an organization without having to move from their office.
- It enables users to send text and images between people using instant messaging.
- In offices, instant messaging allows users to fire off quick questions and answers without the time lag of email or phone-tag.

Problems

- Lack of adequate bandwidth has plagued video communication, resulting in poor-quality images that break up, judder, have shadows, and appear as unnatural images.
- It is difficult to establish eye contact (normally an integral and subconscious part of face-to-face conversations) in virtual worlds, videoconferencing, and videophones.
- Having the possibility of hiding behind a persona, a name, or an avatar in a chatroom gives people the opportunity to behave differently. Sometimes this can result in people becoming aggressive, intrusive, and shifting gender.

(ii) Asynchronous communication

Where communication between participants takes place remotely and at different times. It relies not on time-dependent turn-taking but on participants initiating communication and responding to others when they want or are able to do so.

Examples

- Email, bulletin boards, newsgroups, computer conferencing.

Table 4.1 *(continued)*

New kinds of functionality

- Attachments of different sorts (including annotations, images, videos, music) for email and computer conferencing can be sent.
- Messages can be archived and accessed using various search facilities.

Benefits

- Can be read at any place and any time.
- Greater autonomy and control of when and how to respond, so can attend to it in own time rather than having to take a turn in a conversation at a particular cue.
- Can send the same message to many people.
- Do not have to interact with person so can be easier to say things than when face-to-face, e.g. announcing sudden death of colleague, providing feedback on someone's performance.

Problems

- Flaming can take place, where a user writes an angry email expressed in uninhibited language that is much stronger than normal when interacting with the same person face-to-face. This includes the use of impolite statements, exclamation marks, capitalized sentences or words, swearing, and superlatives. Such 'charged' communication can lead to misunderstandings and bad feelings among the recipients.
- Many people experience message overload, receiving numerous emails and junkmail each day. They find it difficult to cope and may overlook an important message while working through their ever-increasing pile of email—especially if they have not read it for a few days. Various interface mechanisms have been designed to help people manage their email better, including filtering, threading, and the use of signaling to indicate the level of importance of a message (which the sender or recipient can make), through color coding, bold font, or exclamation marks placed beside a message.
- An assumption has evolved that people will read their messages several times a day and reply to them there and then. However, many people have now reverted to treating email more like postal mail, replying when they have the time or inclination to do so.

(iii) CMC combined with other activity

People often talk with each other while carrying out other activities. For example, designing requires people to brainstorm together in meetings, drawing on whiteboards, making notes, and using existing designs. Teaching involves talking with students as well as writing on the board and getting students to solve problems collaboratively. Various meeting and decision support systems have been developed to help people work or learn while talking together.

Table 4.1 *(continued)*

Examples

- Customized electronic meeting rooms have been built that support people in face-to-face meetings, via the use of networked workstations, large public displays, and shared software tools, together with various techniques to help decision-making. One of the earliest systems was the University of Arizona's GroupSystem (see Figure 4.6).
- Different combinations of technologies are beginning to be used to support learning in the classroom and remotely. For example, wireless communication, portable devices, e.g. tablet PCs, and interactive whiteboards are being integrated in classroom settings to allow the teacher and students to learn and communicate with one another in novel interactive ways (see Figure 4.7). More sophisticated and integrated web conferencing tools are also appearing. An example is Macromedia's Breeze, which is a web-based communication system that supports collaborative real-time meetings, instructor-led classes, informational presentations, and e-learning courses.

New kinds of functionality

- Allows new ways of collaboratively creating and editing content.
- Supports effective collaborative learning.
- Integrates different kinds of tools.

Benefits

- Supports talking while carrying out other activities at the same time, allowing multi-tasking—which is what happens in face-to-face settings.
- Greater awareness of other users/learners, enabling each to see how the others are progressing in real time.

Problems

- It can be difficult to see what other people are referring to when in remote locations, especially if there are multiple documents and different users have different documents on their screens.

Table 4.1 *(continued)*

collaborative activities, such as meetings, decision-making, and learning. Although some communication technologies are not strictly speaking computer-based, e.g. phones, video-conferencing, we have included these in the classification of CMC, as most now are display-based and interacted with or controlled via an interface.

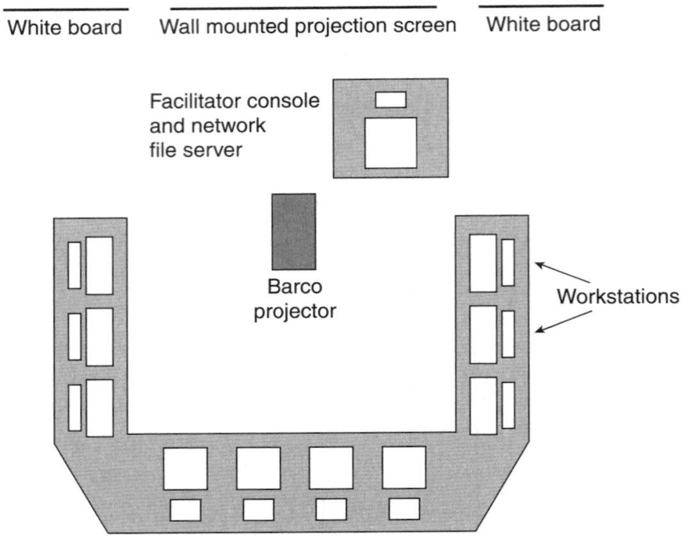

Figure 4.6 *Schematic diagram of a group meeting room, showing relationship of workstation, whiteboards, and video projector*

Figure 4.7 *An ACTIVBoard whiteboard running the Floating World game that enables different students to take control of the front-of-the-class display and collaborate during a classroom seminar*

Activity 4.5

One of the earliest technological innovations (besides the telegraph and telephone) developed for supporting conversations at a distance was the videophone. Despite numerous attempts by the various phone companies to introduce them over the last 50 years (see Figure 4.8), they have failed each time. Why do you think this is so?

Comment

One of the biggest problems with commercial landline videophones is that the bandwidth has been too low, resulting in poor resolution and slow refresh. The net effect is the display of unacceptable images: the person in the picture appears to move in sudden jerks, shadows are left behind when a speaker moves, and it is difficult to read lips or establish eye contact. For cell videophones, network coverage has been a big problem: calls can suddenly hang, leaving the callers talking to a blank screen. They also consume more battery power than audio-only phones, are more bulky to carry, and much more expensive to use.

But perhaps the biggest reason for their lack of uptake is to do with social acceptability: why would anyone want to look at pocket-sized grainy images of the person she is chatting with over the phone? It seems unnatural. We have adapted to talking on the phone while doing something else, such as staring at the ceiling, gesticulating, or watching TV. Many of us do not want to be bothered with having to face a camera on the phone to make sure that the other person can see our face and, moreover, do not want people to see what state we are in, what we are doing, or where we are.

Another innovation has been to develop systems that allow people to communicate and interact with each other in ways not possible in the physical world. Rather than try to imitate or facilitate face-to-face communication, designers have developed new kinds of interactions. For example, ClearBoard was developed to enable facial expressions of participants to be made visible to others by using a transparent board that showed their face to the others (Ishii *et al.*, 1993). HyperMirror was designed to provide an environment in which the participants could feel as if they were in the same virtual place even though they were physically in different places (Morikawa and Maesako, 1998). Mirror reflections of people in different places were synthesized and projected onto a single screen, so that they appeared side-by-side in the same virtual space. In this way, the participants could see both themselves and others in the same seamless virtual space. Observations of people using the system showed how quickly

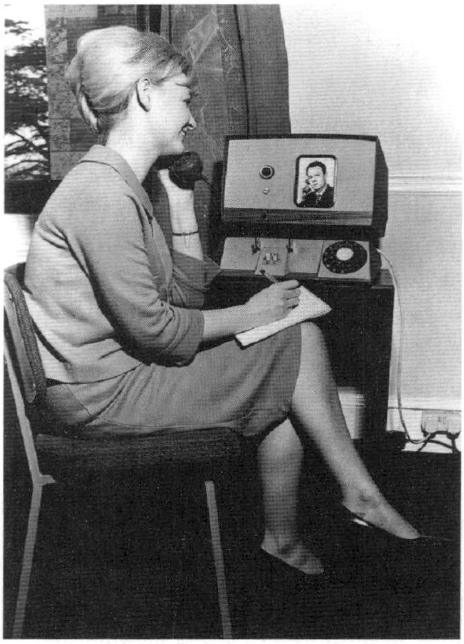

(a)

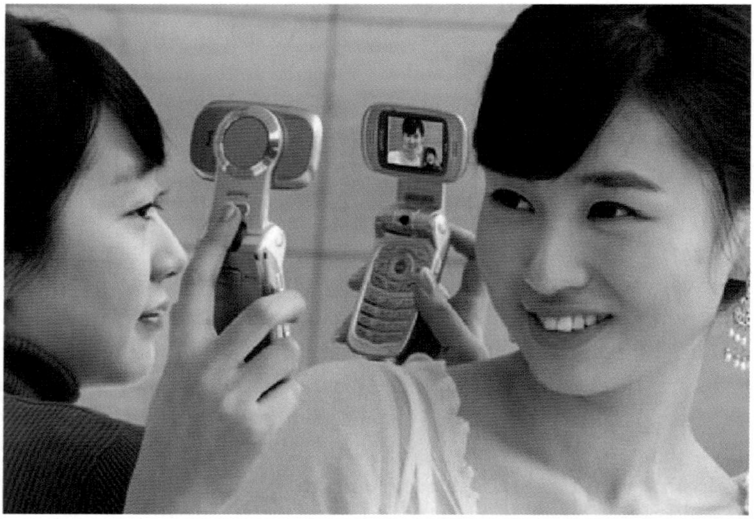

(b)

Figure 4.8 *(a) One of British Telecom's early videophones and (b) a recent mobile 'visualphone' developed in Japan*

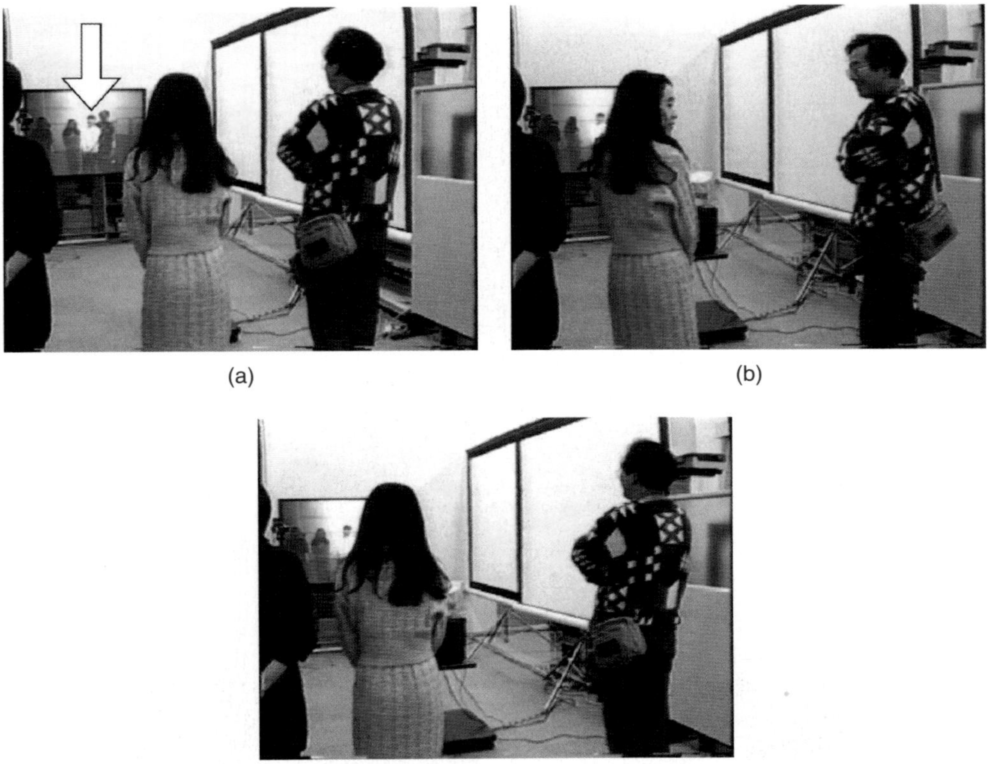

(a) (b) (c)

Figure 4.9 *Hypermirror in action, showing perception of virtual personal space. (a) A woman is in one room (indicated by the arrow on the screen), (b) while a man and another woman are in the other room chatting to each other. They move apart when they notice they are 'overlapping' her and (c) virtual personal space is established*

they adapted to perceiving themselves and others in this way. For example, participants quickly became sensitized to the importance of virtual personal space, moving out of the way if they perceived they were overlapping someone else on the screen (see Figure 4.9).

Another innovative system, called BiReality, developed at Hewlett Packard by Jouppi (2002) uses a teleoperated robotic surrogate to visit remote locations as a substitute for physical travel (see Figure 4.10). The goal was to overcome many of the limitations commonly associated with videoconferencing (discussed in Activity 4.5), by giving the remote person more physical presence at the remote location.

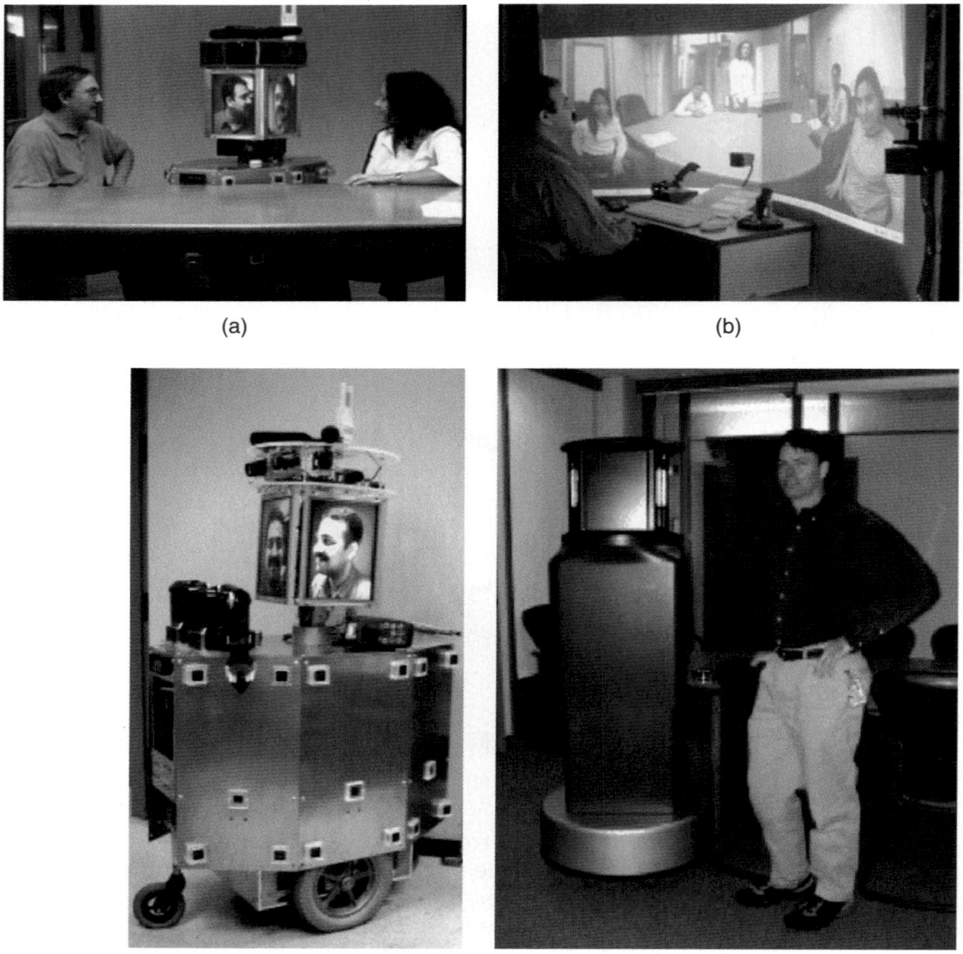

(a) (b) (c) (d)

Figure 4.10 *BiReality: (a) a surrogate robot at a meeting 'sitting' between two physically present people, (b) the remote user's view of the meeting while controlling the surrogate, (c) an early version of the surrogate on the move, and (d) a second-generation surrogate designed to preserve the height and sitting/standing posture of the user (Jouppi, 2002)*

4.2.3 Coordination mechanisms

Coordination takes place when a group of people act or interact together to achieve something. For example, consider what is involved in playing a game of basketball. Teams have to work out how to play with each other and to plan a set of tactics that they think will outwit the other team. For the game to proceed both teams need to follow (and sometimes contravene) the rules of the game. An incredible amount of coordination is required within a team and between the competing teams in order to play.

In general, collaborative activities require us to coordinate with each other, whether playing a team game, moving a piano, navigating a ship, working on a large software project, taking orders and serving meals in a restaurant, constructing a bridge, or playing doubles tennis. In particular, we need to figure out how to interact with one another to progress with our various activities. To help us we use a number of coordinating mechanisms. Primarily, these include:

- verbal and non-verbal communication
- schedules, rules, and conventions
- shared external representations.

Verbal and non-verbal communication

When people are working closely together they talk to each other, issuing commands and letting others know how they are progressing with their part. For example, when two or more people are collaborating together, as in moving a piano, they shout to each other commands like "Down a bit, left a bit, now straight forward" to coordinate their actions with each other. As in a conversation, nods, shakes, winks, glances, and hand-raising are also used in combination with such coordination 'talk' to emphasize and sometimes replace it.

In formal settings, like meetings, explicit structures such as agendas, memos, and minutes are employed to coordinate the activity. Meetings are chaired, with secretaries taking minutes to record what is said and plans of actions agreed upon. Such minutes are subsequently distributed to members to remind them of what was agreed in the meeting and for those responsible to act upon what was agreed.

For time-critical and routinized collaborative activities, especially where it is difficult to hear others because of the physical conditions, gestures are frequently used (radio-controlled communication systems may also be used). Various kinds of hand signals have evolved, with their own set of standardized syntax and semantics. For example, the arm and baton movements of a conductor coordinate the different players in an orchestra, while the arm and baton movements of a ground marshal at an airport signal to a pilot how to bring the plane into its allocated gate.

Activity 4.6

How much communication is non-verbal? Watch a soap opera on the TV and turn down the volume, look at the kinds and frequency of gestures that are used. Are you able to understand what is going on? How do radio soaps compensate for not being able to use non-verbal gestures? How do people compensate when chatting online?

Comment

Soaps are good to watch for observing non-verbal behavior as the actors often exaggerate their gestures and facial expressions to convey their emotions. It is easy to work out what kind of scene is happening from the actors' posture, body movements, gestures, and facial expressions. In contrast, actors on the radio use their voice a lot more, relying on intonation and sound effects to help convey emotions. When chatting online, people use emoticons and conventionally accepted abbreviations, e.g. LOL.

Schedules, rules, and conventions

A common practice in organizations is to use various kinds of schedules to organize the people who are part of it. For example, consider how a university manages to coordinate its people and available resources. A core task is allocating the thousands of lectures and seminars that need to be run each week with the number of rooms available. A schedule has to be devised that allows students to attend the lectures and seminars for their given courses, taking into account numerous rules and constraints. These include:

- A student cannot attend more than one lecture at a given time.
- A professor cannot give more than one lecture or seminar at a given time.
- A room cannot be allocated to more than one seminar or lecture at a given time.
- Only a certain number of students can be placed in a room depending on its size.

Other coordinating mechanisms that are employed by groups working together are rules and conventions. These can be formal or informal. Formal rules, like the compulsory attendance of seminars, writing of monthly reports, and filling in of timesheets, enable organizations to maintain order and keep track of what its members are doing. Conventions, like keeping quiet in a library or removing meal trays after finishing eating in a cafeteria, are a form of courtesy to others.

Shared external representations

Shared external representations are commonly used to coordinate people. We have already mentioned one example, that of shared calendars that appear on users' monitors as graphical charts, email reminders, and dialog boxes. Other kinds that are commonly used include forms, checklists, and tables. These are presented on public noticeboards or as part of other shared spaces. They can also be attached to documents and folders. They function by providing external information on who is working on what, when, where, when a piece of work is supposed to be finished, and to whom it goes next. For example, a shared table of who has completed the checking of files for a design project (see Figure 4.11) provides the necessary information from which other members of the group can at a glance update their model of that project's progress. Importantly, such external representations can be readily updated by annotating. If a project is going to take longer than planned, this can be indicated on a chart or table by extending the line representing it, allowing others to see the change when they pass by and glance up at the whiteboard.

Shared externalizations allow people to make various inferences about the changes or delays with respect to their effect on their current activities. Accordingly, they may need to reschedule their work and annotate the shared workplan. In so doing, these kinds of coordination mechanisms are considered to be tangible, providing important representations of work and responsibility that can be changed and updated as and when needed.

	Gary	Kate & Gary	Mark	Kate	Mark	Mark
Sheet no	copied in	plot file created	checked by Phil	plot sent	plot file created	plot sent mylar
596S6	✓	✓				
S7	✓	✓				
S8	✓					
S9	✓					
S10	✓					

Figure 4.11 *An external representation used to coordinate collaborative work in the form of a printout table showing who has completed the checking of files and who is down to do what*

4.2.4 Designing collaborative technologies to support coordination

Group calendars, electronic schedulers, project management tools, and workflow tools that provide interactive forms of scheduling and planning are some of the main kinds of collaborative technologies that have been developed to support coordination. A specific mechanism that has been implemented is the use of conventions. For example, an early shared workspace system developed in Germany (called POLITeam), that supported email and document sharing to allow politicians to work together at different sites, introduced a range of conventions, such as how folders and files should be organized in the shared workspace. Interestingly, when the system was used in practice, it was found that the conventions were often violated (Mark *et al.*, 1997). For example, one convention that was set up was that users should always type in the code of a file when they were using it. In practice, very few people did this, as pointed out by an administrator: "They don't type in the right code. I must correct them. I must sort the documents into the right archive. And that's annoying."

The tendency of people not to follow conventions can be due to a number of reasons. If following conventions requires additional work that is extraneous to the users' ongoing work, they may find it gets in the way. They may also perceive the convention as an unnecessary burden and 'forget' to follow it all the time. Such 'productive laziness' is quite common. A simple analogy to everyday life is forgetting to put the top back on the toothpaste tube: it is a very simple convention to follow and yet we are all guilty sometimes (or even all the time) of not doing this. While such actions may only take a tiny bit of effort, people often don't do them because they perceive them as tedious and unnecessary. However, the consequence of not doing them can be very annoying to others and make the system much less efficient and workable.

When designing coordination mechanisms it is important to consider how socially acceptable they are to people. Failure to do so can result in the users not using the system in the way intended or simply abandoning it. Getting the right balance between human coordination and system coordination is important. Too much system control and the users will rebel; too little control and the system breaks down. Consider the example of file locking, which is a form of concurrency control. This is used by most shared applications, e.g. file-sharing systems to prevent users from clashing when trying to work on the same part of a shared document or file at the same time. With file locking, whenever someone is working on a file or part of it, it becomes inaccessible to others. Information about who is using the file and for how long may be made available to the other users, to show why they can't work on a particular file. When file-locking mechanisms are used in this way, however, they are often considered too rigid as a form of coordination, primarily because they don't let other users negotiate with the first user about when they can have access to the locked file.

A more flexible form of coordination is to include a social policy of floor control. Whenever a user wants to work on a shared document or file, he must initially request 'the floor.' If no one else is using the specified section or file at that time, then he is given the floor. That part of the document or file then becomes locked, preventing others from having access to it. If other users want access to the file, they likewise make a request for the floor. The current user is then notified and can then let the requester know how long the file will be in use. If not acceptable, the requester can try to negotiate a time for access to the file. This kind of coordination mechanism, therefore, provides more scope for negotiation between users on how to collaborate, rather than simply receiving a point-blank 'permission denied' response from the system when a file is being used by someone else.

Box 4.4
Turning technology inside out: online versus physical coordination mechanisms

Many software applications now exist to support coordination, notably project management systems. From the project manager's perspective, they provide a flexible means of scheduling, distributing, and monitoring collaborative work and enabling them continuously to remind people of deadlines and milestones via the use of email and other kinds of representations. From the perspective of the individuals working in the company, they give them a means of letting others know when they are available for meetings and where they will be.

In practice, however, project management systems that rely exclusively on computer-mediated coordination mechanisms have not been found to be as effective as hoped. This tends to happen when the system is used to coordinate a large number of events or projects. People begin not to take notice of the numerous internal reminders and messages that are sent to them by the system, finding them to be too intrusive, overwhelming, or annoying. This can then lead to missing important meetings and deadlines. A work-around in some organizations has been to print out the schedules and events that have been entered into the project management online database and display them as paper-based external representations (see Whittaker and Schwartz, 1995). A study that looked at the creation and use of shared external representations in collaborative work (Bellotti and Rogers, 1997) found that in several cases, information that is represented online becomes re-represented as a physical entity because the online version often gets lost, forgotten, or overlooked. This was particularly prevalent at new media companies producing web content that needed to be updated regularly. The various groups had to be coordinated across a number of parallel-running, time-critical projects.

At one site, a project coordinator would write up on a physical whiteboard every morning the main projects, schedules, and deadlines relevant for that day fed from the online project management software. When asked why she laboriously wrote down by hand information that could be readily accessed

by everyone over the computer network, she replied that, owing to the multiplication of projects and people working on them, it had become very difficult to keep track of everything that was going on. Moreover, people had become desensitized to the many email reminders that the software application provided, so they often forgot their significance immediately after having acknowledged them. Consequently, everyone (including herself) needed to be reminded of what was urgent and what needed dealing with that day. Placing this critical information on a physical whiteboard in a prominent public place that was clearly distinct from the continuous stream of other online information and messages provided a more effective public reminder of what was urgent and needed doing that day. In essence, the company had resorted to '*turning the technology inside out*.' ■

Activity 4.7

Why are whiteboards so useful for coordinating projects? How might electronic whiteboards be designed to extend this practice?

Comment

Physical whiteboards are very good as coordinating tools as they display information that is external and public, making it highly visible for everyone to see. Furthermore, the information can be easily annotated to show up-to-date modifications to a schedule. Whiteboards also have a gravitational force, drawing people to them. They provide a meeting place for people to discuss and catch up with latest developments.

Electronic whiteboards have the added advantage that important information can be animated to make it stand out. Important information can also be displayed on multiple displays throughout a building and can be fed from existing databases and software, thereby making the project coordinator's work much easier. The boards could also be used to support on-the-fly meetings in which individuals could use electronic pens to sketch out ideas that could then be stored electronically. In such settings they could also be interacted with via wireless handheld computers, allowing information to be 'scraped' off or 'squirted' onto the whiteboard.

4.2.5 Awareness mechanisms

Awareness involves knowing who is around, what is happening, and who is talking with whom (Dourish and Bly, 1992). For example, when we are at a party, we move around the physical space, observing what is going on and who is talking to whom, eavesdropping on others' conversations and passing on gossip to others. A specific kind of awareness is peripheral awareness. This refers to a person's ability to maintain and constantly update a sense of what is going on in the physical and social context, through keeping an eye on what is happening in the periphery of their vision. This might include noting whether people are in a good or bad mood by the way they are talking, how fast the drink and food is being consumed, who has entered or left the room, how long someone has been absent, and whether the lonely guy in the corner is finally talking to someone—all while we are having a conversation with someone else. The combination of direct observations and peripheral monitoring keeps people informed and updated on what is happening in the world.

Similar ways of becoming aware and keeping aware take place in other contexts, such as a place of study, at work, or school. Importantly, this requires fathoming when it is an appropriate time to interact with others to get and pass information on. Seeing a professor slam the office door signals to students that this is definitely not a good time to ask for an extension on an assignment deadline. Conversely, seeing teachers with beaming faces, chatting openly to other students suggests they are in a good mood and therefore this would be a good time to ask them if it would be all right to miss next week's seminar because of an important family engagement. The knowledge that someone is approachable or not rapidly spreads through a company, school, or other institution. People are very eager to pass on both good and bad news to others and will go out of their way to gossip, loitering in corridors, hanging around at the photocopier and coffee machine 'spreading the word.'

In addition to monitoring the behavior of others, people will organize their work and physical environment to enable it to be successfully monitored by others. This ranges from the use of subtle cues to more blatant ones. An example of a subtle cue is when someone leaves their dorm or office door slightly ajar to indicate that they can be approached. A more blatant one is the complete closing of their door together with a 'do not disturb' notice prominently on it, signaling to everyone that under no circumstances should they be disturbed (see Figure 4.12).

Overhearing and overseeing

People who work closely together also develop various strategies for coordinating their work, based on an up-to-date awareness of what the others are doing. This is especially so for inter-dependent tasks, where the outcome of one person's activity is needed for others to be able to carry out their tasks. For example, when putting on a show, the performers will constantly monitor what one another is doing in order to coordinate their performance efficiently.

The metaphorical expression 'closely-knit teams' exemplifies this way of collaborating. People become highly skilled in reading and tracking what others are doing and the information they are attending to. A well-known study of this phenomenon is described by Christian Heath and Paul Luff (1992), who looked at how two controllers worked together in a control room in the London Underground. An overriding observation was that the

Figure 4.12 *An external representation used to signal to others a person's availability*

actions of one controller were tied very closely to what the other was doing. One of the controllers was responsible for the movement of trains on the line (controller A), while the other was responsible for providing information to passengers about the current service (controller B). In many instances, it was found that controller B overheard what controller A was doing and saying, and acted accordingly—even though controller A had not said anything explicitly to him. For example, on overhearing controller A discussing a problem with a train driver over the in-cab intercom system, controller B inferred from the ensuing conversation that there was going to be a disruption to the service and so started announcing this to the passengers on the platform before controller A had even finished talking with the train driver. At other times, the two controllers keep a lookout for each other, monitoring the environment for actions and events which they might have not noticed but may be important for them to know about so that they can act appropriately.

Activity 4.8

What do you think happens when one person of a closely-knit team does not see or hear something or misunderstands what has been said, while the others in the group assume they have seen, heard, or understood what has been said?

Comment

In such circumstances, the person is likely to carry on as normal. In some cases this will result in inappropriate behavior. Repair mechanisms will then need to be set in motion. The knowledgeable

participants may notice that the other person has not acted in the manner expected. They may then use one of a number of subtle repair mechanisms, say coughing or glancing at something that needs attending to. If this doesn't work, they may then resort to explicitly stating aloud what had previously been signaled implicitly. Conversely, the unaware participant may wonder why the event hasn't happened and, likewise, look over at the other people, cough to get their attention, or explicitly ask them a question. The kind of repair mechanism employed at a given moment will depend on a number of factors, including the relationship among the participants, e.g. whether one is more senior than the others—this determines who can ask what, the perceived fault or responsibility for the breakdown, and the severity of the outcome of not acting there and then on the new information.

4.2.6 Designing collaborative technologies to support awareness

The various observations about awareness have led system developers to consider how best to provide awareness information for people who need to work together but who are not in the same physical space. Various technologies have been employed, along with the design of specific applications to convey information about what people are doing and the progress of their ongoing work. As mentioned previously, media spaces and audio–video links have been developed to enable remote colleagues to keep in touch with one another. Some of these systems have also been developed to provide awareness information about remote partners, allowing them to find out what one another is doing. One of the earliest systems was Portholes, developed at Xerox PARC research labs (Dourish and Bly, 1992). The system presented regularly-updated digitized video images of people in their offices from a number of different locations (in the USA and UK). These were shown in a matrix display on people's workstations. Clicking on one of the images had the effect of bringing up a dialog box providing further information about that individual, e.g. name, phone number together with a set of lightweight action buttons, e.g. email the person, listen to a prerecorded audio snippet. The system provided changing images of people throughout the day and night in their offices, letting others see at a glance whether they were in their offices, what they were working on, and who was around (see Figure 4.13). Informal evaluation of the set-up suggested that having access to such information led to a shared sense of community.

The emphasis in the design of these early awareness systems was largely on supporting peripheral monitoring, allowing people to see each other and their progress. Dourish and Bellotti (1992) refer to this as shared feedback. More recent distributed awareness systems provide a different kind of awareness information. Rather than place the onus on participants to find out about each other, they have been designed to allow users to notify each other about specific kinds of events. Thus, there is less emphasis on monitoring and being monitored and more on explicitly letting others know

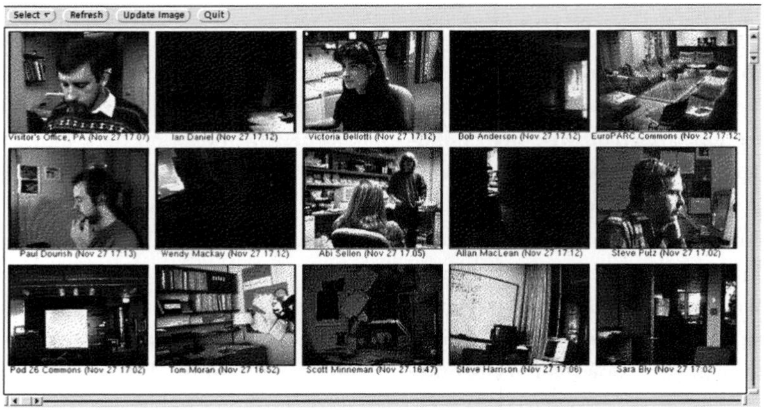

***Figure 4.13** A screen dump of Portholes, showing low resolution monochrome images from offices in the US and UK PARC sites*

about things. Notification mechanisms are also used to provide information about the status of shared objects and the progress of collaborative tasks.

Hence, there has been a shift towards supporting a collective 'stream of consciousness' that people can attend to when they want and likewise provide information for whom they want. An example is Elvin, which is a distributed awareness system that provides a range of client services (Segall and Arnold, 1997). It includes Tickertape, a lightweight messaging system, that shows small color-coded messages scrolling from right to left across a user's screen, together with virtual presence windows, indicating who is online or offline and for how long (see Figure 4.14). This and other Internet instant messaging systems provide a number of functions, including a chat and local organizing tool for shared events, e.g. lunch dates, and announcements, e.g. a party, and an 'always-on' communication tool for people working together on projects but who are not physically collocated.

In addition to presenting awareness information as streaming text messages, more abstract forms of representation have been used. For example, a communication tool called Babble, developed at IBM by David Smith (Erickson *et al.*, 1999), provides a dynamic visualization of the participants in an ongoing chat-like conversation. A large 2D circle called a cookie is depicted with colored marbles on each user's monitor. Marbles inside the cookie convey those individuals active in the current conversation. Marbles outside the cookie convey users involved in other conversations. The more active a participant is in the conversation, the more the corresponding marble is moved towards the center of the cookie. Conversely, the less engaged a person is in the ongoing conversation, the more the marble moves towards the periphery of the cookie (see Figure 4.15). Similarly, Loops, its successor, uses an abstract dynamic representation to convey the participants' activity in a web-based persistent chat system (Halverson *et al.*, 2003).

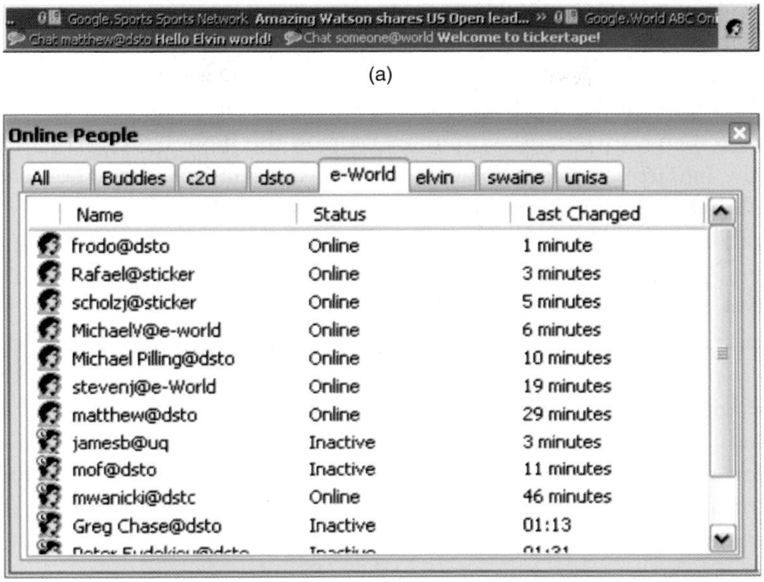

(a)

(b)

Figure 4.14 *Sticker tickertape interface, showing ticker scroller and virtual presence window. Sticker is a newer version of Elvin tickertape*

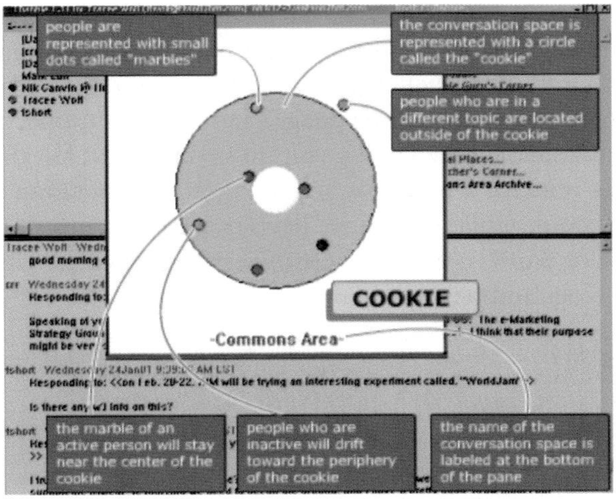

Figure 4.15 *The Babble interface*

4.3 Technology-mediated social phenomena

According to the *New York Times* journalist John Markoff (2005), whenever Catherina Fake, the co-founder of Flickr (the popular photo-sharing service), gets off a plane after a flight she takes a photo of the baggage carousel with her camera phone and sends it to her mother who then views it a few minutes later on the web. This enables her mother to be reassured she has arrived safely. Friends will also take photos using their camera phones to enrich a mutually shared experience, such as a party or concert, where they swap their phones and take pictures of each other and then compare them (Kindberg *et al.*, 2005). Others will send photos taken on their camera phone throughout the day to their family or partner as a form of intimacy.

These examples are indicative of how mobile communication technologies, i.e. cell phones, camera phones, and PDAs, are changing the way millions of people keep in touch, especially the trend towards perpetual communication where day-to-day activities and immediate plans are relayed back and forth—compared with their use of earlier tethered communication technologies. The web has also dramatically changed how people find out about and inform others of events and their news. One of the most significant developments is the proliferation of web-based services that enable people anywhere in the world to share information and content with one another. People are now creating and generating ever-increasing amounts of digital content, e.g. photos, videos, music, news, jokes, games, gossip, information, that web services allow them to easily and freely upload and download to their sites, making it instantly accessible to the rest of the world. As a result, it is now possible for anyone to share and view photos of, say, my nephew and his class on a school trip to Mongolia; read and post up-to-the-minute first-hand accounts of refugees' harrowing experiences in disaster areas; find thousands of recipes on how to make a cheesecake; get recommendations and reviews about the latest movie, hotel, book, restaurant, etc.; find someone who can instantly help them figure out how to get a scrollbar to work on a cell phone using an obscure programming language, and so on. Equally, the same web-based services can enable undesirable views and gossip to be broadcast for all to see; for example, students can ruthlessly criticize a professor and damage his reputation on a public website, e.g. myprofessorsucks.com, while celebrities have become victims of constant surveillance and gossip—their every word, move, and encounter being written about and discussed at length on numerous blogs and news sites.

The social and community web-based services that millions are now using and adapting to share knowledge, views, and personal media include news groups, bulletin boards, buddy lists, blogs, wikis (Internet server programs that allow users to collaborate in the creation of content, such as an online encyclopedia), discussions, and alerts. A number of social network services have also been popularized that enable users to make new friends, find old school chums, keep in touch, and be kept posted of what is happening in their and others' social or business networks, e.g. MySpace or LinkedIn. Online communities have also emerged in every shape and form, from support groups for patients with various illnesses, such as HutchWorld (see Chapter 12), to hobbyists and activists who share common interests, e.g. environmental concerns.

Part of the reason for this phenomenal growth and uptake in the sharing and broadcasting of information, knowledge, and personal content is that many of the web tools have been designed to make it easy for anyone to try them out. Many, too, are freely available. Word of mouth has also greatly accelerated their popularity. But, ultimately, it is about the inherently social nature of human beings; people will always need to collaborate and communicate with one another and the diverse range of applications, web-based services, and technologies that have emerged are enabling them to do so in more extensive and diverse ways.

Assignment

The aim of this activity is for you to analyze the design of a virtual world with respect to how it is designed to support collaboration and communication.

Visit an existing 3D virtual world such as the Palace (thepalace.com), habbo hotel (habbohotel.com), or one hosted by Worlds (worlds.net). Try to work out how they have been designed taking account of the following:

(a) *General social issues*

What is the purpose of the virtual world?
What kinds of conversation mechanisms are supported?
What kinds of coordination mechanisms are provided?
What kinds of social protocols and conventions are used?
What kinds of awareness information is provided?
Does the mode of communication and interaction seem natural or awkward?

(b) *Specific interaction design issues*

What form of interaction and communication is supported, e.g. text/audio/video?
What other visualizations are included? What information do they convey?
How do users switch between different modes of interaction, e.g. exploring and chatting? Is the switch seamless?
Are there any social phenomena that occur specific to the context of the virtual world that wouldn't happen in face-to-face settings, e.g. flaming?

(c) *Design issues*
What other features might you include in the virtual world to improve communication and collaboration?

Summary

In this chapter we have looked at some core aspects of sociality, namely communication and collaboration. We examined the main social mechanisms that people use in different settings in order to collaborate and communicate. A number of collaborative technologies have been designed to support and extend these mechanisms. We looked at representative examples of these, highlighting core interaction design concerns. A particular concern is social acceptability that is critical for the success or failure of the technologies intended to be used by groups of people working or communicating together.

Key Points

- Social aspects are the routine actions and interactions that people engage in at home, work, school, and in public.
- The three main kinds of social mechanisms used to coordinate and facilitate social aspects are conversation, coordination, and awareness.
- Talk and the way it is managed are integral to coordinating social activities.
- Many kinds of computer-mediated communication systems have been developed to enable people to communicate with one another when in physically different locations.
- External representations, rules, conventions, and verbal and non-verbal communication are all used to coordinate activities among people.
- People adapt the social protocols used in face-to-face collaboration when using collaborative technologies.
- Keeping aware of what others are doing and letting others know what you are doing are important aspects of collaboration and socializing.
- Cell phones, web-based social and community services have brought about significant changes in the way people keep in touch.

Further Reading

RHEINGOLD, H. (2002) *Smart Mobs: The Next Social Revolution.* Perseus Publishing. This book is about groups of people who use their cell phones and texting to organize themselves, e.g. set up parties, while on the move. It covers technological issues, privacy issues, and explores the notion of where new technologies are taking human kind.

KATZ, J. and AAKHUS, M. (eds) (2003) *Perpetual Contact: Mobile Communication, Private Talk, Public Performance.* Cambridge University Press. This edited volume presents a collection of papers on mobile communication from around the world, covering how people's lives have changed as a result of untethered communication and what the implications are for society.

DIX, A., FINLAY, J., ABOWD, G. and BEALE, R. (2004) *Human–Computer Interaction*, 3rd edn. Pearson. Chapter 19 provides a comprehensive overview of groupware systems.

PREECE, J. (2000) *Online Communities: Designing Usability, Supporting Sociability.* John Wiley & Sons. This book combines usability and sociability issues to do with designing online communities.

MUNRO, A.J., HOOK, K. and BENYON, D. (eds) (1999) *Social Navigation of Information Space.* Springer-Verlag. Provides a number of papers that explore how people navigate information spaces in real and virtual worlds and how people interact with one another in them.

INTERVIEW with Abigail Sellen

Abigail Sellen is a senior researcher at Microsoft Research in Cambridge, UK. Her work involves carrying out user studies to inform the development of future products. She has a background in cognitive science and human factors engineering, having obtained her doctorate at the University of California, San Diego. Prior to this Abigail worked at Hewlett-Packard Labs in Bristol, UK, Xerox Research Labs in Cambridge, UK, and Apple Computer in Cupertino, California. She has also worked as an academic researcher at the Computer Systems Research Institute at the University of Toronto, Canada and the Applied Psychology Unit in Cambridge, UK. She has written widely on the social and cognitive aspects of paper use, videoconferencing, input devices, human memory, and human error, all with an eye to the design of new technologies.

YR: Could you tell me what you do at Microsoft Research Cambridge?

AS: Sure, I'm in a group at Microsoft Research called 'Computer-Mediated Living' which brings together psychologists, sociologists, computer scientists, hardware engineers and designers. Our goal is to inform the development of new technologies that fit into and enhance everyday life, but that also go beyond the usual metaphors for software and hardware design. You could say that we are trying to go beyond the desktop metaphor to bring technology out of that box and into the everyday world around us. Our focus at the moment is on the home, and on supporting activities related to home (whether these occur at work or on the move).

YR: Right. Could you tell me about user studies, what they are and why you consider them important?

AS: OK. User studies essentially involve looking at how people behave either in their natural habitats or in the laboratory, both with existing technologies and with new ones. I think there are many different questions that these kinds of studies can help you answer. Let me name a few. One question is: who is going to be the potential user for a particular device or service that you are thinking of developing? A second question—which I think is key—is, what is the potential value of a particular product for a user? Once we know this, we can then ask, for a particular situation or task, what features do we want to deliver and how best should we deliver those features? This includes, for example, what would the interface look like? Finally, I think user studies are important to understand how users' lives may change and how they will be affected by introducing a new technology. This has to take into account the social, physical, and technological context into which it will be introduced.

YR: So it sounds like you have a set of general questions you have in mind when you do a user study. Could you now describe how you would do a user study and what kinds of things you would be looking for?

AS: Well, I think there are two different classes of user studies and both are quite different in the ways you go about them. There are evaluation studies, where we take a concept, a prototype or even a developed technology and look at how it is used and then try to modify or improve it based on what we find. The second class of user studies is more about discovering what people's unmet needs may be. This means trying to develop new concepts and ideas for things that people may never have thought of before. This is difficult because you can't necessarily just ask people what they would like or what they would use. Instead, you have to make inferences from studying people in different situations and try to understand from this what they might value.

YR: In the book we mention the importance of taking into account social aspects, such as awareness of others, how people communicate with each other and so on. Do you think these issues are important when you are doing these two kinds of user studies?

AS: Well, yes, and in particular I think social aspects really are playing to that second class of user study I mentioned where you are trying to discover what people's unmet needs or requirements may be. Here you are trying to get rich descriptions about what people do in the context of their everyday lives—whether this is in their working lives, their home lives, or lives on the move. I'd say getting the social aspects understood is often very important in trying to understand what value new products and services might bring to people's day-to-day activities, and also how they would fit into those existing activities.

YR: And what about cognitive aspects, such as how people carry out their tasks, what they remember, what they are bad at remembering? Is that also important to look into when you are doing these kinds of studies?

AS: Yes, if you think about evaluation studies, then cognitive aspects are extremely important. Looking at cognitive aspects can help you understand the nature of the user interaction, in particular what processes are going on in their heads. This includes issues like learning how users perceive a device and how they form a mental model of how something works. Cognitive issues are especially important to consider when we want to contrast one device with another or think about new and better ways in which we might design an interface.

YR: I wonder if you could describe to me briefly research where you have

looked at both cognitive and social aspects.

AS: A good example is a study we did aimed at designing and developing new devices for reading digital documents in workplace settings. When we first set out on this study, before we could begin to think about how to build such devices, we had to begin by asking, "What do we mean by reading?" It turned out there was not a lot written about the different ways people read in their day-to-day lives. So the first thing we did was a very broad study looking at how people read in work situations. The technique we used here was a combination of asking people to fill out a diary about their reading activities during the course of a day and interviewing them at the end of each day. The interviews were based around what was written in the diaries, which turned out to be a good way of unpacking more details about what people had been doing.

That initial study allowed us to categorize all the different ways people were reading. What we found out is that actually you can't talk about reading in a generic sense but that it falls into at least 10 different categories. For example, sometimes people skim read, sometimes they read for the purpose of writing something, and sometimes they read very reflectively and deeply, marking up their documents as they go. What quickly emerged from this first study was that if you're designing a device for reading it might look very different depending on the kind of reading the users are doing. So, for example, if they're reading by themselves, the screen size and viewing angle may not be as important as if they're reading with others. If they're skim reading, the ability to quickly flick through pages is important. And if they're reading and writing, then this points to the need for a pen-based interface. All of these issues become important design considerations.

This study then led to the development of some design concepts and ideas for new kinds of reading devices. At this stage we involved designers to develop different 'props' to get feedback and reactions from potential users. A prop could be anything from a quick sketch to an animation to a styrofoam 3D mockup. Once you have this initial design work, you can then begin to develop working prototypes and test them with realistic tasks in both laboratory and natural settings. Some of this work we have already completed, but the project has had an impact on several different research and development efforts.

YR: Would you say that user studies are going to become an increasingly important part of the interaction design process, especially as new technologies like ubiquitous computing and handheld devices come into being—and where no one really knows what applications to develop?

AS: Yes. I think the main contribution of user studies, say, 15 years ago was in the area of evaluation and usability testing in laboratory settings. One change is that with the advent of mobile and ubiquitous computing, fewer of these technologies can be evaluated or understood in such controlled circumstances. By their very nature they must be useful in many different environments with much more complexity than is present in a laboratory. Our evaluation methods therefore have to adapt too and be oriented more toward evaluation in real world settings and everyday activities. Here we can learn a lot from the methods of sociologists and anthropologists. I think also the role of user studies is shifting from an emphasis on evaluation to more of an emphasis on the invention and development of new product concepts. One of the implications of this is the need to work more closely with people who know how to do design. I think we have a lot to learn from designers and their techniques. The bottom line is drawing on other disciplines is more important than ever for a user studies researcher.

YR: So they are essentially working as a multidisciplinary team. Finally, what is it like to work in a large organization like Microsoft, with so many different departments?

AS: One thing about working for a large organization is that you get a lot of variety in what you can do. I have found that as part of the research laboratory of such an organisation, I get a fair amount of choice in what I do and don't have to be tied to a particular product for any long period of time. If, on the other hand, you work for a smaller organization such as a start-up company, inevitably there is lots of pressure to get things out the door quickly. Things are often very focused so there's less time to spend looking at any one issue deeply. I prefer the flexibility of a large organisation, and, while it may sometimes be more of a challenge, there is still the satisfaction of impacting real products from time to time. ■

5

5.1 Introduction

An overarching goal of interaction design is to develop interactive systems that elicit positive responses from users, such as feeling at ease, being comfortable, and enjoying the experience of using them—be it a washing machine or a flight deck. Designers are also concerned with how to create interactive products that elicit specific kinds of emotional responses in users, such as motivating them to learn, play, be creative, or be social. There has also been much interest in designing websites and Internet applications that people can trust, that make them feel comfortable about divulging personal information or when making a purchase.

Taken together, we refer to this emerging area as the affective aspects of interaction design. In this chapter we look at how and why the design of interactive products causes certain kinds of emotional responses in users. We begin by looking in general at expressive interfaces, examining the role of an interface's appearance to users and how it affects usability. We then examine how interactive products elicit positive effects, e.g. pleasure, and negative responses, e.g. frustration. How technologies are being designed and used to persuade people to change their behavior and attitudes is then covered. Following this, we discuss the controversial topic of anthropomorphism and the implications of designing applications to have human-like qualities. We examine the range of physical and virtual characters that have gained popularity to motivate people to learn, buy, listen and consider how useful and appropriate they are. Finally, we present three models that have been proposed to explain the relationship between affect and user experience: (i) Norman's (2004) emotional design model, (ii) Jordan's (2000) pleasure model for product design, and (iii) McCarthy and Wright's (2004) technology as experience framework.

The main aims of this chapter are to:

- **Explain what expressive interfaces are and the effects they can have on people.**
- **Outline the nature of user frustration and how to reduce it.**
- **Describe how technologies can be designed to change people's attitudes and behavior.**
- **Debate the pros and cons of applying anthropomorphism in interaction design.**
- **Describe the affective aspects used in interface agents and interactive physical toys.**
- **Present models and frameworks of affect that can be applied to interaction design.**
- **Enable you to critique the persuasive impact of an online agent on customers.**

5

Affective aspects

5.2 What are affective aspects?

In general, the term 'affective' refers to the generation of an emotional response. For example, when people are happy they smile. Affective behavior can also trigger an emotional response in others. So, for example, when someone smiles it can cause others to feel good and smile back. Emotional skills, especially the ability to express and recognize emotions, are central to human communication. Most of us are highly skilled at detecting when someone is angry, happy, sad, or bored by recognizing their facial expressions, way of speaking, and other body signals. We are also very good at knowing what emotions to express in a given situation. For example, when someone has just heard he has failed an exam we know it is not a good time to smile and be happy. Instead we try to empathize.

It has been suggested that computers be designed to recognize and express emotions in the same way humans do (Picard, 1998). The term coined for this approach is 'affective computing.' A long-standing area of research in artificial intelligence and artificial life has been the creation of intelligent robots and other computer-based systems that behave like humans and other creatures. One well-known project was MIT's COG, where a group of researchers attempted to build an artificial two-year-old. An offspring of COG was Kismet (Breazeal, 1999), which was designed to engage in meaningful social interactions with humans (see Figure 5.1). Rather than trying to get the system to show an emotion to a user, we consider how interactive systems can be designed to provoke an emotion within the user.

5.3 Expressive interfaces and positive emotions

Expressive forms like emoticons, sounds, icons, and virtual agents have been used at the interface to (i) convey emotional states and/or (ii) elicit certain kinds of emotional responses in users, such as feeling at ease, comfort, and happiness. Icons and animations have been used to indicate the current state of a computer or a cell phone, notably when it is waking up or being rebooted. A classic from the 1980s and 1990s was the happy Mac icon that appeared on the screen of the Apple computer whenever the machine was booted (see Figure 5.2a). The smiling icon conveyed a sense of friendliness, inviting the user to feel at ease and even smile back. The appearance of the icon on the screen was also very reassuring to users, indicating that their computer was working correctly. This was especially true for situations where users had to reboot their computer after it had crashed, and where previous attempts to reboot had failed (usually indicated by a sad icon face—see Figure 5.2b). After 18 years, sadly, the happy Mac icon was laid to rest although the sad Mac icon now shows its face on an iPod if its software needs restoring (see Figure 5.2c). MacOS has since switched to the use of more abstract icons to indicate starting up and busy with a process, showing a swirling clock or a colorful beach ball.

Other ways of conveying the status of a system are through the use of:

- Dynamic icons, e.g. a recycle bin expanding when a file is placed in it.

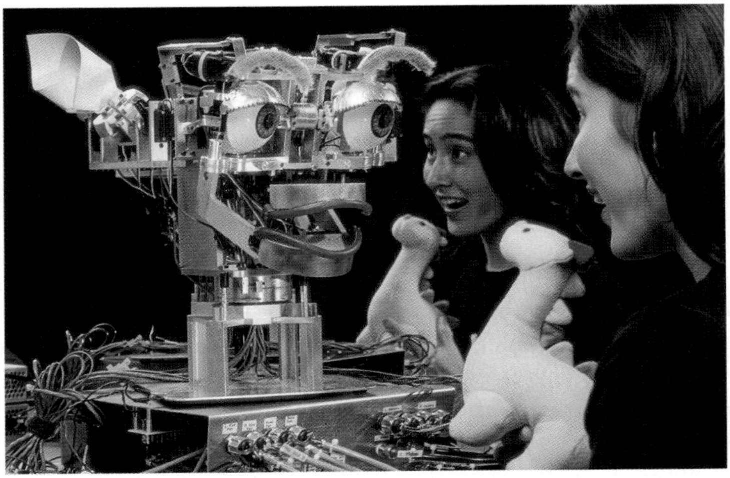

(a)

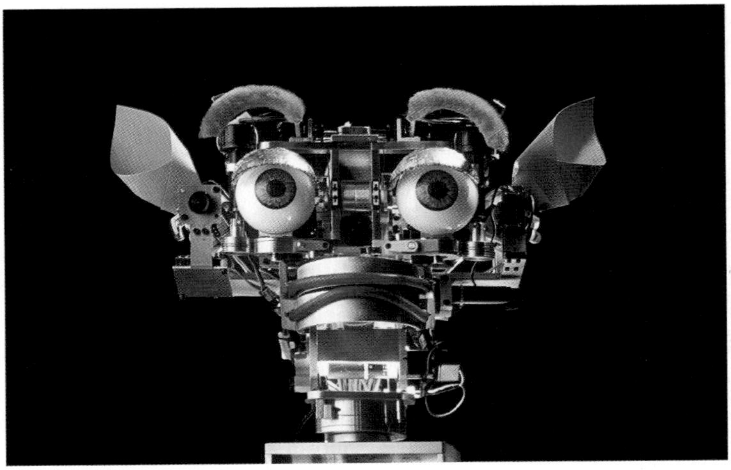

(b)

Figure 5.1 *Kismet the robot expressing (a) surprise and (b) disgust*

- Animations, e.g. a bee flying across the screen indicating that the computer is doing something, such as checking files.
- Spoken messages, using various kinds of voices, telling the user what needs to be done.
- Various sonifications indicating actions and events, e.g. whoosh for window closing, schlook for a file being dragged, ding for new email arriving.

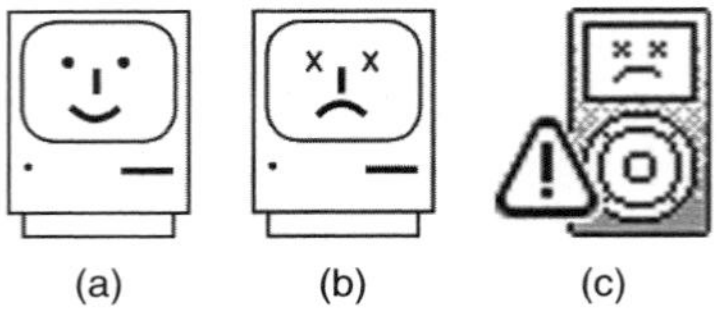

Figure 5.2 *(a) Smiling and sad Apple icons for (b) the classic Mac and (c) the iPod.*

One of the benefits of using expressive embellishments is that they provide reassuring feedback to the user that can be both informative and fun. They can, however, sometimes have the opposite effect on people, who find them intrusive, causing them at times to get annoyed and even angry. This is especially so for 'cutesy' looking ones. How enjoyable they are perceived to be varies considerably across cultures. In South Korea and Japan, for example, cute cartoon characters such as those depicted in Manga comics have huge cult followings. Moreover, their influence has become widespread in the design of websites, video games, cell phone skins, etc. These include the use of large-eyed creatures such as those used in Pokemon and Pikachu games, and bright colors and pastels (Marcus, 2002).

Users themselves have also been inventive in expressing their emotions at the computer interface. One well-known method is the use of emoticons. These are keyboard symbols that are combined in various ways to convey feelings and emotions by simulating facial expressions such as smiling, winking, and frowning on the screen. The meaning of an emoticon depends on the content of the message and where it is placed in the message. For example, a smiley face placed at the end of a message can mean that the sender is happy about a piece of news she has just written about. Alternatively, if it is placed at the end of a comment in the body of the message, it usually indicates that this comment is not intended to be taken seriously. Most emoticons are designed to be interpreted with the viewer's head tilted over to the left (a result of the way the symbols are represented on the screen). Some of the best-known ones are presented in Table 5.1. Nowadays, email and instant messaging users can select from ready-made ones, that are often 3D, very colorful, and cute. An example of a collection of smiley icons that a colleague of mine uses is shown in Figure 5.3.

The style of an interface, in terms of the shapes, fonts, colors, balance, white space, and graphical elements that are used and the way they are combined, can also influence its affectiveness. Use of imagery at the interface can result in more engaging and enjoyable experiences (Mullet and Sano, 1995). Until recently, however, the focus of HCI was primarily on usability, with scant attention being paid to the design of aesthetically pleasing interfaces. Empirical studies showing that the aesthetics of an interface can have a positive effect on people's perception of the system's usability (Tractinsky, 1997, 2000) have begun to change that, and the importance of aesthetics is gaining acceptance within the HCI community. When the 'look and feel' of an interface is pleasing, e.g. beautiful graphics, nice feel to the way the elements have been put together, well-designed fonts, elegant use of images

Emotion	Expression	Emoticon	Possible meanings
Happy	Smile	:) or :D	(i) Happiness, or (ii) previous comment not to be taken seriously
Sad	Mouth down	: (or :-	Disappointed, unhappy
Cheeky	Wink	;) or ; -)	Previous comment meant as tongue-in-cheek
Mad	Brows raised	>:	Mad about something
Very angry	Angry face	>:-(	Very angry, cross
Embarrassed	Mouth open	:O	Embarrassed, shocked
Sick	Looking sick	:x	Feeling ill
Naïve	Schoolboyish look	<:-)	Smiley wearing a dunce's cap to convey that the sender is about to ask a stupid question

Table 5.1 *Some commonly used emoticons*

Figure 5.3 *A collection of graphical smiley icons used by a colleague in MSN messenger*

and color, a good sense of balance, users are likely to be more tolerant, e.g. they may be prepared to wait a few more seconds for a website to download. Furthermore, good-looking interfaces are often more satisfying and pleasurable to use. A key concern, therefore, is to strike a balance between designing pleasurable and usable interfaces (Tractinsky *et al.*, 2000).

Activity 5.1

A question of style or stereotype? Figure 5.4 shows two differently designed dialog boxes. Describe how they differ in terms of style. Of the two, which one do you prefer? Why? Which one do you think Europeans would like the most and which Americans?

Comment

Aaron Marcus, a graphic designer, created the two designs in an attempt to provide appealing interfaces. Dialog box A was designed for white American females while dialog box B was designed for European

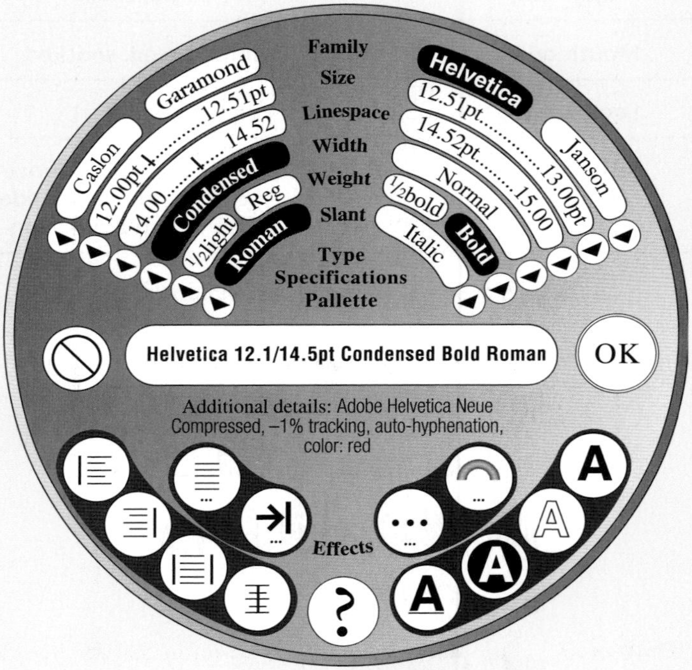

(a)

Figure 5.4 Square and round dialog boxes designed by Aaron Marcus (1993): (a) dialog box designed for white American women; (b) dialog box designed for European adult male intellectuals

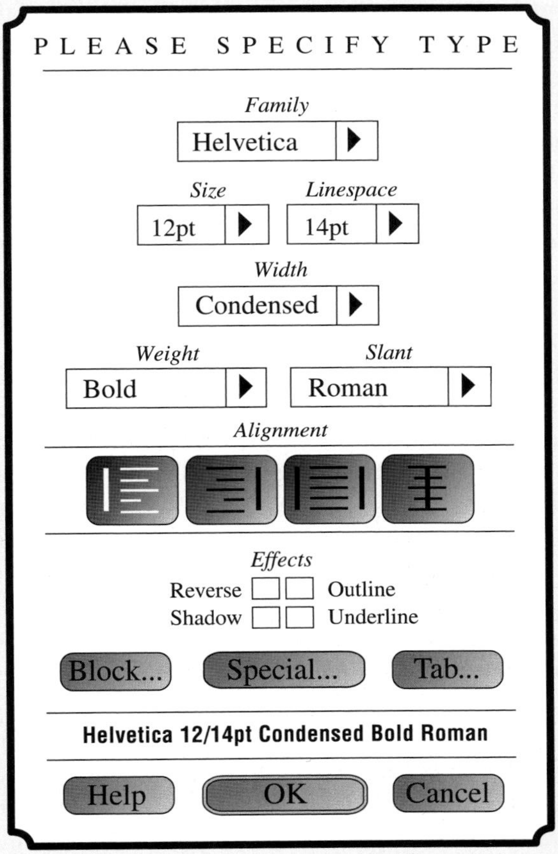

(b)

Figure 5.4 (continued)

adult male intellectuals. The rationale behind Marcus's ideas was that European adult male intellectuals like "suave prose, a restrained treatment of information density, and a classical approach to font selection, e.g. the use of serif type in axial symmetric layouts similar to those found in elegant bronze European building identification signs." In contrast, white American females "prefer a more detailed presentation, curvilinear shapes and the absence of some of the more brutal terms . . . favored by male software engineers."

When the different interfaces were empirically tested by Teasley *et al.* (1994), their results did not support Marcus's assumptions. In particular, they found that the European dialog box was preferred by all and was considered most appropriate for all users. Moreover, the round dialog box designed for women was strongly disliked by everyone. The assumption that women like curvilinear features did not hold in this context. At the very least, displaying the font labels in a circular plane makes them more difficult to read than when presented in the conventionally accepted horizontal plane.

5.4 Frustrating interfaces and negative emotions

In many situations, computer interfaces may *inadvertently* elicit negative emotional responses, such as anger and disgust. This typically happens when something that should be simple to use or set turns out to be complex. The most commonly cited examples are remote controls, VCRs, printers, digital alarm clocks, and digital TV systems (Rourke, 2005). Getting a printer to work with a new digital camera, trying to switch from watching a DVD to the TV, and changing the time on a digital alarm clock in a hotel can be very trying.

This does not mean that developers are unaware of such usability problems. Several methods have been devised to help the novice user get set up and become familiarized with a technology. However, these have sometimes backfired, since the design solution itself has ironically become a source of annoyance and frustration. For example, one technique that was popularized in the 1990s was the use of friendly agents at the interface. The assumption was that novices would feel more at ease with a 'companion' and would be encouraged to try things out, after listening, watching, following, and interacting with it. Microsoft pioneered a class of agent-based software, Bob, aimed at new computer users (many of whom were viewed as computer-phobic). The agents were presented as friendly characters, including a pet dog and a cute bunny. An underlying assumption was that having these kinds of agents on the screen would make users feel more comfortable with using the software. An interface metaphor of a warm, cozy living room, replete with fire and furniture, was also provided (see Figure 5.5)—again intended to convey a comfortable feeling.

However, Bob never became a commercial product. Why do you think not?

Contrary to the designer's expectations, many people did not like the idea of Bob at all, finding the interface too cute and childish. However, Microsoft did not give up on the idea of making their interfaces more friendly and developed other kinds of agents, including the infamous 'Clippy' (a paper clip that has human-like qualities), as part of their Windows 98 operating environment.[1] Clippy typically appeared at the bottom of a user's

[1] On the Mac version of Microsoft's Office 2001, an anthropomorphized Mac computer with big feet and a hand that conveys various gestures and moods replaced Clippy.

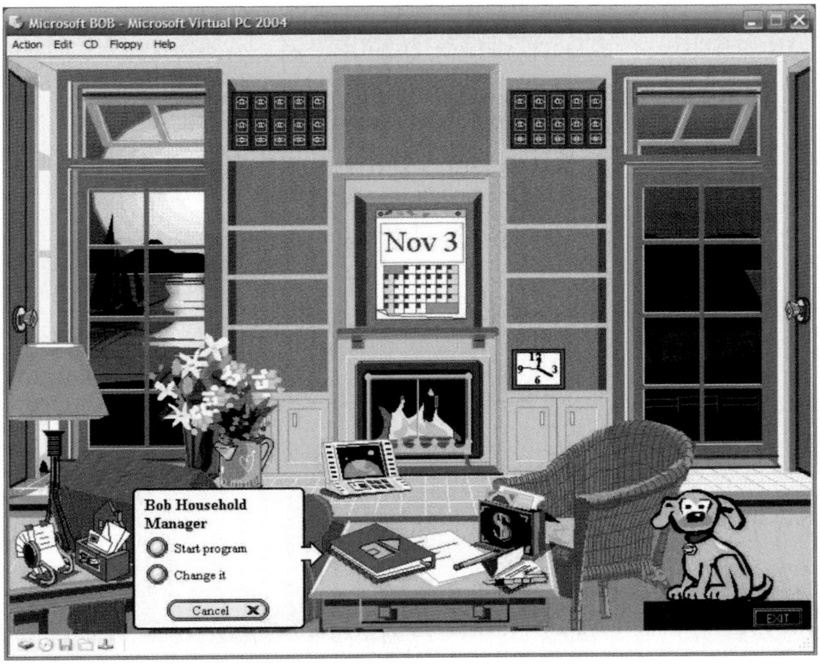

Figure 5.5 *'At home with Bob' software developed for Windows 95. Although now defunct it has been resurrected affectionately to run on a Virtual PC platform*

screen whenever the system 'thought' the user needed help carrying out a particular task (see Figure 5.6). It, too, was depicted as a cartoon character, with a warm personality. This time, Clippy was released as a commercial product but it was not a success. Many Microsoft users found it very trying and intrusive, distracting them from their work. When it was finally retired, numerous websites posted jokes and witty comments, celebrating its demise.

Interfaces, if designed poorly, can make people look stupid, feel insulted or threatened. The effect can be to make them annoyed to the point of losing their temper. There are many reasons why such emotional responses occur:

- When an application doesn't work properly or crashes.
- When a system doesn't do what the user wants it to do.
- When a user's expectations are not met.
- When a system does not provide sufficient information to let the user know what to do.
- When error messages pop up that are vague or obtuse.
- When the appearance of an interface is too noisy, garish, gimmicky, or patronizing.

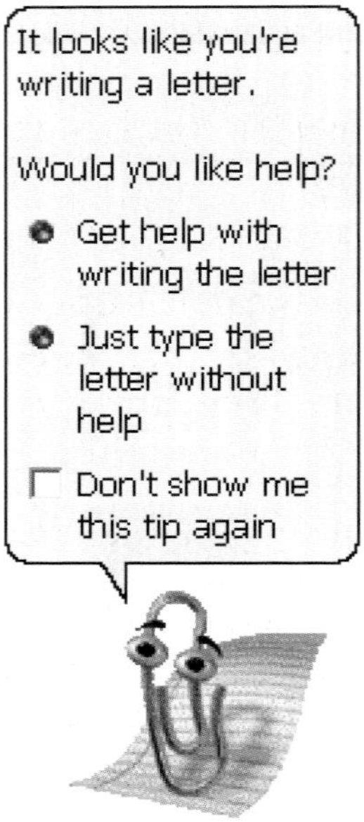

Figure 5.6 *Microsoft's agent Clippy*

- When a system requires users to carry out too many steps to perform a task, only to discover a mistake was made somewhere along the line and they need to start all over again.

Activity 5.2

Provide specific examples for each of the above categories from your own experience, when you have become frustrated with an interactive device, e.g. phone, VCR, vending machine, printer, digital camera, computer. In doing this, write down any further types of frustration that come to mind. Then prioritize these in terms of how annoying they are. Which are the main culprits?

Comment

In the text below we provide examples of common frustrations experienced when using computer systems. The most egregious include unhelpful error messages and excessive housekeeping tasks. You no doubt came up with many more.

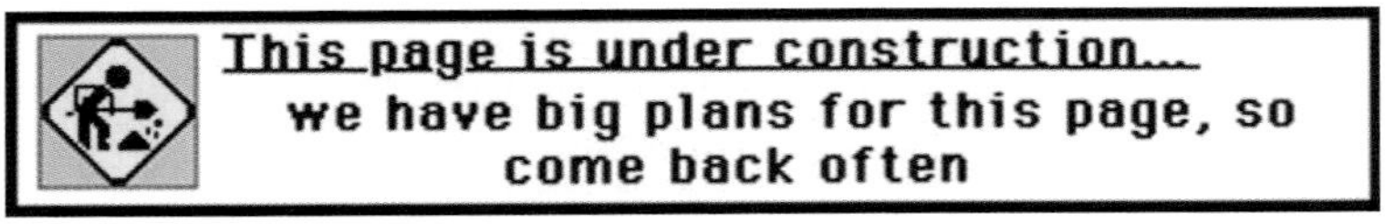

Figure 5.7 *Men at work sign for website 'under construction.'*

Often user frustration is a result of bad design, no design, inadvertent design, or ill-thought-out design. It is rarely caused deliberately. However, the impact of poor design on users can be quite drastic and make them abandon the application or tool.

1. Gimmicks

Frustration can happen when clicking on a link to a website only to discover that it is still 'under construction.' It can be even more annoying when the website displays a road-sign icon of 'men at work' or some other jokey sign (see Figure 5.7). Although the website owner may think such signs amusing, it merely increases the viewer's frustration, having made the effort to go to the website only to be told that it is incomplete.

2. Error messages

Error messages have a long history in computer interface design, and are notorious for their incomprehensibility. For example, Nielsen (1993) describes an early system that was developed, allowing only for one line of error messages. Whenever the error message was too long, the system truncated it to fit on the line, which the users would spend a long time trying to decipher. The full message was available only by pressing the PF1 (help key) function key. While this may have seemed like a natural design solution to the developers, it was not at all obvious to the users. A much better design solution would have been to use the one line of the screen to indicate how to find more information about the current error—"press the PF1 key for explanation".

Threatening error messages can also cause users to get frustrated (see Figure 5.8). Rather than helping them, they can make them panic, especially if subsequently given only two

FLPPS009
FastLane Error!
Your login information is incorrect...
Please verify that you typed in your Last Name, SSN and Password correctly. If you still cannot login, Please contact the FastLane Administrator regarding your access rights.
Return To Previous Page

Figure 5.8 *The error message that the National Science Foundation (NSF) Fastlane website posts up on the web if a user types in his or her personal details for accessing the protected website incorrectly*

chances to rectify the situation, as is often the case after typing in a password incorrectly. Is it really necessary to use bold red with an exclamation mark? Would it not be more pleasant if the message suggested that the user try again?

Box 5.1
Main guidelines on how to design good error messages

Ideally, error messages should be treated as how to fix it messages. Instead of explicating what has happened, they should state the cause of the problem and what the user needs to do to fix it. Shneiderman (1998) has developed a detailed set of guidelines on how to develop helpful messages that are easy to read and understand. Below are some of the main recommendations.

- Rather than condemn users, messages should be courteous, indicating what users need to do to set things right.
- Avoid using terms like FATAL, ERROR, INVALID, BAD, and ILLEGAL.
- Avoid long code numbers and uppercase letters.
- Audio warnings should be under the user's control, since they can cause much embarrassment.
- Messages should be precise rather than vague.
- Messages should provide a help icon or command to allow users to get context-sensitive help.
- Messages should be provided at multiple levels, so that short messages can be supplemented with longer explanations. (Adapted from Shneiderman, 1998)

Activity 5.3

Below are some common error messages expressed in harsh computer jargon that can be quite off-putting. Rewrite them in more usable, useful, and friendly language that would help users to understand the cause of the problem and how to fix it. For each message, imagine a specific context where such a problem might occur.

SYNTAX ERROR

INVALID FILENAME

INVALID DATA

APPLICATION ZETA HAS UNEXPECTEDLY QUIT DUE TO A TYPE 4 ERROR DRIVE ERROR: ABORT, RETRY OR FAIL?

Comment

How specific the given advice can be will depend on the kind of system involved.

Here are suggestions for hypothetical systems.

SYNTAX ERROR—There is a problem with the way you have typed the command. Check for typos.

INVALID FILENAME—Choose another filename that uses only 20 characters or less and is lowercase without any spaces.

INVALID DATA—There is a problem with the data you have entered. Try again, checking that no decimal points are used.

APPLICATION ZETA HAS UNEXPECTEDLY QUIT DUE TO A TYPE 4 ERROR—The application you were working on crashed because of an internal memory problem. Try rebooting and increasing the amount of memory allocated to the application.

DRIVE ERROR: ABORT, RETRY OR FAIL?—There is a problem with reading your disk. Try inserting it again.

Waiting

Websites that take forever to download can be frustrating, especially those that have to load Flash programs. Showing an icon whirring around and the word 'loading' with a slow percentage bar increasing on the splash page can be off-putting, unless the user expects or knows that something good is going to appear. Links that hang and eventually do not load can also be very annoying.

Upgrading software

Another common frustration is upgrading a piece of software. Users now have to go through this housekeeping task on a regular basis, especially if they run a number of applications. More often than not it is time-consuming, requiring the user to do a range of things, such as resetting preferences, sorting out extensions, checking other configurations, and learning new ways of doing things. Often, problems can develop that are not detected until later, when a user tries an operation that worked fine before but mysteriously now fails. A common problem is that settings get lost or do not copy over properly during the upgrade. To add to the frustration, users may also discover that several of their well-learned procedures for carrying out tasks have been substantially changed in the upgrade.

Appearance

People are often frustrated by:

- Websites that are overloaded with text and graphics, making it difficult to find the information desired and slow to access.
- Flashing animations, especially flashing banner ads and pop-up ads, which are very distracting.

- The over-use of sound effects and music, especially when selecting options, carrying out actions, running tutorials, or watching website demos.
- 'Featuritis'—an excessive number of operations, such as the array of buttons on remote controls.
- Childish designs that keep popping up on the screen, such as certain kinds of helper agents.
- Poorly laid out keyboards, pads, control panels, and other input devices that cause users to persistently press the wrong keys or buttons.

5.4.1 Dealing with user frustration

One way of coping with computer-induced frustration is to vent. For example, a typical response to seeing the cursor freeze on the screen is repeatedly to hit the keys on the keyboard. Another way is to flame. When upset or annoyed by a piece of news or something in an email message, people may overreact and respond by writing things in email that they wouldn't dream of saying to someone face-to-face. They often use keyboard symbols to emphasize their anger or frustration, e.g. exclamation marks (!!!!), capital letters (WHY DID YOU DO THAT?), and repeated question marks (??????) that can be quite offensive to those on the receiving end. While such venting behavior can make the user feel temporarily less frustrated, it can be very unproductive and can annoy the recipients. Anyone who has received a flame knows just how unpleasant it can be.

Information that has been designed into the interface to help users carry out tasks includes tips, handy hints, and contextualized advice. Like error messages, this kind of help information needs to be designed to guide users on what to do next when they get stuck and it is not obvious from the interface what to do. The signaling used at the interface to indicate that such online help is available also needs careful consideration. A cartoon-based agent with a catchy tune may seem friendly and helpful the first time round, but can quickly become annoying. A help icon or command that is activated by the users themselves when they want help is often preferable.

Dilemma
Should computers say they're sorry?

A provocative idea is that computers should apologize when they make a mistake. Reeves and Naas (1996), for example, argue that they should be polite and courteous in the same way as people are to one another. While apologizing is normal social etiquette in human behavior, especially when someone makes a mistake, would you agree that computers should be made to behave in the same

way? Would users be as forgiving of computers as they are of one another? For example, what would most users think if, after a system had crashed, it came up with a spoken or written apology such as, "I'm really sorry I crashed. I'll try not to do it again"? Would they think that the computer was being sincere? Would the apology make them forgive the computer in the way they forgive other people, after receiving such an apology? Or would it have no effect at all? Worse still, would users perceive such messages as vacuous statements and regard them simply as condescending, thereby increasing their level of frustration? How else might systems communicate with users when they have committed an error?

5.5 Persuasive technologies

A diversity of technologies is increasingly being used to draw people's attention to certain kinds of information in an attempt to change what they do or think. Pop-up ads, warning messages, reminders, prompts, personalized messages, and recommendations are some of the methods that are being deployed on computer screens. Fogg (2003) has labeled this phenomenon 'persuasive technology'; interactive computing systems are deliberately designed to change people's attitudes and behaviors. Traditionally, media such as magazines, newspapers, pamphlets, radio, and TV have been used to persuade people to join a good cause, give up a bad habit, donate money, or buy a product. For example, a picture of a starving child with bulging eyes staring out at the reader on the front of a newspaper is commonly used by charities. The effect is to pull at the readers' heartstrings, inducing feelings of guilt and, in so doing, spur them on to writing a cheque.

More recently, interactive techniques have been used on the web to entice, cajole, and persuade people to do something they might not have otherwise done. Successful examples include Amazon's 1-click mechanism (see Chapter 1) that makes it so easy and tempting to buy something at their online store, and recommender systems that suggest specific books, hotels, restaurants, etc. a reader might want to try based on their previous purchases, choices, and taste. Splash pages to online shopping sites and color images of gorgeous-looking beach and mountain scenes on travel sites are designed to lure people into making impulse purchases.

In addition to using interactive technologies as a more targeted and personalized form of advertising, Fogg suggests they can be used to change people's behaviors in non-commercial domains, such as safety, preventative healthcare, fitness, personal relationships, and learning. Here, the emphasis is on changing habits or doing something that will improve an individual's well-being through monitoring his or her behavior. For example, Nintendo's Pocket Pikachu (see Figure 5.9) with pedometer attached is designed to motivate children into being more physically active on a consistent basis. The owner of the digital pet that

Figure 5.9 *Pokemon Pikachu: a virtual pet toy with embedded pedometer*

'lives' in the device is required to walk, run, or jump each day to keep it alive. If the owner does not exercise for a week the virtual pet becomes unhappy and eventually dies. This can be a powerful means of persuasion, given that children often become emotionally attached to their virtual pets, especially when they start to care for them.

Similarly, the WaterBot system was developed using a special monitoring and feedback device, but for adults as a way of reducing their usage of water in their homes (Arroyo *et al.*, 2005). There is much evidence to suggest that people are wasteful with water, often leaving the tap running continuously for long periods of time while cleaning their teeth or washing. The research team thought that the use of monitoring technology could help persuade householders to change their behavior to be more conservative in their water usage. To this end, they used the theory of positive reinforcement to inform their design, which states that activities are likely to be repeated if some kind of reward is given occasionally and randomly (similar to the reward system used in slot machines). A sensor-based system was developed where positive auditory messages and chimes were sounded when the tap was turned off. The water was also lit with a random pattern of color as a reward for consistent water-saving behavior (see Figure 5.10). Two illuminated bar graphs were also presented alongside the tap, showing how much water a person had used relative to others in the household. Here, the idea was to encourage peer pressure and for the members of the household to talk to each other about their water usage. Informal feedback of the prototype system in a small number of people's homes suggested that the most effective method of persuasion was the constantly changing bar graph. It drew people's attention to the tap, leading them to make quick comparisons between their's and the others' water consumption. The rewards of chimes and colored water had less impact, especially as their novelty wore off.

A key question is whether the use of novel forms of interactive technologies, e.g. the combination of sensors and dynamically updated information, that monitor, nag, or send personalized messages intermittently to a person are more effective at changing a person's

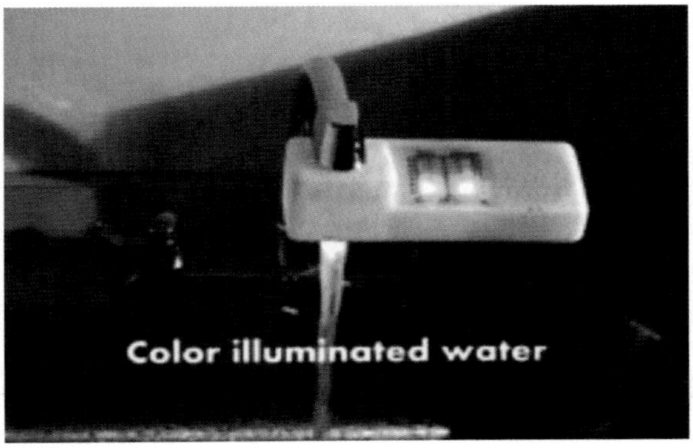

Figure 5.10 *The Waterbot monitoring system showing a continuous visual reminder of a user's water consumption relative to others in the household and illuminated water as a form of reward for using less water*

behavior than non-interactive methods, such as the placement of warning signs, labels, or adverts in prominent positions.

Activity 5.4

Which method is more persuasive for giving up smoking?

There are numerous methods, including hypnosis, that have been developed to help people give up smoking. Many self-help books are also available. Several governments now require tobacco companies to place large and threatening messages on all of their cigarette packs as a way of warning against the dangers of smoking and, in so doing, encourage smokers to give up (see Figure 5.11b). Another method uses a simple monitoring device attached to the top of a pack of cigarettes that counts how many cigarettes someone smokes, providing feedback that will make the smoker more aware of just how many he or she really smokes (smokers will often deceive themselves as to how many cigarettes they actually smoke each day), which in turn, may help them reduce the number they smoke (see Figure 5.11a). Do you think this self-monitoring method is more effective than the use of the 'smoking kills' warning messages and, if so, why?

Comment

When the health warning messages were first introduced they appeared to have a significant shock effect on smokers—especially the guilt-inducing ones which

(a) (b)

Figure 5.11 *(a) A cigarette counter that lights up an LCD display showing the number of cigarettes a person smokes each day. The idea is that people will become aware of how much they really are smoking, which will lead them to take control and reduce the number they smoke. (b) The kind of shocking label required by the British government on all cigarette boxes*

mentioned that smoking can damage a baby during pregnancy and harm the health of those around the smoker. However, the impact can wear off for addicted smokers, who know only too well that it is bad for their health. The counter may prove to be a more effective method in the long run as it dynamically changes in response to the user's behavior, increasing in number whenever a person takes a cigarette from a pack. The accumulating total over a day or week may be sufficiently frightening that it triggers a smoker into deciding to give up.

Box 5.2
The darker side: deceptive technology

Technology is increasingly being used to deceive people into parting with their personal details that allow Internet fraudsters to access their bank accounts and draw money from them. Authentic-looking letters, appearing to be sent from eBay,

PayPal, and various leading banks, are spammed across the world, ending up in people's email boxes with messages such as "During our regular verification of accounts, we couldn't verify your information. Please click here to update and verify your information." Given that many people have an account with one of these corporations, there is a chance that they will be misled and unwittingly follow what is being asked of them, only to discover a few days later they are several thousand dollars worse off. Similarly, letters from supposedly super-rich individuals in far-away countries, offering a share of their assets if the recipient of the email provides them with his bank details, have been persistently spammed worldwide. While many people are becoming increasingly wary of what are known as 'phishing' scams, there are still many vulnerable people who are gullible to such tactics. (Note: The term 'phishing' is a play on the term 'fishing' that refers to the sophisticated way of luring users' financial information and passwords). Moreover, Internet fraudsters are becoming smarter and are always changing their tactics. While the art of deception is centuries old, the increasing, pervasive, and often ingenious use of the web to trick people into divulging personal information may have catastrophic effects on society. ■

5.6 Anthropomorphism in interaction design

A controversial debate in interaction design is whether to exploit anthropomorphism (the propensity people have to attribute human qualities to objects). It is something that people do naturally in their everyday lives and is commonly exploited in the design of technologies, e.g. the creation of human-like animals and plants in cartoon films, the design of toys that have human qualities. The approach is also becoming more widespread in interaction design, through the introduction of agents and interactive toys.

It is well known that people readily attribute human qualities to their pets and their cars, and, conversely, are willing to accept human attributes that have been assigned by others to cartoon characters, robots, and toys. Advertisers are well aware of this phenomenon and often create human-like characters out of inanimate objects to promote their products. For example, breakfast cereals, butter, and fruit drinks have all been transmogrified into characters with human qualities (they move, talk, have personalities, and show emotions), enticing the viewer to buy them. Children are especially susceptible to this kind of 'magic,' as witnessed by their love of cartoons, where all manner of inanimate objects are brought to life with human-like qualities.

The finding that people, especially children, have a propensity to accept and enjoy objects that have been given human-like qualities has led many designers to capitalize on it, most notably in the design of human–computer dialogs modeled on how humans talk to each other. A range of animated screen characters, such as agents, friends, advisors, and virtual pets, have been developed.

Anthropomorphism has also been used in the development of cuddly toys that are embedded with software. Early commercial products like ActiMates™ were designed to encourage children to learn through playing with the cuddly toys. For example, Barney (a cuddly bear ActiMate) attempted to motivate play in children by using human-based speech and movement (Strommen, 1998). The toys were programmed to react to the child and make comments while watching TV together or working together on a computer-based task. In particular, Barney was programmed to congratulate the child whenever she produced a right answer and also to react to the content on screen with appropriate emotions, e.g. cheering at good news and expressing concern at bad news. More recently, interactive dolls, such as those produced by Playmates Toys, have been designed to talk, sense, and understand the world around them, using sensor-based technologies, speech recognition, and various mechanical protractors embedded in their bodies. For example, Amazing Amanda can exhibit a number of facial expressions to convey her feelings. If she is offered something to eat she does not want, e.g. a piece of plastic pizza embedded with an RFID tag that when placed near her mouth is read by a tag reader hidden in her neck, she will contort her face and say "I don't want that" (Figure 5.12).

An underlying argument in favor of the anthropomorphic approach is that furnishing interactive systems with personalities and other human-like attributes makes them more

Figure 5.12 *Playmates Toys interactive doll called Amazing Amanda*

enjoyable and fun to interact with. It is also assumed that they can motivate people to carry out the tasks suggested, e.g. purchasing goods, more strongly than if they are presented in cold, abstract computer language. Being addressed in first person, e.g. "Hello Chris! Nice to see you again. Welcome back. Now what were we doing last time? Oh yes, exercise 5. Let's start again", is much more appealing than being addressed in the impersonal third person ("User 24, commence exercise 5"), especially for children. It can make them feel more at ease and reduce their anxiety. Similarly, interacting with screen characters like tutors and wizards can be much more pleasant than interacting with a cold dialog box or blinking cursor on a blank screen. Typing a question in plain English, using a search engine like Ask (which was based on the well-known fictitious butler Jeeves, who has now been retired), is more natural and personable than thinking up a set of keywords, as required by other search engines.

However, there have been many criticisms of the anthropomorphic approach. Shneiderman (1998), one of the best known critics, has written at length about the problems of attributing human qualities to computer systems. His central argument is that anthropomorphic interfaces, especially those that use first-person dialog and screen characters, are downright deceptive. An unpleasant side-effect is that they can make people feel anxious, resulting in them feeling inferior or stupid. A screen tutor that wags its finger at the user and says, "Now, Chris, that's not right! Try again. You can do better" is likely to feel more offensive than a system dialog box saying, "Incorrect. Try again."

Anthropomorphism can also lead people into a false sense of belief, enticing them to confide in agents called 'software bots' that reside in chatrooms and other electronic spaces, pretending to be conversant human beings. Furthermore, children are no longer required to use their imagination when acting out real-life scenarios, e.g. playing doctors and nurses, but can play with dolls that control the play, telling them their wants and dislikes. By far the most common complaint against computers pretending to have human qualities, however, is that people find them very annoying. Once users discover that a system cannot really converse like a human or does not possess real human qualities (like having a personality or being sincere), they become quickly disillusioned and subsequently distrust it. E-commerce sites that pretend to be caring by presenting an assortment of virtual assistants, receptionists, and other such helpers are seen for what they really are—artificial. Children and adults alike also are quickly bored and annoyed with applications that are fronted by artificial screen characters, e.g. tutor wizards, and simply ignore whatever they might suggest.

A number of studies have investigated people's reactions and responses to computers that have been designed to be more human-like. A body of work reported by Reeves and Nass (1996) has identified several benefits of the anthropomorphic approach. They found that computers that were designed to flatter and praise users when they did something right had a positive impact on how they felt about themselves. For example, an educational program was designed to say, "Your question makes an interesting and useful distinction. Great job!" after a user had contributed a new question to it. Students enjoyed the experience and were more willing to continue working with the computer than were other students who were not praised by the computer for doing the same things. In another study, Walker *et al.* (1994) compared people's responses to a talking-face display and an equivalent text-only one and found that people spent more time with the former than the latter. When given a questionnaire to fill in, the face-display group made fewer mistakes and wrote down more comments. In a follow-up study, Sproull *et al.* (1996) again found that users reacted quite differently to the two interfaces, with users presenting themselves in a more positive light to the talking-face display and generally interacting with it more.

Sproull *et al.*'s studies also revealed, however, that the talking-face display made some users feel disconcerted or displeased. The choice of a stern talking face may have been a large contributing factor. Perhaps a different kind of response would have been elicited if a friendlier smiling face had been used. Nevertheless, a number of other studies have shown that increasing the 'humanness' of an interface is counterproductive. People can be misled into believing that a computer is like a human, with human levels of intelligence. For example, one study investigating users' responses to interacting with agents at the interface represented as human guides found that the users expected the agents to be more human-like than they actually were. In particular, they expected the agents to have personality, emotion, and motivation—even though the guides were portrayed on the screen as simple black and white static icons. Furthermore, the users became disappointed when they discovered the agents did not have any of these characteristics (Oren *et al.*, 1990). In another study comparing an anthropomorphic interface that spoke in the first person and was highly personable ("Hi there, John! It's nice to meet you, I see you are ready now") with a mechanistic one that spoke in the third person ("Press the ENTER key to begin session"), the former was rated by college students as less honest and it made them feel less responsible for their actions (Quintanar *et al.*, 1982).

5.7 Interface agents, virtual pets, and interactive toys

As mentioned in the previous section, a new genre of cartoon and life-like characters has begun appearing on our computer screens—as agents to help us search the web, as e-commerce assistants that give us information about products, as characters in video games, as learning companions or instructors in educational programs, and many more. The best known are videogame stars such as Lara Croft and Super Mario and virtual pets such as Neopets. Other kinds include virtual popstars, virtual talk-show hosts, virtual bartenders, virtual shop assistants, and virtual newscasters (see Figure 5.13). Interactive toy pets, e.g. Aibo, and other artificial anthropomorphized characters, e.g. Pokemon, Creatures, that are intended to be cared for and played with by their owners have also proved highly popular.

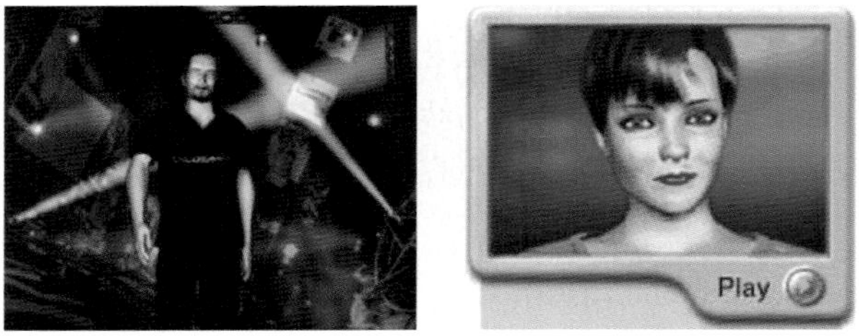

(a) (b)

Figure 5.13 *Examples of (a) an early virtual popstar E-cyas and (b) the first virtual newscaster, Ananova*

One of the earliest groups of agents to be designed that explored the relationship between emotion and behavior was the Woggles (Bates, 1994). The agents were designed to appear on the screen and play games with one another, such as hide and seek. They appeared as different colored bouncy balls with cute facial expressions (see Figure 5.14). Users could change their moods, e.g. from happy to sad, by moving various sliders, which in turn changed their movement, e.g. they bounced less,, facial expression, e.g. they no longer smiled, and how willing they were to play with the other Woggles.

Figure 5.14 *The Woggles*

Box 5.3
Beyond petting?

Bruce Blumberg and his group at MIT develop autonomous animated creatures that live in virtual 3D environments. The creatures are autonomous in that they decide what to do, based on what they can sense of the 3D world, and how they feel, based on their internal states. One of the earliest creatures to be developed was a pet called Silas T. Dog (Blumberg, 1996). The 3D dog looks like a cartoon creature but is designed to behave like a real dog (see Figure 5.15a). For example, he can walk, run, sit, wag his tail, bark, cock his leg, chase sticks, and rub his head on people when he is happy. He navigates through his world by using his 'nose' and synthetic vision. He also has been programmed with various internal goals and needs that he tries to satisfy, including wanting to play and have company. He responds to events in the environment; for example, he becomes aggressive if a hamster enters his patch.

A person can interact with Silas by making various gestures that are detected by a computer-vision system. For example, the person can pretend to throw a stick, which is recognized as an action that Silas responds to. An image of the person is also projected onto a large screen so that he can be seen in relation to Silas (see Figure 5.15b). Depending on his mood, Silas will run after the stick and return it, e.g. when he is happy and playful, or cower and refuse to fetch it, e.g. when he is hungry or sad. Who needs a real pet dog anymore?

Another MIT researcher, Stefan Marti, has developed a physically embodied pet, such as a cuddly squirrel or rabbit cell phone (see Figure 5.16). It is programmed to manage a person's phone calls by answering calls, taking messages, and alerting the owner when it decides it is important enough for him or her to pick up the phone.

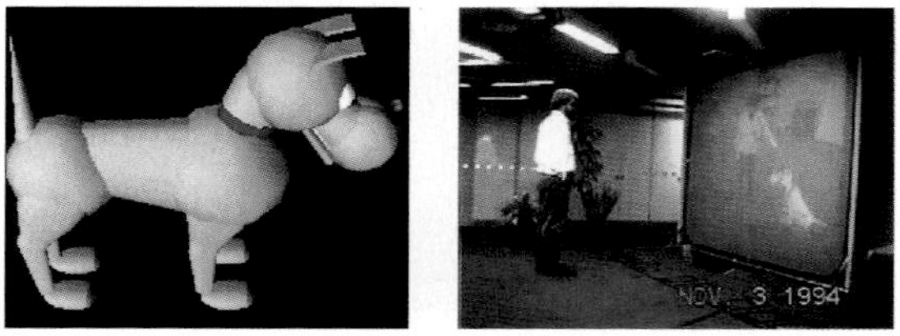

(a) (b)

Figure 5.15 *(a) Silas the virtual dog and (b) with human owner*

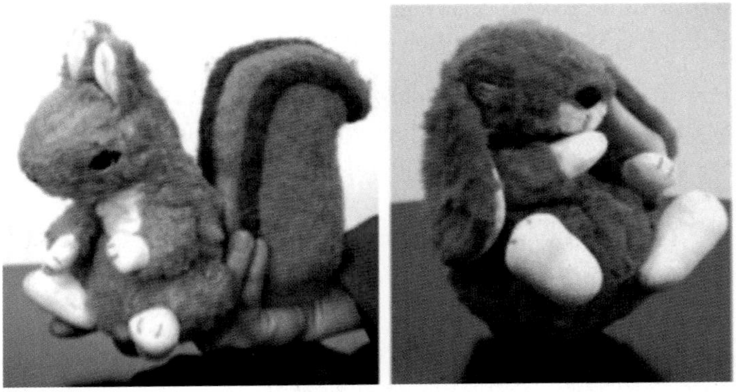

Figure 5.16 Cellular squirrel alert and cellular rabbit sleeping

When it determines that the call is important enough for its owner to answer it waves its arms around and moves its body with a soft shuffling sound—the effect is intended to be more pleasant and less intrusive than that of the harsh ringing tone emitted by a cell or landline phone.

The pet decides whether to alert its owner by listening to the conversation around it, and trying to pick up key subject words that are relevant to what the caller wants to talk about. The number of the caller and the tone of the caller's voice are also evaluated. When the pet starts to move the owner can squeeze one of its upper paws to accept the call that accesses a Bluetooth speakerphone function, or can squeeze a lower paw to send the call to voicemail.

An underlying assumption is that having a cuddly pet screen and signal calls will be less disruptive to ongoing meetings. A study comparing people's responses to being interrupted by the squirrel versus a regular landline ringing, showed that they rated the squirrel as being more friendly, fun, and humorous (Marti and Schmandt, 2005). Most of all they found it cute. ■

Much effort has gone into designing interface agents to be life-like, exhibiting realistic human movements, like walking and running, and having distinct personalities and traits. The design of the characters' appearance, their facial expressions, and how their lips move when talking are all considered important interface design concerns. This has included modeling various conversational mechanisms such as:

- Recognizing and responding to verbal and non-verbal input.
- Generating verbal and non-verbal output.

- Coping with breakdowns, turn-taking, and other conversational mechanisms.
- Giving signals that indicate the state of the conversation as well as contributing new suggestions for the dialog (Cassell, 2000, p. 72).

An example is Rea, who was developed as an embodied real-estate agent with a human-like body that she uses in human-like ways during a conversation (Cassell, 2000). In particular, she uses eye gaze, body posture, hand gestures, and facial expressions while talking (see Figure 5.17). Although the dialog appears relatively simple, it involves a sophisticated underlying set of conversational mechanisms and gesture-recognition techniques. An example of a conversation with Rea is:

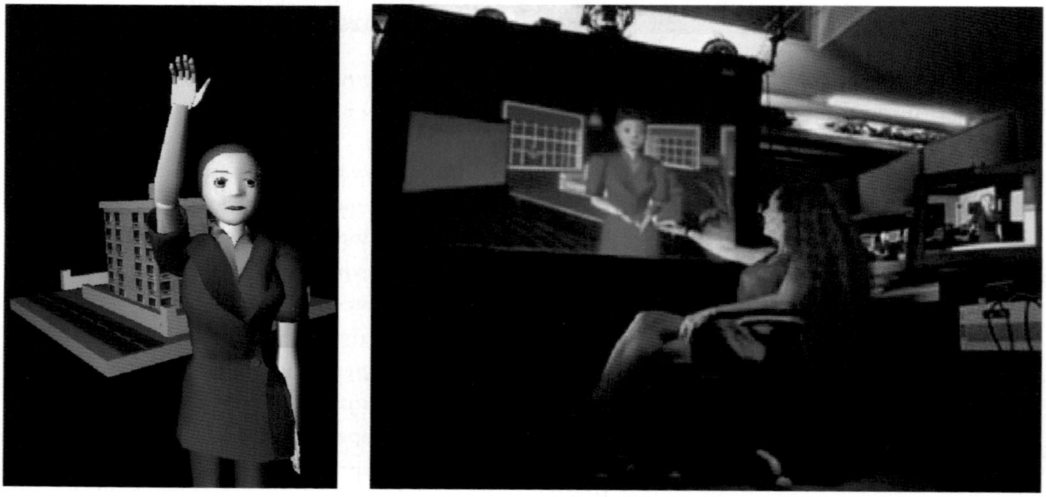

(a) (b)

***Figure 5.17** (a) Rea the life-like realtor and (b) having a conversation with a human*

Mike approaches the screen and Rea turns to face him and says:

"Hello. How can I help you?"

Mike: "I'm looking to buy a place near MIT."

Rea nods, indicating she is following.

Rea: "I have a house to show you" (picture of a house appears on the screen).

"It is in Somerville."

Mike: "Tell me about it."

Rea looks up and away while she plans what to say.

Rea: "It's big."

Rea makes an expansive gesture with her hands.

Mike brings his hands up as if to speak, so Rea does not continue, waiting for him to speak.

Mike: "Tell me more about it."

Rea: "Sure thing. It has a nice garden . . . "

As you can see, the gestures and responses from Rea are human-like although her comments and suggestions are rather simple for an agent trying to sell a house to a customer.

5.8 Models of affective aspects

In Chapters 3 and 4 we described how theories of cognition and communication have been applied to interaction design. Theories of emotion and pleasure are also beginning to appear in interaction design to explain people's responses to and uses of interactive products. Most prominent is Don Norman's (2004), who has shifted his attention from the psychology of design to considering more centrally what he calls 'emotional design.' He argues that our emotional attachment and involvement with products is as important as how easy we find them to use. If we find the look and feel of a product pleasing, we are likely to have a more positive experience.

(i) Emotional design model

Norman and his colleagues, Andrew Ortony and William Revelle (2004), have proposed a model of emotion that explains how emotion and behavior are determined by different levels of the brain. At the lowest level are parts of the brain that are pre-wired to automatically respond to events happening in the physical world. This is called the visceral level. At the next level are the brain processes that control our everyday behavior. This is called the behavioral level. At the highest level are brain processes that contemplate. This is called the reflective level (see Figure 5.18).

The visceral level responds rapidly, making judgments about what is good or bad, safe or dangerous, pleasurable or abhorrent. It also triggers the emotional responses to stimuli, e.g. fear, joy, anger, and sadness that are expressed through a combination of physiological and behavioral responses. For example, on seeing a very large hairy spider running across the floor of the bathroom most people will experience fear, causing them to scream and run away. The behavioral level is the site where most human activities occur; examples include well-learned routine operations such as talking, typing, and driving. The reflective level entails conscious thought where we generalize across events or step back from the routine and the immediate. An example is switching between thinking about the narrative structure and special effects used in a Harry Potter movie and becoming scared at the visceral level when watching the movie.

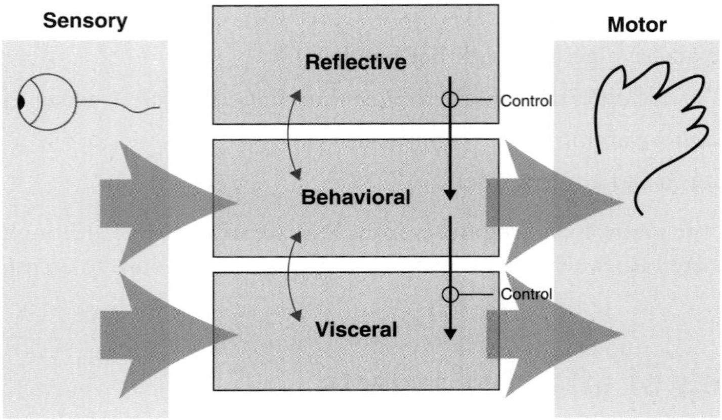

Figure 5.18 *Norman's (2004) model of emotional design showing three levels: visceral, behavioral, and reflective. The arrows refer to how the different levels are affected by each other*

The model makes a number of claims about how we respond to stressful and pleasurable situations. A central claim is that our affective state, be it positive or negative, changes how we think. When we are frightened or angry, the emotional response is to focus on the problem at hand and try to overcome or resolve the perceived danger. Our bodies will respond by tensing our muscles and sweating. In contrast, when we are very happy, such as watching our team win the last game of the championship, the emotional response is to laugh, cheer, and jump about. The body relaxes. When in such a positive state of mind we are assumed to be far less focused, which can even enable us to be more creative.

The model explains how the human brain and the body switch gear to respond appropriately to different events. But how can it be used in interaction design? Can products be designed to make people happy and, in so doing, be more creative? Should this be a high-level goal? According to Norman (2004), when people are happy they are more likely to overlook and cope with minor problems they are experiencing with a device. In contrast, when someone is anxious or angry they are more likely to be less tolerant. So does this mean that designers should be creating products that adapt according to people's different emotional states? When people are feeling angry should an interface be more attentive and informative than when they are happy?

Such an adaptive approach is unrealistic, since people's moods change all the time and it would be difficult to keep abreast of them, let alone know what kind of interface to present to complement them. Instead, Norman takes a more conventional approach to applying the model, suggesting that designers focus on the context and tasks a product is being used for. But Norman's explanation of how this could play out in practice has its problems. On the one hand, he argues that if the product is intended to be used during leisure time and is meant to be fun and enjoyable to use then designers "can get away with more" and not be too worried about how the information appears at the interface. On the other hand, he says that for serious tasks, such as monitoring a process control plant or driving a car, designers need to pay special attention to all the information required to do the task at hand and that the interface should be visible with clear and unambiguous feedback. The bottom line is "things intended to be used under stressful situations require a lot more care, with much more attention to detail."

Activity 5.5

Do you agree with Norman's position about the different amounts of attention that need to be paid to serious versus pleasurable tasks?

Comment

While it is of utmost importance that the technologies used by operators in dangerous and highly stressful situations, such as on a battlefield or in a burning building, are effective, efficient, and informative, why would it not be the case, equally, for other situations? Would people not want to have clear and unambiguous feedback, too, for pleasurable tasks carried out in convivial environments, such as controlling a home entertainment system—especially if they had paid thousands of dollars for it? People can become very frustrated and angry with a TV system that does not give them clear information about when and on which channel a program is supposed to be.

A less controversial application of the model is to think about how to design products in terms of the three levels. Visceral design refers to making products look, feel, and sound good. The designer can use a number of aesthetic techniques such as clean lines, balance, color, shape, and texture. The iPod, featured in Chapter 1, exemplifies this approach. Behavioral design is about use and equates with the traditional values of usability. Reflective design is about taking into account the meaning and personal value of a product in a particular culture. For example, the design of a Swatch watch focuses on reflective aspects, where the aesthetics, the use of cultural images and graphical elements are central. Brilliant colors, wild designs, and art are very much part of the Swatch trademark and are what draw people to buy and wear their watches.

(ii) Pleasure model

Patrick Jordan (2000) has proposed an alternative affective model that focuses more on the pleasurable aspects of our interactions with products. It considers all of the potential benefits that a product can deliver. Based on Lionel Tiger's (1992) framework of pleasure, it proposes four conceptually distinct types of pleasure. These are:

(i) physio-pleasure
(ii) socio-pleasure
(iii) psycho-pleasure
(iv) ideo-pleasure (cognitive).

Physio-pleasure refers to bodily pleasures connected to sensory experiences, e.g. touch, taste, and smell. An example is the tactile pleasure of holding a sleek cell phone while making a call. Socio-pleasure refers to the enjoyment of being in the company of others, such as loved ones, friends, and colleagues. An example is the socio-pleasure of showing photos to one another, via the LCD display on a digital camera, that someone has just taken at a friend's birthday party. Psycho-pleasure refers to people's emotional and cognitive reactions to a product. These are similar to the ones Norman talks about at the behavioral level. An example is the emotionally satisfying experience of shopping on the web using an online site that is both pleasing and easy to use. Ideo-pleasure refers to people's values and is akin to the reflective level of Norman's model. It entails the aesthetics of a product and the cultural and personal values a person attributes to it. For example, a person who buys a hybrid car that runs on a combination of electricity and gas may derive more ideo-pleasure using it because it is saving energy and is cheaper to run.

The pleasure model does not attempt to explain how pleasures happen at a biological or behavioral level, but is intended as a means of framing a designer's thinking about pleasure, highlighting that there are different kinds. It does not prescribe that a product be designed to cover the complete set of pleasures (although this is possible and may be desirable), but that certain ones may be more important to consider for a product. For example, it may be very beneficial to take all of them into account when designing a cell phone for teenagers, but only the psycho and socio aspects when designing a landline phone for use by operators at call centers. What is important is that the benefits of considering a pleasure type or set of types are identified by the design team in the first place.

(iii) Technology as experience framework

McCarthy and Wright (2004) have developed an account of the user experience largely in terms of how it is 'felt' by the user. They recognize that defining experience is incredibly difficult because it is so nebulous and ever-present to us, just as swimming in water is to a fish. Nevertheless, they have tried to capture the essence of human experience by describing it in both holistic and metaphorical terms. These comprise a balance of sensual, cerebral, and emotional 'threads.' Their framework draws heavily from the philosophical writings of Dewey and Pragmatism, which focus on the sense-making aspects of human experience. As Dewey points out: "Emotion is the moving and cementing force. It selects what is congruous and dyes what is selected with its color, thereby giving qualitative unity to materials externally disparate and dissimilar. It thus provides unity in and through the varied parts of experience."

McCarthy and Wright propose four core threads that make up our holistic experiences: compositional, sensual, emotional, and spatio-temporal.

The sensual thread. This is concerned with our sensory engagement with a situation and is similar to the visceral level of Norman's model. It can be equated with the level of absorption people have with various technological devices and applications, most notable being computer games, cell phones, and chatrooms, where users can be highly absorbed in their interactions at a sensory level. These can involve thrill, fear, pain, and comfort.

The emotional thread. Common examples of emotions that spring to mind are sorrow, anger, joy, and happiness. In addition, the framework points out how emotions are intertwined with the situation in which they arise, e.g. a person becomes angry *with* a computer because it does not work properly. Emotions also involve making judgments of value. For example, when purchasing a new cell phone, people may be drawn to the ones that are most cool-looking but be in an emotional turmoil because they are the most expensive. They can't really afford them but they really would like one of them.

The compositional thread. This is concerned with the narrative part of an experience, as it unfolds, and the way a person makes sense of them. For example, when shopping online, the choices laid out to people can lead them in a coherent way to making a desired purchase or they can lead to frustrating experiences resulting in no purchase being made. When in this situation, people ask themselves questions such as "What is this about? Where am I? What has happened? What is going to happen next? What would happen if...?" The compositional thread is the internal thinking we do during our experiences.

The spatio-temporal thread. This refers to the space and time in which our experiences take place and their effect upon those experiences. There are many ways of thinking about space and time and their relationship with one another, for example, we talk of time speeding up, standing still, and slowing down, while we talk of space in terms of public and personal places, and needing one's own space.

So how do you use these concepts to think about designing for affect? The threads are meant as ideas to help designers think and talk more clearly and concretely about the relationship between technology and experience. By describing an experience in terms of the interconnected aspects of experience, the framework can aid thinking about the whole experience of a technology rather than as fragmented aspects, e.g. its usability, its marketability, or utility. For example, when buying clothes online, the framework can be used to capture the whole gamut of experiences, including: the fear or joy of needing to buy a new outfit; the time and place where it can be purchased, e.g. online stores or shopping mall; the tensions of how to engage with the vendor, e.g. the pushy sales assistant or an anonymous website; the value judgment involved in contemplating the cost and how much one is prepared to spend; the internal monologue that goes on where questions are asked such as will it look good on me, what size should I buy, do I have shoes to match, do I need to try it on, how easy will it be to wash, will I need to iron it each time, and how often will I be able to wear it. All of these aspects can be described in terms of the four threads and in so doing highlight which aspects are more important for a given product. For example, if you were to do this exercise for buying a new TV entertainment system versus buying a new MP3 player you might find you would get quite different descriptions, leading ultimately to thinking about their design differently.

CASE STUDY 5.1
Using the 'Technology as Experience' framework

To show how the framework can be used to think about and inform design, two case studies are presented on our website. Both used it to guide their initial ideas for the design of two different websites: (i) an online fundraising site and (ii) a site that reviews men's clothing, intended to appeal to men who do not enjoy shopping.

The first was written by Heather Collins when she was a graduate student. She used primarily the sensory and compositional threads of the framework, leading to insights on how fundraising organizations can maximize their website to tell a compelling story to a potential donor that is balanced in content and emotion. Her design combines elements of storytelling, appropriate emotional triggers, and a welcoming atmosphere to encourage potential donors to act by making a donation, volunteering their time, telling their friends, or attending a related event. Through this process, the donor can create a meaningful connection to a cause or problem directly impacting their community. The personal connection makes the online donation experience pleasurable for the user.

The second was written by Aaron Loehrlein when he was a graduate student. He used all the threads to think about designing a website for a pleasurable experience for clothes shopping among men who ordinarily hate clothes shopping. Because the website is a consumer guide for men's clothes, and not a retail site, it encourages a more relaxed emotional interaction with its users. The website does not present clothes as part of a larger fashion trend, but describes how the clothes are likely to fit into the life of the wearer. The descriptions are meant to provide an entertaining, non-challenging experience by using simple, jargon-free language, familiar metaphors, and sarcastic humor that is never aimed at the wearer. He found the emotional and sensual threads to be particularly useful to design for this.

Assignment

This assignment requires you to write a critique of the persuasive impact of a virtual agent by considering what it would take for a virtual agent to be believable, trustworthy, and convincing.

(a) Look at a website that has a virtual assistant, e.g. Anna at `Ikea.com` or one of the case studies featured by the Digital Animations Group (DAG) at `http://www.dagroupplc.com`, who specialize in developing a variety of online agents) and answer the following:

- What does the virtual agent do?
- What type of agent is it?
- Does it elicit an emotional response from you? If so, what kind?
- What kind of personality does it have?
- How is this expressed?
- What kinds of behavior does it exhibit?
- What are its facial expressions like?
- What is its appearance like? Is it realistic or cartoon-like?
- Where does it appear on the screen?
- How does it communicate with the user (text or speech)?
- Is the level of discourse patronizing or at the right level?
- Is the agent helpful in guiding the user towards making a purchase or finding out something?
- Is it too pushy?
- What gender is it? Do you think this makes a difference?
- Would you trust the agent to the extent that you would be happy to buy a product from it or follow its guidance? If not, why not?
- What else would it take to make the agent persuasive?

(b) Next, look at an equivalent website that does not include an agent but is based on a conceptual model of browsing, e.g. `Amazon.com`. How does it compare with the agent-based site you have just looked at?

- Is it easy to find information?
- What kind of mechanism does the site use to make recommendations and guide the user in making a purchase or finding out information?
- Is any kind of personalization used at the interface to make the user feel welcome or special?
- Would the site be improved by having an agent? Explain your reasons either way.

(c) Finally, discuss which site you would trust most and give your reasons for this.

Summary

This chapter has described the different ways interactive products can be designed (both deliberately and inadvertently) to make people respond in certain ways. The extent to which users will learn, buy a product online, quit a bad habit, or chat with others depends on how convincing the interface is, how comfortable he or she feels when using a product, or how well he or she can trust it. If the interactive product is frustrating to use, annoying, or patronizing, users will easily become angry and despondent, and often stop using it. If, on the other hand, the product is pleasurable, enjoyable to use, and makes people feel comfortable and at ease, then they will continue to use it, make a purchase, return to the website, or continue to learn. This chapter has described various interaction mechanisms that can be used to elicit positive emotional responses in users and ways of avoiding negative ones.

Key Points

- Affective aspects of interaction design are concerned with the way interactive systems engender emotional responses.
- Well-designed interfaces can elicit good feelings in people.
- Aesthetically pleasing interfaces can be a pleasure to use.
- Expressive interfaces can provide reassuring feedback to users as well as be informative and fun.
- Badly designed interfaces often make people frustrated and angry.
- Technologies can be designed to persuade people to change their behaviors or attitudes.
- Anthropomorphism is the attribution of human qualities to objects.
- An increasingly popular form of anthropomorphism is to create agents and other virtual characters as part of an interface.
- Models of affect provide a way of conceptualizing emotional and pleasurable aspects of interaction design.

Further Reading

JORDAN, P.W. (2000) *Designing Pleasurable Products*. Taylor & Francis. This book was written primarily for a product design audience to consider as part of the human factors. However, its applicability to interaction design has meant that it has become a popular book for those wanting to understand more about the relationship between usability and pleasure. It provides many illuminating case studies of the design of products, such as cars, cameras, and clocks. It also provides detailed 'product benefits specifications' that are a form of guidance on how to design and evaluate pleasurable aspects.

FOGG, B.J. (2003) *Persuasive Technology: Using Computers to Change What we Think and Do*. Morgan Kaufmann. This is a very readable and provocative book, explaining how a diversity of technologies can and have been designed to persuade people to change their behavior and attitudes. It presents a conceptual framework of the different types, a host of examples, together with discussing social, ethical, and credibility issues to do with using persuasive technologies.

NORMAN, D. (2004) *Emotional Design: Why we Love (or Hate) Everyday Things*. Basic Books. This book is an easy read while at the same time being thought-provoking. We get to see inside his kitchen and learn about the design aesthetics of his collection of teapots. The book also includes essays on the emotional aspects of robots, computer games, and a host of other pleasurable interfaces.

TURKLE, S. (1995) *Life on the Screen*. Simon and Schuster. This classic covers a range of social impact and affective aspects of how users interact with a variety of computer-based applications. Sherry Turkle discusses at length how computers, the Internet, software, and the design of interfaces affect our identities.

Two early papers on interface agents can be found in Brenda Laurel (ed.) (1990) *The Art of Human–Computer Interface Design*. Addison Wesley:

LAUREL, B. (1990) Interface agents: metaphor with character, pp. 355–366.

OREN, T., SALOMON, G., KREITMAN, K. and **DON, A.** (1990) Guides: characterizing the interface, pp. 367–381.

Excerpts from a lively debate between Pattie Maes and Ben Shneiderman on 'direct manipulation vs. interface agents' can be found in *ACM Interactions Magazine* **4**(6) (1997) 42–61.

6

6.1 Introduction

Until the mid-1990s, interaction designers concerned themselves largely with developing efficient and effective user interfaces for desktop computers aimed at the single user. This involved working out how best to present information on a screen such that users would be able to perform their tasks, including determining how to structure menus to make options easy to navigate, designing icons and other graphical elements to be easily recognized and distinguished from one another, and developing logical dialog boxes that are easy to fill in. Advances in graphical interfaces, speech and handwriting recognition, together with the arrival of the Internet, cell phones, wireless networks, sensor technologies, and an assortment of other new technologies providing large and small displays, have changed the face of human–computer interaction. During the last decade designers have had many more opportunities for designing user experiences. The slew of technological developments has encouraged different ways of thinking about interaction design and an expansion of research in the field. For example, innovative ways of controlling and interacting with digital information have been developed that include gesture-based, tactile-based, and emotion-based interaction. Researchers and developers have also begun combining the physical and digital worlds, resulting in novel interfaces, including 'mixed realities,' 'augmented realities,' 'tangible interfaces,' and 'wearable computing.' A major thrust has been to design new interfaces that extend beyond the individual user: supporting small- and large-scale social interactions for people on the move, at home, and at work.

While making for exciting times, having so many degrees of freedom available within which to design can be daunting. The goal of this chapter is to consider how to design interfaces for different environments, people, places, and activities. To begin with, we give an overview of paradigmatic developments in interaction design. We then present an overview of the major interface developments, ranging from WIMPs (windows, icons, menus, pointer) to wearables. For each one, we outline the important challenges and issues confronting designers, together with illustrative research findings and products.

It is not possible to describe all the different types of interface in one book, let alone one chapter, and so we have necessarily been selective in what we have included. There are many excellent practitioner-oriented handbooks available that cover in more detail design concerns for a particular kind of interface or technology/application (see end of the chapter for examples). These include web, multimedia, and more recently handheld/mobile technology design. Here, we provide an overview of some of the key research and design concerns for a selection of interfaces, some of which are only briefly touched upon while others, that are more established in interaction design, are described in depth. Nevertheless, the chapter is much longer than the others in the book and can be read in sections or simply dipped into to find out about a particular type of interface.

6

Interfaces and interactions

The main aims of this chapter are:

- To introduce the notion of a paradigm and set the scene for how the various interfaces have developed in interaction design.
- To overview the many different kinds of interfaces.
- To highlight the main design and research issues for each of the different interfaces.
- To consider which interface is best for a given application or activity.

6.2 Paradigms

Within interaction design, a paradigm refers to a particular approach that has been adopted by the community of researchers and designers for carrying out their work, in terms of shared assumptions, concepts, values, and practices. This follows from the way the term has been used in science to refer to a set of practices that a community has agreed upon, including:

- The questions to be asked and how they should be framed.
- The phenomena to be observed.
- The way findings from experiments are to be analyzed and interpreted (Kuhn, 1962).

In the 1980s, the prevailing paradigm in human–computer interaction was how to design user-centered applications for the desktop computer. Questions about what and how to design were framed in terms of specifying the requirements for a single 'user' interacting with a screen-based 'interface.' Task analytic and usability methods were developed based on an individual user's cognitive capabilities. The acronym WIMP was used as one way of characterizing the core features of an interface for a single user: this stood for Windows, Icons, Menus, and Pointer. This was later superseded by the GUI (graphical user interface), a term that has stuck with us ever since.

Within interaction design, many changes took place in the mid- to late 1990s. The WIMP interface with its single thread, discrete event dialog was considered to be unnecessarily limiting, e.g. Jacob, 1996. Instead, many argued that new frameworks, tools, and applications were needed to enable more flexible forms of interaction to take place, having a higher degree of interactivity and parallel input/output exchanges. At the same time, other kinds of non-WIMP interfaces were experimented with. The shift in thinking, together with technological advances, led to a new generation of user–computer environments, including virtual reality, multimedia, agent interfaces, pen-based interfaces, eye-movement-based interfaces, tangible interfaces, collaborative interfaces, and ubiquitous computing. The effect of moving interaction design 'beyond the desktop' resulted in many new challenges, questions, and phenomena being considered. New methods of designing, modeling, and analyzing came to the fore. At the same time, new theories, concepts, and ideas entered the stage. A turn to the 'social,' the 'emotional,' and the 'environmental' began shaping what was studied, how it was studied, and ultimately what was designed. Significantly, one of the main frames of reference—the single user—was replaced by a set of others, including people, places, and context.

One of the most influential developments that took place was the birth of ubiquitous computing (Weiser, 1991). A main idea was that the advent of ubiquitous computing (or 'UbiComp' as it is commonly known) would radically change the way people think about and interact with computers. In particular, computers would be designed to be part of the environment, embedded in a variety of everyday objects, devices, and displays (see Figure 6.1). The idea behind Weiser's vision was that a ubiquitous computing device would enter a person's center of attention when needed and move to the periphery of their

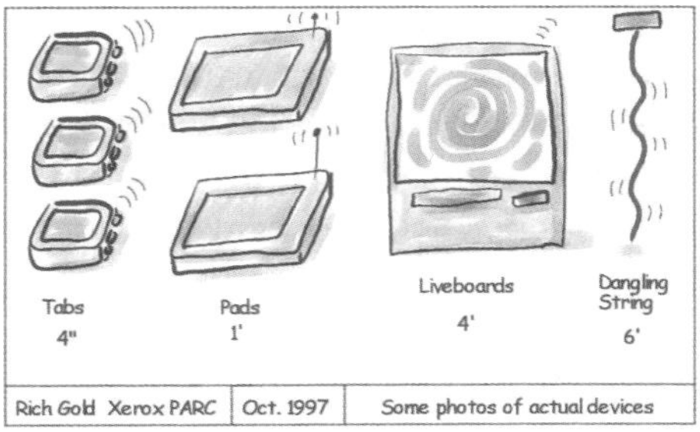

Figure 6.1 *Examples of sketches for the new ubiquitous computing paradigm*

attention when not, enabling the person to switch calmly and effortlessly between activities without having to figure out how to use a computer in performing their tasks. In essence, the technology would be unobtrusive and largely disappear into the background. People would be able to get on with their everyday and working lives, interacting with information and communicating and collaborating with others without being distracted or becoming frustrated with technology.

The grand vision of ubiquitous computing has led to many new challenges, themes, and questions being articulated in interaction design and computer science. These include:

- How to enable people to access and interact with information in their work, social, and everyday lives, using an assortment of technologies.
- How to design user experiences for people using interfaces that are part of the environment but where there are no obvious controlling devices.
- How and in what form to provide contextually-relevant information to people at appropriate times and places to support them while on the move.
- How to ensure that information that is passed around via interconnected displays, devices, and objects, is secure and trustworthy.

The shift in thinking about ubiquitous computing has resulted in many new research and design activities and an extended vocabulary. Other terms, including pervasive computing, the disappearing computer, and ambient intelligence, have evolved that have different emphases and foci (we view them here as overlapping). In the next section, we describe the many new (and old) forms of interfaces that have been developed.

6.3 Interface types

There are many kinds of interface that can be used to design for user experiences. A plethora of adjectives have been used to describe these, including graphical, command, speech, multimodal, invisible, ambient, mobile, intelligent, adaptive, and tangible. Some of the interface types are primarily concerned with a function (e.g. to be intelligent, to be adaptive, to be ambient), while others focus on the interaction style used (e.g. command, graphical, multimedia), the input/output device used (e.g. pen-based, speech-based), or the platform being designed for (e.g. PC, microwave). Here, we describe a selection of established and novel interfaces, outlining their benefits, and main design and research issues. We also include descriptions of illustrative products or prototypes that have been developed for each. The interface types are broken down into three decades loosely ordered in terms of when they were developed (see Table 6.1). It should be noted that this classification is not strictly accurate since some interface types emerged across the decades. The purpose of breaking them down into three sections is to make it easier to read about the many types.

1980s interfaces
- **Command**
- **WIMP/GUI**

1990s interfaces
- **Advanced graphical (multimedia, virtual reality, information visualization)**
- **Web**
- **Speech (voice)**
- **Pen, gesture, and touch**
- **Appliance**

2000s interfaces
- **Mobile**
- **Multimodal**
- **Shareable**
- **Tangible**
- **Augmented and mixed reality**
- **Wearable**
- **Robotic**

Table 6.1 *The selection of interfaces, grouped into three decades, covered in this chapter that have evolved during the last 30 years*

6.3.1 1980s interfaces

In this section we cover command and WIMP/GUI interfaces.

Command interfaces

Command line driven interfaces require the user to type in commands that are typically abbreviations, e.g. ls, at the prompt symbol appearing on the computer display to which the system responds, e.g. by listing current files using a keyboard. Another way of issuing commands is through pressing certain combinations of keys, e.g. Shift+ Alt+ Ctrl. Some commands are also a fixed part of the keyboard, for example, 'delete,' 'enter,' and 'undo,' while other function keys can be programmed by the user as specific commands, e.g. F11 standing for 'print'.

Activity 6.1

If you have not previously had any experience of a command-based interface, ask someone to set up a session for you on a UNIX terminal. Try using the UNIX commands SORT and ctrl D (to stop).

First type at the prompt `sort`

Then type in some names of animals, e.g.

```
Tiger
Elephant
Antelope
Snake
```

Then use the end of input command `^D (Ctrl D)`

What happens on the screen? Do the same for a list of random numbers and see what happens.

Comment

The command SORT alphabetically or numerically sorts the typed input from the keyboard and will display your typed-in list of animals in alphabetical order and your list of numbers in numerical order. The same is true for a list of numbers. It is a very quick and efficient way of sorting and does not require selecting and specifying what to sort in a dialog box (as is required in GUI interfaces).

Advantages of command line based interfaces are their efficiency, precision, and speed. Users can issue a large number of commands that require one-step actions. Histories of interactions can be readily viewed at the prompt, allowing the user to see a trace of their interactions. However, efficiency and speed come at a cost. As you yourself may have experienced, there is a huge overhead in having to learn and remember all the key combinations or abbreviations or names used in a command line based system. While some people are able to remember the meaning of a large number of command names/keys and able to recall them when needed, many users find it difficult. This is especially so for infrequently used commands, where the user has to look them up in a manual or table. This can be time-consuming and break the flow of the interaction. Furthermore, selecting the wrong function key or combination of keys can occur when commands have been designed arbitrarily, e.g. F10 for save, or follow inconsistent rules, e.g. using Ctrl plus first letter of an operation for some commands and not others, such as Ctrl+F keys for Find, and Ctrl+V for Paste.

Box 6.1
Expert use of commands in AutoCAD

AutoCAD LT is a Windows version of a popular drafting package used by a variety of professionals in the building and engineering trade. It is designed to be used by expert draughtsmen/women and offers a sophisticated interface that combines a number of styles. It is a good example of using the different interaction styles for the most appropriate actions. Figure 6.2 illustrates the application's interface. The user has the option of issuing commands using the menus at the top of the screen, the toolbar just below the menus, or by entering the commands directly in the window offered at the bottom (note that this window can be resized, and most expert users keep this portion of the screen to only 3 or 4 lines at most). In addition, entry of point locations on the drawing can be done using a pointing device or by entering coordinates at the command line. The keyboard function keys offer shortcuts for other commands, and there is a set of buttons at the bottom of the screen offering further commands.

The command line portion of the screen has several purposes. First, commands issued using the toolbar, menus, function keys, or pointing device are echoed in the command line window. Second, the user is prompted regarding the appropriate options or other entries needed to complete a command. Third, the command line can be used to enter commands, point locations, or dimensions directly from the keyboard. Fourth, error messages are displayed here.

The two screens shown in Figure 6.2 illustrate some of the steps used to draw the two red squares in the top left of the drawing in Figure 6.2(b) (this was part of the action necessary to add some filing cabinets to the office layout shown). The first screen illustrates some of the commands issued in order to set up a coordinate system in the correct location on the drawing. This is reflected in the first 9 lines of the command line portion of the screen. Note the different responses recorded in the dialog window. The option 'o' was chosen using another menu command, the default for the new origin point was accepted by hitting 'return' at the keyboard. The user then attempted to turn the grid on by pressing the GRID button at the bottom of the screen, but this resulted in the error message "Grid too dense to display." The command 'ucsicon' was typed via the keyboard. This command displays the coordinate origin on the drawing, and the user first turned this 'on' to check that it was in the right place, and then turned it 'off.' Both 'on' and 'off' were typed at the keyboard.

The second screen shows some of the dialog for drawing the two squares. The rectangle and offset commands this time were issued using the toolbar, and the coordinates were entered using the keyboard.

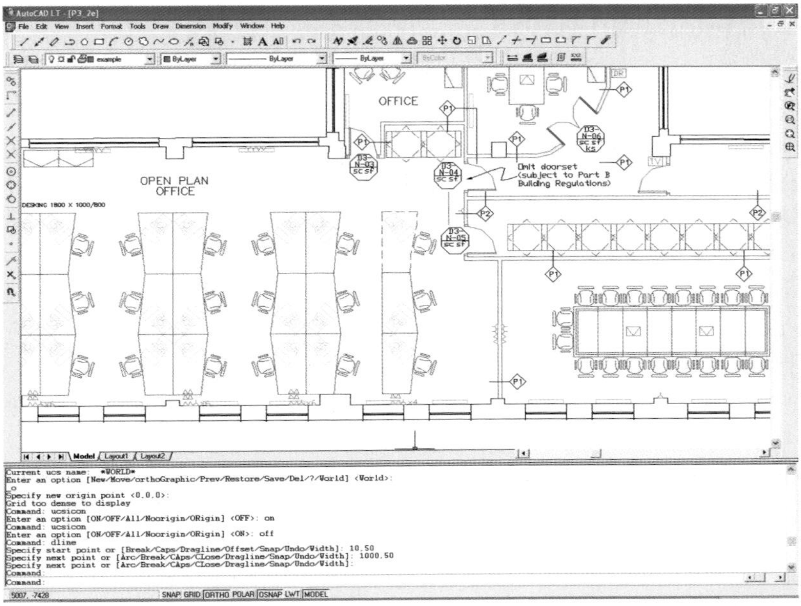

(a)

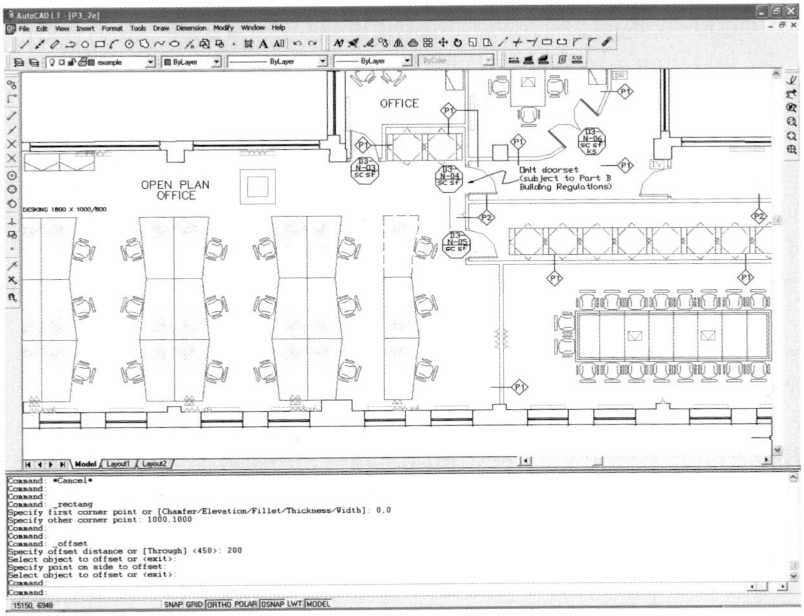

(b)

Figure 6.2 *(a) The first step in drawing the new cabinets is to set up the coordinate system in the correct location. (b) Screen dump showing some of the commands issued in order to draw the red squares at the top of the drawing*

Research and design issues

In the early 1980s, much research investigated ways of optimizing command-based interfaces. The form of the commands (e.g. use of abbreviations, full names, familiar names), syntax (e.g. how best to combine different commands), and organization (e.g. how to structure options) are examples of some of the main areas that have been investigated (Shneiderman, 1998). A further concern was which names to use as commands that would be the easiest to remember. A number of variables were tested, including how familiar users were with the chosen names. Findings from a number of studies, however, were inconclusive; some found specific names were better remembered than general ones (Barnard *et al.*, 1982), others showed names selected by users themselves were preferable (e.g. Ledgard *et al.*, 1981; Scapin, 1981), while yet others demonstrated that high-frequency words were better remembered than low-frequency ones (Gunther *et al.*, 1986).

The most relevant design principle is consistency (see Chapter 1). The method used for labeling/naming the commands should be chosen to be as consistent as possible, e.g. always use first letters of operation when using abbreviations.

Command-line interfaces have been largely superseded by graphical interfaces that incorporate commands as menus, icons, keyboard shortcuts, and pop-up/predictable text commands as part of an application. Where command line interfaces continue to have an advantage is when users find them easier and faster to use than equivalent menu-based systems (Raskin, 2000) and for performing certain operations as part of a complex software package, as we saw in BOX 6.2. They also provide scripting for batch operations and are being increasingly used on the Web, where the search bar acts as a general purpose command line facility, e.g. `www.yubnub.org`. Many programmers prefer managing their files at the DOS/UNIX shell level of an operating system, while using command line text editors, like *vi*, when coding and debugging.

WIMP/GUI interfaces

The Xerox Star interface (described in Chapter 2) led to the birth of the WIMP and subsequently the GUI, opening up new possibilities for users to interact with a system and for information to be presented and represented at the interface. Specifically, new ways of visually designing the interface became possible, that included the use of color, typography, and imagery (Mullet and Sano, 1995). The original WIMP comprises:

- Windows (that could be scrolled, stretched, overlapped, opened, closed, and moved around the screen using the mouse).

- Icons (that represented applications, objects, commands, and tools that were opened or activated when clicked on).
- Menus (offering lists of options that could be scrolled through and selected in the way a menu is used in a restaurant).
- Pointing device (a mouse controlling the cursor as a point of entry to the windows, menus, and icons on the screen).

The first generation of WIMP interfaces was primarily boxy in design; user interaction took place through a combination of windows, scroll bars, checkboxes, panels, palettes, and dialog boxes that appeared on the screen in various forms (see Figure 6.3). Application programmers were largely constrained by the set of widgets available to them, of which the dialog box was most prominent. (A widget is a standardized display representation of a control, like a button or scroll bar, that can be manipulated by the user.)

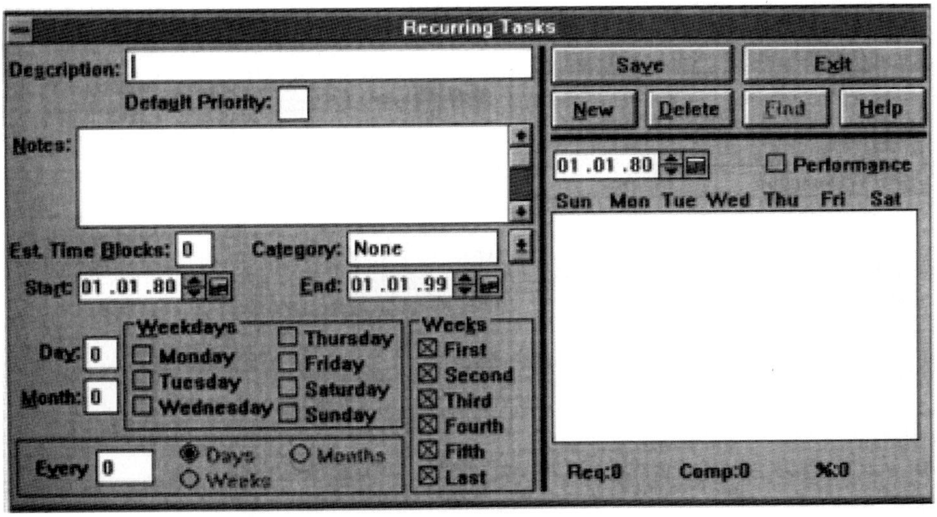

Figure 6.3 The boxy look of the first generation of GUIs. The window presents several checkboxes, notes boxes, and options as square buttons

The basic building blocks of the WIMP are still part of the modern GUI, but have evolved into a number of different forms and types. For example, there are now many different types of icons and menus, including audio icons and audio menus, 3D animated icons, and 2D icon-based menus. Windows have also greatly expanded in terms of how they are used and what they are used for; for example, a variety of dialog boxes, interactive forms, and feedback/error message boxes have become pervasive. In addition, a number of graphical elements that were not part of the WIMP interface have been incorporated into the GUI. These include toolbars and docks (a row or column of available applications and icons of other objects such as open files) and rollovers (where text labels appear next to an icon or part of the screen as the mouse is rolled over it). Here, we give an overview of the design issues concerning the basic building blocks of the WIMP/GUI: windows, menus, and icons.

Window design. Windows were invented to overcome the physical constraints of a computer display, enabling more information to be viewed and tasks to be performed at the same screen. Multiple windows can be opened at any one time, e.g. web pages and word documents, enabling the user to switch between them, when needing to look or work on different documents, files, and applications. Scrolling bars within windows also enable more information to be viewed than is possible on one screen. Scrollbars can be placed vertically and horizontally in windows to enable upwards, downwards, and sideways movements through a document.

One of the disadvantages of having multiple windows open is that it can be difficult to find specific ones. Various techniques have been developed to help users locate a particular window, a common one being to provide a list as part of an application menu. MacOS also provides a function that shrinks all windows that are open so they can be seen side by side on one screen (see Figure 6.4). The user needs only to press one function key and then move the cursor over each one to see what they are called. This technique enables the user to see at a glance what they have in their workspace and also enables them to easily

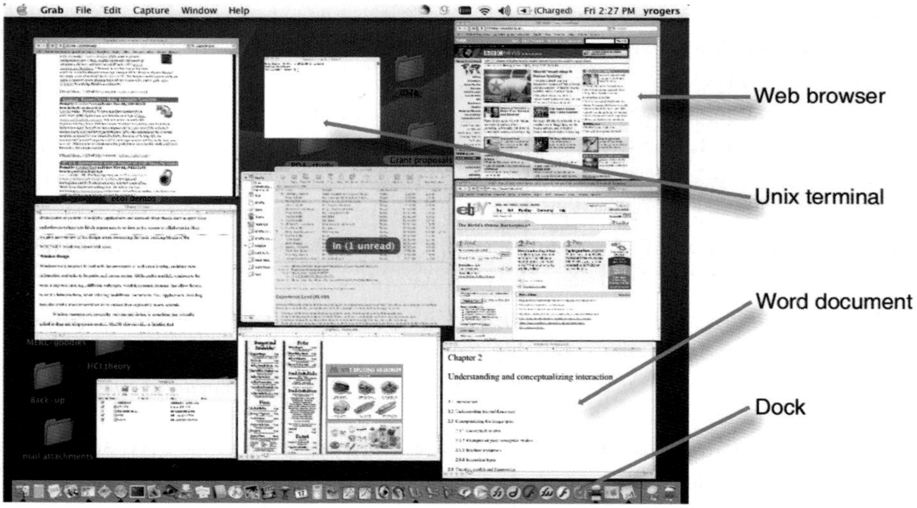

Figure 6.4 *A window management technique provided in MacOS: pressing the F9 key causes all open windows to shrink and be placed side by side. This enables the user to see them all at a glance and be able to rapidly switch between them*

select one to come to the forefront. Another option is to display all the windows open for a particular application, e.g. Word.

A particular kind of window that is commonly used in GUIs is the dialog box. Confirmations, error messages, checklists, and forms are presented through them. Information in the dialog boxes is often designed to guide user interaction, with the user following the sequence of options provided. Examples include a sequenced series of forms (i.e. Wizards) presenting the necessary and optional choices that need to be filled in when choosing a PowerPoint presentation or an Excel spreadsheet. The downside of this style of interaction is that there can be a tendency to cram too much information or data entry fields into one box, making the interface confusing, crowded, and difficult to read (Mullet and Sano, 1995).

Box 6.2
The joys of filling in forms on the web

For many of us, shopping on the Internet is generally an enjoyable experience. For example, choosing a book on Amazon or flowers from Interflora can be done at our leisure and convenience. The part we don't enjoy, however, is filling in the online form to give the company the necessary details to pay for the selected items. This can often be a frustrating and time-consuming experience. It starts with having to create an account and a new password. Once past this hurdle, a new interactive form pops up for the delivery address and credit card details. The standard online form has a fixed format making it cumbersome and annoying to fill in, especially for people whose address does not fit within its constraints. Typically, boxes are provided (asterisked for where they must be filled in) for: address line 1 and address line 2, providing no extra lines for addresses that have more than two lines; a line for the town/city; and a line for the zip code (if the site is based in the USA) or other postal code (if based in another country). The format for the codes is different, making it difficult for non-US residents (and US residents for other country sites) to fill in this part. Further boxes are provided for home, work, and cell phone number, fax number, and email address (is it really necessary to provide all of these?) and credit card type, name of the owner, and credit card number.

One of the biggest gripes about online registration forms is the country of residence box that opens up as a never-ending menu, listing all of the countries in the world in alphabetical order. Instead of typing in the country they live in, users are forced to select the one they are from, which is fine if they happen to live in Australia or Austria but not if they live in Venezuela or Zambia. Some menus place the host site country first, but this can be easily overlooked if the user is primed to look for the letter of their country (see Figure 6.5).

This is an example of where the design principle of recognition over recall (see Chapter 3) does not apply and where the converse is true. A better design might be to have a predictive text option, where users need only to type in the first two or so letters of the country they are from to cause a narrowed down list of choices to appear that they can then select from at the interface.

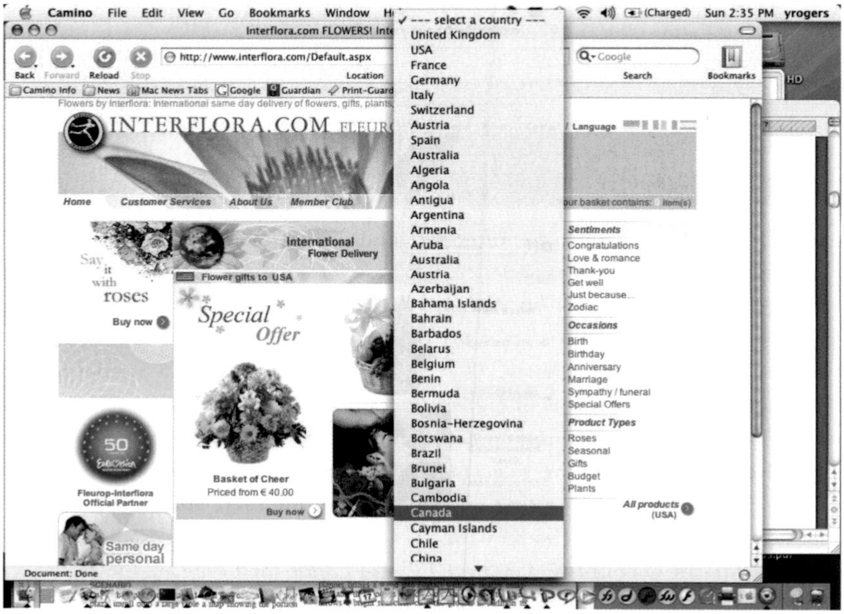

Figure 6.5 *A scrolling menu*

Activity 6.2

Go to the Interflora site (`interflora.co.uk`) and click on the international delivery option at the top of the homepage. How are the countries ordered? Is it an improvement to the scrolling pop-up menu?

Comment

At the time of writing this chapter, eight countries were listed at the top starting with the United Kingdom, then the USA, France, Germany, Italy, Switzerland, Austria, and Spain (see Figure 6.5). This was followed by the remaining set of countries listed in alphabetical order. The reason for having this particular ordering could be that the top eight are the countries who have most customers, with the UK residents using the service the most. More recently, the website had changed to using a table format grouping all the countries in alphabetical order using four columns across the page (see Table 6.2). Do you think this is an improvement? It took me about 8 seconds to select Sri Lanka, having overshot the target the first time I scrolled through, and 6 seconds to scroll through the more recent table (see below) using the web browser scrollbar.

Q	R	S	T
Qatar	**Reunion Islands**	**Saint Pierre et Miquelon**	**Taiwan**
	Romania	**Saudia Arabia**	**Thailand**
	Russia	**Serbia and Montenegro**	**Tonga**
	Republic of Ireland	**Seychelles**	**Trinidad**
		Singapore	**Tunisia**
		Slovakia	**Turkey**
		South Africa	**Turkmenistan**
		Spain	
		Sri Lanka	
		St Lucia	
		St Maarten	

Table 6.2 *An excerpt of the listing of countries in alphabetical order using a table format*

Research and design issues

A key research concern is window management—finding ways of enabling users to move fluidly between different windows (and monitors) and to be able to rapidly switch their attention between them to find the information they need or to work on the document/task within each of them—without getting distracted. Studies of how people use windows and multiple monitors have shown that window activation time (i.e. the time a window is open and interacted with) is relatively short, an average of 20 seconds, suggesting that people switch frequently between different documents and applications (Hutchings *et al.*, 2004). Widgets like the taskbar in the Windows environment are used as the main method of switching between windows.

Microsoft and Apple are also continuously researching new ways of making switching between applications and documents simpler and coming up with new metaphors and organizing principles. An example is the 'galleries' concept (part of Microsoft Office 12), which provides users with a set of options to choose from (instead of a dialog box) when working on a document, spreadsheet, presentation, etc.

To increase the legibility and ease of use of information presented in windows, the design principles of spacing, grouping, and simplicity should be used (discussed in Chapter 3). An early overview of window interfaces—that is still highly relevant today—is Brad Myers's taxonomy of window manager interfaces (Myers, 1988).

Menu design. Just like restaurant menus, interface menus offer users a structured way of choosing from the available set of options. Headings are used as part of the menu to make it easier for the user to scan through them and find what they want. Figure 6.6 presents two different styles of restaurant menu, designed to appeal to different cultures: the American one is organized into a number of categories including starters ("new beginnings"),

Figure 6.6 *Two different ways of classifying menus designed for different cultures*

Figure 6.6 *(continued)*

soups and salads ("greener pastures") and sandwiches, while the Japanese burger menu is presented in three sequential categories: first the main meal, next the side order, and lastly the accompanying drink. The American menu uses enticing text to describe in more detail what each option entails, while the Japanese one uses a combination of appetizing photos and text.

Interface menu designs have employed similar methods of categorizing and illustrating options available that have been adapted to the medium of the GUI. A difference is that interface menus are typically ordered across the top row or down the side of a screen using category headers as part of a menu bar. The contents of the menus are also for the large part invisible, only dropping down when the header is selected or rolled over with a mouse. The various options under each menu are typically ordered from top to bottom in terms of most frequently used options and grouped in terms of their similarity with one another, e.g. all formatting commands are placed together.

There is a number of menu interface styles, including flat lists, drop-down, pop-up, contextual, and expanding ones, e.g. scrolling and cascading. Flat menus are good at displaying a small number of options at the same time and where the size of the display is small, e.g. PDAs, cell phones, cameras, iPod. However, they often have to nest the lists of options within each other, requiring several steps to be taken by a user to get to the list with the desired option. Once deep down in a nested menu the user then has to take the same number of steps to get back to the top of the menu. Moving through previous screens can be tedious.

Expanding menus enable more options to be shown on a single screen than is possible with a single flat menu list. This makes navigation more flexible, allowing for the selection of options to be done in the same window. However, as highlighted in Figure 6.5, it can be frustrating having to scroll through tens or even hundreds of options. To improve navigation through scrolling menus, a number of novel controls have been devised. For example, the iPod provides a physical scrollpad that allows for clockwise and anti-clockwise movement, enabling long lists of tunes or artists to be rapidly scrolled through.

The most common type of expanding menu used as part of the PC interface is the cascading one (see Figure 6.7), which provides secondary and even tertiary menus to appear alongside the primary active drop-down menu, enabling further related options to be selected, e.g. selecting 'track changes' from the 'tools' menu leads to a secondary menu of three options by which to track changes in a Word document. The downside of using expanding menus, however, is that they require precise mouse control. Users can often end up making errors, namely overshooting or selecting the wrong options. In particular, cascading menus require users to move their mouse over the menu item, while holding the mouse pad or button down, and then when the cascading menu appears on the screen to move their cursor over to the next menu list and select the desired option. Most of us (even expert GUI users) have experienced the frustration of under- or over-shooting a menu option that leads to the desired cascading menu and worse, losing it as we try to maneuver the mouse onto the secondary or tertiary menu. It is even worse for people who have poor motor control and find controlling a mouse difficult.

Contextual menus provide access to often-used commands associated with a particular item, e.g. an icon. They provide appropriate commands that make sense in the context of a current task. They appear when the user presses the Control key while clicking on an interface element. For example, clicking on a photo in a website together with holding

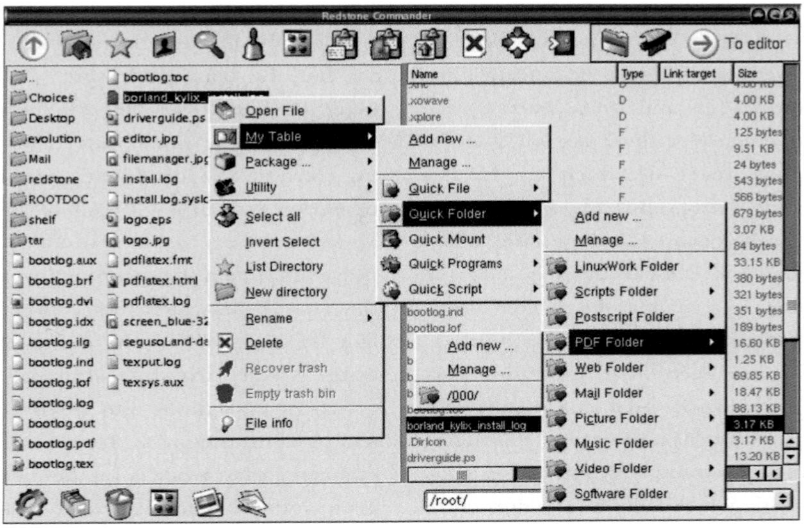

***Figure 6.7** A cascading menu*

down the Control key results in a small set of relevant menu options appearing in an overlapping window, such as 'open it in a new window,' 'save it,' or 'copy it.' The advantage of contextual menus is that they provide a limited number of options associated with an interface element, overcoming some of the navigation problems associated with cascading and expanding menus.

Activity 6.3

Open an application that you use frequently (e.g. wordprocessor, email, web browser) and look at the menu header names (but do not open them just yet). For each one (e.g. File, Edit, Tools) write down what options you think are listed under each. Then look at the contents under each header. How many options were you able to remember and how many did you put in the wrong category? Now try to select the correct menu header for the following options (assuming they are included in the application): replace, save, spelling, and sort. Did you select the correct header each time or did you have to browse through a number of them?

Comment

Popular everyday applications, like wordprocessors, have grown enormously in

terms of the functions they now offer. My current version of Word, for example, has 12 menu headers and 18 toolbars. Under each menu header there are on average 15 options, some of which are hidden under subheadings and only appear when they are rolled over with the mouse. Likewise, for each toolbar there is a set of tools that is available, be it for drawing, formatting, web, table, or borders. I find I can remember best the location of frequently used commands like spelling and replace. However, this is not because I remember which header is associated with which command, but more because of their spatial location. For infrequently used commands, like sorting a list of references into alphabetical order, I spend time flicking through the menus to find the command 'sort.' It is difficult to remember that the command 'sort' should be under the 'table' heading since what I am doing is not a table operation but using a tool to organize a section of my document. It would be more intuitive if the command was under the 'tool' header along with similar tools like 'spelling.' What this example illustrates is just how difficult it can be to group menu options into clearly defined and obvious categories. Some fit into several categories, while it can be difficult to group others. The placement of options in menus can also change between different versions of an application as more functions are added.

Research and design issues

Similar to command names, it is important to decide which are the best terms to use for menu options. Short phrases like 'bring all to front' can be more informative than single words like 'front.' However, the space for listing menu items is often restricted, such that menu names need to be short. They also need to be distinguishable, i.e. not easily confused with one another so that the user does not choose the wrong one by mistake. Operations such as 'quit' and 'save' should also be clearly separated to avoid the accidental loss of work.

The choice of which type of menu to use will often be determined by the application and type of system. Which is best will depend on the number of options that are on offer and the size of the display to present them in. Flat menus are best for displaying a small number of options at one time, while expanding menus are good for showing a large number of options, such as those available in file and document creation/editing applications.

Many guidelines exist for menu design, emphasizing the structuring, the navigation, and the number of items per menu. For example, an excerpt from ISO 9241, a major international standard for interaction design, considers grouping in menu design, as shown in Figure 6.8.

5.2 Grouping options in a menu
Menu options should be grouped within a menu to reflect user expectations and facilitate option search.

5.2.1 Logical groups
If the menu option contains a large number of options (eight or more) and these options can be logically grouped, options should be grouped by function or into other logical categories which are meaningful to users.
EXAMPLE: Grouping the commands in a word-processing system into such categories as customise, compose, edit, print.

5.2.2 Arbitrary groups
If 8 or more options are arranged arbitrarily in a menu panel, they should be arranged into equally distributed groups utilising the following equation:

$$g = \sqrt{n}$$

where

g is the number of groups
n is the number of options on the panel.

EXAMPLE: Given 19 options in a menu panel, arrange them into 4 groups of about 5 options each.

Figure 6.8 *Standard for menu design*

Icon design. The appearance of icons at the interface came about following the Xerox Star project (see Figure 2.1). They were used to represent objects as part of the desktop metaphor, namely, folders, documents, trashcans, and in- and out-trays. An assumption behind using icons instead of text labels is that they are easier to learn and remember, especially for non-expert computer users. They can also be designed to be compact and variably positioned on a screen.

Icons have become a pervasive feature of the interface. They now populate every application and operating system, and are used for all manner of functions besides representing desktop objects. These include depicting tools (e.g. paintbrush), applications (e.g. web browser), and a diversity of abstract operations (e.g. cut, paste, next, accept, change). They have also gone through many changes in their look and feel: black and white, color, shadowing, photorealistic images, 3D rendering, and animation have all been used.

While there was a period in the late 1980s/early 1990s when it was easy to find poorly designed icons at the interface (see Figure 6.9), icon design has now come of age. Interface icons look quite different; many have been designed to be very detailed and animated, making them both visually attractive and informative. The result is the design of GUIs that are highly inviting and emotionally appealing, and that feel alive. For example, Figure 6.10 contrasts the simple and jaggy Mac icon designs of the early 1990s with those that were developed as part of the Aqua range for the more recent operating environment Mac OS X. Whereas early icon designers were constrained by the graphical display technology of

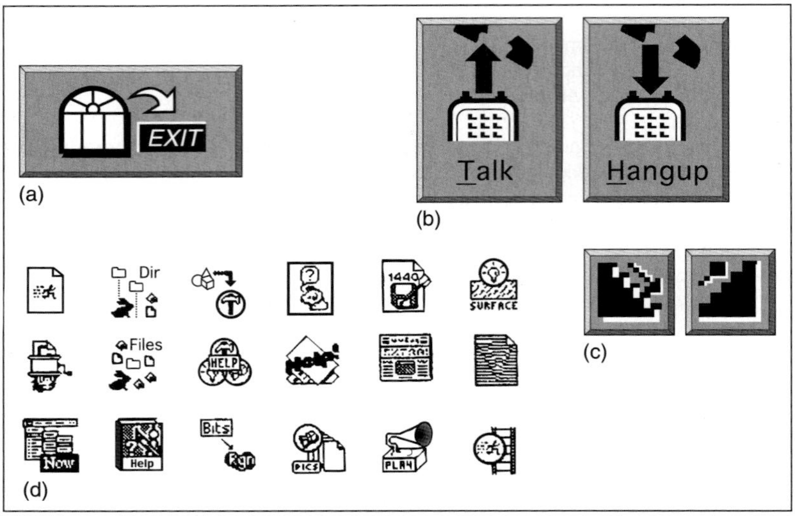

Figure 6.9 *Poor icon set from the early 1990s. What do you think they mean and why are they so bad?*

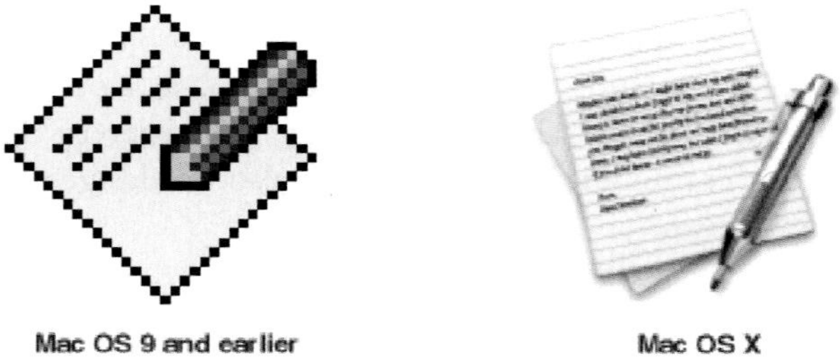

Figure 6.10 *Early and more recent Mac icon designs for the TextEdit application*

the day, they now have more flexibility. For example, the use of anti-aliasing techniques enables curves and non-rectilinear lines to be drawn, enabling more photo-illustrative styles to be developed (anti-aliasing means adding pixels around a jagged border of an object to visually smooth its outline).

Icons can be designed to represent objects and operations at the interface using concrete objects and/or abstract symbols. The mapping between the representation and underlying referent can be similar (e.g. a picture of a file to represent the object file), analogical (e.g. a picture of a pair of scissors to represent 'cut'), or arbitrary (e.g. the use of an X to represent 'delete'). The most effective icons are generally those that are isomorphic since they have direct mapping between what is being represented and how it is represented. Many operations at the interface, however, are of actions to be performed on objects, making it more difficult to represent them using direct mapping. Instead, an effective technique is to use a combination of objects and symbols that capture the salient part of an action through using analogy, association, or convention (Rogers, 1989). For example, using a picture of a pair of scissors to represent 'cut' in a wordprocessing application provides sufficient clues as long as the user understands the convention of 'cut' for deleting text.

The greater flexibility offered by current GUI interfaces has enabled developers to create icon sets that are distinguishable, identifiable, and memorable. For example, different graphical genres have been used to group and identify different categories of icons. Figure 6.11 shows how colorful photo-realistic images have been used, each slanting slightly to the left, for the category of *user* applications, e.g. email, whereas monochrome straight-on and simple images have been used for the class of utility applications, e.g. printer set-up. The former have a fun feel to them, whereas the latter have a more serious look about them.

Figure 6.11 *Contrasting genres of Aqua icons used for the Mac. The top row of icons have been designed for user applications and the bottom row for utility applications*

Another approach has been to develop glossy, logo-style icons that are very distinctive, using only primary colors and symbols, having the effect of making them easily recognizable, such as those developed by Macromedia and Microsoft to represent their popular media applications (see Figure 6.12).

Icons that appear in toolbars or palettes as part of an application or presented on small device displays, e.g. PDAs, cell phones, digital cameras, have much less screen estate available. Because of this, they are typically designed to be simple, emphasizing the outline form of an object or symbol and using only grayscale or one or two colors. They tend to convey the tool and action performed on them using a combination of concrete objects and abstract symbols, e.g. a blank piece of paper with a plus sign representing a new blank

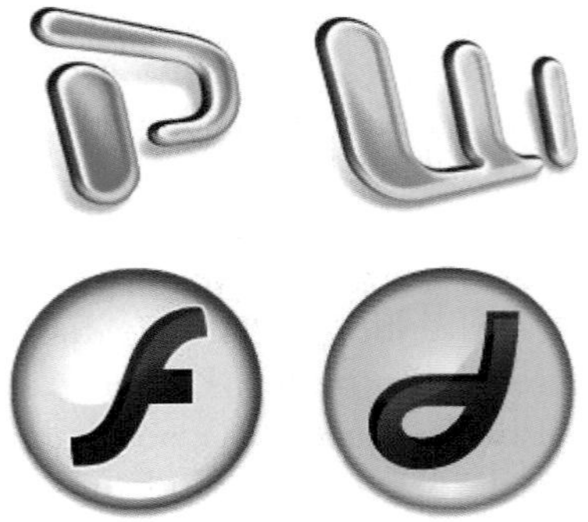

Figure 6.12 Logo-based icons for Microsoft and Macromedia applications (Powerpoint, Word, Dreamweaver, Flash) that are distinctive

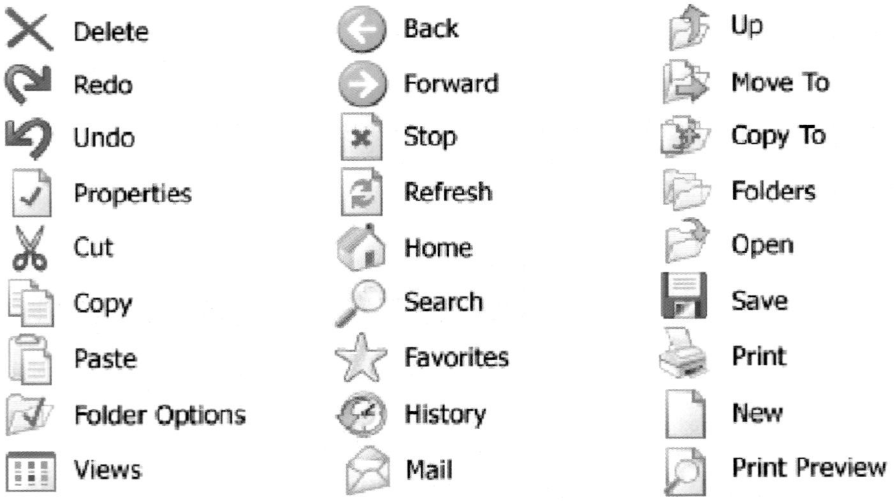

Figure 6.13 Examples of simple and distinguishable icons used in Windows XP toolbar. A combination of objects, abstract symbols, and depictions of tools is used to represent common objects and operations

document, an open envelope with an arrow coming out of it indicating a new message has arrived. Again, the goal should be to design a palette or set of icons that are easy to recognize and distinguishable from one another. Figure 6.13 provides examples of simple toolbar icons from Windows XP.

Activity 6.4

Sketch simple icons to represent the following operations to appear on a digital camera LCD screen:

- Delete last picture taken.
- Delete all pictures stored.
- Format memory card.

Show them to your peers or friends, tell them that they are icons for a new digital camera intended to be really simple to use, and see if they can understand what each represents.

Comment

Figure 6.14 shows Toshiba's icons based on analogy and convention that are presented on the LCD display of the camera. The trashcan, which has become the conventional GUI icon to represent the command 'to delete,' has been used in combination with a representation of a single photo or a stack of photos, indicating what is deleted. The icon (to the left of them) uses a combination of an object and symbol: the image is of a memory card and the arrow conveys a complete circle. (The reason why one occasionally needs to format a memory card is to remove any residual memory files that can accumulate.) A key design issue is to make the three icons distinct from one another, especially the 'delete last photo taken' from the 'delete all saved photos.'

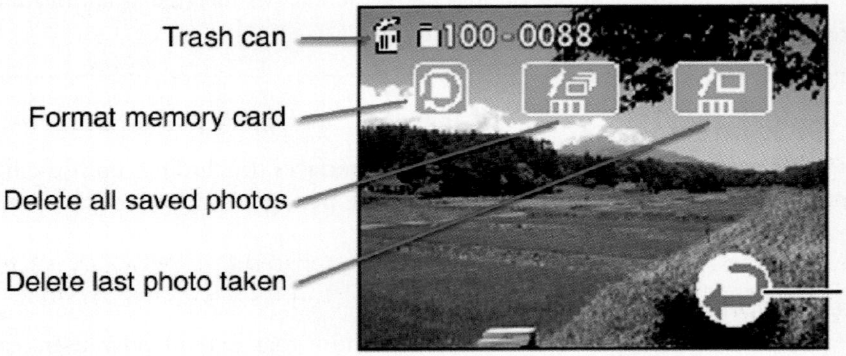

Figure 6.14 Icons used by Toshiba for three of its digital camera operations

Research and design issues

Various books on how to design icons (e.g. Caplin, 2001; Horton, 1994) are now available together with sets of guidelines, standards, and style guides. There are also many icon builders and icon sets, e.g. ClipArt, providing a wealth of resources for designers, so that they do not have to draw or invent icons from scratch. Apple Computer Inc. has always been very good at providing their developers with style guides, explaining why certain designs are preferable to others and how to design icon sets. On its developers' website (`developer.apple.com`), advice is given on how and why certain graphical elements should be used when developing different types of icon. Among the various guidelines, it suggests that different categories of application (e.g. user, utility) should be represented by a different genre (see Figure 6.11) and recommends displaying a tool to communicate the nature of a task, e.g. a magnifying glass for searching, a camera for a photo editing tool. Microsoft has also begun providing more extensive guidance and step-by-step procedures on how to design icons for its applications on its website.

To help disambiguate the meaning of icons, text labels can be used under, above, or to the side of their icons (see Figure 6.13). This method is effective for toolbars that have small icon sets, e.g. those appearing as part of a web browser) but is not as good for applications that have large icon sets, e.g. photo editing or wordprocessing, since the screen can get very cluttered and busy; and conversely, making it sometimes harder and longer to find an icon. To prevent text/icon clutter at the interface, a rollover function can be used, where a text label appears adjacent to or above an icon, after one second of the user holding the cursor over it and for as long as the user keeps the cursor on it. This method allows identifying information to be temporarily displayed when needed.

6.3.2 1990s interfaces

In this section we cover advanced graphical interfaces (including multimedia, virtual reality, and information visualization), speech-based, pen, gesture, and touch interfaces, and appliance interfaces.

Advanced graphical interfaces

A number of advanced graphical interfaces exist now that extend how users can access, explore, and visualize information. These include interactive animations, multimedia, virtual environments, and visualizations. Some are designed to be viewed and used by individuals; others by a group of users who are collocated or at a distance. Many claims have been made about the benefits they bring compared with the traditional GUI. Below we describe two major developments: multimedia and virtual environments, and then briefly touch upon visualizations.

Multimedia. Multimedia, as the name implies, combines different media within a single interface, namely, graphics, text, video, sound, and animations, and links them with various forms of interactivity. It differs from previous forms of combined media, e.g. TV, in that the different media can be interacted with by the user (Chapman and Chapman, 2004). Users can click on hotspots or links in an image or text appearing on one screen that leads them to another part of the program where, say, an animation or a video clip is played. From there they can return to where they were previously or move on to another place.

Many multimedia narratives and games have been developed that are designed to encourage users to explore different parts of the game or story by clicking on different parts of the screen. An assumption is that a combination of media and interactivity can provide better ways of presenting information than can either one alone. There is a general belief that 'more is more' and the 'whole is greater than the sum of the parts' (Lopuck, 1996). In addition, the 'added value' assumed from being able to interact with multimedia in ways not possible with single media (i.e. books, audio, video) is easier learning, better understanding, more engagement, and more pleasure (see Scaife and Rogers, 1996).

One of the distinctive features of multimedia is its ability to facilitate rapid access to multiple representations of information. Many multimedia encyclopedias and digital libraries have been designed based on this multiplicity principle, providing an assortment of audio and visual materials on a given topic. For example, if you want to find out about the heart, a typical multimedia-based encyclopedia will provide you with:

- One or two video clips of a real live heart pumping and possibly a heart transplant operation.
- Audio recordings of the heart beating and perhaps an eminent physician talking about the cause of heart disease.
- Static diagrams and animations of the circulatory system, sometimes with narration.
- Several columns of hypertext, describing the structure and function of the heart.

Hands-on interactive simulations have also been incorporated as part of multimedia learning environments. An early example is the Cardiac Tutor, developed to teach students about cardiac resuscitation, that required students to save patients by selecting the correct set of procedures in the correct order from various options displayed on the computer screen (Eliot and Woolf, 1994). A more recent example is BioBLAST®, a multimedia environment for high school biology classes, that incorporates simulation models based on NASA's research to enable students to develop and test their own designs for a life support system for use on the Moon (see Figure 6.15). The learning environment provides a range of simulators that are combined with online resources.

Multimedia CD-ROMs (and more recently interactive websites) have mainly been developed for training, educational, and entertainment purposes. It is generally assumed that learning (e.g. reading and scientific inquiry skills) and playing can be enhanced through interacting with engaging multimedia interfaces. But what actually happens when users

Figure 6.15 *Screen dump from the multimedia environment BioBLAST*

are given unlimited, easy access to multiple media and simulations? Do they systematically switch between the various media and 'read' all the multiple representations on a particular subject? Or, are they more selective in what they look at and listen to?

Anyone who has interacted with an educational CD-ROM knows just how tempting it is to play the video clips and animations, while skimming through accompanying text or static diagrams. The former are dynamic, easy and enjoyable to watch, whilst the latter are viewed as static, boring, and difficult to read from the screen. For example, in an evaluation of Don Norman's CD-ROM of his work (First Person), students consistently admitted to ignoring the text at the interface in search of clickable icons of the author, which when selected would present an animated video of him explaining some aspect of design (Rogers and Aldrich, 1996). Given the choice to explore multimedia material in numerous ways, ironically, users tend to be highly selective as to what they actually attend to, adopting a 'channel hopping' mode of interaction. While enabling the users to select for themselves the information they want to view or features to explore, there is the danger that multimedia environments may in fact promote fragmented interactions where only part of the media is ever viewed. This may be acceptable for certain kinds of activities, e.g. browsing, but less optimal for others, e.g. learning about a topic. One way to encourage more systematic and extensive interactions (when it is considered important for the activity at hand) is to require certain activities to be completed that entail the reading of accompanying text, before the user is allowed to move on to the next level or task.

Box 6.3
Accessible interactive TV services for all

TV now provides many digital channels, of which sports, news, and movie channels are very popular. In addition, a range of interactive TV services are being offered that enable users to browse the web, customize their viewing choices, play interactive games, do their banking and shopping, and take an active part in a number of broadcast shows, e.g. voting. Besides offering a wide diversity of choices to the general public, there is much potential for empowering disabled and elderly users, by enabling them to access the services from the comfort of their own armchair. But it requires a new sensitivity to 'interactive' design, taking into account specific usability issues for those with impaired motor control, poor vision, and hearing difficulties (Newell, 2003). For example, remote controls need to be designed that can be manipulated with poor dexterity, text/icons need to be readable for those with poor eyesight, while navigation methods need to be straightforward for viewers who are not experienced with multimedia-based interfaces. ■

Activity 6.5

Go to the interactivities section on our accompanying website (`http://www.id-book.com`) and try to design the interface for a cell phone. How did the multimedia representations and interactivity help you to create a design?

Comment

The multimedia interactivity provides a constrained way of completing the task, involving a hands-on physical design activity and the selection of contextually relevant guidelines that are meant to help you think about the rationale behind your choices. However, rather than go through them step-by-step, it can be tempting simply to add a widget component to the template and move on to the next screen without reading or reflecting upon the guidelines. Sometimes, one can be so focused on comparing the visual interface components provided on the right-hand side of the screen that it is easy to forget to look at the left-hand side where the guidelines are.

Research and design issues

A key research question is how to design interactive multimedia to help users explore, keep track of, and integrate the multiple representations of information provided, be it a digital library, a game, or learning material. As mentioned above, one technique is to provide hands-on interactivities and simulations at the interface that require the user to complete a task, solve a problem, or explore different aspects of a topic. Specific examples include electronic notebooks that are integrated as part of the interface, where users can copy, download, or type in their own material; multiple-choice quizzes that give feedback on how the user has done; interactive puzzles where the user has to select and position different pieces in the right combination; and simulation-type games where the user has to follow a set of procedures to achieve some goal for a given scenario. Another approach is to employ 'dynalinking,' where information depicted in one window explicitly changes in relation to what happens in another. This can help users keep track of multiple representations and see the relationship between them (Scaife and Rogers, 1996).

Specific guidelines are available that recommend how best to combine multiple media in relation to different kinds of task, e.g. when to use audio with graphics, sound with animations, and so on for different learning tasks. For example, Alty (1991) suggests that audio information is good for stimulating imagination, movies for action information, text for conveying details, whilst diagrams are good at conveying ideas. From such generalizations it is possible to devise a presentation strategy for learning. This can be along the lines of: first, stimulate the imagination through playing an audio clip; then, present an idea in diagrammatic form; then, display further details about the concept through hypertext. Sutcliffe and his colleagues have also developed guidelines, based on cognitive engineering principles, that recommend how to link different media together to give coherent and comprehensive presentations (Faraday and Sutcliffe, 1997; Sutcliffe, 2003). Quintana *et al.* (2002) have developed a set of guidelines for learner-centered design (LCD) that outline various features that can be used to guide and prompt students in multimedia learning environments. Examples include process maps and flow diagrams.

Virtual reality and virtual environments. Virtual reality and virtual environments are computer-generated graphical simulations, intended to create "the illusion of participation in a synthetic environment rather than external observation of such an environment" (Gigante, 1993, p. 3). Virtual reality (VR) is the generic term that refers to the experience of interacting with an artificial environment, which makes it feel virtually real. The term 'virtual environment' (VE) is used more specifically to describe what has been generated using computer technology (although both terms are used interchangeably). Images are displayed stereoscopically to the users—most commonly through shutter glasses—and objects within the field of vision can be interacted with via an input device like a joystick. The 3D graphics can be projected onto CAVE (Cave Automatic Virtual Environment) floor and wall surfaces (see Figure 2.12), desktop machines, or large shared displays, e.g. IMAX screens.

One of the main attractions of VRs/VEs is that they can provide opportunities for new kinds of experience, enabling users to interact with objects and navigate in 3D space in ways not possible in the physical world or a 2D graphical interface. The resulting user experience can be highly engaging; it can feel as if one really is flying around a virtual world. People can become immersed in and highly captivated by the experience (Kalawsky, 1993). For example, in the Virtual Zoo project, Allison *et al.* (1997) found that people were highly engaged and very much enjoyed the experience of adopting the role of a gorilla, navigating the environment, and watching other gorillas respond to their movements and presence (see Figure 6.16).

(a) (b)

Figure 6.16 *The Virtual Gorilla Project. On the left a student wears a head-mounted display and uses a joystick to interact with the virtual zoo. On the right are the virtual gorillas she sees and which react to her movements*

One of the advantages of VRs/VEs is that simulations of the world can be constructed to have a higher level of fidelity with the objects they represent compared with other forms of graphical interface, e.g. multimedia. The illusion afforded by the technology can make virtual objects appear to be very life-like and behave according to the laws of physics. For example, landing and take-off terrains developed for flight simulators can appear to be very realistic. Moreover, it is assumed that learning and training applications can be improved through having a greater fidelity with the represented world. A sense of 'presence' can also make the virtual setting seem convincing. By presence is meant "a state of consciousness, the (psychological) sense of being in the virtual environment" (Slater and Wilbur, 1997, p. 605), where someone is totally engrossed by the experience, and behaves in a similar way to how he/she would if at an equivalent real event.

Another distinguishing feature of VRs/VEs is the different viewpoints they offer. Players can have a first-person perspective, where their view of the game or environment is through their own eyes, or a third-person perspective, where they see the world through a character visually represented on the screen, commonly known as an avatar. An example of a first-person perspective is that experienced in first-person shooter games such as DOOM, where the player moves through the environment without seeing a representation of themselves. It requires the user to imagine what he/she might look like and decide how best to move around. An example of a third-person perspective is that experienced in the game Tomb Raider, where the player sees the virtual world above and behind the avatar of Lara Croft. The user controls Lara's interactions with the environment by controlling her movements, e.g. making her jump, run, or crouch. Avatars can be represented from behind or from the front, depending on how the user controls its movements. First-person perspectives are typically used for flying/driving simulations and games, e.g. car racing, where it is important to have direct and immediate control to steer the virtual vehicle. Third-person perspectives are more commonly used in games, learning environments, and simulations where it is important to see a representation of self with respect to the environment and others in it. In some virtual environments it is possible to switch between the two perspectives, enabling the user to experience different viewpoints on the same game or training environment.

Early VRs/VEs were developed using head-mounted displays. However, they have been found to be uncomfortable to wear, sometimes causing motion sickness and disorientation. They are also expensive and difficult to program and maintain. Nowadays, desktop VRs/VEs are mostly used; software toolkits are now available that make it much easier to program a virtual environment, e.g. VRML, 3D Alice. Instead of moving in a physical space with a head-mounted display, users interact with a desktop virtual environment—as they would any other desktop application—using mice, keyboards, or joysticks as input devices. The desktop virtual environment can also be programmed to present a more realistic 3D effect (similar to that achieved in 3D movies shown at IMAX cinemas), requiring users to wear a pair of shutter glasses.

Research and design issues

VRs/VEs have been developed to support learning and training for numerous skills. Researchers have designed them to help people learn to drive a vehicle, fly a plane, and perform delicate surgical operations—where it is very expensive and potentially dangerous to start learning with the real thing. Others have investigated whether people can learn to find their way around a real building/place before visiting it by first navigating a virtual representation of it, e.g. Gabrielli *et al.*, (2000). VEs have also been designed to help people practice social skills, speaking skills, and confront their social phobias, e.g. Cobb *et al.*, (2002); Slater *et al.*, (1999). An underlying assumption is that the environment can be designed as a 'safe' place to help people gently overcome their fears (e.g. spiders, talking in public) by confronting them through different levels of closeness and unpleasantness, e.g. seeing a small virtual spider move far away, seeing a medium one sitting nearby, and then finally touching a large one. Studies have shown that people can readily suspend their disbelief, imagining a virtual spider to be a real one or a virtual audience to be a real audience. For example, Slater *et al.* (1999) found that people rated themselves as being less anxious after speaking to a virtual audience that was programmed to respond to them in a positive fashion than after speaking to virtual audiences programmed to respond to them negatively.

Core design issues that need to be considered when developing virtual environments are: what are the most effective ways of enabling users to navigate through them, e.g. first versus third person; how to control their interactions and movements, e.g. use of head and body movements; how best to enable them to interact with information in them, e.g. use of keypads, pointing, joystick buttons; and how to enable users to collaborate and communicate with others in the virtual environment. A central concern is the level of realism to aim for. Is it necessary to design avatars and the environments they inhabit to be life-like, using 'rich' graphics, or can simpler and more abstract forms be used, but which nonetheless are equally capable of engendering a sense of presence? For more on this topic see the dilemma box below.

Guidelines are available for helping to design virtual environments, that focus on how best to support navigation and user control, including where to place landmarks and objects in large-scale environments to ease navigation (Vinson, 1999) and the rules of everyday life that can be contravened, e.g. enabling avatars to walk through virtual walls and buildings (Sutcliffe, 2002).

Dilemma

Realism versus abstraction?

One of the challenges facing interaction designers is whether to use realism or abstraction when designing an interface. This means designing objects either to (i) give the illusion of behaving and looking like real-world counterparts or (ii) appear as abstractions of the objects being represented. This concern is particularly relevant when implementing conceptual models that are deliberately based on an analogy with some aspect of the real world. For example, is it preferable

to design a desktop to look like a real desktop, a virtual house to look like a real house, or a virtual terrain to look like a real terrain? Or, alternatively, is it more effective to design representations as simple abstract renditions, depicting only a few salient features?

One of the main benefits of using realism at the interface is that it can enable people, especially computer phobics and novices, to feel more comfortable when learning an application. The rationale behind this is that such representations can readily tap into people's understanding of the physical world. Hence, realistic interfaces can help users initially understand the underlying conceptual model. In contrast, overly schematic and abstract representations can appear to be too computer-like and may be off-putting to the newcomer. The advantage of more abstract interfaces, however, is that they can be more efficient to use. Furthermore, the more experienced users become, the more they may find 'comfortable' interfaces no longer to their liking. A dilemma facing designers, therefore, is deciding between creating interfaces to make novice users feel comfortable (but more experienced users less comfortable) and designing interfaces to be effective for more experienced users (but maybe harder to learn by novices).

One of the earliest attempts at using realism at the interface was General Magic's office system Magic Cap, which was rendered in 3D. To achieve this degree of realism required using various perceptual cues such as perspective, shadowing, and shading. The result was a rather cute interface (see Figure 6.17). Although their intentions were well-grounded, the outcome was less successful. Many people commented on how childish and gawky it looked, having the appearance of illustrations in a children's picture book rather than a work-based application.

Mullet and Sano (1995) also point out how a 3D rendition of an object like a desk nearly always suffers from both an unnatural point of view and an awkward rendering style that ironically destroy the impression of being in a real physical space. One reason for this is that 3D depictions conflict with the effective use of display space, especially when 2D editing tasks need to be performed. As can be seen in Figure 6.17, these kinds of task were represented as 'flat' buttons that appear to be floating in front of the desk, e.g. mail, program manager, task manager.

For certain kinds of applications, using realism can be very effective for both novices and experienced users. Computer-based games fall into this category, especially those where users have to react rapidly to dynamic events that happen in a virtual world in real time, say flying a plane or playing a game of virtual football. Making the characters in the game resemble humans in the way they look, move, dress, and behave also makes them seem more convincing and lifelike, enhancing the enjoyment and fun factor.

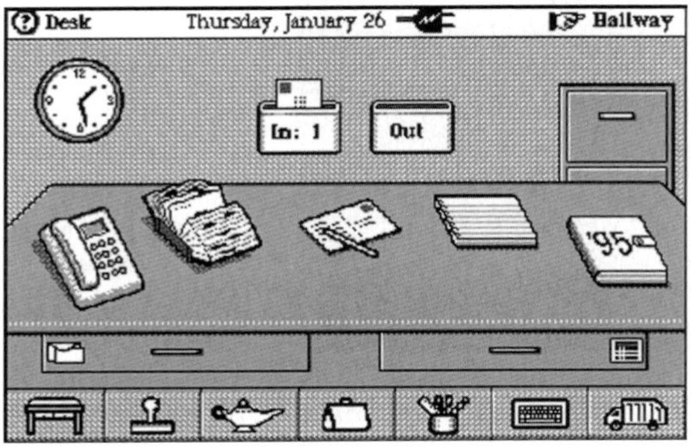

Figure 6.17 *Magic Cap's 3D desktop interface*

Activity 6.6

Many games have been ported from the PC platform to the cell phone. Because of the memory and screen size limitations of the phone device, however, much simpler and more abstract representations have to be used. To what extent does this adaptation of the interface affect the experience of playing the same game?

Comment

The most effective games to have been ported over to the cell phone are highly addictive games that use simple graphics and do not require the user to navigate between different windows. Examples are Snake (see Figure 6.18), Tetris, and Snood, where the goal of the game is to move an object (e.g. a snake, abstract shapes, a shooter) small distances in order to eat food, fill a container, or delete shapes. More complex games, like World of Warcraft—which are very popular on the PC platform—do not port over nearly as well. It is simply too difficult to navigate and engage in the same level of interaction that makes the game enjoyable and addictive when played on a PC. Similar to the debate over text-based command games versus advanced graphical games, the extent to which the interaction style affects the user experience varies in terms of how engaging they are; but both can be equally enjoyable (see Activity 2.7).

Information visualization. Information visualization is a growing field concerned with the design of computer-generated visualizations of complex data that are typically interactive

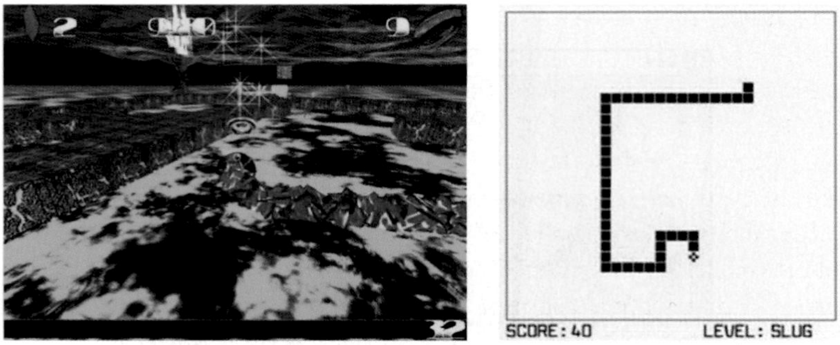

Figure 6.18 *Two screenshots from the game Snake—the one on the left is played on a PC and the one on the right on a cell phone. In both games, the goal is to move the snake (the blue thing and the black squares, respectively) towards targets that pop up on the screen (e.g. the bridge, the star) and to avoid obstacles (e.g. a flower, the end of the snake's tail). When a player successfully moves his snake head over or under a target, the snake increases its length by one blob or block. The longer the snake gets the harder it is to avoid obstacles. If the snake hits an obstacle the game is over. On the PC version there are lots of extra features that make the game more complicated, including more obstacles and ways of moving. The cell phone version has a simple 2D bird's eye representation, whereas the PC version adopts a 3D third-person avatar perspective*

and dynamic. The goal is to amplify human cognition (see Chapter 3), enabling users to see patterns, trends, and anomalies in the visualization and from this to gain insight (Card *et al.*, 1999). Specific objectives are to enhance discovery, decision-making, and explanation of phenomena. Most interactive visualizations have been developed for use by experts to enable them to understand and make sense of vast amounts of dynamically changing domain data or information, e.g. satellite images or research findings, that take much longer to achieve if using only text-based information.

Common techniques that are used for depicting information and data are 3D interactive maps that can be zoomed in and out of and which present data via webs, trees, clusters, scatterplot diagrams, and interconnected nodes (Bederson and Shneiderman, 2003; Chen, 2004). Hierarchical and networked structures, color, labeling, tiling, and stacking are also used to convey different features and their spatial relationships. At the top of Figure 6.19 is a typical treemap, called MillionVis, that depicts one million items all on one screen using the graphical techniques of 2D stacking, tiling, and color (Fekete and Plaisant, 2002). The idea is that viewers can zoom in to parts of the visualization to find out more about certain data points, while also being able to see the overall structure of an entire data set. The treemap has been used to visualize file systems, enabling users to understand why they are running out of disk space, how much space different applications are using, and also for viewing large image repositories that contain Terabytes of satellite images. Similar visualizations have been used to represent changes in stocks and shares over time, using rollovers to show additional information, e.g. Marketmap on `SmartMoney.com`.

The visualization at the bottom of Figure 6.19 depicts the evolution of co-authorship networks over time (Ke *et al.*, 2004). It uses a canonical network to represent spatially the relationships between labeled authors and their place of work. Changing color and thickening lines that are animated over time convey increases in co-authoring over time. For example, the figure shows a time slice of 100 authors at various US academic institutions, in which Robertson, Mackinlay, and Card predominate, having published together many times more than with the other authors. Here, the idea is to enable researchers to readily see connections between authors and their frequency of publishing together with respect to their location over time. (Note: Figure 6.19 is a static screen shot for 1999.) Again, an assumption is that it is much easier to read this kind of diagram compared with trying to extract the same information from a text description or a table.

Research and design issues

Much of the research in information visualization has focused on developing algorithms and interactive techniques to enable viewers to explore and visualize data in novel ways. There has been less research on how visualizations are used in practice and whether they can amplify cognition, enabling people to discover and make better informed decisions, about policy or research. Key design issues include whether to use animation and/or interactivity, what form of coding to use, e.g. color or text labels, whether to use a 2D or 3D representational format, what forms of navigation, e.g. zooming or panning, and what kinds and how much additional information, e.g. rollovers or tables of text, to provide. The type of metaphor to be used is also an important concern, e.g. one based on flying over a geographical terrain or one that represents documents as part of an urban setting. There are, at the time of writing, no clear-cut guidelines on how to design effective visualizations; designers often apply relevant research findings from cognitive psychology (see Chapter 3) and graphical design, e.g. Tufte (1999). An overriding principle is to design a visualization that is easy to comprehend and easy to make inferences from. If too many variables are depicted in the same visualization it can make it much more difficult for the viewer to read and make sense of what is being represented.

Web-based interfaces

Early websites were largely text-based, providing hyperlinks to different places or pages of text. Much of the design effort was concerned with how best to structure information at the interface to enable users to navigate and access it easily and quickly. Jakob Nielsen (2000) adapted his and Ralf Molich's usability guidelines (Nielsen and Molich, 1990) to make them applicable to website design, focusing on simplicity, feedback, speed, legibility, and ease of

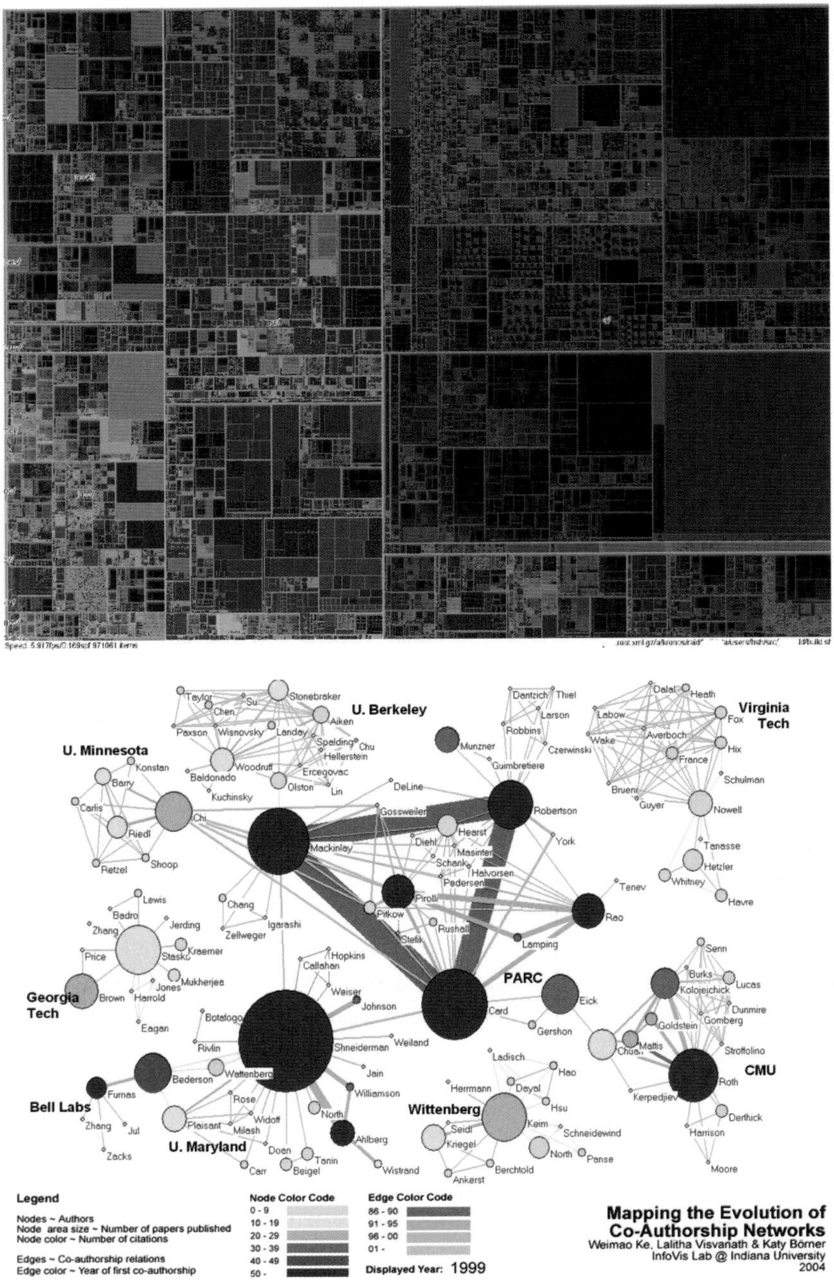

Figure 6.19 *Two types of visualizations, one using flat colored blocks and the other animated color networks that expand and change color over time*

use. He has also stressed how critical download time is to the success of a website. Simply, users who have to wait too long for a page to appear are likely to move on somewhere else. One of Nielsen's recommendations is that it is best to have very few graphics on the homepage of a site but offer users the chance to see pictures of products, or maps, etc., *only* when they explicitly ask for them. This can be achieved by using thumbnails—miniaturized versions of the full picture—as links.

Nielsen has become renowned for his doggedness on insisting that 'vanilla' websites are the most usable and easiest to navigate. True to his word, to this day, Nielsen has resisted including any graphics or photos on his homepage (`useit.com`). Instead he provides a series of hyperlinks to his alertboxes, books, reports, consulting services, and news articles. Other interaction designers, however, do not support his stance, arguing that it is possible to have both aesthetically pleasing and usable sites. A main reason for emphasizing the importance of graphical design is to make web pages distinctive, striking, and pleasurable for the user when they first view them and also to make them readily recognizable on their return.

It is not surprising, therefore, to see that nearly all commercial, public service, and personal websites have adopted more of a 'multi-flavor' rather than a 'vanilla' approach; using a range of graphics, images, and animations on their homepages. Website design took off in a big way in the early 2000s when user-centered editing tools, e.g. Dreamweaver, and programming languages, e.g. php, Flash and XML, emerged providing opportunities for both designers and the general public to create websites to look and behave more like multimedia environments. Groups of technologies, such as Ajax (asynchronous Javascript and XML) also started to appear, enabling applications to be built that are largely executed on a user's computer, allowing the development of reactive and rich graphical user interfaces. Many web-based interactivities and applications have been developed, including online pop quizzes, agents, recommenders, chatrooms, interactive games, and blogs. There is also an increasing number of PC-based applications that have become web-based, such as email, e.g. Gmail, and photo storing and sharing, e.g. Flickr. Web browsers also started to be developed for a range of platforms besides the PC, including interactive TV, cell phones, and PDAs.

Steve Krug (2000) has characterized the debate on usability versus attractiveness in terms of the difference between how designers create websites and how users actually view them. He argues that web designers create sites as if the user was going to pore over each page, reading the finely crafted text word for word, looking at the use of images, color, icons, etc., examining how the various items have been organized on the site, and then contemplating their options before they finally select a link. Users, however, behave quite differently. They will glance at a new page, scan part of it, and click on the first link that catches their interest or looks like it might lead them to what they want. Much of the content on a web page is not read. In his words, web designers are "thinking great literature" (or at least "product brochure") while the user's reality is much closer to a "billboard going by at 60 miles an hour" (Krug, 2000, p. 21). While somewhat of a caricature of web designers and users, his depiction highlights the discrepancy between the meticulous ways designers create their websites with the rapid and less than systematic approach that users take to look at them.

Similar to newspapers, magazines, and TV, working out how to brand a web page to catch and keep 'eyeballs' is central to whether a user will stay on it and, importantly, return to it. We have talked about the need to keep screens uncluttered so that people can find their way around and see clearly what is available. However, there may be occasions when the need to maintain a brand overrides this principle. For example, the website for the Swedish newspaper *Aftonbladet*, while very busy and crowded (see Figure 6.20), was designed to continue the style of the paper-based version, which also has a busy and crowded appearance.

Har du kilon att tappa? Vi är lätta att hitta. ViktKlubb.se

Nu DVD på köpet!

"Med KLM kommer världen närmare."

Grundad 1830 av Lars Johan Hierta. På internet sedan 25 augusti 1994

AFTONBLADET

Startsidan

Fredag 6 maj 2005

Tipsaoss

Nyheter
Sportbladet
Nöje
Tv
Kvinna
Plus i dag
Fimpa!

Aftonbladets marknadsplats

blocket.se

Bilar	98826
Båtar	7870
MC	15084
Bostad	15147
Möbler	36178
Övrigt	166633
Annonsera	

Aftonbladets nr.upplysning

Gratis nummer-upplysning

hitta.se

Bil
Bostad
Böcker
Ekonomi & börs
Föräldrar

Tony Blair ombildar regeringen

Försvarsministern får lämna sin post - utrikesministern och finansministern blir troligen kvar Blair genomför ommöblering i ministären efter knapp valseger.

TV Segerherre - men försvagad

Wolfgang Hansson Blair vann igen - tacka Brown för den segern.

Kuggad kan slippa ny uppkörning

Körkortsaspiranter som kuggas kan bli godkända av bilskolan Vägverket vill starta försöksverksamhet.

Är det ett bra att körskolorna får godkänna kuggade?

Ja Nej Se resultat

Död val strandade på Hönö

Hockey-VM

Finland tappade segern i slut-minuten mot USA Schweiz tog överaskande poäng mot Ryssland.

Tv-nyheter

TV TV-nyheter från Aftonbladet Tony Blair historisk efter tredje valseger.

Bordtennis

Figure 6.20 The front web page of the Aftonbladet newspaper

Advertisers also realize how effective flashing ads and banners can be for promoting their products, similar to the way animated neon light adverts are used in city centers, such as London's Piccadilly Circus. The homepage of many online newspapers, including the *Aftonbladet* is full of flashing banners and cartoon animations, many of which are adverts for other products (see `http://www.aftonbladet.se` for the full animation effects). Music and other sounds have also begun to be used to create a certain mood and captivate users. While online adverts are often garish, distracting, and can contravene basic usability principles, they are good at luring users' attention. As with other media, e.g. TV, newspapers and magazines, advertisers pay significant revenues to online companies to have their adverts placed on their websites, entitling them to say where and how they should appear.

Research and design issues

There are numerous web design handbooks and several web usability books, e.g. Krug (2000); Cooper and Reiman (2003); Spool *et al.* (1997); Nielsen (2000). In addition, there are some good online sites offering guidelines and tips, together with pointers to examples of bad websites. Increasingly, it is the case that today's web interfaces are not that different from GUIs; both need to consider how best to design, present, and structure information and system behavior. The main difference is the web's emphasis on content and the use of hyperlinks for navigation.

Key design issues for websites, which differ from other interfaces, are captured very well by three questions proposed by Keith Instone (quoted in Veen, 2001): Where am I? What's here? Where can I go? Each web page should be designed with these three questions in mind. The answers must be clear to users. Jeffrey Veen (2001) expands on these questions. He suggests that a simple way to view a web page is to deconstruct it into three areas (see Figure 6.21). Across the top would be the answer to "Where am I?" Because users can arrive at a site from any direction (and rarely through the front door, or homepage), telling them where they are is critical. Having an area at the top of the page that 'brands' the page instantly provides that information. Down the left-hand side is an area in which navigation or menus sit. This should allow users to see immediately what else is available on the site, and answers the question "Where can I go?"

The most important information, and the reason a user has come to the site in the first place, is provided in the third area, the content area, which answers the question "What's here?" Content for web pages must be designed differently from standard documents, since

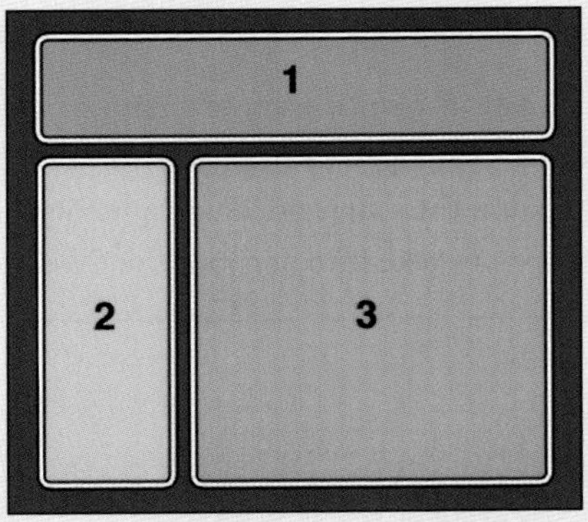

Figure 6.21 *Any web page has three main areas*

the way users read web pages is different. On web pages, content should be short and precise, with crisp sentences. Using headlines to capture the main points of a paragraph is one way to increase the chances of your message getting over to a user who is scanning a page rather than looking at it in detail. Krug (2000) also suggests the importance of breaking up pages into clearly defined areas, making it obvious what is clickable and minimizing noise. He promotes creating a clear visual hierarchy on each page, so it is easy for a user to grasp in a hurry, showing which things are related and what's what (e.g. a link, a search box) and capitalizing on conventions (e.g. using a shopping cart icon on e-commerce sites to indicate the link to make a purchase) rather than reinventing the wheel.

W3C standards and guidelines also exist for web content accessibility (WCAG). By this is meant designing websites for users who have some form of disability. These include:

- Users who may not be able to see, hear, move, or may not be able to process some types of information easily or at all.
- Users who have difficulty reading or comprehending text.
- Users who may not have or be able to use a keyboard or mouse.
- Users who may have a text-only screen, a small screen, or a slow Internet connection.

Website content also needs to be designed for:

- Users who may not speak or understand fluently the language in which the document is written.
- Users who are in a setting where their eyes, ears, or hands are busy or interfered with, e.g. driving to work.
- Users who may have an early version of a browser, a different browser entirely, a voice browser, or a different operating system.

(From Web Content Accessibility Guidelines (WCAG), Version 1.0)

The web has advanced dramatically since the early days of creating HTML homepages. The initial sets of design guidelines developed for the web are currently being rethought, extended, and adapted to take into account the extensive developments. For example, a newer version of the WCAG is being developed to take into account the diversity of new technologies.

CASE STUDY 6.1
Blind users experience the Internet

In this case study Vanessa Evers and Hans Hillen from the University of Amsterdam discuss the redesign of a website's information architecture to provide audio navigation to assist blind users. This study is motivated by previous studies on Internet use with blind participants, which indicate that even with the help of screen readers such as JAWS and Window-eyes, blind users have more difficulty accessing the information on the Internet than seeing users. However, findings by Berry (1999) and others also suggest that blind users feel empowered by the Internet because it allows them to access information even though the linear nature of navigation caused blind users to spend considerable time browsing a web page before deciding on their next action.

Three research questions were asked in this study. First, how do blind users navigate websites? The findings show that blind users adopt different approaches during navigation to compensate for lack of accessibility in web design. Successful blind user navigation depends mostly on the availability of clear landmarks to guide navigation. The second question addressed the problems blind users encounter. Blind users were hindered most by cognitive overload and incomprehensible descriptions. The third question asked whether a high-level representation of a website's information architecture with audio navigation would support blind users well. The findings indicate that blind users do not become aware of the structure of entire websites but focus on identifying landmarks. Once these landmarks have been identified, and a goal achieved, the mental image the user has constructed of the website is limited to the landmarks to reach a particular goal.

The screen below is from a Dutch website, `http://www.aktiebenin.nl`, which was used in this research for navigation tasks by one of the blind participants.

Activity 6.7

Look at the `Nike.com` website and describe the kind of interface used. How does it contravene the design principles outlined by Veen? Does it matter? What kind of user experience is it providing for? What was your experience of engaging with it?

Comment

The Nike website is designed to be more like a cinematic experience and uses rich multimedia elements, e.g. videos, sounds, music, animations, and interactivity. Branding is central. In this sense, it is a far cry from a conventional website and contravenes many of the usability guidelines. Specifically, the site has been designed to entice the visitor to enter the virtual store and watch high quality and innovative movies about Nike Lab, Nike classes, etc. Various multimedia interactivities are embedded into the site to help the viewer move to other parts of the site, e.g. clicking on parts of an image or animation. Screen widgets are also provided, e.g. menus, 'skip over,' and 'next' buttons. It is easy to become immersed in the experience and forget it is a commercial store. It is also easy to get lost and to not know: Where am I? What's here? Where can I go? But this is precisely what Nike wants their visitors to do and enjoy the experience.

Speech interfaces

A speech interface (or voice user interface, VUI) is where a person talks with a system that has a spoken language application, like a train timetable, a travel planner, or a phone service. It is most commonly used for inquiring about specific information, e.g. flight times, or to perform a transaction, e.g. buy a ticket or 'top-up' a cell phone account. It is a specific form of natural language interaction that is based on the interaction type of conversing (see Chapter 2), where users speak and listen to an interface (rather than type at or write on the screen). There are many commercially available speech-based applications that are now being used by corporations, especially for offering their services over the phone. Speech technology has also advanced applications that can be used by people with disabilities, including speech recognition wordprocessors, page scanners, web readers, and speech recognition software for operating home control systems, including lights, TV, stereo, and other home appliances.

Technically, speech interfaces have come of age, being much more sophisticated and accurate than the first generation of speech systems in the early 1990s, which earned a reputation for *mis*hearing all too often what a person said (see cartoon). Actors are increasingly used to record the messages and prompts provided—that are much friendlier, more convincing, and pleasant than the artificially sounding synthesized speech that was typically used in the early systems.

One of the most popular uses of speech interfaces (or SR—speech recognition—as it is now known in the business) is for call routing, where companies use an automated speech system to enable users to reach one of their services. Many companies are replacing the frustrating and unwieldy touchtone technology for navigating their services (which was restricted to 10 numbers and the # and * symbols) with the use of caller-led speech. Callers can now state their needs in their own words (rather than pressing a series of arbitrary numbers), for example, "I'm having problems with my voice mail," and in response are automatically forwarded to the appropriate service (Cohen *et al.*, 2004).

In human conversations we often interrupt each other, especially if we know what we want, rather than waiting for someone to go through a series of options. For example, at a restaurant we may stop the waitress in mid-flow when describing the specials if we know what we want rather then let her go through the whole list. Similarly, speech technology has been designed with a feature called 'barge-in' that allows callers to interrupt a system message and provide their request or response before the message has finished playing. This can be very useful if the system has numerous options for the caller to choose from and the chooser knows already what he wants.

There are several ways a dialog can be structured. The most common is a directed dialog where the system is in control of the conversation, asking specific questions and requiring specific responses, similar to filling in a form (Cohen *et al.*, 2004):

System: Which city do you want to fly to?

Caller: London

System: Which airport, Gatwick, Heathrow, Luton, Stansted or City?

Caller: Gatwick

System: What day do you want to depart?

Caller: Monday week

System: Is that Monday 5th May?

Caller: Yes

Other systems are more flexible, allowing the user to take more initiative and specify more information in one sentence, e.g. "I'd like to go to Paris next Monday for two weeks." The problem with this approach is that there is more chance of error, since the caller might assume that the system can follow all of her needs in one go as a real travel agent can, e.g. "I'd like to go to Paris next Monday for two weeks and would like the cheapest possible flight, preferably leaving Stansted airport and definitely no stop-overs ..." The list is simply too long and would overwhelm the system's parser. Carefully guided prompts can be used to get callers back on track and help them speak appropriately, e.g. "Sorry I did not get all that. Did you say you wanted to fly next Monday?"

Research and design issues

Key research questions are concerned with how to design systems that can recognize speech and keep the conversation on track. Some researchers focus on making it appear natural (i.e. like human conversations) while others are concerned more with how to help people navigate efficiently through a menu system, by enabling them to recover easily from errors (their own or the system's), be able to escape and go back to the main menu (cf. to the undo button of a GUI), and to guide those who are vague or ambiguous in their requests for information or services using prompts. The type of voice actor, e.g. male, female, neutral, or dialect and form of pronunciation are also topics of research. Do people prefer to listen to and are more patient with a female or male voice? What about one that is jolly versus serious?

An extensive set of guidelines by Cohen *et al.* (2004) discusses the pros and cons of using different techniques for structuring the dialog and managing the flow of voice interactions, the different ways of expressing errors, and the use of conversational etiquette.

Pen, gesture, and touchscreen interfaces

Researchers and developers have experimented with a number of input devices besides the standard keyboard/mouse combination to investigate whether more fluid and natural (i.e. physical actions that humans are very familiar with, such as gesturing) ways of interacting with information at the interface can be supported. These forms of input are designed to enable people to write, draw, select, and move objects at an interface using pen-based, e.g. lightpens or styluses, gesture-based, and touch-based methods—all of which are well-honed skills that are developed from childhood. Camera capture and computer vision techniques are used to 'read' and 'recognize' people's arm and hand gestures at a whiteboard or in a room. Touchscreens have also been designed to enable users to use their fingertips to select options at an interface and move objects around an interactive tabletop surface. Using different forms of input can enable more degrees of freedom for user expression and object manipulation; for example, two hands can be used together to stretch and move objects on a touchscreen surface, similar to how both hands are used to stretch an elastic band or scoop together a set of objects. These kinds of two-handed actions are much easier and more natural to do by moving two fingers and thumbs simultaneously at an interface than when using a single pointing device like a mouse.

A successful commercial application that uses gesture interaction is Sony's EyeToy, which is a motion-sensitive camera that sits on top of a TV monitor and plugs into the back of a Sony Playstation. It can be used to play various video games. The camera films the player when standing in front of the TV, projecting her image onto the screen, making her the central character of the video game. The game can be played by anyone, regardless of age or computer experience, simply by moving her legs, arms, head, or any part of the body (see Figure 6.22).

Figure 6.22 *Sony's EyeToy: the image of the player is projected onto the TV screen as part of the game, showing her using her arms and elbows to interact with the virtual game*

Pen-based input is commonly used with PDAs and large displays, instead of mouse or keyboard input, for selecting items and supporting freehand sketching. One of the problems with using pens instead of mice, however, is that the flow of interaction can be more easily interrupted. In particular, it can be more difficult to select menu options that appear along one side of the screen or that require a virtual keyboard to be opened—especially if more than one person is working at the whiteboard. Users often have to move their arms long distances and sometimes have to ask others to get out of the way so they can select a command (or ask them to do it). To overcome these usability problems, Guimbretiere *et al.* (2001) developed novel pen-based techniques for very large wall displays that enable users to move more fluidly between writing, annotating, and sketching content while at the same time performing commands. Thus, instead of having to walk over to a part of the wall to select a command from a fixed menu, users can open up a context-sensitive menu (called a FlowMenu) wherever they were interacting with information at the wall by simply pressing a button on top of the pen to change modes. Using pen-based gestures for PDAs presents different kinds of usability problems. It can sometimes be difficult to see options on the screen because a user's hand can occlude part of it when gesturing. The benefit of using gestures, such as swiping and stroking, is that it supports more direct interaction. These can be mapped onto specific kinds of operations where repeated actions are necessary, e.g. zooming in and out functions for map-based applications.

Being able to recognize a person's handwriting and convert it into text has been a driving goal for pen-based systems. Early research in this area began with Apple Computer's pioneering handheld device, called the Newton (1993). Since then, the newer generation of Tablet PCs have significantly advanced handwriting recognition and conversion techniques, using an active digitizer as part of a special screen that enables users to write directly on the surface, which is then converted into standard typeface text. The process known as 'digital ink' is available for controlling many Windows applications. One of its other uses is to allow users to quickly and easily annotate existing documents, by hand, such as spreadsheets, presentations, and diagrams (see Figure 6.23)—in a similar way to how they would do it using paper-based versions.

A number of gesture-based systems have been developed for controlling home appliances, moving images around a wall, and various forms of entertainment, e.g. interactive games. Early systems used computer vision techniques to detect certain gesture types (e.g. location of hand, movement of arm) that were then converted into system commands. More recent systems have begun using sensor technologies that detect touch, bend, and speed of movement of the hand and/or arm. Figure 6.24 shows Ubi-Finger (Tsukada and Yasumara, 2002), which enables users to point at an object, e.g. a switch, using his/her index finger and then control it by an appropriate gesture, e.g. pushing the finger down as if flicking on the switch. Sign language applications have also been built to enable hearing-impaired people to communicate with others without needing a sign language interpreter (Sagawa *et al.*, 1997).

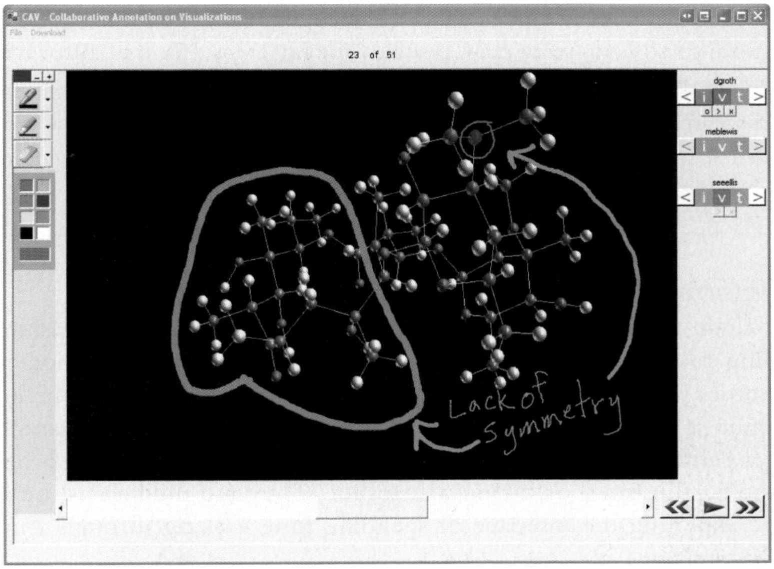

Figure 6.23 *Microsoft's digital ink in action showing how it can be used to annotate a scientific diagram*

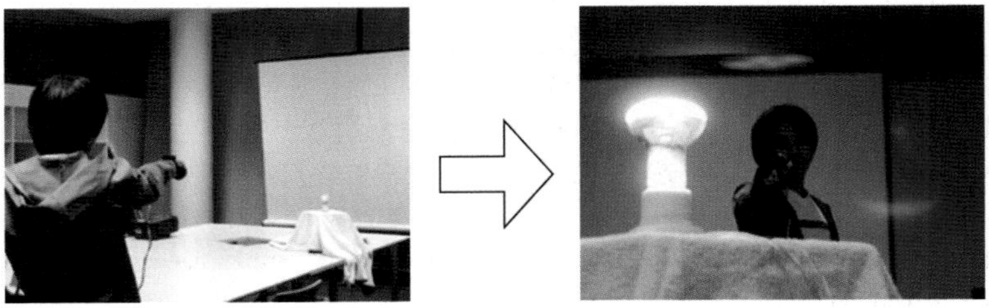

Figure 6.24 *Ubi-Finger: pointing at a light and making the appropriate gesture causes the light to come on*

Research and design issues

Much of the research on gestures has been concerned with the different roles they play in communication, devising methods to distinguish between them for users controlling objects (Baudel and Beaudouin-Lafon, 1993) and how people use gestures to communicate with one another in remote and collocated settings, e.g. Bekker *et al.* (1995); Gutwin and Penner (2002).

A key design concern, when using pens, gestures, and fingers as a form of input, is to consider how a computer system recognizes and delineates the user's gestures. In particular, how does it determine the start and end point of a hand movement and how does it know the difference between a deictic gesture (a deliberate pointing movement) and hand waving (an unconscious gesticulation) that is used to emphasize what is being said verbally?

Appliance interfaces

Appliances include machines for the home, public place, or car (e.g. washing machines, VCRs, vending machines, remotes, photocopiers, printers and navigation systems) and personal consumer products (e.g. MP3 player, digital clock and digital camera). What they have in common is that most people using them will be trying to get something specific done in a short period of time, such as putting the washing on, watching a program, buying a ticket, changing the time, or taking a snapshot. They are unlikely to be interested in spending time exploring the interface or spending time looking through a manual to see how to use the appliance.

Research and design issues

Cooper and Reiman (2003) suggest that appliance interfaces require the designer to view them as transient interfaces, where the interaction is short. All too often, however, designers provide full-screen control panels or an unnecessary array of physical buttons that serve to frustrate and confuse the user and where only a few in a structured way would be much better. Here, the two fundamental design principles of simplicity and visibility are paramount. Status information, such as what the photocopier is doing, what the ticket machine is doing, and how much longer the washing is going to take should be provided in a very simple form and at a prominent place on the interface. A key design question is: as soft displays, e.g. LCD and touchscreens, increasingly become part of an appliance interface, what are the trade-offs with replacing the traditional physical controls, e.g. dials, buttons, knobs?

Activity 6.8

Look at the controls on your toaster (or the one in Figure 6.25 if you don't have one nearby) and describe what each does. Consider how these might be replaced

with an LCD screen. What would be gained and lost from changing the interface in this way?

Comment

Standard toasters have two main controls, the lever to press down to start the toasting and a knob to set the amount of time for the toasting. Many now come with a small eject button intended to be pressed if the toast starts to burn. In Figure 6.25 it is to the left of the timer knob. Some also come with a range of settings for different ways of toasting (e.g. one side, frozen), selected by moving a dial or pressing buttons.

To design the controls to appear on an LCD screen would enable more information and options to be provided, e.g. only toast one slice, keep the toast warm, automatically pop up when the toast is burning. It would also allow precise timing of the toasting in minutes and seconds. However, as has happened with the design evolution of microwave ovens, a downside is that it is likely to increase the complexity of what previously was a set of logical and very simple actions—placing something in an oven and heating it up—making it more difficult to use.

Figure 6.25 *A typical toaster with basic physical controls*

6.3.3 2000s interfaces

In this section we cover mobile, multimodal, shareable, tangible, augmented and mixed reality, wearable and robotic interfaces.

Mobile interfaces

Mobile interfaces are designed for devices that are handheld and intended to be used while on the move, such as PDAs and cell phones. Technologies that support mobile interfaces have become ubiquitous in the last decade. Nearly everyone owns a cell phone, while applications running on PDAs have greatly expanded, and are now commonly used in restaurants to take orders, car rentals to check in car returns, supermarkets for checking stock, on the streets for multi-user gaming, and in education to support life-long learning. There are also smartphones, like the Blackberry device, that is essentially a combined cell phone and PDA (see Figure 6.26).

Figure 6.26 The Blackberry 7780 mobile device. Instead of a keypad it has a set of tiny buttons that is a simple version of the QWERTY keyboard

A number of physical controls have been developed for mobile interfaces, including a roller wheel positioned on the side of a phone (see Figure 6.26) and a rocker dial (see Figure 6.27) positioned on the front of a device—both designed for rapid scrolling of menus; the up/down 'lips' on the face of the phone, and two-way directional keypads and four-way navigational pads that encircle a central push button for selecting options (see Figure 6.27). Softkeys (which usually appear at the bottom of a screen) and silk-screened buttons (icons that are printed on or under the glass of a touchscreen display) have been designed for frequently selected options and for mode changing. New physical controls have also been effectively deployed for specialized handsets, such as those developed for blind users (see Box 6.5).

The preference for and ability to use these control devices varies, depending on the dexterity and commitment of the user when using the handheld device. For example, some people find the rocker device fiddly to use for the fine control required for scrolling through menus on a small screen. Conversely, others are able to master them and find them much faster to use compared with using up and down arrow buttons that have to be pressed each time a menu option is moved through.

Box 6.4
Braille-based cell phones

Cell phones have been developed for blind users that have braille-based interfaces. For example, the ALVA MPO model has eight braille input keys, synthetic speech

output, and a 20-cell refreshable braille display (see Figure 6.27). At each end of the phone are rocker devices that are used to control (i) the speech and (ii) cursor movements and to navigate through menus. To increase or decrease the volume of the speech the user quickly presses the rocker up and down. ■

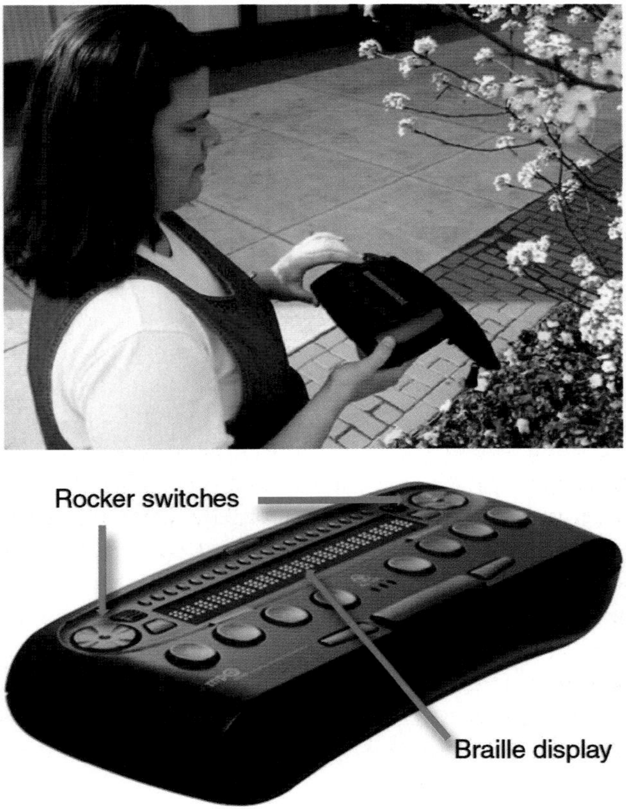

Figure 6.27 *The ALVA MPO model 5500 with refreshable braille display*

Numeric keypads on cell phones have been doubled up as text entry keypads, requiring much thumb activity to send a text message. Many users actually find this a pleasurable challenge rather than a frustrating form of input. To compensate, attachable keyboards and virtual keyboards have been developed. But these require a surface to be used on—restricting their use to when a person is stationary. Predictive text was invented to enable users to select from a range of words and messages offered by the system, having only typed in two or three letters. More recently, faster and more flexible forms of text input have been enabled through the provision of tiny QWERTY keys that appear as hard buttons on cell phones, selected using both thumbs, or soft keyboards that pop up on PDA screens—pecked at with a stylus (see Figure 6.25 showing the Blackberry 7780 and Figure 6.28 of the Treo).

Figure 6.28 *Cell phone interface for the Treo 650 and the Vodaphone Simple Sagem VS1*

Activity 6.9

Which mobile interface in Figure 6.28 do you prefer and which do you think your grandparents would prefer?

Comment

Different types of phones are now being designed for specific user groups, who vary in age, disability, culture, level of experience, and technophobia. The Treo 650 smartphone (shown on the left), with miniature QWERTY keyboard embedded beneath a large color screen and a 4-way navigation pad, is intended largely for those who are experienced technology users, while the Vodaphone Simple

Sagem VS1 shown on the right has been designed for technophobes, providing a simple numerical keypad, simple scrolling menu interface, and only three dedicated buttons for quick access to main screen, messages, and contacts.

Research and design issues

Despite advances made for inputting text, mobile devices still fall short of the speed and efficiency that are attainable using the standard PC QWERTY keyboard/mouse combination. The thought of having to type this book using a mobile interface fills us with horror—it would be like trying to pour a vat of treacle through a funnel. Mobile interfaces can also be quite tricky and cumbersome to use—when compared to the fully-blown GUI—especially for those with poor manual dexterity or 'fat' fingers, making selecting tiny buttons on a cell phone or PDA appear cumbersome (Siek *et al.*, 2005).

Hence, one of the key concerns for mobile interfaces is designing for the small screen real estate and limited control space available. Designers have to think very carefully about what type of dedicated controls (i.e. hard wired) to use, where to place them on the device, and then how to map them onto the software. Applications designed for mobile interfaces need to take into account that navigation will be restricted and text input entry slow, whether using pen or keypad input. To this end, web browsers have been developed that allow users to view and navigate through slimmed-down, largely menu-based and hyperlink-based websites while data entry applications have been customized to have smaller number of menus and predictive form fill-ins. Microsoft has also scaled down the Windows environment (Windows CE) to enable familiar PC applications to run on mobile devices and for data to be readily transferred from them to other computers. Guidelines are now available that focus specifically on how to design graphical and text-based interfaces for mobile devices (e.g. Weiss, 2002). Case study 11.2 presented on our website describes how prototyping can be used for developing mobile interfaces.

Multimodal interfaces

Similar to multimedia interfaces, *multimodal* interfaces follow the 'more is more' principle to provide more enriched and complex user experiences (Bouchet and Nigay, 2004). They do so by multiplying the way information is experienced and controlled at the interface through using different modalities, i.e. touch, sight, sound, speech. Interface techniques that have been combined for this purpose include speech and gesture, eye-gaze and gesture, and pen input and speech (Oviatt *et al.*, 2004).

An assumption is that multimodal interfaces can support more flexible, efficient, and expressive means of human–computer interaction, that are more akin to the multimodal experiences humans experience in the physical world (Oviatt, 2002). Different input/outputs may be used at the same time, e.g. using voice commands and gestures simultaneously to move through a virtual environment, or alternately, e.g. using speech commands followed by gesturing. The most common combination of technologies used for multimodal interfaces are computer speech and vision processing (Deng and Huang, 2004).

So far, there have not been any commercial applications developed that can be said to have multimodal interfaces. Speech-based mobile devices that allow people to interact with information via a combination of speech and touch are beginning to emerge. An example is SpeechWork's multimodal interface developed for one of Ford's SUV concept cars, which allows the occupants to operate on-board systems including entertainment, navigation, cell phone, and climate control by speech. However, despite the claims, in reality, it is just a speech-based system with a built-in touchscreen. It is likely to be some time before commercial applications begin to appear that combine gesture, eye movement, and speech recognition systems, for controlling and managing computer systems.

Box 6.5
Attentive environments

Attentive environments are interfaces that turn user control on its head. Instead of the user controlling the computer, the computer is programmed to attend to the user's needs through anticipating what the user wants to do. In this sense the mode of interaction is much more implicit: where the computer system responds to the user's expressions and gestures. Camera-based techniques are used to detect the user's current state and needs. For example, cameras can detect where people are looking on a screen and decide what to display accordingly. Or they could detect that someone is looking at a TV and turn it on.

But how desirable and usable are such systems? Ultimately, for such systems to be acceptable by people they need to be very accurate and unobtrusive. In particular, they need to be able to determine when someone wants to do something at a given time, e.g. make a phone call or which websites they want to visit at particular times. IBM's Blue Eyes project addressed these concerns by developing a range of computational devices that used non-obtrusive sensing technology, including videos and microphones, to track and identify users' actions and provide feedback via a simple face interface (see Figure 6.29). This information

Figure 6.29 The face of IBM's Blue Eyes

was analyzed with respect to where users were looking, what they were doing, their gestures, and their facial expressions. It was then coded in terms of the user's physical, emotional, or informational state and was then used to determine what information they would like. For example, a Blue Eyes-enabled computer could become active when a user first walks into a room, firing up any new email messages that have arrived. If the user shakes his or her head, it would be interpreted by the computer as "I don't want to read them," and instead it would show a listing of appointments for that day.

Research and design issues

Multimodal systems rely on recognizing aspects of a user's behavior—be it her handwriting, speech, gestures, eye movements, or other body movements. In many ways, this is much harder to accomplish and calibrate than single modality systems that are programmed to recognize one aspect of a user's behavior. The most researched modes of interaction are speech, gesture, and eye gaze tracking. A key research question is what is actually gained from combining different input and outputs and whether talking and gesturing as humans do with other humans is a natural way of interacting with a computer (see Chapter 4). Multimodal design guidelines are beginning to appear, e.g. Reeves (2004).

Shareable interfaces

Shareable interfaces are designed for more than one person to use. Unlike PCs, laptops, and mobile devices—that are aimed at single users—they typically provide multiple inputs and sometimes allow simultaneous input by collocated groups. These include large wall displays, e.g. SmartBoards (see Figure 6.30a), where people use their own pens or gestures, and interactive tabletops, where small groups can interact with information being displayed on the surface using their fingertips. Examples of interactive tabletops include Mitsubishi's DiamondTouch (Dietz and Leigh, 2001, see Figure 6.30b) and Sony's Smartskin (Rekimoto, 2002). The DiamondTouch tabletop is unique in that it can distinguish between different users touching the surface concurrently. An array of antennae is embedded in the touch surface and each one transmits a unique signal. Each user has their own receiver embedded in a mat they stand on or a chair they sit on. When a user touches the tabletop very small signals are sent through the user's body to their receiver, which identifies which antenna has been touched and sends this to the computer. Multiple users can touch the screen at the same time.

An advantage of shareable interfaces is that they provide a large interactional space that can support flexible group working, enabling groups to create content together at the same time. Compared with a collocated group trying to work around a single-user PC—where typically one person takes control of the mouse, making it more difficult for others to take part—large displays have the potential of being interacted with by multiple users, who can point to and touch the information being displayed, while simultaneously viewing the interactions and having the same shared point of reference (Rogers *et al.*, 2004).

Shareable interfaces have also been designed to literally become part of the furniture. For example, Philips (2004) have designed the Café Table that displays a selection of contextually relevant content for the local community. Customers can drink coffee together while browsing digital content by placing physical tokens in a ceramic bowl placed in the center of the table. The Drift Table (see Figure 6.31), developed as part of Equator's Curious Home project, enables people to very slowly float over the countryside in the comfort of their own sitting room (Gaver *et al.*, 2004). Objects placed on the table, e.g. books and mugs, control which part of the countryside is scrolled over, which can be viewed through the hole in the table via aerial photographs. Adding more objects to one side enables faster motion while adding more weight generally causes the view to 'descend,' zooming in on the landscape below.

Roomware has designed a number of integrated interactive furniture pieces, including walls, table, and chairs, that can be networked and positioned together so they can be used in unison to augment and complement existing ways of collaborating (see Figure 6.32). An underlying premise is that the natural way people work together is by congregating around tables, huddling and chatting besides walls and around tables. The Roomware furniture has been designed to augment these kinds of informal collaborative activities, allowing people to engage with digital content that is pervasively embedded at these different locations.

(a)

(b)

Figure 6.30 *(a) A smartboard in use during a meeting and (b) Mitsubishi's interactive tabletop interface, where collocated users can interact simultaneously with digital content using their fingertips*

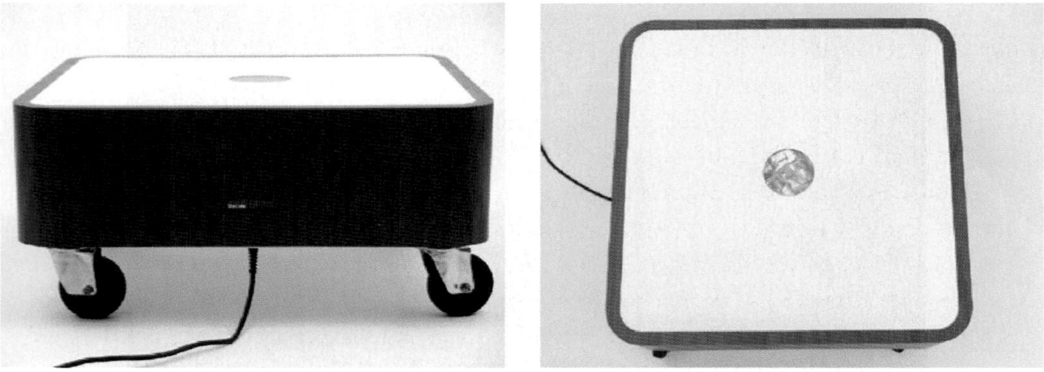

Figure 6.31 *The Drift Table: side and aerial view*

Figure 6.32 *Roomware furniture*

Research and design issues

Early research on shareable interfaces focused largely on interactional issues, such as how to support electronically-based handwriting and drawing, and the selecting and moving of objects around the display (Elrord *et al.*, 1992). The PARCTAB system (Schilit *et al.*, 1993) investigated how information could be communicated between palm-sized, A4-sized, and whiteboard-sized displays using shared software tools, such as Tivoli (Rønby-Pedersen *et al.*, 1993). Since then, there has been continuing interest in developing more fluid and direct styles of interaction with large displays, both wall-based and tabletop, involving freehand and pen-based gestures, e.g. Chen *et al.* (2003); Guimbretiere *et al.* (2001).

A key research issue is whether shareable surfaces can facilitate new and enhanced forms of collaborative interaction compared with what is possible when groups work together using their own devices, like laptops, PCs, and PDAs. One likely benefit is easier sharing and more equitable participation. For example, tabletops have been designed to support more effective joint browsing, sharing, and manipulation of images during decision-making and design activities (Chen *et al.*, 2002; Rogers *et al.*, 2004). Core design concerns include whether size, orientation, and shape of the display have an effect on collaboration. User studies have shown that horizontal surfaces compared with vertical ones support more turn-taking and collaborative working in collocated groups (Rogers and Lindley, 2004), while providing larger-sized tabletops does not improve group working but encourages more division of labor (Ryall *et al.*, 2004). The need for both personal and shared spaces has been investigated to see how best to enable users to move between working on their own and together as a group. Several researchers have begun to investigate the pros and cons of providing users with complementary devices, such as PDAs, that are used in conjunction with the shareable surface. Design guidelines are also beginning to appear for different kinds of shareable surfaces, including tabletops and wall displays, e.g. Scott *et al.*, (2003); O'Hara *et al.* (2004).

Tangible interfaces

Tangible interfaces are a type of sensor-based interaction, where physical objects, e.g. bricks, balls, and cubes, are coupled with digital representations (Ishii and Ullmer, 1987). When a person manipulates the physical object/s, it is detected by a computer system via the sensing mechanism embedded in the physical object, causing a digital effect to occur, such as a sound, animation, or vibration (Fishkin, 2004). The digital effects can take place in a number of media and places, or they can be embedded in the physical object itself. For example, Zuckerman and Resnick's (2005) Flow Blocks (see Figure 6.33) depict changing numbers and lights that are embedded in the blocks, depending on how they are connected together. The flow blocks are designed to simulate real-life dynamic behavior and react when arranged in certain sequences. Another type of tangible interface is where a physical model, e.g. a puck, a piece of clay, or a model, is superimposed on a digital desktop. Moving one of the physical pieces around the tabletop causes digital events to take place on the tabletop. For example, a tangible interface, called Urp, was built to facilitate urban planning; miniature physical models of buildings could be moved around on the tabletop

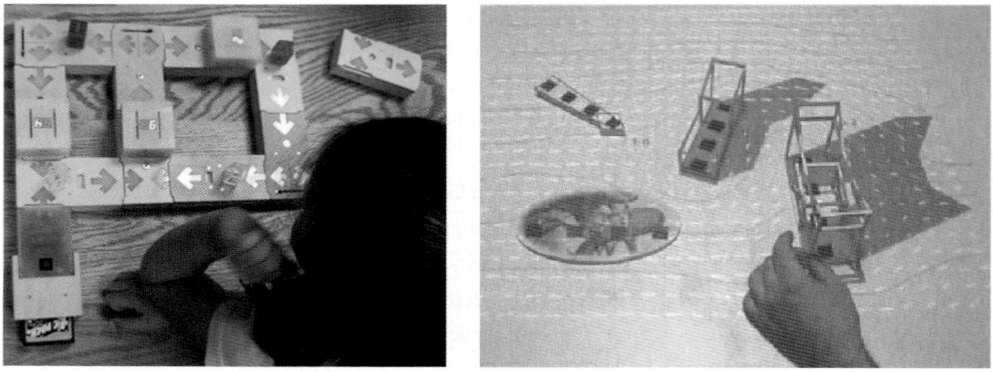

(a) (b)

Figure 6.33 *(a) Tangible Flow Blocks designed to enable children to create structures in time that behave like patterns in life, e.g. chain reactions (Zuckerman and Resnick, 2005); (b) Urp, a tangible interface for urban planning where digital shadows are cast from physical models that are moved around the table surface to show how they vary with different lighting conditions (Ullmar and Ishii, 1999)*

and used in combination with tokens for wind and shadow-generating tools, causing digital shadows surrounding them to change over time and visualizations of airflow to vary (see Figure 6.33b).

Much of the work on tangibles has been exploratory to date. Many different systems have been built, with the aim of encouraging learning, design activities, playfulness, and collaboration. These include planning tools for landscape and urban planning, e.g. Honnecker (2005); Jakob *et al.* (2002); Underkoffler and Ishii (1999). The technologies that have been used to create tangibles include RFID tags (see Chapter 2) embedded in physical objects and digital tabletops that sense the movements of objects and subsequently provide visualizations surrounding the physical objects.

What are the benefits of using tangible interfaces compared with other interfaces, like GUI, gesture, or pen-based? One advantage is that physical objects and digital representations can be positioned, combined, and explored in creative ways, enabling dynamic information to be presented in different ways. Physical objects can also be held in both hands and combined and manipulated in ways not possible using other interfaces. This allows for more than one person to explore the interface together and for objects to be placed on top of each other, beside each other, and inside each other; the different configurations encourage different ways of representing and exploring a problem space. In so doing, people are able to see and understand situations differently, which can lead to greater insight, learning, and problem-solving than with other kinds of interfaces (Marshall *et al.*, 2003).

Research and design issues

Because tangible interfaces are quite different from GUI-based ones, researchers have developed alternative conceptual frameworks that identify their novel and specific features, e.g. Fishkin (2004); Ullmar *et al.* (2005). Rather than think of designing a dialog between user and system, the notion of designing couplings between action and effect is often used (see Box 2.5). A key design concern is what kind of coupling to use between the physical action and effect. This includes determining where the digital feedback is provided in relation to the physical artifact that has been manipulated: for example, should it appear on top of the object (as in Figure 6.33a), beside it, or some other place. The type and placement of the digital media will depend to a large extent on the purpose of using a tangible interface. If it is to support learning then an explicit mapping between action and effect is critical. In contrast, if it is for entertainment purposes, e.g. playing music, storytelling, then it may be better to design them to be more implicit and unexpected. Another key design question is what kind of physical artifact to use to enable the user to carry out an activity in a natural way. Bricks, cubes, and other component sets are most commonly used because of their flexibility and simplicity, enabling people to hold them in both hands and to construct new structures that can be easily added to or changed. Post-it notes and cardboard tokens can also be used for placing material onto a surface that is transformed or attached to digital content, e.g. Klemmer *et al.* (2001); Rogers *et al.* (2006).

As the area of research is in its infancy, design guidance has so far been in terms of implications for using tangible interfaces for specific applications, e.g. learning (O'Malley and Stanton Fraser, 2005).

Augmented and mixed reality interfaces

Other ways that the physical and digital worlds have been bridged include augmented reality, where virtual representations are superimposed on physical devices and objects and mixed reality, where views of the real world are combined with views of a virtual environment (Drascic and Milgram, 1996). One of the precursors of this work was the Digital Desk (Wellner, 1993). Physical office tools, like books, documents, and paper, were integrated with virtual representations, using projectors and video cameras. Both virtual and real documents were combined.

Augmented reality has mostly been experimented with in medicine, where virtual objects, e.g. X-rays and scans, are overlaid on part of a patient's body to aid the physician's understanding of what is being examined or operated on. Figure 6.34(a) shows an overlayed three-dimensional model of a fetus on top of the mother's womb. The aim was to give the doctor 'X-ray vision,' enabling her to 'see inside' the womb (Bajura *et al.*, 1992). Augmented reality has also been used for commercial applications to aid controllers and operators in rapid decision-making. One example is air traffic control, where controllers are provided with dynamic information about the aircraft in their section, that is overlaid on a video screen showing the real planes, etc., landing, taking off, and taxiing. The additional information enables the controllers to easily identify planes that are difficult to make out—especially useful in poor weather conditions. Similarly, head up displays (HUDs) are increasingly being used in military and civil planes to aid pilots when landing during poor weather conditions. A HUD provides electronic directional markers on a fold-down display that appears directly in the field of view of the pilot (see Figure 6.34(b)). Instructions for building or repairing complex equipment, such as photocopiers and car engines, have also been designed to replace paper-based manuals, where drawings are superimposed upon the machinery itself, telling the mechanic what to do and where to do it.

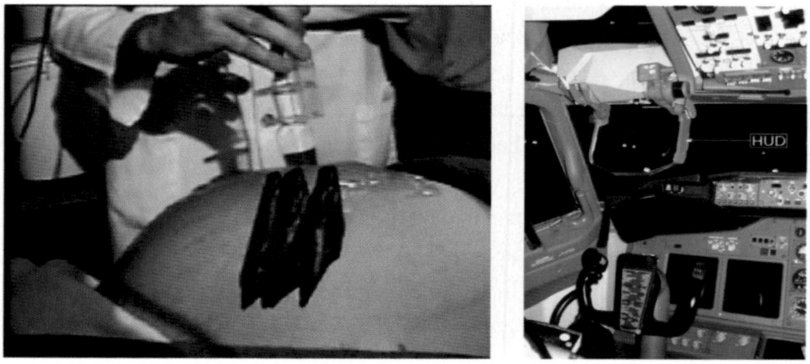

(a) (b)

***Figure 6.34** Two augmented reality applications showing (a) a scanned womb overlaying a pregnant woman's stomach and (b) a head up display (HUD) used in airline cockpits to provide directions to aid flying during poor weather conditions*

Another approach is to augment everyday graphical representations, e.g. maps, with additional dynamic information. Such augmentations can complement the properties of the printed information in that they enable the user to interact with geographically embedded information in novel ways. An illustrative application is the augmentation of paper-based maps with photographs and video footage to enable emergency workers to assess the effects of flooding and traffic (Reitmayr *et al.*, 2005). A camera mounted above the map tracks the map's locations on the surface while a projector augments the maps with projected information from overhead. Figure 6.35 shows areas of flooding that have been superimposed on a map of Cambridge (UK), together with images of the city center captured by cameras.

Figure 6.35 *An augmented map showing the flooded areas at high water level overlayed on the paper map. The PDA device is used to interact with entities referenced on the map*

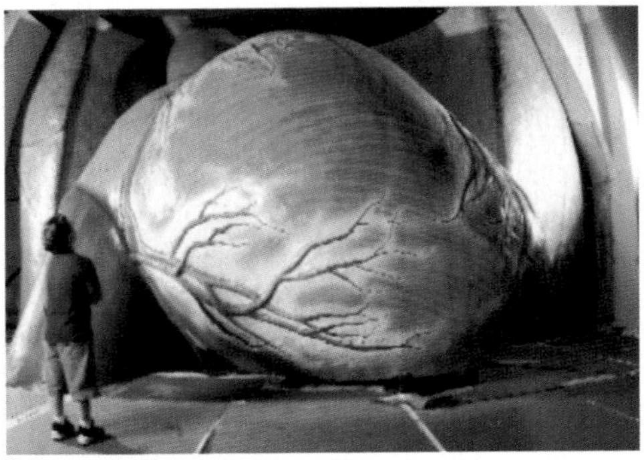

Figure 6.36 *The Healthy Heart interactive installation at the Franklin Institute*

Box 6.6
Larger than life: interactive installations and mixed reality games

Museums and galleries have begun to develop large interactive installations that enable visitors to have a user experience with a difference. Instead of entering a 3D virtual world they enter a 3D physical world that has been augmented with digital interfaces. An example is the healthy heart exhibition at the Franklin Institute in Philadelphia (see Figure 6.36), where a giant size model of the heart can be walked through presenting 3D sounds, lights, and video. One part is an eight-foot-long 'crawl through arteries' device that enables children to pretend they are blood cells navigating through clear and clogged arteries.

Another form of interactive experience is mixed reality games that are played in a blend of physical and virtual worlds using novel interfaces. For example, the Hunting of the Snark adventure game (Rogers *et al.*, 2002) was designed as a series of interlinked mixed reality spaces intended to provoke children's imagination and creativity. Young children (8–10 years old) were given the task of finding as much as they could about an elusive creature called the Snark, by interacting with it in various physical/digital spaces. For example, in the Snooper room they hunt for hidden virtual tokens that can then be transformed into physical counterparts that enable them to interact with the Snark. The physical tokens are used to feed the Snark at a well (see Figure 6.37) fly with it in the air, or walk with it in a cave. The game was inspired by Lewis Carroll's poem in which a group of adventurers describe their encounters with a never really found

Figure 6.37 *Two girls interacting with The Hunting of the Snark mixed reality game: the Snark registers disgust having been fed a physical token of an onion*

fantasy creature. Similarly, in the Snark game, the Snark never shows itself in its entirety, only revealing aspects of itself, e.g. its likes/dislikes, personality, and so forth, depending on what the children do in the different spaces. ■

Research and design issues

A key research concern when designing mixed reality environments and augmented reality is what form the digital augmentation should take and when and where it should appear in the physical environment (Rogers *et al.*, 2005). The information needs to stand out but not distract the person from his ongoing activity in the physical world. For example, ambient sounds need to be designed to be distinct from naturally occurring sounds so that they draw a person's attention without distracting him and then allow him to return to what he was doing. Information that is superimposed on the physical world, e.g. digital information overlaying video footage of a runway to identify vehicles and planes, needs to be simple and easy to align with the real-world objects.

Augmented reality and mixed reality are emerging technologies. Hence, there aren't comprehensive sets of guidelines available. Hix and Gabbard (2002) provide some initial pointers but it must be stressed that the selection of appropriate technologies and interfaces may vary across different application areas. Designing for playful learning experiences is very different from designing for military or medical applications. Ambiguity and uncertainty may be exploited to good effect in mixed reality games but could be disastrous in the latter categories. The type of technology will also determine what guidance will be of relevance. A guideline for the use of an optical see-through display, e.g. shutter glasses or head-mounted display, may not be relevant for a video see-through display. Likewise, a guideline for a mobile augmented reality solution may not be relevant for a fixed display application.

Wearable interfaces

One of the first developments in wearable computing was head- and eyewear-mounted cameras that enabled the wearer to record what he saw and access digital information while on the move (Mann, 1997). Imagine being at a party and being able to access the website of a person whom you have just met, while or after talking to her to find out more about her. The possibility of having instant information before one's very own eyes that is contextually relevant to an ongoing activity and that can be viewed surreptitiously (i.e. without having to physically pull out a device like a PDA) is very appealing.

Since the early experimental days of wearable computing (see Figure 6.38) there have been many innovations and inventions. New display technologies and wireless communication presents many opportunities for thinking about how to embed such technologies on people in the clothes they wear. Jewelry, head-mounted caps, glasses, shoes, and jackets have all been experimented with to provide the user with a means of interacting with digital information while on the move in the physical world. Applications that have been developed include automatic diaries that keep users up-to-date on what is happening and what they need to do throughout the day, and tour guides that inform users of relevant information as they walk through an exhibition and other public places (Rhodes *et al.*, 1999).

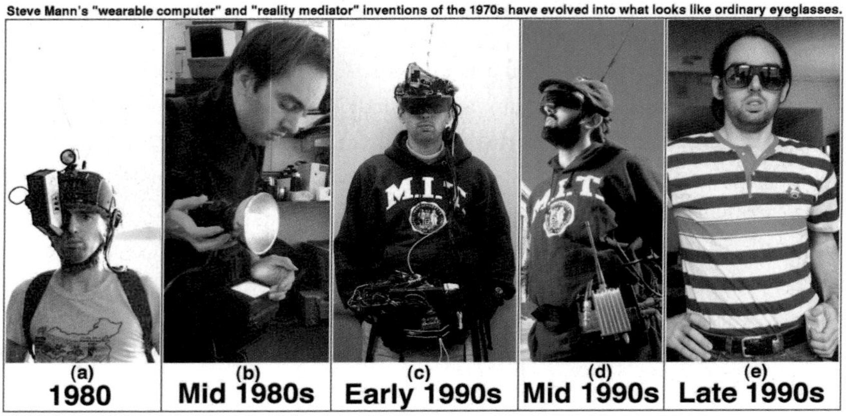

Figure 6.38 *The evolution of wearable computing*

Recent wearable developments include eye glasses that have an embedded miniature LCD display on which digital content from DVD players and cell phones can be seen by the wearer but no one else and a ski jacket with integrated MP3 player controls that enable wearers to simply touch a button on their arm with their glove to change a track (Techstyle News, 2005).

Smart fabrics have also begun to be developed that enable people to monitor their health. For example, The Wearable Health Care System (WEALTHY) prototype contains tiny sensors that can collect information about the wearer's respiration, core and surface skin temperature, position (standing or lying down), and movement. The garment can take advantage of the cell phone network to communicate data with remote sensors, thanks to the integration of a miniaturized GPRS transmitter. The SensVest (see Figure 6.39) has similarly been designed to measure heart rate, body temperature, and movement during sports activities (Knight *et al.*, 2005).

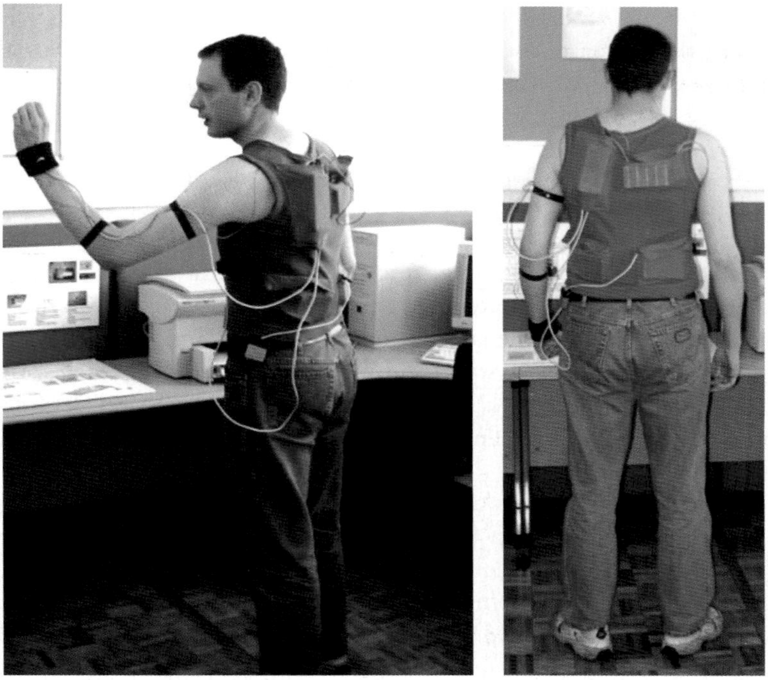

Figure 6.39 *The SensVest prototype developed as part of the EU Lab of Tomorrow project, designed to monitor people playing sports*

Research and design issues

A core design concern—that is specific to wearable interfaces—is comfort. Users need to feel comfortable wearing clothing that is embedded with technology. It needs to be light, small, not get in the way, fashionable, and preferably hidden in the clothing. Another related issue is hygiene—is it possible to wash or clean the clothing once worn? How easy is it to remove the electronic gadgetry and replace it? Where are the batteries going to be placed and how long is their life time? A key usability concern is how does the user control the devices that are embedded in his clothing—is touch, speech, or more conventional buttons and dials preferable?

For health monitoring wearable systems, there is also the trust issue of how reliable and accurate the information being monitored is. A wearer (or carer) does not want to be given false information about the wearer's heart rate or other bodily function, causing undue stress. Two other major concerns are social acceptance and privacy. Is it acceptable in our society for people to be looking up other's details while talking to them and how do people feel about others recording their intimate conversations without necessarily knowing this is happening and what happens subsequently to that information?

Robotic interfaces

Robots have been with us for some time, most notably as characters in science fiction movies, but also playing an important role as part of manufacturing assembly lines, as remote investigators of hazardous locations, e.g. nuclear power stations and bomb disposal, and as search and rescue helpers in disasters, e.g. fires, or far away places, e.g. Mars. Console interfaces have been developed to enable humans to control and navigate robots in remote terrains, using a combination of joysticks and keyboard controls together with camera and sensor-based interactions (Baker *et al.*, 2004). The focus has been on designing interfaces that enable users to effectively steer and move a remote robot with the aid of live video and dynamic maps.

More recently, domestic robots are appearing in our homes as helpers. For example, robots are being developed to help the elderly and disabled with certain activities, such as picking up objects and cooking meals. Pet robots, in the guise of human companions, are being commercialized, having first become a big hit in Japan. A new generation of sociable robots has also been envisioned that will work collaboratively with humans, and communicate and socialize with them—as if they were our peers (Breazeal, 2005).

Several research teams have taken the 'cute and cuddly' approach to designing robots, signalling to humans that the robots are more pet-like than human-like. For example, Mitsubishi has developed Mel the penguin (Sidner *et al.*, 2005) whose role is to host events while the Japanese inventor Takanori Shibata has developed Paro, a baby harp seal, whose role is to be a companion (see Figure 6.40). Sensors have been embedded in the pet robots enabling them to detect certain human behaviors and respond accordingly. For example,

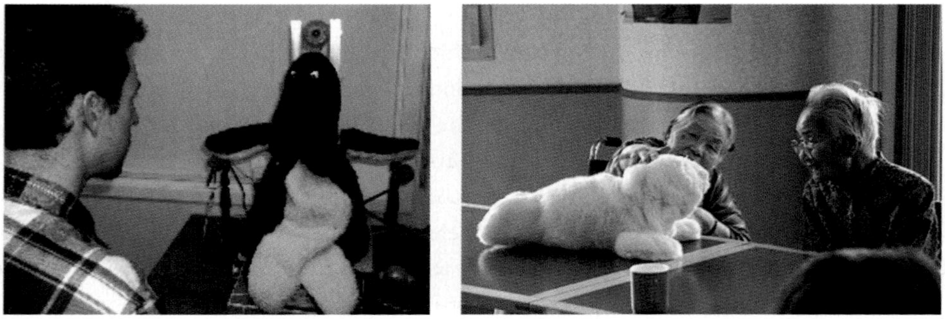

***Figure 6.40** Mel, the penguin robot, designed to host activities and Japan's Paro, an interactive seal, designed as a companion, primarily for the elderly and sick children*

they can open, close, and move their eyes, giggle, and raise their flippers. The robots afford cuddling and talking to—as if they were pets or animals. The appeal of pet robots is thought to be partially due to their therapeutic qualities, being able to reduce stress and loneliness among the elderly and infirm.

Research and design issues

One of the key research questions to consider is what is special about a robotic interface and how it differs from other interfaces we have discussed. Robots are typically designed to exhibit behaviors, e.g. making facial expressions, walking, or talking, that humans will consider to be human or animal-like, e.g. happy, angry, intelligent. While this form of attribution also occurs for PC-based agent interfaces (see Chapter 2), having a physical embodiment—as robots do—can make people suspend their disbelief even more, viewing the robots as pets or humans. This raises the moral question as to whether such anthropomorphism should be encouraged. Should robots be designed to be as human-like as possible, looking like us with human features, e.g. eyes and mouth, behaving like us, communicating like us, and emotionally responding like us (cf. the animated agents approach advocated in Chapter 5)? Or should they be designed to look like robots and behave like robots, e.g. vacuum robots, that serve a clearly defined purpose? Likewise, should the interaction be designed to enable people to interact with the robot as if it was another human being, e.g. talking, gesturing, holding its hand and smiling at it, or should the interaction be designed to be more like human-computer interaction, e.g. pressing buttons, knobs, and dials to issue commands?

For many people, the cute pet approach to robotic interfaces seems preferable to one that aims to design them to be more like fully-fledged human beings. Humans know where they stand with pets and are less likely to be unnerved by them and, paradoxically, are more likely to suspend their disbelief in the companionship they provide.

6.4 Which interface?

In this chapter we have given an overview of the diversity of interfaces that is now available or currently being researched. There are many opportunities to design for user experiences that are a far cry from those originally developed using command-based interfaces in the 1980s. An obvious question this raises is: "but which one and how do you design it?" For the most part, it is likely that much system development will continue for the PC platform, using advanced GUIs, in the form of multimedia, web-based interfaces, and virtual 3D environments. However, in the last decade, mobile interfaces have come of age and many developers are now creating interfaces and software toolkits for designers to enable people to access the web, communicate with one another, interact with information, and use slimmed-down applications while on the move. Speech interfaces are also being used much more for a variety of commercial services. Appliance and vehicle interfaces have become an important area of interaction design. Shareable and tangible interfaces are moving beyond blue-sky research projects and it is likely that soon they will become present in various shapes and forms in our homes, schools, public places, and workplaces. There are many exciting challenges ahead when it comes to the development of multimodal and robotic interfaces.

In many contexts, the requirements for the user experience that have been identified during the design process (to be discussed in Chapter 10) will determine what kind of interface might be appropriate and what features to include. For example, if a health care application is being developed to enable patients to monitor their dietary intake, then a mobile PDA-like device—that has the ability to scan barcodes and take pictures of food items that can be compared with a database—would seem a good interface to use, enabling mobility, effective object recognition, and ease of use. If the goal is to design a work environment to support collocated group decision-making activities then a shareable interactive surface would be a good choice. More novel kinds of interfaces, e.g. mixed reality and tangibles, have so far been primarily experimented with for play and learning experiences, although as the technology develops we are likely to see them being used to support other kinds of work-related and home-based activities.

Given that there are now many alternatives for the same activities it raises the question as to which is preferable for a given task or activity. For example, is multimedia better than tangible interfaces for learning? Is speech as effective as a command-based interface? Is a multimodal interface more effective than a monomodal interface? Will wearable interfaces be better than mobile interfaces for helping people find information in foreign cities? Are virtual environments the ultimate interface for playing games? Or will mixed reality or tangible environments prove to be more challenging and captivating? Will shareable interfaces, such as interactive furniture, be better at supporting communication and collaboration compared with using networked desktop PCs? And so forth. These questions have yet to be answered. In practice, which interface is most appropriate, most useful, most efficient, most engaging, most supportive, etc., will depend on the interplay of a number of factors, including reliability, social acceptability, privacy, ethical and location concerns.

Assignment

In Activity 6.6 we asked you to compare the experience of playing the game of Snake on a PC with a cell phone. For this assignment, we want you to consider the pros and cons of playing the same game using different interfaces. Select three interfaces, other than the GUI and mobile ones, e.g. tangible, wearable, and shareable, and describe how the game could be redesigned for each of these, taking into account the user group being targeted. For example, the tangible game could be designed for young children, the wearable interface for young adults, and the shareable interface for old people.

1. Go through the research and design issues for each interface and consider whether they are relevant for the game setting and what issues they raise. For the wearable interface, issues to do with comfort and hygiene are important when designing the game.
2. Describe a hypothetical scenario of how the game would be played for each of the three interfaces.
3. Consider specific design issues that will need to be addressed. For example, for the shareable surface would it be best to have a tabletop or a wall-based surface? How will the users interact with the snake for each of the different interfaces; by using a pen, fingertips, or other input device? Is it best to have a representation of a snake for each player or one they take turns to play with? If multiple snakes are used, what will happen if one person tries to move another person's snake? Would you add any other rules? And so on.
4. Compare the pros and cons of designing the Snake game using the three different interfaces with respect to how it is played on the cell phone and the PC.

Summary

This chapter has given an overview of the range of interfaces that can now be designed for user experiences. It has described the paradigmatic developments in interaction design and the issues and research questions that these have led to. In so doing, it has highlighted the opportunities and challenges that lie ahead for designers and researchers who are experimenting with and developing innovative interfaces. It has also explicated some of the assumptions behind the benefits of different interfaces—some that are supported, others that are still unsubstantiated. It has presented a number of interaction techniques and structures that are particularly suited (or not) for a given interface type. It has also discussed the dilemmas facing designers when using a particular kind of interface, e.g. abstract versus realism, menu selection versus free-form text input, human-like versus non-human-like. Finally, it has presented pointers to specific design guidelines and exemplary systems that have been designed using a given interface.

Key points

- Many interfaces have emerged post the WIMP/GUI era, including speech, wearable, mobile, and tangible.
- Many new design and research questions need to be considered to guide designers when deciding which of the new generation of interfaces to use and what features to include.
- Web interfaces are becoming more like multimedia-based interfaces.
- An important concern that underlies the design of any kind of interface is how information is represented to the user (be it speech, multimedia, virtual reality, augmented reality, etc.), so that she can make sense of it with respect to her ongoing activity, e.g. playing a game, shopping online or interacting with a pet robot.

Further Reading

Many of the best books on designing interfaces have been developed for the practitioner market. They are often written in a humorous and highly accessible way, replete with cartoons, worldly prescriptions, and figures. They also use modern fonts that make the text very appealing. We recommend:

COOPER, A. and REIMAN, R. (2003) *About Face 2.0: The Essentials of Interaction Design*. John Wiley & Sons. This is a top favorite among designers and has become an international bestseller. It is provocative, laden with humor, has a very personable style while also having extensive coverage of everything you wanted and needed to know about GUI interface design.

JOHNSON, J. (2000) *GUI Bloopers*. Morgan Kaufmann. This has become a classic, covering all the dos and don'ts of software development and web design—full of the author's amusing anecdotes and other designer howlers.

MULLET, K. and SANO, D. (1995) *Designing Visual Interfaces*. SunSoft Press. While a bit dated now, the principles of visual design that are espoused and well illustrated are as relevant to advanced graphical interfaces as they were to the design of early GUI interfaces.
For web interfaces, we suggest:

KRUG, S. (2000) *Don't Make Me Think*. Circle.com Library. This is a very accessible and pithy book.

VEEN, J. (2001) *The Art and Science of Web Design*. New Riders. This has an in-depth coverage of design principles.

SPOOL, J., SCANLON, T., SCHROEDER, W., SNYDER, C. and DEANGELO, T. (1997) *Web Site Usability*. Morgan Kaufmann. While a bit dated, this book provides an extensive evaluation study of different websites, highlighting what works and does not work on different websites.
For speech interfaces:

COHEN, M., GIANGOLA, J. and BALOGH, J. (2004) *Voice User Interface Design*. Addison Wesley. The authors are well known in the field of speech technology and their latest book is a good introduction to the area, covering in equal measure technical and interaction design issues. The accompanying website has a number of speech interfaces that can be played, to bring the examples alive.
For appliance interfaces:

BERGMAN, E. (ed.) (2000) *Information Appliances and Beyond*. Morgann Kaufmann.

7

7.1 Introduction

This chapter presents some techniques for data gathering which are commonly used in interaction design activities. In particular, data gathering is a central part of identifying needs and establishing requirements, and of evaluation.

Within the requirements activity, the purpose of data gathering is to collect sufficient, accurate, and relevant data so that a set of stable requirements can be produced. Within evaluation, data gathering is needed in order to capture users' reactions and performance with a system or prototype.

In this chapter we introduce three main techniques for gathering data. (Some additional techniques relevant only to evaluation are discussed in Chapters 12–15.) In the next chapter we discuss how to analyze and interpret the data collected. These three techniques are interviews, questionnaires, and observation. Interviews involve an interviewer asking one or more interviewees a set of questions which may be highly structured or unstructured; interviews are usually synchronous and are often face-to-face, but they don't have to be. Questionnaires are a series of questions designed to be answered asynchronously, i.e. without the presence of the investigator; these may be on paper, or online. Observation may be direct or indirect. Direct observation involves spending time with individuals observing activity as it happens. Indirect observation involves making a record of the user's activity as it happens to be studied at a later date. All three techniques may be used to collect qualitative or quantitative data.

Although this is a small set of basic techniques, they are flexible and can be combined and extended in many ways. Indeed it is important not to focus on just one data gathering technique but to use them flexibly and in combination so as to avoid biases which are inherent in any one approach.

The way in which each technique is used varies depending on the interaction design activity being undertaken. More detailed descriptions of how the different techniques are used within specific activities of the lifecycle are given in later chapters (Chapter 10 for requirements, and Chapters 12–15 for evaluation). Here we give some basic practical information about each technique.

The main aims of the chapter are to:

- **Discuss how to plan and run a successful data gathering program.**
- **Enable you to plan and run an interview.**
- **Enable you to design a simple questionnaire.**
- **Enable you to plan and execute an observation.**

7

Data gathering

7.2 Four key issues

Data gathering sessions need to be planned and executed carefully. Specific issues relating to the three data gathering techniques are discussed in the following sections, but first we consider four key issues that require attention for a data gathering session to be successful. These four issues are goal setting, the relationship between the data collector and the data provider, triangulation, and pilot studies.

7.2.1 Setting goals

The main reason for gathering data at all is to glean information about something. For example, you might want to understand how technology fits into normal family life, or you might want to identify which of two icons representing a 'send email' action is easier to use, or you might want to find out whether the redesign you are planning for a hand-held meter reader is along the right lines. There are many different reasons for gathering data, and before beginning it is important to identify specific goals for the particular study. The goals that are set will influence the nature of the data gathering sessions, the data gathering techniques to be used, and also the analysis to be performed. Once the goals have been set, then you can concentrate on what data to look for and what to do with it once it is gathered.

The goals may be expressed more or less formally, e.g. using some structured or even mathematical format, or using a simple description such as the ones in the previous paragraph, but whatever the format they should be clear and concise. In interaction design it is more usual to express the goals of data gathering more informally.

7.2.2 The relationship with participants

One significant aspect of any data gathering is the relationship between the person (people) doing the gathering and the person (people) providing the data. Making sure that this relationship is clear and professional will help to clarify the nature of the study. One way in which this can be achieved is to ask participants to sign an informed consent form. The details of this form will vary, but it usually asks the participant to confirm that the purpose of the data gathering and how the data will be used has been explained to them and that they are happy to continue. It also often includes a statement that the participant may withdraw at any time, and that in this case none of their data will be used in the study.

It is common practice in many countries to use an informed consent form when running evaluation sessions, particularly where the participants are members of the public, or are volunteers in a research project (see Box 13.2). In this case, the informed consent form is intended to protect the interests of both the data gatherer and the data provider. The gatherer wants to know that the data she collects can be used in her analysis, presented to interested parties, and published in reports (as appropriate). The data provider wants reassurance that the information he gives will not be used for other purposes, or in any context that would be detrimental to him. This is especially true when disadvantaged groups such as disabled people or children are being interviewed. In the case of children, using an informed consent form reassures parents that their children will not be asked threatening, inappropriate, or embarrassing questions, or be asked to look at disturbing or violent images. In these cases, parents are asked to sign the form.

However, this kind of consent is not generally required when collecting data for the requirements activity where a contract already exists in some form between the data collector and the data provider. For example, consider the situation where a consultant is hired to gather data from a company in order to establish a set of requirements for a new interactive system to support timesheet entry. The employees of this company would be the users of the system, and the consultant would therefore expect to have access to the employees to gather data about the timesheet activity. In addition, the company would expect its employees to cooperate in this exercise. In this case, there is already a contract in place which covers the data gathering activity, and therefore an informed consent form is less likely to be required. As with most ethical issues, the important thing is to consider the situation carefully and make a judgment based on the specific circumstances.

Similarly, incentives for completing a questionnaire might be needed in some circumstances because there is no clear and direct advantage to the respondents, but in other circumstances, respondents may see it as part of their job to complete the questionnaire. For example, if the questionnaires form part of the requirements activity for a new mobile sales application to support sales executives, then it is likely that sales executives will complete a questionnaire about their job if they are told that the new device will impact on their day-to-day lives. In this case, the motivation for providing the required information is clear. However, if you are collecting data to understand how appealing is a new interactive website for school children, different incentives would be appropriate. Here, the advantage for the individuals to complete a questionnaire is not so obvious.

7.2.3 Triangulation

Triangulation is a strategy that entails using more than one data gathering technique to tackle a goal, or using more than one data analysis approach on the same set of data. For example, using observation to understand the context of task performance, interviews to target specific user groups, questionnaires to reach a wider population, and focus groups to build a consensus view is one example of a triangulated data gathering program. Triangulation provides different perspectives and corroboration of findings across techniques, thus leading to more rigorous and defensible findings.

7.2.4 Pilot studies

A pilot study is a small trial run of the main study. The aim is to make sure that the proposed method is viable before embarking on the real study. Data gathering participants can be (and usually are) very unpredictable, even when a lot of time and effort has been spent carefully planning the data gathering session. Plans for a data gathering session should be tested by doing a pilot study before launching into the main study. For example, the equipment and instructions that are to be used can be checked, the questions for an interview or in a questionnaire can be tested for clarity, and an experimental procedure can be confirmed as viable. Potential problems can be identified in advance so that they can be corrected. Distributing 500 questionnaires and then being told that two of the questions were very confusing wastes time, annoys participants, and is an expensive error that could have been avoided by doing a pilot study.

If it is difficult to find people to participate or if access to participants is limited, colleagues or peers can be asked to comment. Getting comments from peers is quick and inexpensive and can be a substitute for a pilot study. It is important to note that anyone involved in a pilot study cannot be involved in the main study. Why? Because they will know more about the study and this can distort the results.

Box 7.1
Data versus information

There is an important difference between data and information. Data is a collection of facts from which conclusions may be drawn, while information is the result of analyzing and interpreting the data. For example, you might want to know whether a particular screen structure has improved the user's understanding of the application. In this case, the data collected might include the time it takes for a set of users to perform a particular task, the users' comments regarding their use of the application, biometric data about the users' heart rate while using the application, and so on. At this stage, all you have is data. In order to get to information, the data needs to be analyzed and the results interpreted. That information can then feed into the requirements or evaluation activity. ■

7.3 Data recording

The most common forms of data recording are taking notes, audio recording, taking photographs, and video recording. These may be used individually or in combination. For example, an interview may be audio recorded and then to help the interviewer in later analysis, a photograph of the interviewee may be taken. Digital still cameras are especially useful as they provide an image immediately and the photograph can be re-taken if necessary. Digicams are also increasingly used to record data directly onto a disk that can be downloaded into a computer package such as iMovie or Premiere. This is much easier, cheaper and more convenient than using analog video cassettes. Questionnaires are usually completed by the participant and therefore are 'self-documenting', i.e. no further data recording needs to be arranged. Participant diary studies are also self-documenting, and interaction logs are usually generated automatically (see Section 7.6.3 for more details). Which data recording techniques are used will depend on the context, time available, and the sensitivity of the situation; the choice of data recording techniques will have an impact on how intrusive the data gathering will be. In most settings, audio taping, photographs, and notes will be sufficient. In others it is essential to collect video data so as to record in detail the intricacies of the activity and its context. Three common data recording approaches are discussed below.

7.3.1 Notes plus still camera

Taking notes is the least technical way of recording data, but it can be difficult and tiring to write and listen or observe at the same time. It is easy to lose concentration, biases creep in, handwriting can be difficult to decipher, and the speed of writing is limited. Working with another person solves some of these problems and provides another perspective. Handwritten notes are flexible in the field or in an interview situation but must be transcribed. However, this transcription can be the first step in data analysis, as the data will be reviewed and organized. A laptop computer can be used instead of handwritten notes, but it is more obtrusive and cumbersome. Even a PDA with keyboard can be distracting because of the key clicks; paper and pen seem to be almost invisible. Digital images or documents can be easily collected (provided permission has been given). If a record of other images and documents is needed, photographs or sketches can be captured.

7.3.2 Audio plus still camera

Audio recording can be a useful alternative to note taking and is less intrusive than video. In observation, it allows observers to be more mobile than with video cameras, and so is very flexible. In an interview, it allows the interviewer to pay more attention to the interviewee rather than be trying to take notes as well as listen. Transcribing a lot of audio data is time-consuming, which may seem daunting, but it isn't always necessary to transcribe all of it—often only sections are needed. Many studies do not need a great level of detail, and instead, recordings are used as a reminder and as a source of anecdotes for reports. It is also surprising how evocative it can be to hear audio recordings of people or places where you have been. If using audio recording as the main or only technique then it is important that the quality is good. It should be checked before the sessions starts.

As above, audio recording can be supplemented with still photographs of artifacts, events, and the environment.

7.3.3 Video

Video has the advantage of capturing both visual and audio data but can be intrusive.

A further problem with using video is that attention becomes focused on what is seen through the lens. It is easy to miss other things going on outside of the camera view. When recording in noisy conditions, e.g. in rooms with fans or air conditioning running or outside when it is windy, the sound can easily get muffled. It is also important to check that the tape is rewound to the beginning, the camera switched on and the lens cap removed.

Activity 7.1

Imagine you are a consultant who is employed to help develop a new computerized garden planning tool to be used by amateur and professional garden designers. Your goal is to find out how garden designers use an early prototype as they walk around their clients' gardens sketching design ideas, taking notes, and asking the clients about what they like and how they and their families use the garden. What are the advantages and disadvantages of the three approaches to data recording discussed above, in this environment?

Comment

Handwritten notes do not require specialist equipment. They are unobtrusive and very flexible but difficult to do while walking around a garden. If it starts to rain there is no equipment to get wet, but notes may get soggy and difficult to read (and write!). Video captures more information, e.g. the landscape, where the designers are looking, sketches, comments, etc., but it is more intrusive and you must hold the camera. It is also difficult if it starts to rain. Audio is a good compromise, but integrating sketches and other artifacts later can be more burdensome.

Garden planning is a highly visual, aesthetic activity, so it would be important to supplement note taking and audio recording with a still camera.

"This is a video of you two watching the video of our vacation."

Such simple checks can go a long way to ensure valuable data is recorded—it is easy to accidentally overlook something in the stress of the moment.

In Table 7.1 we summarize the key features, advantages, and drawbacks of these three combinations of data recording techniques.

Criterion	Notes plus camera	Audio plus camera	Video
Equipment	**Paper, pencil, and camera are easily available.**	**Inexpensive, hand-held recorder with a good microphone. Headset useful for easy transcription.**	**More expensive. Editing, mixing, and analysis equipment needed.**
Flexibility of use	**Very flexible. Unobtrusive.**	**Flexible. Relatively unobtrusive.**	**Needs positioning and focusing camera lens. Obtrusive.**
Completeness of data	**Only get what note taker thinks is important and can record in the time available. Problem with inexperienced evaluators.**	**Can obtain complete audio recording but visual data is missing. Notes, photographs, sketches can augment recording but need coordinating with the recording.**	**Most complete method of data collecting, especially if more than one camera used, but coordination of video material is needed.**
Disturbance to users	**Very low.**	**Low, but microphone needs to be positioned.**	**Medium. Camera needs to be positioned on tripod. Care needed to avoid Hawthorne effect.**
Reliability of data	**May be low. Relies on humans making a good record and knowing what to record.**	**High but external noise, e.g. fans in computers, can muffle what is said.**	**Can be high but depends on what camera is focused on.**
Analysis	**Relatively easy to transcribe. Rich descriptions can be produced. Transcribing data can be onerous or a useful first step in data analysis.**	**Critical discussions can be identified. Transcription needed for detailed analysis. Permanent original record that can be revisited.**	**Critical incidents can be identified and tagged. Software tools are available for detailed analysis. Permanent original record that can be revisited.**

Table 7.1 *Comparison of the three main approaches to data recording*

7.4 Interviews

Interviews can be thought of as a "conversation with a purpose" (Kahn and Cannell, 1957). How like an ordinary conversation the interview can be depends on the type of interview method used. There are four main types of interviews: open-ended or unstructured, structured, semi-structured, and group interviews (Fontana and Frey, 1994). The first three types are named according to how much control the interviewer imposes on the conversation by following a predetermined set of questions. The fourth involves a small group guided by a facilitator.

The most appropriate approach to interviewing depends on the purpose of the interview, the questions to be addressed, and the stage in the lifecycle. For example, if the goal is to gain first impressions about how users react to a new design idea, such as an interactive sign, then an informal, open-ended interview is often the best approach. But if the goal is to get feedback about a particular design feature, such as the layout of a new web browser, then a structured interview or questionnaire is often better. This is because the goals and questions are more specific in the latter case.

7.4.1 Unstructured interviews

Open-ended or unstructured interviews are at one end of a spectrum of how much control the interviewer has over the interview process. They are exploratory and are more like conversations around a particular topic; they often go into considerable depth. Questions posed by the interviewer are open, meaning that there is no particular expectation about the format or content of answers. Open questions are used when you want to explore the range of opinions. For example, "What are the advantages of using a PDA?" Here, the interviewee is free to answer as fully or as briefly as she wishes and both interviewer and interviewee can steer the interview.

It is always advisable to have a plan of the main topics to be covered. Going into an interview without an agenda should not be confused with being open to new information and ideas (see Section 7.4.5 on planning an interview). One of the skills necessary for conducting an unstructured interview is getting the balance right between making sure that answers to relevant questions are obtained, while at the same time being prepared to follow new lines of enquiry that were not anticipated.

A benefit of unstructured interviews is that they generate rich data, i.e. data that gives a deep understanding of the topic, and is often interrelated and complex. In addition, interviewees may mention issues that the interviewer has not considered. But this benefit often comes at a cost. A lot of unstructured data is generated, which can be very time-consuming to analyze. It is also impossible to replicate the process, since each interview takes on its own format. Typically in interaction design, there is no attempt to analyze every interview in detail. Instead, the interviewer makes notes or audio records the session and then goes back through the data afterwards to note the main issues of interest.

7.4.2 Structured interviews

In structured interviews, the interviewer asks predetermined questions similar to those in a questionnaire (see Section 7.5). Structured interviews are useful when the goals are clearly understood and specific questions can be identified. To work best, the questions need to be short and clearly worded. Typically the questions are closed, which means that they require an answer from a predetermined set of alternatives. Responses may involve selecting from a set of options that are read aloud or presented on paper. Closed questions work well for fast interviews when the range of answers is known, and where people tend to be in a rush. In a structured interview the same questions are used with each participant so the study is standardized. Example questions for a structured interview might be:

- Which of the following websites do you visit most frequently: `amazon.com`, `barnes&noble.com`, `google.com`, `msn.com`?
- How often do you visit this website: every day, once a week, once a month, less often than once a month?
- Have you ever purchased anything online?
- If so, how often do you purchase items online: every day, once a week, once a month, less often than once a month?

Questions in a structured interview should be worded exactly the same for each participant, and they should be asked in the same order.

7.4.3 Semi-structured interviews

Semi-structured interviews combine features of structured and unstructured interviews and use both closed and open questions. For consistency the interviewer has a basic script for guidance, so that the same topics are covered with each interviewee. The interviewer starts with preplanned questions and then probes the interviewee to say more until no new relevant information is forthcoming. For example:

> ***Which music websites do you visit most frequently?*** **<Answer mentions several but stresses that she prefers `hottestmusic.com`>**
> ***Why?*** **<Answer says that she likes the site layout>**
> ***Tell me more about the site layout*** **<Silence, followed by an answer describing the site's navigation>**
> ***Anything else that you like about the site?*** **<Answer describes the animations>**
> ***Thanks. Are there any other reasons for visiting this site so often that you haven't mentioned?***

It is important not to pre-empt an answer by phrasing a question to suggest that a particular answer is expected. For example, "You seemed to like this use of color . . . " assumes that this is the case and will probably encourage the interviewee to answer that this is true so as not to offend the interviewer. Children are particularly prone to behave in this way (see Box 7.2 for more on data gathering with children). The body language of the interviewer, for example, whether she is smiling, scowling, looking disapproving, etc., can have a strong influence on whether the interviewee will agree with a question.

Also, the interviewer needs to give the person time to speak and not move on too quickly. Probes are a device for getting more information, especially neutral probes such as, "Do you want to tell me anything else?" The person may also be prompted to help her along. For example, if the interviewee is talking about a computer interface but has forgotten the name of a key menu item, the interviewer might want to remind her so that the interview can proceed productively. Semi-structured interviews are intended to be broadly replicable, so probing and prompting should aim to help the interview along without introducing bias.

Box 7.2
Working with children

Children think and react to situations differently from adults. Sitting a 4-year-old child down in a formal interview situation is unlikely to result in anything other than a wall of silence. If children are to be included in your data gathering sessions, then child-friendly methods are needed to make them feel at ease. For example, for very young children of pre-reading or early reading age, data gathering sessions need to rely on images and chat rather than written instructions or questionnaires. Read *et al.* (2002) have developed a set of 'smileys' for use with children in interviews (see Figure 7.1). Recording children can also pose its problems. Children have a tendency to perform in front of a camera unless it is placed behind them, or they are given time to get used to it being there.

The appropriate techniques to involve children also depend on the goal of the data gathering session. For example, Guha *et al.* (2005) work with children as technology design partners. They focus on children between the ages of 7 and 11. They have found that unexpected innovations result when working as an intergenerational team, i.e. adults and children working together. The method they use is

Figure 7.1 A smileyometer gauge for early readers

called cooperative inquiry (Druin, 2002) and is based on Scandinavian cooperative design practices, participatory design, and contextual inquiry. There are many techniques that can be used in cooperative inquiry, such as sketching ideas and brainstorming, and observational research which has been modified to accommodate children's preferred approaches. For example, the 'mixing ideas' approach (which also works with younger children, aged 5 to 6) involves three stages. In the first stage, each child generates ideas, working one-on-one with an adult. In the second stage, groups of adults and children mix together these ideas. Finally, all the ideas are mixed together to form 'the big idea' (see Figure 7.2). Guha *et al.* report that they are currently developing technology reflecting concepts that emerged from the big idea.

In contrast, the Equator project investigated the use of new technology to encourage children to record and analyse aspects of the environment themselves. For example, Rogers *et al.* (2005) report on the Ambient Wood project which investigates the use of ubiquitous computing and mobile technologies to support learning. In this work, a learning experience was designed that encourages children to explore habitats in a woodland area. Each child was given a PDA and a mobile probing tool (see Figure 7.3), which can collect data about their environment and send it to a central server. The data collected by the probe could be collated and displayed on the PDA in real time, thus giving immediate feedback to their investigations. The child's position was also monitored and location-specific data sent to their PDA, e.g. when they walked past a specific plant. ■

Figure 7.2 *The cut up and remixed big idea*

Figure 7.3 *The probing tool in the Ambient Wood project being used to collect light and moisture readings*

7.4.4 Focus groups

Interviews are often conducted with one interviewer and one interviewee, but it is also common to interview people in groups. One form of group interview that is frequently used in marketing, political campaigning, and social sciences research is the focus group. Normally 3 to 10 people are involved, and the discussion is led by a trained facilitator. Participants are selected to provide a representative sample of the target population. For example, in an evaluation of a university website, a group of administrators, faculty, and students may form three separate focus groups because they use the web for different purposes. In requirements activities it is quite common to hold a focus group in order to identify conflicts in terminology or expectations from different sections within one department or organization.

The benefit of a focus group is that it allows diverse or sensitive issues to be raised that might otherwise be missed. The method assumes that individuals develop opinions within a social context by talking with others. Often questions posed to focus groups seem deceptively simple, but the idea is to enable people to put forward their own opinions in a supportive environment. A preset agenda is developed to guide the discussion, but there is sufficient flexibility for the facilitator to follow unanticipated issues as they are raised. The facilitator guides and prompts discussion and skillfully encourages quiet people to participate and stops verbose ones from dominating the discussion. The discussion is usually recorded for later analysis and participants may be invited to explain their comments more fully.

Focus groups can be very relaxed affairs (for the participants that is), but in some product development methods, focus groups have become very formalized. For example, the workshops (as they are called) used in Joint Application Development (Wood and Silver, 1995) are very structured, and their contents and participants are all prescribed.

Dilemma
What they say and what they do

What users say isn't always what they do. When asked a question, people sometimes give the answers that they think show them in the best light, or they may just forget what happened or how long they spent on a particular activity. For example, in a study looking at the maintenance of telecommunications software, the developers stated that most of their job involved reading documentation, but when observed, it was found that searching and looking at source code was much more common than looking at documentation (Singer *et al.*, 1997).

So, can interviewers believe all the responses they get? Are the respondents giving 'the truth' or are they simply giving the answers that they think the interviewer wants to hear?

It isn't possible to avoid this behavior, but it is important to be aware of it and to reduce such biases by choosing questions carefully, getting a large number of participants or by using a combination of data gathering techniques.

7.4.5 Planning and conducting an interview

Planning an interview involves developing the set of questions or topics to be covered, collating any documentation to give to the interviewee (such as consent form or project description), checking that recording equipment works in advance and you know how to use it, working out the structure of the interview, and organizing a suitable time and place.

Developing interview questions

Questions for an interview may be open or closed. Open questions are best suited to interviews where the goal of the session is exploratory. Closed questions require a list of possible answers, and so they can only be used in a situation where you know the possible answers in advance. It is always possible to have an 'other' option, but the ideal is that this option is not used very often. So whether you choose to use open questions or closed questions depends on what is already known about the topic of investigation and the goal of the interview. An unstructured interview will usually consist entirely of open questions, while a structured interview will usually consist of closed questions. A semi-structured interview may use a combination of both types.

The following guidelines for developing interview questions are derived from Robson (2002):

- Compound sentences can be confusing, so split them into two separate questions. For example, instead of, "How do you like this cell phone compared with previous ones that you have owned?" Say, "How do you like this cell phone?" "Have you owned other cell phones?" If so, "How did you like it?" This is easier for the interviewee to respond to and easier for the interviewer to record.
- Interviewees may not understand jargon or complex language and might be too embarrassed to admit it, so explain them in layman's terms.
- Try to keep questions neutral, for example, if you ask "Why do you like this style of interaction?" this question assumes that the person does like it and will discourage some interviewees from stating their real feelings.

Activity 7.2

Cybelle (see Figure 7.4) is an intelligent agent that guides visitors to the website Agentland which contains information about intelligent agents. As Cybelle is an intelligent agent, it is not straightforward to interact with her, and she can be frustrating. However, she remembers your name between visits, which is friendly.

Figure 7.4 Cybelle the intelligent agent

Cybelle has a variety of facial expressions and although the answers to my questions were often strange, she has an interesting approach to life, and one might almost say that she has personality! To see Cybelle in action, go to the website (`http://www.agentland.com/`) and ask her some questions. You can ask any question you like, about intelligent agents, herself, or anything else. Alternatively, you can do this activity by just looking at the figure and thinking about the questions.

The developers of Cybelle want to find out whether this approach encourages interest in intelligent agents, or whether it turns people away. To this end, they have asked you to conduct some interviews for them.

1. What is the goal of your data gathering session?
2. Suggest ways of recording the interview data.
3. Suggest a set of questions that are suitable for use in an unstructured interview that seek opinions about whether Cybelle would encourage or discourage interest in intelligent agents.
4. Based on the results of the unstructured interviews, the developers of Cybelle have found that two important acceptance factors are whether she is amusing and whether she answers questions on intelligent agents accurately. Write a set of semi-structured interview questions to evaluate these two aspects. Show two of your peers the Cybelle website. Then ask them to comment on your questions. Refine the questions based on their comments.

Comment

1. The goal is to seek opinions about whether Cybelle would encourage or discourage interest in intelligent agents.
2. Taking notes might be cumbersome and distracting to the interviewee, and it would be easy to miss important points. An alternative is to audio record the session. Video recording is not needed as it isn't necessary to see the interviewee. However, it would be useful to have a camera at hand to take shots of the interface in case the interviewee wanted to refer to aspects of Cybelle.
3. Possible questions include: Do you find chatting with Cybelle helpful? Does Cybelle answer your questions on intelligent agents appropriately? In what way(s) does Cybelle affect your interest in intelligent agents?
4. Semi-structured interview questions may be open or closed. Some closed questions that you might ask include:
   - Have you seen Cybelle before?
   - Would you like to find out about intelligent agents from Cybelle?
   - In your opinion, is Cybelle amusing or irritating?

   Some open questions, with follow-on probes, include:
   - What do you like most about Cybelle? Why?
   - What do you like least about Cybelle? Why?
   - Please give me an example where Cybelle amused or irritated you.

It is helpful when collecting answers to list the possible responses together with boxes that can just be checked (i.e. ticked). Here's how we could convert some of the questions from Activity 7.2.

1. Have you seen Cybelle before? (Explore previous knowledge)
   Interviewer checks box ☐ *Yes* ☐ *No* ☐*Don't remember/know*
2. Would you like to find out about intelligent agents from Cybelle? (Explore initial reaction, then explore the response)
   Interviewer checks box ☐ *Yes* ☐ *No* ☐*Don't know*
3. Why?
   If response is "Yes" or "No," interviewer says, "Which of the following statements represents your feelings best?"
   For "Yes," Interviewer checks the box
   ☐ *I don't like typing*
   ☐ *This is fun/cool*
   ☐ *It's going to be the way of the future*
   ☐ *Another reason (Interviewer notes the reason)*

For "No," Interviewer checks the box
☐ *I don't like systems that pretend to be people*
☐ *She doesn't answer my questions clearly*
☐ *I don't like her 'personality'*
☐ *Another reason (Interviewer notes the reason)*

4. In your opinion, is Cybelle amusing or irritating?
Interviewer checks box
☐ *Amusing*
☐ *Irritating*
☐ *Neither*

Running the interview

Before starting, make sure that the aims of the interview have been communicated to and understood by the interviewees, and they feel comfortable. Some simple techniques can help here, such as finding out about their world before the interview so that you can dress, act, and speak in a manner that will be familiar. This is particularly important when working with disadvantaged groups such as disabled people, children, or seriously ill patients.

During the interview, it is better to listen more than to talk, to respond with sympathy but without bias, and even to enjoy the interview (Robson, 2002). Robson suggests the following steps for an interview:

1. An *introduction* in which the interviewer introduces himself and explains why he is doing the interview, reassures interviewees regarding any ethical issues, and asks if they mind being recorded, if appropriate. This should be exactly the same for each interviewee.
2. A *warm-up* session where easy, non-threatening questions come first. These may include questions about demographic information, such as "What area of the country do you live in?"
3. A *main* session in which the questions are presented in a logical sequence, with the more probing ones at the end. In a semi-structured interview the order of questions may vary between participants, depending on the course of the conversation and what seems more natural.
4. A *cool-off period* consisting of a few easy questions (to defuse tension if it has arisen).
5. A *closing* session in which the interviewer thanks the interviewee and switches off the recorder or puts her notebook away, signaling that the interview has ended.

7.4.6 Other forms of interview

Telephone interviews are a good way of interviewing people with whom you cannot meet. You cannot see their body language, but apart from this telephone interviews have much in common with face-to-face interviews.

Online interviews, using either asynchronous communication such as email or synchronous communication such as instant messaging, can also be used. For interviews that involve sensitive issues, answering questions anonymously may be preferable to meeting face-to-face. If, however, face-to-face meetings are desirable but impossible because of geographical distance, video-conferencing systems can be used. Feedback about a product or a process can also be obtained from customer help lines, consumer groups, and online customer communities that provide help and support, e.g. see Box 9.2 on user involvement at Microsoft.

At various stages of design, it is useful to get quick feedback from a few users through short interviews, which are often more like conversations, in which users are asked their opinions.

Retrospective interviews, i.e. interviews which reflect on an activity that was performed in the recent past, are often conducted to check with participants that the interviewer has correctly understood what was happening.

7.4.7 Enriching the interview experience

Interviews often take place in a neutral environment, e.g. a meeting room away from the interviewee's normal desk, and the interview situation provides an artificial context, i.e. separate from normal tasks. In these circumstances it can be difficult for interviewees to give full answers to the questions posed. To help combat this, interviews can be enriched by using props such as prototypes or work artifacts that the interviewee or interviewer brings along, or descriptions of common tasks (examples of these kinds of props are scenarios and prototypes, which are covered in Chapters 10 and 11). These props can be used to provide context for the interviewees and help to ground the data in a real setting. Figure 7.5 illustrates the use of prototypes in a focus group setting.

For example, Jones *et al.* (2004) used diaries as a basis for interviews. They performed a study to probe the extent to which certain places are associated with particular activities and information needs. Each participant was asked to keep a diary in which they entered information about where they were and what they were doing at 30 minute intervals. The interview questions were then based around their diary entries.

7.5 Questionnaires

Questionnaires are a well-established technique for collecting demographic data and users' opinions. They are similar to interviews in that they can have *closed* or *open* questions. Effort and skill are needed to ensure that questions are clearly worded and the data collected can be analyzed efficiently. Clearly worded questions are particularly important when there is no researcher present to encourage the respondent and to resolve any ambiguities or

Figure 7.5 Enriching a focus group with prototypes. Here prototype screens are displayed on the wall for all participants to see

misunderstandings. Well-designed questionnaires are good at getting answers to specific questions from a large group of people, and especially if that group of people is spread across a wide geographical area, making it infeasible to visit them all. Questionnaires can be used on their own or in conjunction with other methods to clarify or deepen understanding. For example, information obtained through interviews with a small selection of interviewees might be corroborated by sending a questionnaire to a wider group to confirm the conclusions. The methods and questions used depend on the context, target audience, data gathering goal, and so on.

The questions asked in a questionnaire, and those used in a structured interview, are similar, so how do you know when to use which technique? Essentially, the difference lies in the motivation of the respondent to answer the questions. If you think that this motivation is high enough to complete a questionnaire without anyone else present, then a questionnaire will be cheaper and easier to organize. On the other hand, if the respondents need some persuasion to answer the questions, it would be better to use an interview format and ask the questions face-to-face through a structured interview. For example, structured interviews are easier and quicker to conduct in situations in which people will not stop to complete a questionnaire, such as at a train station or while walking to their next meeting. One approach which lies between these two is the telephone interview.

It can be harder to develop good questionnaire questions compared with structured interview questions because the interviewer is not available to explain them or to clarify any ambiguities. Because of this, it is important that questions are specific; when possible, closed questions should be asked and a range of answers offered, including a 'no opinion' or 'none of these' option. Finally, negative questions can be confusing and may lead to the respondents giving false information. Some questionnaire designers use a mixture of negative and positive questions deliberately because it helps to check the users' intentions. In contrast, the designers of QUIS (Box 7.3) (Chin *et al.*, 1988) decided not to mix negative and positive statements because the questionnaire was already complex enough without forcing participants to pay attention to the direction of the argument.

Box 7.3
QUIS, Questionnaire for user interaction satisfaction

The Questionnaire for User Interaction Satisfaction (QUIS), developed by the University of Maryland Human–Computer Interaction Laboratory, is one of the most widely used questionnaires for evaluating interfaces (Chin *et al.*, 1988; Shneiderman, 1998a). Although developed for evaluating user satisfaction, it is frequently applied to other aspects of interaction design. An advantage of this questionnaire is that it has gone through many cycles of refinement and has been used for hundreds of evaluation studies, so it is well tried and tested. The questionnaire consists of the following 12 parts that can be used in total or in parts:

- **system experience (i.e. time spent on this system)**
- **past experience (i.e. experience with other systems)**
- **overall user reactions**
- **screen design**
- **terminology and system information**
- **learning (i.e. to operate the system)**
- **system capabilities (i.e. the time it takes to perform operations)**
- **technical manuals and online help**
- **online tutorials**
- **multimedia**
- **teleconferencing**
- **software installation.**

Notice that the third part of QUIS assesses users' overall reactions. Evaluators often use this part on its own because it is short so people are likely to respond. ■

7.5.1 Designing the questionnaire's structure

Many questionnaires start by asking for basic demographic information, e.g. gender, age, place of birth, and details of relevant experience, e.g. the time or number of years spent using computers, or the level of expertise within the domain under study, etc. This background information is useful for putting the questionnaire responses into context. For example, if two respondents conflict, these different perspectives may be due to their level of experience—a group of people who are using the web for the first time are likely to express different opinions regarding websites to another group with five years of web experience. However, only contextual information that is relevant to the study goal needs to be collected. In the website example above, it is unlikely that the person's shoe size will provide relevant context to their responses!

Specific questions that contribute to the data gathering goal usually follow these more general questions. If the questionnaire is long, the questions may be subdivided into related topics to make it easier and more logical to complete.

The following is a checklist of general advice for designing a questionnaire:

- Think about the ordering of questions. The impact of a question can be influenced by question order.
- Consider whether you need different versions of the questionnaire for different populations.
- Provide clear instructions on how to complete the questionnaire. For example, if you want a check put in one of the boxes, then say so. Questionnaires can make their message clear with careful wording and good typography.
- A balance must be struck between using white space and the need to keep the questionnaire as compact as possible. Long questionnaires cost more and deter participation and completion.

Box 7.4 contains an excerpt from a paper questionnaire designed to evaluate users' satisfaction with some specific features of a prototype website for career changers aged 34–59 years.

Box 7.4
An excerpt from a user satisfaction questionnaire used to evaluate a website for career changers

Notice that in the following excerpt most questions involve circling the appropriate response, or checking the box that most closely describes their opinion: these are commonly used techniques. Fewer than 50 participants were involved in this study, so inviting them to write an open-ended comment suggesting recommendations for change was manageable. It would have been difficult to collect this information with closed questions, since good suggestions would undoubtedly have been missed because the evaluator is unlikely to have thought to ask about them.

Participant #:_______________

Please circle the most appropriate selection:

Age Range:	34–39	40–49	50–59	
Gender:	Male	Female		
Career-Change Status:		Exploring	In-Progress	Completed

Internet/Web Experience

Research, Information Gathering	Daily	Weekly	Monthly	Never
Bulletin Board Posting	Daily	Weekly	Monthly	Never
Chat Room Usage	Daily	Weekly	Monthly	Never

Please rate (i.e. check the box to show) agreement or disagreement with the following statements:

Question	Strongly Agree	Agree	Neutral	Disagree	Strongly Disagree
The navigation language on the links is clear and easy to understand					
The website site contains information that would be useful to me					
Information on the website is easy to find					
The "Center Design" presents information in an aesthetically pleasing manner					
The website pages are confusing and difficult to read					
I prefer darker colors to lighter colors for display					
It is apparent from the first website page (homepage) what the purpose of the website is.					

Please add any recommendations for changes to the overall design, language or navigation of the website on the back of this paper.

Thanks for your participation in the testing of this prototype.

From Andrews *et al.*, (2001).

7.5.2 Question and response format

There are several different types of question, each of which requires a particular kind of response. For example, closed questions require an answer from a set of possibilities while open questions are unrestricted. Sometimes many options can be chosen, sometimes respondents need to indicate only one, and sometimes it is better to ask users to locate their answer within a range. Selecting the most appropriate question and response format makes it easier for respondents to be able to answer clearly. Some commonly used formats are described below.

Check boxes and ranges

The range of answers to demographic questionnaires is predictable. Gender, for example, has two options, male or female, so providing the two options and asking respondents to circle a response makes sense for collecting this information (as in Box 7.4). A similar approach can be adopted if details of age are needed. But since some people do not like to give their exact age, many questionnaires ask respondents to specify their age as a range (see Box 7.4). A common design error arises when the ranges overlap. For example, specifying two ranges as 15–20, 20–25 will cause confusion: which box do people who are 20 years old check? Making the ranges 14–19, 20–24 avoids this problem.

A frequently asked question about ranges is whether the interval must be equal in all cases. The answer is that it depends on what you want to know. For example, if you want to collect information for the design of an e-commerce site to sell life insurance, the target population is going to be mostly people with jobs in the age range of, say, 21–65 years. You could, therefore, have just three ranges: under 21, 21–65, and over 65. In contrast, if you wanted to see how the population's political views varied across the generations, you might be interested in looking at 10-year cohort groups for people over 21, in which case the following ranges would be appropriate: under 21, 22–31, 32–41, etc.

Rating scales

There are a number of different types of rating scales that can be used, each with its own purpose (see Oppenheim, 1992). Here we describe two commonly used scales, Likert and semantic differential scales. The purpose of these is to elicit a range of responses to a question that can be compared across respondents. They are good for getting people to make judgments about things, e.g. how easy, how usable, etc., and therefore are important for usability studies.

Likert scales rely on identifying a set of statements representing a range of possible opinions, while semantic differential scales rely on choosing pairs of words that represent the range of possible opinions. Likert scales are more commonly used because identifying suitable statements that respondents will understand is easier than identifying semantic pairs that respondents interpret as intended.

Likert scales. Likert scales are used for measuring opinions, attitudes, and beliefs, and consequently they are widely used for evaluating user satisfaction with products. For example, users' opinions about the use of color in a website could be evaluated with a Likert scale using a range of numbers, as in (1), or with words as in (2):

(1) The use of color is excellent (where 1 represents strongly agree and 5 represents strongly disagree):

1	2	3	4	5
☐	☐	☐	☐	☐

(2) The use of color is excellent:

strongly agree	agree	OK	strongly disagree	disagree
☐	☐	☐	☐	☐

In both cases, respondents could be given a box to tick as shown, or they could be asked to ring the appropriate number or phrase, in which case the boxes are not needed. Designing a Likert scale involves the following three steps:

1. Gather a pool of short statements about the subject to be investigated. For example, "This control panel is easy to use" or "The procedure for checking credit rating is too complex." A brainstorming session with peers in which you identify key aspects to be investigated is a good way of doing this.
2. Decide on the scale. There are three main issues to be addressed here: how many points does the scale need? Should the scale be discrete or continuous? How to represent the scale? See Box 7.5 for more on this topic.
3. Select items for the final questionnaire and reword as necessary to make them clear.

Semantic differential scales. Semantic differential scales are used less frequently than Likert scales, possibly because it is harder to find pairs of words that can be interpreted consistently by participants. They explore a range of bipolar attitudes about a particular item. Each pair of attitudes is represented as a pair of adjectives. The participant is asked to place a cross in one of a number of positions between the two extremes to indicate agreement with the poles, as shown in Figure 7.6. The score for the evaluation is found by summing the scores for each bipolar pair. Scores can then be computed across groups of participants. Notice that in this example the poles are mixed so that good and bad features are distributed on the right and the left. In this example there are seven positions on the scale.

Instructions: for each pair of adjectives, place a cross at the point between them that reflects the extent to which you believe the adjectives describe the home page. You should place *only one cross* between the marks on each line.

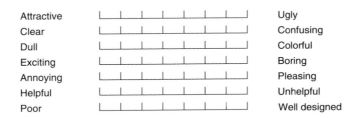

Attractive	|__|__|__|__|__|__|__|	Ugly
Clear	|__|__|__|__|__|__|__|	Confusing
Dull	|__|__|__|__|__|__|__|	Colorful
Exciting	|__|__|__|__|__|__|__|	Boring
Annoying	|__|__|__|__|__|__|__|	Pleasing
Helpful	|__|__|__|__|__|__|__|	Unhelpful
Poor	|__|__|__|__|__|__|__|	Well designed

Figure 7.6 *An example of a semantic differential scale*

Box 7.5
What scales to use—3, 5, 7, or more?

When designing Likert and semantic differential scales, issues that need to be addressed include: how many points are needed on the scale? How should they be presented, and in what form?

Many questionnaires use seven- or five-point scales and there are also three-point scales. Arguments for the number of points go both ways. Advocates of long scales argue that they help to show discrimination, as advocated by the QUIS team (QUIS has a nine-point scale; Box 7.3 (Chin *et al.*, 1988)). Rating features on an interface is more difficult for most people than, say, selecting among different flavors of ice cream, and when the task is difficult there is evidence to show that people 'hedge their bets.' Rather than selecting the poles of the scales if there is no right or wrong, respondents tend to select values nearer the center. The counter-argument is that people cannot be expected to discern accurately among points on a large scale, so any scale of more than five points is unnecessarily difficult to use.

Another aspect to consider is whether the scale should have an even or odd number of points. An odd number provides a clear central point. On the other hand, an even number forces participants to make a decision and prevents them from sitting on the fence.

We suggest the following guidelines:

How many points on the scale?

Use a small number, e.g. 3, when the possibilities are very limited, as in yes/no type answers:

☐	☐	☐
yes	don't know	no

Use a medium-sized range, e.g. 5, when making judgments that involve like/dislike, agree/disagree statements:

- ☐ strongly agree
- ☐ slightly agree
- ☐ agree
- ☐ slightly disagree
- ☐ strongly disagree

Use a longer range, e.g. 7 or 9, when asking respondents to make subtle judgments. For example, when asking about a user experience dimension such as 'level of appeal' of a character in a video game:

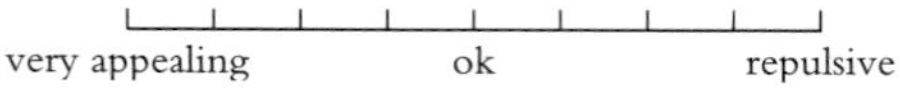

Discrete or continuous?

Use boxes for discrete choices and scales for finer judgments.

What order?

Place the positive end of the scale first and the negative end last. This matches the logical way people think about scoring. For example:

— strongly agree
— slightly agree
— agree
— slightly disagree
— strongly disagree. ■

Activity 7.3

Spot four poorly designed features in Figure 7.7.

Comment

Some of the features that could be improved include:

- Question 2 requests exact age. Many people prefer not to give this information and would rather position themselves in a range.

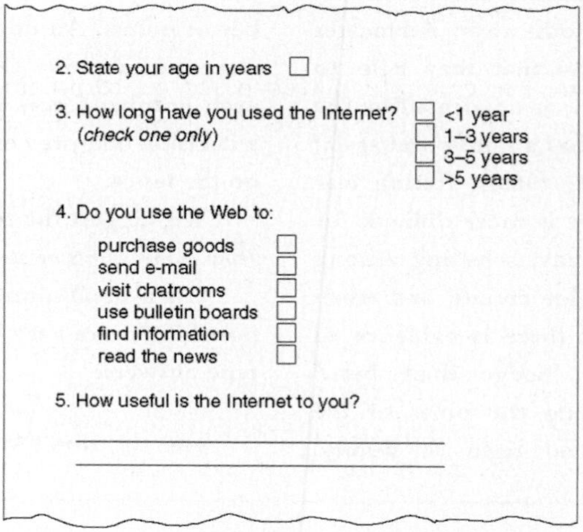
2. State your age in years ☐

3. How long have you used the Internet? (*check one only*)
☐ <1 year
☐ 1–3 years
☐ 3–5 years
☐ >5 years

4. Do you use the Web to:
purchase goods ☐
send e-mail ☐
visit chatrooms ☐
use bulletin boards ☐
find information ☐
read the news ☐

5. How useful is the Internet to you?

Figure 7.7 *A questionnaire with poorly designed features*

- **In question 3, years of experience is indicated with overlapping scales, i.e. 1, <1–3, 3–5, etc. How do you answer if you have 1, 3, or 5 years of experience?**
- **For question 4, the questionnaire doesn't tell you whether you should check one, two, or as many boxes as you wish.**
- **The space left for people to answer the open-ended question 5 is too small, which will annoy some people and deter them from giving their opinions.**

7.5.3 Administering questionnaires

Two important issues when using questionnaires are reaching a representative sample of participants and ensuring a reasonable response rate. For large surveys, potential respondents need to be selected using a sampling technique. However, interaction designers commonly use small numbers of participants, often fewer than 20 users. 100% completion rates are often achieved with these small samples, but with larger or more remote populations, ensuring that surveys are returned is a well-known problem. 40% return is generally acceptable for many surveys, but much lower rates are common. Depending on your audience you might want to consider offering incentives (see Section 7.2.2).

7.5.4 Online questionnaires

Online questionnaires are becoming increasingly common because they are effective for reaching large numbers of people quickly and easily. There are two types: email and web-based. The main advantage of email is that you can target specific users. But unless email is just used to contact potential respondents and point them to a web-based questionnaire, an email questionnaire is likely to be simply an electronic editable version of a paper-based questionnaire, and this loses some of the advantages you get with a web-based questionnaire. For example, a web-based questionnaire can be interactive and can include check boxes, pull-down and pop-up menus, help screens, and graphics, e.g. Figure 7.8. It can also provide immediate data validation and can enforce rules such as select only one response, or certain types of answers such as numerical, which cannot be done in email or with paper. Other advantages of web-based questionnaires include faster response rates and automatic transfer of responses into a database for analysis (Andrews *et al.*, 2003).

The main problem with web-based questionnaires is obtaining a random sample of respondents. As there is no central registry of Internet users, it is not possible to identify the size and demography of the full population being surveyed, and traditional sampling methods cannot be used. This means that the respondents are inevitably self-selecting and

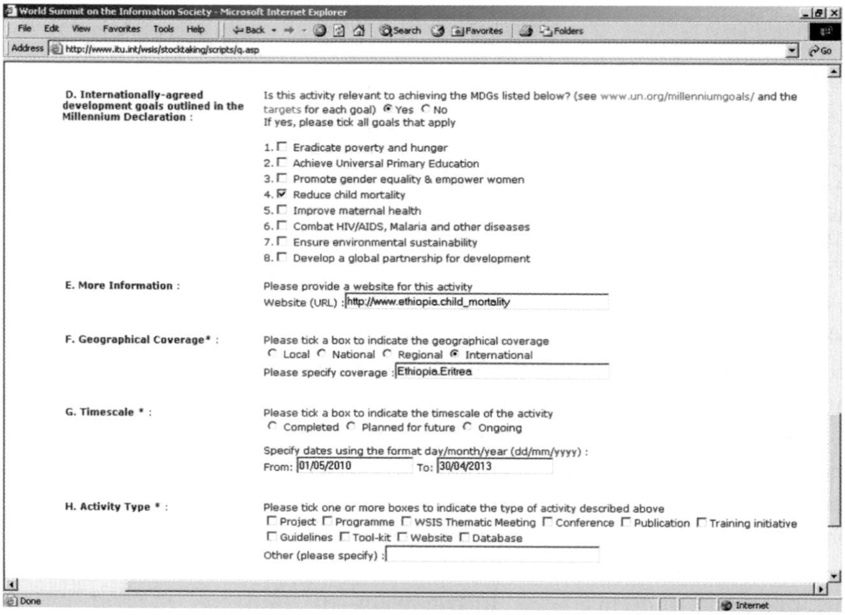

Figure 7.8 *An excerpt from a web-based questionnaire showing pull-down menus*

so the results cannot be generalized to offline populations. This was a criticism of the survey run by Georgia Tech's GVU (Graphic, Visualization and Usability) Centre, one of the first online surveys. This survey collected demographic and activity information from Internet users twice yearly between January 1994 and October 1998. The policy that GVU employed to deal with this difficult sampling issue was to make as many people aware of the GVU survey as possible so that a wide variety of participants were encouraged to respond. However, even these efforts did not avoid biased sampling, since participants were still self-selecting.

Some survey experts instead propose using national census records to sample offline (Nie and Ebring, 2000). The highly regarded PEW surveys select households to poll using random digit samples of telephone numbers, but these are telephone surveys and an equivalently reliable sampling method has not yet been suggested for online surveys. In some countries, web- and mobile phone-based questions are used in conjunction with television to elicit viewers' opinions of programs and political events, e.g. the television program Big Brother. A term that is gaining popularity is *convenience sampling*, which is another way of saying that the sample includes those who were available rather than those selected using scientific sampling.

Designing a web-based questionnaire involves the following steps (Andrews *et al.*, 2003):

1. Devise the questionnaire as if it is to be delivered on paper first, following the general guidelines introduced above.
2. Develop strategies for reaching the target population.
3. Produce an error-free interactive electronic version from the original paper-based one. It may also be useful to embed feedback and pop-up help within the questionnaire.
4. Make the questionnaire accessible from all common browsers and readable from different-sized monitors and different network locations.
5. Make sure information identifying each respondent can be captured and stored confidentially because the same person may submit several completed surveys. This can be done by recording the Internet domain name or the IP address of the respondent, which can then be transferred directly to a database. However, this action could infringe people's privacy and the legal situation should be checked. Another way is to access the transfer and referrer logs from the web server, which provide information about the domains from which the web-based questionnaire was accessed. Unfortunately, people can still send from different accounts with different IP addresses, so additional identifying information may also be needed.
6. Thoroughly pilot test the questionnaire. This may be achieved in four stages: the survey is reviewed by knowledgeable analysts; typical participants complete the survey using a think-aloud protocol (see below); a small version of the study is attempted; a final check to catch small errors is conducted.

There are many online questionnaire templates available on the web that provide a range of choices, including different question types (e.g. open, multiple choice), rating scales (e.g. Likert, semantic differential), and answer types (e.g. radio buttons, check boxes, drop-down menus). The following activity asks you to make use of one of these templates to design a questionnaire for the web.

Activity 7.4

Go to `questionpro.com`, or a similar survey site, that allows you to design your own questionnaire using their set of widgets for a free trial period (`http://www.questionpro.com/buildyoursurvey/` at time of writing).

Create a web-based questionnaire for the set of questions you developed for Activity 7.2 (Cybelle). For each question produce two different designs, for example radio buttons and drop-down menus for one question; for another

question provide a 10-point semantic differential scale and a 5-point scale.

What differences (if any) do you think your two designs will have on a respondent's behavior? Ask a number of people to answer one or other of your questions and see if the answers differ for the two designs.

Comment

You may have found that respondents use the response types in different ways. For example, they may select the end options more often from a drop-down menu than from a list of options that are chosen via radio buttons. Alternatively, you may find no difference and that people's opinions are not affected by the widget style used at the interface. Any differences found, of course, may be due to the variation between individual responses rather than being caused by features in the questionnaire design. To tease the effects apart you would need to ask a large number of participants, e.g. in the order of 50–100, to respond to the questions for each design.

Box 7.6
Do people answer online questionnaires differently to paper and pencil? If so, why?

There has been much research examining how people respond to surveys when using a computer compared with the traditional paper and pencil method. Some studies suggest that people are more revealing and consistent in their responses when using a computer to report their habits and behaviors, such as eating, drinking, and amount of exercise, e.g. Luce *et al.* (2003). Students have also been found to rate their instructors less favorably when online, suggesting they are more honest in their views of their instructors (Chang, 2004). One reason for this is that students may feel less social pressure when filling in a questionnaire at a computer and hence freer to write the truth than when sitting in a classroom, with others around them, filling out a paper-based version.

Another factor that can influence how people answer questions is the way the information is structured on the screen or page, such as the use of headers, the ordering, and the placement of questions. But the potential may be greater for web-based questionnaires since they provide more opportunities than paper ones for manipulating information (Smyth *et al.*, 2004). For example, the use of drop-down menus, radio buttons, and jump-to options may influence how people read and navigate a questionnaire. Research is beginning to investigate how such interactivity affects respondents' behavior when thinking about their replies; for example, Smyth *et al.* (2005) have found that providing forced choice formats results in more options being selected. The initial findings suggest that instead of prescribing a generic design format for all web-based questionnaires, e.g. using only radio buttons or entry check boxes, that the design should be selected based on the purpose of the questionnaire and the types of questions being asked (Gunn, 2002). ■

7.6 Observation

Observation is a useful data gathering technique at any stage during product development. Early in design, observation helps designers understand the users' context, tasks, and goals. Observation conducted later in development, e.g. in evaluation, may be used to investigate how well the developing prototype supports these tasks and goals.

Users may be observed directly by the investigator as they perform their activities, or indirectly through records of the activity that are read afterwards. Observation may also take place in the field, or in a controlled environment. In the former case, individuals are observed as they go about their day-to-day tasks in the natural setting. In the latter case, individuals are observed performing specified tasks within a controlled environment such as a usability laboratory.

Activity 7.5

To appreciate the different merits of observation in the field and observation in a controlled environment, read the scenarios below and answer the questions that follow.

Scenario 1. A usability consultant joins a group who have been given GPS-based phones to test on a visit to Stockholm. Not knowing the restaurants in the area, they use the GPS-based phone to find a list of restaurants within a five-mile radius of their hotel. Several are listed and while the group waits for a taxi, they find the telephone numbers of a couple, call them to ask about their menus, select one, make a booking, and head off to the restaurant. The usability consultant observes some problems keying instructions because the buttons seem small. She also notices that the text on the screen seems rather small, but the person using it is able to get the information needed and call the restaurant. Discussion with the group supports the evaluator's impression that there are problems with the interface, but on balance the device is useful and the group is pleased to get a table at a good restaurant nearby.

Scenario 2. A usability consultant observes how participants perform a preplanned task using the GPS-based phone in a usability laboratory. The task requires the participants to find the telephone number of a restaurant called Matisse. It takes them several minutes to do this and they appear to have problems. The video recording and interaction log suggest that the screen is too small for the amount of information they need to access and this is supported by participants' answers on a user satisfaction questionnaire.

1. In which situation does the observer take the most control?
2. What are the advantages and disadvantages of these two types of observation?
3. When might each type of observation be useful?

Comment

1. The observer takes most control in the second study. The task is predetermined, the participant is instructed what to do, and she is located in a controlled laboratory environment.
2. The advantages of the field study are that the observer saw how the device could be used in a real situation to solve a real problem. She experienced the delight expressed with the overall concept and the frustration with the interface. By watching how the group used the device 'on the move,' she gained an understanding of what they liked and what was lacking. The disadvantage is that the observer was an insider in the group, so how objective could she be? The data is qualitative and while anecdotes can be very persuasive, how useful are they? Maybe she was having such a good time that her judgment was clouded and she missed hearing negative comments and didn't notice some people's annoyance. Another study could be done to find out more, but it is not possible to replicate the exact situation, whereas the laboratory study is easier to replicate. The advantages of the laboratory are that several users performed the same task, so different users' performance could be compared and averages calculated. The observer could also be more objective because she was more of an outsider. The disadvantage is that the study is artificial and says nothing about how the device would be used in the real environment.
3. Both types of study have merits. Which is better depends on the goals of the study. The laboratory study is useful for examining details of the interaction style to make sure that usability problems with the interface and button design are diagnosed and corrected. The field study reveals how the phone is used in a real-world context and how it integrates with or changes users' behavior. Without this study, it is possible that developers might not have discovered the enthusiasm for the phone because the reward for doing laboratory tasks is not as compelling as a good meal!

7.6.1 Direct observation in the field

It can be very difficult for people to explain what they do or to even describe accurately how they achieve a task. So it is very unlikely that an interaction designer will get a full and true story by using interviews or questionnaires. Observation in the field can help fill in details and nuances that are not elicited from the other forms of investigation. It also provides context for tasks, and contextualizing the users and the interactive product provides important information about why activities happen the way they do. However, observation in the field can be complicated and can result in a lot of data that is not very relevant if it is not planned and carried out carefully.

Activity 7.6

1. Find a small group of people who are using any kind of technology, e.g. computers, household, or entertainment appliances, and try to answer the question, "What are these people doing?" Watch for three to five minutes and write down what you observe. When you have finished, note down how you felt doing this, and any reactions in the group of people you observed.

2. If you were to observe the group again, how would you change what you did the first time?

Comment

1. The chances are that you found the experience prompted many uncertainties. For example, were the group talking, working, playing, or something else? How were you able to decide? Did you feel awkward or embarrassed watching? Did you wonder whether you should tell them that you were observing them? What problems did you encounter doing this exercise? Was it hard to watch everything and remember what happened? What were the most important things? Did you wonder if you should be trying to identify and remember just those things? Was remembering the order of events tricky? Perhaps you naturally picked up a pen and paper and took notes. If so, was it difficult to record fast enough? How do you think the people being watched felt? Did they know they were being watched? Did knowing affect the way they behaved? Perhaps some of them objected and walked away. If you didn't tell them, do you think you should have?

2. The initial goal of the observation, i.e. to find out what the people are doing, was vague, and the chances are that it was quite a frustrating experience not knowing what was significant for answering your question and what could be ignored. The questions used to guide observation need to be more focused. For example, you might ask,

what are the people doing with the technology? Is everyone in the group using it? Are they looking pleased, frustrated, serious, happy? Does the technology appear to be central to the users' goals?

All data gathering should have a clearly stated goal, but it is particularly important to have a focus for an observation session because there is always so much going on. On the other hand, it is also important to be able to respond to changing circumstances; for example, you may have planned one day to observe a particular person performing a task, but you are invited to an unexpected meeting which is relevant to your observation goal, and so it makes sense to attend the meeting instead. In observation there is a careful balance between being guided by goals and being open to modifying, shaping, or refocusing the study as you learn about the situation. Being able to keep this balance is a skill that develops with experience.

Dilemma
When should I stop observing?

Knowing when to stop doing any type of data gathering can be difficult for novices, but it is particularly tricky in observational studies because there is no obvious ending. Schedules often dictate when your study ends. Otherwise, stop when you stop learning new things. Two indications of having done enough are when you start to see similar patterns of behavior being repeated, or when you have listened to all the main stakeholder groups and understand their perspectives. ■

Structuring frameworks for observation in the field

During an observation, events can be complex and rapidly changing. There is a lot for observers to think about, so many experts have a framework to structure and focus their observation. The framework can be quite simple. For example, this is a practitioner's framework for use in evaluation studies that focuses on just three easy-to-remember items to look for:

- *The person.* Who is using the technology at any particular time?
- *The place.* Where are they using it?
- *The thing.* What are they doing with it?

Even a simple framework such as this one based on who, where, and what can be surprisingly effective to help observers keep their goals and questions in sight. Experienced observers may, however, prefer more detailed frameworks, such as the one suggested by Colin Robson (2002) which encourages observers to pay greater attention to the context of the activity:

- *Space*. What is the physical space like and how is it laid out?
- *Actors*. What are the names and relevant details of the people involved?
- *Activities*. What are the actors doing and why?
- *Objects*. What physical objects are present, such as furniture?
- *Acts*. What are specific individual actions?
- *Events*. Is what you observe part of a special event?
- *Time*. What is the sequence of events?
- *Goals*. What are the actors trying to accomplish?
- *Feelings*. What is the mood of the group and of individuals?

Activity 7.7

As in Activity 7.6 above, find a small group of people who are using any kind of technology. Observe this group for about 10 minutes and write down your observations, structured using Robson's framework.

Then consider how you feel about this observation exercise compared to the previous one.

Comment

Hopefully you will have felt more confident this second time, partly because it is the second time you've done some observation, and partly because the framework provided you with a structure for what to look at.

Both of the frameworks introduced above are relatively general and could be used in many different types of study, but there are other frameworks that have been developed to focus on particular circumstances. For example, Rogers and Bellotti (1997) suggest a more specific framework to support field studies in conjunction with designing future technologies. They divide their set of questions into two parts: problematizing existing settings and envisioning future settings.

Problematizing existing settings

- **Why is an observation about a work practice or other activity striking?**
- **What are the pros and cons of the existing ways technologies are used in a setting?**
- **How have 'workarounds' evolved and how effective are they?**
- **Why do certain old-fashioned practices, using seemingly antiquated technologies persist, despite more advanced**

technologies being available in the setting?

Envisioning future settings

- **What would be gained and lost through changing current ways of working or carrying out an activity by introducing new kinds of technological support?**
- **What might be the knock-on effects for other practices and activities through introducing new technologies?**
- **How might other settings be enhanced and disrupted through deploying the same kinds of future technologies?**

Degree of participation

Depending on the type of study, the degree of participation within the study environment varies across a spectrum, which can be characterized as 'insider' at one end and 'outsider' at the other (see Figure 7.9). Where a particular study falls along this spectrum depends on its goal and on the practical and ethical issues that constrain and shape it.

An observer who adopts an approach right at the 'outsider' end of the spectrum is called a 'passive observer' and she will not take any part in the study environment at all. It is difficult to be a truly passive observer if you are in the field, simply because you can't avoid interacting with the activities happening around you.

An observer who adopts an approach at the 'insider' end of this spectrum is called a 'participant observer.' This means that he attempts to become a full member of the group he is studying. This can also be a difficult role to play since being an observer requires a certain level of detachment, while being a full participant assumes a different role. As a participant observer it is important to keep the two roles clear and separate, so that observation notes are objective, while participation is also maintained. It may also not be possible to take a full participant observer approach, for other reasons. For example, you may not be skilled enough in the task at hand, the organization/group may not be prepared for you to take part in their activities, or the timescale may not provide sufficient opportunity to become familiar enough with the task to participate fully.

An interesting example of participant observation is provided by Nancy Baym's work (1997) in which she joined an online community interested in soap operas for over a year in order to understand how the community functioned. She told the community what she was doing and offered to share her findings with them. This honest approach gained her their trust, and they offered support and helpful comments. As Baym participated she

Figure 7.9 The degree of participation varies along a spectrum from insider to outsider

learned about the community, who the key characters were, how people interacted, their values, and the types of discussion that were generated. She kept all the messages as data to be referred to later. She also adapted interviewing and questionnaire techniques to collect additional information. She summarizes her data gathering as follows:

> ***The data for this study were obtained from three sources. In October 1991, I saved all the messages that appeared . . . I collected more messages in 1993. Eighteen participants responded to a questionnaire I posted . . . Personal email correspondence with 10 other . . . participants provided further information. I posted two notices to the group explaining the project and offering to exclude posts by those who preferred not to be involved. No one declined to participate.*** **(Baym, 1997, p. 104)**

Using this data, Baym examined the group's technical and participatory structure, its emergent traditions, and its use of technology. As the work evolved, she shared its progress with the group members, who were supportive and helpful.

Activity 7.8

Drawing on your experience of using email, blogs, bulletin boards, or chat rooms, how might participant observation online differ from face-to-face participant observation?

Comment

In online participant observation you don't have to look people in the eye, deal with their skepticism, or wonder what they think of you, as you do in face-to-face situations. What you wear, how you look, and the tone of your voice don't matter. However, what you say (type) or don't say and how you say it are central to the way others will respond to you. When interacting online you only see part of a person's context. You usually can't see how they behave offline, how they present themselves, their body language, how they spend their day, their personalities, who is present but not participating, and so on.

Planning and conducting an observation in the field

The frameworks introduced in the previous section are useful not only for providing focus but also for organizing the observation and data gathering activity. But although choosing a framework is important, it is only one aspect of planning an observation. Other decisions include: the level of participation to adopt; how to make a record of the data; how to gain acceptance in the group being studied; how to handle sensitive issues such as cultural differences or access to private spaces (see Box 7.7 on observation in the home); and how to ensure that the study uses different perspectives (people, activities, job roles, etc.). One way to achieve this last point is to work as a team. This can have several benefits. For instance, each person can agree to focus on different people or different parts of the context thereby covering more ground, observation and reflection can be interweaved more easily when there is more than one observer, and more reliable data is likely to be generated because observations can be compared, and results will reflect different perspectives.

Once in the throes of an observation, there are other issues that need to be considered. For example, it will be easier to relate to some people than others, and it will be tempting to pay attention to those who receive you well but everyone in the group needs to be attended to. Observation is a fluid activity, and it will be necessary to refocus the study as you reflect upon what has been seen. Having observed for a while, interesting phenomena that seem relevant will start to emerge. Gradually ideas will sharpen into questions that guide further observation.

Observing is an intense and tiring activity, but however tired you are, it is important to check the notes and other records and to write up experiences and observations at the end of each day. If this is not done, then valuable information will be lost as the next day's events override your previous day's impressions. Writing a diary or private blog is one way of keeping up, inserting relevant photos. Any documents collected or copied, e.g. minutes of a meeting, or discussion items, should be annotated, describing how they are used and at what stage of the activity. Some observers conducting an observation over several days or weeks take time out of each day to go through their notes and other records.

As notes are reviewed, personal opinion should be separated from observation of what happened, and anything for further investigation should be clearly marked. It is also a good idea to check observations with an informant or members of the group to ensure that you have understood what is happening and that your interpretations are accurate.

Box 7.7
Observation in the home

Home use of technology such as the personal computer, wireless telephones, cell phones, remote controls, and game consoles is growing. Although consumer surveys and similar questionnaires may be able to gather some information about this market, ethnographic studies have been used to gain the extra insight that ensures the products do not just perform needed functions but are also pleasurable and easy to use.

Dray and Mrazek (1996) report on an international study of families' use of technology in which they visited 20 families in America, Germany, and France. They spent at least four hours in each of

the homes, talking with all members of the family, including children of all ages, about their use of computer technology. One aspect of the study they emphasize is the need to develop a rapport with the family. They focused their attention on building a strong positive rapport in the first few minutes of the visit. In all cases, they used food as an icebreaker, by either bringing dinner with them for themselves and the family, or by ordering food to be delivered. This provided a mundane topic of conversation that allowed a natural conversation to be held.

After dinner, they moved to the location of the computer and began by asking the children about their use of the technology. Each family member was engaged in conversation about the technology, and printed samples of work were gathered by the researchers. A protocol designed by the marketing and engineering departments of the company was used to guide the conduct of this part of the study, but after all of the protocol had been covered, families were encouraged to discuss topics they were interested in. Immediately after a visit, the team held a formal debriefing session during which all photographs, videotapes, products, and notes were reviewed and a summary debriefing questionnaire was completed. A thank you letter was later sent to the families.

From this description you can see that a large amount of preparation was required in order to ensure that the study resulted in getting the right data, i.e. in collecting data that was going to answer the relevant questions.

Mateas *et al.* (1996) report on a pilot study that was also aimed at informing the design and development of domestic computing systems. They visited 10 families and they too emphasize the importance of making families feel comfortable with them. In their study, this was partly achieved by bringing a pizza dinner for everyone. After dinner, the adults and the children were separated. The researchers wanted to get an understanding of a typical day in the home. To do this, each family member was asked to walk through a typical day, using a felt board with a layout of their house, and felt rooms, products, activities, and people that could be moved around on the felt house.

From their work they derived a model of space, time, and social communication that differed from the model implied by the standard PC. For example, the standard PC is designed to be used in one location by one user for long periods of uninterrupted time. The studies revealed that, on the other hand, family activity is distributed throughout multiple spaces, is rarely conducted alone, and is not partitioned into long periods of uninterrupted use. In addition, the PC does not support communication among collocated members of the family, which is a key element of family life. They conclude that small, integrated computational appliances supporting multiple collocated users are more appropriate to domestic activity than the single PC.

These two studies, and indeed most studies in the home, focus on western cultures. In contrast, Genevieve Bell from Intel has been conducting studies of domestic technology across South and South East Asia (Bell, 2003; Bell *et al.*, 2005). She emphasizes the importance of spending time with families and using a range of data gathering including observation. She has found significant differences between her experiences with western cultures and those with Asian cultures. For example, there is often not a large range of technologies available in the home, but the home is a hub of social activities and these need supporting. In India, it is often the case that new technologies are linked to communication. In Asia more generally, technologies are used to promote eGovernment,[1] education, and the extended family. She also makes the point that observers have to work hard in order to defamiliarize themselves from the home environment. Everyone is an expert on 'the home,' yet it is important to distance yourself from familiar environments if ethnographic studies are to yield useful insights.

Ethnography

Ethnography has traditionally been used in the social sciences to uncover the social organization of activities, and hence to understand work. Since the early 1990s it has gained credibility in interaction design, and particularly in the design of collaborative systems, e.g. Box 7.8 and Crabtree (2003). A large part of most ethnographic studies is direct observation, but interviews, questionnaires, and studying artifacts used in the activities also feature in many ethnographic studies. Its main distinguishing feature compared to other approaches to data gathering is that it aims to observe a situation without imposing any *a priori* structure or framework upon it, and to view everything as 'strange.'

Ethnography has become popular within interaction design because if products are to be used in a wide variety of environments, designers must know the context and ecology of those environments (Nardi and O'Day, 1999). Bell (2001) observes that ethnographic methods are a way of uncovering people's real desires, of getting insight into their lives and following their own stories and interests; knowing these things allows products to be designed that fit 'intuitively' into people's lives.

The observer in an ethnographic study adopts a participant observer (i.e. insider) role as much as possible. In fact, some ethnographers see participant observation as virtually synonymous with ethnography (Atkinson and Hammersley, 1994). Others view participant observation as just one technique that is used within an ethnographic study along with

[1] eGovernment, or electronic government, is the utilization of electronic technology to streamline or otherwise improve the business of government, often with respect to how citizens interact with it.

informants from the community, interviews with community members, and the study of community artifacts (Fetterman, 1998). Participant observation is simply at one end of the insider–outsider spectrum, and it can be used within various methodological frameworks. For example, participant observation may be used within an action research program of study where one of the goals is to understand the situation by changing and improving it.

Box 7.8
Ethnography in requirements

The MERboard is a tool to support scientists and engineers display, capture, annotate, and share information to support the operation of two Mars Exploration Rovers (MERs) on the surface of Mars. A MER (see Figure 7.10) acts like a human geological explorer by collecting samples, analyzing them, and transmitting results back to the scientists on Earth. The scientists and engineers then collaboratively analyze the data received from the robots, decide what to study next, create plans of action, and send commands to the robots on the surface of Mars. The goal of MERboard is to support this collaboration.

The requirements for MERboard were identified partly through ethnographic fieldwork, observations, and analysis (Trimble *et al.*, 2002). In August 2001, the team of scientists and engineers ran a series of 'field' tests for the MER expedition. These tests simulated the process of receiving data, analyzing it, creating plans, and transmitting them to the MERs. These tests were observed in order to identify gaps in the science process. The main problems stemmed from the scientists' limitations in displaying, sharing, and storing information (see Figure 7.11a). For example, flip charts cannot embed images, cannot easily be

Figure 7.10 Mars Exploration Rover

(a)
(b)

Figure 7.11 (a) The situation before MERboard. (b) A scientist using MERboard to present information

used to share information with team members who are not collocated, are difficult to store and retrieve, and cannot be searched easily. In one incident, participants were seen to raise their laptops in the air for others to view information.

These observations led to the development of MERboard (see Figure 7.11b), which was also inspired by BlueBoard developed by IBM (Trimble *et al.*, 2002). MERboard consists of several 50″ plasma screens with touchscreen overlays backed by a computer; the computers are networked together through a centralized server and database. The interface contains four core applications: a whiteboard for brainstorming and sketching, a browser for displaying information from the web, the capability to display personal information and information across several screens, and a file storage space linked specifically to MERboard. ■

Gathering ethnographic data is not hard. You gather what is available, what is 'ordinary,' what it is that people do, say, how they work. The data collected therefore has many forms: documents, notes of your own, pictures, room layout sketches. Notebook notes may include snippets of conversation and descriptions of rooms, meetings, what someone did, or how people reacted to a situation. Data gathering is opportunistic in that you collect what you can collect and make the most of opportunities as they present themselves. Often, interesting phenomena do not reveal themselves immediately but only later on, so it is important to gather as much as possible within the framework of observation. Initially, time should be spent getting to know the people in the work place and bonding with them. It is critical, from the very beginning, that they understand why you are there, what you hope to achieve, and how long you plan to be there. Going to lunch with them, buying coffee, and bringing small gifts, e.g. cookies, can greatly help this socialization process. Moreover, it may be during one of the informal gatherings that key information is revealed.

Always show interest in the stories, gripes, and explanations that are provided but be prepared to step back if the phone rings or someone else enters the workspace. Most workers will stop mid-sentence if their attention is required elsewhere. Hence, you need to be prepared to switch in and out of their work cycles, moving into the shadow if something happens that needs the worker's immediate attention.

A good tactic is to explain to one of the participants during a quiet moment what you think is happening and then let her correct you. It is important not to appear overly keen or obtrusive. Asking too many questions, taking pictures of everything, showing off your knowledge, and getting in their way can be very off-putting. Putting up cameras on tripods on the first day is not a good idea. Listening and watching while sitting on the sidelines and occasionally asking questions is a much better approach. When you have gained the trust and respect of the participants you can then ask if they mind you setting up a video camera, taking pictures, or using a recorder.

The following is an illustrative list of materials that might be recorded and collected during an ethnographic study (adapted from Crabtree, 2003, p. 53):

- Activity or job descriptions.
- Rules and procedures (etc.) said to govern particular activities.
- Descriptions of activities observed.
- Recordings of the talk taking place between parties involved in observed activities.
- Informal interviews with participants explaining the detail of observed activities.
- Diagrams of the physical layout, including the position of artifacts.
- Photographs of artifacts (documents, diagrams, forms, computers, etc.) used in the course of observed activities.
- Videos of artifacts as used in the course of observed activities.
- Descriptions of artifacts used in the course of observed activities.
- Workflow diagrams showing the sequential order of tasks involved in observed activities.
- Process maps showing connections between activities.

Ethnographic studies traditionally take weeks, months, or even years, but interaction design requires much shorter studies because of the time constraints imposed by development schedules, and several adaptations of ethnography have emerged to tackle this challenge, as in Box 7.9.

Box 7.9
Ethnography in evaluation

Many developers are unsure how to integrate ethnographic evaluation into development cycles. In addition, most developers have a technical training that does not encourage them to value qualitative data. Here is an example where it has been adapted for evaluation.

In a project for the Department of Juvenile Justice, Ann Rose and her colleagues developed a procedure to be used by technical design teams with limited ethnographic training (Rose *et al.*, 1995). This applied form of ethnography acknowledges the comparatively small amounts of time available for any kind of user study. By making the process more structured, the amount of time needed for the study can be reduced. It also emphasizes that taking time to become familiar with the intricacies of a system enhances the evaluator's credibility during the field study and promotes productive fieldwork. The procedures this group advocates are highly structured, and while they may seem contrary to ethnographic practice, this structure helps to make it possible for some development teams to benefit from an applied ethnographic approach. There are four stages, as follows:

1. Preparation
   Understand organization policies and work culture.
   Familiarize yourself with the system and its history.
   Set initial goals and prepare questions.
   Gain access and permission to observe and interview.
2. Field study
   Establish a rapport with managers and users.
   Observe and interview users in their workplace and collect data.
   Follow any leads that emerge from the visits.
   Record your visits.
3. Analysis
   Compile the collected data in numerical, textual, and multimedia databases.
   Quantify data and compile statistics.
   Reduce and interpret the data.
   Refine the goals and processes used.
4. Reporting
   Consider multiple audiences and goals.
   Prepare a report and present the findings. ■

7.6.2 Direct observation in controlled environments

Observing users in a controlled environment most commonly occurs within a usability laboratory and during the evaluation stage of the lifecycle. Observation in a controlled environment inevitably takes on a more formal character than observation in the field, and the user is likely to feel apprehensive. As with interviews discussed in Section 7.4, it is a good idea to prepare a script to guide how the participants will be greeted, be told about the goals of the study and how long it will last, and have their rights explained.

The same basic data recording techniques are used for direct observation in the laboratory and field studies (i.e. capturing photographs, taking notes, collecting video, etc.), but the way in which these techniques are used is different. In the laboratory the emphasis is on the details of what individuals do, while in the field the context is important and the focus is on how people interact with each other, the technology, and their environment. The equipment in the laboratory is usually set up in advance and is relatively static, but in order to avoid participants having to travel to a purpose-built usability laboratory, portable usability laboratories are now available—see Box 7.10.

The arrangement of equipment with respect to the participant is important in a usability laboratory because the details of activity need to be captured. Many usability laboratories, for example, have two or three wall-mounted, adjustable cameras to record users' activities while they work on test tasks. One camera might record facial expressions, another might focus on mouse and keyboard activity, and another might record a broad view of the participant and capture body language. The stream of data from the cameras is fed into a video editing and analysis suite where it is annotated and partially edited.

Box 7.10
Usability laboratory in a box

It is now possible to buy a portable usability laboratory in a suitcase which you can carry around with you. The advantages include that they record straight to hard disk, skipping out the laborious task of encoding video tapes one-by-one; they mix up to four video feeds into a single file, avoiding post hoc synchronization issues; they can be taken anywhere and can be up and running in minutes; they don't require any software installation on the test PC; they are suitable for evaluating mobile devices using the clip-on camera; and are also good for capturing spatially distributed interaction, e.g. ethnographic style observational studies or focus groups. You will read more about this in Chapter 14. ■

The think-aloud technique

One of the problems with observation is that the observer doesn't know what users are thinking, and can only guess from what they see. Observation in the field should not be intrusive as this will disturb the very context you are trying to capture, so asking questions of the participant should be limited. However, in a controlled environment, the observer

Figure 7.12 Home page of Lycos search engine

can afford to be a little more intrusive. The think-aloud technique is a useful way of understanding what is going on in a person's head.

Imagine observing someone who has been asked to evaluate the interface of the web search engine Lycos. The user, who has used the web only once before, is told to find a list of the books written by the well-known biologist Stephen Jay Gould. He is told to type `http://www.lycos.com` and then proceed however he thinks best. He types the URL and gets a screen similar to the one in Figure 7.12.

Next he clicks on the People label just above the search box. He gets a screen similar to the one in Figure 7.13. He is silent. What is going on, you wonder? What is he thinking?

One way around this problem is to collect a think-aloud protocol, a technique developed by Erikson and Simon (1985) for examining people's problem-solving strategies. The technique requires people to say out loud everything that they are thinking and trying to do, so that their thought processes are externalized.

So, let's imagine an action replay of the situation just described, but this time the user has been instructed to think aloud:

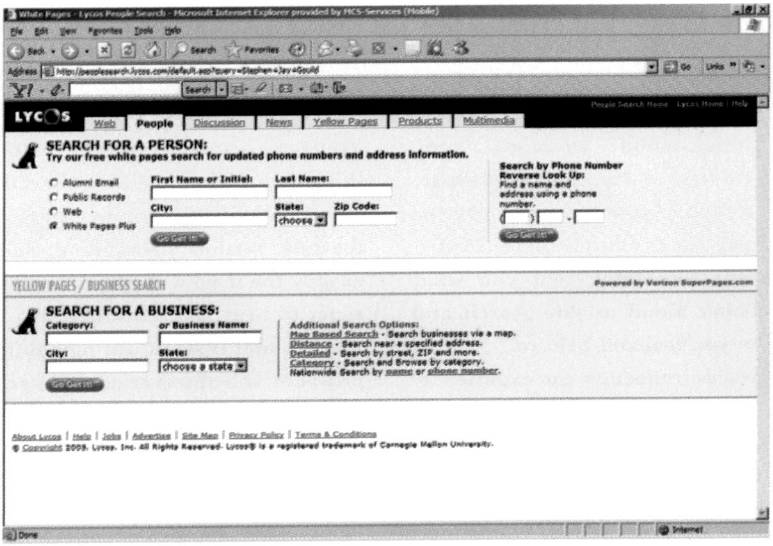

Figure 7.13 The screen that appears in response to choosing the People label

I'm typing in http://www.lycos.com as you told me. **(types)**
Now I press the enter key, right? **(presses enter key)**
(pause and silence)
It's taking a few moments to respond.
Oh! Here it is. **(Figure 7.12 appears)**
Gosh, there's a lot of stuff on this screen, hmmm, I wonder what I do next. **(pauses and looks at the screen)** ***Probably a simple search. What's an advanced search? And there's all these things to choose from?***
I just want to find Stephen Jay Gould, right, so let's go to the People section, and type in his name, then it's bound to have a list of his books? **(pause, moves cursor towards the People label. Positions cursor. Clicks)**
Ah! What's this . . . **(looks at screen and Figure 7.13 appears)**
(silence . . .)

Now you know more about what the user is trying to achieve but he is silent again. You can see that he has gone to the phone book search and that he doesn't realize that he will not find information about Stephen Jay Gould from here. What you don't know is what he is thinking now or what he is looking at. Has he realized where he's gone wrong? Is he confused?

The occurrence of these silences is one of the biggest problems with the think-aloud technique.

Activity 7.9

Try a think-aloud exercise yourself. Go to an e-commerce website, such as `http://www.Amazon.com` or `http://www.BarnesandNoble.com`, and look for something that you want to buy. Think aloud as you search and notice how you feel and behave.

Afterwards, reflect on the experience. Did you find it difficult to keep speaking all the way through the task? Did you feel awkward? Did you stop when you got stuck?

Comment

You probably felt self-conscious and awkward doing this. Some people say they feel really embarrassed. At times you may also have started to forget to speak out loud because it feels like talking to yourself, which most of us don't do normally. You may also have found it difficult to think aloud when the task got difficult. In fact, you probably stopped speaking when the task became demanding, and that is exactly the time when an observer is most eager to hear your comments.

If a user is silent during a think-aloud protocol, the observer could interrupt and remind him to think out loud, but that would be intrusive. Another solution is to have two people work together so that they talk to each other. Working with another person is often more natural and revealing because they talk in order to help each other along. This technique has been found particularly successful with children. It is also very effective when evaluating systems intended to be used synchronously by groups of users, e.g. shared whiteboards.

7.6.3 Indirect observation: tracking users' activities

Sometimes direct observation is not possible because it is obtrusive or observers cannot be present over the duration of the study, and so activities are tracked indirectly. Diaries and interaction logs are two techniques for doing this.

Diaries

In this technique, participants are asked to write a diary of their activities on a regular basis, e.g. what they did, when they did it, what they found hard or easy, and what their reactions were to the situation. For example, Robinson and Godbey (1997) asked participants in their study to record how much time they spent on various activities. These diaries were completed at the end of each day and the data was later analyzed to investigate the impact of television on people's lives.

Diaries are useful when participants are scattered and unreachable in person, for example as in many Internet and web-based projects. Diaries have several advantages: they do not take up much resource, require no special equipment or expertise, and are suitable for long-term studies. In addition, templates, like those used in open-ended online questionnaires, can be created online to standardize entry format and enable the data to go straight into a database for analysis. However, diary studies rely on participants being reliable and remembering to complete them, so incentives may be needed and the process has to be straightforward and quick. Another problem is that participants' memories of events are often exaggerated, e.g. remembering them as better or worse than they really were, or taking more or less time than they actually did.

The use of multiple media in diaries, e.g. photographs, audio clips, etc., is being explored by several researchers. Carter and Mankoff (2005) consider whether capturing events through pictures, audio, or artifacts related to the event affects the results of the diary study. They found that images resulted in more specific recall than other media, but audio was useful for capturing events when taking a picture was too awkward. Also, they found that tangible artifacts such as those in Figure 7.14 are more likely to result in discussion about wider beliefs and attitudes.

A diary study using different media was conducted by Barry Brown and his colleagues, who collected diaries from 22 people to examine when, how, and why they capture different types of information, such as notes, marks on paper, scenes, sounds, moving images, etc. (Brown *et al.*, 2000). The participants were each given a small handheld camera

Figure 7.14 *Some tangible objects collected by participants involved in a study about a jazz festival*

and told to take a picture every time they captured information in any form. The study lasted for seven days and the pictures were used as memory joggers in a subsequent semi-structured interview used to get participants to elaborate on their activities; 381 activities were recorded. The pictures provided useful contextual information. From this data the investigators constructed a framework to inform the design of new digital cameras and handheld scanners.

Interaction logs

Interaction logging involves instrumenting the software to record users' activity in a log that can be examined later. A variety of actions may be recorded, from key presses, mouse or other device movements, to time spent looking at help systems and task flow through software modules. If used in a usability evaluation, then gathering of the data is usually synchronized with video and audio logs to help evaluators analyze users' behavior and understand how users worked on the tasks they set.

Logging the number of visitors to a website is a common application of interaction logs, as the results can be used to justify maintenance and upgrades. For example, if you want to find out whether adding a bulletin board to an e-commerce website increases the number of visits, it is useful to be able to compare traffic before and after the addition of the bulletin board. You can also track how long people stayed at the site, which areas they visited, where they came from, and where they went next by tracking their Internet Service Provider (ISP) address. For example, in a study of an interactive art museum by researchers at the University of Southern California, server logs were analyzed by tracking visitors in this way (McLaughlin *et al.*, 1999). Records of when people came to the site, what they requested, how long they looked at each page, what browser they were using, and what country they were from, etc., were collected over a seven-month period. The data was analyzed using Webtrends, a commercial analysis tool, and the evaluators discovered that the site was busiest on weekday evenings. In another study that investigated lurking behavior in listserver discussion groups, the number of messages posted was compared with list membership over a three-month period to see how lurking behavior differed among groups (Nonnecke and Preece, 2000).

A key advantage of logging activity is that it is unobtrusive provided system performance is not affected, but it also raises ethical concerns about observing participants without their knowledge (see the Dilemma box that follows). Another advantage is that large volumes of data can be logged automatically. However, powerful tools are needed to explore and analyze this data quantitatively and qualitatively. An increasing number of visualization tools are being developed for this purpose; one example is WebLog, which dynamically shows visits to websites, as illustrated in Figure 7.15 (Hochheiser and Shneiderman, 2001). A further example is shown in Figures 8.6 and 8.7.

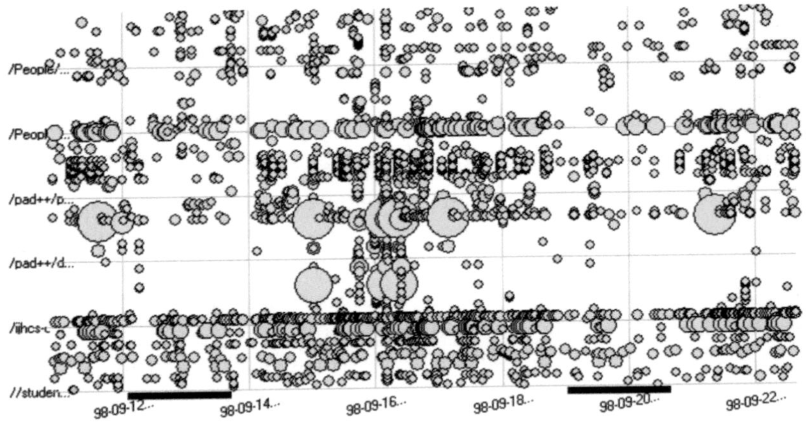

Figure 7.15 *A display from WebLog, time versus URL. The requested URL is on the y-axis, with the date and time on the x-axis. The dark lines on the x-axis correspond to weekends. Each circle represents a request for a single page, and the size of the circle indicates the number of bytes delivered for a given request. (Color indicates the http status response)*

While logging software can provide very useful data for website developers and application designers, it also has had some unfortunate negative side effects in Spyware, see Box 7.11.

Dilemma
They don't know we are watching. Shall we tell them?

If you have appropriate algorithms and sufficient computer storage, large quantities of data about Internet usage can be collected and users need never know. This information could be very valuable for many different reasons, but if we tell users that we are logging their behavior they may object or change their behavior. So, what should we do? It depends on the context, how much personal information is collected, and how the information will be used. Many companies now tell you that your computer activity and phone calls may be logged for quality assurance and other purposes. Most people do not object to this practice. However, should we be concerned about logging personal information (e.g. discussions about health or financial information)? Should users be worried? How can we exploit the ability to log user behavior when visiting websites without overstepping a person's civil rights? Where should we draw the line?

Box 7.11
Spyware: user logging without users knowing

A staggering number of PCs across the world have been infected by spyware; one independent survey found that nearly 90% of consumer machines have been hit (Webroot, cited in Hines, 2005). These are programs that are secretly deposited on computers that then roam around collecting information about users' browsing patterns, without letting them know. The logged data is then used to launch pop-up ads that target users, redirect web searches, and more insidiously steal users' personal information. Among the most popular programs are adware, keystroke loggers, and system monitors. Is this a desirable, ethical, or acceptable way of using data logging? What can be done about it?

Many people are beginning to change their online behavior, having learnt that spyware usually hijacks shareware and file-sharing programs they have downloaded from the web. They stop visiting such sites for fear that they harbor the spyware. ■

7.7 Choosing and combining techniques

It is usual to combine data gathering techniques in any one data gathering program in order to triangulate findings. Choosing which data gathering techniques to use depends on a variety of factors pertaining to the focus of the study, the participants involved, the nature of the technique, and the resources available. There is no 'right' technique or combination of techniques, but the decision will need to take all of these factors into account. Table 7.2 provides some information to help choose a set of techniques for a specific project. It lists the kind of information you can get, e.g. answers to specific questions, and the kind of data it yields, e.g. mostly qualitative or mostly quantitative. It also includes some advantages and disadvantages for each technique.

The focus of the study

The techniques used must be compatible with the goal of the study, i.e. they must be able to gather appropriate data. For example, the data to be collected may be implicit knowledge or it may be explicit, observable behavior; it may be opinion or it may be facts; it may be formal documented rules or it may be informal work-arounds and heuristics; it may be publicly accessible information or it may be confidential, and so on. The kind of data you want will probably be influenced by where you are in the development cycle. For example, at the beginning of the project you may not have any specific questions that need answering, so it is better to spend time exploring issues through interviews and observation rather than sending out questionnaires.

Technique	Good for	Kind of data[2]	Advantages	Disadvantages
Interviews	Exploring issues.	Some quantitative but mostly qualitative.	Interviewer can guide interviewee if necessary. Encourages contact between developers and users.	Time-consuming. Artificial environment may intimidate interviewee.
Focus groups	Collecting multiple viewpoints.	Some quantitative but mostly qualitative.	Highlights areas of consensus and conflict. Encourages contact between developers and users.	Possibility of dominant characters.
Questionnaires	Answering specific questions.	Quantitative and qualitative.	Can reach many people with low resource.	The design is crucial. Response rate may be low. Responses may not be what you want.
Direct observation in the field	Understanding context of user activity.	Mostly qualitative.	Observing actual work gives insights that other techniques can't give.	Very time-consuming. Huge amounts of data.

(continued)

Table 7.2 *Overview of data gathering techniques and their use*

[2] For a discussion of qualitative and quantitative see Section 8.2.

Technique	Good for	Kind of data[2]	Advantages	Disadvantages
Direct observation in a controlled environment	**Learning about procedures, regulations and standards.**	**Quantitative and qualitative.**	**Can focus on the details of a task without interruption.**	**Results may have limited use in the normal environment because the conditions were artificial.**
Indirect observation	**Observing users without disturbing their activity; data captured automatically.**	**Quantitative (logging) and qualitative (diary).**	**User doesn't get distracted by the data gathering; automatic recording means that it can extend over long periods of time.**	**A large amount of quantitative data needs tool support to analyze (logging); participants' memories may exaggerate (diary).**

Table 7.2 *(continued)*

The task being investigated will also have dimensions that influence the techniques to use. For example, Olson and Moran (1996) suggest a task can be characterized along three dimensions: is it a set of sequential steps or a rapid overlapping series of subtasks; does it involve a lot of information and complex displays, or little information and simple representations; is the task to be performed by a layman or by a trained professional?

The participants involved

The characteristics of the target user group for the product will affect the kind of data gathering technique used. For example, techniques used for data gathering from young children may be very different from those used with adults (see Box 7.2). If the participants are in a hurry to catch a plane, they will not be receptive to a long interview; if their job involves interacting with people then they may be comfortable in a focus group, and so on.

The location and accessibility of participants also needs to be considered. It may be attractive to run a focus group for a large set of stakeholders, but if they are spread across a wide geographical area, it is unlikely to be practical. Similarly, the time participants need to give their undivided attention to the session is significant, e.g. an interview requires a higher level of active engagement while an observation allows the participant to continue with her normal activity.

Depending on what is motivating the participants to take part, it may be better to conduct interviews rather than to issue a questionnaire. It may also be better to conduct a focus group in order to widen consultation and participation, thereby enhancing feelings of ownership and expectations of the users.

The nature of the technique

We have already mentioned the issue of participants' time and the kind of data to be collected, but there is also the issue of whether the technique requires specialist equipment or training, and whether available investigators have the appropriate knowledge and experience. For example, how experienced is the investigator at conducting ethnographic studies, or in handling video data?

Available resources

The resources available will influence the choice, too. For example, sending out questionnaires nationwide requires sufficient time, money, and people to do a good design, pilot it, issue it, collate the results, and analyze them. If there is only three weeks and no-one on the team has designed a questionnaire before, then this is unlikely to be a success.

Activity 7.10

For each of the situations below, consider what kinds of data gathering would be appropriate and how you might use the different techniques introduced above. You should assume that you are at the beginning of the development and that you have sufficient time and resources to use any of the techniques.

1. **You are developing a new software system to support a small accountant's office. There is a system running already with which the users are reasonably happy, but it is looking dated and needs upgrading.**
2. **You are looking to develop an innovative device for diabetes sufferers to help them record and monitor their blood sugar levels. There are some products already on the market, but they tend to be large and unwieldy. Many diabetes sufferers rely on manual recording and monitoring methods involving a ritual with a needle, some chemicals, and a written scale.**
3. **You are developing a website for a young persons' fashion e-commerce site.**

Comment

1. **As this is a small office, there are likely to be few stakeholders. Some period of observation is always important to understand the context of the new and the old system. Interviewing the staff rather than giving them questionnaires is likely to be appropriate because there aren't very many of them, and this will yield richer data and give the developers a chance to meet the users. Accountancy is regulated by a variety of laws and it would also pay to look at documentation to understand some of the constraints from this direction. So we would suggest a series of interviews with the main users to understand the positive and negative features of the existing system, a short observation session to understand the context of the system, and a study of documentation surrounding the regulations.**
2. **In this case, your user group is spread about, so talking to all of them is infeasible. However, it is important to interview some, possibly at a local diabetic clinic, making sure that you have a representative sample. And you would need to observe the existing manual operation to understand what is required. A further group of stakeholders would be those who use or have used the other products on the market. These stakeholders can be questioned to find out the problems with the existing devices so that the new device can improve on them. A questionnaire sent to a wider group in order to back up the findings from the interviews would be appropriate, as might a focus group where possible.**
3. **Again, you are not going to be able to interview all your users. In fact, the user group may not be very well defined. Interviews backed up by questionnaires and focus groups would be appropriate. Also, in this case, identifying similar or competing sites and evaluating them will help provide information for producing an improved product.**

Assignment

The aim of this assignment is for you to practice data gathering. Assume that you have been employed to improve an interactive product such as a mobile phone, an iPOD, a VCR, a photocopying machine, computer software, or some other type of technology that interests you. You may either redesign this product, or create a completely new product. To do the assignment you will need to find a group of people or a single individual prepared to be your user group. These could be your family, your friends, or people in your class or local community group.

For this assignment you should:

(a) Clarify the basic goal of 'improving the product' by considering what this means in your circumstances.

(b) Watch the group (or person) casually to get an understanding of issues that might create challenges for you doing this assignment and information that might enable you to refine your goals.

(c) Explain how you would use each of the three data gathering techniques: interview, questionnaire, and observation in your data gathering program. Explain how your plan takes account of triangulation.

(d) Consider your relationship with your user group and decide if an informed consent form is required (Box 13.2 will help you to design your own if needed).

(e) Plan your data gathering program in detail:

  (i) Decide what kind of interview you want to run, and design a set of interview questions for your study. Decide how you will record data, then acquire and test any equipment needed and run a pilot study.

  (ii) Decide whether you want to include a questionnaire in your data gathering program, and design appropriate questions for it. Run a pilot study to check your questionnaire.

  (iii) Decide whether you want to use direct or indirect observation and where on the outsider–insider spectrum of observers you wish to be. Decide how you will record data, then acquire and test any equipment needed and run a pilot study.

(f) Carry out your study but limit its scope. For example, only interview two or three people or plan only two half-hour observation periods.

(g) Reflect on your experience and suggest what you would do differently next time.

Keep the data you have gathered as this will form the basis of the assignment in Chapter 8.

Summary

This chapter has presented three main data gathering methods that are commonly used in interaction design: interviews, questionnaires, and observation. It has described in detail the planning and execution of each. In addition, four key issues of data gathering were presented, and how to record the data gathered was discussed.

Key points

- All data gathering sessions should have clear goals.
- Each planned data gathering session should be tested by running a pilot study.
- Triangulation involves a combination of data gathering techniques.
- Data may be recorded using handwritten notes, audio or video recording, a camera, or any combination of these.
- There are three styles of interviews: structured, semi-structured, and unstructured.
- Questionnaires may be paper-based, email, or web-based.
- Questions for an interview or questionnaire can be open or closed. Closed questions require the interviewee to select from a limited range of options. Open questions accept a free-range response.
- Observation may be direct or indirect.

- In direct observation, the observer may adopt different levels of participation ranging from 'insider' (participant observer) to 'outsider' (passive observer).
- Choosing appropriate data gathering techniques depends on the focus of the study, the participants involved, the nature of the technique, and the resources available.

Further Reading

ANDREWS, D., NONNECKE, B. and PREECE, J. (2003) Electronic survey methodology: a case study in reaching hard-to-involve internet users. *International Journal of Human–Computer Interaction* **16**(2): 185–210. This paper provides a comprehensive review of electronic survey design issues, based on recent literature. It then goes on to describe a case study from online communities showing how the quality criteria identified from this literature can be implemented.

OPPENHEIM, A.N. (1992) *Questionnaire Design, Interviewing and Attitude Measurement.* Pinter Publishers. This text is useful for reference. It provides a detailed account of all aspects of questionnaire design, illustrated with many examples.

ROBSON, C. (2002) *Real World Research*, 2nd edn. Blackwell Publishing. This book provides comprehensive coverage of data gathering (and analysis) techniques and how to use them.

BLY, S. (1997) Field work: is it product work? *Interactions* Jan/Feb: 25–30. This article provides additional information to supplement the interview with Sara Bly. It gives a broad perspective on the role of participant observation in product development.

BOGDEWIC, S.P. (1992) Participant observation. In *Doing Qualitative Research*, B.F. Crabtree and W.L. Miller (eds). Sage, pp. 45–69. This chapter provides an introduction to participant observation.

FETTERMAN, D.M. (1998). *Ethnography: Step by Step*, 2nd edn (Vol. 17). Sage. This book provides an introduction to the theory and practice of ethnography and is an excellent guide for beginners. In addition, it has a useful section on computerized tools for ethnography.

FULTON SURI, J. (2005) *Thoughtless Acts?* Chronicle Books, San Francisco. This intriguing little book invites you to consider how people react to their environment. It is a good introduction to the art of observation.

INTERVIEW with Sara Bly

Sara Bly is a user-centered design consultant who specializes in the design and evaluation of distributed group technologies and practices. As well as having a Ph.D. in computer science, Sara is one of the pioneers in the development of rich, qualitative observational techniques for gathering data to analyze group interactions and activities that inform technology design. Prior to becoming a consultant, Sara managed the Collaborative Systems Group at Xerox Palo Alto Research Center (PARC). While at PARC, Sara also contributed to ground-breaking work on shared drawing, awareness systems, and systems that used non-speech audio to represent information, and to the PARC Media Space project, in which video, audio, and computing technologies were uniquely combined to create a trans-geographical laboratory.

JP: Sara, tell us about your work and what especially interests you.
SB: I'm interested in the ways that qualitative studies, particularly based on ethnographic methods, can inform design and development of technologies. My work spans the full gamut of user-centered design, from early conceptual design through iterative prototypes to final product deployment. I've worked on a wide range of projects from complex collaborative systems to straightforward desktop applications, and a variety of new technologies. My recent projects include a study of how people save and use the information they encounter while reading, a home projector with integrated DVD and an exploration of how people solve problems in home networks.

JP: Why do you think qualitative methods are so important for data gathering?
SB: I strongly believe that technical systems are closely bound with the social setting in which they are used. An important part of design and evaluation is to look 'beyond the task.' Too often we think of computer systems in isolation from the rest of the activities in which the people are involved. It's important to be able to see the interface in the context of ongoing practice. Usually the complexities and 'messiness' of everyday life do not lend themselves to constraining the data gathering to very specific and narrow questions. Qualitative methods are

particularly helpful for exploring complex systems that involve several tasks, embedded in other activities that include multiple users.

JP: Can you give me an example?
SB: I was part of a team exploring how people encounter and save published material in the form of paper and electronic clippings. We conducted twenty artifact interviews in homes and offices. We weren't surprised to find that everyone has clippings of some form and they often share them. However, we were somewhat surprised to find that these shared clippings did more than provide a simple exchange of information. In fact, the content itself did not always have immediate value to the recipient. The data that particularly intrigued me was that the clippings could be a form of social bonding. Several recipients described some of their clippings as an indication that the giver was 'thinking of' them. This came from the open-ended interviews we had with people who were describing a range of materials they read and clippings they receive.[3]

JP: Collaborative applications seem particularly difficult to understand out of context.
SB: Yes, you have to look at collaborative systems integrated within an organizational culture in which working relationships are taken into account. We know that work practice impacts system design and that the introduction of a new system impacts work practice. Consequently, the system and the practice have to evolve together. Understanding the task or the interface is impossible without understanding the environment in which the system is or will be used.

JP: Much of what you've described involves various forms of observation. How do you collect and analyze this data?
SB: It's important that qualitative methods are not seen as just *watching*. Any method we use has at least three critical phases. First, there is the initial assessment of the domain and/or technology and the determination of the focal points to address. Second is the data collection, analysis, and representation, and third, the communication of the findings with the research or development team. I try to start with a clear understanding of what I need to focus on in the field. However, I also try hard not to start with assumptions about what will be true. So, I start with a *well-defined* focus but *not* a hypothesis. In the field (or even in the lab), I primarily use interviews and observations with some self-reporting that often takes the form of diaries, etc. The data typically consist of my notes, the audio and/or videotapes from interviews and observation time, still pictures, and as many artifacts as I can appropriately gather, e.g. a work document covered with post-its, a page from an old calendar. I also prefer to work with at least one other colleague so that there is a minimum of two perspectives on the events and data.

JP: It sounds like keeping track of all this data could be a problem. How do you organize and analyze it?
SB: Obviously it's critical not to end with the data collection. Whenever possible, I do

[3]Further information about this work is in Marshall and Bly (2004).

immediate debriefs after each session in the field with my colleagues, noting individually and collectively whatever jumped out at us. Subsequently, I use the interview notes (from everyone involved) and the tapes and artifacts to construct as much of a picture of what happened as possible, without putting any judgment on it. For example, in a recent study six of us were involved in interviews and observations. We worked in pairs and tried to vary the pairings as often as possible. Thus, we had lots of conversations about the data and the situations before we ever came together. First, we wrote up the notes from each session (something I try to do as soon as possible). Next we got together and began looking across the data. That is, we created representations of important events (tables, maps, charts) together. Because we collectively had observed all the events and because we could draw upon our notes, we could feed the data from each observation into each finding. Oftentimes, we create collections, looking for common behaviors or events across multiple sessions. A collection will highlight activities that are crucial in addressing the original focal points of the study. Whatever techniques we use, we always come back to the data as a reality and validity check.

JP: Is it difficult to get development teams and managers to listen to you? How do you feed your findings back?

SB: As often as possible, research and development teams are involved in the process along the way. They participate in setting the initial focal points for gathering data, occasionally in observation sessions, and as recipients of a final report. My goal with any project is to ensure that the final report is not a handoff but rather an interactive session that offers a chance to work together on what we've found.

JP: What are the main challenges you face?

SB: It's always difficult to conduct a field study with as much time and participation as would be ideal. Most development cycles are short and collecting the field data is just one of many necessary steps. So it's always a challenge to do a qualitative study that is timely, useful, and yet based on solid methodology.

The real gnawing question for me is how to get valuable data in the context of the customer's own environment and experience when either the activities are not easily observable and/or the system is not fully developed and ready to deploy. For example, a client recently had a prototype interface for a system that was intended to provide a new approach to person-to-person calls. It was not possible to give it to people to use outside the lab but using the interface only made sense in the context of actual real-world interactions. So, while we certainly could do a standard usability study of the interface, this approach wouldn't get at the questions of how well the product would fit into an actual work situation. What kinds of data can we hope to get in that situation that will inform us reliably about real world activity?

Of course there are always 'day-to-day' challenges; that's what makes the work so much fun to do! For instance, in the clipping study mentioned earlier, we expected that people would be likely to forget many of their clippings. How do we uncover the forgotten? We pushed to look at different rooms and different places (file drawers, piles by the sofa, the refrigerator), often discovering a clipping ourselves that we could then explore in conversation. We didn't want to rely on asking participants to predetermine what clippings they had.

In a more recent study of reading, one of our participants regularly reads in bed. How do we gather realistic data in that situation while not compromising our participant? In this case, we set up a videocamera that our participant turned on himself. He just let a tape run out each day so that he could fall asleep as normally as possible.

JP: Finally, what about the future? Any comments?

SB: I think the explosion of digital technologies is both exciting and overwhelming. We now have so much new information constantly available and so many new devices to master that it's hard to keep up. The digital home is now even more complex than the digital office. This makes design more challenging—there are more complex activities, more diverse users and more conflicting requirements to pull together. To observe and understand this growth is a challenge that will require all the techniques at our disposal. I think an increasingly important aspect of new interfaces and interaction procedures will be not only how well they support performance, satisfaction, and experience, but how well a user is able to grasp a conceptual model that allows them to transition from current practices to new ones.

8

8.1 Introduction

The kind of analysis that can be performed on a set of data will be influenced by the goals identified at the outset, and the data actually gathered. Broadly speaking, you may take a qualitative analysis approach or a quantitative analysis approach, or a combination of qualitative and quantitative. The last of these is very common as it supports triangulation and provides flexibility.

Most analysis, whether it is quantitative or qualitative, begins with initial reactions or observations from the data. This might involve identifying patterns or calculating simple numerical values such as ratios, averages, or percentages. This initial analysis is followed by more detailed work using structured frameworks or theories to support the investigation.

Interpretation of the findings often proceeds in parallel with analysis, but there are different ways to interpret results and it is important to make sure that the data supports your conclusions. A common mistake is for the investigator's existing beliefs or biases to influence the interpretation of results. Imagine that through initial analysis of your data you have discovered a pattern of responses to customer care questionnaires which indicates that inquiries from customers that are routed through the Sydney office of an organization take longer to process than those routed through the Moscow office. This result can be interpreted in many different ways. Which do you choose? You may conclude that the customer care operatives in Sydney are less efficient, or you may conclude that the customer care operatives in Sydney provide more detailed responses, or you may conclude that the technology supporting the processing of inquiries needs to be updated in Sydney, or you may conclude that customers reaching the Sydney office demand a higher level of service, and so on. In order to determine which of these potential interpretations is more accurate, it would be appropriate to look at other data such as customer inquiry details, and maybe interviews with staff.

Another common mistake is to make claims that go beyond what the data can support. This is a matter of interpretation and of presentation. The words 'many' or 'often' or indeed 'all' need to be used very carefully when reporting conclusions. An investigator should remain as impartial and objective as possible if the conclusions are to be believed, and showing that your conclusions are supported by your results is an important skill to develop.

Finally, finding the best way to present your findings is equally skilled, and depends on your goals but also on the audience for whom the results were produced. For example, in the requirements activity you might choose to present your findings using a formal notation, while reporting the results of an evaluation to the team of developers might involve a summary of problems found, supported by video clips of users experiencing those problems.

In this chapter we will introduce a variety of methods and describe in more detail how to approach data analysis using some of the common approaches taken in interaction design.

8

Data analysis, interpretation, and presentation

The main aims of this chapter are to:

- **Discuss the difference between qualitative and quantitative data and analysis.**
- **Enable you to be able to analyze data gathered from questionnaires.**
- **Enable you to be able to analyze data gathered from interviews.**
- **Enable you to be able to analyze data gathered from observation studies.**
- **Make you aware of the kind of software packages that are available to help your analysis.**
- **Identify some of the common pitfalls in data analysis, interpretation, and presentation.**
- **Enable you to be able to interpret and present your findings in a meaningful and appropriate manner.**

8.2 Qualitative and quantitative

Quantitative data is data that is in the form of numbers, or that can easily be translated into numbers. For example, the number of years' experience the interviewees have, the number of projects a department handles at a time, or the number of minutes it takes to perform a task. Qualitative data is data that is difficult to measure, count, or express in numerical terms in a sensible fashion (it may be possible to record or express qualitative data in a numerical form, but that does not mean it is sensible to do so—see Box 8.1).

It is sometimes assumed that certain forms of data gathering will only result in quantitative data and others will only result in qualitative data. However, this is a fallacy. All the forms of data gathering discussed in the previous chapter may result in qualitative and quantitative data. For example, on a questionnaire, questions about the participant's age, or number of software packages they use a day, will result in quantitative data, while any 'comments' fields will result in qualitative data. In an observation, quantitative data you may record includes the number of people involved in a project, or how many hours a participant spends trying to sort out a problem they encounter, while notes about the level of frustration, or the nature of interactions between team members, is qualitative data.

Quantitative analysis uses numerical methods to ascertain the magnitude, amount, or size of something, for example, the attributes, behavior, or opinions of the participants. For example, in describing a population, a quantitative analysis might conclude that the average person is 5 feet 11 inches tall, weighs 180 pounds, and is 45 years old. Qualitative analysis focuses on the nature of something and can be represented by themes, patterns, and stories. For example, in describing the same population, a qualitative analysis might conclude that the average person is tall, thin, and middle-aged.

Box 8.1
Use and abuse of numbers

Numerical information can be used and abused in many ways, and if you are not comfortable dealing with numbers, it is always better to ask for help from someone who is, because it is easy to misrepresent your data. Any qualitative data can be turned into a set of numbers, which in turn can be manipulated in a wide variety of ways, and then interpreted with respect to your goals. People tend to believe that numbers offer a stronger or clearer conclusion, and so there is a strong temptation to use numbers, even though, on reflection, you would probably realize that their use is unwarranted. For example, assume that you have collected a set of interviews from sales representatives regarding the use of a new mobile product for reporting sales queries. One way of turning this data into a numerical form would be to count the number of words uttered by each of your interviewees.

You might then draw conclusions about how strongly the sales representatives feel about the mobile devices, e.g. the more they had to say about the product, the stronger they feel about it. But do you think this is a wise way to analyze the data? This set of quantitative data is unlikely to be of much use in answering your study questions.

Other, less obvious abuses include translating small population sizes into percentages. For example, saying that 50% of users take longer than 30 minutes to place an order through an e-commerce website carries a different meaning than saying that two out of four users had the same problem. It is better not to use percentages unless the number of data points is at least over 10, and even then it is appropriate to use both percentages and raw numbers, to make sure that your claim is not misunderstood.

Numbers are infinitely malleable, and make a very convincing argument, but before adding a set of numbers together, finding an average, calculating a percentage, or performing any other kind of numerical translation on your data, stop and think about whether what you are doing makes sense in the context.

It is also possible to perform perfectly legitimate statistical calculations on a set of data and still to present misleading results by not making the context clear, or by choosing the particular calculation that gives the most favorable result (Huff, 1991).

There are times when translating non-numerical data into a numerical or ordered scale is perfectly appropriate, and this is a common approach in interaction design. However, you need to be careful that any translations you apply will not misrepresent your data. ■

8.2.1 The first steps in analyzing data

Having performed data gathering sessions, there is some initial processing of the data normally required before data analysis can begin in earnest. There are many different combinations of data, but here we discuss typical data collected through interviews, questionnaires, and observation sessions. This information is summarized in Table 8.1.

Interviews. Raw interview data is usually in the form of audio recordings and interviewer notes. The notes need to be written up and expanded as soon as possible after the interview has taken place so that the interviewer's memory is clear and fresh. The audio recording may be used to help in this process, or it may be transcribed (i.e. written out) for more detailed analysis. Transcription takes significant effort, as people talk more quickly than most people can type (or write), and the recording is not always very clear, requiring the tape to be repeatedly rewound and replayed. It is therefore worth considering whether or not to transcribe the whole interview, or just sections of it that are relevant to your investigation.

Interviews are sometimes video recorded, especially if the interviewee is given a task to perform, or props are used to prompt discussion. The audio channel of the video data may also be transcribed.

Closed questions are usually treated as quantitative data and analyzed using simple quantitative analysis (see below). For example, a question that asks for the respondent's age range can easily be analyzed to find out the percentage of respondents in each range. More complicated statistical techniques are needed to identify relationships between question responses that can be generalized, such as being able to say that men over the age of 35 all believe that buttons on cell phones are too small.

Open questions result in qualitative data which might be searched for categories or patterns of response.

Questionnaires. Raw data from questionnaires consists of the respondents' answers to the questions, and these may be in written format, or for online surveys, the data is likely to be in a database. It may be necessary to clean up the data by removing entries where the respondent has misunderstood a question.

The data can be filtered according to respondent subpopulations, e.g. everyone under 16, or according to question, e.g. to understand respondents' reactions to color. This allows analyses to be conducted on subsets of the data, and hence to draw detailed conclusions for more specific goals. This is made easier by the use of a simple tool such as a spreadsheet, as discussed below.

As for interviews, closed questions are likely to be analyzed quantitatively and open questions qualitatively.

Observation. This kind of data gathering can result in a wide variety of raw data including observer's notes, photographs, data logs, think-aloud protocols, video and audio recordings. All this raw data presents a rich picture of the activity under observation, but it can also make it difficult to analyze unless a structured framework is adopted. Initial data processing here would include writing up and expanding notes, transcribing elements of the audio and video recordings, and the think-aloud protocols. For observation in a controlled environment, initial processing might also include synchronizing different data recordings.

Transcriptions and observer's notes are most likely to be analyzed using qualitative approaches, while photographs provide contextual information. Data logs and some elements of the observer's notes would probably be analyzed quantitatively.

Throughout this initial processing, patterns and themes in the data may present themselves. It is useful to make a note of these initial impressions to use as a basis for further, more detailed analysis, but don't rely on these initial impressions alone as you may be unintentionally biased by them.

	Usual raw data	Example qualitative data	Example quantitative data	Initial processing steps
Interviews	Audio recordings. Interviewer notes. Video recordings.	Responses to open questions. Video pictures. Respondent's opinions.	Age, job role, years of experience. Responses to closed questions.	Transcription of recordings. Expansion of notes.
Questionnaires	Written responses. Online database.	Responses to open questions. Responses in 'further comments' fields. Respondent's opinions.	Age, job role, years of experience. Responses to closed questions.	Clean up data. Filter into different data sets.
Observation	Observer's notes. Photographs. Audio and video recordings. Data logs. Think-aloud.	Records of behavior. Description of a task as it is undertaken. Copies of informal procedures.	Demographics of participants. Time spent on a task. The number of people involved in an activity.	Expansion of notes. Transcription of recordings. Synchronization between data recordings.

***Table 8.1** Data gathered and typical initial processing steps for the main data gathering techniques*

8.3 Simple quantitative analysis

Explaining statistical analysis requires several books on its own. We will not try to explain statistics in any detail, although some basic statistical terms and use of statistics are discussed further in Chapter 14. Here, we introduce some simple quantitative analysis techniques you can use effectively in an interaction design context. The techniques explored here are averages and percentages. Percentages are useful for standardizing the data, particularly if you want to compare two or more large sets of responses.

Averages and percentages are fairly well-known numerical measures. However, there are three different types of 'average' and which one you use changes the meaning of your results. These three are: mean, median, and mode. Mean refers to the commonly understood interpretation of average, i.e. add together all the figures and divide by the number of figures you started with. Median and mode are less well-known but are very useful. The median is the middle value of the data when the numbers are ranked. The mode is the most commonly occurring number. For example, in a set of data (2, 3, 4, 6, 6, 7, 7, 7, 8), the median is 6 and the mode is 7, while the mean is $50/9 = 5.56$. In this case, the difference between the different averages is not that great. However, consider the set (2, 2, 2, 2, 450). Now the median is 2, the mode is 2, and the mean is $458/5 = 91.6$!

Before any analysis can take place, the data need to be collated into analyzable data sets. Quantitative data can usually be translated into rows and columns, where one row equals one record, e.g. respondent or interviewee. If these are then entered into a spreadsheet such as Excel, this makes simple manipulations and data set filtering easier. Before entering data in this way, it is important to decide how you will represent the different possible answers. For example, a 'don't know' answer and no answer at all are different responses that need to be distinguished. Also, if dealing with options from a closed question, such as job role, there are two different possible approaches which affect the analysis. One approach is to have a column headed 'job role' and to enter the job role as it is given to you by the respondent or interviewee. The alternative approach is to have a column for each possible answer. The latter approach lends itself more easily to automatic summaries. Note, however, that this option will only be open to you if the original question was designed to collect the appropriate data (see Box 8.2).

Box 8.2
How question design affects data analysis

Activity 7.2 asked you to suggest some interview questions that you might ask a colleague to help evaluate Cybelle. We shall use this example here to illustrate how different question designs affect the kinds of analysis that can be performed, and the kind of conclusions that can be drawn.

Assume that you have asked the question: "How do you feel about Cybelle?" Responses to this will be varied and may include that she is pretty, wears nice clothes, is life-like, is intelligent, is amusing, is helpful, and so on. There are many possibilities, and the responses would need to be treated qualitatively.

This means that analysis of the data must consider each individual response. If you have only 10 or so responses then this may not be too bad, but if you have many more then it becomes harder to process the information, and harder to summarize your findings. This is typical of open-ended questions—answers are not likely to be homogeneous and so will need to be treated individually. In contrast, answers to a closed question, which gives respondents a fixed set of alternatives to choose from, can be treated quantitatively. So, for example, instead of asking "How do you feel about Cybelle?," assume that you have asked: "In your opinion, is Cybelle amusing or irritating?" This clearly reduces the number of options and you would then record the response as 'irritating,' 'amusing,' or 'neither.'

When entered in a spreadsheet, or a simple table, initial analysis of this data might look like the following:

Respondent	Amusing	Irritating	Neither
A	1		
B		1	
C		1	
...			
Z			1
Total	14	5	7

Based on this, we can then say that 14 out of 26 (54%) of our respondents found Cybelle amusing, 5 out of 26 (19%) found her irritating, and 7 out of 26 (27%) found her neither amusing nor irritating.

Another alternative which might be used in a questionnaire is to phrase the question in terms of a Likert scale, such as the one below. This again alters the kind of data and hence the kind of conclusions that can be drawn:

In your opinion, Cybelle is amusing:

strongly agree	agree	neither	disagree	strongly disagree
☐	☐	☐	☐	☐

Then this data could be analyzed using a simple spreadsheet or table:

Respondent	Strongly agree	Agree	Neither	Disagree	Strongly disagree
A		1			
B	1				
C				1	
...					
Z					1
Total	5	7	10	1	3

In this case we have changed the kind of data we are collecting, and cannot, based on this second set, say anything about whether respondents found Cybelle irritating, as we have not asked that question. We can only say that, for example, 4 out of 26 (15%) disagreed with the statement that Cybelle is amusing (and of those 3 (11.5%) strongly disagreed). ■

For simple collation and analysis, spreadsheet software such as Excel is often used as it is commonly available, well-understood, and it offers a variety of numerical manipulations and graphical representations. Initial analysis might involve finding out averages, and identifying any 'outliers,' i.e. values that are significantly different from the others. Producing a graphical representation of the data helps to get an overall view of the data and any patterns it contains.

For example, consider the set of data shown in Table 8.2 which is extracted from a set of data collected during an evaluation study of an e-commerce website. The overall goal of the study was to identify areas of the website that are problematic for users, and at what point in the transaction the user is likely to abandon the process. The data gathering methods used were questionnaire, observation of a controlled task, and data logging. The data in this table shows the experience of the users and the number of errors made by each user trying to complete the task. This data was captured in a spreadsheet and the totals and averages were calculated automatically once the data had been entered. Then the graphs in Figure 8.1 were generated using a spreadsheet package. From these we

	Internet use					
User	< once a day	once a day	once a week	2 or 3 times a week	once a month	Number of errors made
1		1				4
2	1					2
3			1			1
4	1					0
5				1		2
6		1				3
7	1					2
8		1				0
9					1	3
10	1					2
11				1		1
12			1			2
13		1				4
14		1				2
15						1
16				1		1
17		1			1	0
18		1				0
Totals	4	7	2	3	2	30
					Mean	1.67 (to 2 decimal places)

Table 8.2 *Data gathered during a study of an e-commerce site*

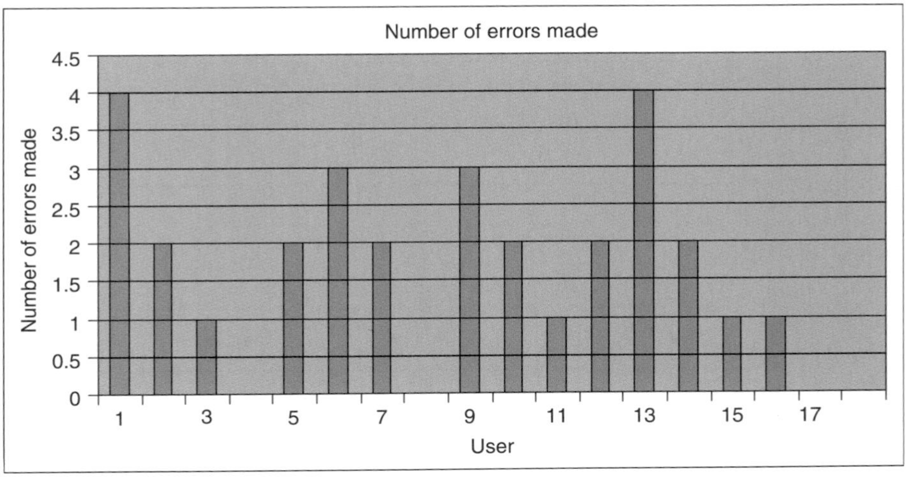

(a)

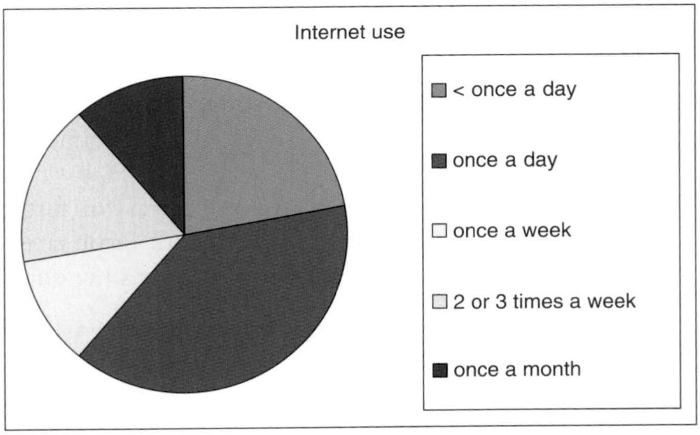

(b)

Figure 8.1 *Graphical representations of the data in Table 8.2. (a) The distribution of errors made. Take note of the scale used in these graphs as seemingly large differences may be much smaller in reality. (b) The spread of Internet experience within the participant group*

can get an overall view of the data set. In particular, we can see that there are no significant outliers in the error rate data. Note that you may choose to present the data to your target audience using these graphical representations, or you may not. The point here is that it is valuable to use them for your own data analysis, whatever happens to them afterwards.

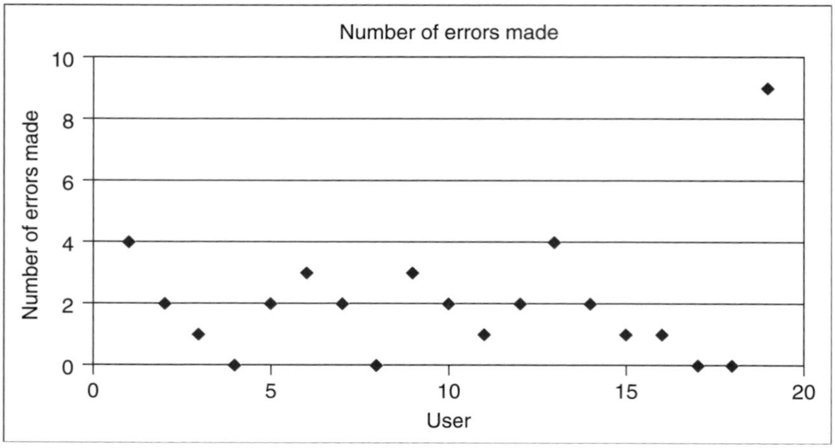

Figure 8.2 *Using a scatter diagram helps to identify outliers in your data quite quickly*

If we add one more user to Table 8.2 with an error rate of 9, we can see in Figure 8.2 how using a scatter graph helps to identify outliers. Outliers are usually removed from the larger data set because they distort the general patterns, however, they may also be interesting cases to investigate further to see if there are special circumstances surrounding this user and their session.

These initial investigations also help to identify other areas for further investigation. For example, is there something special about the users with error rate 0, or something distinctive about the performance of those who use the Internet only once a month?

Activity 8.1

The data in the table below represents the time taken for a group of users to select and buy an item from an online shopping website.

1. **Calculate the mean, median, and mode values for this data.**
2. **Comment on how values differ and consider which of these averages you might choose to report in your study findings.**
3. **Using a spreadsheet application to which you have access, generate a bar graph and a scatter diagram to give you an overall view of the data. Using these diagrams, make two initial observations about the data that might form the basis of further investigation.**

User	A	B	C	D	E	F	G	H	I	J	K	L	M	N	O	P	Q	R	S
Time to complete (mins)	15	10	12	10	14	13	11	18	14	17	20	15	18	24	12	16	18	20	26

Comment

1. The mean is:
   15 + 10 + 12 + 10 + 14 + 13 + 11 + 18+
   14 + 17 + 20 + 15 + 18 + 24 + 12 + 16+
   18 + 20 + 26
   divided by 19 = 303/19 = 15.95 (to 2 decimal places).
   The median is calculated by ranking the values first:
   10, 10, 11, 12, 12, 13, 14, 14, 15, 15, 16, 17, 18, 18, 18, 20, 20, 24, 26
   The median then is 15 and the mode is 18.
2. In this example, the mean and median are close together—15.95 and 15 respectively—and the mode is a bit higher at 18. Each of these averages reports on a different feature of the data, and hence highlights a different point about the participants' performance. The most common completion time is 18 minutes, but this information on its own doesn't say anything about the range of completion times. The middle point of completion times is 15 minutes, but this on its own doesn't say how wide that range is. The mean of 15.95 minutes may indicate that all participants completed the task in exactly this time, or that the range of performance times was between one minute and 285 minutes, or any of a wide range of other combinations. Any one of these averages, taken on its own, gives a partial picture of the data collected. In order to communicate a more accurate, rounded view of the data, it would be better to report all three averages.
3. The first graph is a bar graph:

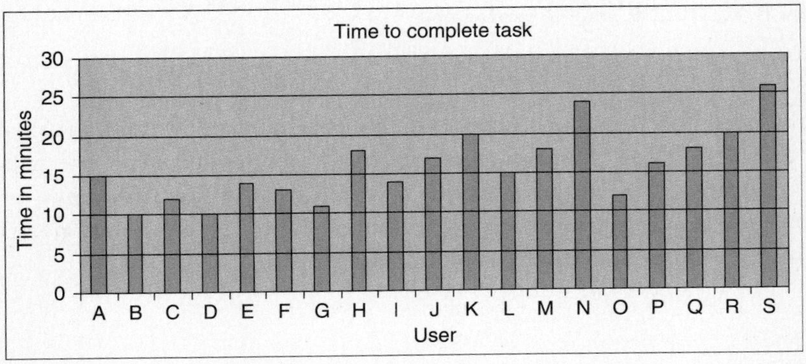

The scatter diagram for this data is:

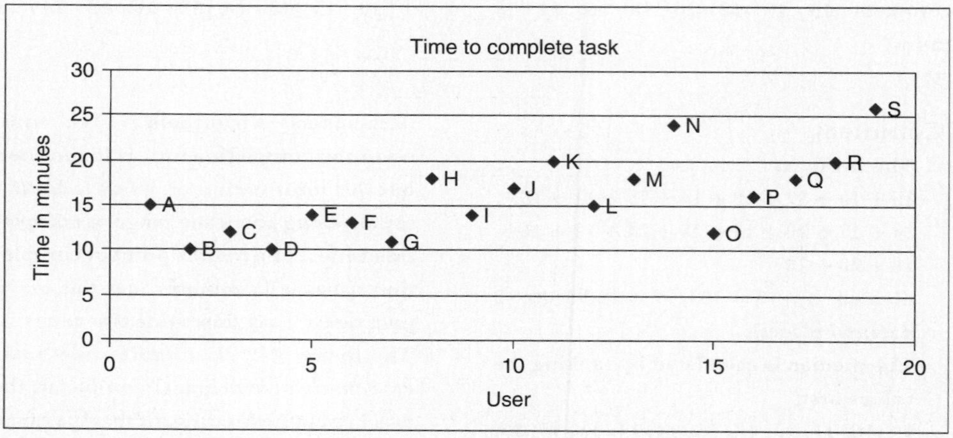

From these two diagrams there are two areas for further investigation. First of all, the values for user N (24) and user S (26) are higher than the others and could be looked at in more detail. In addition, there appears to be a trend that the users at the beginning of the testing time (particularly users B, C, D, E, F, and G) performed faster than those towards the end of the testing time. This is not a clear-cut situation as O also performed well, and I, L, and P were almost as fast, but there may be something about this later testing time that has affected the results, and it is worth investigating further.

It is fairly straightforward to compare two sets of results, e.g. from the evaluation of two interactive products, using these kinds of graphical representations of the data. Semantic differential data can also be analyzed in this way and used to identify trends, provided the format of the question is appropriate. For example, the following question was asked in a questionnaire to evaluate two different phone designs:

For each pair of adjectives, place a cross at the point between them that reflects the extent to which you believe the adjectives describe the phone design. Please place only one cross between the marks on each line.

Annoying						*Pleasing*
Easy to use						*Difficult to use*
Value-for-money						*Expensive*
Attractive						*Unattractive*
Secure						*Not secure*
Helpful						*Unhelpful*
Hi-tech						*Lo-tech*
Robust						*Fragile*
Inefficient						*Efficient*
Modern						*Dated*

Tables 8.3 and 8.4 show the tabulated results from 100 respondents who replied to the questionnaire. Note that the responses have been translated into five possible categories, numbered from 1 to 5, based on where the respondent marked the line between each pair of adjectives. It is possible that respondents may have intentionally put a cross closer to one side of the box than the other, but it is acceptable to lose this nuance in the data provided the original data is not lost, and any further analysis could refer back to it. It is always important to keep any data you collect so that it can be used to confirm or refute any suggestions later—as well as being able to use it for further data analysis.

Phone 1	1	2	3	4	5	
Annoying	35	20	18	15	12	**Pleasing**
Easy to use	20	28	21	13	18	**Difficult to use**
Value-for-money	15	30	22	27	6	**Expensive**
Attractive	37	22	32	6	3	**Unattractive**
Secure	52	29	12	4	3	**Not secure**
Helpful	33	21	32	12	2	**Unhelpful**
Hi-tech	12	24	36	12	16	**Lo-tech**
Robust	44	13	15	16	12	**Fragile**
Inefficient	28	23	25	12	12	**Efficient**
Modern	35	27	20	11	7	**Dated**

Table 8.3

Phone 2	1	2	3	4	5	
Annoying	24	23	23	15	15	Pleasing
Easy to use	37	29	15	10	9	Difficult to use
Value-for-money	26	32	17	13	12	Expensive
Attractive	38	21	29	8	4	Unattractive
Secure	43	22	19	12	4	Not secure
Helpful	51	19	16	12	2	Unhelpful
Hi-tech	28	12	30	18	12	Lo-tech
Robust	46	23	10	11	10	Fragile
Inefficient	10	6	37	29	18	Efficient
Modern	3	10	45	27	15	Dated

Table 8.4

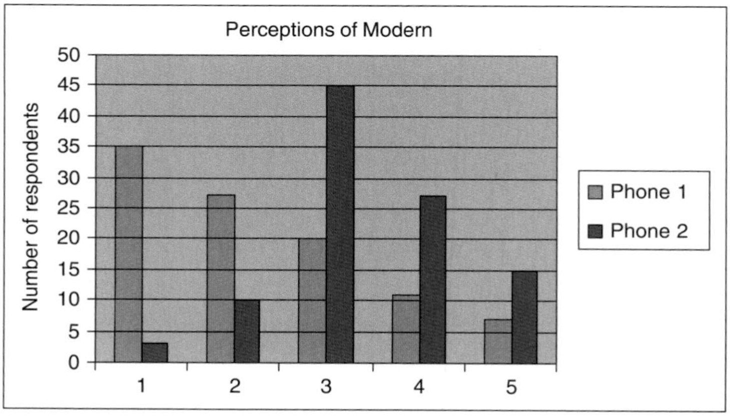

Figure 8.3 *A graphical comparison of two phone designs according to whether they are perceived as 'modern' or 'dated'*

The graph in Figure 8.3 shows how the two phone designs varied according to the respondents' perceptions of how modern the design is. This graphical notation shows clearly how the two designs compare.

Data logs that capture users' interactions with a system can also be analyzed and represented graphically, thus helping to identify patterns in behavior. Also, more sophisticated manipulations and graphical images can be used to highlight patterns in collected data. Box 8.3 describes how data logs of an online computer game were used to identify patterns of interactions. This example also shows how observational data can be used to interpret quantitative data.

The examples given in this section have largely focused on data sets which have more than 10 records, i.e. respondents or interviewees. If only a small number of records are collected, then it may be more important to analyze the individual records in more depth than to identify trends. In this case, tabulating the data for ease of presentation may be sufficient.

Box 8.3
Identifying interaction patterns in log data from a massively multiplayer online role-playing game

Massively Multiplayer Online Role-Playing Games (MMORPGs) involve hundreds of thousands of players interacting on a daily basis within a virtual world, and working towards achieving certain targets. While the challenges offered by these games are often the same as those in a single-player environment, the attraction of MMORPGs is the ability to join a community of gamers, to gain a reputation within that community, and to share gaming experiences directly. Several recent games have been designed so that players have to collaborate in order to progress.

Ducheneaut and Moore (2004) wanted to investigate how successful MMORPGs are at encouraging interactivity between players. To do this, they analyzed data logs and video recordings of player-to-player interactions in the game Star Wars Galaxies (SWG), complemented by a three-month ethnography of the same environment. The ethnography was achieved by the researchers joining the SWG community as players and using the system regularly over three months. During this time, they identified two locations within the virtual world which were heavily used by other players—the cantina and starport in Coronet City. The cantina is where entertainers can be found and players often go to recover from battle fatigue; players have to go to the starport in order to travel between locations, and shuttles fly about every 9 minutes. See Figure 8.4.

To collect a log of player interactions, they then created two characters and placed them, one in each location, for a month. Using the game's '/log' command, they recorded all public utterances and gestures from these locations. In all, 26 days of data were recorded, with 21 hours a day. This resulted in 100 mb of data and represented a total of 5493 unique players in the two locations. A purpose-built parser was used to extract the most interesting data from the logs and to identify who was interacting with whom, in what way (gesture or chat), where, when, and what was the content of the interaction (text chat or 'social' command). In this context, a 'gesture' may be a smile, greet, clap, cheer, etc., and a 'social' is a particular

Figure 8.4 *The cantina in SWG's Coronet City*

kind of gesture which is non-directional such as flex. They then analyzed the data for patterns of behavior. One finding was that a small number of players were frequently present in one location while there were many others who visited for only a short time. The median number of days a player was present was 2, while the average was 3.5; only 2% of the total number of players were present more than half the time. Another aspect they investigated was the activity within the cantina over the course of a day. Figure 8.5 shows a summary graph of activity in the cantina for the 26 days. This shows a fairly even distribution of activity throughout the day, with gestures representing about one-third of the events and public messages representing two-thirds.

Their analysis of the 10 most popular gestures is summarized below:

Gesture	% of total (cantina)	Gesture	% of total (starport)
Smile	18.13	Thank	15.95
Cheer	9.57	Bow	12.29
Clap	7.77	Wave	9.81
Wave	6.27	Flail	8.17
Wink	4.22	Smile	7.89
Grin	3.72	Nod	7.03
Nod	3.23	Salute	2.48
Bow	3.22	Pet	1.95
Thank	2.51	Puke	1.89
Greet	2.40	Cheer	1.56

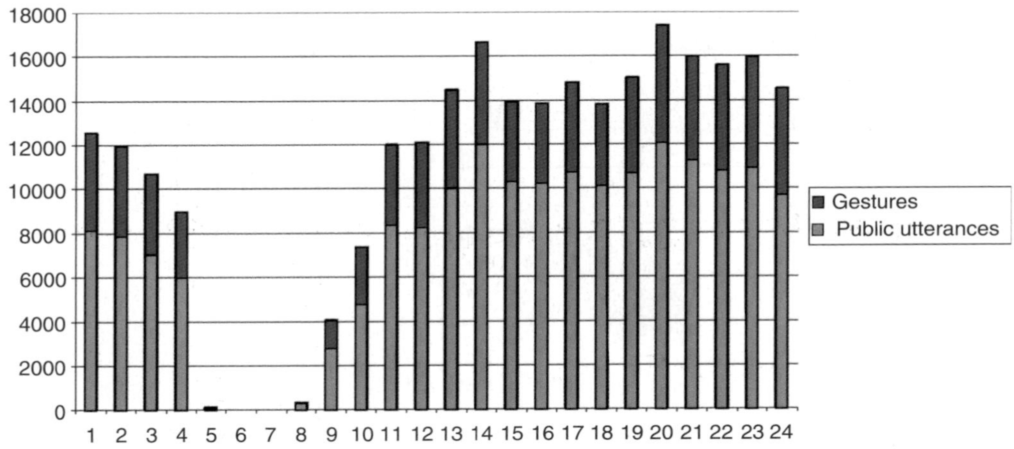

***Figure 8.5** Summary of the activity in the cantina over the course of a day. (The gap between 4 a.m. and 7 a.m. is due to a regular server reboot during this time)*

These two kinds of analysis are helpful to get an overview of the different players' interactions but do not indicate the richness of social interaction each player is engaged with. So Ducheneaut and Moore analyzed the interactions on three dimensions for each player: the number of gestures received, the number of gestures made, and the number of public utterances made. Having done so, they concluded that the average player goes into the cantina, makes about one gesture to another player, exchanges about four sentences with him or her, and receives one gesture in return. This conclusion was arrived at from taking averages across the data, but in order to get a clearer view of interactions, they plotted dimensions for each individual set of data on a graph. This is reproduced in Figure 8.6. The x-axis represents the number of gestures received, the y-axis represents the number of gestures made, and the size of the 'dot' is proportional to the number of public utterances made by the player. This graphical representation illustrated an unexpected finding—that the majority of players do not interact very much. Another set of players make a large number of utterances but make or receive no gestures. Yet another (smaller) set of players gesture and talk a lot, but receive few gestures in return.

The researchers concluded that these last two kinds of behavior are due to the player programming their avatar to repeat actions even when the player is not logged on. This kind of behavior is not truly interactive as it is designed simply to advance the player within the game (one way of gaining points is to repeatedly perform activities related to the avatar's

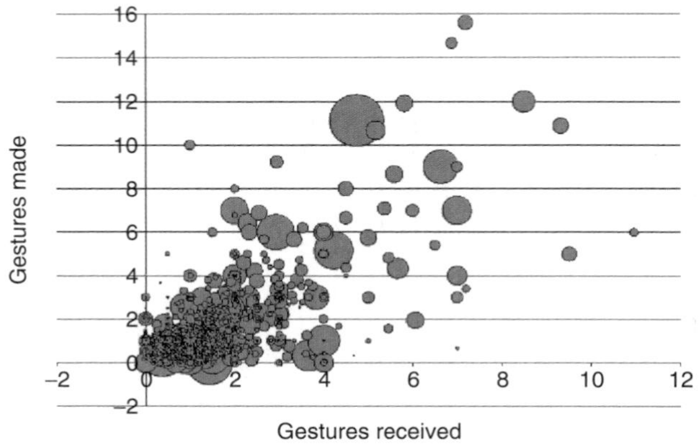

Figure 8.6 Interaction profiles of players in the cantina

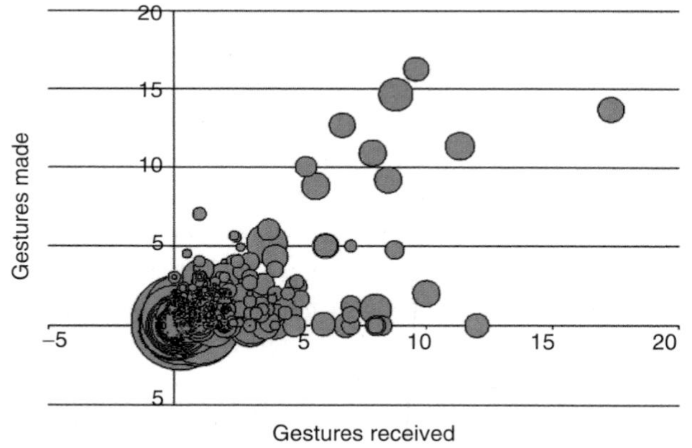

Figure 8.7 Interaction profiles of players in the starport

profession). This behavior then affects the social atmosphere of the cantina because other players are unhappy about the false kind of interaction.

Bubbles to the right of this graph represent players who interact a lot—making and receiving gestures, and chatting. These players are engaging in the kind of social interaction that the designers of SWG want to promote.

A similar analysis was performed for the starport (Figure 8.7), but a different

pattern of interactions was found. A large number of players made and received no gestures, but made a lot of public utterances. The ethnographic data helped researchers to interpret this finding too—the starport was a good place to advertise as there were many people gathered waiting for a shuttle. Another set of players at the starport said very little; the researchers believe that these were people looking for trainers to give them a particular skill they needed in order to progress in the game. ■

8.4 Simple qualitative analysis

As with quantitative analysis, the first step in qualitative analysis is to gain an overall impression of the data and to start looking for patterns. Some patterns will have emerged during the data gathering itself, and so you may already have some idea of the kinds of pattern to look for, but it is important to confirm and re-confirm findings to make sure that initial impressions are not biasing analysis. For observation data, the guiding framework will have given some structure to the data. For example, the framework for observation from Goetz and LeCompte (1984) introduced in Chapter 7, will have resulted in a focus on questions such as "Who is present," "What is happening" and "Where is it happening." Using this framework you may notice that when someone from the accounts department comes to the administration office to meet staff members, then there is a lot of interest and everyone from the office attends the meeting. However, when visitors from other departments come to the administration office, or when accounts meetings are held in the accounts office, there is less interest. Using Robson's framework, patterns relating to physical objects, people's goals, sequences of events, and so on are likely to emerge.

There are three simple types of qualitative analysis that we discuss here: identifying recurring patterns and themes, categorizing data, and analyzing critical incidents. These are not mutually exclusive and can each be used with the others.

8.4.1 Identifying recurring patterns or themes

As you become more familiar with the data, recurring themes or patterns will emerge. An example is noticing that most senior managers interviewed express frustration at the lack of up-to-date information they have from the marketing department.

Nearly all data analysis begins with identifying patterns or themes. This is true when working with quantitative and qualitative data. Sometimes the patterns or themes form the primary set of findings for the analysis and sometimes they are just the starting point for more detailed investigation of the data. Patterns in quantitative data may be identified through graphical representation (as discussed above), but identifying themes in qualitative data requires the researcher to be immersed in the data. Themes emerge and evolve over this time.

The study goals provide an orienting focus for the formulation of themes. For example, consider a survey to evaluate whether the information displayed on a train travel website is adequate and sufficient. Several of the respondents add comments to the survey suggesting that, as well as the origin and destination stations, the station stops in between should also be displayed. This is a theme relevant to the study goals and would be reported as a main theme. In another part of the survey, under 'further comments' you might notice that several respondents comment that the company's logo is distracting. Although this too is a theme in the data, it is not directly relevant to the study's goals and may be reported only as a minor theme.

One aspect of this form of analysis is to keep clear and consistent records of what has been found, and a close description of themes or patterns that are emerging. If the description is not specific enough then you may end up with a set of observations that do not address the goals. If the description is too specific then you may find that you have lots of themes, each with only one or two pieces of evidence.

Studying the data, focusing on the study goals, and keeping clear records of the analysis as it progresses are important. Box 8.4 and Case Study 8.1 describe studies where themes have been identified from qualitative data and reported as a significant part of their results. The results in Box 8.4 were arrived at by immersion in the data; the box for Case Study 8.1 illustrates the use of a specific technique for ordering data—the affinity diagram.

Note that patterns and themes in your data may relate to a variety of aspects: to behavior, to your user group, to places or situations where certain events happen, and so on. Each of these kinds of theme may be relevant to your goals. For example, descriptions of typical users (personas) may be an outcome of data analysis that focuses on patterns of participant characteristics.

Box 8.4
Themes in European culture

Bell (2001) reports on ethnographic research in Italy, Germany, France, the UK, and Spain that focused on European culture. She and her team visited 45 households from small towns, cities, and major metropolitan centers. The aim of the study was to understand what people do and don't do in their homes, how a household relates to the wider community, what technologies were present, and how they were used. The work they conducted informed the design of existing products and pointed to new product opportunities such as computing in public spaces.

Figure 8.8 Bell interviewing a German family

The researchers used an approach which allowed them to track important cultural values—in each country they started by visiting a small town, then moved to a city, and then to a larger metropolitan area. In this way, they could initially understand the daily rhythm of life in the country in a manageable context before moving to the more complex situations. They assumed that any patterns which were observed in all three different contexts were likely to be significant. Taking an ethnographic stance, the researchers tried to do everything that native people would normally do. They followed people around and asked lots of questions about what life was like and what people do. Four significant themes (called 'domains' by the researchers) were identified from this work: togetherness, media experiences, consumption habits, and life outside of the home.

Togetherness. Family, kinship, and community were found to be very significant in Europe. For example, the importance of the family eating together was a recurrent theme in the interviews and in the team's observations. Other occasions also promote social gatherings, such as sporting events and leisure activities. The researchers noted that sometimes people spend time together simply watching television. They found an emphasis on face-to-face social time throughout their studies, and the willingness of people to expend effort to maintain this 'togetherness.'

Media experiences. The researchers found that many different kinds of media play a variety of roles in European life—both consumption and production of content. For example, they found people painting, playing musical instruments, sketching and drawing in nearly every population center they visited. Television and print media also play an important role. Television is talked about explicitly by European families for its educational role. The researchers found print media of various kinds (magazines, newspapers, catalogues, pricelists, etc.) in the European homes they visited, and also observed rituals of reading and use of these materials, for example buying more than one daily newspaper in order to gain different perspectives on the news articles.

Consumption habits. "Food shopping is a really important part of daily life in most European countries." Europeans frequent a wide variety of shops and have a distinct preference for very fresh food. The open-air market is a particularly important part of French daily life, and the preparation, cooking, and consumption of the food is highly valued. In addition to purchasing items, shopping is also a social activity which connects people to their communities.

Life outside of the home. The researchers were struck by the variety of spaces outside the home where people socialized, and by the diversity of behaviors they observed. For example, people talk, flirt, play games, admire, create art, listen to music, eat, dance, swim, walk, and 'hang out' in gardens, parks, bars, pubs, cafes, promenades, markets, boulevards, and plazas. How often people frequent these places, and what they do there, changes with age and life stage. ■

CASE STUDY 8.1
Using ethnographic data to understand Indian ATM usage

This case study focuses on an investigation into the use of ATMs (Automated Teller Machines) in Mumbai, India. It illustrates the use of ethnographic data to answer questions such as: "What is the general attitude towards ATMs use?" and "What problems do people face when using ATMs?"

The project involved data collection through field observations and semi-structured interviews with early ATM adopters, bank customers who do not use the ATM, and customers who used the ATM for the first time during this study. Over 40 interviews were recorded, and photographs and videos were taken where possible. In addition, user profiles representing six different social classes were generated. Together with observations of ATM usage the project collected a considerable amount of data.

The project's use of affinity diagrams to help analyze the information that they collected is described by De Angeli *et al.* (2004). The affinity diagram (see Figure 8.9 for an example) which is used in contextual design (Beyer and Holtzblatt, 1998) aims to organize individual ideas and insights into a hierarchy showing common structures and themes. Notes are grouped together

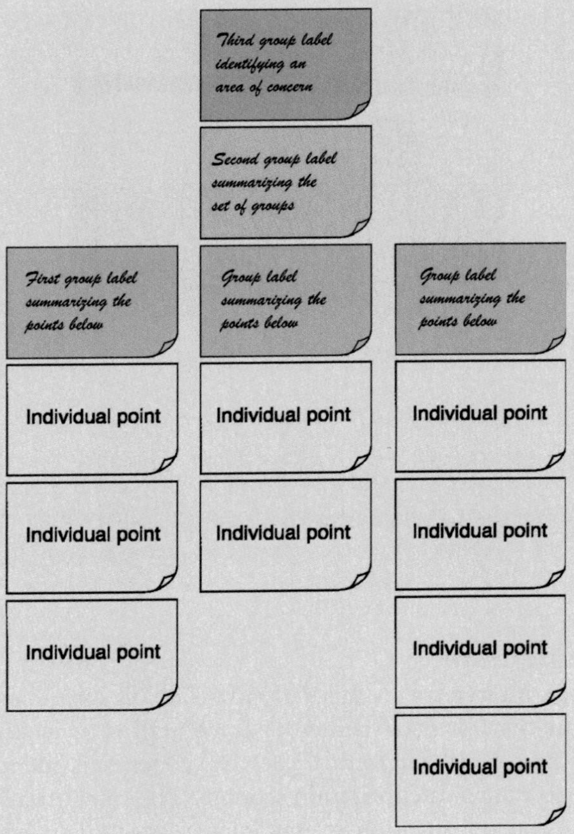

***Figure 8.9** The structure of an affinity diagram*

because they are similar in some fashion. The groups are not predefined, but must emerge from the data. The process was originally introduced into the software quality community from Japan, where it is regarded as one of the seven quality processes. The affinity diagram is built by a process of induction. One note is put up first, and then the team searches for other notes that are related in some way.

The affinity diagram organized the insights, ideas, and cultural influences gathered during the interviews and observations into a set of 10 top-level categories including perceptions of ATMs, banking habits, what people do while waiting in banks, and social and language barriers to banking (see Figure 8.10). Using the affinity diagram technique also highlighted some opposite behaviors. For example, two women who both wanted to avoid temptation

Figure 8.10 *Building the affinity diagram of Indian ATM usage*

(that of spending too much money) had different attitudes to the ATM. One used the ATM routinely but only to draw out enough cash to cover her immediate requirements. The other felt that having 24-hour access to cash was too much of a temptation in itself.

8.4.2 Categorizing data

Transcripts of meetings, interviews, or think-aloud protocols can be analyzed at a high level of detail, such as identifying stories or themes, or at a fine level of detail in which each word, phrase, utterance, or gesture is analyzed. Either way, elements identified in the data are usually categorized first using a categorization scheme. The categorization scheme may arise from the data itself, if the investigation is exploratory, as it might be in the requirements activity, or it might originate elsewhere in a well-recognized categorization scheme, or a combination of these two approaches may be used. The principle here is that the data is divided up into elements and each element is then categorized.

Which categories to use is largely determined by the goal of the study. One of its most challenging aspects is determining meaningful categories that are orthogonal—i.e. do not overlap each other in any way. Another is deciding on the appropriate granularity for the categories, e.g. at word, phrase, sentence, or paragraph level; this is also dependent on the goal of the study and the data being analyzed.

The categorization scheme used must be reliable so that the analysis can be replicated. This can be demonstrated by training a second person to use the categories. When training is complete, both people analyze the same data sample. If there is a large discrepancy between the two analyses, either training was inadequate or the categorization is not working and needs to be refined. Talking to those applying the categorization scheme can determine the source of the problem, which is usually with the categorization. If so, then the categorization scheme needs to be revised and re-tested. However, if the individuals do not seem to know how to carry out the process then they probably need more training.

When a high level of reliability is reached, it can be quantified by calculating the *inter-rater reliability*. This is the percentage of agreement between the two researchers, defined as the number of items that both people categorized in the same way, expressed as a percentage of the total number of items examined. It provides a measure of the efficacy of the technique and the rigor of the category definition.

To illustrate categorization, we present an example derived from a set of studies looking at the use of different navigation aids in an online educational setting (Armitage, 2004). These studies involved observing users working through some online educational material (about evaluation methods), using the think-aloud technique. The think-aloud protocol was recorded and then transcribed before being analyzed from various perspectives, one of which was to identify usability problems that the participants were having with the online environment (Nestor Navigator, Zeiliger *et al.* (1997)). An excerpt from the transcription is shown in Figure 8.11.

> I'm thinking that it's just a lot of information to absorb from the screen. I just I don't concentrate very well when I'm looking at the screen. I have a very clear idea of what I've read so far . . . but it's because of the headings I know OK this is another kind of evaluation now and before it was about evaluation which wasn't anyone can test and here it's about experts so it's like it's nice that I'm clicking every now and then coz it just sort of organises the thoughts. But it would still be nice to see it on a piece of paper because it's a lot of text to read.
>
> Am I supposed to, just one question, am supposed to say something about what I'm reading and what I think about it the conditions as well or how I feel reading it from the screen, what is the best thing really?
>
> *Observer— What you think about the information that you are reading on the screen . . . you don't need to give me comments . . . if you think this bit fits together.*
>
> There's so much reference to all those previously said like I'm like I've already forgotten the name of the other evaluation so it said unlike the other evaluation this one like, there really is not much contrast with the other it just says what it is may be . . . so I think I think of. . .
>
> May be it would be nice to have other evaluations listed to see other evaluations you know here, to have the names of other evaluations other evaluations just to, because now when I click previous I have to click it several times so it would be nice to have this navigation, extra links.

Figure 8.11 *Excerpt from a transcript of a think-aloud protocol when using an online educational environment. Note the prompt from the observer about half way through*

This excerpt was analyzed using a categorization scheme derived from a set of negative effects of a system on a user given in van Rens (1997) and was iteratively extended to accommodate the specific kinds of interaction observed in these studies. The categorization scheme is shown in Figure 8.12.

1. Interface Problems

- **1.1.** Verbalisations show evidence of dissatisfaction about an aspect of the interface.
- **1.2.** Verbalisations show evidence of confusion/uncertainty about an aspect of the interface.
- **1.3.** Verbalisations show evidence of confusion/surprise at the outcome of an action.
- **1.4.** Verbalisations show evidence of physical discomfort.
- **1.5.** Verbalisations show evidence of fatigue.
- **1.6.** Verbalisations show evidence of difficulty in seeing particular aspects of the interface.
- **1.7.** Verbalisations show evidence that they are having problems achieving a goal that they have set themselves, or the overall task goal.
- **1.8.** Verbalisations show evidence that the user has made an error.
- **1.9.** The participant is unable to recover from error without external help from the experimenter.
- **1.10.** The participant makes a suggestion for redesign of the interface of the electronic texts.

2. Content Problems

- **2.1.** Verbalisations show evidence of dissatisfaction about aspects of the content of the electronic text.
- **2.2.** Verbalisations show evidence of confusion/uncertainty about aspects of the content of the electronic text.
- **2.3.** Verbalisations show evidence of a misunderstanding of the electronic text content (the user may not have noticed this immediately).
- **2.4.** The participant makes a suggestion for re-writing the electronic text content.

Identified problems should be coded as **[UP, ≪ problem no. ≫]**.

Figure 8.12 *Criteria for identifying usability problems from verbal protocol transcriptions*

This scheme developed and evolved as the transcripts were analyzed. Figure 8.13 shows the excerpt above coded using this categorization scheme. Note that the transcript is divided up using square brackets to indicate which element is being identified as showing a particular usability problem.

A rigid categorization scheme means that the data is structured only according to the prespecified categories. However, where a significant set of data cannot be categorized, the scheme can be extended. In this case the categorization scheme and the categorization itself develop in parallel, with the scheme evolving as more analysis is done.

Having categorized the data, the results can be used to answer the study goals. In the example above, the study allowed the researchers to be able to quantify the number of usability problems encountered overall by participants, the mean number of problems per

[I'm thinking that it's just a lot of information to absorb from the screen. **UP 1.1][** I just I don't concentrate very well when I'm looking at the screen **UP 1.1]**. I have a very clear idea of what I've read so far . . . [but it's because of the headings **UP 1.1]** I know OK this is another kind of evaluation now and before it was about evaluation which wasn't anyone can test and here it's about experts so it's like it's nice that I'm clicking every now and then coz it just sort of organises the thoughts. [But it would still be nice to see it on a piece of paper **UP 1.10]** [because it's a lot of text to read **UP 1.1]**.

Am I supposed to, just one question, am supposed to say something about what I'm reading and what I think about it the conditions as well or how I feel reading it from the screen, what is the best thing really?

Observer— What you think about the information that you are reading on the screen . . . you don't need to give me comments . . . if you think this bit fits together.

[There's so much reference to all those previously said **UP2.1] [** like I'm like I've already forgotten the name of the other evaluation so it said unlike the other evaluation this one like, there really is not much contrast with the other it just says what it is may be . . . so I think I think of . . . **UP 2.2]**

[May be it would be nice to have other evaluations listed to see other evaluations you know here, to have the names of other evaluations other evaluations **UP 1.10]** just to, [because now when I click previous I have to click it several times **UP 1.1, 1.7]** [so it would be nice to have this navigation, extra links **UP 1.10]**.

Figure 8.13 *The excerpt in Figure 8.11 coded using the categorization scheme in Figure 8.12*

participant for each of the test conditions, and the number of unique problems of each type per participant. This also helped to identify patterns of behavior and recurring problems. Having the think-aloud protocol meant that the overall view of the usability problems could take context into account.

Activity 8.2

The following is another think-aloud extract from the same study. Using the categorization scheme in Figure 8.12, code this extract for usability problems. Remember to put brackets around the complete element of the extract that you are coding.

Well, looking at the map, again there's no obvious start point, there should be something highlighted that says "start here."

Ok, the next keyword that's highlighted is evaluating, but I'm not sure that's where I want to go straight away, so I'm just going to go back to the introduction.

Yeah, so I probably want to read about usability problems before I start looking at evaluation. So, I, yeah. I would have thought that the links in each one of the pages would take you to the next logical point, but my logic might be different to other people's. Just going to go and have a look at usability problems.

Ok, again I'm going to flip back to the introduction. I'm just thinking if I was going to do this myself I would still have a link back to the introduction, but I would take people through the logical sequence of each one of these bits that fans out, rather than expecting them to go back all the time.

Going back ... to the introduction. Look at the types. Observation, didn't really want to go there. What's this bit [pointing to Types of UE on map]? Going straight to types of...

Ok, right, yeah, I've already been there before. We've already looked at usability problems, yep that's ok, so we'll have a look at these references.

I clicked on the map rather than going back via introduction, to be honest I get fed up going back to introduction all the time.

Comment

Coding transcripts is not easy, and you may have had some difficulties doing this, but this activity will have given you an idea of the kind of decisions that need to be taken. As with much data analysis, it gets easier with practice. Our coded extract is below:

[Well, looking at the map, again there's no obvious start point **UP 1.2, 2.2]**, [there should be something highlighted that says "start here" **UP 1.1, 1.10]**.

Ok, the next keyword that's highlighted is evaluating, but **[**I'm not sure that's where I want to go straight away **UP 2.2]**, so I'm just going to go back to the introduction.

Yeah, so I probably want to read about usability problems before I start looking at evaluation. So, I, yeah. **[**I would have thought that the links in each one of the pages would take you to the next logical point, but my logic might be different to other people's **UP 1.3]**. Just going to go and have a look at usability problems.

Ok, again I'm going to flip back to the introduction. **[**I'm just thinking if I was going to do this myself I would still have a link back to the introduction, but I would take people through the logical sequence of each one of these bits that fans out, rather than expecting them to go back all the time **UP 1.10]**.

Going back ... to the introduction. **[**Look at the types. Observation, didn't really want to go there. What's this bit [pointing to Types of UE on map]? **UP 2.2]** Going straight to types of...

Ok, right, yeah, I've already been there before. We've already looked at usability problems, yep that's ok, so we'll have a look at these references.

I clicked on the map rather than going back via introduction, [to be honest I get fed up going back to introduction all the time. **UP 1.1]**

The example above used a form of content analysis. Content analysis typically involves categorizing the data and then studying the frequency of category occurrences. For example, Maria Ebling and Bonnie John (2000) developed a hierarchical content classification for analyzing data when evaluating a graphical interface for a distributed file system.

An informal version of content analysis is often used as the first stage in identifying software objects from descriptions of the domain. In this approach, nouns and verbs are identified and scrutinized to see if they represent significant classes.

Another way of analyzing a transcript is to use discourse analysis. Discourse analysis focuses on the dialog, i.e. the meaning of what is said, and how words are used to convey meaning. Discourse analysis is strongly interpretive, pays great attention to context, and views language not only as reflecting psychological and social aspects but also as constructing it (Coyle, 1995). An underlying assumption of discourse analysis is that there is no objective scientific truth. Language is a form of social reality that is open to interpretation from different perspectives. In this sense, the underlying philosophy of discourse analysis is similar to that of ethnography. Language is viewed as a constructive tool and discourse analysis provides a way of focusing upon how people use language to construct versions of their worlds (Fiske, 1994).

Small changes in wording can change meaning, as the following excerpts indicate (Coyle, 1995):

> ***Discourse analysis is what you do when you are saying that you are doing discourse analysis . . .***
>
> ***According to Coyle, discourse analysis is what you do when you are saying that you are doing discourse analysis . . .***

By adding just three words, "According to Coyle," the sense of authority changes, depending on what the reader knows about Coyle's work and reputation.

Conversation analysis is a very fine-grained form of discourse analysis. In conversation analysis the semantics of the discourse are examined in fine detail, and the focus is on how conversations are conducted. This technique is used in sociological studies and examines how conversations start, how turn-taking is structured, and other rules of conversation. This analysis technique has been used to analyze interactions on the Internet, e.g. in chatrooms, bulletin boards, and virtual worlds, and has started to influence designers' understanding about users' needs in these environments. It can also be used to compare conversations that take place through different media, e.g. face-to-face versus email.

8.4.3 Looking for critical incidents

Data gathering sessions for interaction design usually result in a lot of data. Analyzing all of that data in any detail would be very time-consuming, and is often not necessary. We have already suggested that themes, patterns and categories can be used to identify areas where detailed analysis is appropriate. Another approach is to use the 'critical incident technique.'

The critical incident technique is a flexible set of principles that emerged from work carried out in the United States Army Air Forces where the goal was to identify the critical requirements of 'good' and 'bad' performance by pilots (Flanagan, 1954). It has two basic principles: "(a) reporting facts regarding behaviour is preferable to the collection of interpretations, ratings and opinions based on general impressions; (b) reporting should be limited to those behaviours which, according to competent observers, make a significant contribution to the activity" (Flanagan, 1954, p. 355). In the interaction design context, the use of well-planned observation sessions as discussed in Chapter 7 satisfies the first principle. The second principle is referring to critical incidents, i.e. incidents which are significant or pivotal to the activity being observed, in either a desirable or an undesirable way.

In interaction design, critical incident analysis has been used in a variety of ways, but the main focus is to identify specific incidents that are significant, and then to focus on these and analyze them in detail, using the rest of the data collected as context to inform their interpretation. These may be identified by the users, through a retrospective discussion of a recent event, or they may be identified by an observer either through studying video footage, or from observation of the event in real time. For example, in an evaluation study a critical incident may be signalled by times when users were obviously stuck—usually marked by a comment, silence, looks of puzzlement, etc. Jurgen Koenemann-Belliveau *et al.* (1994) used this approach to compare the efficacy of two versions of a Smalltalk programming manual for supporting novice programmers. They examined breakdowns or problems in achieving a programming task and identified possible threats of incidents, and they were able to trace through a sequence of incidents and achieve a more holistic understanding of the problem. For example, they found that they needed to emphasize how objects interact in teaching object-oriented programming.

Another example is reported in Curzon *et al.* (2002). They identified a set of critical incidents through field trials of an in-car navigation device. One example incident in this context was "On one journey, the system gave directions to turn right when the destination was to the left. Its route was to go round the block to go in the other direction. A car following ignored this turn and went the more obvious way, arriving first."

Activity 8.3

Set yourself or a friend the task of identifying the next available theatre or cinema performance you'd like to attend in your local area. As you perform this task, or watch your friend do it, make a note of critical incidents associated with the activity. Remember that a critical incident may be a positive or a negative event.

Comment

In my local area, information about entertainment is available through the local paper, the Internet, ringing up local cinemas or theaters, or by visiting the local library where they stock leaflets about the entertainment on in the area. When I asked my daughter to attempt this task, I noticed several critical incidents including the following:

1. **After searching around the house for a while, she found a copy of the local paper for the correct week.**
2. **The local paper she had found did not have details of the cinema that she wanted to visit.**
3. **When trying to book the cinema tickets by phone she discovered that she needed a credit card which she doesn't have, and so she had to give me the phone!**

As with data gathering, it is common practice to employ more than one complementary data analysis approach. For example, following a critical incident analysis, themes may be identified around the circumstances that caused the incident to occur, and then discourse analysis may be conducted to understand the detail. Analyzing video material brings its own challenges; we address video analysis in Box 8.5.

Box 8.5
Analyzing video material

One approach to analyzing video data is interaction analysis (IA), outlined by Jordan and Henderson (1995). They describe it as an in-depth microanalysis of how people interact with one another, their physical environment, and the documents, artifacts, and technologies in that environment. A focus is on the patterns and anomalies in people's routine interactions and the events that unfold throughout time. These are described in terms of the turns people take in talking and physical actions they perform, e.g. writing. The approach also looks to see if there are seamless transitions between events, e.g. handovers between shift workers, or there is some awkwardness or something does not happen, e.g. one shift worker forgets to pass on information to another. Other approaches to analyzing and interpreting video data are distributed cognition and grounded theory, covered in Section 8.5. Here, again, the emphasis is on revealing phenomena that are important to an ongoing activity. Ethnographically and anthropologically informed analyses of human and social conduct in work, home, and everyday spaces are also popular, e.g. Heath and Luff (1994).

A good way to start a video analysis is to watch what has been recorded all the way through while writing a high-level narrative of what happens, noting down where in the video there are any potentially interesting events. How you decide which is an interesting event will depend on what is being observed. For example, if you are studying the interruptions that occur in an open plan office, you would include each time a person breaks off from an ongoing activity, e.g. phone rings, someone walks into their cubicle, email arrives. If it is a study of how pairs of students use a collaborative learning tool then activities such as turn-taking, sharing of input device/s, speaking over one another, and 'fighting' over shared objects would be appropriate to record.

Chronological and video time is used to index and number events. These may not be the same, since videotape can run at different speeds to real time. Labels for certain routine events are also used, e.g. lunchtime, coffee break, staff meeting, doctor's round. Spreadsheets are used to record the classification and description of events, together with annotations and notes of how the events began, how they unfold, and how they end.

Video can be augmented with captured screens or logged data of people's interactions with a computer display. There are various logging and screen capture tools, e.g. Camtasia or SnagIt, available for this purpose that enable you to play back the interactions as a movie, showing screen objects being opened, moved, selected, and so on. These can then be played in parallel with the video to provide different perspectives on the talk, physical interactions, and the system's responses that occur. Having a combination of data streams can enable more detailed and fine-grained patterns of behavior to be interpreted. ■

8.5 Tools to support data analysis

It would be possible to analyze even large data sets using only manual techniques, however most people would agree that it is quicker, easier, and more accurate to use a software tool of some kind. We introduced the idea of using a simple spreadsheet application in Section 8.3, but there are other more sophisticated tools available—some of which support the organization and manipulation of the data, and some of which are focused on performing statistical tests.

New tools are developed and existing ones are enhanced on a regular basis, so we do not attempt to provide a comprehensive survey of this area. Instead, we discuss the kind of support available, and describe briefly some of the more popular tools used in interaction design.

For qualitative data, there are two broad types of package available. The first supports the categorization and theme-based analysis of data. These typically provide facilities to associate labels (categories, themes, etc.) with sections of data, search the data for key words or phrases, investigate the relationships between different themes or categories, and help to develop the coding scheme further; some packages can also generate graphical representations. The second supports the quantitative analysis of text-based data. These help with techniques such as content analysis which focus on the number of occurrences of words, or words with similar meanings. Some of these provide very sophisticated mechanisms to show the occurrence and co-occurrence of words or phrases. Both types of package provide searching, coding, project management, writing and annotating, and report generation facilities. Although it is useful to distinguish between these two types of package, software that is primarily focused on quantitative analysis now also includes some coding facilities, and vice versa, and so the distinction is very blurred.

More detail regarding software tools to support the analysis of qualitative data can be found through the CAQDAS Networking Project, based at the University of Surrey (`http://caqdas.soc.surrey.ac.uk/`).

One popular example of the first type of package is N6 (formerly NUD*IST), which supports the annotation and coding of textual data. Using N6, field notes can be searched for key words or phrases and a report printed listing every occasion the word or phrase is used. The information can also be printed out as a tree showing the relationship of occurrences. Similarly, N6 can be used to search a body of text to identify specific predetermined categories or words for content analysis. Like all software packages, N6 has advantages and disadvantages, but it is particularly powerful for handling very large sets of data. Nvivo is another package developed by the same people as N6, and this provides more sophisticated facilities for exploring, merging, and manipulating codes and data. Both packages can generate output for statistical packages such as SPSS.

SPSS (Statistical Package for the Social Sciences) is one of the more popular quantitative analysis packages that supports the use of statistical tests. SPSS is a sophisticated package which assumes that the user knows and understands statistical analysis. As we pointed out above, many of the qualitative data analysis tools produce output that can be fed into a statistical analysis package such as SPSS, facilitating the quantitative analysis of qualitative data. SPSS offers a wide range of statistical tests for things such as frequency distributions, rank correlations (to determine statistical significance), regression analysis, and cluster analysis.

Box 8.6 briefly describes the Observer Video-Pro tool which is designed to help the analysis of video data.

Box 8.6
The Observer Video-Pro: an automated data analysis tool

The Observer Video-Pro provides the following features (Noldus, 2000):

- **During preparation of a video tape recording, a *time code generator* adds a time code to each video frame.**
- **During a data collection session, a *time***

code reader retrieves the time code from the tape, allowing frame-accurate event timing independent of the playback speed of the video cassette recorder (VCR).

- Each keyboard entry is firmly anchored to the video frame displayed at the instant the evaluator presses the first key of a behavior code or free-format note. The evaluator can also use a mouse to score events.
- Observational data can be reviewed and edited, with synchronized display of the corresponding video images.
- For optimal visual feedback during coding, the evaluator can display the video image in a window on the computer screen.
- The VCR can be controlled by the computer, allowing software-controlled 'jog,' 'shuttle,' and 'search' functions.
- Video images can be captured and saved as disk files for use as illustrations in documents, slides for presentations, etc.
- Marked video episodes can be copied to an Edit Decision List for easy creation of highlight tapes. ■

Activity 8.4

What does the Observer Video-Pro tool allow you to search for in the data collected?

Comment

Depending on how the logs have been annotated, using the Observer Video-Pro product you can search the data for various things including the following:

Video time—a specific time, e.g. 02:24:36.04 (hh:mm:ss.dd).

Marker—a previously entered free-format annotation.

Event—a combination of actor, behavior, and modifiers, with optional wildcards, e.g. the first occurrence of "glazed look" or "Sarah approaches Janice".

Text—any word or alphanumeric text string occurring in the coded event records or free-format notes.

8.6 Using theoretical frameworks

Structuring the analysis of qualitative data around a theoretical framework can lead to additional insights that go beyond the results found from the simple techniques introduced earlier. This approach also relies less on the study goals to focus analysis. However, these frameworks are quite sophisticated and using them requires investment to make sure that the framework is understood and applied appropriately. This section discusses three frameworks that are commonly used in interaction design to structure the analysis of data gathered in the field, such as ethnographic data: grounded theory, distributed cognition, and activity theory.

8.6.1 Grounded theory

Grounded theory is an approach to qualitative data analysis that aims to develop theory from the systematic analysis and interpretation of empirical data, i.e. the theory derived is grounded in the data. The approach was originally developed by Glaser and Strauss (1967) and since has been adopted by several researchers, with some adaptations to different circumstances. In particular, Glaser and Strauss have individually (and with others) developed the theory in slightly different ways, but the aim of this approach remains the same. Glaser (1992) provides further information about the differences and areas of controversy.

The aim of grounded theory is to develop a theory that fits a set of collected data. By 'theory' is meant in this context: "a set of well-developed concepts related through statements of relationship, which together constitute an integrated framework that can be used to explain or predict phenomena" (Strauss and Corbin, 1998). Development of a 'grounded' theory progresses through alternating data collection and data analysis: first data is collected and analyzed to identify categories, then that analysis leads to the need for further data collection, which is analyzed, and more data is then collected. Data gathering is hence driven by the emerging theory. This approach continues until no new insights emerge and the theory is well-developed. During this process, the researcher needs to maintain a balance between objectivity and sensitivity. Objectivity is needed to maintain accurate and impartial interpretation of events; sensitivity is required to notice the subtleties in the data and identify relationships between concepts.

The thrust of the analysis undertaken is to identify and define the properties and dimensions of relevant categories and then to use these as the basis for constructing a theory. Category identification and definition is achieved by 'coding' the data, i.e. marking it up according to the emerging categories. According to Strauss and Corbin (1998), this coding has three aspects, which are iteratively performed through the cycle of data collection and analysis:

(i) *Open coding.* Open coding is the process through which categories, their properties, and dimensions are discovered in the data. This process is similar to our discussion of categorization above, including the question of granularity of coding (at the word, line, sentence, conversation level, etc.).

(ii) *Axial coding.* Axial coding is the process of systematically fleshing out categories and relating them to their subcategories.

(iii) *Selective coding.* Selective coding is the process of refining and integrating categories to form a larger theoretical scheme. The categories are organized around one central category that forms the backbone of the theory. Initially, the theory will contain only an outline of the categories but as more data is collected, they are refined and developed further.

Grounded theory says little about what data collection techniques should be used, but focuses instead on the analysis. Strauss and Corbin (1998) encourage the use of written records of analysis and diagrammatic representations of categories (which they call memos and diagrams). These memos and diagrams evolve as data analysis progresses. The following analytic tools are used to help stimulate the analyst's thinking and identify and characterize relevant categories:

- The use of questioning (not questioning your participants, but questioning the data): questions can help an analyst to generate ideas or consider different ways of looking at the data. It can be useful to ask questions when analysis appears to be in a rut.
- Analysis of a word, phrase, or sentence: considering in detail the meaning of an utterance can also help to trigger different perspectives on the data.
- Further analysis through comparisons: comparisons may be made between objects or between abstract categories. In either case, comparing one with the other brings alternative interpretations. Sharp *et al.* (2005) take this idea further and use metaphor as an analysis technique with qualitative data.

One of the things that distinguishes a grounded theory approach to data gathering and analysis from ethnographic approaches is that researchers are encouraged to draw on their own theoretical backgrounds to help inform the study, provided that they are alert to the possibility of unintentional bias.

An example of applying the grounded theory approach to qualitative data analysis

Sarker *et al.* (2001) used the grounded theory approach to develop a model of collaboration in virtual teams. The virtual teams used in the study were made up of students from two universities—one in Canada and one in the United States of America. Each team consisted of four to five members from each university. Each team was given the task of studying a business systems problem, producing a systems design for it, and developing a working prototype. The projects themselves lasted about 14 weeks and a total of 12 teams participated in the study. The team members could communicate directly with each other using various technologies such as email, videoconferencing, telephone, and fax. The main communication channel, however, was Webboard, a collaborative message board tool supporting threaded discussions, email discussions, chat rooms, instant messaging, calendar, whiteboard, blogging, and so on. Using Webboard meant that communication was more public, and could be recorded more easily.

All communication data through Webboard was automatically saved, minutes of any videoconferences, telephone calls, or Internet chat sessions undertaken were posted on Webboard, and the team members were also asked to provide any additional emails they received or sent to other team members. In addition to this data, the team's final project reports, individual team members' reflections on the lessons learned through the project, feedback on fellow team members' performance, and comments on the virtual project itself were all collected and used as data for the study.

As soon as the teams were formed, informal data analysis began and two of the researchers became participant observers in the project teams, developing sensitivity to the project and its goals. They also began to reflect on their own backgrounds to see what theoretical frameworks they could draw on.

Open coding. This was done initially on a line-by-line basis, but later coding was done at the message level, while other documents such as reports and reflections were coded at document level. Over 200 categories were generated, and as these were refined, some informal axial coding was also done. Table 8.5 shows two messages posted at the beginning of a project, and illustrates how these messages were coded during the open coding process.

Sarker *et al.* note that codes emerged and continued to be refined over the life of the project. Also, a significant number of the codes that were ultimately used in the theory

Message	Post date, week #, time	Sample codes generated (underlined) and notes
Hi there in UB, I'm Henry. I just wanted to say hello and provide you with the rest of our group members' email address. [Names and email addresses] Well, I guess we'll see each other on Saturday at the videoconference.	1/22/98, week 1, 1:41:52 PM	1. <u>Leadership</u>—<u>initiative</u> to represent. 2. Establishing team's <u>co-presence</u> on the Internet. 3. Implying <u>preference</u> for <u>communication technology</u> (email). 4. Implying <u>technology</u> (VC) can bridge the <u>time and space</u> gap.
Hello UB. Just letting you know that you are free to email us anytime. I might be getting an ICQ account going so that if any of you are into real-time chat and wish to communicate that way, it might be something to try . . .	1/26/98, week 1, 2:56:37 PM	1. UB members' <u>identity</u> viewed at an <u>aggregate level</u> (as in msg. #1). 2. <u>Collapsing/bridging</u> across <u>time boundaries.</u> 3. <u>Invitation.</u> 4. Implying <u>preference for communication technology.</u> 5. <u>Properties of communication technology/medium</u> (real-time, synchronous?). 6. <u>Novelty of technology</u>, recognizing the need to try/<u>explore.</u>

Table 8.5 *An illustration of open coding*

building were recurrent, for example, preference for technology and time gaps/boundaries. Finally, some of the key categories were identified when considering messages as one unit and looking at comparable strips in other data segments.

Through constant comparison of data across categories, the names of categories were refined, merged, and changed over time.

Axial coding. Sarker *et al.* found the suggestions in Strauss and Corbin about how to relate subcategories too constraining. They instead used a two-step process for axial coding:

1. The major categories, e.g. technology, norms, social practices, stages of team development, and frames of reference, were hierarchically related to subcategories. For example, the category technology was linked to the subcategories purpose of technology, nature of ownership, accessibility (by time, location, cost, awareness), future potential, degree of novelty, and interconnectedness. At the next level, purpose of technology was linked to information sharing, triggering, and so on (see Figure 8.14). During this process, the researchers returned to open coding and refined categories further.
2. For each major category researchers created a description (called a 'memo') that attempted to integrate as many of the categories and subcategories as possible. These memos also

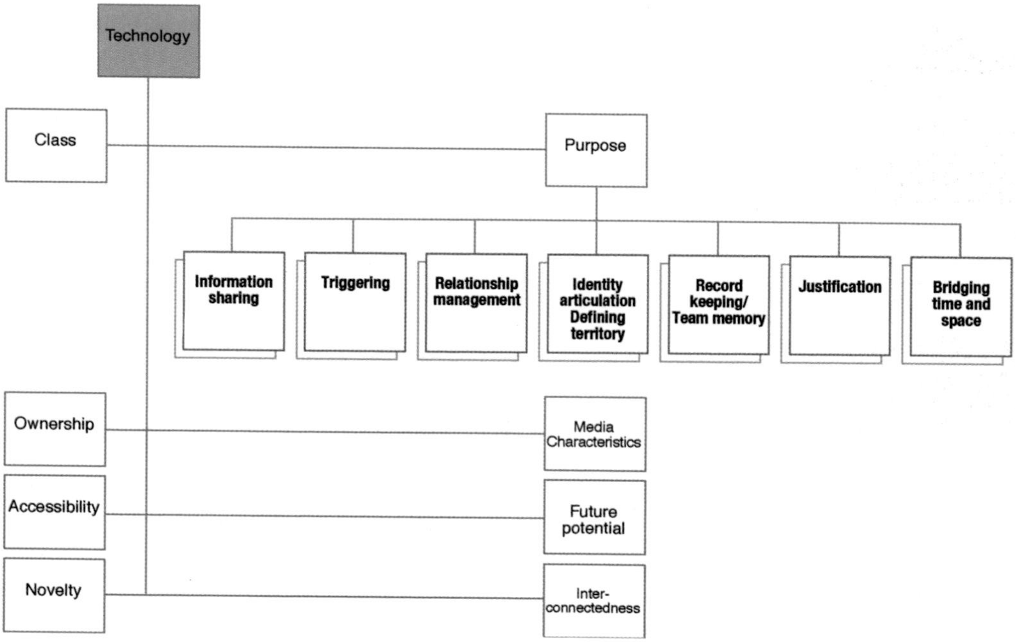

Figure 8.14 *Axial coding for the technology category*

Collaboration across time and space requires mediation by technology for both symbolic and substantive purposes. Substantive purposes include sharing information, record-keeping, managing relationships, pacing and triggering of activities in collaboration. Some symbolic uses of technology involve the articulation of the self and group identity and legitimising different courses of action by appealing to the use of technology.

Different classes of technology provide different capabilities, some of them different to the features of technology as defined from the designers' or the implementers' point of view. For example, we wanted Webboard to be a public record... students have extended this use by creating a local enclave for information exchange with local members in a domain traditionally thought of as being public. The Webboard has also become a project archive, conserving team memory through the documentation of agendas, minutes, project steps, and deliverables.

Figure 8.15 *An excerpt from an early draft of an integrative memo for the technology category*

evolved as analysis progressed. Figure 8.15 contains an excerpt from an early draft memo for the technology category.

Selective coding. This stage of coding involves linking the categories and subcategories into a theory, and as theory building is quite complex, we only present an overview of the process here.

Sarker *et al.* wanted to develop a theory of virtual teams, and so they used two approaches from their background to help them. One of these approaches (Couch, 1996) emphasizes the concepts that a theory of human conduct must use. The other focuses on social structure (Giddens, 1984). Using these two approaches, the category 'stages of team development' was chosen as the core category for the grounded theory to be built from this data set, and other categories were linked around it. This theory was further elaborated upon through discussions and reading of theory, and evolved into a theory of how virtual teams develop over time. More details can be found in Sarker and Sahay (2003).

How useful is a grounded theory approach to analysis?

A grounded theory approach to analysis emphasizes the important role of empirical data in the derivation of theory. It has become increasingly popular in interaction design to answer specific questions and design concerns.

For example, Adams *et al.* (2005) describe their use of grounded theory to investigate how technology can empower or exclude its users due to interactions between social context, system design, and implementation. They studied the introduction and use of digital libraries in four settings over a four-year period, collecting data from a total of 144 users. Focus groups and interviews were the primary data collection techniques. They concluded that where technology is integrated with the communities and their practice, through an information intermediary, perceptions of empowerment were increased; where technology is deployed within communities, yet with poor design and support, technologies were perceived as complex and threatening; and where technology was designed in isolation from the communities, users were either unaware of the technology or perceived it as complex or threatening.

Dourish *et al.* (2004) used semi-structured interviews and grounded theory to examine how people answer the question "Is this system secure enough for what I want to do now?," in the context of ubiquitous and mobile technologies. This qualitative approach was used to explore the issues before moving on to develop more detailed questions, but their conclusions included suggested design modifications to take this perspective on security into account.

8.6.2 Distributed cognition

We introduced the distributed cognition approach in Chapter 3, as a theoretical account of the distributed nature of cognitive phenomena across individuals, artifacts, and internal and external representations (Hutchins, 1995). Here, we illustrate how to conduct a distributed cognition analysis by providing a worked example.

Typically, a distributed cognition analysis results in an event-driven description which emphasizes information and its propagation through the cognitive system under study. The cognitive system under study might be one person's use of a computational tool, such as a calculator; two people's joint activities when designing the layout for the front page of a newspaper, using a shared authoring tool, or more widely, a large team of software developers and programmers, examining how they coordinate their work with one another, using a variety of mediating artifacts, such as schedules, clocks, to-do lists, and shared files.

The granularity of analysis varies depending on the activities and cognitive system being observed and the research or design questions being asked. For example, if the goal is to examine how a team of pilots fly a plane—with a view to improving communication between them—then the focus will be on the interactions and communications that take place between them and their instruments, at a fine level of granularity. If the goal is to understand how pilots learn how to fly—with a view to developing new training materials—then the focus will be at a coarser grain of analysis, taking into account the cultural, historical, and learning aspects involved in becoming a pilot.

The description produced may cover a period of a day, an hour, or only minutes, depending on the study's focus. For the longer periods, verbal descriptions are primarily used. For the shorter periods, micro-level analyses of the cognitive processes are meticulously plotted using diagrammatic forms and other graphical representations. The rationale for performing the finer levels of analysis is to reveal practices and discrepancies that would go unnoticed using coarser grains of analysis, but which reveal themselves as critical to the work activity.

Ed Hutchins emphasizes that an important part of doing a distributed cognition analysis is to have a deep understanding of the work domain that is being studied. He even recommends, where possible, that the investigators take steps to learn 'the trade' under study and become an accomplished pilot or sailor (as he has done himself in both cases). This can take a team of researchers several months and even years to accomplish and in most cases this is impractical for a research or design team to do.

Alternatively, it is possible to spend a few weeks immersed in the culture and setting of a specific team to learn enough about the organization and its work practices to conduct a focused analysis of a particular cognitive system. For example, I spent six weeks with an engineering team, where I was able to learn enough about their work practice to gain a good understanding of how they worked together on projects, how they coordinated their work with each other, and how the technologies that were used mediated their work activities. I was then able to document and analyze a number of problems they were experiencing through the introduction of new networking technology. Using the distributed cognition framework, I described how seemingly simple communication problems led to large delays and recommended how the situation could be improved (Rogers, 1993, 1994).

Performing a distributed cognition analysis

It should be stressed that there is not one single way of doing a distributed cognition analysis, nor is there an off-the-shelf manual that can be followed. A good way to begin analyzing and interpreting the data collected is to describe the official work practices, in terms of the routines and procedures followed, and the workarounds that teams develop when coping with the various demands placed upon them at different times during their work. In so doing, any breakdowns, incidents, or unusual happenings should be highlighted, especially where it was discovered that excessive time was being spent doing something, errors were made using a system, or a piece of information was passed on incorrectly to someone else or misheard. While writing these observations down it is good to start posing specific research questions related to them, e.g. "Why did X not let Y know the printer was broken when he came back from his break?" and to contemplate further, e.g. "Was it a communication failure, a problem with being overloaded at the time, or a technology problem?"

It is at this point that knowledge of the theory of distributed cognition can help in interpreting and representing the observations of a work setting (see Chapter 3 and Hutchins, 1995). It provides an analytic framework and a set of concepts to describe what is happening at a higher level of abstraction. Problems can be described in terms of the communication pathways that are being hindered or the breakdowns arising due to information not propagating effectively from one representational state to another (see Box 8.7). The framework can reveal where information is being 'distorted,' resulting in poor communication or inefficiency. Conversely, it can show when different technologies and the representations displayed via them are effective at mediating certain work activities and how well they are coordinated.

Box 8.7
Distributed cognition concepts

A distributed cognition analysis involves producing a detailed description of the domain area at varying levels of granularity. At the micro-level, a small set of cognitive terms are used to depict the representations employed in a cognitive activity and the processes acting upon them. The terms are intended to steer the analysis towards conceptualizing problems in terms of distributed information and representations. This level of description can also directly lead to recommendations, suggesting how to change or redesign an aspect of the cognitive system, such as a display or a socially mediated practice. The main terms used are:

The cognitive system—**the interactions among people, the artifacts they use, and the environment they are working in.**

The communicative pathways—**the channels by which information is passed between people, e.g. phone, email, physical gesture.**

Propagation of representational states—**how information is transformed across different media. Media refers to external artifacts (e.g. instruments, maps, paper notes) and internal representations (e.g. human memory). These can be socially mediated (e.g. passing on a message verbally), technologically mediated (e.g. pressing a key on a computer), or mentally mediated (e.g. reading the time on a clock).** ■

An example of applying the distributed cognition approach: call centers

Ackermann and Halverson's research (Ackermann and Halverson, 2000; Halverson, 2002) has used the distributed cognition framework to understand, at a cognitive level, how call centers work. Call centers have greatly increased during the last 10 years—now fronting many organizations, including banks, computer companies, postal services, and government offices. Their main function is to field phone-based queries, offering help and advice to customers about their products, services, etc.

The aim of Ackermann and Halverson's study was to find out how the operators of a typical call center manage the fast-paced and information-intensive process they are engaged in and, in particular, how they answer queries and what information resources they use to achieve this. Their study lasted 18 months, where they collected large amounts of data, including observations, videos, and semi-structured interviews. From their assortment of data, they initially described the domain area and what the phone operators do to accomplish their work. They also noted the unusual demands placed upon the operators and the methods and workarounds they used.

One of the first things they noted is that call center operators are under a lot of pressure. They need to begin forming their answers within 45–60 seconds of answering a call. This can be very demanding, given the diversity of questions that can be asked and the round-about way of talking some callers adopt. However, they also observed that many of the queries the operators encounter are similar, enabling the operators to classify them into types and develop 'routines' for finding the information needed for a given type. At a finer level of analysis, Ackermann and Halverson decided to focus on the routines. They observed over 300 calls, taped 60 of them, and chose to analyze 10 in detail. The 10 were transcribed, covering the actions taken and the conversations that took place. One example of 'Joan' is used in their write up of the study to illustrate what is involved in a typical routine.

To begin, they drew a schematic bird's eye view of Joan's workplace, illustrating the physical set-up (see Figure 8.16). The figure shows how the different workspaces are related to each other and the various resources that are used during calls. What stands out immediately from the figure is the way the resources are spread out, requiring Joan to walk from her desk to a shared table for every call. While keeping her fit, it also reveals that certain types of information have to be 'carried' between the different locations.

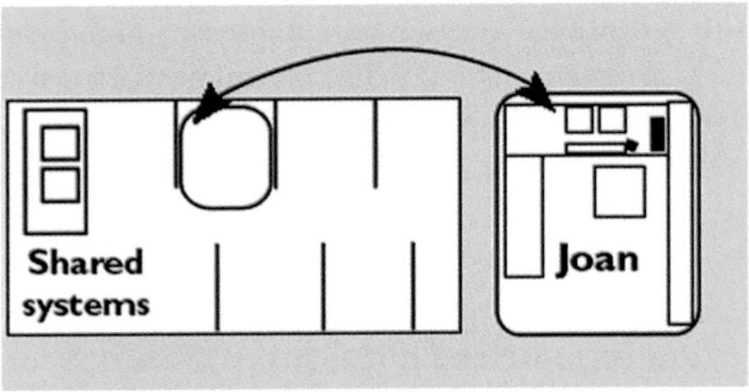

Figure 8.16 *Joan's workplace and the shared resources used by the operators. The left-hand diagram shows how the cubicles are positioned in relation to one another and the right-hand diagram is a blown-up schematic of Joan's space*

The representations and technologies that are used at Joan's desk and elsewhere are then described. These include software applications, monitors, the telephone, manuals, lists, scraps of paper, and post-it notes. The way that incoming calls are handled is also highlighted: pointing out how the telephone system allocates incoming calls to the next available operator.

The type of call that is then analyzed is one of the most common, which in this call center concerns employment verification. Ackermann and Halverson describe a specific example that is representative of many others. A caller (a mortgage lender) wishes to find out whether one of its customers is actually employed by Company X and so calls the call center to verify this. Joan, who receives the call, looks up this information using a database (EMPLOY) that can only be accessed at the shared terminal that is 3 meters away from her desk. For every call she has to disconnect her headset from the phone, and walk to the central table to access the database to find out the information needed. In addition, Joan has to enter a record for every call using a computer-based tracking system (CAT) that is accessed via the terminal on her desk. When she answers the call, she has at the same time to close out the one she was previously working on. While doing this, she asks the caller for details about the person in question. This she types into the new record (the overlapping of tasks is noted by the analysts as being significant). Joan then writes this down on a piece of paper. The reason for this duplication of the same information is that she needs to carry it over to the EMPLOY system. The information (including a social security number) is too much to remember and would be easy to get mixed up or forgotten while walking over to the other terminal. She walks over to the EMPLOY system with the piece of paper and copies the information into the software, to enable her to get the new information she needs. She writes this down on the same piece of paper. She then returns to her desk and relays this new piece of information back to the caller, while completing the details of the call in the record on the CAT system (the overlapping of tasks at this stage is noted by the analysts as also being significant).

Having described the seemingly simple task in prose, Halverson and Ackermann re-represent the short sequence of events in a diagrammatic form, making explicit how the various media support the way the information is propagated across different representational states. The diagram reveals the different cognitive memories that are used during the various transformations (see Figure 8.17), including Joan's and the caller's, indicating how they are transformed from working memory to long-term memory. Importantly, by representing this common routine using the notation, nine different memories were revealed as being involved in the propagation of representational states. This is a large number and shows how the routine task is far from simple, involving a complex set of overlapping steps.

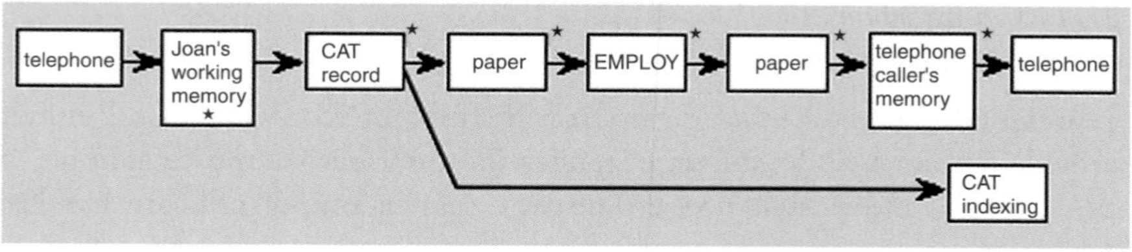

Figure 8.17 A diagram showing the propagation of representational states for the employee verification process. The boxes show the different representational states for different media (e.g. telephone, paper, Joan's memory) and the arrows show the transformations on these. The asterixes indicate where Joan's working memory is also involved

Through examining the diagram and revisiting their textual descriptions, Ackermann and Halverson were able to reflect upon the implications of the many overlapping tasks Joan has to accomplish, some simultaneously. They subsequently performed an even finer grain of analysis, examining how the multiple memories are interleaved at a physical level, noting the actual physical movements involved in each change in representation state, e.g. when Joan moved and clicked the mouse, alongside what was said at that point. Another notation was used for this purpose.

How useful is distributed cognition?

What is gained from conducting a detailed distributed cognition analysis such as this one? To a manager or outsider, the routine call would appear to involve a simple request and yet Ackermann and Halverson's analysis reveals it to be a complex cognitive task. An outcome of performing their micro-level analysis was to make explicit the nature of the complexity: showing how memories are distributed and interwoven; sometimes they belong to an individual, e.g. Joan's note written down on a piece of paper, and other times they are part of the system, e.g. the call handling procedure embedded in the telephone system. Furthermore, it describes systematically how a piece of information is propagated through multiple representational states, being verbally, physically, and mentally transformed, that has implications for the redesign of the supporting systems. It identifies the cognitive workload that is involved when different resources have to be used and coordinated for the same task.

What are the design implications? Simply enabling the EMPLOY database to be accessed at the same terminal as the CAT system would seem like an obvious solution. However, the information still needs to be propagated between applications and the cutting and pasting editing functions may not be compatible between the different applications. Moreover, the operator may be put under even more pressure to complete a call in even less time, if it is perceived that the operators no longer have to walk anywhere to access information resources. However, this perspective does not take into account the amount of cognitive effort required to access and enter information via different information systems.

Performing a detailed distributed cognition analysis enables researchers and designers to explore the trade-offs and likely outcomes of potential solutions and in so doing suggest a more grounded set of cognitive requirements, e.g. types of information resources, that are considered suitable for specific kinds of activities. Clearly, such a painstaking level of analysis and the expertise required in the interpretation is very costly. In the commercial world, where deadlines and budgets are always looming, it is unlikely to be practical. However, in large-scale and safety critical projects, where more time and resources are available, it can be a valuable analytic tool to use.

8.6.3 Activity theory

Activity theory (AT) is a product of Soviet psychology that explains human behavior in terms of our practical activity with the world. It originated as part of the attempt to produce a Marxist psychology, an enterprise usually associated with Vygotsky (e.g. 1926/1962) and later Leontiev (e.g. 1978, 1989). In the last 20–30 years, versions of AT have become popular elsewhere, particularly in Scandinavia, Germany, and now growing in the USA and UK. The newer 'versions' of AT have been popular in research investigating 'applied' problems, particularly those to do with work, technology, and education.

Activity theory provides a framework that focuses analysis around the concept of an 'activity' and helps to identify tensions between the different elements of the system. For example, Wendy Mackay *et al.* (2000) analyzed a 4-minute excerpt from a video of users working with a new software tool. They identified 19 shifts in attention between different parts of the tool interface and the task at hand. In fact, some users spent so much time engaged in these shifts that they lost track of their original task. Using the theory helped evaluators to focus on relevant incidents.

AT outlines two key models: one which outlines what constitutes an 'activity' and one which models the mediating role of artifacts.

The individual model

AT models activities in a hierarchical way. At the bottom level are 'operations,' routinized behaviors that require little conscious attention, e.g. rapid typing. At an intermediate level are 'actions,' behavior that is characterized by conscious planning, e.g. producing a glossary. The top level is the activity, and that provides a minimum meaningful context for understanding the individual actions, e.g. writing an essay (see Figure 8.18). There may be many different operations capable of fulfilling an action, and many actions capable of serving the same activity.

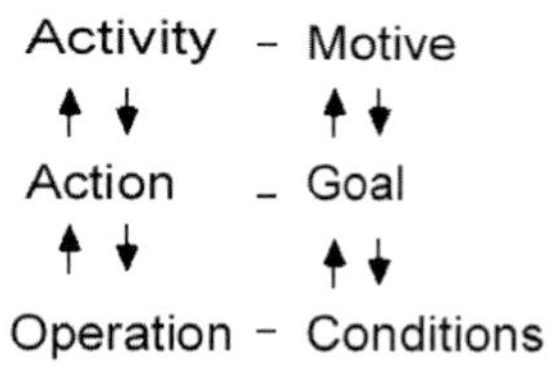

***Figure 8.18** The original activity theory model*

Activities can be identified on the basis of the motives that elicit them, actions on the basis of conscious goals that guide them, and operations by the conditions necessary to attain the goals. However, there is an intimate and fluid link between levels. Actions can become operations as they become more automatic and operations can become actions when an operation encounters an obstacle, thus requiring conscious planning. Similarly there is no strict demarcation between action and activity. If 'motive' changes then an activity can become an action. It is also important to realize that activities are not self-contained. Activities relate to others while actions may be part of different activities, and so on.

The role of artifacts

Artifacts can be physical, such as a book or a stone, or they can be abstract, such as a system of symbols or a set of rules. Physical artifacts have physical properties that cause humans to respond to them as direct objects to be acted upon. They also embody a set of social practices, their design reflecting a history of particular use. Leontiev describes the process of learning what these inherent properties are as one of 'appropriation,' signifying the active nature of the learning that is needed. The kind of learning involved is one of identifying and participating in the activity appropriate to the artifact. Consider an infant learning to feed with a spoon. Leontiev (1981) observed that, at first, the infant carries the spoon to its mouth as though it were handling any other object, not considering the need to hold it horizontal. Over time, with adult guidance, the spoon is shaped in the way it is because of the social practice—the activity—of feeding and, in turn, the infant's task is to learn that relationship—to discover what practice(s) the object embodies. By contrast a spoon dropped into the cage of a mouse, say, will only ever have the status of just another physical object—no different from that of a stone.

The idea of abstract artifacts follows from the idea of 'mediation,' i.e. a fundamental characteristic of human development is the change from a direct mode of acting on the world to one that is mediated by something else. In AT, the artifacts involved in an activity mediate between the elements of it.

AT also emphasizes the social context of an activity. Even when apparently working alone, an individual is still engaged in activities that are given meaning by a wider set of practices.

The classic view of an activity has a subject (who performs the activity) and an object (on which the activity is performed). Recent developments in AT, particularly by Engeström (e.g. 1999) and Nardi (e.g. 1996), have widened the focus from the 'individual' triangle of a single activity (subject, activity, and object) to include supra-individual concepts—tools, rules, community, and division of labor. By tool is meant the artifacts, signs, and means that mediate the subject and object; by community is meant those who share the same object; by rules is meant a set of agreed conventions and policies covering what it means to be a member of that community (set by laws, parents, managers, boards, etc.); and by division of labor is meant the primary means of classifying the labor in a workplace, e.g. manager, engineer, receptionist. The extended versions allow consideration of networks of interrelated activities—forming an 'activity system' (see Figure 8.19).

Performing an analysis driven by activity theory

AT does not present a clear methodological prescription for the description or analysis of behavior as a set of procedures to be followed. The conceptual model (Figure 8.18) is the main framework that is used to describe levels within an activity. This means that identifying elements will be highly dependent on individual interpretation. Christiansen (1996, p. 177)

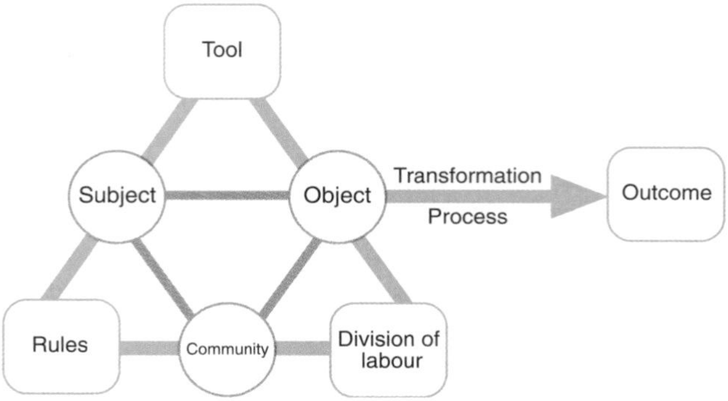

Figure 8.19 *Engeström's (1999) activity system model. The tool element is sometimes referred to as the mediating artifact*

summarizes: "Methodologically . . . the ideal data for an application of AT consist of longitudinal ethnographic observation, interviews and discussion in real-life settings, supplemented by experiments." She continues that you "cannot interview people directly through rote questions but must interpret their actions and opinions after some careful reflection," which is a difficult process. Nevertheless, the original and later versions of the AT framework have become popular amongst researchers and some practitioners as a way of identifying needs for new tools and to analyze problems that are present in a work or other setting.

One of the biggest problems with doing an AT analysis is working out when something should be described as a top-level activity and when something is better described as a lower-level action. In Figure 8.20, completing a software project is considered to be a top-level activity, while programming a module as an action. However, equally, programming a module could be viewed as an activity—if that was the object of the subject (person).

Activity level	- Building a house	- Completing a software project	- Carrying out research into a topic
Action level	- Fixing the roofing - Transporting bricks by truck	- Programming a module - Arranging a meeting	- Searching for references - Participating in a conference - Writing a report
Operation level	- Hammering - Changing gears when driving	- Using operating system commands - Selecting appropriate programming language constructs	- Using logical syllogisms - Selecting appropriate wording

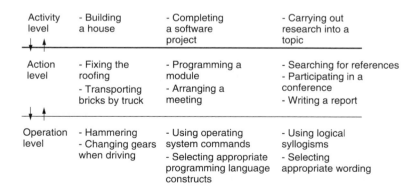

Figure 8.20 *Examples of activities, actions, and operations*

An example of applying the activity system approach: customer support center

To illustrate how AT can be used to interpret a work setting, we describe how it was used by Collins *et al.* (2002), who together with a small in-house IT support team, set out to identify the tools needed by customer support engineers whose job it is to document solutions to customer problems. The version of AT they used was the popular Engeström one (Figure 8.19). The domain chosen overlaps with the call center analyzed using the distributed cognition approach. We have selected these two projects on purpose to show the different emphases between the two approaches.

Documenting solutions to customer problems was identified as the activity to be focused on. This was seen in the wider context of knowledge management—a concept that has received much attention in recent years. The primary method of data collection was through interview: 32 employees were interviewed for one to one-and-a-half hours each. The interviews were transcribed and documented with notes and artifacts produced by the interviewees during the conversation. These were then annotated in terms of particular elements of the activity system, e.g. rules, object. Examples of subjects were frontline and backline engineers who deal with the calls; examples of tools were a knowledge repository tool with documented answers and the computer network used to run it on.

The analysts noted the tensions that the interviewees had talked about within or between elements, e.g. subject versus rules. These provided them with talking points by which to consider the system dynamics together with opportunities for thinking about new tools to support the customer support people. Examples of within and between element tensions include:

- *Community*—limited communication across stakeholder groups contributes to a lack of appreciation among the backline engineers of the needs of frontline customer support engineers.
- *Tool*—combination of a new knowledge repository tool and the physical computer from which it ran (the hardware and network on which the tool ran were not fast enough to enable timely access to the desired knowledge).
- *Division of labor versus subject*—workload balance and focus was lacking for the backline engineers who were expected to handle the majority of customer calls that do not currently have documented solutions the frontline staff can handle.
- *Subject versus rules*—the organization has a set of explicit and implicit rules for rating the knowledge documents. However, there was considerable conflict between the subjects involved in authoring and annotating them as to which was the most important. As a consequence, many did not use the rating system.

In presenting the results, excerpts from the interviews are used to back up many of the identified tensions, for example, an answer to the question "When you're talking to a customer, do you do documentation in real time" was "I try to. This is the best way, but it's real hard to get all that down. A lot of times I summarize it or if I can get another call while I am finishing up this call . . . if another one is coming, I'll answer the phone and start working on it. I'll then have to go back and work from memory to update this other call. It's not a good habit to get into. If the phone is ringing, it's ringing, you know.''

How useful is activity theory?

Many examples of tensions were identified in Collins' *et al.* analysis. Hence they built up a picture of the company by, firstly, identifying the core elements in the customer support center in terms of rules, objects, etc., and then assigning examples of tensions and conflict within and between them. Using these as discussion points, the team were able to suggest specific improvements to the knowledge management tool being developed, including:

- Delay in retrieval of relevant documents must be reconciled with user expectations for speed.
- Software tools must support individual user preferences for communication media, e.g. email, instant messaging.

Performing an AT analysis enables researchers and designers to identify the tensions in a workplace leading to specific needs for new technological tools. It can be difficult, however, getting to grips with the concepts and being able to determine how to label the points raised in the interviews. Expertise and a good background in the Soviet version of activity theory are recommended to become competent in it. Similar to the distributed cognition approach, in the commercial world, where deadlines and budgets are always looming, it is unlikely to be practical. As with distributed cognition, where more time and resources are available, it can be a valuable analytic tool.

Activity 8.5

Give some examples of how this activity theory (AT) analysis differs from and is similar to the distributed cognition (DC) analysis of the call center in the previous section.

Comment

Some of the main differences and similarities are:

1. **AT focuses on describing the tensions between parts of the AT system, using quotes to back them up, whereas a DC analysis focuses on drilling down on the way representations and technologies are used for a given distributed activity.**
2. **AT provides a set of concepts by which to label and instantiate specific observations for an activity system, whereas DC represents the sequence of events (often in a diagrammatic form) making explicit how the various media**

support the way information is propagated across different representational states.

3. **Both AT and DC analyses reveal problems with existing technologies leading the analysts to suggest design recommendations for improving the existing set-up.**
4. **The AT analysis used a large number of interviews and in-house team discussions to collect and articulate their data, whereas the DC analysis used data collected from a combination of observations and interviews.**
5. **The AT analysis provided specific requirements for a particular software tool being developed, whereas the DC analysis explored the trade-offs and likely outcomes of potential solutions suggesting a grounded set of cognitive requirements.**

8.7 Presenting the findings

The best way to present findings depends on the audience, and the original goals of the study. However, it also is dependent on the data gathering and analysis techniques used.

In the previous sections of this chapter, you met many different ways of presenting findings—as numbers, through various graphical devices, in tables, in textual descriptions, as a set of themes or categories, and so on. These representations may be used directly to report your findings, provided they are appropriate for your audience and your purpose, or they may be used as background evidence for a different form of representation.

Broadly speaking, data gathering and analysis in interaction design is carried out for one of two purposes: to derive requirements for an interactive product, or to evaluate an interactive product under development. These two purposes have their own needs in terms of the notations to use and the information to be highlighted, but they also have similarities in terms of the choices to be made for presentation. For example, they usually involve reporting findings to a technical design team who will act on the findings.

In this section, we discuss three kinds of presentation style that we have not focused on as yet: using rigorous notations, using stories, and summarizing. There are other ways of presenting findings, but these are representative of the main options. In addition, these are not mutually exclusive and are often used in combination.

8.7.1 Rigorous notations

A number of rigorous notations have been developed to analyze, capture, and present information for interaction design. The term 'rigorous' is not intended to imply 'formal' or 'rigid,' but simply to say that the notations have clear syntax and semantics. For example, the work models promoted in contextual design (Beyer and Holtzblatt, 1998) use simple but clear conventions for representing flows, breakdowns, individual roles, and so on. The modeling language UML (Unified Modeling Language) has stricter and more precise syntax to be followed and is more often used to specify internal software designs (although it has also been used and extended in the context of user interface design, e.g. Van Den Bergh and Coninx, 2005).

Advantages of using a rigorous notation are that it gives you clear guidance on what to look for in the findings and what to highlight, and that it forces you to be precise. Disadvantages include: that by highlighting specific elements, it inevitably also downplays or ignores other aspects, and that the precision expressed by the notation may be lost on an audience if they don't know the notation well. Producing diagrams in these notations inevitably requires further analysis of the findings in order to identify the specific characteristics and properties that the notation highlights.

To overcome their disadvantages, rigorous notations are usually used in combination with stories or other more easily accessible formats.

8.7.2 Using stories

Storytelling is an easy and intuitive approach for people to communicate ideas and experiences. It is no surprise, then, that stories (also sometimes called narratives) are used extensively in interaction design both to communicate findings of investigative studies, and as the basis for further development such as product design or system enhancements.

Storytelling may be employed in three different ways. First, participants, i.e. interviewees, questionnaire respondents, and those you have observed, may have told stories of their own during data gathering. These stories can be extracted, compared, and may be used to communicate findings to others, e.g. as anecdotes to bring a summary report to life.

Second, stories about participants may be employed. For example, in reporting her findings about European culture, Bell (2001) presents general themes and overall findings, but then illustrates these with specific stories about participants she observed. For example, one of the themes from her observations was that food shopping is important in European cultures. To illustrate the importance of the local market in France, she tells the following story:

> ***Patrice lives with her husband Frederico and their two small children in a tiny village in Brittany. In her early 30s, Patrice has retired from working in the company she and her husband started. She now runs her household and looks after her kids and husband. Like many other European women we interviewed, she expressed serious reservations about catalog shopping, saying "I like to touch and see things before I buy them." And although she lives just a five-minute drive from a town with a large supermarket, Patrice chooses to shop in the local produce markets, which cycle through southern Brittany. It is important to buy what is locally seasonally available: "it just tastes better," Patrice says.***

Including these kinds of specific stories gives credibility and adds weight to the summary claim. Making a multimedia presentation of the story by adding video or audio excerpts and photographs will illustrate the story further. This kind of approach can be particularly effective if presenting data from an evaluation study that involves observation, as it is hard to contest well-chosen video excerpts of users interacting with technology or anecdotes from interview transcripts.

Third, stories may be constructed from smaller anecdotes or repeated patterns that are found in the data. In this case, stories provide a way of rationalizing and collating data to form a representative account of a product's use or a certain type of event.

Any stories collected through data gathering may be used as the basis for constructing scenarios. Scenarios are hypothesized stories about people and their daily life. They are a powerful technique for interaction design and can be used throughout the lifecycle. See Chapters 10 and 11 for more information on scenarios.

8.7.3 Summarizing the findings

Clearly written reports with an overview at the beginning and a detailed content list make for easy reading and a good reference document. Including anecdotes, quotations, pictures, and video clips helps to bring the study to life, stimulate interest, and make the written description more meaningful. Some teams emphasize quantitative data, but its value depends on the type of study. Often both qualitative and quantitative data analysis are used because they provide alternative perspectives.

Some audiences are likely to be more interested in the headline findings than in the details of stories or precise specifications. These may be high-level managers, the set of users who acted as participants in studies, or product designers who want to use the results to develop a new product. Whoever they are, being able to present a summary of the findings is important. This is where numbers and statistical values (if you have any) can be really powerful. However, in these summaries it is important not to overstate your findings—if 8 out of 10 users preferred design A over design B, this does not mean that design A is 80% more attractive than design B. If you found 800 out of 1000 users preferred design A then you have more evidence to suggest that design A is better, but there are still other factors to take into account. In general, be wary of using words such as 'most,' 'all,' 'majority,' 'none,' and be careful when writing justifications to ensure that they reflect the data.

Activity 8.6

Consider each of the findings below and the associated summary statement about it. For each one, comment on whether the finding supports the statement.

1. *Finding:* 2 out of 4 people who filled in the questionnaire ticked the box that said they prefer not to use the ring back facility on their cell phone.

***Statement:* Half of the users don't use the ringback facility.**

2. *Finding:* Joan who works in the design department was observed one day walking for 10 minutes to collect printout from the high-quality colour printer.

   Statement: Significant time is wasted by designers who have to walk a long distance to collect printout.
3. *Finding:* A data log of 1000 hours of interaction with a website recorded during January, February, and March records 8 hours spent looking at the helpfiles.

   Statement: The website's helpfiles were used less than 1% of the time during the first quarter of the year.

Comment

1. The questionnaire didn't ask if they use the ring back, just whether they preferred to use the ring back facility. In addition, 2 users out of 4 is a very small number of participants and it would be better to state the actual numbers.
2. Observing one designer on one day having to walk to get printout does not mean that this is a general problem. There may be other reasons why this happened on this day, and other information is needed to make a clear statement.
3. This statement is justified as the log was recorded for a significant period of time, and using percentages to represent this finding is appropriate as the numbers are so large.

Assignment

The aim of this assignment is for you to practice data analysis and presentation. Assume that you are to present the findings of your data gathering assignment from Chapter 7 to a group of peers, e.g. through a seminar.

(a) Review the data you have gathered and identify any qualitative data and any quantitative data in your data set.

(b) Is there any qualitative data that could sensibly and helpfully be translated into quantitative measures? If so, do the translation and add this data to your quantitative set.

(c) Consider your quantitative data.

  (i) Decide how best to enter your quantitative data into your spreadsheet software. For example, you need to consider how to handle answers to closed questions. Then enter the data and generate some graphical representations. As you are likely to have very few records, i.e. respondents or interviewees, in your data set, you will have to think carefully about what if any graphical representations will provide meaningful summaries of your findings.

  (ii) Is there any data for which simple measures such as percentages or averages will be helpful? If so, calculate the three different types of average.

(d) Consider your qualitative data.
  (i) Based on your refinement of the study question 'improving the product,' identify some themes from your qualitative data, e.g. what features of the product cause people difficulties, did any of your participants suggest alternative designs or solutions? Refine your themes and collate extracts of data which support the theme.
  (ii) Identify any critical incidents in your data. This may arise from interview or questionnaire responses, or from observation. Describe these incidents carefully and choose one or two to analyze in more depth, focusing on the context in which they occurred.

(e) Collate your findings as a presentation and deliver them to a group of your peers.

(f) Review your presentation and any questions you received from your peers and consider where your analysis and presentation could be improved.

Summary

This chapter has described in detail the difference between qualitative and quantitative data and between qualitative or quantitative analysis.

Quantitative and qualitative data can be analyzed for patterns and trends using simple techniques and graphical representations. Qualitative data may be analyzed using a variety of approaches including identifying categories or themes, and using theoretical frameworks, such as grounded theory, distributed cognition and activity theory.

It was noted that presenting the results is just as important as analyzing the data, hence it is important to make sure that any summary or claim arising from the analysis is carefully contextualized, and can be justified by the data.

Key points

- The kind of data analysis that can be done depends on the data gathering techniques used.
- Qualitative and quantitative data may be collected from any of the main data gathering techniques: interviews, questionnaires, and observation.
- Quantitative data analysis for interaction design usually involves calculating percentages and averages.
- There are three different kinds of average: mean, mode, and median.
- Graphical representations of quantitative data help in identifying patterns, outliers, and the overall view of the data.
- Qualitative data analysis may be framed by theories. Three such theories are grounded theory, activity theory, and distributed cognition.

Further Reading

HUFF, D. (1991) *How to Lie with Statistics*. Penguin Books. This wonderful little book illustrates the many ways in which numbers can be misrepresented. Unlike some (many) books on statistics, the text is easy to read and amusing.

STRAUSS, A. AND CORBIN, J. (1998) *Basics of Qualitative Research: Techniques and Procedures for Developing Grounded Theory*, 2nd edn. Sage. This presents a readable and practical account of applying the grounded theory approach. It is not tailored specifically to interaction design and therefore requires some interpretation. It is a good discussion of the basic approach.

ROGERS, Y. (2006) Distributed cognition and communication. In *The Encyclopedia of Language and Linguistics*, 2nd edn, K. Brown (ed.). Elsevier, pp. 731–733. (A version can also be downloaded from Yvonne Rogers' website.) This chapter provides a readable introduction to the background and application of distributed cognition.

KUUTTI, K. (1996) Activity theory as a potential framework for human–computer interaction. In *Context and Consciousness*, B.A. Nardi (ed.). MIT Press. pp. 17–44. This provides a digestible description of activity theory and how it can be applied in HCI.

9

9.1 Introduction

Design is a practical and creative activity, the ultimate intent of which is to develop a product that helps its users achieve their goals. In previous chapters, we looked at different kinds of interactive products, issues that need to be taken into account when doing interaction design, some of the theoretical basis for the field, and techniques for gathering and analyzing data to understand users' goals. In this chapter we start to explore *how* we can design and build interactive products.

Chapter 1 defined interaction design as being concerned with "designing interactive products to support the way people communicate and interact in their everyday and working lives." But how do you go about doing this?

Developing a product must begin with gaining some understanding of what is required of it, but where do these requirements come from? Whom do you ask about them? Underlying good interaction design is the philosophy of user-centered design, i.e. involving users throughout development, but who are the users? Will they know what they want or need even if we can find them to ask? For an innovative product, users are unlikely to be able to envision what is possible, so where do these ideas come from?

In this chapter, we raise and answer these kinds of questions and discuss user-centered design and the four basic activities of the interaction design process that were introduced in Chapter 1. We also introduce a lifecycle model of interaction design that captures these activities.

The main aims of this chapter are to:

- **Consider what 'doing' interaction design involves.**
- **Explain some advantages of involving users in development.**
- **Explain the main principles of a user-centered approach.**
- **Ask and provide answers for some important questions about the interaction design process.**
- **Introduce the idea of a lifecycle model to represent a set of activities and how they are related.**
- **Describe some lifecycle models from software engineering and HCI and discuss how they relate to the process of interaction design.**
- **Present a lifecycle model of interaction design.**

9

The process of interaction design

9.1 Introduction

9.2 What is involved in interaction design?

9.3 Some practical issues

9.4 Lifecycle models: showing how the activities are related

9.2 What is involved in interaction design?

The previous chapters have introduced you to many exciting ideas, approaches, theories, and opinions about interaction design, but what does it mean to actually 'do' interaction design? The following activity is intended to start you thinking about this by asking you to produce an initial design for an interactive product.

Activity 9.1

Imagine that you want to design a travel planner for yourself. You might use this system to plan your route, check visa requirements, book flights or train tickets, investigate the facilities at your destination, and so on. Assume that the system is destined to run on a desktop system for the purposes of this activity.

1. **Make a list of the user experience and usability goals for the system.**
2. **Outline the initial screen or two for this system, showing its main functionality and its general look and feel. Spend about five minutes on this.**
3. **Having produced an outline, now spend five minutes reflecting on how you went about tackling this activity. What did you do first? Did you have any particular artifacts or experience to base your design upon? What process did you go through?**

Comment

1. **The three main usability goals I would like for my system are efficiency, effectiveness, and safety. I'm not so bothered about whether the system is easy to learn or memorable as I am likely to use it regularly, and I am prepared to put the time in to learn something that supports me well. When I look at the list of user experience goals, there are definitely some that I don't wish to be associated with my travel organizer, such as annoying, frustrating, and challenging! I want it to be helpful and satisfying. Being fun or engaging would be additional bonuses to me I think, as the main purpose of using the system is to plan my travel.**
2. **The initial screens I produced are shown in Figure 9.1. The first screen prompts me for the four main items of information I usually have at the top of my mind: where am I going, when am I going there, how do I want to get there, and do I need to organize accommodation? The second screen then shows the kind of response I would like the system to give if I'm trying to go to York by train: it gives me train times from my local station on the specified date (straight through trains only, as I prefer that), and the range of accommodation available in York. I can then find out more about the trains and the accommodation by drilling down further.**

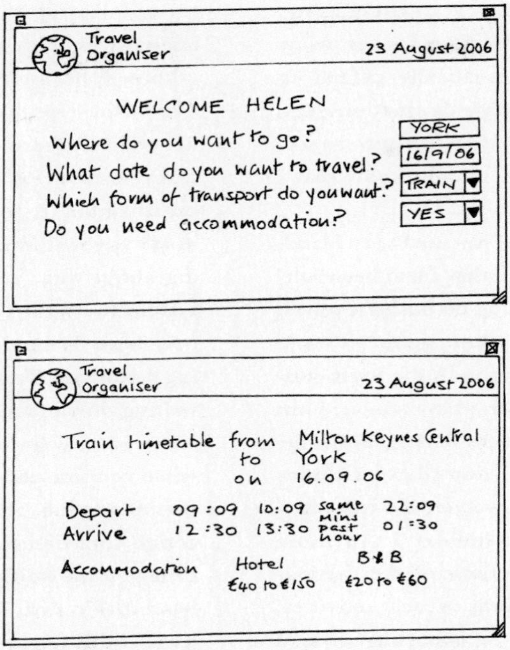

Figure 9.1 *Initial sketches of the travel organizer*

3. The first thing that came into my head when I started doing this was the myriad of resources I currently use to plan my travel. For example, travel agents will arrange accommodation, visas, guided tours, etc., for me; I can look at paper-based or electronic timetables for journey routes and times, ring up automated timetable readers, operators who will give me travel advice, embassies who will also give me travel advice about their own country, websites to identify cheap flights, and so on. There is a long list. I then thought it would be good to combine the advantages of all of these into one system that could then be tailored to me. For example, so that the first airline offered for any flights is my favorite airline, and the starting point for my journeys is defaulted to my normal train station or airport. The next thing I focused on was the dialog I would have with the system. Hence, my sketches focus on questions the system might ask me and my responses. One of the things that occurred to me as I was producing this sketch is that the location I need to enter will depend on the kind of transport I choose, and the kind of help I need will also depend on the kind of transport I want to use. On the other hand, I would want the system to know that I am unlikely to

want to drive in my car to Hong Kong, which is several thousand miles away, so it should automatically default to travel by air for some destinations, and similarly if there is no airport near a destination then it should know that I would not want to fly.

The 'look and feel' seemed very bland, and I then realized that I had been subconsciously focusing on business travel, which usually is about getting to and from a given location in the most convenient and comfortable manner; I am unlikely to be concerned about the location itself as I don't have a choice of destination. However, if I was planning travel for a holiday I am more likely to want pictures of the destination and descriptions of local activities, restaurants, historic sites, and so on. I might also want to enter my choices in a different way, focusing on the kind of holiday or location I want to travel to, and leaving the system to suggest alternatives. This led me to reconsider (although not redraw) my ideas.

The exact steps taken to create a product will vary from designer to designer, from product to product, and from organization to organization. In this activity, you may have started by thinking about what you would like such a system to do for you, or you may, like me, have been thinking about existing resources. Sketching something, or writing down concrete lines, squiggles, and words, helps to focus the mind on what you are designing, the details of the interaction, and the kinds of interaction your design will support. All the time you were doing this, you will have been making choices between alternatives, exploring your requirements in more detail, and refining your ideas about what you would like a travel organizer to do for you.

There are many fields of design, for example, graphic design, architectural design, industrial and software design, and although each discipline has its own interpretation of 'designing,' there are three fundamental activities that are recognized in all design: understanding the requirements, producing a design that satisfies those requirements, and evaluating the design. Interaction design also involves these activities, and in addition we focus attention very clearly on users and their goals. For example, we investigate the artifact's use and target domain by taking a user-centered approach to development, we seek users' opinions and reactions to early designs, and we involve users appropriately in the development process itself. This means that users' concerns direct the development rather than just technical concerns, and for interaction design, the three fundamental activities of design listed above are extended to include an activity of producing a version of the design that users can interact with.

So design involves work on requirements, designing a solution, producing an interactive version of the solution, and evaluating it. But design is also about trade-offs, about balancing conflicting requirements. One common form of trade-off when developing a system to offer advice is deciding how much choice will be given to the user and how much direction the system should offer. Often the division will depend on the purpose of the system, e.g. for business travel or for holiday travel. Getting the balance right requires experience, but it also requires the development and evaluation of alternative solutions.

Generating alternatives is a key principle in most design disciplines, and one that should be encouraged in interaction design. As Linus Pauling once said: "The best way to get a good idea, is to get lots of ideas." This is not necessarily easy, however, and unlike many design disciplines, interaction designers are not generally trained to generate alternative designs. The good news is that the ability to brainstorm and contribute alternative ideas can be learned. For example, Kelley (2001) describes seven secrets for better brainstorms, including sharpen the focus (have a well-honed problem statement), playful rules (to encourage ideas), and get physical (use visual props). He also discusses six ways to kill a brainstorm, including do it off-site and write everything down. Danis and Boies (2000) found that using techniques from graphic design that encouraged the generation of alternative designs stimulated innovative interactive systems design.

Involving users and others in the design process means that the designs and potential solutions need to be communicated to people other than the original designer. This requires the design to be captured and expressed in some suitable form that allows review, revision, and improvement. There are many ways of doing this, one of the simplest being to produce a series of sketches. Other common approaches are to write a description in natural language, to draw a series of diagrams, and to build prototypes. A combination of these techniques is likely to be the most effective. When users are involved, capturing and expressing a design in a suitable format is especially important since they are unlikely to understand jargon or specialist notations. In fact, a form that users can interact with is most effective, and building prototypes of one form or another (see Chapter 11) is an extremely powerful approach (see Box 9.1).

In the rest of this section, we explore in more depth the significance and practicality of involving users in design, i.e. using a user-centered approach, and consider again the four activities of interface design that were introduced in Chapter 1.

Box 9.1
The value of prototyping

I learned the value of a prototype through a very effective role-playing exercise. I was on a course designed to introduce new graduates to different possible careers in industry. One of the themes was production and manufacturing and the aim of one group exercise was to produce a notebook. Each group was told that it had 30 minutes to deliver 10 books to the person in charge. Groups were given various pieces of paper, scissors, sticky tape, staples, etc., and told to organize ourselves as best we could. So my group set to work organizing ourselves into a production line, with one of us cutting up the paper, another stapling the pages together, another sealing

the binding with the sticky tape, and so on. One person was even in charge of quality assurance. It took us less than 10 minutes to produce the 10 books, and we rushed off with our delivery. When we showed the person in charge, he replied, "That's not what I wanted, I need it bigger than that." Of course, the size of the notebook wasn't specified in the description of the task, so we found out how big he wanted it, got some more materials, and scooted back to produce 10 more books. Again, we set up our production line and produced 10 books to the correct size. On delivery we were again told that it was not what was required: he wanted the binding to work the other way around. This time we got as many of the requirements as we could and went back, developed one book, and took that back for further feedback and refinement before producing the 10 required.

If we had used prototyping as a way of exploring our ideas and checking requirements in the first place, we could have saved so much effort and resource! ■

9.2.1 The importance of involving users

The description above emphasizes the need to involve users in interaction design, but why is it important? In the past, developers would often talk to managers or to 'proxy users,' i.e. people who role-played as users, when eliciting requirements. While a proxy user can provide useful information, they will not have the same perspective as someone who performs the task every day, or who will use the intended product on a regular basis. For example, several years ago, I was involved with a system to process and record financial transactions from the foreign exchange ('forex') dealers in a large international bank. The users of this system took the handwritten transaction records completed by the 'forex' dealers and entered the details into the system. The system then validated the transaction and communicated a confirmation to the relevant parties. When the requirements for this system were developed, no-one from the development team spoke to the end-users of the system; the requirements were identified by higher-level managers. Although the system was successfully used to support the task, the end-users had developed several 'work-arounds.' For example, the system required both buyer code and buyer name to be entered, but it was quite common for the dealers to write only the buyer name on their transaction chitty. It would have been simple to design the system to support entry of transactions based on names or codes, but this wasn't done—both fields were required. This wasted a lot of time as the users had to identify the codes manually.

The best way to ensure that development continues to take users' activities into account is to involve real users throughout development. In this way, developers can gain a better understanding of users' goals, leading to a more appropriate, more usable product. However, two other aspects that have nothing to do with functionality are equally as important if the product is to be usable and used: expectation management and ownership.

Expectation management is the process of making sure that the users' views and expectations of the new product are realistic. The purpose of expectation management is to ensure that there are no surprises for users when the product arrives. If users feel they have been 'cheated' by promises that have not been fulfilled, then this will cause resistance and maybe rejection. Expectation management is relevant whether you are dealing with an organization introducing a new software system or a company developing a new interactive toy. In both cases, the marketing of the new arrival must be careful not to misrepresent the product. How many times have you seen an advert for something you thought would be really good to have, but when you see one, discover that the marketing 'hype' was a little exaggerated? I expect you felt quite disappointed and let down. Well, this is the kind of feeling that expectation management tries to avoid.

It is better to exceed users' expectations than to fall below them. This does not mean just adding more features, however, but that the product supports the users' goals more effectively than they expect. Involving users throughout development helps with expectation management because they can see from an early stage what the product's capabilities are and what they are not. They will also understand better how it will affect their jobs and lives, and what they can expect to do with the product; they are less likely to be disappointed. Users can also see the capabilities develop and understand, at least to some extent, why the features are the way they are.

Adequate and timely training is another technique for managing expectations. If you give people the chance to work with the product before it is released, either by training them on the real system or by offering hands-on demonstrations of a pre-release version, then they will understand better what to expect when the final product is released.

A second reason for user involvement is ownership. Users who are involved and feel that they have contributed to a product's development are more likely to feel a sense of 'ownership' towards it and be receptive to it when it finally emerges.

9.2.2 Degrees of user involvement

Different degrees of user involvement may be implemented in order to manage expectations and to create a feeling of ownership. At one end of the spectrum, users may be co-opted to the design team so that they are major contributors. For any one user, this may be on a full-time basis or a part-time basis, and it may be for the duration of the project or for a limited time only. There are advantages and disadvantages to each situation. If a user is co-opted full-time for the whole project, their input will be consistent and they will become very familiar with the system and its rationale. However, if the project takes many years they may lose touch with the rest of the user group, making their input less valuable. If a user is co-opted part-time for the whole project, she will offer consistent input to development while remaining in touch with other users. Depending on the situation, this will need careful management as the user will be trying to learn new jargon and handle unfamiliar material as a member of the design team, yet concurrently trying to fulfill the demands of their original job. This can become very stressful for the individuals. If a number of users from each user group are co-opted part-time for a limited period, input is not necessarily consistent across the whole project, but careful coordination between users can alleviate this problem. In this case, one user may be part of the design team for six months, then another takes over for the next six months, and so on.

At the other end of the spectrum, users may be kept informed through regular newsletters or other channels of communication. Provided they are given a chance to feed into the development process through workshops or similar events, this can be an effective approach to expectation management and ownership. In a situation with hundreds or even thousands of users it would not be feasible to involve them all as members of the team, and so this might be the only viable option.

If a large number of users is available, then a compromise situation is probably the best. Representatives from each user group may be co-opted onto the team on a full-time basis, while other users are involved through design workshops, evaluation sessions, and other data-gathering activities.

The individual circumstances of the particular project affect what is realistic and appropriate. If your end-user groups are identifiable, e.g. you are developing a product for a particular company, then it is easier to involve them. If, however, you are developing a product for the open market, it is unlikely that you will be able to co-opt a user to your design team, and so an alternative approach is needed. For example, Box 9.2 explains how Microsoft involves users in its developments.

One of the reasons often cited for not involving users in development is the amount of time it takes to organize, manage, and control such involvement. This issue may appear particularly acute in developing systems to run on the Internet, where ever-shorter timescales are being forced on teams—in this fast-moving area, projects lasting three months or less are common. You might think, therefore, that it would be particularly difficult to involve users in such projects. However, Braiterman *et al.* (2000) report two case studies showing how to involve users successfully in large-scale but very short multidisciplinary projects, belying the claim that involving users can waste valuable development time.

The first case study was a three-week project to develop the interaction for a new web shopping application. The team included a usability designer, an information architect, a project manager, content designers, and two graphic designers. In such a short timeframe, a long research phase and detailed prototyping sessions were impossible, so the team produced a hand-drawn paper prototype of the application that was revised daily in response to customer testing. The customers were asked to perform tasks with the prototype, which was manipulated by one of the team in order to simulate interaction, e.g. changing screens. After half the sessions were conducted, the team produced a more formal version of the prototype in Adobe Illustrator. They found that customers were enthusiastic about using the paper prototype and were keen to offer improvements. These improvements ranged from changes to terminology to task flow and page design changes such as the addition of full product descriptions and instructional information on shipment dates.

Box 9.2
How Microsoft involves users

Microsoft involves its users throughout development in a variety of ways, from product and feature identification to feature development and testing, and via the customer support call centers.

Microsoft bases feature selection and prioritization on a technique called 'activity-based planning.' This technique involves studying what users do to achieve a certain activity like writing a letter, and using the results of the study to choose product features. Each new release of a software product is limited to supporting about four new major activities. Each of these proposed new activities can be broken down into sub-activities, and these mapped against features already existing in the software. Any new features required are noted. If a feature can support more than one activity, then it is placed higher in the priority list. The techniques used to gather customer data for activity-based planning do not appear to be prescribed in any way, and can vary from visiting customers through to asking them to use an instrumented version of the software, i.e. a version that records the actions they take. Microsoft also employs contextual inquiry (see chapter 10) to learn about their customers' work, although they find that it can be time-consuming and the results ambiguous.

Because the world of applications software changes so rapidly, developers need to continually observe and test with users. Throughout the development phase, usability tests are carried out in Microsoft's usability lab. Each time a developer believes that a feature is finished, then it is scheduled for testing in the usability lab. A group of about 10 users 'off the street' are invited into the lab to perform certain tasks, while their behavior is observed and their performance recorded. The data is then analyzed and the findings fed back into development. This results in thorough testing of all features. As an example, an early version of Office 4.0 went through over 8000 hours of usability testing.

Once a product is complete, it is used internally by Microsoft staff (who are selected users and atypical, but are using it in a realistic working environment); then it may be released in a beta version to selected customers.

Microsoft has millions of customers around the world, about 30% of whom call their customer support lines with problems and frustrations resulting from poor features or software errors. This data about customer behavior and their problems with the products is a further source of information that is fed back into product development and improvement. ■

(Cusumano and Selby, 1995)

The second case study involved the development of a website for a video game publisher over three months. In order to understand what attracts people to such gaming sites, the multidisciplinary team felt they needed to understand the essence of gaming. To do this, they met 32 teenage gamers over a 10-day period, during which they observed and interviewed them in groups and individually. This allowed the team to understand something of the social nature of gaming and gave insights into the gamers themselves. During design, the team also conducted research and testing sessions in their office lab. This led them to develop new strategies and web designs based on the gamers' habits, likes, and dislikes.

Box 9.3 describes a situation in which users were asked to manage a software development project. There were hundreds of potential users, and so in addition, users became design team members on a full- and part-time basis; regular design workshops, debriefings, and training sessions were also held.

How actively users should be involved is a matter for debate. Some studies have shown that too much user involvement can lead to problems. This issue is discussed in the Dilemma box below.

Box 9.3
Users as project team leaders

The Open University (OU) in the UK is a large distance education university with many thousands of students enrolled each year in a variety of courses (undergraduate, graduate, vocational, and professional) in a variety of subjects (Technology, Languages, Education, etc.). The courses are presented through paper-based and electronic media including DVDs with video and audio resources. It has a network of centers through which it supports and distributes courses to students throughout the UK and Europe. The OU employs about 3000 academic and other full-time staff and about 6000 part-time and counseling staff. The University has around 200,000 students and customers for its education packs, and manages a network of distributors operating in over 30 countries. Such an operation requires considerable computerized support: in 1993 approximately 54 major systems of varying sizes were held on mainframe UN-LX host/workstations, VAX hosts, or PCs.

Traditionally, the systems had been built by an in-house software development team, who, due to resource constraints, sometimes needed to make business decisions although their expertise was in technical issues, not in the business side of the University. When it was time to redevelop these information systems, the OU decided that a new approach to development was required: users were to have a much more significant role.

Development was divided into a number of areas, each with its own project team and its own schedule. Consistency across the areas was maintained through the development of a GUI interface standard style guide that ensured all systems had the same look and feel (style guides are discussed in Chapter 6). Users were involved in development on a number of different levels, typically 30–80% of their time. For example, in one area (Area E), one user was appointed full-time to manage the project team, two others joined the project team part-time for a limited period (about 18 months each), one user was consulted on a regular basis, and a wider set of users were involved through workshops and prototyping sessions. The project team also included technically trained analysts and developers.

When asked for the most successful and the least successful aspects of the project, both users and technical developers agreed that the most successful had been getting users involved in development. They said that this had made the system closer to what the users wanted. The users' reactions were not all favorable, however. One user commented that, because users were part of the team for only a limited time, they did not see the development through from the beginning, but saw only some of the phases, and that this led to lack of continuity. Another user commented on the fact that the business had changed faster than the software could be developed, and hence the system had to be changed. Another group of users who were consulted mainly through workshops and prototyping sessions did not feel that their needs had been adequately addressed.

One of the user project managers had this to say:

> *The most successful thing has been getting people to go back to basics. We didn't look at existing systems and say, "We want the same thing but with go-faster stripes." We've examined what the University wants from the area. The most disappointing part has been that increased user involvement has not brought about ownership of the system by user areas. There was an expectation that we could move away from the traditional view of, "This is a computer system devised by computer people for you to use." In practice it's been far more difficult to get users to make decisions; they tend to say, "That's part of development. You decide."*

This lack of ownership was commented upon by users and developers alike. One of the analysts commented:

> *The user-led aspect has resulted in [the system's][1] greatest successes and greatest failures. User project managers do not have a systems background. Depending on their character they can be open to ideas or very blinkered. If they come from a user area with a system already it can be hard for them to see beyond their current system.* ■
>
> *(M880, 2000)*

[1] When reporting raw data such as quotations anonymously, it is common practice to replace specific words or phrases that might compromise anonymity with similar words enclosed in square brackets to indicate that they are not the speaker's original words.

Dilemma
Too much of a good thing?

Involving users in development is a good thing. Or is it? And how much should they become involved? Box 9.3 describes a project in which users were appointed as project managers and were actively involved in development throughout. But are users qualified to lead a technical development project? And does this matter, provided there is sufficient technical expertise in the team?

Involving users at any level incurs costs, whether in terms of time for communication, or for workshops, or time spent explaining technical issues. Detailed user studies may also require the use of recording equipment and the subsequent cost of transcription and analysis. What evidence is there that user involvement is productive, or that it is worth putting the required level of resources into development? Research by Keil and Carmel (1995) indicates that the more successful projects do have direct links to users and customers. Kujala and Mäntylä (2000) performed some empirical work to investigate the costs and benefits of user studies early in product development. They concluded that user studies do in fact produce benefits that outweigh the costs of conducting them.

On the other hand, Heinbokel *et al.* (1996) suggest that a high user involvement has some negative effects. They found that projects with high user participation showed lower overall success, fewer innovations, a lower degree of flexibility, and low team effectiveness, although these effects were noticeable only later in the project (at least 6–12 months into the project). In short, projects with a high level of user participation tended to run less smoothly. They identified four issues related to communication among users and developers that they suggest caused problems. First, as the project progressed, users developed more sophisticated ideas, and they wanted them to be incorporated late in the project. Second, users were fearful of job losses or worsening job conditions and this led to a tendency for participation to be not constructive. Third, users were unpredictable and not always sympathetic to software development matters. For example, they asked for significant changes to be made just as testing was due to start. Fourth, user orientation in the designers may lead to higher aspirations and hence higher levels of stress.

Webb (1996) too has concerns about user involvement, but Scaife *et al.* (1997) suggest that it is not the fact of user involvement that is in question, but how and at what stage in development they should get involved. ■

9.2.3 What is a user-centered approach?

Throughout this book, we emphasize the need for a user-centered approach to development. By this we mean that the real users and their goals, not just technology, should be the driving force behind development of a product. As a consequence, a well-designed system will make the most of human skill and judgment, will be directly relevant to the work in hand or other activity, and will support rather than constrain the user. This is less of a technique and more of a philosophy.

In 1985, Gould and Lewis (1985) laid down three principles they believed would lead to a "useful and easy to use computer system:"

1. *Early focus on users and tasks.* This means first understanding *who* the users will be by directly studying their cognitive, behavioral, anthropomorphic, and attitudinal characteristics. This requires observing users doing their normal tasks, studying the nature of those tasks, and then involving users in the design process.
2. *Empirical measurement.* Early in development, the reactions and performance of intended users to printed scenarios, manuals, etc., is observed and measured. Later on, users interact with simulations and prototypes and their performance and reactions are observed, recorded, and analyzed.
3. *Iterative design.* When problems are found in user testing, they are fixed and then more tests and observations are carried out to see the effects of the fixes. This means that design and development is iterative, with cycles of 'design, test, measure, and redesign' being repeated as often as necessary.

These three principles are now accepted as the basis for a user-centered approach (e.g. see Mao *et al.*, 2005), but when Gould and Lewis wrote their paper, they were not accepted by most developers. In fact, they comment in their paper how 'obvious' these principles are, and remark that when they started recommending these to designers, the designers' reactions implied that these principles were indeed obvious. However, when they asked designers at a human factors symposium for the major steps in software design, most of them did not cite most of the principles—in fact, only 2% mentioned all of them. So maybe they had 'obvious' merit, but were not so easy to put into practice. The Olympic Messaging System (OMS) (Gould *et al.*, 1987) was the first reported large computer-based system to be developed using these three principles. Here a combination of techniques was used to elicit users' reactions to designs, from the earliest prototypes through to the final product. In this case, users were mainly involved in evaluating designs. The OMS is discussed further in Chapter 12.

Below, we discuss these principles in more detail.

Early focus on users and tasks

This principle can be expanded and clarified through the following five further principles:

1. *Users' tasks and goals are the driving force behind the development.* In a user-centered approach to design, while technology will inform design options and choices, it should not be the driving force. Instead of saying, "Where can we deploy this new technology?," say, "What technologies are available to provide better support for users' goals?"
2. *Users' behavior and context of use are studied and the system is designed to support them.* This is about more than just capturing the tasks and the users' goals. How people perform their tasks is also significant. Understanding behavior highlights priorities, preferences, and implicit intentions. One argument against studying current behavior is that we are looking to improve work, not to capture bad habits in automation. The implication is that exposing designers to users is likely to stifle innovation and creativity, but experience tells us that the opposite is true (Beyer and Holtzblatt, 1998). In addition, if something is designed to support an activity with little understanding of the real work involved, it is likely to be incompatible with current practice, and users don't like to deviate from their learned habits if operating a new device with similar properties (Norman, 1988).
3. *Users' characteristics are captured and designed for.* When things go wrong with technology, we often say that it is our fault. But as humans, we are prone to making errors and we have certain limitations, both cognitive and physical. Products designed to support humans should take these limitations into account and should limit the mistakes we make. Cognitive aspects such as attention, memory, and perception issues were introduced in Chapter 3. Physical aspects include height, mobility, and strength. Some characteristics are general, such as that about one man in 12 has some form of color blindness, but some characteristics may be associated more with the job or particular task at hand. So, as well as general characteristics, we need to capture those specific to the intended user group.
4. *Users are consulted throughout development from earliest phases to the latest and their input is seriously taken into account.* As discussed above, there are different levels of user involvement and there are different ways in which to consult users. However involvement is organized, it is important that users are respected by designers.
5. *All design decisions are taken within the context of the users, their work, and their environment.* This does not necessarily mean that users are actively involved in design decisions. In her interview at the end of this chapter, Gillian Crampton Smith points out that it is not a good idea for users to be designers. As long as designers remain aware of the users while making their decisions, then this principle will be upheld. Keeping this context in mind can be difficult, but an easily accessible collection of gathered data is one way to achieve this. Some design teams set up a specific design room for the project where data and informal records of brainstorming sessions are pinned on the walls or left on the table.

Activity 9.2

Assume that you are involved in developing a new e-commerce site for selling garden plants. Suggest ways of applying the above principles in this task.

Comment

To address the first three principles, you would need to find out about potential users of the site. As this is a new site, there is no immediate set of users to consult. However, the tasks and goals, behavior, and characteristics of potential users of this site can be identified by investigating how people shop in existing online and physical shopping situations—for example, shopping through interactive television, through other online sites, in a garden center, in the local corner shop, and so on. For each of these, you will find advantages and disadvantages to the shopping environment and you will observe different behaviors. By looking at behavior and patterns in a physical garden center, you can find out a lot about who might be interested in buying plants, how these people choose plants, what criteria are important, and what their buying habits are. From existing online shopping behavior, you could determine likely contexts of use for the new site. There may be occasions when online shopping behavior conflicts with physical shopping behavior, e.g. someone in the garden center likes to smell the flowers before buying their seeds, while online decisions are based upon the descriptions and pictures of the plants. In this case, as a designer you will need to interpret your findings to create a suitable balance, and evaluate any solution you suggest.

For the fourth principle, there is no easily tapped set of users available, you could try to recruit people you believe to be representative of the group. These people may be involved in workshops or in evaluation sessions, possibly in a physical shopping environment. Valuable input can be gained in targeted workshops, focus groups, and evaluation sessions. The last principle could be supported through the creation of a design room to house all the data collected.

Empirical measurement

Specific usability and user experience goals should be identified, clearly documented, and agreed upon at the beginning of the project. They can help designers to choose between alternative designs and to check on progress as the product is developed. Identifying specific goals up front means that the product can be empirically evaluated at regular stages as it is developed, to ensure that the final product is as intended.

Iterative design

Iteration allows designs to be refined based on feedback. As users and designers engage with the domain and start to discuss requirements, needs, hopes, and aspirations, then different insights into what is needed, what will help, and what is feasible will emerge. This leads to a need for iteration, for the activities to inform each other and to be repeated. However good the designers are and however clear the users may think their vision is of the required artifact, it will be necessary to revise ideas in light of feedback, several times. This is particularly true if you are trying to innovate. Innovation rarely emerges whole and ready to go. It takes time, evolution, trial and error, and a great deal of patience. Iteration is inevitable because designers never get the solution right the first time (Gould and Lewis, 1985).

9.2.4 Four basic activities of interaction design

Four basic activities for interaction design were introduced in Chapter 1, some of which you will have engaged in when doing Activity 9.1. These are: identifying needs and establishing requirements for the user experience, developing alternative designs that meet those requirements, building interactive versions of the designs so that they can be communicated and assessed, and evaluating what is being built throughout the process and the user experience it offers. They are fairly generic activities and can be found in other design disciplines too. For example, in architectural design (RIBA[2], 1988) basic requirements are established in a work stage called 'inception,' alternative design options are considered in a 'feasibility' stage, and 'the brief' is developed through outline proposals and scheme design. During this time, prototypes may be built or perspectives may be drawn to give clients a better indication of the design being developed. Detail design specifies all components, and working drawings are produced. Finally, the job arrives on site and building commences.

We will be expanding on each of the basic activities of interaction design in the following chapters. Here we give only a brief introduction to each.

Identifying needs and establishing requirements for the user experience

In order to design something to support people, we must know who our target users are and what kind of support an interactive product could usefully provide. These needs form the basis of the product's requirements and underpin subsequent design and development. This activity is fundamental to a user-centered approach, and is very important in interaction design. Understanding these needs is gleaned through data gathering and analysis, which

---

[2]RIBA (Royal Institute of British Architects) is the professional organization for architects of the built environment in the UK.

were discussed in Chapters 7 and 8. The requirements activity is discussed further in Chapter 10.

Developing alternative designs that meet those requirements

This is the core activity of designing: actually suggesting ideas for meeting the requirements. This activity can be broken up into two sub-activities: conceptual design and physical design. Conceptual design involves producing the conceptual model for the product, and a conceptual model describes what the product should do, what it should look like and how it should behave. Physical design considers the detail of the product including the colors, sounds, and images to use, menu design, and icon design. Alternatives are considered at every point. You met some of the ideas for conceptual design in Chapter 2, and some more design issues for specific interface types in Chapter 6; we go into more detail about how to design an interactive product in Chapter 11.

Building interactive versions of the designs

Interaction design involves designing interactive products. The most sensible way for users to evaluate such designs, then, is to interact with them. This requires an interactive version of the designs to be built, but that does not mean a software version is required. There are different techniques for achieving 'interaction,' not all of which require a working piece of software. For example, paper-based prototypes are very quick and cheap to build and are very effective for identifying problems in the early stages of design, and through role-playing users can get a real sense of what it will be like to interact with the product. This aspect is also covered in Chapter 11.

Evaluating what is being built throughout the process and the user experience it offers

Evaluation is the process of determining the usability and acceptability of the product or design that is measured in terms of a variety of criteria including the number of errors users make using it, how appealing it is, how well it matches the requirements, and so on. Interaction design requires a high level of user involvement throughout development, and this enhances the chances of an acceptable product being delivered. In most design situations you will find a number of activities concerned with quality assurance and testing to make sure that the final product is 'fit-for-purpose.' Evaluation does not replace these activities, but complements and enhances them. We devote Chapters 12 to 15 to the important subject of evaluation.

The activities of developing alternative designs, building interactive versions of the design, and evaluation are intertwined: alternatives are evaluated through the interactive versions of the designs and the results are fed back into further design. This iteration is one of the key characteristics of a user-centered approach.

9.3 Some practical issues

Before we consider how these activities of interaction design can be pulled together into a coherent process, we want to consider some questions highlighted by the discussion so far. These questions must be answered if we are going to be able to 'do' interaction design in practice. These are:

- Who are the users?
- What do we mean by needs?
- How do you generate alternative designs?
- How do you choose among alternatives?

9.3.1 Who are the users?

With all this emphasis on users and user involvement in the interaction design process, a fairly basic question to ask is "Who are the users?"

Identifying the users may seem like a straightforward activity, but in fact there are many interpretations of 'user,' and involving the right users is crucial to successful user-centered design. The most obvious definition is those people who interact directly with the product to achieve a task. Most people would agree with this definition; however, there are others who can also be thought of as users. For example, Holtzblatt and Jones (1993) include in their definition of 'users' those who manage direct users, those who receive products from the system, those who test the system, those who make the purchasing decision, and those who use competitive products. Eason (1987) identifies three categories of user: primary, secondary, and tertiary. Primary users are those likely to be frequent hands-on users of the system; secondary users are occasional users or those who use the system through an intermediary; and tertiary users are those affected by the introduction of the system or who will influence its purchase.

The trouble is that there is a surprisingly wide collection of people who all have a stake in the development of a successful product. These people are called *stakeholders*. Stakeholders are "people or organizations who will be affected by the system and who have a direct or indirect influence on the system requirements" (Kotonya and Sommerville, 1998). Dix *et al.* (2004) make an observation that is very pertinent to a user-centered view of development, that "It will frequently be the case that the formal 'client' who orders the system falls very low on the list of those affected. Be very wary of changes which take power, influence or control from some stakeholders without returning something tangible in its place."

Generally speaking, the group of stakeholders for a particular product is going to be larger than the group of people you would normally think of as users, although it will of course include users. Based on the definition above, we can see that the group of stakeholders includes the development team itself as well as its managers, the direct users and their managers, recipients of the product's output, people who may lose their jobs because of the introduction of the new product, and so on.

For example, consider again the travel organizer in Activity 9.1. According to the description we gave you, the user group for the system has just one member: you. However, the stakeholders for the system would also include the people you are going to see, the airlines you book flights with, staff in the hotels you might stay at, a wide selection of companies and staff members who have an interest to make sure that any information you are given is correct, and even the restaurants on the route chosen for your journey, since the route suggested by the system will determine whether or not you drive past certain restaurants and shops. This last point may seem a little exaggerated for just one system, but if you think of others also using a similar travel organizer (after all, having put the time and effort into designing one, why not capitalize on it and sell a few!), then you can see how influential the system may turn out to be.

The net of stakeholders is really quite wide. It is not necessary to involve all of the stakeholders in a user-centered approach, but it is important to be aware of the wider impact of any product you are developing. Identifying the stakeholders for your project means that you can make an informed decision about who should be involved and to what degree.

Activity 9.3

Who do you think are the stakeholders for the check-out system of a large supermarket?

Comment

First, there are the check-out operators. These are the people who sit in front of the machine and pass the customers' purchases over the bar code reader, receive payment, hand over receipts, etc. Their stake in the success and usability of the system is fairly clear and direct. Then you have the customers, who want the system to work properly so that they are charged the right amount for the goods, receive the correct receipt, and are served quickly and efficiently. Also, the customers want the check-out operators to be satisfied and happy in their work so that they don't have to deal with a grumpy assistant. Outside of this group, you then have supermarket managers and supermarket owners, who also want the assistants to be happy and efficient and the customers to be satisfied and not complaining. They also don't want to lose money because the system can't handle the payments correctly. Other people who will be affected by the success of the system include other supermarket employees such as warehouse staff, supermarket suppliers, supermarket owners' families, and local shop owners whose business would be affected by the success or failure of

the system. We wouldn't suggest that you should ask the local shop owner about requirements for the supermarket check-out system. However, you might want to talk to warehouse staff, especially if the system links in with stock control or other functions.

9.3.2 What do we mean by 'needs?'

If you had asked someone in the street in the late 1990s what she 'needed,' I doubt that the answer would have included interactive television, or a ski jacket with integrated MP3 player, or a robot pet. If you presented the same person with these possibilities and asked whether she would buy them if they were available, then the answer may have been more positive. When we talk about identifying needs, therefore, it is not simply a question of asking people, "What do you need?" and then supplying it, because people don't necessarily know what is possible (see Suzanne Robertson's interview at the end of Chapter 10 for "un-dreamed-of" requirements). Instead, we have to approach it by understanding the characteristics and capabilities of the users, what they are trying to achieve, how they achieve it currently, and whether they would achieve their goals more effectively and have a more enjoyable experience if they were supported differently.

There are many dimensions along which a user's characteristics and capabilities may vary, and that will have an impact on the product's design. You have met some of the cognitive ones in Chapter 3. A person's physical characteristics may also affect the design: size of hands may affect the size and positioning of input buttons, and motor abilities may affect the suitability of certain input and output devices; height is relevant in designing a physical kiosk, for example; and strength in designing a child's toy—a toy should not require too much strength to operate, but may require strength greater than expected for the target age group to change batteries or perform other operations suitable only for an adult. Cultural diversity and experience may affect the terminology the intended user group is used to, or how nervous about technology a set of users may be, or how a facility is used (we discuss user requirements in more detail in Chapter 10).

If a product is a new invention, then it can be difficult to identify the users and representative tasks for them, e.g. before microwave ovens were invented, there were no users to consult about requirements and there were no representative tasks to identify. Those developing the oven had to imagine who might want to use such an oven and what they might want to do with it.

It may be tempting for designers simply to design what they would like to use themselves, but their ideas would not necessarily coincide with those of the target user group, because they have different experiences and expectations. It is *imperative* that representative users from the real target group be consulted. For example, Netpliance developed a new Internet Appliance, i.e. a product that would seamlessly integrate all the services necessary for the user to achieve a specific task on the Internet (Isensee *et al.*, 2000). They took a user-centered approach and employed focus group studies and surveys to understand their customers' needs. The marketing department led these efforts, but developers observed the focus groups to learn more about their intended user group. Isensee *et al.* (p. 60) observe that, "It is always tempting for developers to create products they would want to use or similar to what they have done before. However, in the Internet appliance space, it was essential to develop for a new audience that desires a simpler product than the computer industry has previously provided."

Whether the product is a new invention or not, it is always useful to start by understanding similar behavior that is already established. Apart from anything else, introducing something new into people's lives, especially a new 'everyday' item such as a microwave oven, requires a culture change in the target user population, and it takes a long time to effect a culture change. For example, before cell phones were so widely available there were no users and no representative tasks available for study, *per se*. But there were standard telephones and so understanding the tasks people perform with, and in connection with, standard telephones was a useful place to start. Apart from making a telephone call, users also look up people's numbers, take messages for others not currently available, and find out the number of the last person to ring them. These kinds of behavior have been translated into memories for the telephone, answering machines, and messaging services for mobiles. In order to maximize the benefit of e-commerce sites, traders have found that referring back to customers' non-electronic habits and behaviors can be a good basis for enhancing e-commerce activity (CHI Panel, 2000; Lee *et al.*, 2000).

Focusing on people's goals and on usability and user experience goals is a more promising approach to interaction design than focusing on people's needs and expecting them to be able to tell us the requirements for a product. Techniques for data gathering to investigate these goals and to establish requirements are discussed more in Chapters 7 and 10.

9.3.3 How do you generate alternative designs?

A common human tendency is to stick with something that we know works. We probably recognize that a better solution may exist out there somewhere, but it is very easy to accept this one because we know it works—it is 'good enough.' Settling for a solution that is good enough is not, in itself, necessarily 'bad,' but it may be undesirable because good alternatives may never be considered, and considering alternative solutions is a crucial step in the process of design. But where do these alternative ideas come from?

One answer to this question is that they come from the individual designer's flair and creativity. While it is certainly true that some people are able to produce wonderfully inspired designs while others struggle to come up with any ideas at all, very little in this world is completely new. Normally, innovations arise through cross-fertilization of ideas from different applications, the evolution of an existing product through use and observation, or straightforward copying of other, similar products. For example, if you think of something commonly believed to be an 'invention,' such as the steam engine, this was in fact inspired by the observation that the steam from a kettle boiling on the stove lifted the lid. Clearly there was an amount of creativity and engineering involved in making the jump from a boiling kettle to a steam engine, but the kettle provided the inspiration to translate experience gained in one context into a set of principles that could be applied in another. As an example of evolution, consider the wordprocessor. The capabilities of suites of office software have gradually increased from the time they first appeared. Initially, a wordprocessor was just an electronic version of a typewriter, but gradually other capabilities, including the spell-checker, thesaurus, style sheets, graphical capabilities, etc., were added.

So, although creativity and invention are often wrapped in mystique, we do understand something of the process and of how creativity can be enhanced or inspired. We know, for instance, that browsing a collection of designs will inspire designers to consider alternative perspectives, and hence alternative solutions. The field of case-based reasoning (Maher and Pu, 1997) emerged from the observation that designers solve new problems by drawing on knowledge gained from solving previous similar problems. As Schank (1982, p. 22) puts it, "An expert is someone who gets reminded of just the right prior experience to help him in processing his current experiences." And while those experiences may be the designer's own, they can equally well be others'.

Another approach to creativity has been taken by Maiden *et al.* (2004). They have been running creativity workshops to generate innovative requirements in an air traffic management (ATM) application domain. Their idea is to introduce experts in different fields into the workshop, and then invite stakeholders to identify analogies between their own field and this new one. For example, they invited a textile expert to discuss Indian textile design and a musician to discuss modern music composition. Although not obviously analogical domains, they sparked creative ideas for the air traffic management application. For example, participants reported that one textile design was 'elegant,' i.e. simple, beautiful, and symmetrical. They then transferred these properties to a key area of the ATM domain—that of aircraft conflict resolution. They explored the meaning of elegance within this context, and realized that elegance is perceived differently by different controllers. From this they generated the requirement that the system should be able to accommodate different air traffic controller styles during conflict resolution.

A more pragmatic answer to this question, then, is that alternatives come from looking at other, similar designs, and the process of inspiration and creativity can be enhanced by prompting a designer's own experience and by looking at others' ideas and solutions. Deliberately seeking out suitable sources of inspiration is a valuable step in any design process. These sources may be very close to the intended new product, such as competitors' products, or they may be earlier versions of similar systems, or something completely different.

Activity 9.4

Consider again the travel organizer introduced at the beginning of the chapter. Reflecting on the process again, what do you think inspired your outline design? See if you can identify any elements within it that you believe are truly innovative.

Comment

For my design, I was heavily influenced by existing sources of travel information, and what I see as the flaws in them. For example, having to always enter my home train station when I go to the online timetable (and never remembering that there are two different stations that have to be distinguished) is a hassle. I thought it would be good to have the system remember that piece of information, together with other personal details, such as always ordering a vegetarian meal on a flight.

Some of the things you might have been thinking about include your existing paper-based timetables, brochures, and tickets. Maybe you regularly use a website to book flights or accommodation; there are many different kinds available. I'm not sure how innovative my ideas were, but the key thing for me was to have the application tailor its advice to me and my habits. However, there are probably other aspects that make your design somehow unique to you and which may be innovative to a greater or lesser degree.

Having said this, under some circumstances the scope to consider alternative designs may be limited. Design is a process of balancing constraints and constantly trading off one set of requirements with another, and the constraints may be such that there are very few viable alternatives available. As another example, if you are designing a software system to run under the Windows operating system, then elements of the design will be prescribed because you must conform to the Windows 'look and feel,' and to other constraints intended to make Windows programs consistent for the user. Style guides and standards are discussed in Chapter 6.

If you are producing an upgrade to an existing system, then you may face other constraints, such as wanting to keep the familiar elements of it and retain the same 'look and feel.' However, this is not necessarily a rigid rule. For example, Kent Sullivan reports that when designing the Windows 95 operating system to replace the Windows 3.1 and Windows for Workgroups 3.11 operating systems, they initially focused too much on consistency with the earlier versions (Sullivan, 1996).

Box 9.4
A box full of ideas

The innovative product design company IDEO was introduced in Chapter 1. Underlying some of their creative flair is a collection of weird and wonderful engineering housed in a large flatbed filing cabinet called the TechBox (see Figure 9.2). The TechBox holds around 200 gizmos and interesting materials,

Figure 9.2 *The TechBox at IDEO*

divided into categories: "Amazing Materials," "Cool Mechanisms," "Interesting Manufacturing Processes," "Electronic Technologies," and "Thermal and Optical." Each item has been placed in the box because it represents a neat idea or a new process. Staff at IDEO take along a selection of items from the TechBox to brainstorming meetings. The items may be chosen because they provide useful visual props or possible solutions to a particular issue, or simply to provide some light relief.

Each item is clearly labeled with its name and category, but further information can be found by accessing the TechBox's online catalog. Each item has its own page detailing what the item is, why it is interesting, where it came from, and who has used it or knows more about it. For example, the page in Figure 9.3 relates to a metal injection-molding technique.

Other items in the box include an example of metal-coated wood, materials with and without holes that stretch, bend,

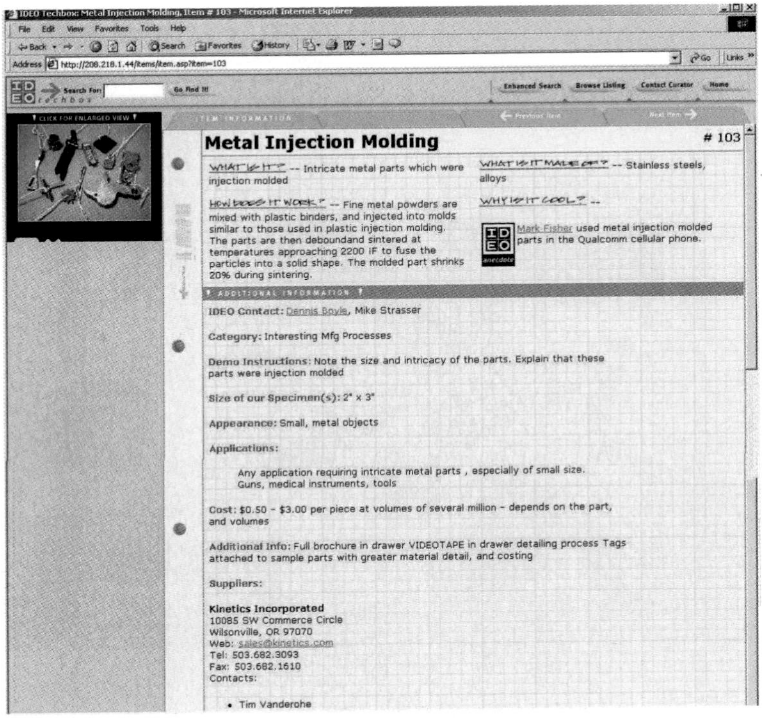

Figure 9.3 *The web page for the metal injection molding*

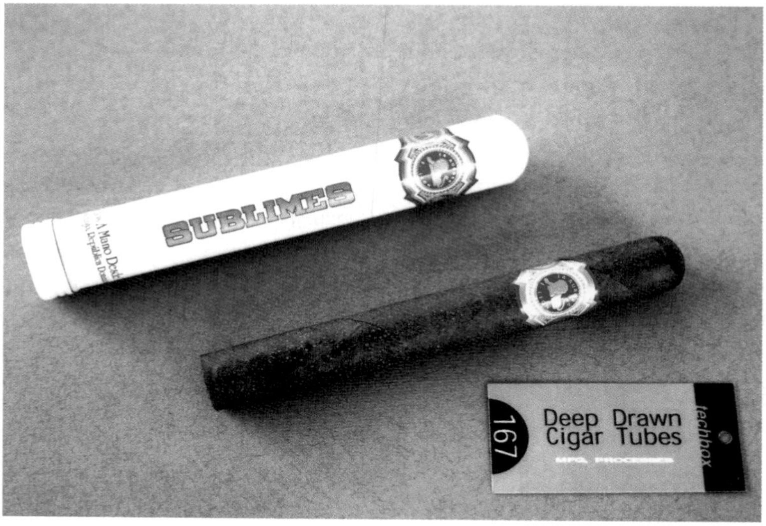

(a)

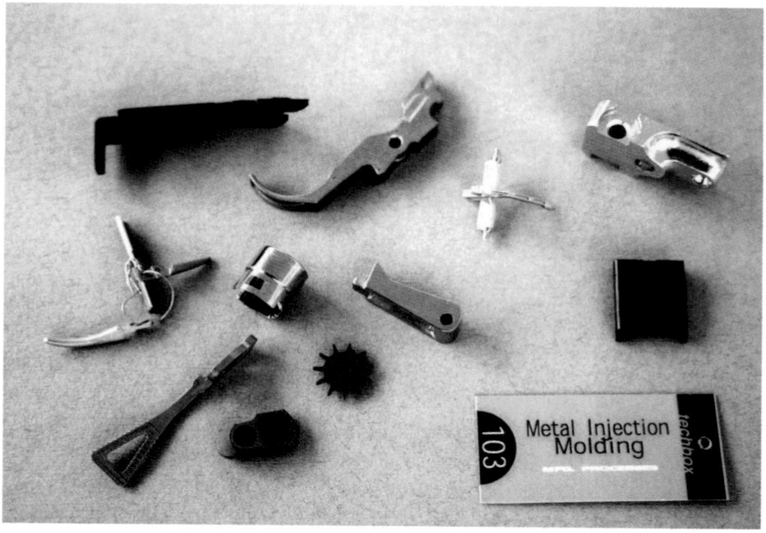

(b)

Figure 9.4 *Items from the TechBox used in the design of a medical product. (a) Deep Draw—a metal-forming process to generate close-ended cylindrical parts; (b) Metal Injection Molding—a molding and sintering process to produce complex metal parts in high numbers; (c) Flexy Battery—a lithium polymer cell from Varta that is very thin (intended for Smart Cards) and can be formed into cylindrical shapes*

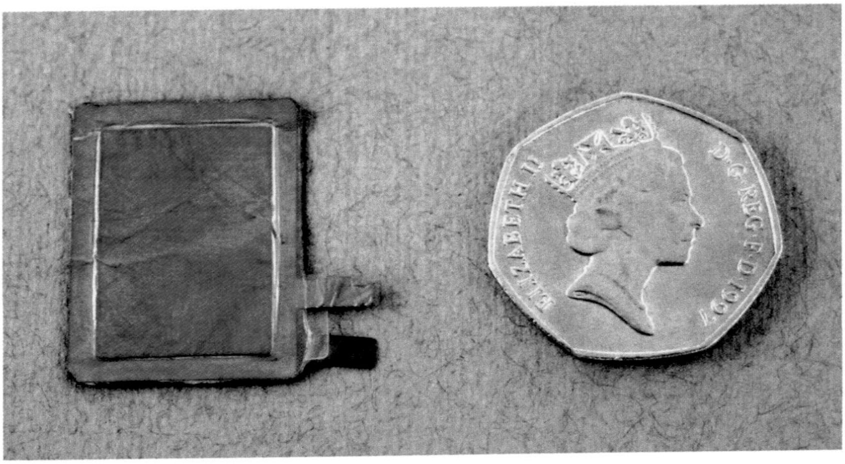

(c)

Figure 9.4 (continued)

and change shape or color at different temperatures.

Each TechBox has its own curator who is responsible for maintaining and cataloging the items and for promoting its use within the office. Anyone can submit a new item for consideration and as items become commonplace, they are removed from the TechBox to make way for the next generation of fascinating contraptions.

How are these things used? Here is an example from Patrick Hall at the London IDEO office.

IDEO was asked to review the design of a mass-produced hand-held medical product that was deemed to be too big. As well as brainstorming and other conventional idea-generation methods, I was able to immediately pick out items which I knew about from having used the TechBox in the past: Deep Draw; Fiber-Optic Magnifier; Metal Injection Molding; Flexy Battery (see Figure 9.4). Further browsing and searching using the keywords search engine highlighted in-mold assembly and light-intensifying film.

The associated web pages for these items enabled me to learn more about these items immediately and indicated who to talk to in IDEO to find out more, and the details of vendors to approach. The project ended at the feasibility phase, with the client pursuing the technologies I had suggested. Only the fiber-optic magnifier proved (immediately) not to be worth pursuing (because of cost). ■

Dilemma
Copying for inspiration: is it legal?

Designers draw on their experience of design when approaching a new project. This includes the use of previous designs that they know work, both designs they have created themselves and those that others have created. Others' creations often spark inspiration that also leads to new ideas and innovation. This is well known and understood. However, the expression of an idea is protected by copyright, and people who infringe that copyright can be taken to court and prosecuted. Note that copyright covers the expression of an idea and not the idea itself. This means, for example, that while there are numerous wordprocessors all with similar functionality, this does not represent an infringement of copyright as the idea has been expressed in different ways, and it is the expression that has been copyrighted. Copyright is free and is automatically invested in the author of something, e.g. the writer of a book or a programmer who develops a program, unless he signs the copyright over to someone else. Authors writing for academic journals are often asked to sign over their copyright to the publisher of the journal. Various limitations and special conditions can apply, but basically, the copyright is no longer theirs. People who produce something through their employment, such as programs or products, may have in their employment contract a statement saying that the copyright relating to anything produced in the course of that employment is automatically assigned to the employer and does not remain with the employee.

On the other hand, patenting is an alternative to copyright that does protect the idea rather than the expression. There are various forms of patenting, each of which is designed to allow the inventor the chance to capitalize on an idea. It is unusual for software to be patented, since it is a long, slow, and expensive process, although there have been some examples of patenting business processes. For example, Amazon, the online bookstore, has patented its 'one-click' purchasing process, which allows regular users simply to choose a book and buy it with one mouse click (US Patent No. 5960411, September 29, 1999). This is possible because the system stores its customers' details and 'recognizes' them when they access the site again.

More recently there has been a lot of activity to try and work around copyright issues. For example, it is now possible to publish works under a licensing agreement that offers some of your rights to any member of the public but only on certain conditions (see `www.creativecommons.org`). In the Open Source software development movement, software code is freely

distributed and can be modified, incorporated into other software, and redistributed under the same open source conditions. No royalty fees are payable on any use of open source code.

So the dilemma comes in knowing when it is OK to use someone else's work as a source of inspiration and when you are infringing copyright or patent law. The issues around this question are complex and detailed, and well beyond the scope of this book, but more information and examples of law cases that have been brought successfully and unsuccessfully can be found in Bainbridge (2004). ■

9.3.4 How do you choose among alternative designs?

Choosing among alternatives is about making design decisions: Will the device use keyboard entry or a touch screen? Will the device provide an automatic memory function or not? These decisions will be informed by the information gathered about users and their tasks, and by the technical feasibility of an idea. Broadly speaking, though, the decisions fall into two categories: those that are about externally visible and measurable features, and those that are about characteristics internal to the system that cannot be observed or measured without dissecting it. For example, externally visible and measurable factors for a building design include the ease of access to the building, the amount of natural light in rooms, the width of corridors, and the number of power outlets. In a photocopier, externally visible and measurable factors include the physical size of the machine, the speed and quality of copying, the different sizes of paper it can use, and so on. Underlying each of these factors are other considerations that cannot be observed or studied without dissecting the building or the machine. For example, the number of power outlets will be dependent on how the wiring within the building is designed and the capacity of the main power supply; the choice of materials used in a photocopier may depend on its friction rating and how much it deforms under certain conditions.

In an interactive product there are similar factors that are externally visible and measurable and those that are hidden from the users' view. For example, exactly why it takes 30 seconds for a web page to load, or why it takes an hour for a cell phone text message to arrive, will be influenced by technical decisions made when the web page or cell phone software was constructed. From the users' viewpoint the important observation is the fact that it does take 30 seconds to load or an hour to arrive.

In interaction design, the way in which the users interact with the product is considered the driving force behind the design and so we concentrate on the externally visible and measurable behavior. Detailed internal workings are important only to the extent that they affect the external behavior. This does not mean that design decisions concerning a system's internal behavior are any less important; however, the tasks that the user will perform should influence design decisions no less than technical issues.

So, one answer to the question posed above is that we choose between alternative designs by letting users and stakeholders interact with them and by discussing their experiences, preferences, and suggestions for improvement. This is fundamental to a user-centered approach to development. This in turn means that the designs must be available in a form that can be reasonably evaluated with users, not in technical jargon or notation that seems impenetrable to them.

One form traditionally used for communicating a design is documentation, e.g. a description of how something will work or a diagram showing its components. The trouble is that a static description cannot capture the dynamics of behavior, and for an interaction device we need to communicate to the users what it will be like to actually operate it.

In many design disciplines, *prototyping* is used to overcome potential client misunderstandings and to test the technical feasibility of a suggested design and its production. Prototyping involves producing a limited version of the product with the purpose of answering specific questions about the design's feasibility or appropriateness. Prototypes give a better impression of the user experience than simple descriptions can ever do, and there are different kinds of prototyping that are suitable for different stages of development and for eliciting different kinds of information. Prototyping is discussed in detail in Chapter 11.

Another basis on which to choose between alternatives is 'quality,' but this requires a clear understanding of what 'quality' means. People's views of what is a quality product vary, and it is not always written down. Whenever we use anything we have some notion of the level of quality we are expecting, wanting, or needing. Whether this level of quality is expressed formally or informally does not matter. The point is that it exists and we use it consciously or subconsciously to evaluate alternative items. For example, if you have to wait too long to download a web page, then you are likely to give up and try a different site—you are applying a certain measure of quality associated with the time taken to download the web page. If one PDA makes it easy to perform a critical function while another involves several complicated key sequences, then you are likely to buy the former rather than the latter. You are applying a quality criterion concerned with efficiency.

Now, if you are the only user of a product, then you don't necessarily have to express your definition of 'quality' since you don't have to communicate it to anyone else. However, as we have seen, most projects involve many different stakeholder groups, and you will find that each of them has a different definition of quality and different acceptable limits for it. For example, although all stakeholders may agree on targets such as "response time will be fast" or "the menu structure will be easy to use," exactly what each of them means by this is likely to vary. Disputes are inevitable when, later in development, it transpires that 'fast' to one set of stakeholders meant "under a second," while to another it meant "between 2 and 3 seconds." Capturing these different views in clear unambiguous language early in development takes you halfway to producing a product that will be regarded as 'good' by all your stakeholders. It helps to clarify expectations, provides a benchmark against which products of the development process can be measured, and gives you a basis on which to choose among alternatives.

The process of writing down formal, verifiable—and hence measurable—usability criteria is a key characteristic of an approach to interaction design called *usability engineering*. This has emerged over many years and with various proponents (Whiteside *et al.*, 1988; Nielsen, 1993). Usability engineering involves specifying quantifiable measures of product performance, documenting them in a usability specification, and assessing the product against them. One way in which this approach is used is to make changes to subsequent versions of a system based on feedback from carefully documented results of usability tests for the earlier version. We shall return to this idea later when we discuss evaluation.

Activity 9.5

Consider the travel organizer that you designed in Activity 9.1. Suggest some usability criteria that you could use to determine the organizer's quality. Use the usability goals introduced in Chapter 1: effectiveness, efficiency, safety, utility, learnability, and memorability. Be as specific as possible. Check your criteria by considering exactly what you would measure and how you would measure its performance.

Then try to do the same thing for the user experience goals introduced in Chapter 1; these relate to whether a system is satisfying, enjoyable, motivating, rewarding, and so on.

Comment

Finding measurable characteristics for some of these is not easy. Here are some suggestions, but you may have found others. Where possible criteria must be measurable and specific.

- ***Effectiveness*: identifying measurable criteria for this goal is particularly difficult since it is a combination of the other goals. For example, does the system support you in traveling to places, booking accommodation, and so on. In other words, is the organizer used?**
- ***Efficiency*: when you ask for recommendations from the organizer, what is the response time for identifying a suitable hotel or flight details?**
- ***Safety*: how often does data get lost or do you choose the wrong option? This may be measured, for example, as the number of times this happens per hour of use.**
- ***Utility*: how many functions offered by the organizer are used every week, how many every month, how many every two months? How many tasks are difficult to complete in a reasonable time because functionality is missing or the**

organizer doesn't support the right subtasks?

- ***Learnability*: how long does it take for a novice user to be able to do a series of set tasks, e.g. book a hotel room in Paris for a particular date, identify appropriate flights from Sydney to Wellington, find out whether you need a visa to go to China?**
- ***Memorability*: if the organizer isn't used for a month, how many functions can you remember how to perform? How long does it take you to remember how to perform your most frequent task?**

Finding measurable characteristics for the user experience criteria is even harder, though. How do you measure satisfaction, fun, motivation, or aesthetics? What is entertaining to one person may be boring to another; these kinds of criteria are subjective, and so cannot be measured as objectively.

9.4 Lifecycle models: showing how the activities are related

Understanding what activities are involved in interaction design is the first step to being able to do it, but it is also important to consider how the activities are related to one another so that the full development process can be seen. The term *lifecycle model*[3] is used to represent a model that captures a set of activities and how they are related. Sophisticated models also incorporate a description of when and how to move from one activity to the next and a description of the deliverables for each activity. The reason such models are popular is that they allow developers, and particularly managers, to get an overall view of the development effort so that progress can be tracked, deliverables specified, resources allocated, targets set, and so on.

Existing models have varying levels of sophistication and complexity. For projects involving only a few experienced developers, a simple process would probably be adequate. However, for larger systems involving tens or hundreds of developers with hundreds or thousands of users, a simple process just isn't enough to provide the management structure and discipline necessary to engineer a usable product. So something is needed that will provide more formality and more discipline. Note that this does not mean that innovation is lost or that creativity is stifled. It just means that a structured process is used to provide a more stable framework for creativity.

However simple or complex it appears, any lifecycle model is a simplified version of reality. It is intended as an abstraction and, as with any good abstraction, only the amount

[3]Sommerville (2006) uses the term 'process model' to mean what we call a lifecycle model, and refers to the waterfall model as the software lifecycle. Pressman (1992) talks about paradigms. In HCI the term 'lifecycle model' is used more widely. For this reason, and because others use 'process model' to represent something that is more detailed than a lifecycle model (e.g. Comer, 1997), we have chosen to use lifecycle model.

of detail required for the task at hand will be included. Any organization wishing to put a lifecycle model into practice will need to add detail specific to its particular circumstances and culture. For example, Microsoft wanted to maintain a small-team culture while also making possible the development of very large pieces of software. To this end, they have evolved a process that has been called 'synch and stabilize,' as described in Box 9.5.

In the next subsection, we introduce our view of what a lifecycle model for interaction design might look like that incorporates the four activities of interaction design and the three principles of user-centered design discussed above. Depending on the kind of product being developed, it may not be possible or appropriate to follow this model for every element of the product, and it is certainly true that more detail would be required to put the lifecycle into practice in a real project.

Many other lifecycle models have been developed in fields related to interaction design, such as software engineering and HCI, and our model is evolved from these ideas. To put our interaction design model into context we include here a description of seven lifecycle models, four from software engineering and three from HCI, and consider how they relate to it.

Box 9.5
How Microsoft builds software

Software for Microsoft products is very complex, consisting of millions of lines of code. For example, Windows XP contains around 40 million lines of code. Over a two-and-a-half-year period from the beginning of 1993, two researchers, Michael Cusumano and Richard Selby, were given access to Microsoft project documents and key personnel for study and interview. Their aim was to build up an understanding of how Microsoft produces software. Rather than adopt the structured software engineering practices others have followed, Microsoft's strategy has been to cultivate entrepreneurial flexibility throughout its software teams. In essence, it has tried to scale up the culture of a loosely structured, small software team. "The objective is to get many small teams (three to eight developers each) or individual programmers to work together as a single relatively large team in order to build large products relatively quickly while still allowing individual programmers and teams freedom to evolve their designs and operate nearly autonomously" (p. 54).

In order to maintain consistency and to ensure that products are eventually shipped, the teams synchronize their activities daily and periodically stabilize the whole product. Cusumano and Selby have therefore labeled Microsoft's unique process "synch and stabilize." Figure 9.5 shows an overview of this process, which is divided into three phases: the planning phase, the development phase and the stabilization phase.

Planning Phase Define product vision, specifications, and schedule

- **Vision Statement** Product and program management use extensive customer input to identify and priority-order product features.
- **Specification Document** Based on vision statement, program management and development group define feature functionality, architectural issues, and component interdependencies.
- **Schedule and Feature Team Formation** Based on specification document, program management coordinates schedule and arranges feature teams that each contain approximately 1 program manager, 3–8 developers, and 3–8 testers (who work in parallel 1:1 with developers).

Development Phase Feature development in 3 or 4 sequential subprojects that each results in a milestone release

Program managers coordinate evolution of specification. Developers design, code, and debug. Testers pair with developers for continuous testing.

- **Subproject I** First 1/3 of features (Most critical features and shared components)
- **Subproject II** Second 1/3 of features
- **Subproject III** Final 1/3 of features (Least critical features)

Stabilization Phase Comprehensive internal and external testing, final product stabilization, and ship

Program managers coordinate OEMs and ISVs and monitor customer feedback. Developers perform final debugging and code stabilization. Testers recreate and isolate errors.

- **Internal Testing** Thorough testing of complete product within the company.
- **External Testing** Thorough testing of complete product outside the company by "beta" sites, such as OEMs, ISVs, and end users.
- **Release preparation** Prepare final release of "golden master" disks and documentation for manufacturing.

***Figure 9.5** Overview of the synch and stabilize development approach*

The planning phase begins with a vision statement that defines the goals of the new product and the user activities to be supported by the product. (Microsoft uses a method called activity-based planning to identify and prioritize the features to be built.) The program managers together with the developers then write a functional specification in enough detail to describe features and to develop schedules and allocate staff. The feature list in this document will change by about 30% during the course of development, so the list is not fixed at this time. In the next phase, the development phase, the feature list is divided into three or four parts, each with its own small development team, and the schedule is divided into sequential subprojects, each with its own deadline (milestone). The teams work in parallel on a set of features and synchronize their work by putting together their code and finding errors on a daily and weekly basis. This is necessary because many programmers may be working on the same code at once. For example, during the peak development of Excel 3.0, 34 developers were actively changing the same source code on a daily basis.

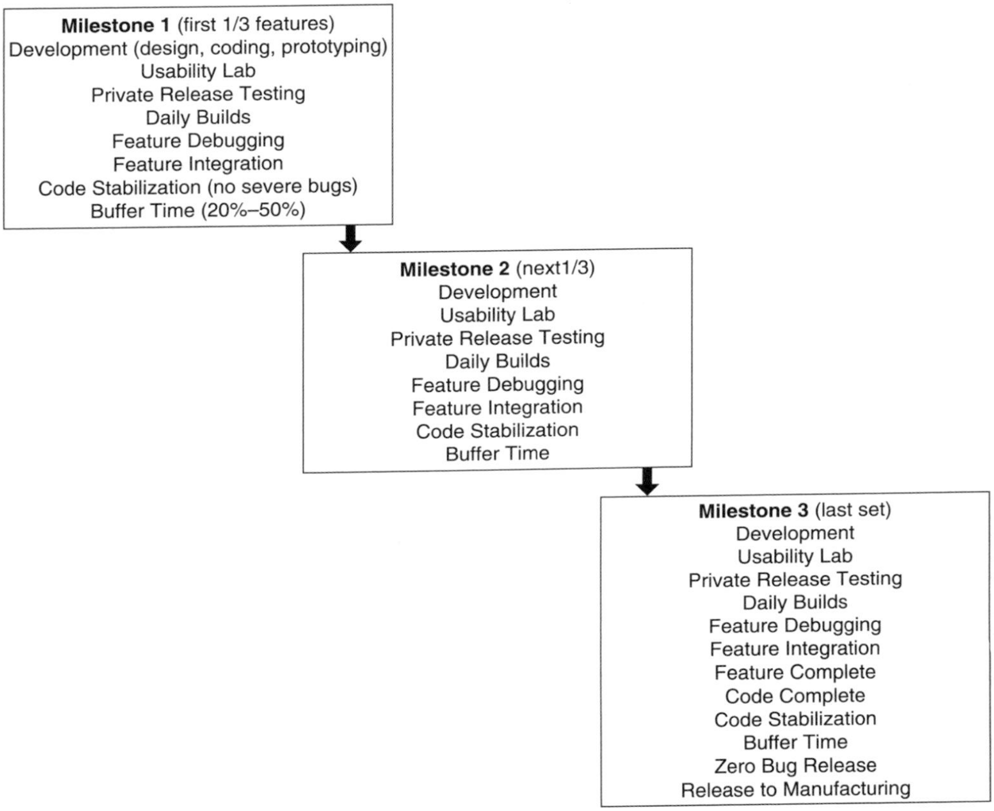

Figure 9.6 *Milestones in the synch and stabilize approach (each taking two to four months)*

At the end of a subproject, i.e. on reaching a milestone, all errors are found and fixed, thus stabilizing the product, before moving on to the next subproject and eventually to the final milestone, which represents the release date. Figure 9.6 shows an overview of the milestone structure for a project with three subprojects. This synch-and-stabilize approach has been used to develop Excel, Office, Publisher, Windows operating systems, Word, and Works, among others. Although the research for this book was conducted over a decade ago, we understand that these practices are still current. ■

(Cusumano and Selby, 1997)

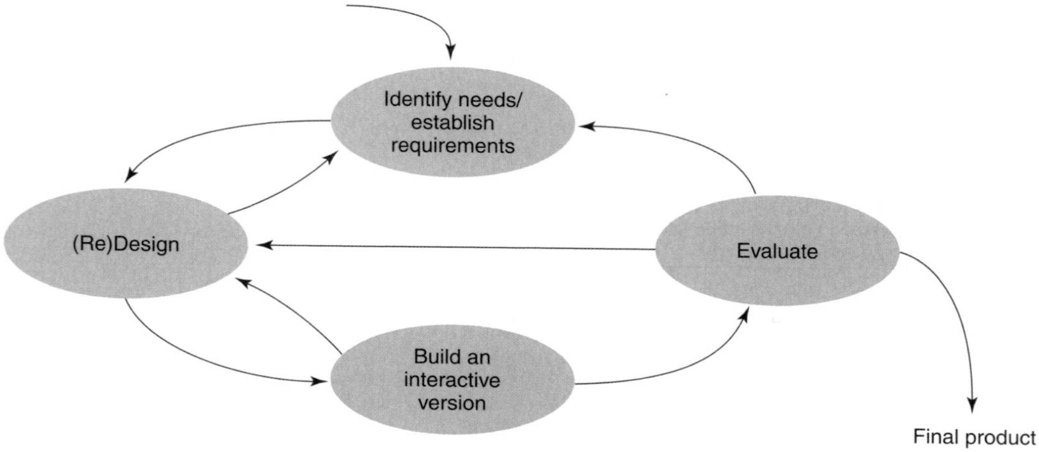

Figure 9.7 *A simple interaction design lifecyle model*

9.4.1 A simple lifecycle model for interaction design

We see the activities of interaction design as being related as shown in Figure 9.7. This model incorporates iteration and encourages a user focus. While the outputs from each activity are not specified in the model, you will have seen from our discussion earlier in this chapter the importance of specifying measurable usability criteria.

The model is not intended to be prescriptive; that is, we are not suggesting that this is how all interactive products are or should be developed. It is based on our observations of interaction design and on information we have gleaned in the research for this book. It has its roots in the software engineering and HCI lifecycle models described below, and it represents what we believe is practiced in the field.

Most projects start with identifying needs and establishing requirements. The project may have arisen because of some evaluation that has been done, but the lifecycle of the new (or modified) product can be thought of as starting at this point. From this activity, some alternative designs are generated in an attempt to meet the needs and requirements that have been identified. Then interactive versions of the designs are developed and evaluated. Based on the feedback from the evaluations, the team may need to return to identifying needs or refining requirements, or it may go straight into redesigning. It may be that more than one alternative design follows this iterative cycle in parallel with others, or it may be that one alternative at a time is considered. Implicit in this cycle is that the final product will emerge in an evolutionary fashion from a rough initial idea through to the finished product. Exactly how this evolution happens may vary from project to project, and we return to this issue in Chapter 11. The only factor limiting the number of times through the cycle is the resources available, but whatever the number is, development ends with an evaluation activity that ensures the final product meets the prescribed user experience and usability criteria.

9.4.2 Lifecycle models in software engineering

Software engineering has spawned many lifecycle models, including the waterfall, the spiral, and rapid applications development (RAD). Before the waterfall was first proposed in 1970, there was no generally agreed approach to software development, but over the years since then, many models have been devised, reflecting in part the wide variety of approaches that can be taken to developing software. We choose to include these specific lifecycle models for two reasons: first, because they are representative of the models used in industry and they have all proved to be successful; and second, because they show how the emphasis in software development has gradually changed to include a more iterative, user-centered view.

We also include here a discussion of a more recent addition to software engineering methods—the family of 'agile' development methods. These methods don't favor one particular lifecycle model (although some have their own lifecycle, or development rhythm), but aim to be able to react to change quickly, and embed principles of iteration, communication, and feedback, hence having characteristics sympathetic to user-centered approaches.

The waterfall lifecycle model

The waterfall lifecycle was the first model generally known in software engineering and forms the basis of many lifecycles in use today. This is basically a linear model in which each step must be completed before the next step can be started (see Figure 9.8). For example, requirements analysis has to be completed before design can begin. The names given to these steps varies, as does the precise definition of each one, but basically, the lifecycle starts with some requirements analysis, moves into design, then coding, then implementation, testing, and finally maintenance. One of the main flaws with this approach is that requirements change over time, as businesses and the environment in which they operate change rapidly. This means that it does not make sense to freeze requirements for months, or maybe years, while the design and implementation are completed.

Some feedback to earlier stages was acknowledged as desirable and indeed practical soon after this lifecycle became widely used (Figure 9.8 does show some limited feedback between phases). But the idea of iteration was not embedded in the waterfall's philosophy. Some level of iteration is now incorporated in most versions of the waterfall, and review sessions among developers are commonplace. However, the opportunity to review and evaluate with *users* was not built into this model.

The spiral lifecycle model

For many years, the waterfall formed the basis of most software developments, but in 1988 Barry Boehm (1988) suggested the spiral model of software development (see Figure 9.9).

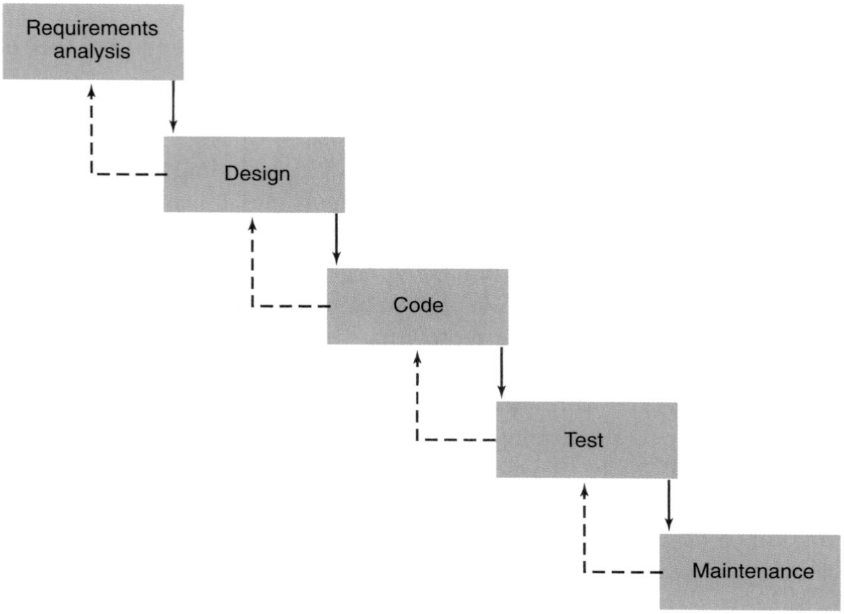

Figure 9.8 *The waterfall lifecycle model of software development*

Two features of the spiral model are immediately clear from Figure 9.9: risk analysis and prototyping. The spiral model incorporates them in an iterative framework that allows ideas and progress to be repeatedly checked and evaluated. Each iteration around the spiral may be based on a different lifecycle model and may have different activities.

In the spiral's case, it was not the need for user involvement that inspired the introduction of iteration but the need to identify and control risks. In Boehm's approach, development plans and specifications that are focused on the risks involved in developing the system drive development rather than the intended functionality, as was the case with the waterfall. Unlike the waterfall, the spiral explicitly encourages alternatives to be considered, and steps in which problems or potential problems are encountered to be readdressed.

A more recent version of the spiral, called the WinWin spiral model (Boehm *et al.*, 1998), explicitly incorporates the identification of key stakeholders and their respective 'win' conditions, i.e. what will be regarded as a satisfactory outcome for each stakeholder group. A period of stakeholder negotiation to ensure a 'win–win' result is included.

Rapid Applications Development (RAD)

During the 1990s the drive to focus upon users became stronger and resulted in a number of new approaches to development. The Rapid Applications Development (RAD) approach

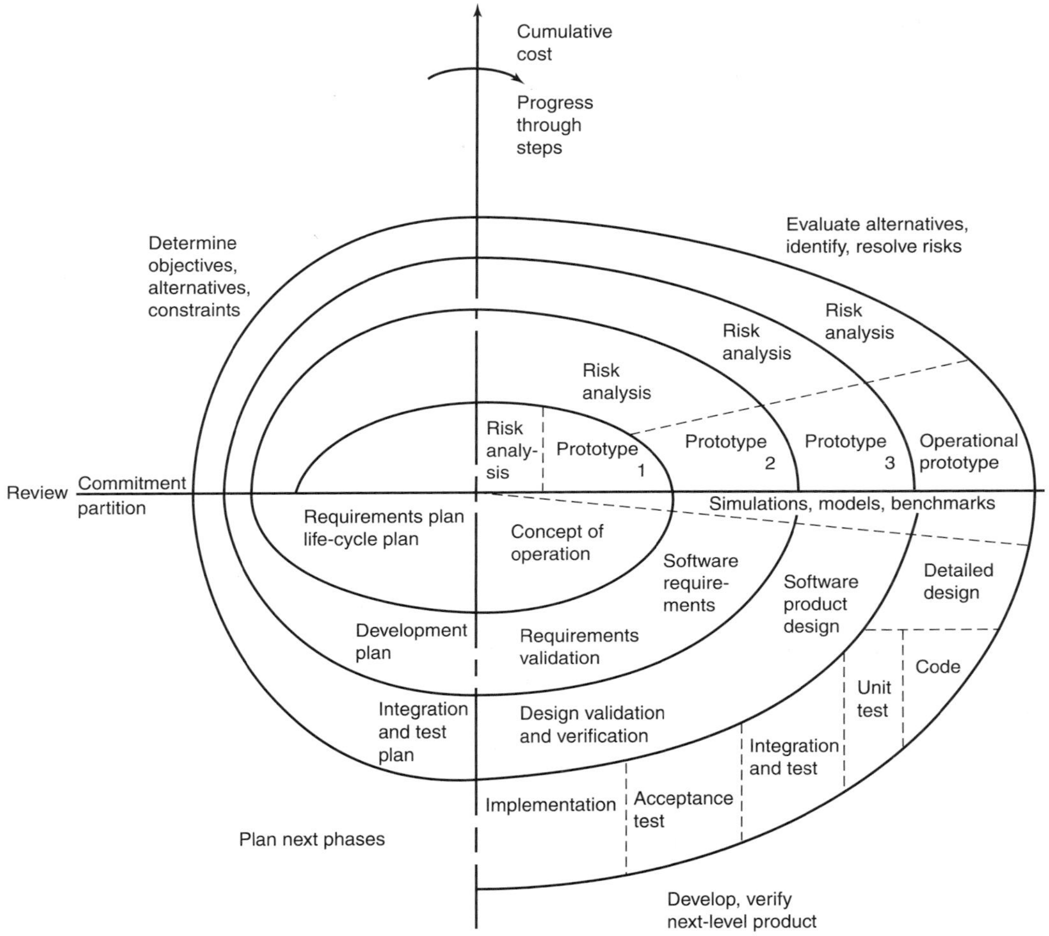

Figure 9.9 *The spiral lifecycle model of software development*

(Millington and Stapleton, 1995) attempts to take a user-centered view and to minimize the risk caused by requirements changing during the course of the project. The ideas behind RAD began to emerge in the early 1990s, also in response to the inappropriate nature of the linear lifecycle models based on the waterfall. Two key features of a RAD project are:

- Time-limited cycles of approximately six months, at the end of which a system or partial system must be delivered. This is called time-boxing. In effect, this breaks down a large project into many smaller projects that can deliver products incrementally, and enhances flexibility in terms of the development techniques used and the maintainability of the final system.

- JAD (Joint Application Development) workshops in which users and developers come together to thrash out the requirements of the system (Wood and Silver, 1995). These are intensive requirements gathering sessions in which difficult issues are faced and decisions are made. Representatives from each identified stakeholder group should be involved in each workshop so that all the relevant views can be heard.

A basic RAD lifecycle has five phases (see Figure 9.10): project initiation, JAD workshops, iterative design and build, engineer and test final prototype, implementation review. The popularity of RAD has led to the emergence of an industry-standard RAD-based method called DSDM (Dynamic Systems Development Method). This was developed by a non-profit-making DSDM consortium made up of a group of companies that recognized the need for some standardization in the field. The first of nine principles stated as underlying DSDM is that "active user involvement is imperative." The DSDM lifecycle is more complicated—see Figure 9.11. It involves five phases:

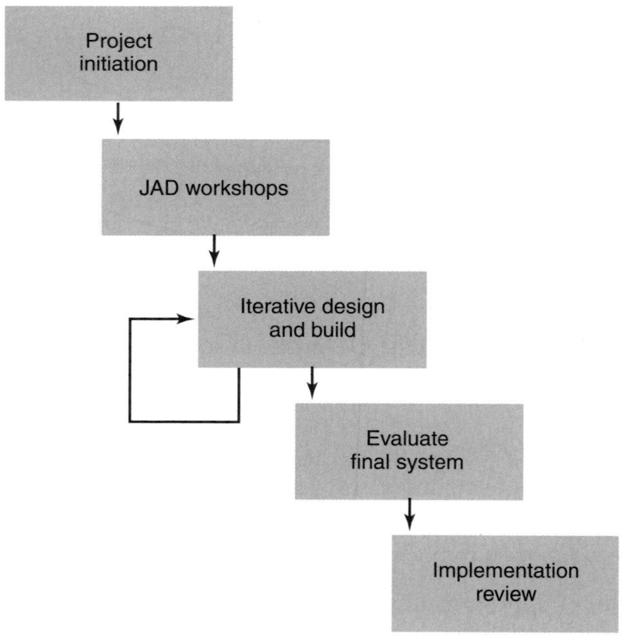

Figure 9.10 *A basic RAD lifecycle model of software development*

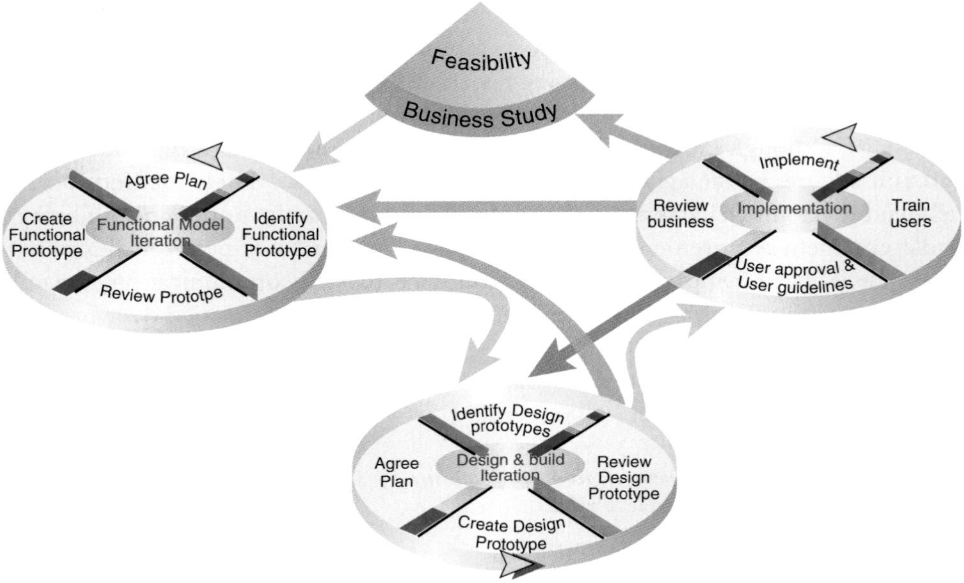

Figure 9.11 *The DSDM lifecycle model*

feasibility study, business study, functional model iteration, design and build iteration, and implementation. This is only a generic process and must be tailored for a particular organization.

Activity 9.6

How closely do you think the RAD and DSDM lifecycle models relate to the interaction design lifecycle model described in Section 9.4.1?

Comment

RAD and DSDM explicitly incorporate user involvement, evaluation, and iteration. User involvement, however, appears to be limited to the JAD workshop, and iteration appears to be limited to the design and build phase. The philosophy underlying the interaction design lifecycle model is present, but the flexibility appears not to be. Our interaction design process would be appropriately used within the design and build stage.

Agile development

Agile software development methods began to emerge in the late 1990s. The most well-known of these are eXtreme Programming (Beck, 2000), Crystal (Cockburn, 2005), Scrum (Schwaber and Beedle, 2002), and Adaptive Software Development (ASD) (Highsmith, 2000). DSDM, although established before the agile movement, is also regarded as an agile method as it adheres to the agile manifesto (reproduced below). These methods differ, but they all exhibit certain characteristics. For example, they stress the importance of being able to handle emergent requirements, and of striking a good balance between flexibility and structure. They also all emphasize collaboration, face-to-face communication, streamlined processes to avoid unnecessary activities, and the importance of practice over process, i.e. of getting work done.

The opening statement for the *Manifesto for Agile Software Development* (`http://www.agilemanifesto.org/`) is:

> ***We are uncovering better ways of developing software by doing it and helping others do it. Through this work we have come to value:***
>
> Individuals and interactions over processes and tools
> Working software over comprehensive documentation
> Customer collaboration over contract negotiation
> Responding to change over following a plan

This manifesto is underpinned by a series of principles, which range from communication with the business through to excellence of coding and maximizing the amount of work done. The agile approach to development is particularly interesting from the point of view of interaction design because it incorporates tight iterations and feedback, and collaboration with the customer (e.g. Armitage, 2004; Sharp *et al.*, 2006). For example, in eXtreme[4] Programming (XP), each iteration is between one and three weeks, with a product of value being delivered at the end of each iteration. Also, XP stipulates that the customer should be on-site with developers, and that the customer is an end-user (although in practice this is rarely achieved). Because of these similarities, several companies have integrated agile methods with interaction design practices to produce better quality products. Box 9.6 describes one example of this.

---

[4]The method is called 'extreme' because it pushes a key set of good practices to the limit, i.e. it is good practice to test often, so in XP the development is test-driven and a complete set of tests is executed many times a day, it is good practice to talk to people about their requirements, so rather than having weighty documentation, XP reduces documentation to a minimum, thus forcing communication, and so on. Kent Beck says that it is called extreme because if he called it 'moderate programming', no-one would ever take any notice of it!

Box 9.6
Integrating user-centered design and agile development

Toronto-based company Alias (now part of Autodesk) produce 2D and 3D graphics applications for a variety of markets including video, film, games, automotive design, and interactive media. Their products have been used to create special effects for many award-winning films such as *Spider-Man* and *Lord of the Rings: Return of the King*. One of their products is called Alias SketchBook Pro. This application is used for 2D sketching and is a sketching, annotating, and presentation application designed to run on the Tablet PC or any PC with a digitizer tablet. The kinds of images produced by SketchBook Pro are illustrated in Figure 9.12. The detail in this box relates to the development of SketchBook Pro v2.0.

At the same time that this application was being envisioned, Alias' product development group wanted to adopt an agile approach, but they also needed to accommodate their customer input methods within the agile lifecycle. The methods they most commonly use are contextual inquiry, interviews, usability tests, surveys (questionnaires or structured interviews), and beta tests. These beta tests (called 'previews' for SketchBook) are conducted when a set of features has been completed. The interaction designers in the group found that the methods for collecting customer data did not need to change for agile development, but the frequency and timing of collection did need to change.

The agile approach adopted by the Alias team used a combination of ASD, Scrum meetings, and many elements of eXtreme Programming. Alias have always been very careful about identifying exactly who their target audience is, i.e. who are the people who will do the kind of sketching and annotating that the product will support, and have many years' experience of collecting customer input. However, the timing and incorporation of this input into the development cycle was not ideal and the activity was often squeezed. To counteract this, interaction designers would often start to develop features before the full set of features for the product was confirmed, which meant that there was more time for customer input, but designed features were sometimes not implemented in the final product.

As a consequence of the agile approach, the development team went from developers working individually on separate features in parallel, to all developers working together on a smaller set of features in a short timescale. One of the principles of agile development is early and continuous delivery of valuable software, hence demanding that customer input be obtained often.

Figure 9.12 *Some sample images produced from SketchBook Pro v2.0*

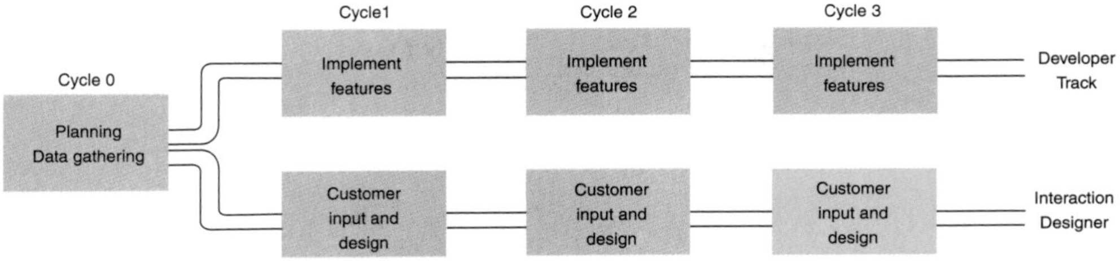

Figure 9.13 *Cycle 0 and its relationship to later cycles*

The team organized feature implementation and customer input and design as two interrelated tracks (see Figure 9.13).

Cycle 0 is the 'speculate' phase of ASD. During this time, the team investigated (with their users) the top features that needed to be added for v2.0 of the product. Cycle 1 was a little different from subsequent cycles because the interaction designers had not had any time to do any design, but the developers were waiting to code. To get around this, the team identified some important features that did not require very much design input, but would take time to implement.

For subsequent cycles, three activities were conducted by the interaction designers in parallel with the developers. In Cycle n, usability tests were conducted on the features implemented in Cycle $n-1$, features for implementation in Cycle $n+1$ were designed, prototyped, and tested with their carefully selected set of users, and customer input data was collected for the features to be implemented in Cycle $n+2$ (see Figure 9.14).

Overall the interaction designers worked very tightly with the developers during design and implementation to make sure that they designed something that could be implemented and also that what was implemented was what had been designed. The interaction designers felt that there were three big advantages to this process. First, no design time was wasted on features that would not be implemented. Second, usability testing (for one set of features) and contextual inquiry (for the next set) could be done on the same customer visit, thus saving time. Third, the interaction designers received timely feedback from all sides—both users and developers. More importantly, they had time to react to that feedback because of the agile way of working. For example, the schedule could be changed if something was going to take longer to develop than first thought, or a feature could be dropped if it became apparent from the users that something else had higher priority.

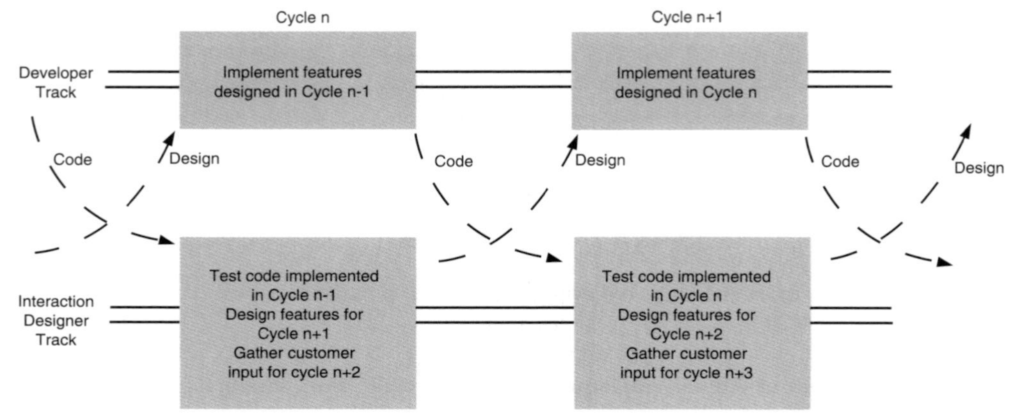

***Figure 9.14** The parallel interaction design and implementation tracks*

9.4.3 Lifecycle models in HCI

One of the traditions from which interaction design has emerged is the field of HCI (human–computer interaction). Fewer lifecycle models have arisen from this field than from software engineering and, as you would expect, they have a stronger tradition of user focus. We describe three of these here. The first one, the Star, was derived from empirical work on understanding how designers tackled HCI design problems. This represents a very flexible process with evaluation at its core. In contrast, the second one, the usability engineering lifecycle, shows a more structured approach and hails from the usability engineering tradition. The third lifecycle model is enshrined in an international standard, ISO 13407 *Human-centered design processes for interactive systems*, and is therefore the result of international collaboration and agreement.

The Star lifecycle model

About the same time that those involved in software engineering were looking for alternatives to the waterfall lifecycle, so too were people involved in HCI looking for alternative ways to support the design of interfaces. In 1989, the Star lifecycle model was proposed by Hartson and Hix (1989) (see Figure 9.15). This emerged from some empirical work they did looking at how interface designers went about their work. They identified two different modes of activity: analytic mode and synthetic mode. The former is characterized by such notions as top-down, organizing, judicial, and formal, working from the systems view towards the user's view; the latter is characterized by such notions as bottom-up, free-thinking, creative, and *ad hoc*, working from the user's view towards the systems view. Interface designers move from one mode to another when designing. A similar behavior has been observed in software designers (Guindon, 1990).

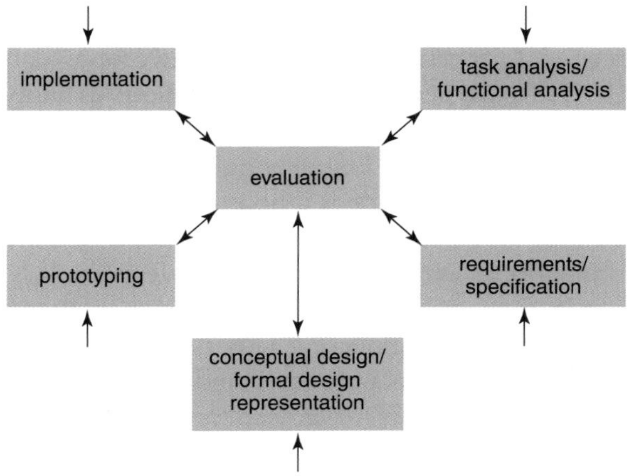

Figure 9.15 *The Star lifecycle model*

Unlike the lifecycle models introduced above, the Star lifecycle does not specify any ordering of activities. In fact, the activities are highly interconnected: you can move from any activity to any other, provided you first go through the evaluation activity. This reflects the findings of the empirical studies. Evaluation is central to this model, and whenever an activity is completed, its result(s) must be evaluated. So a project may start with requirements/specification, or it may start with evaluating an existing situation, or by analyzing existing tasks, and so on.

Activity 9.7

The Star lifecycle model has not been used widely and successfully for large projects in industry. Consider the benefits of lifecycle models introduced above and suggest why this may be.

Comment

One reason may be that the Star lifecycle model is extremely flexible. This may be how designers work in practice, but as we commented above, lifecycle models are popular because "they allow developers, and particularly managers, to get an overall view of the development effort so that progress can be tracked, deliverables specified, resources allocated, targets set, and so on." With a model as flexible as the Star lifecycle, it is difficult to control these issues without substantially changing the model itself.

The usability engineering lifecycle

The Usability Engineering Lifecycle in Figure 9.16 was proposed by Deborah Mayhew in 1999 (Mayhew, 1999). Many people have written about usability engineering, and as Mayhew herself says, "I did not invent the concept of a Usability Engineering Lifecycle. Nor did I invent any of the Usability Engineering tasks included in the lifecycle ... " However, what her lifecycle does provide is a holistic view of usability engineering and a detailed description of how to perform usability tasks, and it specifies how usability tasks can be integrated into traditional software development lifecycles. It is therefore particularly helpful for those with little or no expertise in usability to see how the tasks may be performed alongside more traditional software engineering activities. For example, Mayhew has linked the stages with a general development approach (rapid prototyping) and a specific method (object-oriented software engineering (OOSE, Jacobson *et al.*, 1992)) that have arisen from software engineering.

The lifecycle itself has essentially three tasks: requirements analysis, design/testing/development, and installation, with the middle stage being the largest and involving many subtasks (see Figure 9.16). Note the production of a set of usability goals in the first task. Mayhew suggests that these goals be captured in a style guide that is then used throughout the project to help ensure that the usability goals are adhered to.

This lifecycle follows a similar thread to our interaction design model but includes considerably more detail. It includes stages of identifying requirements, designing, evaluating, and building prototypes. It also explicitly includes the style guide as a mechanism for capturing and disseminating the usability goals of the project. Recognizing that some projects will not require the level of structure presented in the full lifecycle, Mayhew suggests that some substeps can be skipped if they are unnecessarily complex for the system being developed.

Activity 9.8

Study the usability engineering lifecycle and identify how this model differs from our interaction design lifecycle model described in Section 9.4.1, in terms of the iterations it supports.

Comment

One of the main differences between Mayhew's model and ours is that in the former the iteration between design and evaluation is contained within the second phase. Iteration between the design/test/development phase and the requirements analysis phase occurs only after the conceptual model and the detailed designs have been developed, prototyped, and evaluated one at a time. Our version models a return to the activity of identifying needs and establishing requirements after evaluating any element of the design.

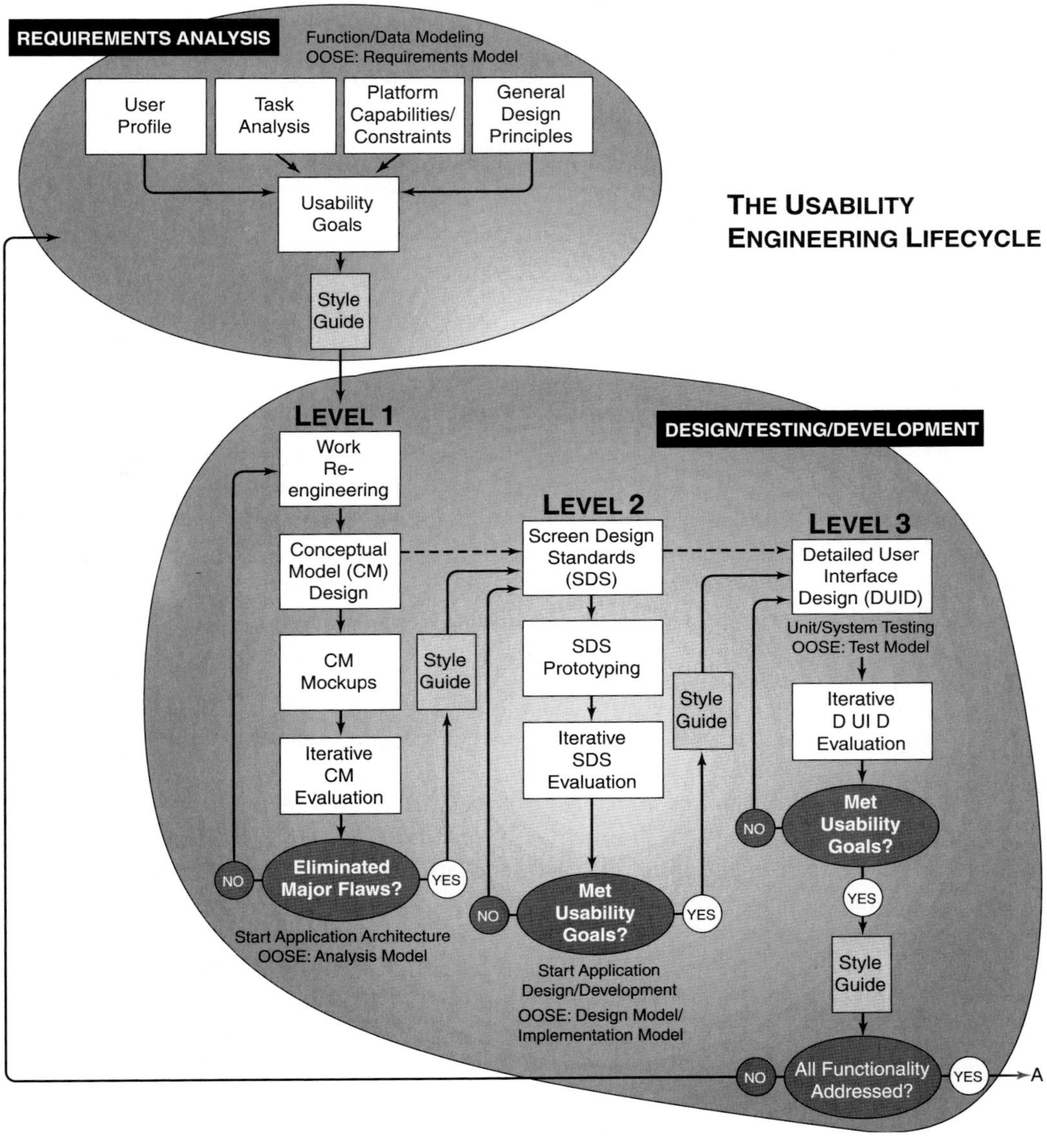

Figure 9.16 *The Usability Engineering Lifecycle*

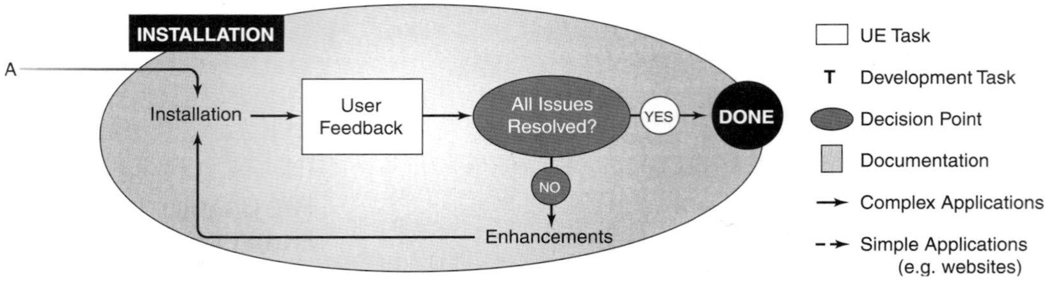

Figure 9.16 *(continued)*

ISO 13407 Human-centered design processes for interactive systems

ISO 13407 is an international standard providing guidance on human-centered design activities throughout the lifecycle of an interactive product. It addresses the planning and management of human-centered design and is concerned with both hardware and software components. It does not cover specific design approaches in any detail, and is complementary to another standard, ISO 9241, which does cover this area.

The standard identifies four principles of human-centered design:

1. The active involvement of users and a clear understanding of user and task requirements. The standard claims that the involvement of users provides a valuable source of information, and that the effectiveness of involvement increases as the level of interaction between developers and users increases.
2. An appropriate allocation of function between users and technology. The standard emphasizes that this decision should not be a simple matter of identifying what the technology is capable of doing, and then allocating all other activities to the human. Instead this decision should be based on several factors including relative competence of technology and humans in terms of reliability, flexibility of response, and user well-being.
3. The iteration of design solutions.
4. Multi-disciplinary design. The standard suggests a wide range of potential roles to be included in the team, although it emphasizes that the team need not be large as one member may take on a variety of roles.

It specifies four human-centered design activities as being central to a system development project:

1. To understand and specify the context of use.
2. To specify the user and organizational requirements.
3. To produce design solutions.
4. To evaluate designs against requirements.

The lifecycle model suggested by this standard is shown in Figure 9.17. This process should iterate from the earliest stage of the project through to project completion when the product meets its requirements.

In addition, the start of this lifecycle should be prefaced by a planning phase which identifies the design activities and how they will be integrated into other system development activities, who is responsible for these activities, procedures for establishing and documenting feedback and communication, and milestones and timescales to allow for feedback to be incorporated into the project schedule.

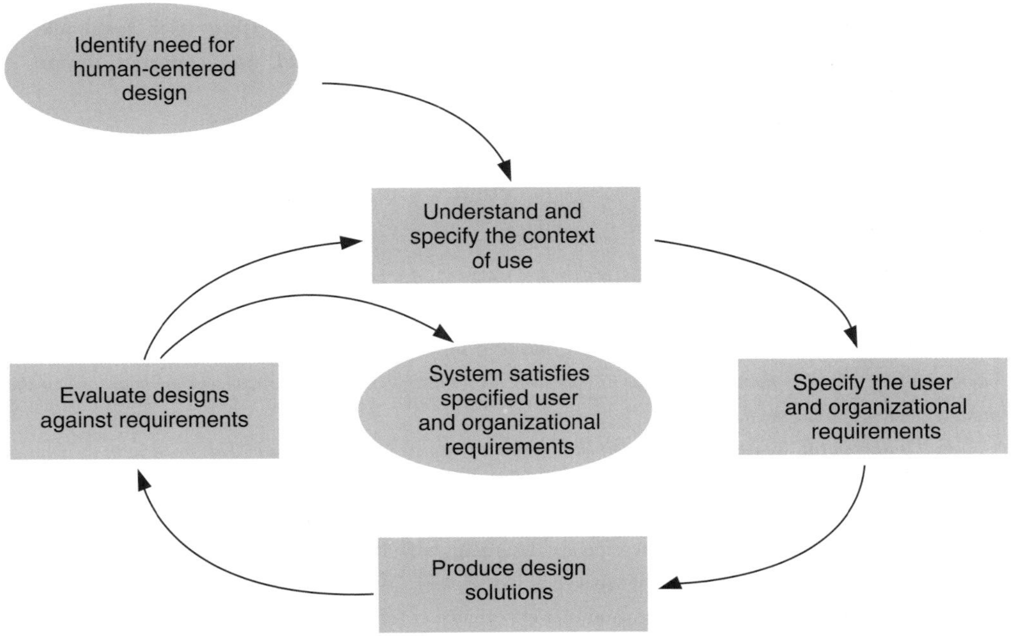

Figure 9.17 *The ISO 13407 human-centered design lifecycle model*

Dilemma
How agile should user-centered design become?

Earlier in this chapter, we have discussed examples where user feedback has been successfully incorporated into short product lifecycles. Box 9.6 describes a situation where agile development and user-centered design have been integrated to great advantage. But Mao *et al.* (2005) found that experienced UCD practitioners regard field studies (including contextual inquiry) as the most important element of user-centered design. In many user-centered design projects, there is a dedicated period of user research during which the users and their context are investigated through field studies, before starting to develop a product. With agile development and other shorter project lifecycles, a different balance needs to be struck. But this then leads to several questions and a dilemma: how much field study data is needed before product development starts? How much time should be allocated to gathering this data, and how much time should be spent on prototyping and getting user feedback? How agile should user-centered design become? ■

Assignment

Nowadays, timepieces (such as clocks, wristwatches, etc.) have a variety of functions. They not only tell the time and date but they can speak to you, remind you when it's time to do something, and provide a light in the dark, among other things. Mostly, the interface for these devices, however, shows the time in one of two basic ways: as a digital number such as 23:40 or through an analog display with two or three hands—one to represent the hour, one for the minutes, and one for the seconds.

In this assignment, we want you to design an innovative timepiece for your own use. This could be in the form of a wristwatch, a mantelpiece clock, an electronic clock, or any other kind of clock you fancy. Your goal is to be inventive and exploratory. We have broken this assignment down into the following steps to make it clearer:

(a) Think about the interactive product you are designing: what do you want it to do for you? Find three to five potential users and ask them what they would want. Write a list of requirements for the clock, together with some usability criteria and user experience criteria based on the definitions in Chapter 1.

(b) Look around for similar devices and seek out other sources of inspiration that you might find helpful. Make a note of any findings that are interesting, useful, or insightful.

(c) Sketch out some initial designs for the clock. Try to develop at least two distinct alternatives that both meet your set of requirements.

(d) Evaluate the two designs, using your usability criteria and by role playing an interaction with your sketches. Involve potential users in the evaluation, if possible. Does it do what you want? Is the time or other information being displayed always clear? Design is iterative, so you may want to return to earlier elements of the process before you choose one of your alternatives.

Summary

In this chapter, we have looked at user-centered design and the process of interaction design, i.e. what is user-centered design, what activities are required in order to design an interactive product, and how lifecycle models show the relationships between these activities. A simple interaction design lifecycle model consisting of four activities was introduced and issues surrounding the involvement and identification of users, generating alternative designs, and evaluating designs were discussed. A range of lifecycle models from software engineering and HCI were introduced.

Key Points

- The interaction design process consists of four basic activities: identifying needs and establishing requirements, developing alternative designs that meet those requirements, building interactive versions of the designs so that they can be communicated and assessed, and evaluating them.
- User-centered design rests on three principles: early focus on users and tasks, empirical measurement and iterative design. These principles are also key for interaction design.
- Involving users in the design process helps with expectation management and feelings of ownership, but how and when to involve users is a matter of dispute.
- Before you can begin to establish requirements, you must understand who the users are and what their goals are in using the product.
- Looking at others' designs provides useful inspiration and encourages designers to consider alternative design solutions, which is key to effective design.
- Usability criteria, technical feasibility, and users' feedback on prototypes can all be used to choose among alternatives.
- Prototyping is a useful technique for facilitating user feedback on designs at all stages.
- Lifecycle models show how development activities relate to one another.
- The interaction design lifecycle model is complementary to lifecycle models from other fields.

Further Reading

GREENBAUM, J. and KYNG, M. (eds) (1991) *Design at Work: Co-operative Design of Computer Systems*. Lawrence Erlbaum. This book is a good collection of papers about the co-design of software systems: both why it is worthwhile and experience of how to do it.

HIGHSMITH, J. (2002) *Agile Software Development Ecosystems*. Addison Wesley. This book introduces the main agile methods and their proponents. Highsmith explains the motivation behind the agile approach to development and extracts some common themes. The book includes some case studies, and how you the reader can go about developing your own agile method that suits your own particular environment.

KELLEY, T. with LITTMAN, J. (2004) *The Art of Innovation*. Profile Books. Tom Kelley is general manager of IDEO. In this book, Kelley explains some of the innovative techniques used at IDEO, but more importantly he talks about the culture and philosophy underlying IDEO's success. There are some useful practical hints in here as well as an informative story about building and maintaining a successful design company.

MAYHEW, D.J. (1999) *The Usability Engineering Lifecycle*. Morgan Kaufmann. This is a very practical book about product user interface design. It explains how to perform usability tasks throughout development and provides useful examples along the way to illustrate the techniques. It links in with two software development-based methods: rapid prototyping and object-oriented software engineering.

SOMMERVILLE, I. (2006) *Software Engineering* (8th edn). Addison-Wesley. If you are interested in pursuing the software engineering aspects of the lifecycle models section, then this book provides a useful overview of the main models and their purpose.

NIELSEN, J. (1993) *Usability Engineering*. Morgan Kaufmann. This is a seminal book on usability engineering. If you want to find out more about the philosophy, intent, history, or pragmatics of usability engineering, then this is a good place to start.

INTERVIEW with Gillian Crampton Smith

In 1991 Gillian Crampton Smith founded the Computer Related Design Department at the Royal College of Art—a program to enable artist-designers to develop and apply their traditional skills and knowledge to the design of all kinds of interactive products and systems. Between 2001 and 2006 she was director of the brand new Interaction Design Institute Ivrea (near Turin), an institute for teaching and research funded by Telecom Italia and Olivetti, where she worked to develop connections between the disciplines of technology, design, and business. In 2006 she moved to the IUAV University of Architecture and Design in Venice to continue the work started at Ivrea.

GC: I believe that things should work but they should also delight. In the past, when it was really difficult to make things work, that was what people concentrated on. But now it's much easier to design and build software and hardware that is robust and reliable. We have an amazing range of technologies but they're often not well designed for people—and they're certainly not very enjoyable to use. If we think about other things in our life, our clothes, our furniture, the things we eat with, we choose them because they have a meaning beyond their practical use. Good design is partly about working really well, but it's also about what something looks like, what it reminds us of, what it refers to in our broader cultural environment. It's this side that interactive systems are only just beginning to address—how they can become a true part of culture. They are not just tools for professionals any more, but an environment in which we live.

HS: How do you think we can improve things?

GC: The parallel with architecture is interesting. In architecture, a great deal of time and expense is put into the initial design; with software this is rarely the case: on the whole not much money or time is put into the initial design stages. If you think of the big software engineering companies, how many people work on the design side rather than on the implementation side?

HS: When you say design do you mean conceptual design, or task design, or something else?

GC: I mean all phases of design. Firstly there's research—finding out about people, their needs and desires. This is not necessarily limited to finding out about what they want, because if we're designing new things, they are probably things people don't even know they could have. At the Royal College of Art we developed ways of working with users—to be inspired by them, and not constrained by what they know is possible.

The second stage is thinking, "What should this thing we are designing do?" You could call this conceptual design, deciding the idea of what the product is. A third stage is thinking how do you represent it—what mental model of what it is do you want to conjure up in the mind of the user—and how do you give it form? And then the fourth stage is actually crafting the interface—exactly what color is this pixel? Is this type the right size, or do you need a size bigger? How much can you get on a screen?—all those things about the details that make the difference between something graceful or awkward.

One of the problems companies have is that the feedback they get is: "I wish it did x." Software looks as if it's designed, not with a basic model of how it works that is then expressed on the interface, but as a load of different functions that are strung together. The desktop interface, although it has great advantages, encourages the idea that you have a menu and you can just add a few more bits when people want more things. In today's word processors, for instance, there isn't a clear conceptual model about how it works, or an underlying theory people can use to reason about why it is not working in the way they expect.

HS: So in trying to put more effort into the design aspect of things, do you think we need different people in the team?

GC: Yes. People in the software field tend to think that designers are people who know how to do the pretty bits at the end which, of course, they do. But a graphic designer, for instance, is somebody who also thinks at a more strategic level, "What message needs to be communicated? and to whom?" and then, "What is the best way to give form to a message like that?" The part you see is the beautiful design, the lovely poster or record sleeve, or elegant book, but behind that is a lot of thinking about how to communicate ideas via a particular medium.

HS: If you've got people from different disciplines, have you experienced difficulties in communication?

GC: Absolutely. People from different disciplines have different values, so different results and different approaches are valued. People have different temperaments, that have led them to the different fields in the first place, and they've been trained in different ways. In my view the big difference between the way engineers are trained and the way designers are trained is that engineers are trained to focus in on a solution from the beginning whereas designers are trained first to focus out and only when they have explored a lot of different ideas to focus in. This is very hard for both the engineers and the designers because the designers are thinking the engineers are trying to home in much too quickly on a solution without considering enough alternatives; and the engineers can't bear the designers faffing about! Each is trained to get their results in a completely different way.

HS: Is your idea to make each more tolerant of the other?
GC: Yes, my idea is not to try to make renaissance people, as I don't think it's feasible. Very few people can do everything well. The ideal team is made up of people who are really confident and good at what they do and open-mined enough to realize there are very different approaches. There's the scientific approach of the HCI specialists, the engineering approach, the design approach. All three are different and that's their value—you don't want everybody to be the same. The best combination is where you have engineers who understand and appreciate design and designers who understand and appreciate engineering.

It's important that people know their limitations too. If you realize that you need an ergonomist, then you go and find one and you hire them to consult for you. So you need to know what you don't know as well as what you do.

HS: What other aspects of traditional design do you think help with interaction design?
GC: The ability to visualize things. It allows people to make quick prototypes or models or sketches so that a group of people can talk about something concrete. It's an invaluable aid to the process. And making things that people like is one of the things that good designers have a feel for.

HS: Do you mean aesthetically like or like in its whole sense?
GC: In its whole sense. Obviously there's the aesthetic of what something looks like or feels like but there's also the aesthetic of how it works. You can talk about an elegant way of doing something as well as an elegant look.

HS: Another trait I've seen in designers is being protective of their design.
GC: This is both a vice and a virtue. In order to keep a design coherent you need to keep a grip on the whole and to push it through as a whole. Otherwise it can happen that people try to make this a bit smaller and cut bits out of that, and so on, and before you know where you are the original coherence of the design is lost. It is quite difficult for a team to hold a coherent vision of a design. If you think of other design fields, like film-making, for instance, there is one director and everybody accepts that the director's role is to hold the vision; all the other roles are essential—cameraman, producer, scriptwriter, but it is the director who makes all the elements work together to make something powerful. One of the things that's wrong with products like Microsoft Word, for instance, is that there's no single powerful organizing idea in it that makes you think, "Oh yes, I understand how this all fits together."

Design is always a balance between things that work well and things that look good. The ideal design satisfies everything, but in most designs you have to make trade-offs. If you're making a game it's more important that people enjoy it and that it looks good than to worry if some of it's a bit difficult. If you're making a fighter cockpit then the most important thing is that pilots don't fall out of the sky, and so this informs the trade-offs you make. The question is, who decides how to decide the criteria for the trade-offs that inevitably need to be made. This is not a matter of engineering: it's a matter of values—cultural, emotional, aesthetic.

HS: I know this is a controversial issue for some designers. Do you think users should be part of the design team?

GC: No, I don't. I think it's an abdication of responsibility. Users should definitely be involved as a source of inspiration, suggesting ideas, evaluating proposals—saying, "Yes, we think this would be great" or "No, we think this is an appalling idea." But in the end, if designers aren't better than the general public at designing things, what are they doing as designers? ■

10

10.1 Introduction

An interaction design project may aim to replace or update an established system, or it may aim to develop a totally innovative product with no obvious precedent. There may be an initial set of requirements, or the project may have to begin by producing a set of requirements from scratch. Whatever the initial situation and whatever the aim of the project, the users' needs, requirements, aspirations, and expectations have to be discussed, refined, clarified, and probably re-scoped. This requires an understanding of, among other things, the users and their capabilities, their current tasks and goals, the conditions under which the product will be used, and constraints on the product's performance.

As we discussed in Chapter 9, identifying users' needs is not as straightforward as it sounds. Establishing requirements is also not simply writing a wish list of features. Given the iterative nature of interaction design, isolating requirements activities from design activities and from evaluation activities is a little artificial, since in practice they are all intertwined: some design will take place while requirements are being established, and the design will evolve through a series of evaluation–redesign cycles. However, each of these activities can be distinguished by its own emphasis and its own techniques.

This chapter provides a more detailed overview of identifying needs and establishing requirements. We introduce different kinds of requirements and explain some useful techniques.

The main aims of this chapter are to:

- **Describe different kinds of requirements.**
- **Enable you to identify examples of different kinds of requirements from a simple description.**
- **Explain how different data gathering techniques (those introduced in Chapter 7 and others) may be used during the requirements activity.**
- **Enable you to develop a 'scenario,' a 'use case,' and an 'essential use case' from a simple description.**
- **Enable you to perform hierarchical task analysis on a simple description.**

10

Identifying needs and establishing requirements

10.2 What, How, and Why?

10.2.1 What are we trying to achieve in the requirements activity?

There are two aims. One aim is to understand as much as possible about the users, their work, and the context of that work, so the system under development can support them in achieving their goals; this we call "identifying needs." Building on this, our second aim is to produce, from the needs identified, a set of stable requirements that form a sound basis to move forward into thinking about design. This is not necessarily a major document nor a set of rigid prescriptions, but you need to be sure that it will not change radically in the time it takes to do some design and get feedback on the ideas. Because the end goal is to produce this set of requirements, we shall sometimes refer to this as the requirements activity.

10.2.2 How can we achieve this?

This whole chapter is devoted to explaining how to achieve these aims, but first we give an overview of where we're heading.

At the beginning of the requirements activity, we know that we have a lot to find out and to clarify. At the end of the activity we will have a set of stable requirements that can be moved forward into the design activity. In the middle, there are activities concerned with data gathering, analysis, interpretation, and presentation, with the aim of capturing the findings in a form that can be expressed as requirements. Broadly speaking, these activities progress in a sequential manner: first gather some data, then analyze and interpret it, then extract some requirements from it, but it gets a lot messier than this, and the activities influence one another as the process iterates. One of the reasons for this is that once you start to analyze data, you will find that you need to gather some more data to clarify or confirm your findings. Another reason is that the way in which you present your requirements may affect your analysis, since it will enable you to identify and express some aspects more easily than others (as discussed in Section 8.7). For example, using a notation which emphasizes the data characteristics of a situation will lead the analysis to focus on this aspect rather than, for example, on task structure. Remember from Chapter 7 that it is valuable to triangulate data gathering and analysis and to use a complementary set of techniques. As we discuss below, there are different kinds of requirements, and each can be emphasized or de-emphasized by the different techniques.

Identifying needs and establishing requirements is itself an iterative activity in which the subactivities inform and refine one another. It does not last for a set number of weeks or months and then finish. In practice, requirements evolve and develop as the stakeholders interact with designs and see what is possible and how certain facilities can help them. And as shown in the lifecycle model in Chapter 9, the activity itself will be repeatedly revisited.

10.2.3 Why bother? The importance of getting it right

Much has been written about the significant cost of fixing errors late in the software development cycle rather than early, during the requirements activity. For example, Davis (1995) identifies insufficient user communication, poor specifications, and insufficient analysis as contributors to poor cost estimation. Boehm and Basili (2001) present a top ten list of software defect reduction findings, the first of which states that "finding and fixing a software problem after delivery is often 100 times more expensive than finding and fixing it during the requirements and design phase." Taylor (2000) investigated the causes of IT project failure. The article admits that "there is no single cause of IT project failure," but requirements issues figured highly in the findings. Others too have identified requirements errors as being a major source of severe problems, e.g. Jones (2000); Weinberg, (1997). Although this research does not specifically focus on interactive products, software is a significant element in most kinds of interactive products, and so these findings are very relevant here. The cartoon below illustrates very well what can go wrong if requirements are not clearly articulated.

10.2.4 Why *establish* requirements?

The activity of understanding what a product should do has been given various labels—for example, requirements gathering, requirements capture, requirements elicitation, requirements analysis, and requirements engineering. The first two imply that requirements exist out there and we simply need to pick them up or catch them. 'Elicitation' implies that 'others' (presumably the clients or users) know the requirements and we have to get them to tell us. Requirements, however, are not that easy to identify. You might argue that, in some cases, customers must know what the requirements are because they know the tasks that need supporting, and may have asked for a product to be built in the first place. However, they may not have articulated requirements as yet, and even if they have an initial set of requirements, they probably have not explored them in sufficient detail for development to begin.

The term 'requirements analysis' is normally used to describe the activity of investigating and analyzing an initial set of requirements that have been gathered, elicited, or captured. Analyzing the information gathered is an important step, since it is this interpretation of the facts, rather than the facts themselves, that inspires the design. Requirements engineering is a better term than the others because it recognizes that developing a set of requirements is an iterative process of evolution and negotiation, and one that needs to be carefully managed and controlled.

We chose the term *establishing* requirements to represent the fact that requirements arise from data gathering, analysis, and interpretation activities and have been established from a sound understanding of the users' needs. This also implies that requirements can be justified by and related back to the data collected.

10.3 What are requirements?

Before we go any further, we need to explain what we mean by a requirement. Intuitively, you probably have some understanding of what a requirement is, but we should be clear. A requirement is a statement about an intended product that specifies what it should do or how it should perform. One of the aims of the requirements activity is to make the requirements as specific, unambiguous, and clear as possible. For example, a requirement for a website might be that the time to download any complete page is less than 5 seconds. Another less precise example might be that teenage girls should find the site appealing. In the case of this latter example, further investigation would be necessary to explore exactly what teenage girls would find appealing. Requirements come in many different forms and at many different levels of abstraction, but we need to make sure that the requirements are as clear as possible and that we understand how to tell when they have been fulfilled. The example requirement shown in Figure 10.1 is expressed using a format called a 'shell' from the Volere process (Robertson and Robertson, 2006), which you'll hear more about later in this chapter and in Suzanne Robertson's interview at the end of this chapter. This shell

Requirement #: **75** Requirement Type: **9** Event/use case #: **6**

Description: **The product shall issue an alert if a weather station fails to transmit readings.**

Rationale: **Failure to transmit readings might indicate that the weather station is faulty and needs maintenance, and that the data used to predict freezing roads may be incomplete.**

Source: **Road Engineers**
Fit Criterion: **For each weather station the product shall communicate to the user when the recorded number of each type of reading per hour is not within the manufacturer's specified range of the expected number of readings per hour.**

Customer Satisfaction: **3** Customer Dissatisfaction: **5**
Dependencies: **None** Conflicts: **None**
Supporting Materials: **Specification of Rosa Weather Station**
History: **Raised by GBS, 28 July 99**

Volere

***Figure 10.1** An example requirement using the Volere shell*

requires quite a bit of information about the requirement itself, including something called a 'fit criterion,' which is a way of measuring when the solution meets the requirement. In Chapter 9 we emphasized the need to establish specific usability criteria for a product early on in development, and this part of the shell encourages this.

10.3.1 Different kinds of requirements

In software engineering, two different kinds of requirements have traditionally been identified: functional requirements, which say what the system should do, and non-functional requirements, which say what constraints there are on the system and its development. For example, a functional requirement for a word processor may be that it should support a variety of formatting styles. This requirement might then be decomposed into more specific requirements detailing the kind of formatting required, such as formatting by paragraph, by character, and by document, down to a very specific level such as that character formatting must include 20 typefaces, each with bold, italic, and standard options. A non-functional requirement for a wordprocessor might be that it must be able to run on a variety of platforms such as PCs, Macs, and Unix machines. Another might be that the target platform is expected to have at least 1.0 GB RAM. A different kind of non-functional requirement would be that it must be delivered in six months' time. This represents a constraint on the development activity itself rather than on the product being developed.

If we consider interactive products in general, other kinds of non-functional requirements become relevant such as physical size, weight, color, and production feasibility. For example, when the PalmPilot was developed (Bergman and Haitani, 2000), an overriding requirement was that it should be physically as small as possible, allowing for the fact that it needed to incorporate batteries and an LCD display. In addition, there were extremely tight constraints on the size of the screen, and that had implications for the number of pixels available to display information. For example, formatting lines or certain typefaces may become infeasible to use if they take up even one extra pixel. Figure 10.2 shows two screen shots from the PalmPilot development. As you can see, removing the line at the left-hand side of the display in the top window released sufficient pixels to display the missing 's' in the bottom window.

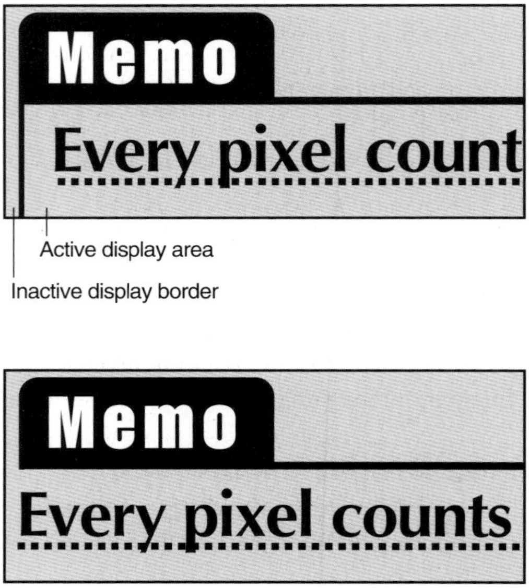

Figure 10.2 *Every pixel counts*

Interaction design involves understanding the functionality required and the constraints under which the product must operate or be developed. However, instead of referring to all requirements that are not functional as simply 'non-functional' requirements, we prefer to refine this into further categories. The following is not an exhaustive list of the different requirements we need to be looking out for (see the figure in Suzanne Robertson's interview at the end of this chapter for a more detailed list), nor is it a distinct categorization, however, it does illustrate the variety of requirements that need to be captured.

Functional requirements capture what the product should do. For example, a functional requirement for a robot working in a car assembly plant might be that it should be able to accurately place and weld together the correct pieces of metal. Understanding the functional requirements for an interactive product is fundamental.

Data requirements capture the type, volatility, size/amount, persistence, accuracy, and value of the required data. All interactive products have to handle greater or lesser amounts of data. For example, if the system under consideration is to operate in the share-dealing application domain, then the data must be up-to-date and accurate, and is likely to change many times a day. In the personal banking domain, data must be accurate, must persist over many months and probably years, is very valuable, and there is likely to be a lot of it.

Environmental requirements or *context of use* refer to the circumstances in which the interactive product will be expected to operate. Four aspects of the environment must be considered when establishing requirements. First is the physical environment, such as how much lighting, noise, and dust is expected in the operational environment. Will users need to wear protective clothing, such as large gloves or headgear, that might affect the choice of interface type? How crowded is the environment? For example, an ATM operates in a very public physical environment. Using speech to interact with the customer is therefore likely to be problematic.

The second aspect of the environment is the social environment. The issues raised in Chapter 4 regarding the social aspects of interaction design, such as collaboration and coordination, need to be explored in the context of the current development. For example, will data need to be shared? If so, does the sharing have to be synchronous, e.g. does everyone need to be viewing the data at once, or asynchronous, e.g. two people authoring a report take turns in editing and adding to it? Other factors include the physical location of fellow team members, e.g. do collaborators have to communicate across great distances?

The third aspect is the organizational environment, e.g. how good is user support likely to be, how easily can it be obtained, and are there facilities or resources for training? How efficient or stable is the communications infrastructure? How hierarchical is the management? And so on.

Finally, the technical environment will need to be established: for example, what technologies will the product run on or need to be compatible with, and what technological limitations might be relevant?

Box 10.1
Underwater PCs

Developing a PC for undersea divers to take underwater has one major environmental factor: it is surrounded by water! However, waterproofing is not the main issue for the designers at WetPC, a company who have produced such a system. The interface has proved to be more of a problem. Divers typically have only one hand free to operate the computer, and are likely to be swimming and moving up and down in the water at the same time. So a traditional interface design is no good.

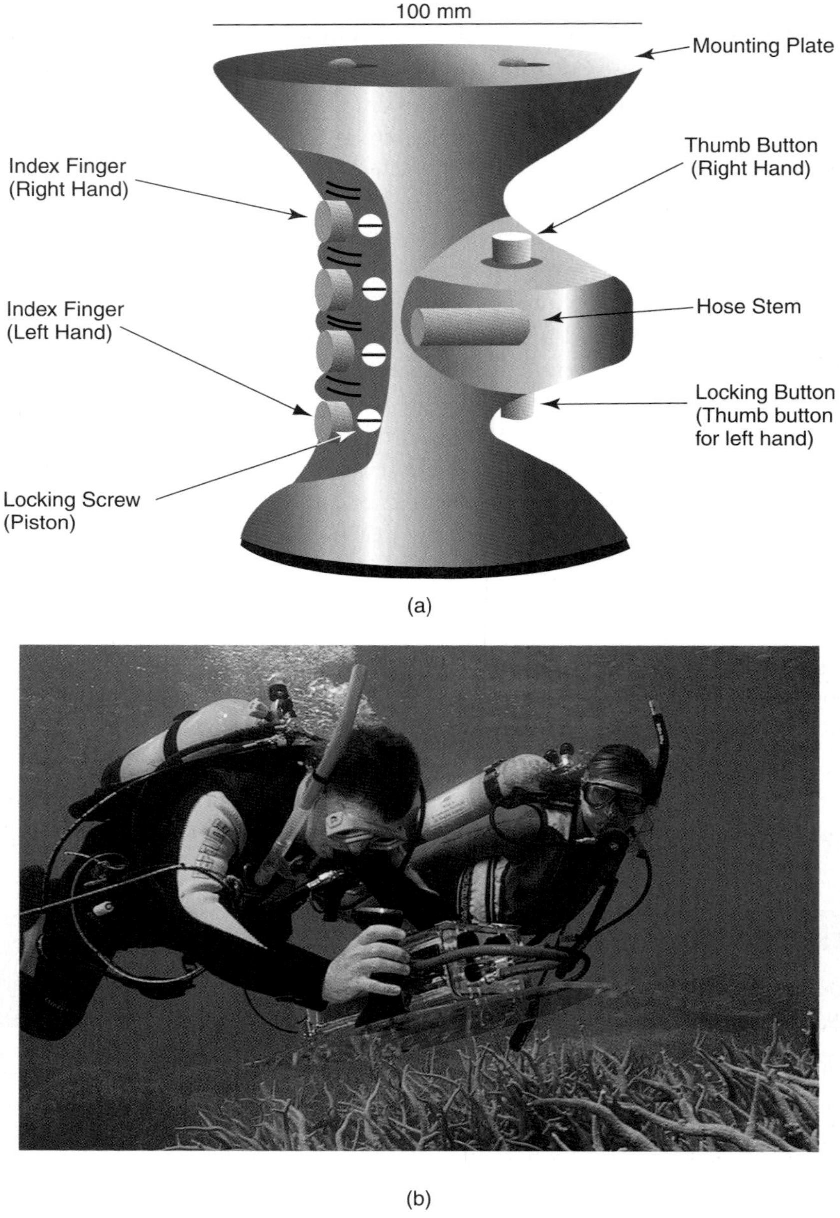

Figure 10.3 *(a) The KordGrip interface; (b) the KordGrip in use under water*

Early prototypes of the computer used voice recognition, but the bubbles made too much noise and distorted the sound. Tracker balls were also inappropriate because the divers are not working on a flat surface. So the main developer at WetPC, Bruce Macdonald, devised a 'keyboard' called a KordGrip that has five keys (see Figure 10.3a). Combinations of keys represent different symbols, so that divers can choose items from menus. They can perform operations such as controlling a camera and sending messages. The system is also linked to a GPS system that tells the divers where they are. This makes it much easier to mark the location of mines and other underwater discoveries. ■

User characteristics capture the key attributes of the intended user group. In Chapter 9 we mentioned the relevance of a user's abilities and skills, and these are an important aspect of user requirements. But in addition to these, a user may be a novice, an expert, a casual, or a frequent user. This affects the ways in which interaction is designed. For example, a novice user will require step-by-step instructions, probably with prompting, and a constrained interaction backed up with clear information. An expert, on the other hand, will require a flexible interaction with more wide-ranging powers of control. Other attributes that may affect the design are: the users' nationality, educational background, preferences, personal circumstances, physical or mental disabilities, and so on. Boxes 10.2 and 10.3 provide more information on national culture and accessibility. The collection of attributes for a 'typical user' is called a *user profile*. Any one product may have a number of different user profiles.

In order to bring the user profiles to life, they are often transformed into a number of 'personas' (Cooper, 1999). Personas are rich descriptions of typical users of the product under development that the designers can focus on and design the product for. They don't describe

Box 10.2
National culture

As globalization spreads, the importance of the impact that national culture has on interaction design has increased. This impact varies from relatively obvious concerns such as the natural language used (e.g. Spanish or Japanese), through aesthetic concerns (e.g. the use of colors), to semantic features (e.g. the use of appropriate structures and images). All of these issues are important and can make a difference between a product being used and enjoyed or it being offensive and ignored. Various definitions of culture have been suggested, and there is not one generally agreed view, but it usually involves words such as 'values,' 'beliefs,' 'norms,' and 'behavior.' One definition we like is that culture is "programming

of the mind" (Hofstede and Hofstede, 2005).

One of the most influential pieces of work on characterizing national culture differences was carried out by a management theorist called Geert Hofstede around 1970. He was given access to responses from a survey of IBM employees in over 50 countries worldwide and from this he identified four 'dimensions' of national culture: power distance (PD), individualism (IND), masculinity–femininity (MAS), and uncertainty avoidance (UA). As a result of work done in Hong Kong at a later date by a Canadian, Michael Bond, a fifth dimension was added which deals with time-orientation.

- Power distance defines the extent to which inequality in power is accepted and considered as normal by less powerful members of society. In his studies, Hofstede found that Austria had the lowest PD score and Malaysia the highest.
- Individualism is the degree to which an individual acts as part of a group or as an individual independent of the group. In an individualistic culture, everyone is expected to look after herself and her immediate family; in a collectivist culture the collective is more highly valued than the individual. In his studies Hofstede found that Guatemala had the lowest IND score and the USA the highest.
- The MAS dimension relates to gender roles and reveals any tendencies in the culture towards 'masculine' values of assertiveness, competitiveness, and materialism, or towards 'feminine' values of nurturing, and the quality of life and relationships. In his studies he found that Sweden had the lowest score, showing that gender roles were not rigidly adhered to and Japan had the highest.
- Uncertainty avoidance is concerned with whether a society is uncomfortable with uncertainty, preferring predictability and stability, or it welcomes unpredictability as providing new opportunities and challenges. In his studies Hofstede found that Singapore had the lowest UA score, indicating a desire to explore the unknown, and Greece the highest, indicating that Greeks value certainty.
- Long term orientation (LTO) describes a culture associated with perseverance, thrift, the acceptance of many truths, the ability to accept change, and tendency to look to the future. A culture with short-term orientation seek stability, a single truth, and results in the short term. Asian countries such as China score highest on this dimension, while Western cultures score lowest.

Although influential, Hofstede's work does have limitations. For example, he admits that the people involved in designing the original questionnaire were all from Western cultures. In addition, his studies and conclusions have been discussed and challenged over the intervening years, e.g. the stereotype that European Americans are more individualistic than people from other ethnic groups has been challenged by Oyserman *et al.* (2002). ■

Box 10.3
Accessibility

The area of 'accessibility' refers to the degree to which an interactive product is usable by people with disabilities[1]. But what does it mean to be disabled? Definitions vary, but the following captures the main points. A person is considered to be disabled if:

- They have a mental or physical impairment.
- The impairment has an adverse effect on their ability to carry out normal day-to-day activities.
- The adverse effect is substantial and long-term (meaning it has lasted for 12 months, or is likely to last for more than 12 months or for the rest of their life).

Whether or not a person is considered to be disabled changes over time with age, or as recovery from an accident progresses. In addition, severity and impact of an impairment can vary over the course of a day or in different environmental conditions.

It is quite common, when people first consider the topic of accessibility and interaction design, to consider it largely in terms of a specific physical disability, such as the need for a wheelchair, or loss of sight. However, it is often the case that a person with disabilities will have more than one disability, and in addition, there is a wide range of disabilities such as:

- Color-blindness. The inability to distinguish between two colors affects approximately 1 in 10 men and 1 in 200 women. This has an impact on the use of color for highlighting or distinguishing interface elements.
- Dyslexia. Although usually associated with difficulties in reading and writing, there are many different forms of dyslexia, some of which affect the way in which people comprehend the totality of concepts. A relatively simple interaction design decision that can cause difficulties for people with dyslexia is the contrast between foreground and background text or images.
- Physical impairments range from conditions such as tremor or shaking, weakness, pain, reduced control of limbs, and inability to sit upright to short or missing limbs.

Disabilities such as these and others will affect the kinds of interfaces that are appropriate for a user group, and the detailed design of interfaces that will meet user experience and usability goals. For example, the accessibility of web-based systems has received much attention; the section on research and design issues for web-based interfaces in Chapter 6 discusses standards and guidelines that have been developed to support web content accessibility. ■

[1]The accepted terminology when discussing disabilities varies between countries. For example, 'people with disabilities' is preferred in the US, while 'disabled people' is preferred in the UK. In this book we have followed the publisher's policy of using the US terminology.

real people, but are synthesized from a number of real users who have been involved in data gathering exercises. Personas are described with rigor and with detail, and they are defined by the goals of that persona, so each persona has a unique set of goals. Basing a persona on a job description or a job title is not appropriate as goals often differ between people even within the same job role, and people with very different job roles may have the same goals for this particular product. For example, personas for a device to alert an amateur runner when he has burned a certain number of calories would focus on different exercising routines, fitness levels, fashion preferences, and so on rather than on the runner's job role.

As well as goals, a persona will include a description of the pretend user's skills, attitudes, tasks, and environment. These are all defined specifically, so instead of describing someone simply as a competent sailor, include detail such as that he has completed a Day Skipper qualification and has over 100 hours of sailing experience in and around European waters. Each persona has a name, often a photograph, and some personal details such as what they do in the evening. It is the addition of precise, credible details that helps designers to see the personas as real potential users, and hence as people they can design for.

Including user experience goals for personas is useful too as it adds context, bringing the intended user to life. For example, imagine you're designing an educational game to help teenagers learn about science, and have chosen user experience goals of 'exciting' and 'enjoyable.' Introducing a specific character called Damian as a possible end-user, with details of his likes and dislikes, strengths and weaknesses, and aspirations, allows the designer to relate the new game to a concrete situation, and imagine how Damian might react to a particular feature, or game character, and so on. The persona should not be idealized, but include realistic characteristics, such as that Damian suffers from Attention Deficit Disorder, and the challenges that brings.

Usually a product will require a small set of personas rather than just one. It is difficult to give a specific number for how many personas are needed, but it may be helpful to choose one primary persona who represents a large section of the intended user group. The persona in Box 10.4 was developed for an intranet project and illustrates the kind of information that might be included.

Box 10.4
Example persona

Bob is 52 years old and works as a mechanic with an organization offering road service to customers when their car breaks down. He has worked in the job for the past 12 years and knows it well. Many of the younger mechanics ask Bob for advice when they meet up in the depot as he always knows the answer to tricky

mechanical problems. Bob likes sharing his knowledge with the younger guys, as it makes him feel a valued part of the team.

Bob works rolling day and night shifts and spends his shifts attending breakdowns and lockouts (when customers lock their keys in the car). About 20% of the jobs he attends are complex and he occasionally needs to refer to his standard issue manuals. Bob tries to avoid using the manuals in front of customers as he thinks it gives the impression he doesn't know what he's doing.

Bob has seen many changes over the years with the company and has tried his best to move with the times. However he found it a bit daunting when a new computer was installed in his van several years ago, and now he has heard rumors that the computer is going to be upgraded to one with a bigger screen that's meant to be faster and better.

Bob's been told that he will be able to access the intranet on the new computer. He has heard about the intranet and saw it once in an early version on his manager's computer. He wonders if he will be able to find out what's going on in the company more easily, especially as customers seem to know more about the latest company news than he does when he turns up at a job. This can be embarrassing and has been a source of frustration for Bob throughout his time with the company.

Bob wonders if he will be able to cope with the new computer system. He doesn't mind asking his grandchildren for help when he wants to send an email to his brother overseas, but asking the guys at work for help is another story.

***Source:* from** `http://www.steptwo.com.au/papers/kmc_personas/` **(12.11.05)**

Usability goals and user experience goals were described in Chapter 1. These are another kind of requirement, and should be captured together with appropriate measures. In Chapter 9 we introduced the idea of usability engineering, an approach in which specific measures for the usability goals of the product are established and agreed upon early in the development process and are then revisited, and used to track progress as development proceeds. This both ensures that usability is given due priority and facilitates progress tracking. Usability goals include: effectiveness, efficiency, safety, utility, learnability, and memorability. If we are to follow the philosophy of usability engineering and meet these usability goals, then we must identify the appropriate requirements. The same is true for some user experience goals, such as making products that are fun, enjoyable, pleasurable, aesthetically pleasing, and motivating. It is harder to identify quantifiable measures that allow us to track these qualities, but an understanding of how important each of these is to the current development should emerge as we learn more about the intended product.

There are two different perspectives that can be taken when identifying measures for these goals—one focuses on objective measures of the user's performance while the other focuses on the user's perceptions of the interaction. This difference will be discussed further in Chapter 14.

Activity 10.1

Suggest some key requirements in each category above (functional, data, user characteristics, usability goal, and user experience goal) for each of the following scenarios:

1. **An interactive product for use in a university's self-service cafeteria that allows users to pay for their food using a credit system.**
2. **An interactive product to control the functioning of a nuclear power plant.**
3. **An interactive product to support distributed design teams, e.g. for car design.**

Comment

You may have come up with alternative suggestions; these are indicative of the kinds of answer we might expect.

1. ***Functional*: the product will calculate the total cost of purchases.**

   ***Data*: the product must have access to the price of products in the cafeteria.**

   ***Environmental*: cafeteria users will be carrying a tray and will most likely be in a reasonable rush. The physical environment will be noisy and busy, and users may be talking with friends and colleagues while using the product.**

   ***User characteristics*: the majority of users are likely to be under 25 and comfortable dealing with technology.**

   ***Usability goals*: the product needs to be easy to learn so that new users can use it immediately, and memorable for more frequent users. Users won't want to wait around for the system to finish processing, so it needs to be efficient and safe to use, i.e. able to deal easily with user errors.**

   ***User experience goals*: of the user experience goals listed in Chapter 1, I feel that those most likely to be relevant here are satisfying, helpful, and enhancing sociability. The last of these may be difficult to implement in this kind of environment, but a cafeteria is a sociable place, and so a system that enhances that would be welcome. While some of the other goals are not inappropriate, it is not essential for this product to, for example, be cognitively stimulating.**

2. ***Functional*: the product will be able to monitor the temperature of the reactors.**

   ***Data*: the product will need access to temperature readings.**

   ***Environmental*: the physical environment is likely to be uncluttered and to impose few restrictions on the console itself unless there is a need to wear protective clothing (depending on where the console is to be located).**

User characteristics: the user is likely to be a well-trained engineer or scientist who is competent to handle technology.

Usability goals: the system needs to exhibit all of the usability goals. You wouldn't want a safety-critical system like this being anything other than effective, efficient, safe, easy to learn and remember how to use, and with good utility. For example, outputs from the system, especially warning signals and gauges, must be clear and unambiguous.

User experience goals: on the other hand, none of the user experience goals is particularly relevant here. You certainly wouldn't want the product to be surprising, annoying, provocative, or challenging, although there's nothing wrong with it being aesthetically pleasing or enjoyable.

3. *Functional*: the product will be able to communicate information between remote sites.

   Data: the product must have access to design information that will be captured in a common file format (such as AutoCAD).

   Environmental: physically distributed over a wide area. Files and other electronic media need to be shared. The product must comply with available communication protocols and be compatible with network technologies.

   User characteristics: professional designers, who may be worried about technology but who are likely to be prepared to spend time learning a system that will help them perform their jobs better. The design team is likely to be multi-lingual.

   Usability goals: all of the usability goals will be relevant here, but maybe safety is one of the key requirements. Keeping transmission error rate low is likely to be of high priority.

   User experience goals: working collaboratively across distances can be challenging, so a system that is motivating, supportive of creativity, and enhancing sociability will fit well with its purpose.

CASE STUDY 10.1
Universal usability: Web Fun for individuals with Down Syndrome

In this case study by Assadour Kirijian and Matthew Myers, from A.K.A. New Media Inc. in Toronto, Canada, usability consultants and specialists in Down Syndrome worked with individuals with Down Syndrome to create a set of online tools to help individuals with Down Syndrome learn and practice the basic skills required to use the Internet. The goals of these tools are to enable individuals with Down Syndrome to take better advantage of the entertainment and educational benefits that the Internet can provide. The suite of software that they created is known as Web Fun Central.

The skills that are supported by Web Fun Central are deemed particularly important for people with Down Syndrome in their late teens who are likely to experience increased isolation as they leave high school and enter adulthood. In the course of this growing isolation, they also tend to lose some of their reading, writing, and communication skills.

The specific target group is middle-functioning (reading level grade 3 or 4) young adults aged 14–20 with Down Syndrome. From their analysis of this user population, the development team discovered that these users tended to: love music; love pop-culture; be easily led; be easily frustrated; enjoy accomplishing things; not like change; and be reward-oriented.

Web Fun Central would enable them to learn how to use the Internet for communication and entertainment, which in turn might help them maintain reading and writing skills. The interactive learning process itself lays the groundwork for the opportunity to introduce more advanced technological concepts and Internet functions in the future, and the game segments provide an enjoyable means for the user to practice the skills learned.

The case study describes how the development team worked with individuals with Down Syndrome to understand and analyze the needs of people with Down Syndrome. Together they designed, evaluated, and refined prototypes until they developed the final product.

These screens are from an application called Web World, one of the modules in Web Fun Central that teaches basic web navigation skills to individuals with Down Syndrome. (Kirijian *et al.*, in Lazar, 2007)

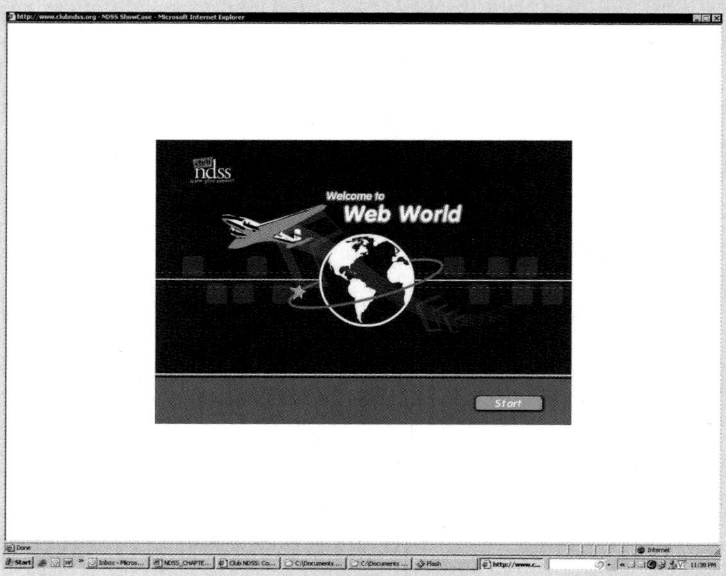

10.4 Data gathering for requirements

The overall purpose of data gathering in the requirements activity is to collect sufficient, relevant, and appropriate data so that a set of stable requirements can be produced. Even if a set of initial requirements exists, data gathering will be required to expand, clarify, and confirm those initial requirements. Data gathering needs to cover a wide spectrum of issues because the different kinds of requirement we need to establish are quite varied, as we saw above. We need to find out about the tasks that users currently perform and their associated goals, the context in which the tasks are performed, and the rationale for the current situation.

You met three common forms of data gathering in Chapter 7: interviews, questionnaires, and observation. Below, we first consider how these three techniques are used in the requirements activity, and then we introduce two other techniques—studying documentation and researching similar products—and their use in establishing requirements. Box 10.5 describes a very different approach aimed at prompting inspiration rather than simple data gathering.

Box 10.5
An artist-designer approach to users

An alternative approach to understanding users and their needs was taken in a European Union-funded project called the Presence Project (Gaver *et al.*, 1999). This

work arose from research looking at novel interaction techniques to increase the presence of elderly people in their local community. Three different groups were studied: one in Oslo, Norway; one near Amsterdam, The Netherlands; and one near Pisa, Italy. One of the problems with designing for an unknown culture is that it can be difficult to understand or appreciate the needs of that culture. Rather than take a more traditional approach of questionnaires, interviews, or ethnographic studies, this project used "cultural probes." These probes consisted of a wallet containing a variety of items: eight to ten postcards, about seven maps, a disposable camera, a photo album, and a media diary (see Figure 10.4). The intent was for the recipients to look through the wallet and answer questions associated with certain probes that they contained, then to return the items directly to the researchers when they had finished with them.

The postcards had pictures on the front and questions on the back, and were pre-addressed and stamped so that they could be easily returned. Questions included "Please tell us a piece of advice or insight that has been important to you," "What place does art have in your life?," and "Tell us about your favorite device." The maps and associated inquiries were designed to find out about the participants' attitudes towards their environment. They were printed on various textured papers and were in the form of folding envelopes, also to facilitate their return. On local maps, participants were asked to mark sites where they would go to meet people, to be alone, to daydream, and where they would like to go, but can't. On a map of the world, they were asked to mark places where they had been.

Participants were asked to use the camera to take pictures of their home, what they will wear today (whenever 'today' was), the first person you see today, something desirable, and something boring. In the photo album they were asked to tell the researchers their story in pictures. The media diary was to record their use of television and radio.

The approach taken by these researchers was not to identify specific user needs but to seek inspiration that would lead to new opportunities, new pleasures, new forms of sociability, and new cultural forms. Hence they were seeking inspiration rather than requirements.

The probes were returned over a period of a month or so, at different rates and in different quantities for each group. The data were not analyzed *per se*, but the resulting designs reflect what the designers learned.

For the Dutch site, they proposed building a network of computer displays with which the elderly could help inhabitants communicate their values and attitudes about the culture.

For the Norwegians, they proposed that the elders should lead a community-wide conversation about social issues, publishing questions from the library that would be sent for public response to electronic systems in cafes, trams, or public spaces.

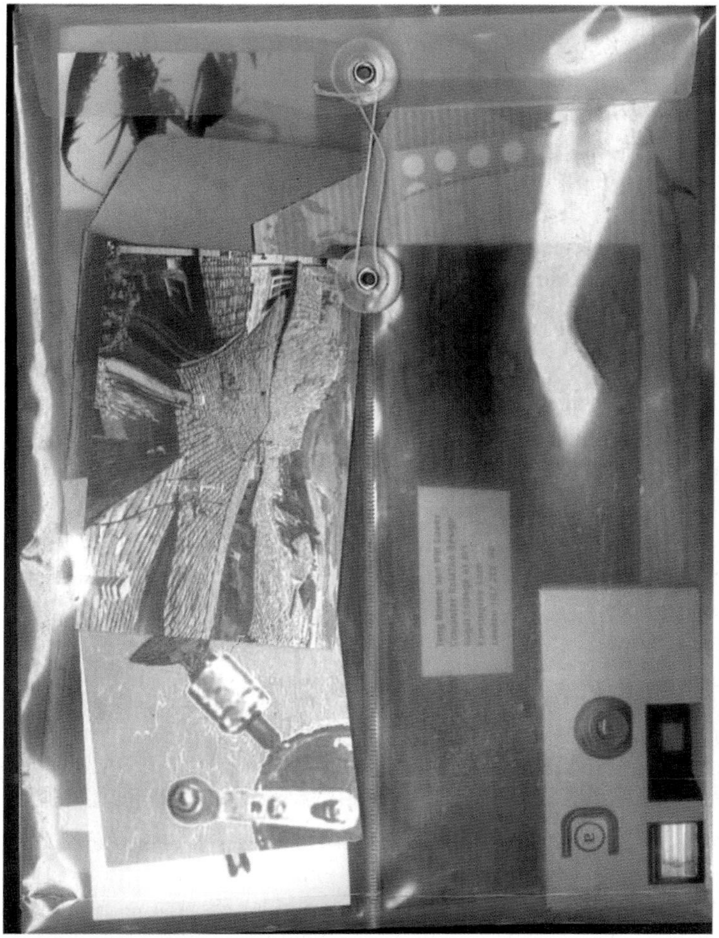

Figure 10.4 A cultural probe package

For the Italian village near Pisa, they plan to create social and pastoral radioscapes allowing them to create flexible communications networks and to listen to the surrounding countryside.

"What we learned about the elders is only half the story, however. The other half is what the elders learned from the probes. They provoked the groups to think about the roles they play and the pleasures they experience, hinting to them that our designs might suggest new roles and new experiences." (Gaver *et al.*, 1999, p. 29). ■

Interviews. Interviews are good at getting people to explore issues, and semi-structured or unstructured interviews are often used early on to elicit scenarios (see Section 10.6.1 below). In the context of establishing requirements, it is equally important for development team members to meet stakeholders and for users to feel involved. This on its own may be sufficient motivation to arrange interviews.

Focus groups. Focus groups are good at gaining a consensus view and highlighting areas of conflict and disagreement during the requirements activity. On a social level it also helps for stakeholders to meet designers and each other, and to express their views in public. It is not uncommon for one set of stakeholders to be unaware that their understanding of an issue or a process is different from another's even though they are in the same organization.

The generic idea of a focus group has been tailored for use within the requirements activity and requirements workshops have grown in popularity. The workshops themselves have been developed to have significant structure, evolving in some cases from the earlier JAD idea (see Chapter 9). This does not mean that each requirements workshop is the same, but the workshop structure is carefully planned attendees are carefully chosen, and specific deliverables are produced. Gottesdiener (2002) suggests a very useful, practical approach to requirements workshops that emphasizes planning and deliverables but also collaboration and facilitation. Another form of workshop that has emerged to help identify requirements is described in Box 10.6.

Box 10.6
Future technology workshops

Future Technology Workshops (FTWs) encourage users to postulate future uses of technology and provide a transition from current to future thinking. It is an example of a structured workshop designed to elicit requirements and to inspire users' participation in design. FTWs use props that encourage play and construction, such as modeling clay, paper, glue, sequins, wool, and pins; catalogs of existing relevant technologies are also available. An FTW lasts for a day and is broken down into seven sessions:

- ***Session 1 — Imagineering (10–15 minutes).*** **This first session is a brainstorm to identify a set of new activities that people would like to be able to perform in the future, based around the design task at hand. The purpose of the session is to set the scene and get the participants to think in terms of the future, with respect to both the technology and the needs satisfied by it.**

- *Session 2 — Modeling (40–50 minutes).* The participants are divided into groups, asked to select some of the ideas from the first session, and build a model that will demonstrate how the relevant activities are performed. The focus for this session is on future activities performed using futuristic, envisioned technology. Figure 10.5 illustrates a model built by children aged 13–14 during a session to envisage new ways of interacting with images. This photograph shows the children's designed examples of future imaging technology—a 'SpyCam' (an unobtrusive wireless camera that you could wear and would allow other people to view on a remote screen what you are seeing) and a 'RoboCam' (a tiny wireless camera that could be attached to a pet or a toy car).
- *Session 3 — Role Play (30 minutes).* The groups are asked to exchange models and then devise and enact a scenario demonstrating how the model might be used. The purpose of this session is to get participants to act as if the future technologies were already available to help them perform futuristic activities, and to make the participants' ideas of their envisioned designs more tangible.
- *Session 4 — Retrofit (30 minutes).* The groups are asked to modify their scenarios so that they use only existing technologies. The purpose of this session is explore new activities that existing technologies might support.
- *Session 5 — Everyday (10–15 minutes).* The group is asked to discuss how existing technology is used to perform current activities and to identify relevant problems and shortcomings of the existing technologies.
- *Session 6 — Futurefit (50–60 minutes).* The group is asked to look at the current activities and problems that were produced in the previous session and discuss how they think those current activities will be performed in the future. The facilitator prompts them to think in relation to the models they had built earlier.
- *Session 7 — Requirements (15–20 minutes).* The whole group is asked to produce a set of requirements for each model, based on their experience of the previous sessions and their needs.

From the initial workshop held to investigate new digital imaging technologies shown in Figure 10.5, a working prototype of the SpyCam was produced. Figure 10.6 shows a child wearing the wireless SpyCam attached to a pair of glasses. She is wearing a blindfold and the other children are guiding her by watching the image from her SpyCam on a remote screen and giving her directions through a walkie talkie. ■

(Vavoula *et al.*, 2002; Vavoula and Sharples, 2003)

Figure 10.5 An example model built during an FTW to envisage new ways of interacting with images

Figure 10.6 A working prototype produced from the ideas generated in an initial FTW

Questionnaires. Questionnaires may be used for getting initial responses that can then be analyzed to choose people to interview or to get a wider perspective on particular issues that have arisen elsewhere. For example, a questionnaire might be used in order to gauge whether a new university helpline would be welcomed by students. This questionnaire could ask for impressions and opinions about current support services and whether the respondent is prepared to be interviewed further. Or the questionnaire might be used to get opinions and views about specific suggestions for the kind of help that would be most appreciated.

Direct observation. In the requirements activity, observation of participants in their natural setting is used to understand the nature of the tasks and the context in which they are performed. Sometimes the observation is carried out by trained observers who record their findings and report them back to the design team, and sometimes the observation is carried out by or with a member of the design team.

Indirect observation. Diaries and interaction logging are used less often within the requirements activity. Interaction logging on an existing system may be used to provide some data about how a task is performed currently, but the information is too tightly coupled with details of the existing computer support to be particularly helpful if a completely new system is planned.

Studying documentation. Manuals and other documentation are a good source of data about the steps involved in an activity and any regulations governing a task. Such documentation should not be used as the only source, however, as everyday practices may augment them and may have been devised by those concerned to make the procedures work in a practical setting. Taking a user-centered view of development means that we are interested in the everyday practices rather than an idealized account.

Studying documentation is good for understanding legislation and getting some background information on the work. It also doesn't involve stakeholder time, which is a limiting factor on the other techniques.

Researching similar products. In Chapter 9 we talked about looking at similar products in order to generate alternative designs. Another reason to look at similar products is to help prompt requirements. For example, when developing an image editor for a mobile device, Kangas and Kinnunen (2005) report that they looked at PC image editing software in order to gain an understanding of the kinds of features and interaction that such a package might offer. Similarly, Chisnell and Brown (2004) performed competitive evaluation of other health plan websites to see what they were doing.

The choice of data gathering techniques for the requirements activity is influenced by several factors including the nature of the task, the participants, the analyst, and the resources available (see Chapter 7 for a more detailed discussion of these factors). It is usual for more than one data gathering technique to be used in order to triangulate the findings. For example, observation to understand the context of task performance, interviews to target specific user groups, questionnaires to reach a wider population, and focus groups to build a consensus view. There is no 'right' choice or combination as this will depend on the specific circumstances and resources. Many different combinations are used in practice. Box 10.7 provides examples of just some of these. Note that some examples include evaluating prototypes as part of the requirements activity. This serves to highlight the close relationship between requirements, design, and evaluation, as illustrated in our interaction design process in Chapter 9—the distinction between these phases is blurred and depends mainly on emphasis.

Box 10.7
Combining data gathering in requirements activities

Diary and interview. **Jones *et al.* (2004) were investigating location-aware community systems, and as they wanted to explore people's personal experiences of everyday activities, they felt that a diary study would be appropriate. Informants were asked to enter where they were and what they were doing every 30 minutes for a day. The diary entries were analyzed and then semi-structured interviews were conducted in order to probe the participants further, asking them to elaborate on the diaries.**

Ethnographic interviews, focus groups with props, and questionnaires. **Stevens *et al.* (2003) report the research and design of a system called the Living Memory Box (see Figure 10.7) for collecting, archiving, and annotating memories of family life. Initially they focused on parents wanting to save memories of their children growing up. They conducted ethnographic interviews with 13 parents of children ranging from four weeks to 29 years old. Parents felt that current storage methods are inadequate, despite the different media available to save memories, e.g. video, audio, artwork, etc., and that there is a lack of storage facilities for anything other than physical objects, e.g. photo albums. Findings from the interviews included: remove the work from collecting, annotating, and revisiting memories; make the inclusion of physical objects a primary feature; develop natural interaction, e.g. voice and touch; enable storytelling so that the memory can be saved intact.**

The team used visual models and scenarios to develop the design. This helped them to develop prototypes which were taken to a set of focus groups. The week before attending the focus group, participants were asked to answer a set of questions with pictures or words. These questions focused on the participants' current memorabilia and their storage. In the focus groups, participants were asked about their answers and the prototype system was demonstrated. At the end of the two-hour session feedback was elicited through discussion and via a questionnaire.

Figure 10.7 The Living Memory Box

Documentation, interview, online survey, group discussion. Oostveen and van den Besselaar (2004) describe the development of a smart-card-based system that would support mobile European citizens in achieving various administrative transactions between countries. For example, moving from one country to another requires a set of bureaucratic operations to be performed, largely concerned with exchanging documentation. This system would enable the citizen to download the required information onto a smart card and use this electronic 'document' in the new country. In-depth interviews with expatriates from different countries allowed them to catalog the problems mobile Europeans encounter. Interviews with civil servants and various intermediaries whose jobs involve helping such people were also held. In order to check the relevance of the interview results to a wider set of potential users, they then set up an online survey. The administrative processes were investigated through group discussions which were held in different countries between technology designers and administrative experts; potential solutions were also discussed in these workshops. Documentation was studied to underpin the other requirements activities.

Focus groups, interviews, and evaluations. **Liu *et al.* (2005) report on some research into expanding the use of ATMs in China. This study was conducted in order to identify factors that might affect requirements for ATM design, identify problems or issues with current ATMs in China, and identify appropriate ways in which to increase adoption. They used three different approaches to data gathering: focus groups were used to share good and bad experiences of ATM use, interviews were carried out in a shopping center with 100 participants to find out how widely applicable the findings were from the focus groups, and evaluations of existing ATMs were conducted to uncover confusions and error rates.** ■

10.4.1 Contextual inquiry

Contextual inquiry (Holtzblatt and Jones, 1993) is one of seven parts of contextual design (Beyer and Holtzblatt, 1998), which is a structured approach to the collection and interpretation of data from fieldwork with the intention of building a software-based product. Contextual design involves the production of five different models of work.

We include contextual inquiry in this chapter as it is a popular technique for uncovering requirements, and in particular in uncovering requirements relating to the context of use. It is not always used along with the complete contextual design method, and in addition focused contextual inquiry sessions can be conducted more rapidly than extensive user research. For example, Kangas and Kinnunen (2005) conducted interviews with only six to eight people before moving to create a prototype for their mobile application.

Contextual inquiry is an approach that emerged from the ethnographic approach to data gathering. It is tailored to gather data that can be used in design and it follows an apprenticeship model: the designer works as an apprentice to the user. The most typical format for contextual inquiry is a contextual interview, which is a combination of observation, discussion, and reconstruction of past events. Contextual inquiry rests on four main principles: context, partnership, interpretation, and focus.

The context principle emphasizes the importance of going to the workplace and seeing what happens. The partnership principle states that the developer and the user should collaborate in understanding the work; in a traditional interviewing or workshop situation, the interviewer or workshop leader is in control, but in contextual inquiry the spirit of partnership means that the understanding is developed through cooperation.

The interpretation principle says that the observations must be interpreted in order to be used in design, and this interpretation should also be developed in cooperation between the user and the developer. For example, I have a set of paper cards stuck on my screen at work. They are covered in notes; some list telephone numbers and some list commands for the software I use. Someone coming into my office might interpret these facts in a number of ways: that I don't have access to a telephone directory; that I don't have a user manual for my software; that I use the software infrequently; that the commands are particularly difficult to remember. The best way to interpret these observations is to discuss them with me. In fact, I do have a telephone directory, but I keep the numbers on a note to save me the trouble of looking them up in the directory. I also have a telephone with a memory, but it isn't clear to me how to put the numbers in memory, so I use the notes instead. The commands are there because I often forget them and waste time searching through menu structures.

The fourth principle, the focus principle, is related to our discussions in Chapter 7 about keeping the data gathering focused on your goals. In contextual inquiry, as in an unstructured interview, for example, it is easy for the discussion to wander off target. To help avoid this, a project focus is established to guide the interviewer, which will then be augmented by the individual's own focus that arises from their perspective and background.

Activity 10.2

How does the contextual inquiry interview compare with the interviews introduced in Chapter 7?

Comment

We introduced structured, unstructured, and semi-structured interviews in Chapter 7. Contextual inquiry could be viewed as an unstructured interview, but it has other characteristics not normal for an unstructured interview. A contextual inquiry interview is conducted at the interviewee's place of work, while normal work continues. Contextual inquiry specifically incorporates other data gathering techniques as well, such as observation.

Normally, each member of the team developing the interactive product conducts at least one contextual inquiry session. Data is collected in the form of notes and perhaps audio and video recording, but a lot of information is in the observer's head. It is important to review the experience and to start documenting the findings as soon as possible after the session. Contextual inquiry is usually followed by an interpretation session in which a number of models are generated: an affinity diagram, the work flow model, the sequence model, the artifact model, the cultural model, and the physical model. More detail about these models and how to generate them is in Beyer and Holtzblatt (1998).

10.4.2 Data gathering guidelines for requirements

General advice for data gathering was given in Chapter 7, but there are a few more specific guidelines worthy of note when gathering data for requirements.

- Focus on identifying the stakeholders' needs. This may be achieved by studying their existing behavior and support tools, or by looking at other products, such as a competitor's product or an earlier release of your product under development.
- Involve all the stakeholder groups. It is very important to make sure that you get the views of all the right people. This may seem an obvious comment, but it is easy to overlook certain sections of the stakeholder population if you're not careful. We were told about one case where a large distribution and logistics company reimplemented their software systems and were very careful to involve all the clerical, managerial, and warehouse staff in their development process, but on the day the system went live, the productivity of the operation fell by 50%. On investigation it was found that the bottleneck was not in their own company, but in the suppliers' warehouses that had to interact with the new system. No one had asked them how they worked, and the new system was incompatible with their working routines.
- Involving only one representative from each stakeholder group is not enough, especially if the group is large. Everyone you involve in data gathering will have their own perspective on the situation, the task, their job, and how others interact with them. If you only involve one representative stakeholder then you will only get a narrow view.
- Support the data gathering sessions with suitable props, such as task descriptions and prototypes if available. Since the requirements activity is iterative, prototypes or descriptions generated during one session may be reused or revisited in another with the same or a different set of stakeholders. Using props will help to jog people's memories and act as a focus for discussions.

10.5 Data analysis, interpretation, and presentation

Methods and approaches for analysis, interpretation, and presentation of data were discussed in Chapter 8. These are applicable during the requirements activity. However, the aim here is to structure and record descriptions of requirements. Using a format such as the Volere shell (Figure 10.8) highlights the kinds of information to look for and is a good first step in data analysis for requirements. Note that many of the entries are concerned with traceability. For example, who raised the requirement and where can more information about it be found. This information may be captured in documents or in diagrams drawn during analysis. Providing links with raw data as captured on video or audio recordings can be harder, although just as important. Haumer *et al.* (2000) have developed a tool that records concrete scenarios using video, speech, and graphic media, and relates these recorded observations to elements of a corresponding design. This helps designers to keep track of context and usage information while analyzing and designing for the system.

In parallel with producing Volere shells, the different kinds of requirements will start to emerge. These are best investigated using other, more formal techniques and notations. For example, functional requirements have traditionally been analyzed and documented

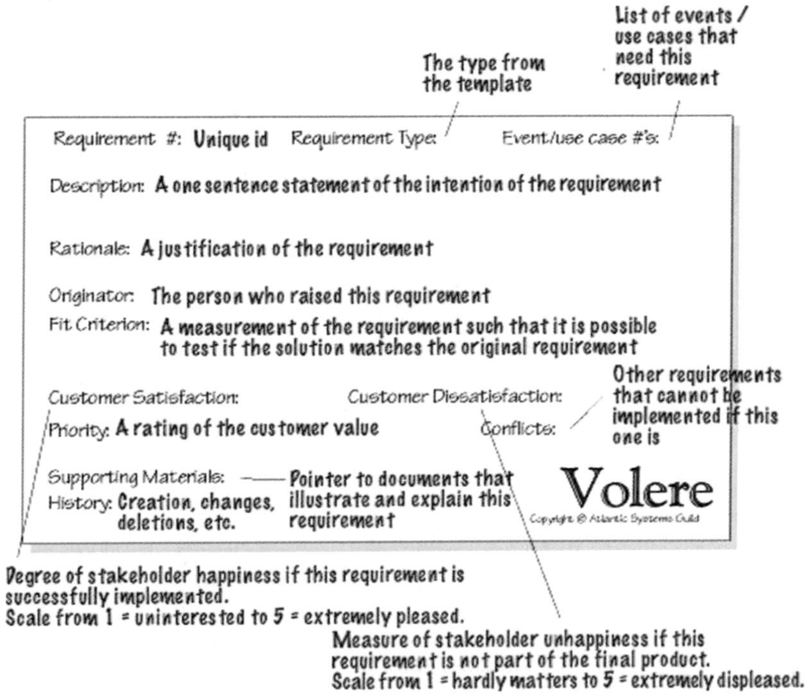
List of events / use cases that need this requirement
The type from the template
Requirement #: Unique id
Requirement Type:
Event/use case #'s:
Description: A one sentence statement of the intention of the requirement
Rationale: A justification of the requirement
Originator: The person who raised this requirement
Fit Criterion: A measurement of the requirement such that it is possible to test if the solution matches the original requirement
Other requirements that cannot be implemented if this one is
Customer Satisfaction:
Customer Dissatisfaction:
Priority: A rating of the customer value
Conflicts:
Supporting Materials:
Pointer to documents that illustrate and explain this requirement
History: Creation, changes, deletions, etc.
Volere
Copyright © Atlantic Systems Guild
Degree of stakeholder happiness if this requirement is successfully implemented.
Scale from 1 = uninterested to 5 = extremely pleased.
Measure of stakeholder unhappiness if this requirement is not part of the final product.
Scale from 1 = hardly matters to 5 = extremely displeased.

Figure 10.8 *The Volere shell for requirements*

using data-flow diagrams, state charts, work-flow charts, etc. (see, e.g. Sommerville, 2006). Data requirements can be expressed using entity-relationship diagrams, for example. If the development is to take an object-oriented approach, then functional and data requirements are combined in class diagrams, with behavior being expressed in state charts and sequence diagrams, among others. Examples of two such diagrams representing a portion of a holiday booking system are given in Figure 10.9. These diagrams can be linked to the requirements through the "Event/use case" field in the shell in Figure 10.8.

We don't go into the detail of how specialized diagrams such as these might be developed, as whole books are dedicated to them. Instead, we describe four techniques that have a user-centered focus and are used to understand users' goals and tasks: scenarios, use cases, essential use cases, and task analysis. All of them may be produced as a result of data gathering sessions, and their output used as props in subsequent data gathering sessions.

The requirements activity is iterated a number of times before a set of stable requirements evolves. As more analysis techniques are applied, a deeper understanding of requirements will emerge and the requirements descriptions will expand and clarify.

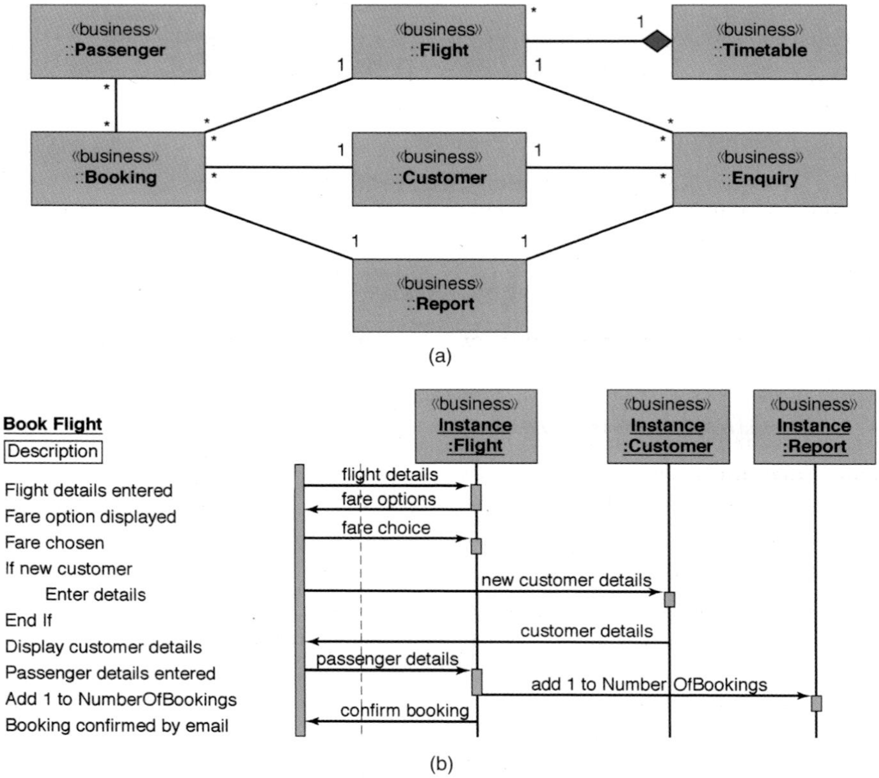

Figure 10.9 *(a) Class diagram and (b) sequence diagram that might be used to analyze and capture static structure and dynamic behavior (respectively) if the system is being developed using an object-oriented approach*

Dilemma
How formal should your notation be?

Many forms of notation are used in design activities. Each discipline has its own set of symbols, graphs, and mnemonics that communicate precisely and clearly among people from the same discipline. But, in the early stages of design, designers are well known for their 'back-of-an-envelope' sketches that capture the essence of an idea. At what stage should these sketches be transformed into more formal notations?

When we have identified needs and established requirements, they must be documented somehow. Whether this is in a purely textual form, or in prototypical form, or more formal box and line notations, or a programming language, our findings need to be captured. When Verplank (1994) speaks about producing software-based prototypes, he talks emphatically about the importance of allowing ideas to flourish before they are formalized in the computer medium. Once cast in this way, we "get sucked into thinking that the design already works and all we have to do is fix it." The same could be said of formal paper-based notations. In interaction design, we have many notations to choose from, arising from the various disciplines that underpin our field (see Figure 1.4). How quickly should we formalize our ideas in structured notation, and for how long should we leave the ideas fluid and flexible?

A counterargument to Verplank's position is that trying to write our findings in a more structured fashion also helps us to understand better what we've found and what's missing. The problem is that any notation has its strengths and weaknesses, and we must be aware of these when we commit our ideas to a specific notation so that our thinking and our ideas don't become too influenced by the foibles of the notation itself.

Yet again, there is also a question of who the requirements are being captured for. If users are to read and understand them, then the notation shouldn't contain technical jargon or symbols. On the other hand, if it is for communicating precise meaning within a team of developers, a more formal, specialized notation may be more appropriate.

Choosing the medium for the message can affect how the message is received and hence the meaning that is communicated, so it's important to get the medium right. ■

10.5.1 Brainstorming for innovation

So far we have focused on how requirements may emerge directly from the data gathered. However, establishing a suitable set of requirements is likely to also involve innovation. Brainstorming is not a technique specific to interaction design, or to any other discipline, and is a generic technique used to generate, refine, and develop ideas. It is widely used in interaction design specifically for generating alternative designs (as discussed in Chapter 9) or for suggesting new and better ideas for supporting users.

Various 'rules' have been suggested for making a brainstorming session successful, some of which we list below. For requirements, two key success factors are firstly that the participants should know the users' goals that the product is to support, and secondly that no ideas should be criticized or debated (Robertson and Robertson, 2006; Kelley, 2001). Some other suggestions for successful requirements brainstorms are:

1. Include participants from a wide range of disciplines, with a broad range of experience (Robertson and Robertson, 2006; Kelley, 2001).
2. Don't ban 'silly stuff' (Kelley, 2001). Unconventional ideas often turn into really useful requirements (Robertson and Robertson, 2006).
3. Use catalysts for further inspiration. Build one idea on top of another (Robertson and Robertson, 2006). Kelley (2001) also suggests jumping back to an earlier idea, or considering alternative interpretations when energy levels start to flag. If you get stuck, use a word pulled randomly from a dictionary to prompt ideas related to the product (Robertson and Robertson, 2006).
4. Keep records. Robertson and Robertson (2006) suggest that every idea should be captured, without censoring. Kelley (2001) suggests that you number them so that you can jump around and refer back to ideas more easily. He also suggests that the walls and tables in the room be covered in paper and that participants be encouraged to sketch, mind-map, and diagram ideas, including keeping the flow of ideas, as spatial memory is very strong and this can facilitate recall.
5. Sharpen the focus (Kelley, 2001). Start the brainstorm with a well-honed problem. This will get the brainstorm off to a good start and makes it easier to pull people back to the main topic if the session wanders.
6. Use warm-up exercises. The group will require 'warming up' if they haven't worked together before, most of the group don't brainstorm regularly, or the group is distracted by other pressures (Kelley, 2001). Warm-up exercises might take the form of word games, or the exploration of physical items related or unrelated with the problem at hand. For example, see the use of the TechBox discussed in Chapter 9.

10.6 Task description

Descriptions of business tasks have been used within software development for many years. During the 1970s and 1980s, 'business scenarios' were commonly used as the basis for acceptance testing, i.e. the last testing stage before the customer paid the final fee installment and 'accepted' the system. In more recent years, due to the emphasis on involving users earlier in the development lifecycle and the large number of new interactive products now being developed, task descriptions are used throughout development, from early requirements activities through prototyping, evaluation, and testing. Consequently, more time and effort has been put into understanding how best to structure and use them.

As shown by Alexander and Maiden's (2004) collection of scenarios, stories, and use cases, there are many different flavors of task descriptions, and they can be used for different purposes, emphasizing different elements of the product being developed. For example, Alexander and Maiden use a structuring framework that distinguishes task descriptions according to four views which are made up of nine facets including method of description (e.g. text, graphics, image or prototype, and formal, informal, or semi-formal notation), context (e.g. organizational environment and system interaction), and role (descriptive, exploratory, or explanatory).

We shall introduce three of the more common description types here: scenarios, use cases, and essential use cases. Each of these may be used to describe either existing tasks or envisioned tasks with a new product. They are not mutually exclusive and are often used in combination to capture different perspectives or to document different stages during the development lifecycle.

In this section and the next, we use two main examples to illustrate the application of techniques. These are a library catalog service and a shared travel organizer. The library catalog is similar to any you might find in a public or university library, and allows you to access the details of books held in the library: for example, to search for books by a particular author, or by subject, to identify the location of a book you want to borrow, and to check on a member's current loans and status.

The shared travel organizer is to support a group of people in exploring a joint holiday. This might be used by groups of friends or family members and could be located in a travel agent's office or other public space. The travel organizer would help the users to explore different kinds of destination, travel, and accommodation options, offer advice for visa and vaccination requirements, and identify a set of possible holidays that meet the group's requirements.

10.6.1 Scenarios

A scenario is an "informal narrative description" (Carroll, 2000). It describes human activities or tasks in a story that allows exploration and discussion of contexts, needs, and requirements. It does not explicitly describe the use of software or other technological support to achieve a task. Using the vocabulary and phrasing of users means that the scenarios can be understood by the stakeholders, and they are able to participate fully in the development process. In fact, the construction of scenarios by stakeholders is often the first step in establishing requirements.

Imagine that you have just been invited along to talk to a group of users who perform data entry for a university admissions office. You walk in, and are greeted by Sandy, the supervisor, who starts by saying something like:

> ***Well, this is where the admissions forms arrive. We receive about 50 a day during the peak application period. Brian here opens the forms and checks that they are complete, that is, that all the documentation has been included. You see, we require copies of relevant school exam results or evidence of work experience before we can process the application. Depending on the result of this initial inspection, the forms get passed to . . .***

Telling stories is a natural way for people to explain what they are doing or how to achieve something. It is therefore something that stakeholders can easily relate to. The focus of such stories is also naturally likely to be about what the users are trying to achieve, i.e. their goals. Understanding why people do things as they do and what they are trying to achieve in the process allows us to concentrate on the human activity rather than interaction with technology.

This is not to say that the human activity should be preserved and reflected in any new product we are trying to develop, but understanding what people do now is a good starting point for exploring the constraints, contexts, irritations, facilitators, and so on under which the humans operate. It also allows us to identify the stakeholders and the products involved in the activity. Repeated reference to a particular form, book, behavior, or location indicates that this is somehow central to the activity being performed and that we should take care to understand what it is and the role it plays.

A scenario that might be generated by potential users of a library catalog service is given below:

> ***Say I want to find a book by George Jeffries. I don't remember the title but I know it was published before 1995. I go to the catalog and enter my user password. I don't understand why I have to do this, since I can't get into the library to use the catalog without passing through security gates. However, once my password has been confirmed, I am given a choice of searching by author or by date, but not the combination of author and date. I tend to choose the author option because the date search usually identifies too many entries. After about 30 seconds the catalog returns saying that there are no entries for George Jeffries and showing me the list of entries closest to the one I've sought. When I see the list, I realize that in fact I got the author's first name wrong and it's Gregory, not George. I choose the entry I want and the system displays the location to tell me where to find the book.***

In this limited scenario of existing system use, there are some things of note: the importance of getting the author's name right, the annoyance concerning the need to enter a password, the lack of flexible search possibilities, and the usefulness of showing a list of similar entries when an exact match isn't clear. These are all indicators of potential design choices for the new catalog system. The scenario also tells us one (possibly common) use of the catalog system: to search for a book by an author when we don't know the title.

The level of detail present in a scenario varies depending on where in the development process they are being used. During requirements it is a good idea for scenarios to emphasize the context, the usability and user experience goals, and the tasks the user is performing. The inclusion of dramatic or emotional elements in scenarios has been found to increase software developers' understanding of context (Strøm, 2006). When used in combination with detailed personas, this kind of scenario can improve the developers' appreciation of the user experience.

Often scenarios are generated during workshop, interview, or brainstorming sessions to help explain or discuss some aspect of the user's goals. They can be used to imagine potential uses of a product as well as to capture existing behavior. They are not intended to capture a full set of requirements, but are a very personalized account, offering only one perspective.

A longer scenario for the shared travel organizer that was elicited in an informal interview is included below. This describes how one function of the system might work:

to identify potential holiday options. Note that this scenario includes details about some typical users and their needs. This is the kind of information that you might glean from a requirements interview.

> *The Thomson family enjoy outdoor activity holidays and want to try their hand at sailing this year. There are four members of the family: Sky who is 10 years old, Eamonn who is 15 years old, Claire who is 35, and Will who is 40. While out on a shopping trip they call by at the travel agents in their local town to start exploring the possibilities, although they only have an hour to spare. The travel organizer is located in a quiet corner of the agents' office, where there are comfortable seats and play things for young children. They all gather around the organizer and enter their initial set of requirements — a sailing holiday for four novices. The stand-alone console is designed so that all members of the family can interact easily and comfortably with it. The system's initial suggestion is that they should consider a flotilla holiday, where several novice crews go sailing together and provide mutual support for first-time sailors. Sky and Eamonn aren't very happy at the idea of going on holiday with a group of other people and take some convincing that this would be good. The travel organizer shows them some descriptions of these holidays from other children their ages who have been on flotillas and they are all very positive. So eventually, they all agree that this would be a good idea, and accept this recommendation. The system then asks for various further details such as choice of destination. The Thomsons have been to the Mediterranean several times, and would like to return. The system confirms that there are several places in the Mediterranean that are suitable for first-time sailors and that flotilla holidays can be arranged there. As time is running short, Will suggests that they take the current suggestions away with them and consider them at home. The travel organizer prints out a summary of the different options they have considered, and the favorite suggestion so far.*

An example of a futuristic scenario, devised by Symbian, showing one vision of how wireless devices might be used in the future is shown in Figure 10.10.

A businesswoman traveling to Paris from the US
A businesswoman is traveling from San Francisco to Paris on a business trip.
Upon arrival at the airport, the location-sensitive Smartphone notifies the airline that she will be checking in shortly, and an airline employee immediately finds her and takes her baggage. Her on-screen display shows that her flight is on time and provides a map to her gate. On her way to the gate she downloads tourist information such as maps and events occurring in Paris during her stay.
Once she finds her seat on the plane, she begins to review all the information she has downloaded. She notices than an opera is playing in Paris that she has been wanting to see, and she books her ticket. Her Smartphone can make the booking using her credit card number, which it has stored in its memory. This means that she does not need to reenter the credit card number each time she uses wCommerce (i.e. wireless commerce), facilities. The security written into the software of the Smartphone protects her against fraud.
The Smartphone stores the opera booking along with several emails that she writes on the plane. As soon as she steps off the plane, the Smartphone makes the calls and automatically sends the emails.
As she leaves the airport, a map appears on her Smartphone's display, guiding her to her hotel.

***Figure 10.10** A scenario showing how two technologies, a Smartphone and wCommerce (wireless commerce), might be used*

In this chapter, we refer to scenarios only in their role of helping to establish requirements. They have a continuing role in the design process that we shall return to in Chapter 11. Indeed, as Alexander and Maiden (2004) show, scenarios have a role to play throughout the lifecycle, and Rosson and Carrol (2002) explain an approach called scenario-based usability engineering that illustrates the use of scenarios within a usability engineering framework.

Capturing scenarios of existing behavior and goals helps in determining new scenarios and hence in gathering data useful for establishing the new requirements. The next activity is intended to help you appreciate how a scenario of existing activity can help identify the requirements for a future application to support the same user goal.

Activity 10.3

Write a scenario of how you would currently go about choosing a new car. This should be a brand new car, not a second-hand car. Having written it, think about the important aspects of the task, your priorities and preferences. Then imagine a new interactive product that supports you in your goal and takes account of these issues. Write a futuristic scenario showing how this product would support you.

Comment

The following example is a fairly generic view of this process. Yours will be different, but you may have identified similar concerns and priorities.

> ***The first thing I would do is to observe cars on the road and identify ones that I like the look of. This may take some weeks. I would also try to identify any consumer reports that will include an assessment of car performance. Hopefully, these initial activities will result in me identifying a likely car to buy. The next stage will be to visit a car showroom and see at first hand what the car looks like, and how comfortable it is to sit in. If I still feel positive about the car, then I'll ask for a test drive. Even a short test drive helps me to understand how well the car handles, how noisy is the engine, how smooth are the gear changes, and so on. Once I've driven the car myself, I can usually tell whether I would like to own it or not.***

From this scenario, it seems that there are broadly two stages involved in the task: researching the different cars available, and gaining first-hand experience of potential purchases. In the former, observing cars on the road and getting actual and maybe critical information about them has been highlighted. In the latter, the test drive seems to be quite significant.

For many people buying a new car, the smell and touch of the car's exterior and interior, and the driving experience itself are often the most influential factors in choosing a particular model. Other more factual attributes such as fuel

consumption, amount of room inside, colors available, and price may rule out certain makes and models, but at the end of the day, cars are often chosen according to how easy they are to handle and how comfortable they are inside. This makes the test drive a vital part of the process of choosing a new car.

Taking these comments into account, we've come up with the following scenario describing how a new 'one-stop shop' for new cars might operate. This product makes use of immersive virtual reality technology that is already used for other applications such as designing buildings and training bomb disposal experts.

> *I want to buy a new car, so I go down the street to the local 'one-stop car shop.' The shop has a number of booths in it, and when I go in I'm directed to an empty booth. Inside there's a large seat that reminds me of a racing car seat, and in front of that a large display screen, keyboard, and printer. As I sit down, the display jumps into life. It offers me the options of browsing through video clips of new cars which have been released in the last two years, or of searching through video clips of cars by make, by model, or by year. I can choose as many of these as I like. I also have the option of searching through and reading or printing consumer reports that have been produced about the cars I'm interested in. I spend about an hour looking through materials and deciding that I'd like to experience a couple that look promising. I can of course go away and come back later, but I'd like to have a go with some of those I've found. By flicking a switch in my armrest, I can call up the options for virtual reality simulations for any of the cars I'm interested in. These are really great as they allow me to take the car for a test drive, simulating everything about the driving experience in this car, from road holding, to windscreen display, and front pedal pressure to dashboard layout. It even recreates the atmosphere of being inside the car.*

Note that the product includes support for the two research activities mentioned in the original scenario, as well as the important test drive facility. This would be only a first cut scenario, which would then be refined through discussion and further investigation.

Activity 10.4

What is the difference between a scenario and a persona?

Comment

A persona describes the attributes of a person and aspects of their personality. A scenario describes activities and context of use but can also include a 'day in the life' of a person.

CASE STUDY 10.2
Establishing Requirements for a mobile learning system

MobiLearn was a European-funded research and development project that explored new ways of using mobile environments to meet the needs of learners working by themselves and with others. It developed a new m-learning architecture to support the creation, brokerage, delivery, and tracking of learning and information content, using ambient intelligence, location-dependence, personalization, multimedia, instant messaging (text, video), and distributed databases. Establishing the requirements for such a project was a complex task, involving many methods and notations.

MobiLearn revolved around three different learning scenarios: one focused on museum visitors, one focused on MBA students, and one focused on first aid workers. Data to establish the requirements was gathered using FTWs (see Box 10.6), questionnaires, direct observation, and interviews. The requirements were captured using the Volere shell but the project team found that the shell needed to be tailored by adding two fields: title and status.

This case study explains the project's use of scenarios and the Volere shell to document and evolve a set of requirements. It also discusses some of the issues faced by large distributed project teams.

10.6.2 Use cases

Use cases also focus on user goals, but the emphasis here is on a user–system interaction rather than the user's task itself. They were originally introduced through the object-oriented community in the book *Object-Oriented Software Engineering* (Jacobson *et al.*, 1992). Although their focus is specifically on the interaction between the user (called an 'actor') and a software system, the stress is still very much on the user's perspective, not the system's. The term 'scenario' is also used in the context of use cases. In this context, it represents one path through the use case, i.e. one particular set of conditions. This meaning is consistent with the definition given above in that they both represent one specific example of behavior.

A use case is associated with an actor, and it is the actor's goal in using the system that the use case wants to capture. In this technique, the main use case describes what is called the 'normal course,' i.e. the set of actions that the analyst believes to be most commonly performed. So, for example, if through data gathering we have found that most users of the library go to the catalog to check the location of a book before going to the shelves, then the normal course for the use case would include this sequence of events. Other possible sequences, called alternative courses, are then listed at the bottom of the use case.

A use case for retrieving the visa requirements using the travel organizer, with the normal course being that information about the visa requirements is available, might be:

1. The system displays options for investigating visa and vaccination requirements.
2. The user chooses the option to find out about visa requirements.
3. The system prompts user for the name of the destination country.
4. The user enters the country's name.
5. The system checks that the country is valid.
6. The system prompts the user for her nationality.
7. The user enters her nationality.
8. The system checks the visa requirements of the entered country for a passport holder of her nationality.
9. The system displays the visa requirements.
10. The system displays the option to print out the visa requirements.
11. The user chooses to print the requirements.

Alternative courses:

6. If the country name is invalid:
   6.1 The system displays an error message.
   6.2 The system returns to step 3.
8. If the nationality is invalid:
   8.1 The system displays an error message.
   8.2 The system returns to step 6.
9. If no information about visa requirements is found:
   9.1 The system displays a suitable message.
   9.2 The system returns to step 1.

Note that the number associated with the alternative course indicates the step in the normal course that is replaced by this action or set of actions. Also note how specific the use case is about how the user and the system will interact.

Use cases may be described graphically. Figure 10.11 shows the use case diagram for the travel organizer example. The actor 'Travel agent' is associated with the use case 'Update holiday details.' Another actor for the travel organizer is the 'Holidaymaker,' such as the Thomson family members above. Actors may be associated with more than one use case, so for example the actor 'Holidaymaker' is associated with a use case 'Identify potential holiday options' as well as the 'Retrieve visa requirements' use case. Each use case may also be associated with more than one actor. Note that an actor represents a role, so when Jasmine, who works for the travel agency, is looking for holidays for herself, she adopts the actor role of Holidaymaker, but in her role as travel agent she will adopt the Travel agent actor role.

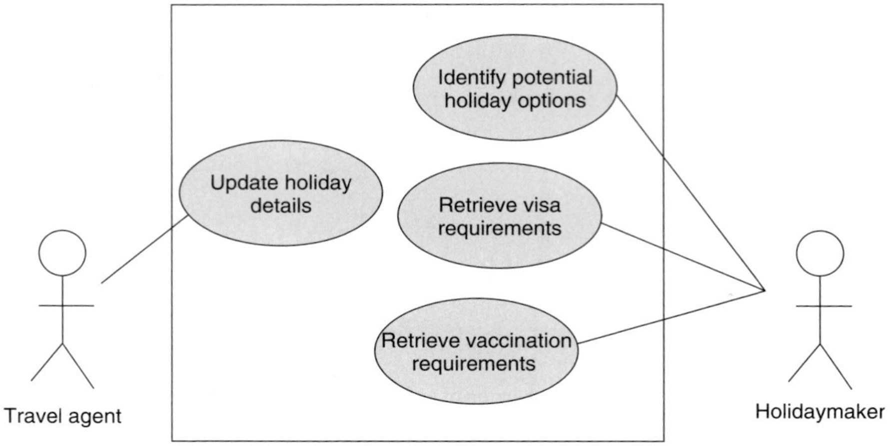

Figure 10.11 *Use case diagram for the travel organizer showing four use cases and two actors*

This kind of description has a different style and a different focus from the scenarios described in Section 10.6.1. The layout is more formal, and the structure of 'good' use cases has been discussed by many, e.g. Cockburn (2000); Bittner and Spence (2002); Ben Achour (1999). The description also focuses on the user–system interaction rather than on the user's activities; thus a use case presupposes that technology is being used. This kind of detail is more useful at conceptual design stage than during requirements or data gathering, but use cases have been found to help some stakeholders express their views on how existing systems are used and how a new system might work.

To develop a use case, first identify the actors, i.e. the people or other systems that will be interacting with the system under development. Then examine these actors and identify their goal or goals in using the system. Each of these will be a use case.

Activity 10.5

Consider the example of the library catalog service. One use case is 'Locate book,' and this would be associated with the 'Library member' actor.

1. **Identify one other main actor and an associated use case, and draw a use case diagram for the library catalog system.**
2. **Write out the use case for 'Locate book' including the normal and some alternative courses. You may assume that the normal course is for users to**

go to the catalog to find the location, and that the most common path to find this is through a search by author.

Comment

1. One other main actor is the 'Librarian.' A use case for the 'Librarian' would be 'Update catalog.' Figure 10.12 is the associated use case diagram. There are other use cases you may have identified.
2. The use case for 'Locate book' might be something like this:
   1. The system prompts for user name and password.
   2. The user enters his or her user name and password into the catalog system.
   3. The system verifies the user's password.
   4. The system displays a menu of choices.
   5. The user chooses to locate book.
   6. The system displays the search menu.
   7. The user chooses to search by author.
   8. The system displays the search author screen.
   9. The user enters the author's name.
   10. The system displays search results.
   11. The user chooses the required book.
   12. The system displays details of chosen book.
   13. The user notes location.
   14. The user quits catalog system.

Alternative courses:

4. If user password is not valid:
   - 4.1 The system displays error message.
   - 4.2 The system returns to step 1.
5. If user knows the book details:
   - 5.1 The user chooses to enter book details.
   - 5.2 The system displays book details screen.
   - 5.3 The user enters book details.
   - 5.4 The system goes to step 12.

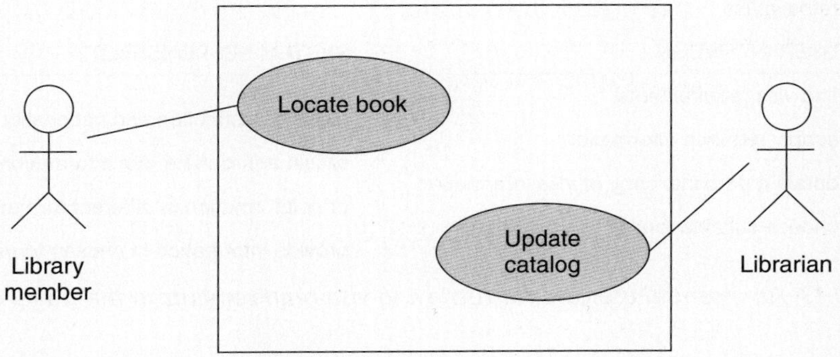

Figure 10.12 Use case diagram for the library catalog service

10.6.3 Essential use cases

Essential use cases were developed by Constantine and Lockwood (1999) to combat what they see as the limitations of both scenarios and use cases as described above. Scenarios are concrete stories that concentrate on realistic and specific activities. They therefore can obscure broader issues concerned with the wider organizational view. On the other hand, traditional use cases contain certain assumptions, including the fact that there is a piece of technology to interact with, and also assumptions about the user interface and the kind of interaction to be designed.

Essential use cases represent abstractions from scenarios, i.e. they represent a more general case than a scenario embodies, and try to avoid the assumptions of a traditional use case. An essential use case is a structured narrative consisting of three parts: a name that expresses the overall user intention, a stepped description of user actions, and a stepped description of system responsibility. This division between user and system responsibilities can be very helpful during conceptual design when considering task allocation and system scope, i.e. what the user is responsible for and what the system is to do.

An example essential use case based on the visa requirements example given above is shown in Figure 10.13. Note that the steps are more generalized than those in the use case in Section 10.6.2, while they are more structured than the scenario in Section 10.6.1. For example, the second user intention does not say anything about choosing options or system prompts, it simply states that the user supplies the required information. This could be achieved in a variety of ways including scanning a passport, accessing a database of personal information based on fingerprint recognition, and so on. The point is that at the time of creating this essential use case, there is no commitment to a particular interaction design. Essential use cases would normally be developed before the more detailed use case.

retrieveVisa

USER INTENTION	SYSTEM RESPONSIBILITY
find visa requirements	
	request destination and nationality
supply required information	
	obtain appropriate visa information
obtain a personal copy of visa information	
	offer information in different formats
choose suitable format	
	provide information in chosen format

***Figure 10.13** An essential use case for retrieving visa requirements in the travel organizer*

Instead of actors, essential use cases are associated with user roles. One of the differences is that an actor could be another system, whereas a user role is just that: not a particular person, and not another system, but a role that a number of different people may play when using the system. Just as with actors, though, producing an essential use case begins with identifying user roles.

Activity 10.6

Construct an essential use case 'locateBook' for the user role 'Library member' of the library catalog service discussed in Activity 10.5.

Comment

Note here that we don't talk about passwords, but merely state that the users need to identify themselves. This could be done using fingerprinting, or retinal scanning, or any other suitable technology. The essential use case does not commit us to technology at this point. Neither does it specify search options or details of how to initiate the search.

locateBook

USER INTENTION	SYSTEM RESPONSIBILITY
identify self	
	verify identity
	request appropriate details
offer known details	
	offer search results
note search results	
quit system	
	close

10.7 Task analysis

Task analysis is used mainly to investigate an existing situation, not to envision new products. It is used to analyze the underlying rationale and purpose of what people are doing: what are they trying to achieve, why are they trying to achieve it, and how are they going about it? The information gleaned from task analysis establishes a foundation of existing practices on which to build new requirements or to design new tasks.

Task analysis is an umbrella term that covers techniques for investigating cognitive processes and physical actions, at a high level of abstraction and in minute detail. In practice, task analysis techniques have had a mixed reception. The most widely used version is Hierarchical Task Analysis (HTA), and this is the technique we introduce in this chapter. Another well-known task analysis technique called GOMS (Goals, Operations, Methods, and Selection rules) that models procedural knowledge (Card *et al.*, 1983) is described in Chapter 15.

10.7.1 Hierarchical task analysis

Hierarchical Task Analysis (HTA) was originally designed to identify training needs (Annett and Duncan, 1967). It involves breaking a task down into subtasks and then into sub-subtasks and so on. These are then grouped together as plans that specify how the tasks might be performed in an actual situation. HTA focuses on the physical and observable actions that are performed, and includes looking at actions that are not related to software or an interactive product at all. The starting point is a user goal. This is then examined and the main tasks associated with achieving that goal are identified. Where appropriate, these tasks are subdivided into subtasks.

Consider the library catalog service, and the task of borrowing a book. This task can be decomposed into other tasks such as accessing the library catalog, searching by name, title, subject, or whatever, making a note of the location of the book, going to the correct shelf, taking it down off the shelf (provided it is there), and finally taking it to the check-out counter. This set of tasks and subtasks might be performed in a different order depending on how much is known about the book, and how familiar the user might be with the library and the book's likely location. Figure 10.14 shows these subtasks and some plans for different paths through those subtasks. Indentation shows the hierarchical relationship between tasks and subtasks.

Note how the numbering works for the task analysis: the number of the plan corresponds to the number of the step to which the plan relates. For example, plan 2 shows how the subtasks in step 2 can be ordered; there is no plan 1 because step 1 has no subtasks associated with it.

An alternative expression of an HTA is a graphical box-and-line notation. Figure 10.15 shows the graphical version of the HTA in Figure 10.14. Here the subtasks are represented by named boxes with identifying numbers. The hierarchical relationship between tasks is shown using a vertical line. If a task is not decomposed any further then a thick horizontal line is drawn underneath the corresponding box.

0. In order to borrow a book from the library
1. go to the library
2. find the required book
   - 2.1 access library catalog
   - 2.2 access the search screen
   - 2.3 enter search criteria
   - 2.4 identify required book
   - 2.5 note location
3. go to correct shelf and retrieve book
4. take book to checkout counter

plan 0: do 1-3-4. If book isn't on the shelf expected, do 2-3-4.
plan 2: do 2.1-2.4-2.5. If book not identified do 2.2-2.3-2.4-2.5.

Figure 10.14 *An HTA for borrowing a book from the library*

Plans are also shown in this graphical form. They are written alongside the vertical line emitting from the task being decomposed. For example, in Figure 10.15 plan 2 is specified next to the vertical line from box 2: "find required book."

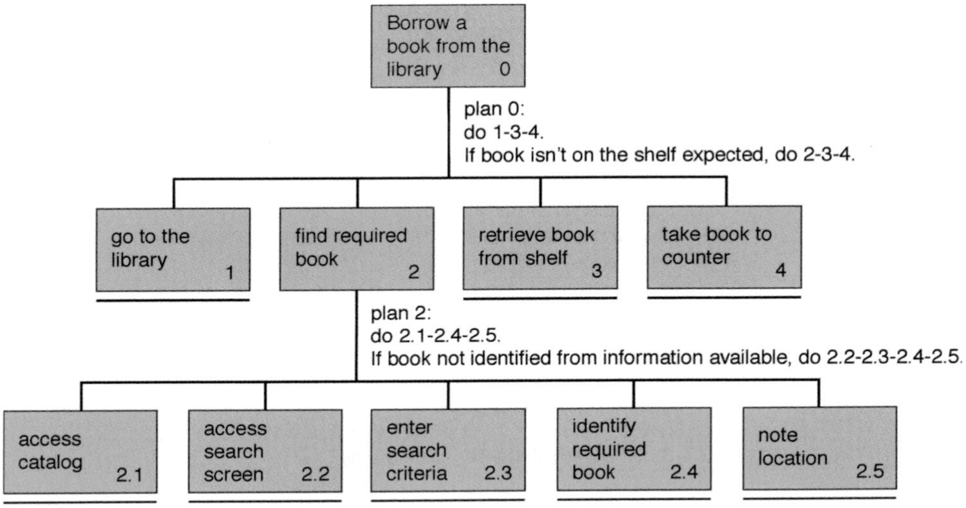

Figure 10.15 *A graphical representation of the task analysis for borrowing a book*

Activity 10.7

Consider the travel organizer again and the task of identifying potential holiday options. Perform hierarchical task analysis for the goal of identifying a holiday. Include all plans in your answer. Express the task analysis textually and graphically.

Comment

The main tasks involved in this are to compile a set of initial criteria (e.g. a sailing holiday for novices), find out any constraints on the holiday, such as possible dates and facilities required at the destination (e.g. child crêche), identify potential holidays that fit the criteria (e.g. a flotilla holiday around the Greek Islands with BoatsRUs), decide on the preferred holiday, and book the holiday. Identifying potential holidays can be decomposed into other tasks such as looking for suitable destinations, looking at a destination's facilities, identifying holiday companies who operate to the chosen destination, and checking availability of potential holiday on preferred dates. At any point while identifying potential holidays,

the holiday options can be printed out. The textual version of the HTA is shown below. Figure 10.16 shows the corresponding graphical representation.

0. In order to identify potential holiday options:
1. Compile a set of initial criteria.
2. Compile a set of constraints.
3. Identify potential holiday.
   3.1 Identify potential destinations.
   3.2 Investigate facilities at potential destination.
   3.3 Identify holiday companies operating at potential destinations.
   3.4 Check availability of potential holiday.
   3.5 Print holiday option details.
4. Decide on preferred holiday.
5. Book holiday.

plan 0: do 1-2-3. Repeat 3 until several potential holidays are available or no more potential holidays can be found. If one or more potential holidays is available, do 4–5. If no potential holidays are available, repeat plan 0.
plan 3: do 3.1-3.2-3.3–3.4 or do 3.1-3.3-3.2–3.4 or do 3.1-3.3-3.4-3.2. If potential holiday available do 3.5.

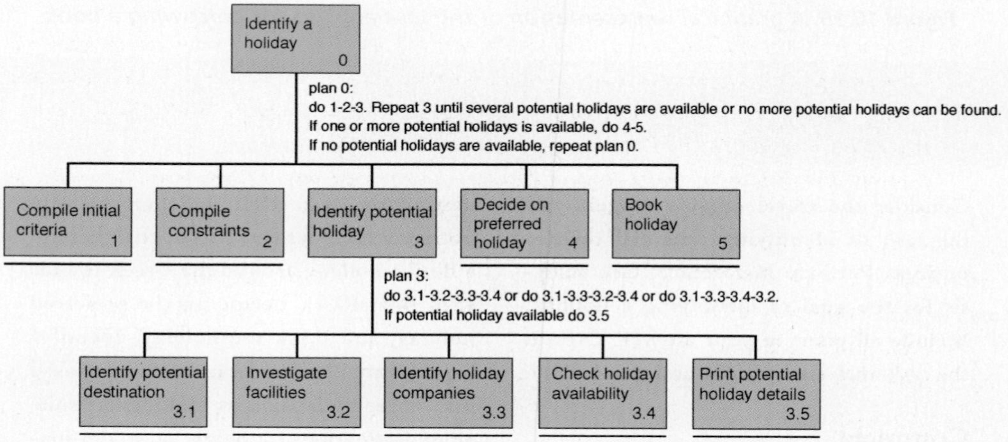

***Figure 10.16** A graphical representation of the holiday HTA*

Activity 10.8

What do you think are the main problems with using task analysis on real problems? Think of more complex tasks such as scheduling delivery trucks, or organizing a large conference.

Comment

Real tasks are very complex. One of the main problems with task analysis is that it does not scale very well. The notation soon becomes unwieldy, making it difficult to follow. Imagine what it would be like to produce a task analysis in which there were hundreds or even thousands of subtasks.

A second problem is that task analysis is limited in the kinds of task it can model. For example, it cannot model tasks that are overlapping or in parallel, nor can it model interruptions. Most people work through interruptions of various kinds, and many significant tasks happen in parallel.

Assignment

This assignment is the first of four assignments that together take you through the complete development lifecycle for an interactive product. This assignment requires you to use techniques described in this chapter for identifying needs and establishing requirements. You will also need to draw on techniques from Chapters 7 and 8. The further three assignments are at the end of Chapters 11, 14, and 15.

The overall assignment is for you to design and evaluate an interactive website for booking tickets online for events like concerts, the theater, and the cinema. This is currently an activity that, in many instances, can be difficult or inconvenient to achieve using traditional means, e.g. waiting for ages on the phone to get hold of an agent, queuing for hours in the rain at a ticket office. Although some online booking sites are available, they often do not offer the best seats and can be difficult to operate.

For this assignment, you should:

(a) Identify users' needs for this website. You could do this in a number of ways. For example, you could observe people using ticket agents, think about your own experience of purchasing tickets, look at existing websites for booking tickets, interview friends and family about their experiences, and so on. Record your data carefully.

(b) Based on your user requirements, choose two different user profiles and produce one persona and one main scenario for each, capturing how the user is expected to interact with the system.

(c) Perform a task analysis on the main task associated with the ticket booking system, i.e. booking a ticket.

(d) Based on this analysis, produce a use case for the main task of booking a ticket.

(e) Using the data gathered in part (a) and your subsequent analysis, identify different kinds of requirements for the website, according to the headings introduced in Section 10.3 above. Write up the requirements in the style of the Volere shell.

Summary

In this chapter, we have looked in more detail at the importance of the requirements activity, and how to identify users' needs and establish requirements for interaction design. The data gathering techniques introduced in Chapter 7 can be used in various combinations to gather requirements data. In addition, contextual inquiry, studying documentation, and researching similar products are commonly used techniques. Scenarios, use cases, and essential use cases are helpful techniques for beginning to document the findings from the data gathering sessions. Task analysis is a little more structured, but does not scale well.

Key Points

- Getting the requirements right is crucial to the success of the interactive product.
- There are different kinds of requirements: functional, data, environmental (context of use), user characteristics, usability goals and user experience goals. Every product will have requirements under each of these headings.
- The most commonly used data gathering techniques for this activity are: questionnaires, interviews, focus groups, direct observation, indirect observation, studying documentation, researching similar products and contextual inquiry.
- Descriptions of user tasks such as scenarios, use cases, and essential use cases help users to articulate existing work practices. They also help to express envisioned use for new products.
- Task analysis techniques help to investigate existing systems and current practices.

Further Reading

ROBERTSON, S. and ROBERTSON, J. (2006) *Mastering the Requirements Process*, 2nd edn. Addison-Wesley. In this book, Robertson and Robertson explain a useful framework for software requirements work (see also the interview with Suzanne Robertson at the end of this chapter).

CONSTANTINE, L.L. and LOCKWOOD, L.A.D. (1999) *Software for Use*. Addison-Wesley. This very readable book provides a concrete approach for modeling and analyzing software systems. The approach has a user-centered focus and contains some useful detail. It also includes more information about essential use cases.

JACOBSON, I., BOOCH, G. and RUMBAUGH, J. (1992) *The Unified Software Development Process*. Addison-Wesley. This is not an easy book to read, but it is the definitive guide for developing object-oriented systems using use cases and the modeling language Unified Modeling Language (UML).

GOTTESDIENER, E. (2002) *Requirements by Collaboration: workshops for defining needs.* Addison-Wesley. This refreshing book provides some good, solid advice for planning and running requirements workshops.

DIAPER, D. and STANTON, N. (2004) *The Handbook of Task Analysis for Human–Computer Interaction.* Lawrence Erlbaum Associates. This collection of articles covers the wide diversity of task analysis, including the foundations of task analysis, cognitive approaches, formal notations, and industry experiences. This is not a book to read cover to cover, but is more of a reference book.

LAZAR, J. (ed.) (2007) *Universal Usability: Designing Information Systems for Diverse User Populations.* John Wiley & Sons. This book provides an interesting selection of case studies that demonstrate how developers can design for diverse populations to ensure universal usability.

SOMMERVILLE, I. (2006) *Software Engineering,* 8th edn. Addison-Wesley. If you are interested in pursuing notations for functional and data requirements, then this book introduces a variety of notations and techniques used in software engineering.

INTERVIEW
with Suzanne Robertson

Suzanne Robertson is a principal of The Atlantic Systems Guild, an international think tank producing numerous books and seminars whose aim is to make good ideas to do with systems engineering more accessible. Suzanne is particularly well known for her work in systems analysis and requirements related activities including the development of the Volere requirements techniques.

HS: What are requirements?
SR: Well the problem is that 'requirements' has turned into an elastic term. Requirements is an enormously wide field and there are so many different types of requirements. One person may be talking about budget, somebody else may be talking about interfacing to an existing piece of software, somebody else may be talking about a performance requirement, somebody else may be talking about the calculation of an algorithm, somebody else may be talking about a data definition, and I could go on for hours as to what requirement means. What we advise people to do to start with is to look for something we call 'linguistic integrity' within their own project. When all people who are connected with the project are talking about requirements, what do they mean? This gets very emotional, and that's why we came up with our framework. We gathered together all this experience of different types of requirements, tried to pick the most common organization, and then wrote them down in a framework.

HS: Please would you explain your framework? (The version discussed in this interview is shown in the figure on page 526. The most recent version may be downloaded from `www.systems-guild.com`.)
SR: Imagine a huge filing cabinet with 27 drawers, and in each drawer you've got a category of knowledge that is related to requirements. In the very first drawer for example you've got the goals, i.e. the reason for doing the project. In the second drawer you've got the stakeholders. These are roles because they could be played by more than one person, and one person may play more than one role. You've got the client who's going to pay for the development, and the customer who's making the decision about buying it. Then you've got stakeholders like the project leader, the developers, the requirements engineers, the designers, the quality people, and the testers. Then you've

got the less obvious stakeholders like surrounding organizations, professional bodies, and other people in the organization whose work might be affected by the project you're doing, even if they're never going to use the product.

HS: So do you find the stakeholders by just asking questions?
SR: Yes, partly that and partly by using the domain model of the subject matter, which is in drawer 9, as the driver to ask more questions about the stakeholders. For example, for each one of the subject matter areas, ask who have we got to represent this subject matter? For each one of the people that we come across, ask what subject matter are we expecting from them?

Drawer 3 contains the end users. I've put them in a separate drawer because an error that a lot of people make when they're looking for requirements is that the only stakeholder they talk about is the end user. They decide on the end user too quickly and they miss opportunities. So you end up building a product that is possibly less competitive or relevant. I keep them a bit fuzzy to start with, and as you start to fix on them then you can go into really deep analysis about them: What is their psychology? What are their characteristics? What's their subject-matter knowledge? How do they feel about their work? How do they feel about technology? All of these things help you to come up with the most competitive non-functional requirements for the product.

HS: How do you resolve conflict between stakeholders?
SR: Well, part of it is to get the conflicts out in the open up front, so people stop blaming each other, but that certainly doesn't resolve it. One of the ways is to make things very visible all the way through and to keep reminding people that conflict is respectable, that it's a sign of creativity, of people having ideas. The other thing that we do is that in our individual requirements (that is atomic requirements), which end up living in drawers 9 to 17 of this filing cabinet, we've got a place to say "Conflict: Which other requirement is this in conflict with?" and we encourage people to identify them. Sometimes these conflicts resolve themselves because they're on people's back burners, and some of the conflicts are resolved by people just talking to one another. We have a continuing process of cross-checking requirements and looking for conflicts and if we find some that are just not sorting themselves out, then we stop and have a serious negotiation.

In essence, it's bubbling the conflicts up to the surface. Keep on talking about them and keep them visible. De-personalize it as much as you can. That helps.

HS: What other things are associated with these atomic requirements?
SR: Each one has a unique number and a description that is as close as you can get to what you think the thing means. It also has a rationale that helps you to figure out what it really is. Then the next component is the fit criterion, which is, "If somebody came up with a solution to this requirement, how would you know whether or not it satisfies the requirement?" So this

means making the requirement quantifiable, measurable. And it's very powerful because it makes you think about the requirement. One requirement quite often turns into several when you really try and quantify it. It also provides a wonderful opportunity for involving testers, because at that point if you write the fit criterion you can get a tester and ask whether this can be used as input to writing a cost-effective test. Now this is different from the way we usually use the testers, which is to build tests that test our solutions. Here I want to get them in much earlier, I want them to test whether this requirement really is a requirement.

HS: So what's in drawers 18 through 27?

SR: Well here you can get into serious quarrels. The overall category is 'project issues,' and people often say they're not really requirements, and they aren't. But if the project is not being managed according to the real work that's being done, in other words the contents of the drawers, then the project goes off the rails. In project issues we create links so that a project manager can manage the project according to what's happening to the requirements.

In the last drawer we have design ideas. People say when you're gathering requirements you should not be concerned with how you're going to solve the problem. But mostly people tell you requirements in the form of a solution anyway. The key thing is to learn how to separate the real requirements from solution ideas, and when you get a solution idea, pop it in this drawer. This helps requirements engineers, I think, because we are trained to think of solutions, not to dig behind and find the real problem.

HS: How do you go about identifying requirements?

SR: For too long we've been saying the stakeholders should give us their requirements: we'll ask them and they'll give them to us. We've realized that this is not practical—partly because there are many requirements people don't know they've got. Some requirements are conscious and they're usually because things have gone wrong or they'd like something extra. Some requirements are unconscious because maybe people are used to it, or maybe they haven't a clue because they don't see the overall picture. And then there are undreamed-of requirements that people just don't dream they could ever have, because we've all got boundaries based on what we think technology is capable of doing or what we know about technology or what our experience is. So it's not just asking people for things, it's also inventing requirements. I think that's where prototyping comes in and scenario modeling and storyboarding and all of those sorts of techniques to help people to imagine what they could have.

If you're building a product for the market and you want to be more competitive you should be inventing requirements. Instead of constricting yourself within the product boundary, say, "Can I push myself out a bit further? Is there something else I could do that isn't being done?"

HS: So what kinds of techniques can people use to push out further?

SR: One of the things is to learn how to imagine what it's like to be somebody else, and this is why going into other fields, for example family therapy, is helpful. They've learned an awful lot about how to imagine you might be somebody else. And that's not something that software engineers are taught in college normally and this is why it's very healthy for us to be bringing together the ideas of psychology and sociology and so on with software and systems engineering. Bringing in these human aspects—the performance, the usability features, the 'look and feel' features—that's going to make our products more competitive.

I always tell people to read a lot of novels. If you're having trouble relating to some stakeholders, for example, go and read some Jane Austen and then try to imagine what it would have been like to have been the heroine in *Pride and Prejudice*. What would it have been like to have to change your clothes three times a day? I find this helps me a lot, it frees your mind and then you can say, "OK, what's it really like to be that other person?" There's a lot to learn in that area.

HS: So what you're saying really is that it's not easy.

SR: It's not easy. I don't think there's any particular technique. But what we have done is we have come up with a lot of different 'trawling' techniques, along with recommendations, that can help you.

HS: Do you have any other tips for gathering requirements?

SR: It's important for people to feel that they've been heard. The waiting room (drawer number 26) was invented because of a very enthusiastic high-level stakeholder in a project we were doing. She was very enthusiastic and keen and very involved. Wonderful! She really gave us tremendous ideas and support. The problem was she kept having ideas, and we didn't know what to do. We didn't want to stop her having ideas, on the other hand we couldn't always include them because then we would never get anything built. So we invented the waiting room. All the good ideas we have we put in there and every so often we go into the waiting room and review the ideas. Some of them get added to the product, some are discarded, and some are left waiting. The psychology of it is very good because the idea's in the waiting room, everyone knows it's in there, but it's not being ignored. When people feel heard, they feel better and consequently they're more likely to cooperate and give you time. ■

The Template

PROJECT DRIVERS

1. The Purpose of the Product
2. Client, Customer and other Stakeholders
3. Users of the Product

PROJECT CONSTRAINTS

4. Mandated Constraints
5. Naming Conventions and Definitions
6. Relevant Facts and Assumptions

FUNCTIONAL REQUIREMENTS

7. The Scope of the Work
8. The Scope of the Product
9. Functional and Data Requirements

NON-FUNCTIONAL REQUIREMENTS

10. Look and Feel Requirements
11. Usability Requirements
12. Performance Requirements
13. Operational Requirements
14. Maintainability and Portability Requirements
15. Security Requirements
16. Cultural and Political Requirements
17. Legal Requirements

PROJECT ISSUES

18. Open Issues
19. Off-the-Shelf Solutions
20. New Problems
21. Tasks
22. Cutover
23. Risks
24. Costs
25. User Documentation and Training
26. Waiting Room
27. Ideas for Solutions

The Volere Requirements Specification Template © Atlantic Systems Guild.

11

11.1 Introduction

Design activities begin once some requirements have been established. The design emerges iteratively, through repeated design–evaluation–redesign cycles involving users. Broadly speaking, there are two types of design: conceptual and physical. The former is concerned with developing a conceptual model that captures what the product will do and how it will behave, while the latter is concerned with details of the design such as screen and menu structures, icons, and graphics. We discussed physical design issues relating to different types of interfaces in Chapter 6 and so we do not return to this in detail here, but refer back to Chapter 6 as appropriate.

For users to evaluate the design of an interactive product effectively, designers must produce an interactive version of their ideas. In the early stages of development, these interactive versions may be made of paper and cardboard, while as design progresses and ideas become more detailed, they may be polished pieces of software, metal, or plastic that resemble the final product. We have called the activity concerned with building this interactive version prototyping and construction.

There are two distinct circumstances for design: one where you're starting from scratch and one where you're modifying an existing product. A lot of design comes from the latter, and it may be tempting to think that additional features can be added, or existing ones tweaked, without extensive investigation, prototyping, or evaluation. It is true that if changes are not significant then the prototyping and evaluation activities can be scaled down, but they are still invaluable activities that should not be skipped.

In Chapter 10, we discussed some ways to identify user needs and establish requirements. In this chapter, we look at the activities involved in progressing a set of requirements through the cycles of prototyping to construction. We begin by explaining the role and techniques of prototyping and then explain how prototypes may be used in the design process. Tool support plays an important part in development, but tool support changes so rapidly in this area that we do not attempt to provide a catalog of current support. Instead, we discuss the kinds of tools that may be of help and categories of tools that have been suggested.

The main aims of this chapter are to:

- **Describe prototyping and different types of prototyping activities.**
- **Enable you to produce simple prototypes from the models developed during the requirements activity.**
- **Enable you to produce a conceptual model for a product and justify your choices.**
- **Explain the use of scenarios and prototypes in design.**
- **Discuss the range of tool support available for interaction design.**

11

Design, prototyping, and construction

11.2 Prototyping and construction

It is often said that users can't tell you what they want, but when they see something and get to use it, they soon know what they don't want. Having collected information about work and everyday practices, and views about what a system should and shouldn't do, we then need to try out our ideas by building prototypes and iterating through several versions. And the more iterations, the better the final product will be.

11.2.1 What is a prototype?

When you hear the term *prototype*, you may imagine something like a scale model of a building or a bridge, or maybe a piece of software that crashes every few minutes. But a prototype can also be a paper-based outline of a screen or set of screens, an electronic 'picture,' a video simulation of a task, a three-dimensional paper and cardboard mockup of a whole workstation, or a simple stack of hyperlinked screen shots, among other things.

In fact, a prototype can be anything from a paper-based storyboard through to a complex piece of software, and from a cardboard mockup to a molded or pressed piece of metal. A prototype allows stakeholders to interact with an envisioned product, to gain some experience of using it in a realistic setting, and to explore imagined uses.

For example, when the idea for the PalmPilot was being developed, Jeff Hawkin (founder of the company) carved up a piece of wood about the size and shape of the device he had imagined. He used to carry this piece of wood around with him and pretend to enter information into it, just to see what it would be like to own such a device (Bergman and Haitani, 2000). This is an example of a very simple (some might even say bizarre) prototype, but it served its purpose of simulating scenarios of use.

Ehn and Kyng (1991) report on the use of a cardboard box with the label 'Desktop Laser Printer' as a mockup. It did not matter that, in their setup, the printer was not real. The important point was that the intended users, journalists and typographers, could experience and envision what it would be like to have one of these machines on their desks. This may seem a little extreme, but in 1982 when this was done, desktop laser printers were expensive items of equipment and were not a common sight around the office.

So a prototype is a limited representation of a design that allows users to interact with it and to explore its suitability.

11.2.2 Why prototype?

Prototypes are a useful aid when discussing ideas with stakeholders; they are a communication device among team members, and are an effective way to test out ideas for yourself. The activity of building prototypes encourages reflection in design, as described by Schön (1983) and as recognized by designers from many disciplines as an important aspect of the design process. Liddle (1996), talking about software design, recommends that prototyping should always precede any writing of code.

Prototypes answer questions and support designers in choosing between alternatives. Hence, they serve a variety of purposes: for example, to test out the technical feasibility of an idea, to clarify some vague requirements, to do some user testing and evaluation, or to check that a certain design direction is compatible with the rest of the system development. Which of these is your purpose will influence the kind of prototype you build. So, for example, if you are trying to clarify how users might perform a set of tasks and whether your proposed design would support them in this, you might produce a paper-based mockup. Figure 11.1 shows a paper-based prototype of the design for a handheld device to help an autistic child communicate. This prototype shows the intended functions and buttons, their positioning and labeling, and the overall shape of the device, but none of the buttons actually work. This kind of prototype is sufficient to investigate scenarios of use and to decide, for example, whether the buttons are appropriate and the functions sufficient, but not to test whether the speech is loud enough or the response fast enough.

Heather Martin and Bill Gaver (2000) describe a different kind of prototyping with a different purpose. When prototyping audiophotography products, they used a variety of different techniques including video scenarios similar to the scenarios we introduced in Chapter 10, but filmed rather than written. At each stage, the prototypes were minimally specified, deliberately leaving some aspects vague so as to stimulate further ideas and discussion.

11.2.3 Low-fidelity prototyping

A low-fidelity prototype is one that does not look very much like the final product. For example, it uses materials that are very different from the intended final version, such as paper and cardboard rather than electronic screens and metal. The lump of wood used to prototype the PalmPilot described above is a low-fidelity prototype, as is the cardboard-box laser printer.

Low-fidelity prototypes are useful because they tend to be simple, cheap, and quick to produce. This also means that they are simple, cheap, and quick to modify so they support the exploration of alternative designs and ideas. This is particularly important in early stages of development, during conceptual design for example, because prototypes that are used for exploring ideas should be flexible and encourage rather than discourage exploration and modification. Low-fidelity prototypes are never intended to be kept and integrated into the final product. They are for exploration only.

Storyboarding. Storyboarding is one example of low-fidelity prototyping that is often used in conjunction with scenarios, as described in Chapter 10. A storyboard consists of a series of sketches showing how a user might progress through a task using the product under development. It can be a series of sketched screens for a GUI-based software system, or a series of scene sketches showing how a user can perform a task using an interactive device. When used in conjunction with a scenario, the storyboard

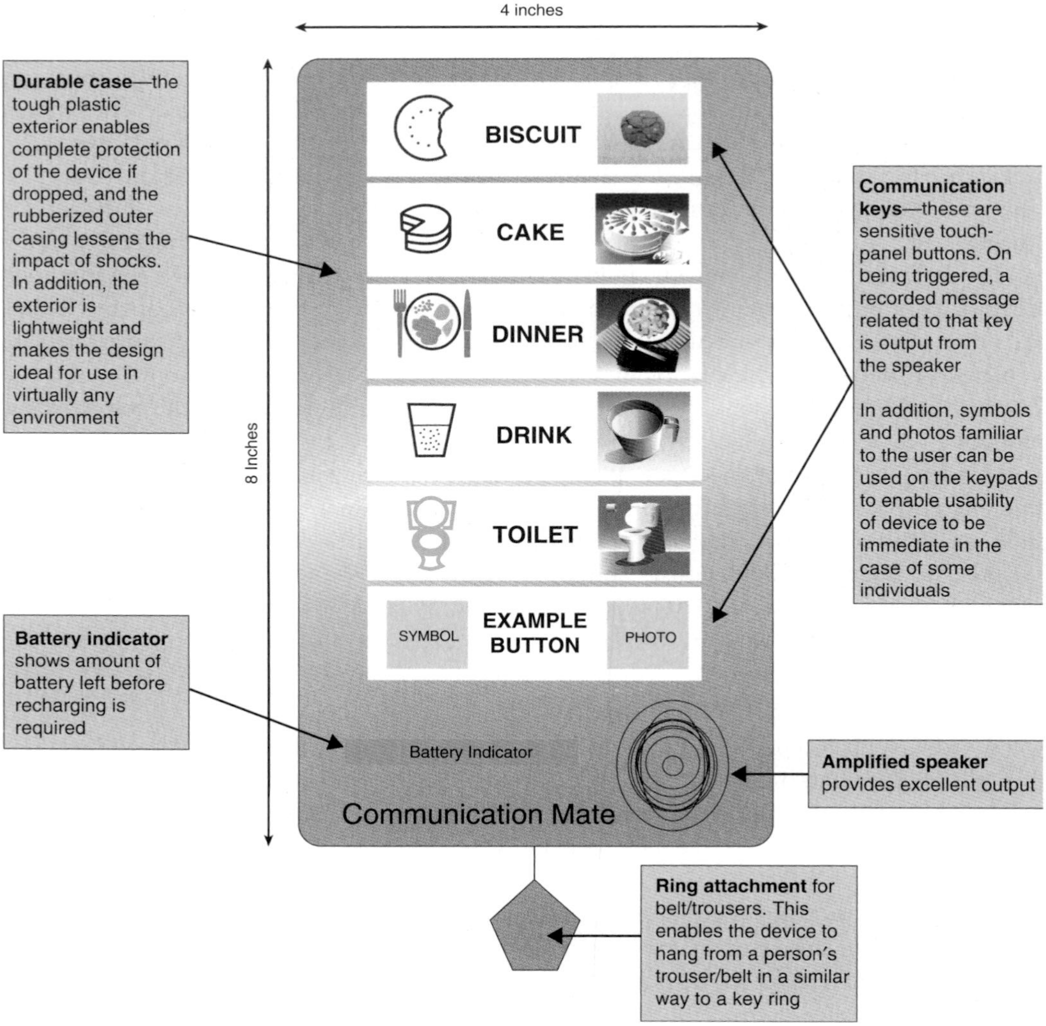

Figure 11.1 *A paper-based prototype of a handheld device to support an autistic child*

brings more detail to the written scenario and offers stakeholders a chance to role-play with the prototype, interacting with it by stepping through the scenario. The example storyboard shown in Figure 11.2 (Hartfield and Winograd, 1996) depicts a person using a new system for digitizing images. This example does not show detailed drawings of the

Figure 11.2 *An example storyboard*

screens involved, but it describes the steps a user might go through in order to use the system.

Sketching. Low-fidelity prototyping often relies on sketching, and many people find it difficult to engage in this activity because they are inhibited about the quality of their drawing. Verplank (1989) suggests that you can teach yourself to get over this inhibition by devising your own symbols and icons for elements you might want to sketch, and practice using them. They don't have to be anything more than simple boxes, stick figures, and stars. Elements you might require in a storyboard sketch, for example, include 'things' such as people, parts of a computer, desks, books, etc., and actions such as give, find, transfer, and write. If you are sketching an interface design, then you might need to draw various icons, dialog boxes, and so on. Some simple examples are shown in Figure 11.3. Try copying these and using them. The next activity requires other sketching symbols, but they can still be drawn quite simply.

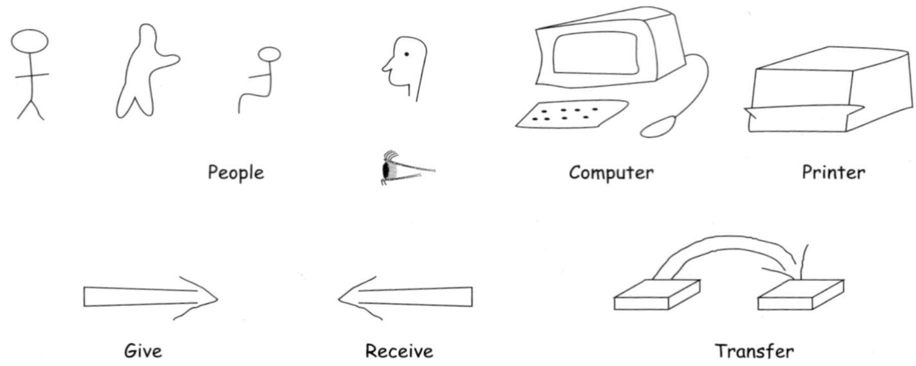

***Figure 11.3** Some simple sketches for low-fidelity prototyping*

Activity 11.1

Produce a storyboard that depicts how to fill a car with gas (petrol).

Comment

Our attempt is shown in Figure 11.4.

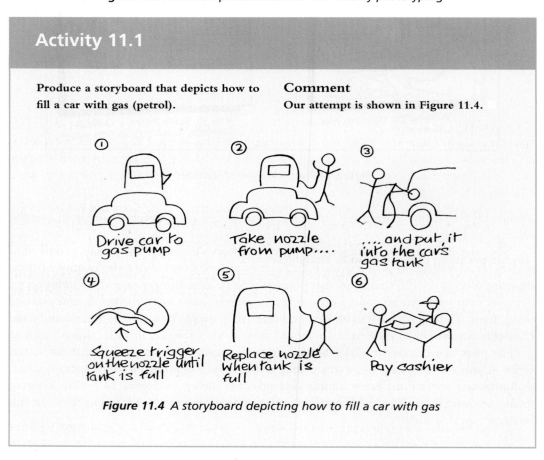

1
Drive car to gas pump
2
Take nozzle from pump....
3
...., and put it into the cars gas tank
4
Squeeze trigger on the nozzle until tank is full
5
Replace nozzle when tank is full
6
Pay cashier

***Figure 11.4** A storyboard depicting how to fill a car with gas*

Prototyping with index cards. Using index cards (small pieces of cardboard about 3 × 5 inches) is a successful and simple way to prototype an interaction, and is used quite commonly when developing websites. Each card represents one screen or one element of a task. In user evaluations, the user can step through the cards, pretending to perform the task while interacting with the cards. A more detailed example of this kind of prototyping is given in Section 11.6.2.

Wizard of Oz. Another low-fidelity prototyping method called Wizard of Oz assumes that you have a software-based prototype. In this technique, the user sits at a computer screen and interacts with the software as though interacting with the product. In fact, however, the computer is connected to another machine where a human operator sits and simulates the software's response to the user. The method takes its name from the classic story of the little girl who is swept away in a storm and finds herself in the Land of Oz (Baum and Denslow, 1900). The Wizard of Oz is a small shy man who operates a large artificial image of himself from behind a screen where no-one can see him. The Wizard of Oz style of prototyping has been used successfully for various systems, including PinTrace, a robotic system that helps surgeons to position orthopedic 'pins' accurately during the surgery of hip fractures (Molin, 2004).

11.2.4 High-fidelity prototyping

High-fidelity prototyping uses materials that you would expect to be in the final product and produces a prototype that looks much more like the final thing. For example, a prototype of a software system developed in Visual Basic is higher fidelity than a paper-based mockup; a molded piece of plastic with a dummy keyboard is a higher-fidelity prototype of the PalmPilot than the lump of wood.

If you are to build a prototype in software, then clearly you need a software tool to support this. Common prototyping tools include Flash, Visual Basic, and Smalltalk. These are also fully-fledged development environments, so they are powerful tools, but building prototypes using them can also be straightforward.

In a classic paper, Marc Rettig (1994) argues that more projects should use low-fidelity prototyping because of the inherent problems with high-fidelity prototyping. He identifies these problems as:

- They take too long to build.
- Reviewers and testers tend to comment on superficial aspects rather than content.
- Developers are reluctant to change something they have crafted for hours.
- A software prototype can set expectations too high.
- Just one bug in a high-fidelity prototype can bring the testing to a halt.

High-fidelity prototyping is useful for selling ideas to people and for testing out technical issues. However, the use of paper prototyping and other ideas should be actively encouraged

Type	Advantages	Disadvantages
Low-fidelity prototype	• Lower development cost. • Evaluate multiple design concepts. • Useful communication device. • Address screen layout issues. • Useful for identifying market requirements. • Proof-of-concept.	• Limited error checking. • Poor detailed specification to code to. • Facilitator-driven. • Limited utility after requirements established. • Limited usefulness for usability tests. • Navigational and flow limitations.
High-fidelity prototype	• Complete functionality. • Fully interactive. • User-driven. • Clearly defines navigational scheme. • Use for exploration and test. • Look and feel of final product. • Serves as a living specification. • Marketing and sales tool.	• More expensive to develop. • Time-consuming to create. • Inefficient for proof-of-concept designs. • Not effective for requirements gathering.

Table 11.1 *Relative effectiveness of low- vs. high-fidelity prototypes (Rudd et al., 1996)*

for exploring issues of content and structure. Further advantages and disadvantages of the two types of prototyping are listed in Table 11.1.

Powerpoint is often used for prototyping because it balances the provisionality of paper with the polished appearance of software prototypes. A Powerpoint prototype has characteristics of high and low fidelity.

11.2.5 Compromises in prototyping

By their very nature, prototypes involve compromises: the intention is to produce something quickly to test an aspect of the product. The kind of questions or choices that any one prototype allows the designer to answer is therefore limited, and the prototype must be designed and built with the key issues in mind. In low-fidelity prototyping, it is fairly clear that compromises have been made. For example, with a paper-based prototype an obvious compromise is that the device doesn't actually work! For software-based prototyping, some of the compromises will still be fairly clear; for example, the response speed may be slow, or the exact icons may be sketchy, or only a limited amount of functionality may be available.

Box 11.1
Prototyping cultures

"The culture of an organization has a strong influence on the quality of the innovations that the organization can produce." (Schrage, 1996, p. 193)

This observation is drawn mainly from product-related organizations, but also applies to software development. There are primarily two kinds of organizational culture for innovation: the specification culture and the prototyping culture. In the former, new products and development are driven by written specifications, i.e. by a collection of documented requirements. In the latter, understanding requirements and developing the new product are driven by prototyping. Large companies such as IBM or AT&T that have to gather and coordinate a large amount of information tend to be specification-driven, while smaller entrepreneurial companies tend to be prototype-driven. Both approaches have potential disadvantages. A carefully prepared specification may prove completely infeasible once prototyping begins. Similarly, a wonderful prototype may prove to be too expensive to produce on a large scale.

David Kelley (Schrage, p. 195) claims that organizations wanting to be innovative need to move to a prototype-driven culture. Schrage sees that there are two cultural aspects to this shift. First, scheduled prototyping cycles that force designers to build many prototypes are more likely to lead to a prototype-driven culture than allowing designers to produce *ad hoc* prototypes when they think it appropriate. Second, rather than innovative teams being needed for innovative prototypes, it is now recognized that innovative prototypes lead to innovating teams! This can be especially significant when the teams are cross-functional, i.e. multidisciplinary. ■

(Schrage, 1996)

Two common compromises that often must be traded against each other are breadth of functionality provided versus depth. These two kinds of prototyping are called *horizontal prototyping* (providing a wide range of functions but with little detail) and *vertical prototyping* (providing a lot of detail for only a few functions).

Other compromises won't be obvious to a user of the system. For example, the internal structure of the system may not have been carefully designed, and the prototype may contain 'spaghetti code' or may be badly partitioned. One of the dangers of producing running prototypes, i.e. ones that users can interact with automatically, is that they may believe that the prototype is the system. The danger for developers is that it may lead them to consider fewer alternatives because they have found one that works and

"THEN IN HERE WE DO A CLAY MOCK-UP OF THE COMPUTER MODEL"

that the users like. However, the compromises made in order to produce the prototype must not be ignored, particularly the ones that are less obvious from the outside. We still have to produce a good-quality system and good engineering principles must be adhered to.

A different point is made by Holmquist (2005), who points out that the design team themselves must be careful not to inadvertently design something that is not technically feasible. Claiming that a mobile device will be able to detect the state of its user automatically and modify its behavior accordingly is fairly simple to do when you only have a paper prototype to play with, however, having a paper model does not mean that a claimed feature can be implemented. This is one reason why it is important to have technical and design knowledge in an interactive design team.

11.2.6 Construction: from design to implementation

When the design has been around the iteration cycle enough times to feel confident that it fits requirements, everything that has been learned through the iterated steps of prototyping and evaluation must be integrated to produce the final product.

Although prototypes will have undergone extensive user evaluation, they will not necessarily have been subjected to rigorous quality testing for other characteristics such as robustness and error-free operation. Constructing a product to be used by thousands or millions of people running on various platforms and under a wide range of circumstances requires a different testing regime than producing a quick prototype to answer specific questions.

The dilemma box below discusses two different development philosophies. One approach, called *evolutionary prototyping*, involves evolving a prototype into the final product. An alternative approach, called *throwaway prototyping*, uses the prototypes as stepping stones towards the final design. In this case, the prototypes are thrown away and the final product is built from scratch. If an evolutionary prototyping approach is to be taken, the prototypes should be subjected to rigorous testing along the way; for throw-away prototyping such testing is not necessary.

Dilemma
Prototyping to throw away

Low-fidelity prototypes are never intended to be kept and integrated into the final product. But when building a software-based system, developers can choose to do one of two things: either build a prototype with the intention of throwing it away after it has fulfilled its immediate purpose, or build a prototype with the intention of evolving it into the final product.

Above, we talked about the compromises made when producing a prototype, and we commented that the 'invisible' compromises, concerned with the structure of the underlying software must not be ignored. However, when a project team is under pressure to produce the final product and a complex prototype exists that fulfills many of the requirements, or maybe a set of vertical prototypes exists that together fulfill the requirements, it can become very tempting to pull them together and issue the result as the final product. After all, many hours of development have probably gone into developing the prototypes, and evaluation with the client has gone well, so isn't it a waste to throw it all away? Basing the final product on prototypes in this way will simply store up testing and maintenance problems for later on: in short, this is likely to compromise the quality of the product.

Evolving the final prototype into the final product through a defined process of evolutionary prototyping can lead to a robust final product, but this must be clearly planned and designed for from the beginning. Building directly on prototypes that have been used to answer specific questions through the development process will not yield a robust product. As Constantine and Lockwood (1999) observe, "Software is the only engineering field that throws together prototypes and then attempts to sell them as delivered goods."

On the other hand, if your device is an innovation, then being first to market with a 'good enough' product may be more important for securing your market position than having a very high-quality product that reaches the market two months after your competitors'.

11.3 Conceptual design: moving from requirements to first design

Conceptual design is concerned with transforming needs and requirements into a conceptual model. Designing the conceptual model is fundamental to interaction design, yet the idea of a conceptual model can be difficult to grasp. One of the reasons for this is that conceptual models take many different forms and it is not possible to provide a definitive detailed characterization of one. Instead, conceptual design is best understood by exploring and experiencing different approaches to it, and the purpose of this section is to provide you with some concrete suggestions about how to go about doing this.

In Chapter 2 we said that a conceptual model is an outline of what people can do with a product and what concepts are needed to understand how to interact with it. The former will emerge from the current functional requirements; possibly it will be a subset of them, possibly all of them, and possibly an extended version of them. The concepts needed to understand how to interact with the product depend on a variety of issues related to who the user will be, what kind of interaction will be used, what kind of interface will be used, terminology, metaphors, application domain, and so on. The first step in getting a concrete view of the conceptual model is to steep yourself in the data you have gathered about your users and their goals and try to empathize with them. From this, a picture of what you want the users' experience to be when using the new product will emerge and become more concrete. This process is helped by considering the issues in this section, and by using scenarios (introduced in Chapter 10) and prototypes (introduced in Section 11.2) to capture and experiment with ideas. All of this is also informed by the requirements activity and must be tempered with technological feasibility.

There are different ways to achieve this empathy. For example, Beyer and Holtzblatt (1998), in their method *Contextual Design*, recommend holding review meetings within the team to get different peoples' perspectives on the data and what they observed. This helps to deepen understanding and to expose the whole team to different aspects. Ideas will emerge as this extended understanding of the requirements is established, and these can be tested against other data and scenarios, discussed with other design team members and prototyped for testing with users. Other ways to understand the users' experience are described in Box 11.2.

Ideas for a conceptual model may emerge during data gathering, but remember what Suzanne Robertson said in her interview at the end of Chapter 10: you must separate the real requirements from solution ideas.

Key guiding principles of conceptual design are:

- Keep an open mind but never forget the users and their context.
- Discuss ideas with other stakeholders as much as possible.
- Use low-fidelity prototyping to get rapid feedback.
- Iterate, iterate, and iterate.

Before explaining how scenarios and prototyping can help, we explore in more detail some useful perspectives to help develop a conceptual model.

Box 11.2
How to really understand the users' experience

Some design teams go to great lengths to ensure that they come to empathize with, not just understand, the users' experience. We know from learning things ourselves that 'learning by doing' is more effective than being told something or just seeing something. Buchenau and Suri (2000) describe an approach they call *experience prototyping*, which is intended to give designers some of the insight into a user's experience that can only come from first-hand knowledge. For example, they describe a team designing a chest-implanted automatic defibrillator. A defibrillator is used with victims of cardiac arrest when their heart muscle goes into a chaotic arrythmia and fails to pump blood, a state called fibrillation. A defibrillator delivers an electric shock to the heart, often through paddle electrodes applied externally through the chest wall; an implanted defibrillator does this through leads that connect directly to the heart muscle. In either case, it's a big electric shock intended to restore the heart muscle to its regular rhythm that can be powerful enough to knock people off their feet.

This kind of event is completely outside most people's experience, and so it is difficult really to understand what the user's experience is likely to be for this kind of device. You can't fit a prototype pacemaker to each member of the design team and simulate fibrillation in them! This makes it difficult for designers to gain the insight they need. However, you can simulate some critical aspects of the experience, one of which is the random occurrence of a defibrillating shock. To achieve this, each team member was given a pager to take home over the weekend (elements of the pack are shown in Figure 11.5). The pager message simulated the occurrence of a defibrillating shock. Messages were sent at random, and team members were asked to record where they were, who they were with, what they were doing, and what they thought and felt knowing that this represented a shock. Experiences were shared the following week, and example insights ranged from anxiety around everyday happenings such as holding a child and operating power tools, to being in social situations at a loss how to communicate to onlookers what was happening. This first-hand experience brought new insights to the design effort.

Another instance in which designers tried hard to come to terms with the user experience is the Third Age suit, developed at ICE, Loughborough University (see Figure 11.6). This suit was designed

Figure 11.5 The patient kit for experience prototyping

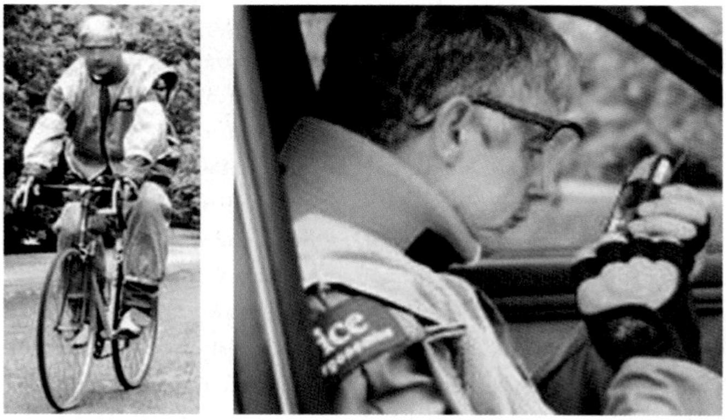

(a) (b)

Figure 11.6 The Third Age suit: (a) riding a bike and (b) using a cell phone

so that car designers could experience what it might be like to be in an older body. The suit restricts movement in the neck, arms, legs, and ankles in a way that simulates the mobility problems typically experienced by someone over 55 years of age. For example, when operating the foot pedals in a car, many 'third agers' (as they are called) lack the flexibility in their ankles to be able to rest their heel on the floor and operate the pedals by flexing their ankle. Thus they have to lift their whole foot up and push it down each time they operate the pedal, which puts much more stress on their leg muscles. ■

11.3.1 Developing an initial conceptual model

Some elements of a conceptual model will derive from the requirements for the product. For example, the requirements activity will have provided information about the concepts involved in a task and their relationships, e.g. through task descriptions and analysis. Immersion in the data and attempting to empathize with the users as described above will, together with the requirements, provide information about the product's user experience goals, and give you a good understanding of what the product should be like. In this section we discuss approaches which help in pulling together an initial conceptual model. In particular, we consider:

- Which interface metaphors would be suitable to help users understand the product?
- Which interaction type(s) would best support the users' activities?
- Do different interface types suggest alternative design insights or options?

In all the discussions that follow, we are not suggesting that one way of approaching a conceptual design is right for one situation and wrong for another; they all provide different ways of thinking about the product and hence aid in generating potential conceptual models. Box 11.3 describes another way of thinking about different conceptual models, and introduces the idea that some are based on process and others are based on product.

Interface metaphors. As mentioned in Chapter 2, interface metaphors combine familiar knowledge with new knowledge in a way that will help the user understand the system. Choosing suitable metaphors and combining new and familiar concepts requires a careful balance between utility and fun, and is based on a sound understanding of the users and their context. For example, consider an educational system to teach six-year-olds mathematics. You could use the metaphor of a classroom with a teacher standing at the blackboard. But if you consider the users of the system and what is likely to engage them, you will be more likely to choose a metaphor that reminds the children of something they enjoy, such as a ball game, the circus, a playroom, etc.

Erickson (1990) suggests a three-step process for choosing a good interface metaphor. The first step is to understand what the system will do. Identifying functional requirements was discussed in Chapter 10. Developing partial conceptual models and trying them out may be part of the process. The second step is to understand which bits of the system are likely to cause users problems. Another way of looking at this is to identify which tasks or subtasks cause problems, are complicated, or are critical. A metaphor is only a partial mapping between the software and the real thing upon which the metaphor is based. Understanding areas in which users are likely to have difficulties means that the metaphor can be chosen to support those aspects. The third step is to generate metaphors. Looking for metaphors in the users' description of the tasks is a good starting point. Also, any metaphors used in the application domain with which the users may be familiar may be suitable.

When suitable metaphors have been generated, they need to be evaluated. Again, Erickson (1990) suggests five questions to ask.

1. How much structure does the metaphor provide? A good metaphor will require structure, and preferably familiar structure.
2. How much of the metaphor is relevant to the problem? One of the difficulties of using metaphors is that users may think they understand more than they do and start applying inappropriate elements of the metaphor to the system, leading to confusion or false expectations.
3. Is the interface metaphor easy to represent? A good metaphor will be associated with particular visual and audio elements, as well as words.
4. Will your audience understand the metaphor?
5. How extensible is the metaphor? Does it have extra aspects that may be useful later on?

In the group travel organizer introduced in Chapter 10, one obvious metaphor we could use is a printed travel brochure. This is familiar to everyone, and we could combine that familiarity with facilities suitable for an electronic 'brochure' such as hyperlinks and searching. Having thought of this metaphor, we need to apply the five questions listed above.

1. Does it supply structure? Yes, it supplies structure based on the familiar paper-based brochure. This is a book and therefore has pages, a cover, some kind of binding to hold the pages together, an index, and table of contents. Travel brochures are often structured around destinations but are also sometimes structured around activities, particularly when the company specializes in activity holidays. However, a traditional brochure focuses on the details of the holiday and accommodation and has little structure to support visa or vaccination information (both of which change regularly and are therefore not suitable to include in a printed document).
2. How much of the metaphor is relevant? Having details of the accommodation, facilities available, holiday plan, and supporting illustrations is relevant for the travel organizer, so the content of the brochure is relevant. Also, structuring that information around holiday types and destinations is relevant, but preferably both sets of grouping could be offered. But the physical nature of the brochure, such as page turning, is less relevant. The travel organizer can be more flexible than the brochure and should not try to emulate the book nature of the brochure. Finally, the brochure is printed maybe once a year and cannot be kept up-to-date with the latest changes whereas the travel organizer should be capable of offering the most recent information.
3. Is the metaphor easy to represent? Yes. The holiday information could be a set of brochure-like 'pages.' Note that this is not the same as saying that the navigation through the pages will be limited to page-turning.
4. Will your audience understand the metaphor? Yes.
5. How extensible is the metaphor? The functionality of a paper-based brochure is fairly limited. However, it is also a book, and we could borrow facilities from electronic books (which are also familiar objects to most of our audience), so yes, it can be extended.

Activity 11.2

Another possible interface metaphor for the travel organizer is the travel consultant. A travel consultant takes a set of holiday requirements and tailors the holiday accordingly, offering maybe two or three alternatives, but making most of the decisions on the travelers' behalf. Ask the five questions above of this metaphor.

Comment

1. Does the travel consultant metaphor supply structure? Yes, it supplies structure because the key characteristic of this metaphor is that the travelers specify what they want and the consultant goes and researches it. It relies on the travelers being able to give the consultant sufficient information to be able to search sensibly rather than leaving him to make key decisions.
2. How much of the metaphor is relevant? The idea of handing over responsibility to someone else to search for suitable holidays may be appealing to some users, but might feel uncomfortable to others. On the other hand, having no help at all in sifting through potential holidays could become very tedious and dispiriting. So maybe this metaphor is relevant to an extent.
3. Is the metaphor easy to represent? Yes, it could be represented by a software agent, or by having a sophisticated database entry and search facility. But the question is: would users like this approach?
4. Will your audience understand the metaphor? Yes.
5. How extensible is the metaphor? The wonderful thing about people is that they are flexible, hence the metaphor of the travel consultant is also pretty flexible. For example, the consultant could be asked to bring just a few options for the users to consider, having screened out inappropriate ones; alternatively the consultant could be asked to suggest 50 or 100 options!

Box 11.3
Process-oriented versus product-oriented conceptual models

Mayhew (1999) characterizes conceptual models in terms of their focus on products or on process.

The difference between these two kinds of conceptual model concerns the drivers for the design activity. For a

UTILITY CUSTOMER SERVICE

Service Requests
- Change Service
- Cancel Service
- Install New Service
  - Add Customer Info
  - Select Service
  - Check Credit
  - Quote Rate
  - Schedule Install

Billing Questions
- View Bill
- Change Bill
- Sales—Offer Service Options

Maintenance Requests
- Report Problem
- Schedule Maintenance
- View Maintenance History

Info Requests
- Show Services
- Show Products
- Show Installation Procedures

Here is a possible design presenting these work processes through a process-oriented Conceptual Model:

Conceptual Model—Utility Customer Service

Application Window

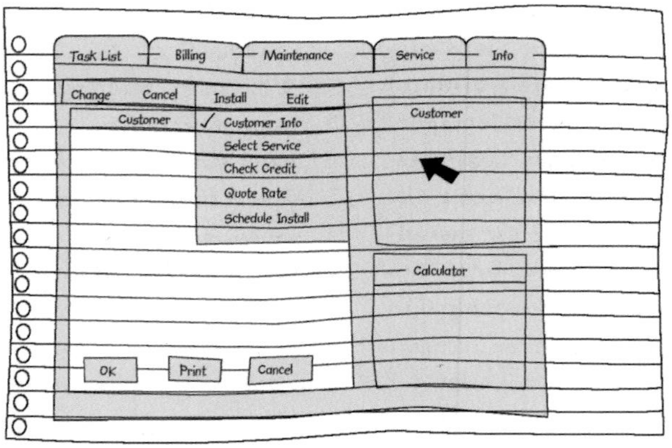

The presentation rules followed in this design are as follows (this design is not complete; it simply provides some examples of components of a process-oriented model).

The overall application is represented as a tab metaphor. *Highest-level processes* (e.g., billing questions, maintenance requests) are represented by tabs, and each tab represents a work space for that process. The tabbed work space includes a main window where that process is carried out, plus two "common windows," where tools common across all highest-level processes are maintained.

Second-level subprocesses are represented by selections in the menu bar within each tab, and third-level subprocesses by selections in pull-downs from the menu bar.

Structured subprocesses are controlled through dimming of subprocesses in pull-downs (until earlier sub-processes are completed, later subprocesses are dimmed out and unselectable).

Completed subprocesses are designated with a check mark.

Common activities available across highest-level processes (i.e., Customer, Calculator) are presented as separate, dedicated windows within the tabbed work spaces.

All windows are dialog boxes—that is, they cannot be minimized. They are all unresizable and unscrollable, but are movable and modeless. The main dialog box represents subprocesses, and it changes contents as the user moves through the subprocesses in sequence to complete a given subprocess and process.

Different windows have different background colors. Note that the active tabbed workspace itself is dark gray, the main subprocess dialog box is white, and all common dialog boxes are light gray.

Figure 11.7 *An example of a process-oriented conceptual model* product-oriented application, the main products and the tools needed to create them form the main structure of the application. For a process-oriented application, it is the list of process steps that forms the system's basis. Mayhew suggests the following issues must be addressed during conceptual design, whether the application is primarily product-oriented or process-oriented:

- Products or processes must be clearly identified. For example, what documents are to be generated and what other tools are required to produce them? In a process-oriented model, what processes are to be supported?
- A set of presentation rules must be designed. For example, urgent tasks must be placed on the desktop, while less urgent tasks may be accessible through the menu bar. If designing for a GUI, design rules and guidelines come with the particular platform.
- Design a set of rules for how windows will be used.
- Identify how major information and functionality will be divided across displays.
- Define and design major navigational pathways. This will draw on the task analysis earlier, and leads to a structure for the tasks. Don't over-constrain users, make navigation easy, and provide facilities so that they always know where they are.
- Document alternative conceptual design models in sketches and explanatory notes.

An example conceptual model based on this approach is shown in Figure 11.7. This is a process-based model, and so it is structured around the processes and subprocesses the system is to support. ■

(Mayhew, 1999)

Interaction types. In Chapter 2 we introduced four different types of interaction: instructing, conversing, manipulating, and exploring. Which is best suited to your current design depends on the application domain and the kind of product being developed. For example, a computer game is most likely to suit a manipulating style, while a drawing package has aspects of instructing and conversing.

Most conceptual models will include a combination of interaction types, and it is necessary to associate different parts of the interaction with different types. For example, consider the travel organizer. One of the users' tasks is to find out the visa regulations for a particular destination; this will require an instructing approach to interaction. No dialog is necessary for the system to show the required information, the user simply has to enter a predefined set of information, e.g. origin of passport and destination. On the other hand, the users' task of trying to identify a holiday for a group of people may be conducted more like a conversation. We can imagine that the user begins by selecting some characteristics of the holiday and some time constraints and preferences, then the organizer will respond with several options, and the user will provide more information or preferences and so on. This is much more like a conversation. (You may like to refer back to the scenario of this task in Chapter 10 and consider how well it matches this type of interaction.) Alternatively, for users who don't have any clear requirements yet, they might prefer to be able to explore the information before asking for specific options.

Activity 11.3

Consider the library catalog system introduced in Chapter 10. Identify tasks associated with this product that would be best supported by each of the interaction types instructing, conversing, manipulating, and exploring.

Comment

Here are some suggestions. You may have identified others:

1. **Instructing: the user wants to see details of a particular book, such as publisher and location.**
2. **Conversing: the user wants to identify a book on a particular topic but doesn't know exactly what is required.**
3. **Manipulating: the library books might be represented as icons that could be interrogated for information or manipulated to represent the book being reserved or borrowed.**
4. **Exploring: the user is looking for interesting books, with no particular topic or author in mind.**

Interface types. Considering different interfaces at this stage may seem premature, but it has both a design and a practical purpose. When thinking about the conceptual model for a product, it is important not to be unduly influenced by a predetermined interface type. Different interface types prompt and support different perspectives on the product under development and suggest different possible behaviors. Therefore considering the effect of different interfaces on the product at this stage is one way to prompt alternatives.

Before the product can be prototyped, some candidate alternative interfaces will need to have been chosen. These decisions will depend on the constraints on the product, arising from the requirements you have established. For example, input and output devices will be influenced particularly by user and environmental requirements. Therefore, considering interfaces here also takes one step towards producing practical prototypes.

To illustrate this, we consider a subset of the interfaces introduced in Chapter 6, and the different perspectives they bring to the travel organizer:

- *WIMP/GUI interface.* This is the traditional desktop interface which uses windows, icons, menus, and a pointing device. It would certainly be possible to build the travel organizer around this model, but having a separate keyboard and mouse in a public space may not be practical because of potential risk of damage. WIMP systems also tend not to be very exciting and engaging, but a system to support people going on holiday to have a good time should be exciting and fun.

- *Shareable interface.* The travel organizer has to be shareable as it is intended to be used by a group of people. The design issues for shareable interfaces which were introduced in Chapter 6 will need to be considered for this system.
- *Tangible interface.* Tangible interfaces are a form of sensor-based interaction, where blocks or other physical objects are moved around. Thinking about a travel organizer in this way conjures up an interesting image of people collaborating, maybe with the physical objects representing themselves traveling, but there are practical problems of having this kind of interface in a public place, as the objects may be lost or damaged.
- *Advanced graphical interface.* These interfaces include multimedia presentations, virtual environments, and interactive animations. If this kind of interface were used then the system could provide moving images and virtual experiences representing the holiday and the destination for the users. Giving users the chance to experience more than two-dimensional descriptions and photographs would be a very exciting prospect indeed!

Activity 11.4

Consider the library catalog system and pick out two interface types from Chapter 6 that might provide a different perspective on the design.

Comment

Library catalog systems tend to be built around the WIMP/GUI style of interface, so it is worth exploring other styles to see what insights they may bring. We had the following thoughts, but you may have had others.

The library catalog is likely to be used only in certain places, such as the library itself or perhaps in an office. However, it might be useful to be mobile around the library while searching for a book or journal. The mobile interface therefore presents some interesting alternative ideas such as using bar code readers or positioning technology to help identify locations, or books, or to inform users about sections of the library they are in. Any interfaces that require speech or that make a noise would not be appropriate in this quiet environment, also complex presentation styles (such as multimedia or multimodal) might make the task of finding the book you want more complex than it needs to be. A web-based interface may be appropriate.

11.3.2 Expanding the initial conceptual model

Considering the issues in the previous section helps the designer to produce a set of initial conceptual model ideas. These ideas must be thought through in more detail and expanded before being prototyped or tested with users. For example, you have to decide more concretely what concepts need to be communicated between the user and the product and how they are to be structured, related, and presented. This means deciding which functions the product will perform (and which the user will perform), how those functions are related, and what information is required to support them. Although these decisions must be made, remember that they are made only tentatively to begin with and may change after prototyping and evaluation.

What functions will the product perform? Understanding the tasks the product will support is a fundamental aspect of developing the conceptual model, but it is also important to consider more specifically what functions the product will perform, i.e. how the task will be divided up between the human and the machine. For example, in the travel organizer example, the system may suggest specific holidays for a given set of people, but is that as far as it should go? Should it automatically put the holidays on hold, or wait until told that this holiday is suitable? Developing scenarios, essential use cases, and use cases for the system will help clarify the answers to these questions. Deciding what the system will do and what must be left for the user is sometimes called task allocation. The trade-off between what the product does and what to keep in the control of the user has cognitive implications (see Chapter 3), and is linked to social aspects of collaboration (see Chapter 4). In addition, if the cognitive load is too high for the user, then the device may be too stressful to use. On the other hand, if the product takes on too much and is too inflexible, then it may not be used at all.

Another aspect concerns the functions the hardware will perform, i.e. what functions will be 'hard-wired' into the product and what will be left under software control, and thereby possibly indirectly in the control of the human user? This leads to considerations of the product's architecture, although you would not expect necessarily to have a clear architectural design at this stage of development.

How are the functions related to each other? Functions may be related temporally, e.g. one must be performed before another, or two can be performed in parallel. They may also be related through any number of possible categorizations, e.g. all functions relating to telephone memory storage in a cell phone, or all options for accessing files in a wordprocessor. The relationships between tasks may constrain use or may indicate suitable task structures within the product. For example, if a task is dependent on completion of another task, then you may want to restrict the user to performing the tasks in strict order.

If task analysis has been performed on relevant tasks, the breakdown will support these kinds of decisions. For example, in the travel organizer example, the task analysis performed in Section 10.1 shows the subtasks involved and the order in which the subtasks can be performed. Thus, the system could allow potential holiday companies to be found before or after investigating the destination's facilities. It is, however, important to identify the potential holiday companies before looking for holiday availability.

What information needs to be available? What data is required to perform a task? How is this data to be transformed by the system? Data is one of the categories of requirements we aim to identify and capture through the requirements activity. During conceptual design, we need to consider these requirements and ensure that our model provides the information necessary to perform the task. Detailed issues of structure and display, such as whether to use an analog display or a digital display, will more likely be dealt with during the physical design activity, but implications arising from the type of data to be displayed may impact conceptual design issues. Information visualization was discussed in Section 6.2.3.

For example, in the task of identifying potential holiday options for a set of people using the travel organizer, the system needs to be told what kind of holiday is required, available budget, preferred destinations (if any), preferred dates and duration (if any), how many people it is for, and any special requirements (such as physical disability) that this group has. In order to perform the function, the system must have this information and also must have access to detailed holiday and destination descriptions, holiday availability, facilities, restrictions, and so on.

Physical design involves considering more concrete, detailed issues of designing the interface, such as screen or keypad design, which icons to use, how to structure menus, etc.

11.4 Physical design: getting concrete

There is no rigid border between conceptual design and physical design. Producing a prototype inevitably means making some detailed decisions, albeit tentatively. Interaction design is inherently iterative, and so some detailed issues will come up during conceptual design; similarly, during physical design it will be necessary to revisit decisions made during conceptual design. Exactly where the border lies is not relevant. What is relevant is that the conceptual design should be allowed to develop freely without being tied to physical constraints too early, as this might inhibit creativity.

Design is about making choices and decisions, and the designer must strive to balance environmental, user, data, and usability requirements with functional requirements. These are often in conflict. For example, a PDA must provide adequate functionality but the size of screen and use of keyboard are constrained by the fact that it is a portable device. This means that the display of information is limited and the number of unique function keys is also limited, resulting in restricted views of information and the need to associate multiple functions with function keys.

There are many aspects to the physical design of interactive products, and we can't cover them all in this book. Chapter 6 introduced you to several interface types and their associated design issues. You will notice from this chapter that a plethora of guidelines for all types of design are available, and their number is growing. In addition, there are guidelines and regulations covering design for certain kinds of user. Box 11.4 describes some pointers for designing telephones for elderly people; Box 11.5 discusses issues concerning culturally-sensitive design.

The way we design the physical interface of the interactive product should not conflict with the user's cognitive processes involved in achieving the task. In Chapter 3, we introduced a number of these processes, such as attention, perception, memory, and so on, and we must design the physical form with these human characteristics very much in mind. For example, to help avoid memory overload, the interface should list options instead of making us remember a long list of possibilities. A wide range of guidelines, principles, and rules has been developed to help designers ensure that their products are usable.

Box 11.4
Designing telephones for the elderly and disabled

The British Royal National Institute for the Blind (RNIB), together with the British Department of Trade and Industry and British Telecommunications, have compiled a brochure to explain the different impairments affecting many telephone user groups, together with a set of suggested telephone features that could greatly enhance the accessibility of devices for such user groups. They identify 15 impairments and 44 features that could be added to telephones to make their use more pleasant. The impairments include cognitive impairment, weak grip, limited dexterity, speech impairment, hearing impairment, and hand tremor (Gill and Shipley, 1999). Features that could make a difference to these user groups include:

- Guarded or recessed keys to help prevent pressing the wrong key by mistake.
- Sidetone reduction, which reduces the amount of noise picked up from the environment and mixed with incoming speech at the earpiece.
- Allowing the user to adjust the amount of pressure needed to select a key. Apart from the more obvious consequences of too much or too little pressure, unsuitable key pressure may produce muscle spasms in some users.
- Audio and tactile key feedback to indicate when a key has been pressed.

The ALVA MPO braille-based cell phone was described in Box 6.5. This phone represents an advance in cell phones for people with visual impairments, although it does not cater for all of these guidelines. ■

Box 11.5
Designing for different cultures

Throughout the book, you will find interaction design examples relating to different cultures, e.g. Indian midwives, Chinese ATM users, European travelers, American and British online shoppers, and so on. As companies and communities stretch around the world, designing systems, particularly websites, for a wide ranges of cultures has become more important. Building on the cultural dimensions proposed by Hofstede (see Chapter 10), Aaron Marcus and Emilie West Gould (2000) have suggested how these dimensions are reflected in the design of websites. For example, websites designed for countries with high 'power distance' are likely to focus on expertise, authority, certificates, leaders, and official stamps, while low power distance countries will focus more on social and moral order, customers, citizens, and freedom. Countries with high 'uncertainty avoidance' will be designed around simple, clear metaphors, navigation schemes to avoid users getting lost, and redundant cues to reduce ambiguity. Low uncertainty avoidance cultures emphasize complexity with maximal choice, acceptance of 'risk' associated with getting lost, less control of navigation, and multiple links with coding in color, sound, and typography.

An alternative approach to taking explicit account of differences in national culture is to develop an international site. The following guidelines are intended to help international design (Esselink, 2000).

1. Be careful about using images that depict hand gestures or people.
2. Use generic icons.
3. Choose colors that are not associated with national flags or political movements.
4. Ensure that the product supports different calendars, date formats, and time formats.
5. Ensure that the product supports different number formats, currencies, weights and measurement systems.
6. Ensure that the product supports international paper sizes, envelope sizes, and address formats.
7. Avoid integrating text in graphics as they cannot be translated easily.
8. Allow for text expansion when translated from English. ■

Dilemma
One global website or many local websites?

One choice that multinational companies have to make when designing their websites is whether to attempt to produce one site that will appeal across all cultures or to tailor each country's website to the local culture. This is more than just translating the site into different languages, as different cultures around the world respond differently to a whole range of attitudes and priorities. The list of guidelines in Box 11.5 illustrates this. It could be argued that trying to create one website image that is appealing to most cultures is very difficult, e.g. what does a generic icon look like? Yet creating different images for each culture is resource-intensive and might run the risk of diluting the brand. The website for Coca-Cola (`www.cocacola.com`), a brand which has a worldwide image, has links to a different local website for each of over 80 countries from Malawi to New Zealand and from Russia to the Seychelles. On the other hand, Pepsi, who also have a worldwide image, do not have such links from their website (`www.pepsi.com`). If you were going to design a website for a multinational company, what would you do?

11.5 Using scenarios in design

In Chapter 10, we introduced scenarios as informal stories about user tasks and activities. They are a powerful mechanism for communicating among team members and with users. We stated in Chapter 10 that scenarios could be used and refined through different data-gathering sessions, and they can be used to check out alternative designs at any stage.

Scenarios can be used to explicate existing work situations, but they are more commonly used for expressing proposed or imagined situations to help in conceptual design. Often, stakeholders are actively involved in producing and checking through scenarios for a product. Bødker identifies four roles that have been suggested for scenarios (Bødker, 2000, p. 63):

- As a basis for the overall design.
- For technical implementation.
- As a means of cooperation within design teams.
- As a means of cooperation across professional boundaries, i.e. as a basis of communication in a multidisciplinary team.

In any one project, scenarios may be used for any or all of these. Box 11.6 details how different scenarios were used throughout the development of a speech-recognition system. More specifically, scenarios have been used as scripts for user evaluation of prototypes, providing a concrete example of a task the user will perform with the product. Scenarios can also be used as the basis of storyboard creation (see below), and to build a shared understanding among team members of the kind of system being developed. Scenarios are good at selling ideas to users, managers, and potential customers. For example, the scenario presented in Figure 10.9 was designed to sell ideas to potential customers on how a product might enhance their lifestyles.

An interesting idea also proposed by Bødker is the notion of *plus* and *minus scenarios*. These attempt to capture the most positive and the most negative consequences of a particular proposed design solution (see Figure 11.8), thereby helping designers to gain a more comprehensive view of the proposal.

Scenario 3: Hyper-wonderland

This scenario addresses the positive aspects of how a hypermedia solution will work.

The setting is the Lindholm construction site sometime in the future.

Kurt has access to a portable PC. The portables are hooked up to the computer at the site office via a wireless modem connection, through which the supervisors run the hypermedia application.

Action: During inspection of one of the caissons[1] *Kurt takes his portable PC, switches it on and places the cursor on the required information. He clicks the mouse button and gets the master file index together with an overview of links. He chooses the links of relevance for the caisson he is inspecting.*

Kurt is pleased that he no longer needs to plan his inspections in advance. This is a great help because due to the 'event-driven' nature of inspection, constructors never know where and when an inspection is taking place. Moreover, it has become much easier to keep track of personal notes, reports etc. because they can be entered directly on the spot.

The access via the construction site interface does not force him to deal with complicated keywords either. Instead, he can access the relevant information right away, literally from where he is standing.

A positive side effect concerns his reachability. As long as he has logged in on the computer, he is within reach of the secretaries and can be contacted when guests arrive or when he is needed somewhere else on the site. Moreover, he can see at a glance where his colleagues are working and get in touch with them when he needs their help or advice.

All in all, Kurt feels that the new computer application has put him more in control of things.

[1] Used in building to hold water back during construction.

Scenario 4: Panopticon

This scenario addresses the negative aspects of how a hypermedia solution will work.

The setting is the Lindholm construction site sometime in the future.

Kurt has access to a portable PC. The portables are hooked up to the computer at the site office via a wireless modem connection, through which the supervisors run the hypermedia application.

Action: During inspecting one of the caissons Kurt starts talking to one of the builders about some reinforcement problem. They argue about the recent lab tests, and he takes out his portable PC in order to provide some data which justify his arguments. It takes quite a while before he finds a spot where he can place the PC: either there is too much light, or there is no level surface at a suitable height. Finally, he puts the laptop on a big box and switches it on. He positions the cursor on the caisson he is currently inspecting and clicks the mouse to get into the master file. The table of contents pops up and from the overview of links he chooses those of relevance — but no lab test appears on the screen. Obviously, the file has not been updated as planned.

Kurt is rather upset. This loss of prestige in front of a contractor engineer would not have happened if he had planned his inspection as he had in the old days.

Sometimes. he feels like a hunted fox especially in situations where he is drifting around thinking about what kind of action to take in a particular case. If he has forgotten to log out, he suddenly has a secretary on the phone: "I see you are right at caisson 39, so could you not just drop by and take a message?"

All in all Kurt feels that the new computer application has put him under control.

Figure 11.8 *Example plus and minus scenarios*

Activity 11.5

Consider an in-car navigation system ('sat nav') for planning routes, and suggest one plus and one minus scenario. For the plus scenario, try to think of all the possible benefits of the system. For the minus scenario, try to imagine everything that could go wrong.

Comment

***Scenario 1*. This plus scenario shows some potential positive aspects of an in-car navigation system.**

Beth is in a hurry to get to her friend's house. She jumps into the car and switches on her in-car navigation system. The display appears quickly, showing her local area and indicating the current location of her car with a bright white dot. She calls up the memory function of the device and chooses her friend's address. A number of her frequent destinations are stored like this in the device, ready for her to pick the one she wants. She chooses the 'shortest route' option and the device thinks for a few seconds before showing her a bird's-eye view of her route. This feature is very useful because she can get an overall view of where she is going.

Once the engine is started, the display reverts to a close-up view to show the details of her journey. As she pulls away from the pavement, a calm voice tells her to "drive straight on for half a mile, then turn left." After half a mile, the voice says again "turn left at the next junction." As Beth has traveled this route many times before, she doesn't need to be told when to turn left or right, so she turns off the voice output and relies only on the display, which shows sufficient detail for her to see the location of her car, her destination and the roads she needs to use.

***Scenario 2*. This minus scenario shows some potential negative aspects of an in-car navigation system.**

Beth is in a hurry to get to her friend's house. She gets in her car and turns on the in-car navigation system. The car's battery is faulty so all the information she had entered into the device has been lost. She has to tell the device her destination by choosing from a long list of towns and roads. Eventually, she finds the right address and asks for the quickest route. The device takes ages to respond, but after a couple of minutes displays an overall view of the route it has found. To Beth's dismay, the route chosen includes one of the main roads that is being dug up over this weekend, so she cannot use the route. She needs to find another route, so she presses the cancel button and tries again to search for her friend's address through the long list of towns and roads. By this time, she is very late.

Box 11.6
Using scenarios throughout design

Scenarios were used throughout the design of a speech-recognition system (Karat, 1995). The goal of the project was to produce a product that used speech-recognition technology, so there was no defined set of user requirements to start with. The system offered speech-to-text dictation capabilities and also speech command capabilities for an application running on the same platform.

Initially, scenarios were used to set the direction of the project: discussions revolved around whether the scenario was correct or not, i.e. whether people would want to use the device to achieve the suggested task. Then scenarios were used to sketch out screens and an early user guide. Discussions at this point included checking what information was needed on the screen at what time, and also deciding what components needed to be built. Use-oriented scenarios, i.e. scenarios suggesting how the device might be used, formed the basis of early design meetings that resulted in a shared understanding of what facilities the system might include. An example scenario from basic direction setting was, "Imagine taking away the keyboard and mouse from your current workstation and describe doing everything through voice commands."

Once the basic direction was agreed, further scenarios were generated to discuss the components of the system. These scenarios focused on typical use of speech commands so that vocabulary could be tracked. An example scenario for discussing vocabulary and system components was as follows.

Overall task: Open system editor, find file REPORT.TXT, change font to Times 16, save changes, and exit the editor.

This scenario was then broken down into a specific word list as follows:

Voice scenario steps: "system_editor" "open" "open" "file" "find" "r" "e" "p" "open" "font" "times" "16" "ok" "save" "close"

A short user guide was developed early on, in parallel with the initial scenario development. User guide scenarios were generated by thinking about the kinds of question a user might need to answer, for example, "What is a speech manager?" "How do I know what I can say?"

Once early prototypes were developed, scenarios together with additional tasks were used as a basis for user testing. One of the problems was that people were unsure of what they could say, and although the system included a "What can I say?" module, this itself proved difficult to use. An example scenario used in testing was "Change the background color of the icon for the communications folder to red."

Scenarios in the form of video prototypes were taken to potential customers

later in the project for feedback. The feedback they received was mostly in scenario form too, and the scenarios extracted were fed back into the design process. For example, one of the scenarios collected was, "I would like to walk around while I dictate." This could be accommodated by making mobility a factor when selecting the microphone.

Collecting feedback in the form of scenarios continued later in the project, and these informed both the design of the product and the associated documentation. ■

11.6 Using prototypes in design

We introduced different kinds of prototype and reasons for prototyping in Section 11.2. In this section we illustrate how prototypes may be used in design, and specifically we demonstrate one way in which prototypes may be generated from the output of the requirements activity, as described in this book: producing a storyboard from a scenario and a card-based prototype from a use case. Both of these are low-fidelity prototypes and they may be used as the basis to develop more detailed interface designs and higher-fidelity prototypes as development progresses.

11.6.1 Generating storyboards from scenarios

A storyboard represents a sequence of actions or events that the user and the system go through to achieve a task. A scenario is one story about how a product may be used to achieve the task. It is therefore possible to generate a storyboard from a scenario by breaking the scenario into a series of steps which focus on interaction, and creating one scene in the storyboard for each step. The purpose for doing this is two-fold. First, to produce a storyboard that can be used to get feedback from users and colleagues. Second, to prompt the design team to consider the scenario and the use of the system in more detail. For example, consider the scenario for the travel organizer developed in Chapter 10. This can be broken down into six main steps:

1. The Thomson family gather around the organizer and enter a set of initial requirements.
2. The system's initial suggestion is that they consider a flotilla holiday but Sky and Eamonn aren't happy.
3. The travel organizer shows them some descriptions of the holidays written by young people.
4. The system asks for various further details.
5. The system confirms that there are places in the Mediterranean.
6. The travel organizer prints out a summary.

The first thing to notice about this set of steps is that it does not have the detail of a use case, and is not intended to be a use case. We are simply trying to identify the key events or activities associated with the scenario. The second thing to notice is that some of these events are focused solely on the travel organizer's screen and some are concerned with the environment. For example, the first one talks about the family gathering around the organizer, while the third and fourth are focused on the travel organizer and the information it is outputting. We therefore could produce a storyboard that focuses on the screens or one that is focused on the environment. Either way, sketching out the storyboard will prompt us to think about issues concerning the travel organizer and its design.

For example, the scenario says nothing about the kind of input and output devices that the system might use, but drawing the organizer forces you to think about these things. There is some information about the environment within which the system will operate, but again drawing the scene makes you stop and think about where the organizer will be. You don't have to make any decisions about, e.g. using a trackball, or a touch screen or whatever, but you are forced to think about it. When focusing on the screens, the designer is prompted to consider issues including what information needs to be available and what information needs to be output. This all helps to explore design decisions and alternatives, but is also made more explicit because of the drawing act.

We chose to draw a storyboard that focuses on the environment of the travel organizer, and it is shown in Figure 11.9. While drawing this, various questions relating to the environment arose in my mind such as how can the interaction be designed for all the family? Will they sit or stand? How confidential should the interaction be? What kind of documentation or help needs to be available? What physical components does the travel organizer need? And so on. In this exercise, the questions it prompts are just as important as the end product.

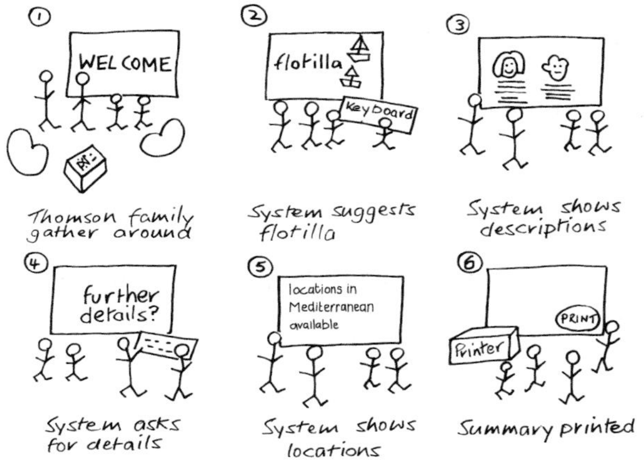

Figure 11.9 The storyboard for the travel organizer focusing on environmental issues

Note that although we have used the scenario as the main driver for producing the storyboard, there is other information from the requirements activity that also informs the development.

Activity 11.6

In Activity 10.3, you developed a futuristic scenario for the one-stop car shop. Using this scenario, develop a storyboard that focuses on the environment of the user. As you are drawing this storyboard, write down the design issues you are prompted to consider.

Comment

We used the scenario in the comment for Activity 10.3. This scenario breaks down into five main steps: the user arrives at the one-stop car shop; the user is directed into an empty booth; the user sits down in the racing car seat and the display comes alive; the user can print off reports and can take a virtual reality drive in their chosen car. The storyboard is shown in Figure 11.10. Issues that occurred to me as I drew this storyboard included where to locate the printer, what kind of virtual reality equipment is needed, what input devices are needed: a keyboard or touchscreen, a steering wheel, clutch, accelerator and brake pedals? How like the car controls do the input devices need to be? You may have thought of other issues.

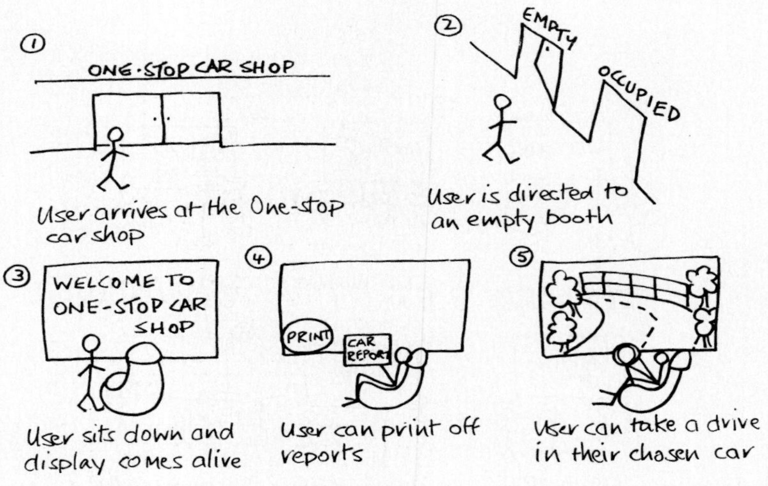

Figure 11.10 The storyboard generated from the one-stop car shop scenario in Chapter 10

11.6.2 Generating card-based prototypes from use cases

The value of a card-based prototype lies in the fact that the screens or screen elements can be manipulated and moved around in order to simulate interaction (either with a user or without). Where a storyboard focusing on the screens has been developed, this can be translated into a card-based prototype and used in this way. Another way to produce a card-based prototype is to generate one from a use case output from the requirements activity.

For example, consider the use case generated for the travel organizer in Chapter 10. This focused on the visa requirements part of the system. For each step in the use case, the travel organizer will need to have an interaction component to deal with it, e.g. a button or menu option, or a display screen. By stepping through the use case, it is possible to build up a card-based prototype to cover the required behavior. For example, the cards in Figure 11.11 were developed by considering each of the steps in the use case. Card one covers step 1. Card two covers steps 2, 3, 4, 5, 6, and 7. Card three covers steps 8, 9, 10, and

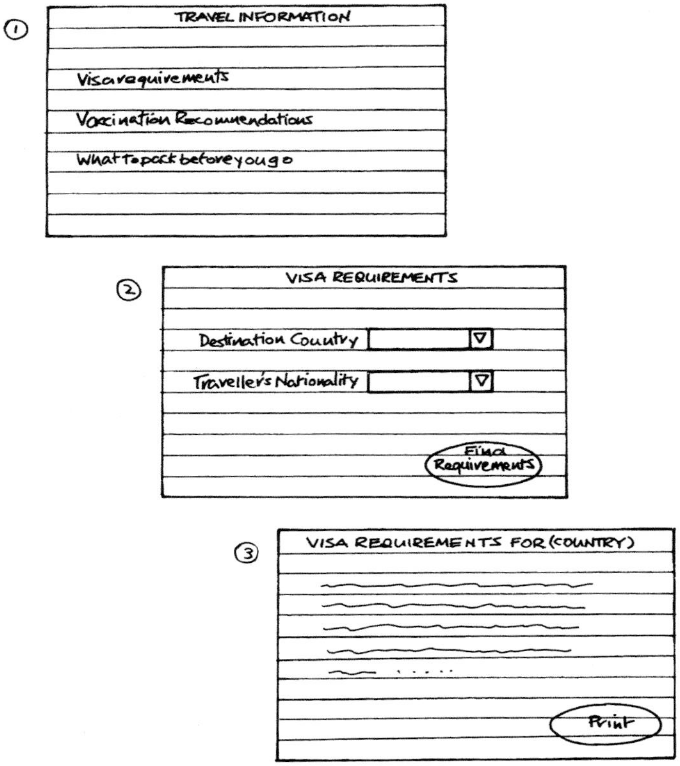

Figure 11.11 *Cards one to three*

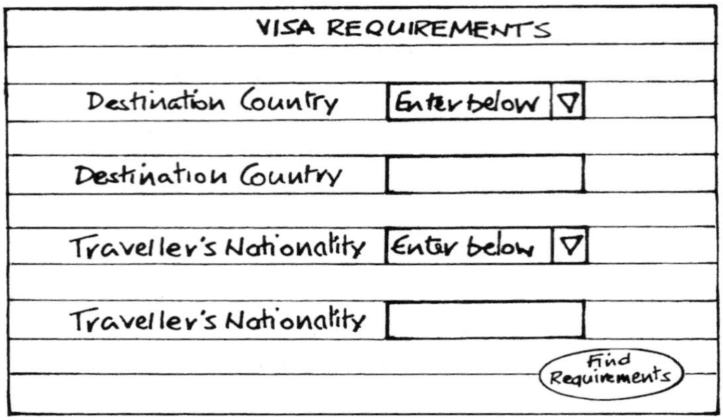

Figure 11.12 *Card four from the above*

11—notice the print button that is drawn into card three to allow for steps 10 and 11. As with the storyboards, drawing concrete elements of the interface like this forces the designer to think about detailed issues so that the user can interact with the prototype. In card two you will see that I chose to use a drop-down menu for the country and nationality. This is to avoid mistakes. However, the flaw in this is that I may not catch all of the countries in my list, and so an alternative design could also be incorporated where the user can choose an 'enter below' option and then type in the country or nationality (see Figure 11.12).

These cards can then be shown to potential users of the system to get their informal feedback. Remember that the more often you show developing ideas to potential users, the more likely it is that the design will fulfill its goals.

Activity 11.7

Produce a card-based prototype for the library catalog system and the task of locating a book as described by the use case in Activity 10.5. You may also like to ask one of your peers to act as a user and step through the task using the prototype.

Comment

Three of the cards from our prototype are shown in Figure 11.13. Note that in putting these cards together, we have not included a separate search author screen (as implied by step 8 of the use case), but have included other search options for the user to choose. In checking the interaction with users, it may be decided that having a separate screen is better.

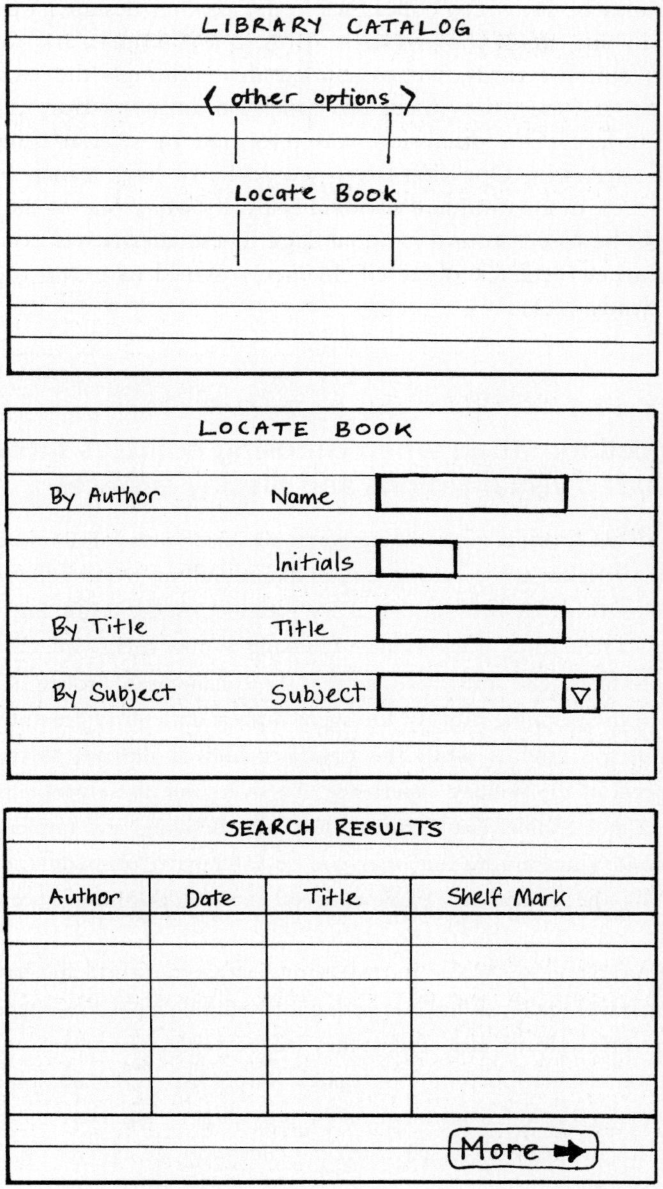

Figure 11.13 *A card-based prototype for locating a book in the library catalog system*

Card-based prototypes may be shown to users to gain informal feedback. Equally importantly, they may be shown to colleagues to get another designer's perspective on the emerging design. In this case, I showed these cards to a colleague, and through discussion of the application and the cards, we concluded that although the cards represent one interpretation of the use case, they focus too much on an interaction model that assumes a WIMP/GUI interface. Our discussion was informed by several things including the storyboard and the scenario. One alternative would be to have a map of the world, and users can indicate their destination and nationality by choosing one of the countries on the map; another might be based around national flags. These alternatives could be prototyped using cards and further feedback obtained. In fact, a world map was used in the eSpace project (see Case Study 11.1).

CASE STUDY 11.1

Supporting collaboration when choosing holidays through the design of shared visualizations and display surfaces

The goal of the eSPACE project was to help agents and customers collaborate more effectively when developing complex, tailor-made products like round the world holidays, hi-fi systems, insurance portfolios, fitted kitchens, or digital TV packages. At the beginning of the project an in-depth six-month field study was conducted looking at how agents and customers plan and build up travel products. The study revealed that the collaborative process is often hampered by asymmetries in the planning process: the agent finds it difficult to communicate and share information about the product while the customer finds it difficult to piece together all the different aspects of the holiday experience. To overcome these problems an innovative workspace, called the 'eTable' (see Figure 11.14), was designed and implemented that uses interactive dynamic visualizations and user-centric interactive planning tools. The designs were informed by the conceptual framework of external cognition (Scaife and Rogers, 1996).

The eTable prototype was placed in trade shows across the world and has been evaluated in use at a leading travel agency. It has met with overwhelmingly positive responses. Customers come away with a much clearer idea of what they will be doing. Consultants are able to explore options with customers in a much more integrated way. One consultant commented that the eTable enabled her to 'draw the customer in' by providing an attractive vicarious experience of the holiday. "It's much easier to sell when the client can see everything, they get excited when it starts taking shape."

Figure 11.14 The eSpace project

Box 11.7
Design patterns for HCI

Design patterns have become popular in software engineering since the early 1990s. Patterns capture experience, but they have a different structure and a different philosophy from other forms of guidance, such as the guidelines we introduced earlier, or specific methods. One of the intentions of the patterns community is to create a vocabulary, based on the names of the patterns, that designers can use to communicate with one another and with users. Another is to produce a literature in the field that documents experience in a compelling form.

The idea of patterns was first proposed by Christopher Alexander, a British architect who described patterns in architecture. His hope was to capture the 'quality without a name' that is recognizable in something when you know it is good.

But what is a pattern? One simple definition is that it is a solution to a problem in a context. What this means is that a pattern describes a problem, a solution, and where this solution has been found to work. This means that users of the pattern

can see not only the problem and solution, but also understand when and where it has worked before and access a rationale for why it worked. This helps designers in adopting it (or not) for themselves.

Patterns on their own are interesting, but not as powerful as a pattern language. A pattern language is a network of patterns that reference one another and work together to create a complete structure.

The application of patterns to interaction design has grown steadily since the late 1990s. For example, Jan Borchers (2001) describes three pattern languages for interactive music exhibits: one for music, one for HCI, and one for software engineering, all of which have arisen from his experience of designing music exhibits.

A more recent example comes from a case study at Yahoo!, where they wanted to communicate standards in order to increase consistency, predictability, and usability across their various product teams, and to increase productivity by preventing developers from 'reinventing the wheel.' They developed an interaction design pattern repository and a process for submitting and reviewing patterns. This pattern repository is growing. ■

11.6.3 Prototyping physical design

Moving forward from a card-based prototype, you can expand the cards to generate a more detailed software or paper-based prototype. To do this, you would take one or more cards and translate them into a sketch that included more detail about input and output technology, icon usage, error messages, menu structures, and any style conventions needed for consistency with other products. Also, issues such as interface layout, information display, attention, memory, etc., would be considered at this stage.

If the prototype remains paper-based then it may consist of a set of sketches representing the interface and its different states, or it may be more sophisticated using post-it notes, masking tape, acetate sheets, and various other paper products that allow the prototype to be 'run' by a person pretending to be the computer. In this set-up, the user sits in front of the paper representation of the interface and interacts with the interface as though it was real, pressing buttons, choosing options, etc., but instead of the system reacting automatically and changing the display according to the user's input, a human places the next screen, or modified message display, or menu drop-down list, etc., in front of the user. Snyder (2003) provides a lot of practical information for creating this kind of prototype and running these sessions. She suggests that a minimum of four people are required to evaluate this form of prototype: the 'computer,' a user, a facilitator who conducts the session, and one or more observers. Figure 11.15 illustrates this kind of session. Here you see the user (on the left) interacting with a prototype while the 'computer' (on the right) simulates the system's behavior. Further information about paper prototyping is in Case Study 11.2.

Figure 11.15 The 'computer' highlights a term the user has just clicked on

Box 11.8
Involving users in design: participatory design

The idea of participatory design emerged in Scandinavia in the late 1960s and early 1970s. There were two influences on this early work: the desire to be able to communicate information about complex systems, and the labor union movement pushing for workers to have democratic control over changes in their work. In the 1970s, new laws gave workers the right to have a say in how their working environment was changed, and such laws are still in force today. A fuller history of the movement is given in Ehn (1989) and Nygaard (1990).

Several projects at this time attempted to involve users in design and tried to focus on work rather than on simply producing a product. One of the most discussed is the UTOPIA project, a cooperative effort between the Nordic Graphics Workers Union and research institutions in Denmark and Sweden to design computer-based tools for text and image processing.

Involving users in design decisions is not simple, however. Cultural differences can become acute when users and designers are asked to work together to produce a specification for a system. Bødker *et al.* (1991) recount the following scene from the UTOPIA project:

Late one afternoon, when the designers were almost through with a long presentation of a proposal for the user interface of an integrated text and image processing system, one of the typographers commented on the lack of information about typographical code-structure. He didn't think that it was a big error (he was a polite person), but he just wanted to point out that the computer scientists who had prepared the proposal had forgotten to specify how the codes were to be presented on the screen. Would it read "<bf/" or perhaps just "\b" when the text that followed was to be printed in boldface?

In fact, the system being described by the designers was a WYSIWYG (what you see is what you get) system, and so text that needed to be in bold typeface

En lokal fackklubb
förbereder sig för ny teknik:
– Ritningama begriper vi inte
Vi gör attrapper och provar

Sort machine mock-up. The headline reads: "We did not understand the blueprints, so we made our own mock-ups."

Figure 11.16 *A newspaper cutting showing a parcel-sorting machine mockup*

would appear as bold (although most typographic systems at that time did require such codes). The typographer was unable to link his knowledge and experience with what he was being told. In response to this kind of problem, the project started using mockups. Simulating the working situation helped workers to draw on their experience and tacit knowledge, and designers to get a better understanding of the actual work typographers needed to do. An example mockup for a computer-controlled parcel-sorting system, from another project, is shown in Figure 11.16 (Ehn and Kyng, 1991). The headline of this newspaper clipping reads, "We did not understand the blueprints, so we made our own mockups." ■

CASE STUDY 11.2
Paper prototyping as a core tool in the design of cell phone user interfaces

Paper prototyping is increasingly being used by cell phone companies as a core part of their design process. This approach is replacing the old adage of 'throwing the technology at users to see if it sticks.' There is much competition in the cell phone industry demanding ever more new concepts. Mobile devices are feature-rich. They now include mega-pixel cameras, music players, media galleries, and downloaded applications and more. This requires designing complex interactions, but which are clear to learn and use. Paper prototyping offers a rapid way to work through every detail of the interaction design across multiple applications.

Cell phone projects involve a range of disciplines—all with their own viewpoint on what the product should be. A typical project may include programmers, project managers, marketing experts, commercial managers, handset manufacturers, user experience specialists, visual designers, content managers, and network specialists. Paper prototyping provides a vehicle for everyone involved to be part of the design process—considering the design from multiple angles in a collaborative way.

The case study on the website describes the benefits of using paper prototyping from a designers' viewpoint while considering the bigger picture of its impact across the entire project lifecycle. It starts by explaining the problem space and how paper prototyping is used as an integrated part of UI design projects for European and US-based mobile operator companies. The case study uses project examples to illustrate the approach and explains step-by-step how the method can be used to include a range of stakeholders in the design process—regardless of their skill set or background. The case study offers exercises so you can experiment with the approach yourself.

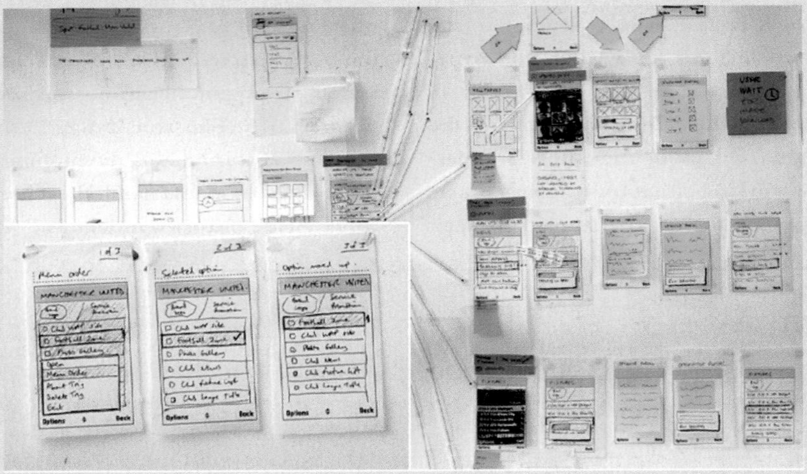

***Figure 11.17** Prototype developed for cell phone user interface*

As well as considering information relating to the product's usability and user experience goals, physical design prototypes draw on design guidelines for potential interface types, like those discussed in Chapter 6. For example, consider the travel organizer system. For this, we need a shareable interface and from the design issues discussed in Chapter 6, we know that a horizontal surface encourages more collaboration than a vertical one; we also know that a large interface leads to a break-up in this collaboration. So, a horizontal (i.e. table) interface appears to be most appropriate at this stage. Scott *et al.* (2003) have studied these kinds of system and generated a set of eight design guidelines tailored just for tabletop displays. They are summarized briefly in Table 11.2.

Some of these guidelines are particularly interesting to consider in the context of the travel organizer. For example, guideline two addresses the user's behavior of switching between different activities. In a drawing package, for example, the user is normally required to explicitly signal when moving from the activity of pointing, to writing text, to drawing a box, etc., yet if you observe people interacting without software there is usually a much more fluid transition between activities. In the travel organizer, users will be spending a lot of time choosing alternatives, e.g. selecting a destination or holiday and wanting to find out more about it. They will also need to enter text, e.g. to give their names or to initiate searches. One possible way to support this would be to have a touchscreen so

1. ***Support Interpersonal Interaction:*** **technology designed to support group activities must support the fundamental mechanisms people use to collaborate. Some of these were discussed in Chapter 4.**
2. ***Support Fluid Transitions between Activities*****: technology should not impose excessive overhead on switching between activities such as writing, drawing, and manipulating artifacts.**
3. ***Support Transitions between Personal and Group Work*****: people are adept at rapidly moving between individual and group work when collaborating. With a traditional table, people often identify distinct areas for personal use, and this may help to support transition from individual to group working.**
4. ***Support Transitions between Tabletop Collaboration and External Work*****: the system should provide an easy way to integrate work done external to the tabletop environment.**
5. ***Support the Use of Physical Objects*****: items placed on a table include work-related items such as reports and design plans and personal items such as coffee cups. Tabletop systems should support these familiar practices.**
6. ***Provide Shared Access to Physical and Digital Objects*****: sharing an object supports collaboration more easily than if each participant has their own copy of the object. If people are at different positions around the table then orientation of an object can become an issue, e.g. it may be upside down for some participants.**
7. ***Consideration for the Appropriate Arrangements of Users*****: people gather around a table in different locations, in relation to each other and in relation to the items on the table. The kind of activity and the items on the table affect the most appropriate positions for individuals, e.g. text or pictures may be upside down for some attendees.**
8. ***Support Simultaneous User Actions*****: at a standard table, participants can interact with an item on the table simultaneously. Turn-taking in such a situation, while possible, feels cumbersome.**

Table 11.2 *Design guidelines for tabletop displays (Scott et al., 2003)*

that people can point at what they want, and to support hand-writing recognition with touchscreen technology. This would be simple and easy to use, as touchscreens only need a finger or other similar implement; the main disadvantage is that touchscreens are not very accurate.

Guideline seven is relevant to table location and how it would be oriented within the travel agent's office. For example, if it was against the wall then users would only be able to access it from the front and sides. This has advantages as a lot of the display material will be textual or photographic, which makes most sense if you see it the right way up. This might also restrict the number of people who can gather comfortably around the device, depending on its size, and how friendly members of the group want to be with each other.

Activity 11.8

Consider guidelines three and five, and discuss their application within the context of the travel organizer. It might help you to think about how you and your peers interact around an ordinary table. Does the shape of the table make a difference? How does the interaction vary?

Comment

These were our thoughts, but yours may be different.

If you look at people collaborating on a task around a table, they often have their own personal table space as well as interacting with the wider shared table space. How might this be achieved for the travel organizer? What kind of personal space might be needed? One possibility would be to divide up the surface so that parts of the display can be partitioned off to make a separate screen area for each individual. In this context, users might then be looking at other information away from the main focus of the group, and may be exploring alternative holidays on their own. In much the same way that people exploring their email through a laptop is distracting from the wider meeting, this could also be disruptive from the main goal of the group. However, providing an area for people to take notes and print them off later would be helpful.

Guideline five is about supporting the use of physical objects. But what physical objects might the users of the travel organizer have with them? Some of these are not relevant to the task, e.g. shopping bags, but they will need to be taken care of, i.e. stored somewhere. Other objects such as travel brochures or books or maps, which are relevant to the task, need somewhere to stand so that they can be seen and used as appropriate.

11.7 Tool support

The tools available to support the activities described here range from development environments that support prototyping through sketching tools, environments to support icon and menu design to widget libraries and so on.

For example, researchers at Berkeley (Newman *et al.*, 2003) have been developing a tool to support the informal sketching and prototyping of websites. This tool, now called DENIM, is a pen-based sketching tool that allows designers to sketch sites at different levels of refinement—overall site map, sequence of pages (like our card-based prototypes), and individual page. DENIM links these different levels of sketching together through zooming. Once created, pages can be linked to each other as with web links, and the prototype can then be run to show how the pages link together. All the while, the prototype maintains the

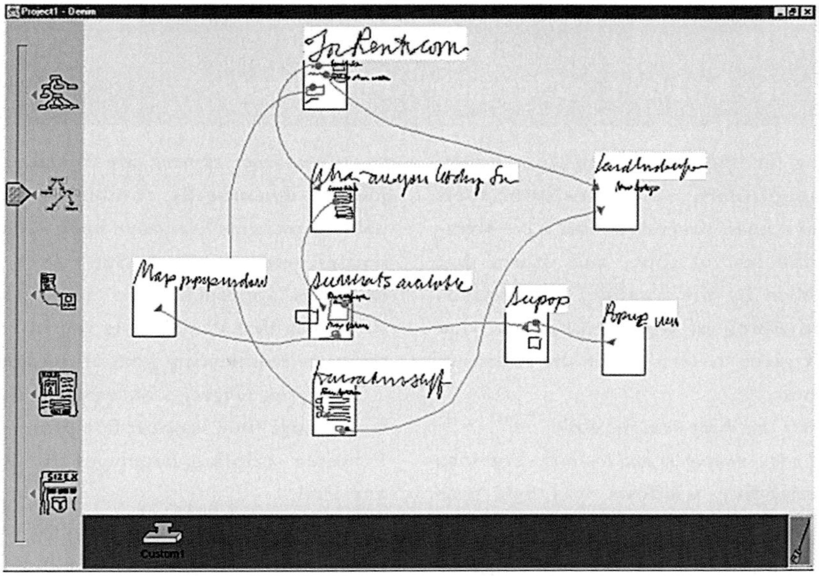

Figure 11.18 *An example screen from the tool DENIM that supports the development and running of sketchy prototypes in early design*

'sketchy' look. Figure 11.18 shows a screen from DENIM illustrating the individual pages and the links between them (green lines). The pages are at different stages of development, with some being blank while others have text, images, and links sketched onto them.

User interface software tools support developers by reducing the amount of code that has to be written in order to implement elements of the user interface such as windows and widgets, and to tie them all together. Box 11.9 summarized the successes and failures of these tools through the twentieth century, but Myers *et al.* (2002) go on to suggest some changes for user interface tools of the future. Most desktop applications built today were constructed using user interface software tools, but new tools and techniques are needed for constructing other interfaces such as very small (e.g. mobile) or very large (e.g. tabletop) displays. For example, the standard menu designs and widgets built into user interface tools are inappropriate for very small or very large displays; using a stylus instead of a mouse and keyboard relies on different interaction techniques from standard GUI applications, as do multi-modality interfaces. The need to rapidly prototype and evaluate devices as well as applications will affect the kinds of tools developers need. Tools to cater for the higher sophistication of users, the aging population (and therefore reduced dexterity of users), and end-user programming activities will also be needed. Maybe even tools that enforce the design of usable interfaces will be developed and deployed.

Box 11.9
Successes and failures for user interface tools

Looking at the history of user interface design tools, we can see some tools that have been successful and have withstood the test of time, and others that have fallen by the wayside. Understanding something of what works and what doesn't gives us lessons for the future of such tools.

Tools that have been successful are:

Window managers and toolkits. The idea of overlapping windows was first proposed by Alan Kay (Kay, 1969). These have been successful because they help to manage scarce resources: screen space and human perceptual and cognitive resources such as limited visual field and attention.

Event languages that are designed to program actions based on external events: for example, when the left mouse button is depressed, move the cursor here. These have worked because they map well to the direct manipulation graphical user interface style.

Interactive graphical tools or interface builders, such as Visual Basic. These allow the easy construction of user interfaces by placing interface elements on a screen using a mouse. They have been successful because they use a graphical means to design a graphical layout, i.e. you can build a graphical screen layout by grabbing and placing graphical elements without touching any program code.

Component systems are based on the idea of dynamically combining individual components that have been separately written and compiled. Sun's Java Beans uses this approach. One reason for its success is that it addresses the important software engineering goal of modularity.

Scripting languages have become popular because they support fast prototyping. Example scripting languages are Python and Perl.

Hypertext allows elements of a document to be linked in a multitude of ways, rather than the traditional linear layout. Most people are aware of hypertext links because of their use on the web.

Object-oriented programming. This programming approach is successful in interface development because the objects of an interface such as buttons and other widgets can so readily be cast as objects in the language.

Promising approaches that have not caught on are:

Technology has changed so fast that in some cases the tools to support the development of certain technologies have failed to keep up with the rapidly changing requirements. Good ideas that have fallen by the wayside include:

User interface management tools (UIMS). The idea behind UIMS was akin to the idea behind database management systems. Their purpose was to abstract away the details of interface implementation to allow developers to specify and manipulate interfaces at a higher level of abstraction. This separation turned out to be undesirable, as it is not always appropriate to be able to understand and manipulate interface elements only at a high level of abstraction.

Formal language based tools. Many systems in the 1980s were based on formal language concepts such as state transition diagrams and parsers for context-free grammars. These failed to catch on because: the dialog-based interfaces for which these tools were particularly suited were overtaken by direct manipulation interfaces; they were very good at producing sequential interfaces, but not at expressing unordered sequences of action; and they were difficult to learn even for programmers.

Constraints. Tools that were designed to maintain constraints, i.e. relationships among elements of an interface such as that the scroll bar should always be on the right of the window, or that the color of one item should be the same as the color of other items. These systems have not caught on because they can be unpredictable. Once constraints are set up, the tool must find a solution to maintain them, and since there is more than one solution, the tool may find a solution the user didn't expect.

Model-based and automatic techniques. The aim of these systems was to let developers specify interfaces at a high level of abstraction and then for an interface to be automatically generated according to a predefined set of interpretation rules. These too have suffered from problems of unpredictability, since the generation of the interfaces relies on heuristics and rules that are themselves unpredictable in concert. ■

(Myers *et al.*, 2002)

Assignment

This assignment continues work on the web-based ticket reservation system introduced at the end of Chapter 10. The work will be continued in the assignments for Chapters 14 and 15.

(a) Based on the information gleaned from the assignment in Chapter 10, suggest three different conceptual models for this system. You should consider each of the aspects of a conceptual model discussed in this chapter: interface metaphor, interaction style, interface style, activities it will support, functions, relationships between functions, and information requirements. Of these conceptual models, decide which one seems most appropriate and articulate the reasons why.

(b) Produce the following prototypes for your chosen conceptual model:

  (i) Using the scenarios generated for the ticket reservation system, produce a storyboard for the task of booking a ticket for one of your conceptual models. Show it to two or three potential users and get some informal feedback.

(ii) Now develop a card-based prototype from the use case for the task of booking a ticket, also incorporating feedback from part (i). Show this new prototype to a different set of potential users and get some more informal feedback.

(iii) Using a software-based prototyping tool (e.g. Visual Basic or Director) or web authoring tool (e.g. Dreamweaver), develop a software-based prototype that incorporates all the feedback you've had so far. If you do not have experience in using any of these, create a few HTML web pages to represent the basic structure of your website.

(c) Consider the web page's detailed design. Sketch out the application's main screen (homepage or data entry). Consider the screen layout, use of colors, navigation, audio, animation, etc. While doing this, use the three main questions introduced in Chapter 6 as guidance: Where am I? What's here? Where can I go? Write one or two sentences explaining your choices, and consider whether the choice is a usability consideration or a user experience consideration.

Summary

This chapter has explored the activities of design, prototyping, and construction. Prototyping and scenarios are used throughout the design process to test out ideas for feasibility and user acceptance. We have looked at different forms of prototyping, and the activities have encouraged you to think about and apply prototyping techniques in the design process.

Key Points

- Prototyping may be low fidelity (such as paper-based) or high fidelity (such as software-based).
- High-fidelity prototypes may be vertical or horizontal.
- Low-fidelity prototypes are quick and easy to produce and modify and are used in the early stages of design.
- There are two aspects to the design activity: conceptual design and physical design.
- Conceptual design develops an outline of what people can do with a product and what concepts are needed to understand how to interact with it, while physical design specifies the details of the design such as screen layout and menu structure.
- We have explored three approaches to help you develop an initial conceptual model: interface metaphors, interaction styles, and interface styles.
- An initial conceptual model may be expanded by considering which functions the product will perform (and which the user will perform), how those functions are related, and what information is required to support them.
- Scenarios and prototypes can be used effectively in design to explore ideas.
- There is a wide variety of support tools available to interaction designers.

Further Reading

SNYDER, C. (2003) *Paper Prototyping.* Morgan Kaufmann. This book provides some useful practical guidance for creating paper-based prototypes and 'running' them to get feedback from users and others.

CARROLL, J.M. (ed.) (1995) *Scenario-based Design.* John Wiley & Sons, Inc. This volume is an edited collection of papers arising from a three-day workshop on use-oriented design. The book contains a variety of papers including case studies of scenario use within design, and techniques for using them with object-oriented development, task models, and usability engineering. This is a good place to get a broad understanding of this form of development.

MYERS, B., HUDSON, S.E. and PAUSCH, R. (2002) Past, present and future of user interface software tools. Chapter 10 in *Human–Computer Interaction in the New Millennium*, J.M. Carroll (ed.). Addison-Wesley. This paper is an updated version of a previous paper in *ACM Transactions on Computer–Human Interaction.* It presents an interesting description of user interface tools and their future, expanding on the information given in Box 11.9.

WINOGRAD, T. (1996) *Bringing Design to Software.* Addison-Wesley and ACM Press. This book is a collection of articles all based on the theme of applying ideas from other design disciplines in software design. It has a good mixture of interviews, articles, and profiles of exemplary systems, projects, or techniques. Anyone interested in software design will find it inspiring.

TIDWELL, J. (2005) *Designing Interfaces: Patterns for Effective Interaction* O'Reilly. This book is about designing interfaces in detail. It includes patterns for doing user research, information architecture, organizing widgets on an interface, and navigation, among other things.

INTERVIEW with Karen Holtzblatt

Karen Holtzblatt is the originator of Contextual Inquiry, a process for gathering field data on product use, which was the precursor to Contextual Design, a complete method for the design of systems. Together with Hugh Beyer, the codeveloper of Contextual Design, Karen Holtzblatt is cofounder of InContext Enterprises, which specializes in process and product design consulting.

HS: What is Contextual Design?

KH: If you're going to build something that people want, there are basically three large steps that you have to go through. The first question that you ask as a company is, "What in the world matters to the customer or user such that if we make something, they're likely to buy it and use it?" So the question is "What matters?" Now once you identify what the issues are, every corporation will have the corporate response of how to change the human practice with technology to improve it. This is the 'vision.' Finally you have to work out the details and structure the vision into a product or system or website or handheld application .... In any design process, whether it's formalized or not, every company must do these things. They have to find out what matters, they have to vision their corporate response, and then they have to structure it into a system.

Contextual Design has team and individual activities that bring them through those processes in an orderly fashion so that you can deliver a reliable result that works for people. So you could say that Contextual Design is a set of techniques to be used in a customer-centered design process with design teams. It is also a set of practices that help people engage in creative and productive design thinking with user data and it helps them co-operate and design together.

HS: What are the steps of Contextual Design?

KH: In the 'what matters' piece, we go out into the field, we talk with people about their work or life practice as they do it: that's Contextual Inquiry and that's a one-on-one, two to two-and-a-half-hour field interview. Then we interpret that data with a cross-functional team, and we model the activities with five work models: The flow model showing communication and coordination, the cultural model showing influences between people, both from law, and from geography, the physical model looking at the physical environment's role in organizing activity, the sequence model showing the steps of a task or business process, and the artifact model showing the things people use and how they are used. We also capture individual points on virtual post-it notes. After the interpretation session, every person we interviewed has a set of models and a set of post-its. Our next step is to consolidate all that data because you don't want to be designing from one person, from yourself, or from any one interview; we need to look at the structure of the practice itself. The consolidation step means that we end up with an affinity diagram and five consolidated models showing the issues *across* the target population.

At that point, we have modeled the work practice as it is and we have now six communication devices that the team can dialog with. Each one of them poses a point of view on which to have the conversation 'what matters?'

Now the team moves into that second activity, which is "what should our corporate response be?" We have a visioning process that is a very large group story-telling process to reinvent the practice given technological possibility and the core competency of the business. After that, we develop storyboards driven by the consolidated data and the vision. At this point we have not done a systems design; we have redesigned the practice. In Contextual Design we redesign the practice first, seeing the technology as it will appear within the work or life activity that will change.

To structure the system we start by rolling the storyboards into a User Environment Design (UED)—the structure of the system itself, independent of the user interface and the object model or implementation. The UED operates like a software floor plan that structures the movement inside the product. This is used to drive the user interface design, which is mocked up in paper and tested and iterated with the user. When it has stabilized, the UED, the storyboards, and the user interface drive development of the object model. Finally, we do visual design and mock the whole system up in an interactive environment and test that too. In this way we deal with interaction design, visual design and branding testing as well.

This is the whole process of Contextual Design, a full front-end design process. Because it is done with a cross-functional team, everyone in the organization knows what they're doing at each point: they know how to select the data, they know how to work in groups to get all these different steps done. So not only do you end up with a set of design thinking techniques that help you to design, you have an organizational process that helps the organization actually do it.

HS: How did the idea of Contextual Design emerge?

KH: Contextual Design started with the invention of Contextual Inquiry in a post-doctoral internship with John Whiteside at Digital in about 1987. At the time, usability testing and usability issues had been around maybe eight years or so and he was asking the question, "Usability identifies about 10 to 20% of the fixes at the tail end of the process to make the frosting on the cake look a little better to the user. What would it take to really figure out what people want in the product and system?" Contextual Inquiry was my answer to that question. After that, I took a job with Lou Cohen's Quality group at DEC, where I picked up the affinity diagram idea. Also at that time, Pelle Ehn and Kim Madsen were talking about Morten Kyng's ideas on paper mock-ups and I added paper prototyping with post-its to check out the design. Sandy Jones and I worked out the lower level details of Contextual Inquiry then Hugh and I hooked up. He's a software and object-oriented developer. We started working with teams and we noticed that they didn't know how to go from the data to the design and they didn't know how to structure the system to think about it. So then we invented more of the work models and the UED.

So the Contextual Design method came from looking at the software development practice; we evolved every single step of this process based on what people needed. The whole process was worked out with real people doing real design in real companies. So, where did it come from? It came from dialog with the problem.

HS: What are the main problems that organizations face when putting Contextual Design into practice?

KH: The question is, "What does organizational change look like?" because that's what we're talking about. The problem is that people want to change and they don't want to change. What we communicate to people is that organizational change is piecemeal. In order to own a process you have to say what's wrong with it, you have to change it a little bit, you have to say how whoever invented the process is wrong and how the people in the organization want to fix it, you have to make it fit with your organizational culture and issues. Most people will adopt the field-data gathering first and that's all they'll do and they'll tell me that they don't have time for anything else and they don't need anything else, and that's fine. And then they'll wake up one day and they'll say, "We have all this qualitative stuff and nobody's using it . . . maybe we should have a debriefing session." So then they have debriefing sessions. Then they wake up later on and they say, "We don't have any way of structuring this information . . . models are a good idea." And basically they reconstruct many aspects of the Contextual Design process as they hit the next problem—of course adding their own flavor and twists and things they learned along the way.

Now it's not quite that clean, but my point is that organizational adoption is about people making it their own and taking on the parts, changing them, doing what they can. You have to get somebody to do something and then once they do something it snowballs.

From an organization change perspective it is nice that Contextual Design generates paper and a design room as part of the process. The design room creates a talk event, and the talk event pulls everyone in because they want to know what you're doing. Then if they like the data, others feel left out, and because they feel left out they want to do a project and they want to have a room for themselves as well.

The biggest complaint about Contextual Design is that it takes too long. Some of that is about time, some of it is about thought. You have people who are used to coding and now have to think about field data. They're not used to that. So for that reason we wrote Rapid CD—to help people see how to pick and choose techniques from Contextual Design in short amounts of time.

HS: You have recently published a book on Rapid CD. What are the compromises that you made when integrating Contextual Design into a shortened product lifecycle?

KH: The most important thing to understand about Contextual Design and in point of fact any user-centred design approach is that time is completely dependent on scope. The second factor, which is actually secondary to scope, is the number of models that you use to represent the data.

Rapid CD creates guidelines to help you identify a small enough scope so that you can get user data into projects quickly. If you have a small tight scope then it's going to take less time because you're going to interview fewer users, and you're going to have a less extensive design. Limiting your product or system to one to four job types means that your scope is going to be small, and then after the visioning process you can prioritize scope again. At that point you may end up prioritising out roles and aspects of the vision that can be addressed later. The next phase of Rapid CD is working out the details of the design through paper prototyping and visual design and so on. This phase is again completely dependent on scope. If we already started with one to four roles, you're not going to have more than that so you can keep the number of screens to be developed small enough to manage quickly. The difference between this process and a normal Contextual Design process is that you are limiting scope and as a result you can do it with fewer people and in less time.

The second thing that we do in Rapid CD is we limit the number of models. One thing that we cut out is the UED. We eliminate the UED because we've limited the scope and if we're doing something simple like a webpage where you already have the idea of a webmap (which is effectively a UED), or you're doing the next version of a particular product which means you already have system structure, then you can go from having the data and the vision to mocking up some user interfaces. So we eliminate the UED without feeling that we're losing quality because we've reduced scope. One model we don't cut out at all is the affinity diagram because it's the best organisation and structure for understanding the issues. Finally, depending on the problem and how Contextual Design is being used we may or may not have sequence models (task analysis) as part of Rapid CD.

To make it easy for people we characterised Rapid CD into three smaller processes: Lightning Fast, Lightning Fast Plus, and Focused Rapid CD. With Lightning Fast you use Contextual Design up to the end of the visioning process and then follow your normal process to work out the detailed design. It appears shorter because we're just using Contextual Design for the requirements gathering phase and to conceptualise the product or process.

In Lightning Fast Plus you do the visioning process and work up your ideas your way, then you mock up your interfaces, and take them out and test them with users. Any time you're not testing with the user you're at risk. So in Lightning Fast Plus we're skipping storyboarding, extensive modeling, and the UED.

In Focused Rapid CD you do sequence consolidation for a task analysis, vision a solution, then storyboarding, paper mock-ups, and testing. So Focused Rapid CD eliminates the UED and the rest of the models. Focused Rapid CD says if you have a task or a small process then you really need to do consolidated sequences, in other words, you need to do task analysis. In typical web-page design you don't need sequences unless you're doing transactions. If all you're doing is an information environment, you don't need sequences. But any time you need to do task analysis then the recommendation would be that you use Focused Rapid CD.

HS: What's the future direction of Contextual Design?

KH: Every process can always be tweaked. I think the primary parts of Contextual Design are there. There are interesting directions in which it can go, but there's only so much we can get our audience to buy.

I think that for us there are two key things that we're doing. One is we're starting to talk about design and what design is, so we can talk about the role of design and design thinking. And we are still helping train everyone who wants to learn. But the other thing we're finding is that sometimes the best way to support the client is to do the design work for them. So we have the design wing of the business where we put together the Contextual Design teams. What clients really like is our hybrid design process where we create a cross company team and do the work together—they learn and we get the result.

A new challenge for Contextual Design is its role in Six Sigma process redefinition work. We believe that qualitative approaches to business process redesign works well with quantitative approaches like Six Sigma. Our initial work on this has shown that Contextual Design uncovers root causes and processes to address much much faster than typical process mapping. And our visioning process helps redesign process and technology together—so that they inform each other instead of trying to deal with one at a time. We hope to have more stories about these successes in the future.

But for most organizations looking to adopt a customer-centered design process, the standard Contextual Design is enough for now, they have to get started. And because Contextual Design is a scaffolding, they can plug other processes into it, as we suggest with Rapid CD. Most organizations haven't got a backbone for customer-centered design, and Contextual Design is a good backbone to start with.

12

12.1 Introduction

Imagine you have designed a website for sharing music, gossip, and photos among teenagers. You have used Flash to prototype your first design and implemented the core functionality. How would you find out whether it would appeal to teenagers and if they will use it? You would carry out an evaluation study.

Evaluation is integral to the design process. It collects information about users' or potential users' experiences when interacting with a prototype, computer system, a component of a computer system, or a design artifact, e.g. screen sketch, in order to improve its design. It focuses on both the usability of the system, e.g. how easy it is to learn and to use, and on the users' experience when interacting with the system, e.g. how satisfying, enjoyable, or motivating the interaction is.

The web's presence and, more recently, the proliferation of cell phones and other small digital devices like iPods, has heightened awareness about usability, but many designers still assume that if they and their colleagues can use the product and find it attractive, others will too. The problem with this argument is that designers are often not like the target user population. For example, a 24-year-old software developer is likely to have different characteristics from a retired 86-year-old teacher with little computer experience. Without evaluation, designers cannot be sure that their design is usable by the target user population, and that it is what users want.

There are many different evaluation methods, some of which involve users directly, while others call indirectly on an understanding of users' needs and psychology. Sometimes evaluation is done in a laboratory and other times in natural work or leisure settings. This chapter starts by discussing why evaluation is important, what needs to be evaluated, where that evaluation should take place, and when in the product lifecycle evaluation is needed. We introduce some terms that are used in this and other books you may read. We then introduce three evaluation approaches and key evaluation methods, and examine six short evaluation case studies which illustrate them. For each one we look at the aim of the evaluation, at what stage the evaluation was done during design, the techniques that are used to collect and analyze the data, and the challenges that the evaluators encountered. The chapter ends with a discussion of what we learn from the case studies.

The specific aims of this chapter are to:

- **Illustrate how observation, interviews, and questionnaires that you encountered in Chapters 7 and 8 are used in evaluation.**
- **Explain the key concepts and terms used in evaluation.**
- **Introduce three main evaluation approaches and key evaluation methods within the context of real evaluation studies.**

- Examine how the approaches and methods are used for different purposes at different stages of the design process.
- Discuss some of the practical challenges that evaluators have to consider when doing evaluation.

12 Introducing evaluation

12.2 The why, what, where, and when of evaluation

Users want interactive products to be easy to learn, effective, efficient, safe, and satisfying to use. Being entertaining, attractive, challenging, and enjoyable is also important for the success of websites, games, toys, and other consumer products. Achieving this requires the product to be evaluated, and running effective evaluations involves understanding not only why evaluation is important but also what aspects to evaluate, where evaluation should take place, and when to evaluate.

12.2.1 Why evaluate?

Evaluation is needed to check that users can use the product and that they like it, particularly if the design concept is new. Furthermore, nowadays users look for much more than just a usable system, they look for a pleasing and engaging experience. "*'User experience' encompasses all aspects of the end-user's interaction . . . the first requirement for an exemplary user experience is to meet the exact needs of the customer, without fuss or bother. Next comes simplicity and elegance which produces products that are a joy to own, a joy to use*" Nielsen Norman Group (`www.nngroup.com`). "*Websites must be usable as well as aesthetically pleasing*" (Badre, 2002, pp. 6–7).

From a business and marketing perspective there are also good reasons for investing in evaluation, these include: designers get feedback about their early design ideas; major problems are fixed before the product goes on sale; designers focus on real problems rather than debating what each other likes or dislikes about the product.

"It's the latest innovation in office safety. When your computer crashes, an air bag is activated so you won't bang your head in frustration."

12.2.2 What to Evaluate

The wide diversity of interactive products gives rise to a range of features that evaluators must be able to evaluate. For example, developers of a new web browser may want to know if users find items faster with their product, whereas developers of a creativity support tool for teaching story-writing may ask if students develop more engaging, emotionally satisfying stories. Government authorities may ask if a computerized system for controlling traffic lights results in fewer accidents. Makers of a toy may ask if six-year-olds can manipulate the controls and whether they are engaged by its furry case and pixie face, and whether the toy is safe for them to play with. A company that develops personal, digital music players may want to know if the size, color, and shape of the casing is liked by people from different age groups living in different countries. A new company may want to assess market reaction to its new homepage design.

Activity 12.1

Think of examples of the following systems and write down the usability and user experience features that are important for the success of each:

1. **a wordprocessor**
2. **a personal music player (i.e. like iPod)**
3. **a website that sells clothes**
4. **an online patient support community.**

Comment

1. **It must be as easy as possible for the intended users to learn and to use and it must be satisfying. Note that wrapped into this are characteristics such as consistency, reliability, predictability, etc., that are necessary for ease of use.**
2. **A personal music player must also have all the above characteristics and it must be possible to record, organize, and find music easily. In addition, the physical design, e.g. color, shape, size, position of keys, etc., must be usable and attractive, e.g. pleasing feel, shape, and color.**
3. **A website that sells clothes needs to have the basic usability features too. In particular, navigation through the system needs to be straightforward and well supported. In addition, the website must be attractive, with good graphics of the clothes—who would want to buy clothes they can't see or that look unattractive? Trust is also a big issue in online shopping, so a well-designed, secure procedure for taking customer credit card details is essential; it must not only be clear but must take into account the need to provide feedback, protect the users' financial information, and engender trust.**
4. **An online patient support group must support the exchange of factual and emotional information. As well as the standard usability features, it needs to enable patients to express emotions, possibly using emoticons, other symbols, sending personal pictures, sounds, or flowers. For example, some 3D environments enable users to represent themselves on the screen as avatars that can jump, wave, look happy or sad, move close to another person, or move away.**

From these examples, you can see that the success of many interactive products depends on much more than usability. Aesthetic, emotional, engaging, and motivating qualities are important too.

12.2.3 Where to evaluate

Some features, such as the sequence of links on a website, are generally best evaluated in a laboratory, because it is easier for the evaluators to control the evaluation process and to make sure that the evaluation focuses on specific aspects of the system. Similarly, testing the size of the keys on a cell phone can be done in a laboratory. Other aspects, such as whether children enjoy playing with a collaborative toy, or whether an online dating system is emotionally satisfying, can be evaluated more effectively in natural settings, because evaluators can see what children do with the toy when left to their own devices, and can assess the emotional expressions of the adults in the dating system example. Likewise, evaluating how a cell phone is used and liked by different users such as busy business executives, or teenagers, involves observing how the users use the phone in their normal lives and talking to them about it.

Activity 12.2

Identify one adult and one teenager who is prepared to talk with you about their cell phone usage; these may be family or friends. Ask them questions such as: Do they always carry the cell-phone switched on? Do they give their number to others freely or is the number only made available to a restricted group of people? Do they have a large phone book of numbers stored in the phone? Is having the latest model important? What functionality do they use? Is the size, feel, color, ring-tone, and casing important to them? Is their phone a fashion object?

Comment

You are likely to have found quite different patterns of use between the adult and the teenager. Typically teenagers are avid cell phone users; they carry their cell phone everywhere and are frequently in contact with their friends and family. Often their calls are concerned with coordinating social activities. For example, it is quite common to hear comments such as: "I just got off the Metro and I'll be at Starbucks in a few minutes. What about you?" Having a new cell phone model can bring kudos, and so does having a modern case. Members of this user group often feel anxious when separated from their cell phone because they feel isolated. Comments like: "If you don't have a cell phone you can get left out" are common. The physical appearance of the phone may also be important. "I had to use my Mum's old phone which is a real brick. It was so embarrassing!"

In contrast, many adults use their phones for purposes other than social activities such as work commitments, checking up on their spouses and children, and for keeping in touch when they are traveling.

12.2.4 When to evaluate

At what stage in the product lifecycle evaluation takes place depends on the type of product itself. For example, the product being developed may be a brand-new concept or an upgrade of an existing product. If the product is new, then considerable time is usually invested in market research and establishing user requirements. Once these requirements have been established, they are used to create a design artifact such as initial sketches, a series of screens, or a prototype of the design ideas. These are then evaluated to see if the designers have interpreted the users' requirements correctly and embodied them in their designs appropriately. The designs will be modified according to the evaluation feedback and a new set of prototypes will be developed and then evaluated.

When a product is upgraded there is usually less scope for change than when designing a new product, and attention is focused on improving specific aspects of the product's design such as how to navigate through a website. Some products, such as office systems, go through many versions, and successful products may reach double-digit version numbers. If the product is being upgraded then evaluation is not necessarily dependent on establishing a set of requirements, and evaluation may be the first step in redesign.

Evaluations that are done to assess the success of a finished product, such as those needed to satisfy a funding agency that its money has been used well or to check that a standard is being upheld, are known as *summative evaluations*. Agencies such as the National Institute of Standards and Technology (NIST) in the USA, the International Standards Organization (ISO), and the British Standards Institute (BSI) set standards by which products may be evaluated.

When evaluations are done during design to check that the product continues to meet users' needs they are know as *formative evaluations*. Formative evaluations cover a broad span of design, from the development of early sketches and prototypes through to tweaking and perfecting an almost finished design, and then maintaining the product, which may involve several upgrades.

In the case studies in Section 12.5 we examine evaluations that have been performed during:

1. Early design of an artifact to clarify design ideas.
2. Evaluation of a working prototype.
3. Refining or maintaining a product.
4. Exploration of a new design concept.

Box 12.1
The language of evaluation

Analytical evaluation: an approach to evaluation that does not involve end-users. Heuristic evaluation, walkthroughs, and modeling are forms of analytical evaluation.

Controlled experiment: a study that is performed in a laboratory which is controlled by the evaluator. Aspects controlled typically include the task that participants are asked to perform, the environment in which the study occurs, and the amount of time available to complete the study.

Field study: a study that is done in a natural environment such as at home as opposed to a study in a controlled setting such as a laboratory.

Formative evaluation: an evaluation that is done during design to check that the product continues to meet users' needs.

Heuristic evaluation: an approach to evaluation in which knowledge of typical users is applied, often guided by heuristics, to identify usability problems.

Predictive evaluation: an approach to evaluation in which theoretically based models are used to predict user performance.

Summative evaluation: an evaluation that is done when the design is complete to assess whether it meets required standards such as those set by a standards agency like NIST or BSI.

Usability laboratory: a laboratory that is designed for usability testing.

User studies: any evaluation that involves users directly, either in their natural environments, or in the laboratory.

Usability study: an evaluation that is performed to examine the usability of a design or system.

Usability testing: an evaluation approach to evaluation that involves measuring users' performance and evaluating their satisfaction with the system in question on certain tasks in a laboratory setting.

User testing: an evaluation approach where users are asked to perform certain tasks using a system or prototype in an informal or laboratory setting. ■

12.3 Evaluation approaches and methods

At a general level, we describe evaluation studies as taking one of three main evaluation approaches. Each of these is based on a distinct set of values and assumptions as to how evaluation should be conducted. At a more detailed level, we consider a set of evaluation methods some of which are based on the data gathering techniques introduced in Chapter 7, but tailored for evaluation purposes.

12.3.1 Approaches

The three main evaluation approaches are: (1) usability testing; (2) field studies; and (3) analytical evaluation. Each of these approaches has several methods associated with it. The methods used in evaluation are: observing users, asking users, e.g. through interviews and questionnaires, asking experts, user testing, inspections, and modeling users' performance. Some approaches use the same methods. For example, usability testing and field studies both involve observing users and asking users but the conditions under which they are used, and the ways in which they are used, are different.

1. Usability testing

Usability testing was the dominant evaluation approach in the 1980s (Whiteside *et al.*, 1998), and remains important, particularly at later stages of design for ensuring consistency in navigation structure, use of terms, and how the system responds to the user. Usability testing involves measuring typical users' performance on typical tasks. This is generally done by noting the number and kinds of errors that the users make and recording the time that it takes them to complete the task. As the users perform these tasks, they are watched and recorded on video and their interactions with the software are recorded, usually by logging input to and output from the system. User satisfaction questionnaires and interviews are also used to elicit users' opinions.

The defining characteristic of usability testing is that the test environment and the format of the testing is controlled by the evaluator (Mayhew, 1999; Hackos and Reddish, 1998; Koyani *et al.*, 2003). Quantifying users' performance is a dominant theme in usability testing. Typically, tests take place in a laboratory or in laboratory-like conditions where the user is isolated from the normal day-to-day interruptions. Visitors are not allowed and telephone calls are stopped, and there is no possibility of talking to colleagues, checking email, or doing any of the other tasks that most of us rapidly switch among in our normal lives.

Usability testing has been particularly important for the development of standard products that go through many generations, such as wordprocessing systems, databases, and spreadsheets. In this case, the findings from a usability test are summarized in a usability specification so that developers can test future prototypes or versions of the product against it. Optimal performance levels and minimal levels of acceptance are generally specified and current levels noted. Changes in the design can then be implemented. This is called 'usability engineering.'

User testing methods that form the heart of usability testing are discussed in more detail in Chapter 14.

2. Field studies

The distinguishing feature of field studies is that they are done in natural settings with the aim of understanding what people do naturally and how products mediate their activities. More specifically, they can be used to: (1) help identify opportunities for new technology;

(2) establish the requirements for design; (3) facilitate the introduction of technology, or how to deploy existing technology in new contexts; and (4) evaluate technology (Bly, 1997; Holtzblatt, 2005). Each of these will be illustrated in the examples described in Section 12.5.

Chapter 7 introduced you to the data gathering techniques of interviews and observation, which are the basic techniques of field studies. As you will recall, the data takes the form of events and conversations that are recorded as notes, or by audio or video recording, and later analyzed using a variety of methods. Artifacts are also collected and questionnaires may also be administered. More details on field studies are presented in Chapter 14.

3. Analytical evaluation

In analytical evaluation two categories of evaluation methods are considered: inspections, which include heuristic evaluation and walkthroughs, and theoretically based models, which are used to predict user performance. In heuristic evaluations knowledge of typical users is applied, often guided by heuristics, e.g. guidelines and standards, to identify usability problems. Walkthroughs, as the name suggests, involve experts in walking through scenarios with prototypes of the application. A key feature for analytical evaluations is that users need not be present (Nielsen and Mack, 1994; Nielsen and Tahir, 2002).

Heuristics are based on common-sense knowledge and usability guidelines, e.g. always provide clearly marked exits and use consistent terms. They were originally developed for screen-based applications but these have now been adapted to make new sets of heuristics for evaluating web-based products, mobile devices, collaborative technologies, and computerized toys. Care is needed in using heuristics because designers are sometimes led astray by findings from heuristic evaluations that turn out not to be as accurate as they seemed at first (Cockton *et al.*, 2002).

Cognitive walkthroughs, which were the first walkthroughs developed, involve simulating a user's problem-solving process at each step in the human–computer dialog, and checking to see how users progress from step to step in these interactions (Nielsen and Mack, 1994). A key feature of cognitive walkthroughs is that they focus on evaluating designs for ease of learning. Other types of walkthroughs have also been developed, and in Chapter 15 you will learn about pluralistic walkthroughs.

Models have been used primarily for comparing the efficacy of different interfaces for the same application, and the optimal arrangement and location of features on the interface base. For example, the keystroke level model provides numerical predictions of user performance and Fitts' Law predicts the time it takes to reach a target using a pointing device. There is more about analytical evaluation in Chapter 15.

Combining approaches

We have presented each evaluation approach separately, which implies that they are used independently of each other, which is sometimes true. However, this is often not the case. Combinations of approaches are used to get a broad understanding of the efficacy of a design. For example, sometimes the controlled studies performed in a usability laboratory are combined with observations intended to find out how users typically use the product in their natural environment. Figure 12.1 illustrates one way in which usability testing and field studies may be combined in one program of evaluation.

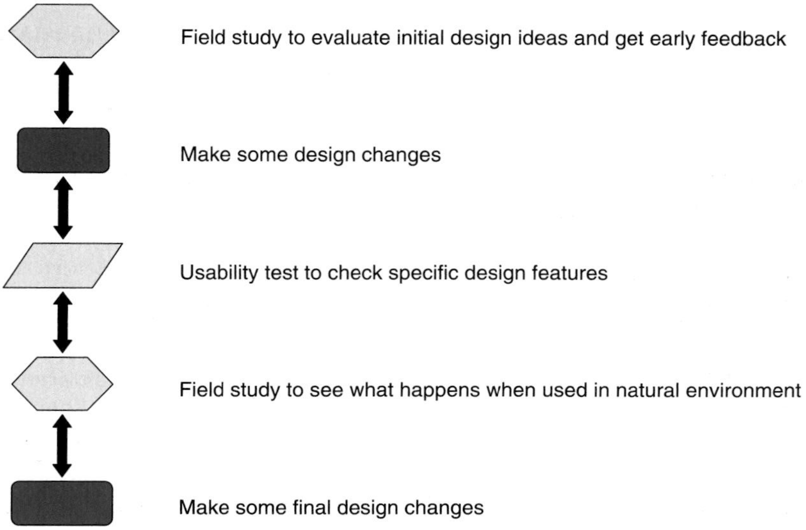
Field study to evaluate initial design ideas and get early feedback
Make some design changes
Usability test to check specific design features
Field study to see what happens when used in natural environment
Make some final design changes

***Figure 12.1** Example of the way usability testing and field studies can complement each other*

Opportunistic evaluations

Evaluations may be detailed studies or opportunistic investigations. The latter are generally done early in the design process to provide designers with feedback quickly about a design idea. Getting this kind of feedback early in the design process is an essential ingredient of successful design because it confirms whether it is worth proceeding to develop an idea into a prototype. Typically, these early evaluations are informal and do not require many resources. For example, the designers may go to a few local users and ask their opinions. Getting feedback this early in design can help save time and money if an idea needs to be modified or abandoned. In fact, opportunistic evaluations with users can be conducted often in addition to more formal evaluations.

Table 12.1 summarizes the key aspects of each evaluation approach for the following issues:

- the role of users
- who controls the process and the relationship between evaluators and users during the evaluation

Evaluation paradigms	Usability testing	Field studies	Analytical
Role of users	To carry out set tasks.	Natural behavior.	Users generally not involved.
Who controls	Evaluators strongly in control.	Evaluators try to develop relationships with users.	Expert evaluators.
Location	Laboratory.	Natural environment.	Laboratory-oriented but often happens on customer's premises.
When used	With a prototype or product.	Most often used early in design to check that users' needs are being met or to assess problems or design opportunities.	Expert reviews (often done by consultants) with a prototype, but can occur at any time. Models are used to assess specific aspects of a potential design.
Type of data	Quantitative. Sometimes statistically validated. Users' opinions collected by questionnaire or interview.	Qualitative descriptions often accompanied with sketches, scenarios, quotes, other artifacts.	List of problems from expert reviews. Quantitative figures from model, e.g., how long it takes to perform a task using two designs.
Fed back into design by...	Report of performance measures, errors etc. Findings provide a benchmark for future versions.	Descriptions that include quotes, sketches, anecdotes, and sometimes time logs.	Reviewers provide a list of problems, often with suggested solutions. Times calculated from models are given to designers.
Philosophy	Applied approach based on experimentation, i.e., usability engineering.	May be objective observation or ethnographic.	Practical heuristics and practitioner expertise underpin expert reviews. Theory underpins models.

Table 12.1 *Characteristics of different evaluation approaches*

- the location of the evaluation
- when the evaluation is most useful
- the type of data collected and how it is analyzed
- how the evaluation findings are fed back into the design process
- the philosophy and theory that underlies the evaluation approaches.

12.3.2 Methods

The main methods used in evaluation are: observing users; asking users their opinions; asking experts their opinions; testing users' performance; and modeling users' task performance to predict the efficacy of a user interface. Observation studies, questionnaires, and interviews underpin the first three of these methods, and these were discussed in Chapter 7. In this chapter we discuss how these techniques are used in evaluation. Testing users' performance will be discussed in Chapter 14; asking experts their opinions and modeling users' task performance to predict the efficacy of a user interface will both be discussed in Chapter 15. The relationship between evaluation approaches and evaluation methods is shown in Table 12.2.

12.4 Evaluation case studies

The following six short case studies illustrate the use of these evaluation methods and introduce you to some of the challenges that evaluators face. Each case study is followed by an activity which is designed to encourage you to explore these issues yourself.

12.4.1 Evaluating early design ideas for a mobile device for rural indian nurses

This case study illustrates how a field study based on observation and interviews was used in an early evaluation of design ideas for a mobile record-keeping system for use by auxiliary nurses in India. It also provides examples of some of the issues that have to be taken into account when working with users from a different culture.

A research team from the former Apple Research Laboratory (ARL) spent several months with auxiliary nurse midwives (ANMs) in rural India in 1995/6. They were trying to understand how ANMs go about their daily tasks and whether and how digital technology could help to improve both the service they give to their patients and their own job satisfaction (Grisedale *et al.*, 1997). A diary entry by one of the researchers describes the work of a typical nurse midwife.

> ***This morning I am following Padma, the local nurse midwife, on her house calls in Narwar, a farming village in Rajasthan. It is a hot dry day, and the local traffic, consisting of a few stray cattle and bristly pigs, lie slumped in troughs of dust trying to keep cool. We come to the gate of the Sharma household and are greeted by three women who welcome us. ''Namaste'' they say, and***

	Evaluation paradigms		
Methods	**Usability testing**	**Field studies**	**Analytical**
Observing users	**Video and interaction logging, which can be analyzed to identify errors, investigate routes through the software, or calculate performance time.**	**Observation is the central part of any field study. In ethnographic studies evaluators immerse themselves in the environment. In other types of studies the evaluator looks on objectively.**	**N/A**
Asking users	**User satisfaction questionnaires are administered to collect users' opinions. Interviews may also be used to get more details.**	**The evaluator may interview or discuss what she sees with participants. Ethnographic interviews are used in ethnographic studies.**	**N/A**
Asking experts	**N/A**	**N/A**	**Experts use heuristics early in design to predict the efficacy of an interface.**
User testing	**Testing typical users on typical tasks in a controlled laboratory-like setting is the cornerstone of usability testing.**	**N/A**	**N/A**
Modeling users' task performance	**N/A**	**N/A**	**Models are used to predict the efficacy of an interface or compare performance times between versions.**

Table 12.2 *The relationship between evaluation approaches and methods*

> ***adjust their veils. The yard outside the house is the center of communal activity. It is formed from compacted earth and adorned with chalk drawings. Blankets are brought for us to sit on. Water is served in metal cups, drawn from a ceramic urn at the side of the house. Three generations of women are living in the house.***
>
> ***Today, Padma is performing a routine post natal examination on the newest member of the family, baby Rao, whom she delivered three months ago. Padma reaches into her bag to consult her diary, which she keeps close by her. She talks with the women about Rao, and lays him on a low wooden bed to take a closer look at him. He has black hair and dark eyes, and on his forehead a crescent moon has been drawn, to protect him from the spirits.***
>
> ***(Grisedale et al., 1997, p. 471)***

The goal of the design project was to develop a prototype of a mobile data-capture system to record health records. The system would need to be suitable for use by health care workers like Padma working in the kinds of environments described in the diary story. For such a system to be successful it would have to be suitable for people with minimal exposure to computers and require low-tech support. Typically each of around 350,000 ANMs is responsible for 3500 to 9000 people whom they visit on foot or by bicycle or moped. Each ANM covers three to five villages, some of which may be quite isolated. Their work generally includes: treating minor injuries and ailments, referring people to the local hospital, providing ante- and post-natal care, vaccinating people, malaria testing, and motivating villagers to use contraceptives. Each ANM receives two years of basic health-care training with refresher courses once they are working in the field.

Record-keeping is a major part of an ANM's job. She keeps a record of her daily activities which she then compiles into weekly and monthly reports. The kind of data recorded includes: number of wells in each village and when they have been treated to prevent malaria, weddings, the number of people in each household, the name of the head of house and the date when she last visited. For every eligible couple she records details about contraception and for each individual she records any illnesses, vaccinations, medication given, referrals, operations, etc. In addition she monitors all pregnancies, births, infant mortalities, and abortions. She also attends and records birth details such as gender and weight. At the time of the study, these records were typically not kept accurately and often bore little relation to reality, but there was no limit to the number of records that were kept. The ANMs completed forms rapidly and recorded figures by hand. The forms were often incorrect or incomplete because they didn't have time, or they didn't understand how to complete them, or villagers did not give accurate descriptions. From these observations the following design goals for the new product were identified:

- Translating the paper-based record keeping into an electronic format in a way that would fit into the working life of an ANM.
- Designing a view onto the data that would be meaningful for the ANM since the format of the device could not provide a 1:1 mapping of the forms that were currently used because the screen size was too small.

- Providing a navigational structure that felt natural for the ANMs.
- Providing a lightweight way for entering information.

Each of the design goals was used to develop prototype designs that could be evaluated with the ANMs. During field visits the evaluators used picture cards that showed the activities of the ANMs. These cards helped them to overcome the language barrier and develop a shared understanding of the ANM's tasks. They also developed an early mockup of a household overview as shown in Figure 12.2. A graphical language was needed that made sense to the ANMs, and which was sensitive to the cultural conventions of the community. For example, these users did not have experience of interface widgets such as scroll-bars and buttons. Developing appropriate icons was achieved by looking at training magazines that took account of cultural norms. For example, naked bodies were not shown and pregnant women were shown clothed with a diagram of the fetus drawn on top of their clothing.

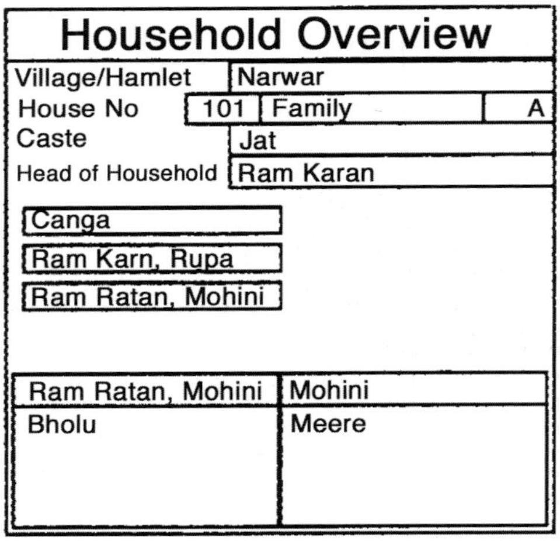

***Figure 12.2** Mockup of a household overview*

The evaluation involved showing the designs to the ANMs, observing their reactions, and talking to them (i.e. informally interviewing them) to get suggestions for modifying the icons so that they distinguished between different circumstances, such as a pregnant woman and a woman who is not pregnant, a child with a disease and a healthy child, but did not offend the users. Figure 12.3 shows examples of some of these icons. The feedback collected from the evaluation enabled the team to improve the icon design.

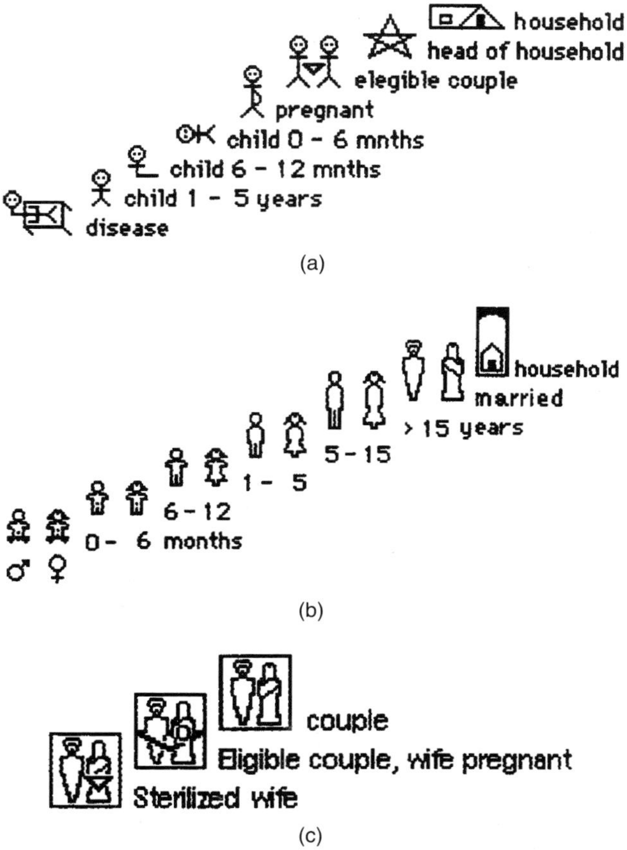

Figure 12.3 *(a) Icons drawn by ANMs in the Punjab; (b) icons representing people by gender and age; (c) icons modified by the team to represent state of patients*

Activity 12.3

1. The account above does not say how the data was recorded. What form of data recording would you have used?
2. Based on this case study and on the information in Chapter 10, how does the use of interviews and observation differ between the requirements activity and evaluation?
3. What kind of practical problems might the evaluators have encountered that

would influence their evaluation procedures?

Comment

1. **There are several ways that the data could have been recorded. However, carrying video recorders is unlikely to be practical in the circumstances, and choosing a simple approach is more likely to be feasible. Taking notes is the simplest approach, and audio-recording may also have been possible. From their report it seems likely that Grisedale *et al.* relied on notes.**
2. **In evaluation, attention is focused on getting feedback about an actual artifact. In the requirements activity, the focus is broader than this and encompasses a wider view of the product under development. In this case study, evaluation was carried out very early in the design process and focused on icon sketches. Establishing the requirements and evaluating prototypes was closely tied. Furthermore, in small teams like this one the same people often do both design and evaluation.**
3. **This case study illustrates some practical issues when designing for people from another culture, for example communicating with users who speak a different language, the need to be sensitive to different norms, e.g. pictures of naked bodies were not acceptable, the need to spend time understanding the lifestyle of the users, which was very different from that of the design team. Other practical considerations would have included environmental conditions, such as dust and heat.**

12.4.2 Evaluating cell phones for different world markets

This case study describes how evaluators use field studies of already existing devices in order to understand how to modify the product for a different market. It discusses how differences in cultural behavior can impact the way an evaluation is conducted and highlights the practical issues that evaluators may face, particularly when working with cell phones and other mobile devices.

Jan Blom and Jaakko Lehikoinen work for Nokia in Finland; Jan Chipchase is a research manager in Tokyo. They evaluate Nokia phone designs for customers worldwide which sometimes involves evaluating prototypes that are eight years ahead of what appears on a particular country's market (Blom *et al.*, 2005). Their evaluations can be thought of as discovery research.

In 2004 the half billion Nokia phones sold were purchased by people from almost every country in the world. Evaluations were needed in emerging markets in China, India, and Brazil. In order to capture and secure these markets the evaluators had to examine cross-cultural differences, sometimes involving people with poor literacy, so that products could be tailored to local needs. Doing cross-cultural research poses its own logistical challenges. Is it better to attempt to blend with cultural norms or to be an outsider? These researchers have learned that being an outsider gives them an excuse for asking blatant questions which would be unacceptable from someone of the same culture.

Unlike devices for narrow, clearly defined user groups, cell phones are used by a wide variety of people in different situations and environments. For example, a cell phone conversation may start on public transport and be completed after the person arrives home. These changes in environment can provide challenges for data gathering. For example, users may not want evaluators to come into their homes or other private places or to observe them making personal phone calls or sending private messages.

Typical methods used to capture data for these kinds of evaluations include *photo diaries* obtained by shadowing people. Collecting this kind of data can be problematic because the user may move from a well-lit room to a dark place where flash photography draws unwanted attention. Evaluators must also be prepared for changing circumstances, so it's a good idea to carry coins, notes in local currency, energy bars, drinks, pens, a power plug adapter, spare batteries, DVDs, cassettes, mini-tripod, clean clothing, waterproof clothing, sun screen, pre-paid travel cards, printed copies of contact information, medication, and other things that support coping with the unexpected. Furthermore, cell phones are used intermittently but over long periods of time. This can cause tensions because researchers may need to be uncomfortably close to participants for prolonged periods. There are also the obvious problems of not speaking the same language, and security issues. Taking pictures and video recording is likely to be a sensitive issue in some situations, such as airports and train stations with heightened tension due to terrorist attacks. Riding in a taxi can present challenges. Is there enough room? Where should the observer sit? Will additional fare be needed? An alternative of shadowing moving vehicles by bike brings other challenges such as the evaluator needing to be a competent bike rider.

Activity 12.4

1. **Which evaluation method was used and how was the data collected?**
2. **What was the prototype the researchers used?**
3. **Would you consider this evaluation to be early in design or late in design? Explain your answer.**
4. **We are not told much about what the evaluators were looking to find out. What kind of questions do think might have driven the evaluations?**

Comment

1. The method used was primarily observation and there was probably also some informal interviewing, although we are not told this. We are told that the data was collected using

photo diaries in which the evaluator recorded a series of actions in photographs.

2. The prototype used was a phone that was developed for a different market. We can assume from this that the design team anticipated being able to tailor the phone for these markets rather than having to create a completely different design.
3. This evaluation can be regarded as early in the design of a cell phone for a particular market outside of Europe. On the other hand, since the prototype was a working phone, another perspective suggests that the evaluation is happening late in the design process.
4. The evaluators wanted to see how the phone could be tailored for use in a different culture. This would have involved observing several factors including whether the physical casing, size of keys, and overall size and shape of the phone, was liked by people from different cultures. They might also have focused on whether people like to communicate by speaking as in the USA or by sending text messages (i.e. texting) as in many parts of Europe. If the latter, then short-cuts and the ability for personally tailoring the system might be needed to make text entry easier. Other cultural and social issues that would also have been of interest include what kind of emotional signals and moods do people want to communicate via their phone calls, is telling jokes, expressing trust and personal warmth in phone calls important in this culture?

12.4.3 Evaluating affective issues: challenge and engagement in a collaborative immersive game

The success of collaborative entertainment technology depends on more than the productivity and performance measures that are at the heart of usability testing. For these systems to be successful they must engage and challenge users. New ways of evaluating these aspects are therefore needed and, in this case study (Mandryk and Inkpen, 2004), we see how physiological responses can be used to evaluate users' experiences with a collaborative immersive game.

Emerging technologies offer exciting new opportunities for co-located entertainment experiences as growth in the sales of games indicates. Like board games, many of these collaborative immersive games are highly interactive. Evaluating the success of such games depends on being able to identify how well they challenge and entertain users. The traditional focus of usability testing is on performance rather than user experience, and so evaluating these aspects presents a challenge. Regan Mandryk and Kori Inkpen (2004) conjectured that physiological indicators can be used to measure objectively a player's experience with entertainment technology. They have developed such measures, and tested their efficacy through an experiment to evaluate participants' experience of playing an online ice-hockey game.

They worked with ten subjects who were university students with a passion for playing computer games. They set up two conditions of play. In one condition players played the

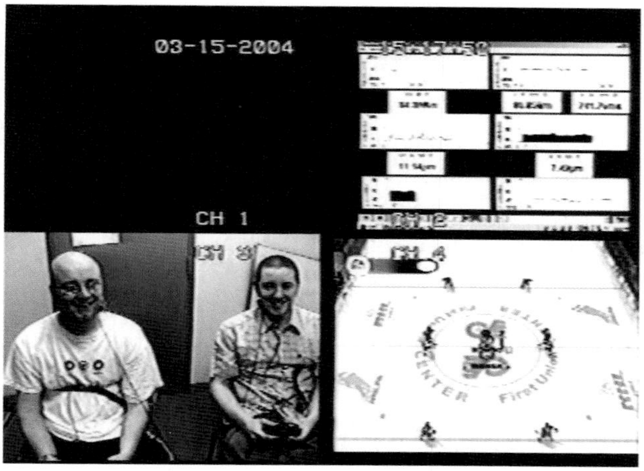

Figure 12.4 The display shows the physiological data (top right), two participants, and a screen of the game they played

game against a friend via the computer, and in the other condition each player played against the computer. During each gaming session they placed sensors on their subjects to collect physiological data. These included measures of the moisture produced by sweat glands in the hands and feet, changes in heart rate and breathing rate. In addition they videoed participants and asked them to complete user satisfaction questionnaires at the end of the session. In order to reduce the effects of learning, half of the participants played first against a friend and then against the computer, and the other half played against the computer first. Figure 12.4 shows the set-up for recording data while the participants were playing the game.

Results from the user satisfaction questionnaire revealed that the mean ratings on a 1–5 scale for each item indicated that playing against a friend was the favored experience (Table 12.3).

Data recorded from the physiological responses was compared for the two conditions and in general revealed higher levels of excitement when players played against a friend than when they played against the computer. The physiological recordings were also compared across players and, in general, indicated the same trend. Figure 12.5 shows a comparison for two players.

Because of individual differences in physiological data it was not possible to directly compare the means of the two sets of results: subjective questionnaires and physiological measures. However, by normalizing the results it was possible to correlate the results across individuals. This indicated that the physiological data gathering and analysis methods used in this research appear to offer promise for evaluating levels of challenge and engagement, which are prime measures of the success of collaborative immersive entertainment technology. Although not perfect, these measures offer a way of going beyond traditional usability testing to get a deeper understanding of user experience goals.

	Playing against computer		Playing against friend	
	Mean	St. Dev.	Mean	St. Dev.
Boring	2.3	0.949	1.7	0.949
Challenging	3.6	1.08	3.9	0.994
Easy	2.7	0.823	2.5	0.850
Engaging	3.8	0.422	4.3	0.675
Exciting	3.5	0.527	4.1	0.568
Frustrating	2.8	1.14	2.5	0.850
Fun	3.9	0.738	4.6	0.699

Table 12.3 *Mean subjective ratings given on a user satisfaction questionnaire using a five-point scale, in which 1 is lowest and 5 is highest for the 10 players. Identifying strongly with an experience state is indicated by a higher mean. The standard deviation indicates the spread of the results around the mean. Low values indicate little variation in participants' responses, high values indicate more variation*

Activity 12.5

1. What challenges might other evaluators face when using the physiological measures described in the case study?
2. How might these challenges be overcome?

Comment

1. Collecting physiological data requires special equipment and expertise to use it effectively so that participants are not alarmed or harmed (see Figure 12.4). Data analysis also requires different skills from those of most trained usability specialists.
2. It is relatively easy and cheap to develop small sensing devices, and it is possible that if these measures become more widely accepted, then less obtrusive, non-invasive devices for collecting physiological data will become more widely available.

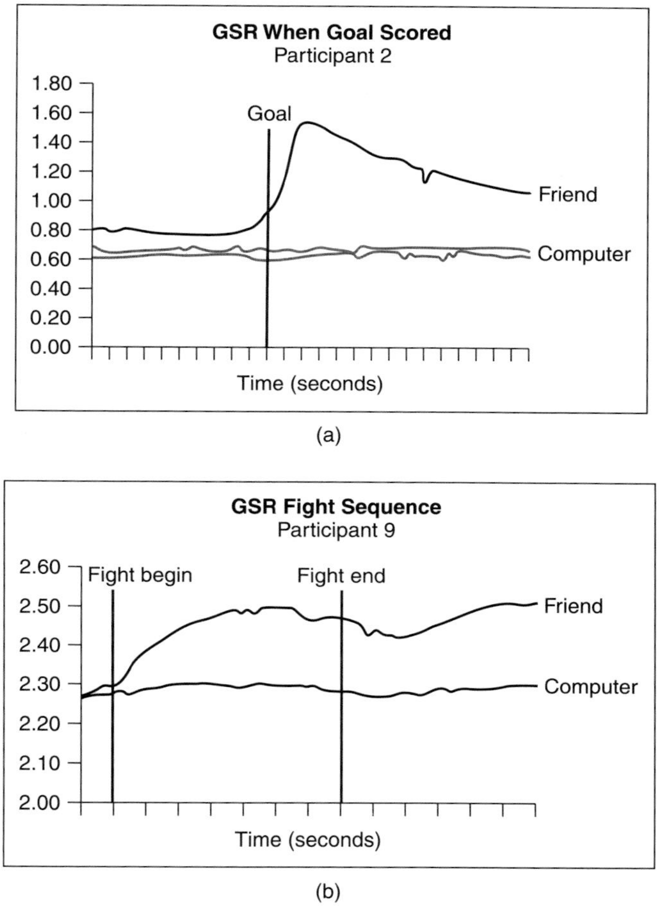

Figure 12.5 *(a) A participant's skin response when scoring a goal against a friend versus against the computer and (b) another participant's response when engaging in a hockey fight against a friend versus against the computer*

12.4.4 Improving a design: the HutchWorld patient support system

This study shows how usability testing can be done late in the design of a system to identify problems that have been overlooked by designers. You will also read about how the evaluators conducted field studies to evaluate the system while dealing with the constraints of working with sick people in a hospital environment.

HutchWorld is a distributed virtual community developed in a collaboration between Microsoft's Virtual Worlds Research Group, and librarians and clinicians at the Fred Hutchinson Cancer Research Center in Seattle, Washington (Cheng *et al.*, 2000). The system enables cancer patients, their caregivers, family, and friends to chat, tell their stories, discuss their experiences and coping strategies, and gain emotional and practical support from one another. Because this population is often isolated for fear of infection during treatment, being a cancer patient can be a lonely and frightening experience, which is also emotionally demanding on family and friends. The motivation for developing this system was to make HutchWorld a useful, engaging, easy-to-use, and emotionally satisfying environment for its users. It also had to provide privacy when needed and foster trust among participants.

A common approach to evaluation in a large project like HutchWorld is to begin by carrying out a number of informal studies. Typically, this involves asking a small number of users to comment on early prototypes. These findings are then fed back into the iterative development of the prototypes. Then, more formal evaluations are conducted in controlled environments and in natural settings (i.e. field studies). In this case study we focus on the evaluations that were done with the working prototypes.

Before developing this product, the team needed to learn about the patients' experience at the Fred Hutchinson Center. For instance, what is the typical treatment process, what resources are available to the patient community, and what are the needs of the different user groups within this community? Some patients were very sick, others suffered from bouts of depression. Patients varied along other dimensions, such as education and experience with computers, age, and gender. They came from different cultural backgrounds with different expectations. The team needed to work out what kind of virtual environment patients wanted. What would they do there? How would people interact? What should it look like? Therefore, they interviewed potential users from all the stakeholder groups—patients, caregivers, family, friends, clinicians, and social support staff––and observed their daily activity in the clinic and the hospital. They also read the latest research literature, talked to experts and former patients. After much discussion, they decided to make the design resemble the outpatient clinic lobby of the Fred Hutchinson Cancer Research Center. By using this real-world metaphor, they hoped that the users would easily infer what functionality was available in HutchWorld from their knowledge of the real clinic. A synchronous chat environment was selected because the team thought that this would be more realistic and personal than an asynchronous environment. They also decided to include 3D photographic avatars (i.e. representations of users) so that users could easily recognize each other. Figure 12.6 shows the preliminary design with examples of the avatars. You can also see the outpatient clinic lobby, the auditorium, the virtual garden, and the school. Outside the world, at the top right-hand side of the screen, is a list of commands in a palette and a list of participants. On the right-hand side at the bottom is a picture of a participant's avatar, and underneath the window is the textual chat window. Participants can move their avatars and interact with objects in the environment.

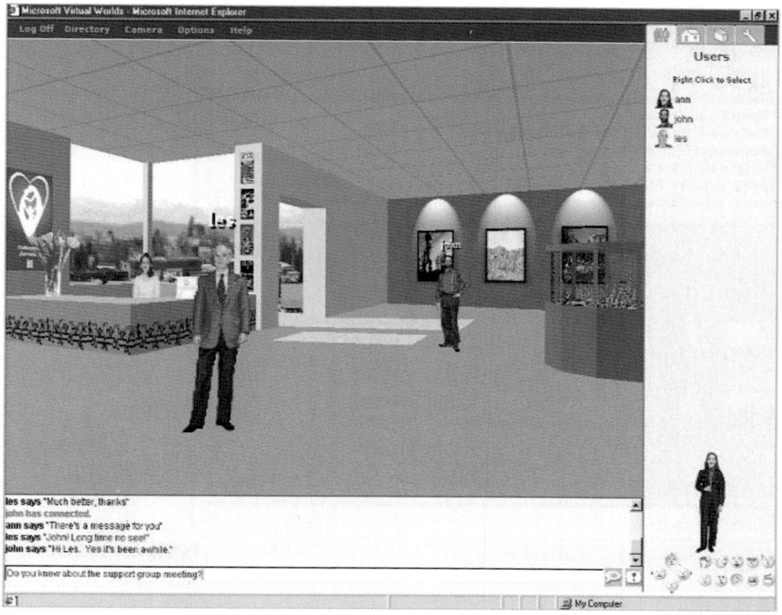

Figure 12.6 *The preliminary design showing a view of the entrance into HutchWorld*

The prototype was evaluated informally by interviewing users and observing their reactions. Once the basic design was determined the evaluators set up six computers in the Fred Hutchinson Center. These were managed by hospital staff and made available to patients. The evaluators focused on two aspects: they observed how and when patients used the system, how they interacted with it, and the kinds of problems that they experienced.

From these observations the evaluators realized that the user community was small, and there were never enough participants in the chat room for successful communication—a concept known as *critical mass* (Markus, 1987). Furthermore, many patients preferred asynchronous communication, which does not require an immediate response. Patients and their families used the email, journals, discussion lists, and the discussion boards. They also played games and searched the web.

Based on these findings the lobby was fully developed (Figure 12.7) and the software was redesigned to support asynchronous communication. HutchWorld became more like a portal that provided access to information-retrieval tools, communication tools, games, and other types of entertainment. Email, a bulletin board, a text-chat, and a web page creation tool, and a way of checking to see if anyone was around to chat in the 3D world were also provided.

The evaluators examined the usability of the revised system to get answers to such questions as: Is the system easy to learn to use? Can users find what they need? Can they send messages or chat? Do they recognize what the icons mean? Are menu names intuitive?

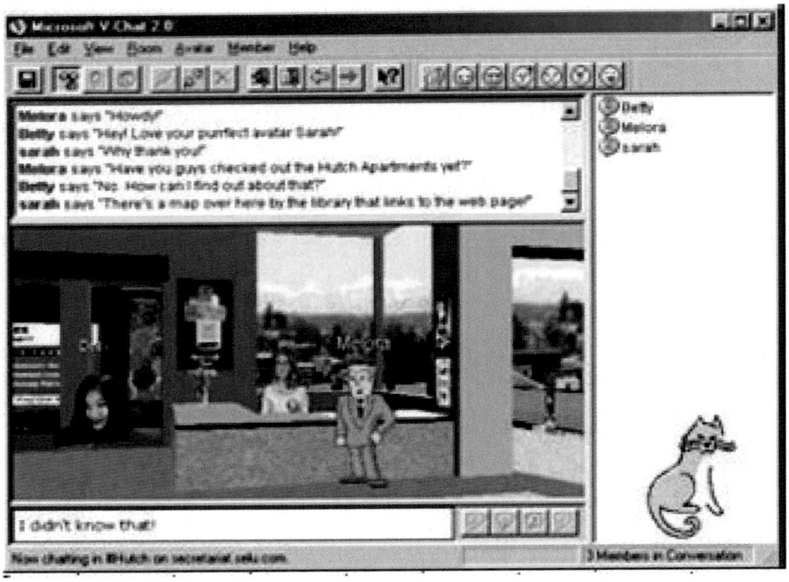

Figure 12.7 Prototype showing the lobby

They did this by developing specific tasks for the users to complete in Microsoft's usability labs, which are specially designed for evaluating usability. Seven participants (four male and three female) participated in the tests. Four participants had used chat rooms before and three were regular users and they all had browsed the web.

Each participant was introduced to the session and given five minutes to explore HutchWorld. They worked independently and while they explored they were asked to provide a running commentary about what they were looking at, what they were thinking, and what they found confusing. This commentary was recorded on video and so were the screens that they visited, so that the evaluators watching through a one-way mirror had a record of the participants' activities for later analysis. When the five-minute exploration period ended, the participants were asked to complete a series of tasks that were designed to test particular features of the HutchWorld interface. These tasks focused on how participants:

- Dealt with their virtual identity; that is, how they represented themselves and were perceived by others.
- Communicated with others.
- Got the information they wanted.
- Found entertainment.

Figure 12.8 shows some of the structured tasks. Notice that the instructions are short, clearly written, and specific.

A. Point to the 3 dimensional (3D) view of HutchWorld.
B. Point at your self in the 3D view of HutchWorld.
C. Get a map view in the 3D view of HutchWorld.
D. Walk around in the 3D view: go forward, turn left and turn right.
E. Change the color of your shirt.
F. Change some information about your self, such as where you are from.

Figure 12.8 *Example of the structured tasks—your identity in HutchWorld*

During the study, a member of the development team role-played being a participant so that the real participants would be sure to have someone with whom to interact. The evaluator also asked the participants to fill out a short questionnaire after completing the tasks, with the aim of collecting their opinions about their experiences with HutchWorld. The questionnaire asked:

- What did you *like* about HutchWorld?
- What did you *not like* about HutchWorld?
- What did you find confusing or difficult to use in HutchWorld?
- How would you suggest improving HutchWorld?

By running these usability tests, the evaluators collected masses of data that they had to make sense of by systematic analysis. The findings from this and similar evaluations are usually extensive so the following discussion provides only a snapshot of what was learned from the evaluation.

Some participants' problems started right at the beginning of the five-minute exploration. The login page referred to 'virtual worlds' rather than the expected HutchWorld and, even though this might seem trivial, it was enough to confuse some users. This isn't unusual; developers tend to overlook small things like this, which is why evaluation is so important. Usability testing is particularly useful for identifying these kinds of problems, which are usually easy to fix but can cause users much frustration if left. Fortunately, most participants read the welcome message and used the navigation list, and over half used the chat buttons, managed to move around the 3D world, and read the overview. The five-minute free-exploration data was also analyzed to determine what people thought of HutchWorld.

The evaluators analyzed the users' performance on the tasks in detail and also how participants rated different features on a scale of 1–3 where 1 = easy, 2 = OK, 3 = difficult, and bold = needed help. Any activity that received an average rating above 1.5 across participants was considered in need of improvement. Figure 12.9 shows a fragment of the analysis summary.

The evaluation team reviewed the data and drew up a table of issues, noting whether each was a priority to fix. Table 12.4 shows how some of the issues were ranked in priority. There were just five high-ranking problems that absolutely had to be fixed:

Participant number:	1	2	3	4	5	6	Average
Background Information							
sex	F	M	M	F	F	F	4F, 2M
age	25	43	36	31	33	52	36.7
years of college	0	4	0	0	4	2	1.7
hours of chat use in past year	18	26	52	104	130	260	98.3
hours of web use in past year	130	728	728	1040	520	1560	784.3
Structured Tasks							
change color of shirt	2	1	1	2	1	1	1.3
change information about self		1	1	2	2	2	1.6
get a map view of world	1	3	2	1	3	3	2.2
find out who is currently on	4	2	1	1	1	3	2.0
find out where another is from	1	1	1	1	1	1	1.0
chat to other person	1	1	1	1	1	1	1.0

Figure 12.9 *Summary of part of the analysis in which users rated HutchWorld*

Issue#	Issue Priority	Issue	Recommendation
1	high	Back button sometimes not working.	Fix back button.
2	high	People are not paying attention to navigation buttons.	Make navigation buttons more prominent.
3	low	Fonts too small, hard to read for some people.	Make it possible to change fonts. Make the font colors more distinct from the background color.
4	low	When navigating, people were not aware overview button would take them back to the main page.	Change the overview button to a home button, change the wording of the overview page accordingly.
5	medium	"Virtual worlds" wording in login screen confusing.	Change wording to "HutchWorld".
6	high	People frequently clicking on objects in 3D view expecting something to happen.	Make the 3D view have links to web pages. For example, when people click on the help desk the browser area should show the help desk information.
7	low	People do not readily find map view button.	Make the icon on the map view button more map-like.

Table 12.4 *Usability issues ranked according to importance*

Issue#	Issue Priority	Issue	Recommendation
8	medium	Moving avatar with mouse took some getting used to.	Encourage the use of the keyboard. Mention clicking and dragging the avatar in the welcome.
9	low	People wanted to turn around in 3D view, but it was awkward to do so.	Make one of the chat buttons a button that lets you turn around.
10	medium	Confusion about the real world/virtual world distinction.	Change wording of overview description, to make clear Hutch-World is a "virtual" place made to "resemble" the FHCRC, and is a place where anybody can go.
11	high	People do not initially recognize that other real people could be in Hutch World, that they can talk to them and see them.	Change wording of overview description, to make clear HutchWorld is a place to "chat" with others who are "currently in" the virtual HutchWorld.
12	high	People not seeing/finding the chat window. Trying to chat to people from the people list where other chat-like features are (whisper, etc.)	Make chat window more prominent. Somehow link chatlike features of navigation list to chat window. Change wording of chat window. Instead of type to speak here, type to chat here.
13	low	Who is here list and who has been here list confused.	Spread them apart more in the people list.
14	medium	Difficulty in finding who is here.	Change People button to "Who is On" button.
15	low	Went to own profile to make someone a friend.	Let people add friends at My profile
16	low	Not clear how to append/reply to a discussion in the bulletin board.	Make an append button pop up when double clicking on a topic. Change wording from "post a message" to "write a message" or "add a message".
17	low	Bulletin board language is inconsistent.	Change so it is either a bulletin board, or a discussion area.

Table 12.4 *(continued)*

- The back button did not always work.
- People were not paying attention to navigation buttons, so they needed to be more prominent.
- People frequently clicked on objects in the 3D view and expected something to happen. A suggestion for fixing this was to provide links to a web page.
- People did not realize that there could be other real people in the 3D world with whom they could chat, so the wording in the overview description had to be changed.
- People were not noticing the chat window and instead were trying to chat to people in the participant list. The team needed to clarify the instructions about where to chat.

After dealing with these problems the software was evaluated again with six new participants, two males and four females. These tests followed the same general format as those just described but this time they tested multiple users at once, to ensure that the virtual world supported multi-user interactions. The tests were also more detailed and focused and, of course, there were still usability problems to be fixed. This raises the question of "when has enough testing been done?," which we explore in the Dilemma box.

Dilemma
When is it time to stop testing?

Was HutchWorld good enough after these evaluations? When has enough testing been done? This frequently asked question is difficult to answer. Few developers have the luxury of testing as thoroughly as they would like. Since every test you do will reveal some area where improvement can be made, you cannot assume that there will be a time when the system is perfect: no system is ever perfect. Normally, schedule and budget constraints determine when testing has to stop. Joseph Dumas and Ginny Redish, established usability consultants, point out that for iterative design and testing to be successful, each test should take as little time as possible while still yielding useful information and without burdening the team (Dumas and Redish, 1999).

The next step was to evaluate whether there were problems when HutchWorld was used by cancer patients and caregivers in the real world setting of the Fred Hutchinson Cancer Research Center. Focus groups and informal observation enabled the evaluators to examine patterns of use and to see who used which parts of the system, when, and why. (For those interested in finding out about this part of the study or reading a more detailed account of the whole study, you will find this information on our book website.) ■

Activity 12.6

1. The case study does not say much about early evaluation to test the design shown in Figure 12.6. What would you have done to evaluate this early design?
2. The evaluators recorded the gender of participants and noted their previous experience with similar systems. Why is this important?
3. Why do you think it was important to give participants a five-minute exploration period?
4. The evaluators collected participants' opinions. What kinds of concerns do you think participants might have about using HutchWorld? Hints: personal information, medical information, communicating feelings, etc.
5. Which evaluation methods were used early in design, which were used late in design, and which were used during both early and late design phases.

Comment

1. We would have based the evaluation on informal discussion with users such as patients, medical staff, relatives, friends, caregivers, physicians, and hospital administrators. We would also have spent time observing what happened in the hospital.
2. It is possible that men and women react differently in certain circumstances. Experience of using computers is likely to be an important influence on how the users would react to the system, so knowing how much previous experience users have with different types of software enables evaluators to make informed judgments about their performance. For example, experts and novices tend to behave differently.
3. The evaluators wanted to see how participants reacted to the system and whether or not they could logon and get started. The exploration period gave the participants time to get used to the system before doing the set tasks.
4. Comments and medical details are personal and people want privacy. Participants might be concerned about whether the medical information they get via the computer and from one another is accurate. Participants might be concerned about how clearly and accurately they are communicating because non-verbal communication is reduced online.
5. As in the previous case studies, observation and interviews were used early in design. Late in design, once a functional prototype or working system was developed and the project was nearing completion, more formal usability tests were performed. Two types of tests were done: usability tests in Microsoft's laboratory, and field studies of how people used the product in the Fred Hutchinson Center.

From the usability test data the evaluators could see when users got stuck or confused or failed to complete the task and how long it took them. Questionnaires and interviews were used to collect information about the users' satisfaction with the system. In the field studies, users were observed and their opinions were sought via questionnaires and interviews. Observation, individual or focus group interviews, and questionnaires were used to evaluate the software both early on and later in design.

12.4.5 Multiple methods help ensure good usability: the olympic messaging system (OMS)

This case study describes a system that was highly visible and carried with it IBM's reputation. Therefore it had to function well. Consequently, the design team contained some of the most creative designers and evaluators of the time and no expense was spared. This case study is a classic, though now old, and we are including it to illustrate how a range of methods can be used to evaluate different aspects of a system.

The 1984 Olympic Message System (OMS) was a voice mail system, developed by IBM so that Olympic Games contestants, their families, and friends could send and receive messages (Gould *et al.*, 1987, 1990). Listeners could hear the message exactly as it was spoken. The OMS could be used from almost any push-button phone system around the world. While this may not sound amazing by today's standards, in 1983 it was innovative. The OMS worked in 12 languages and the kiosks and dialog are shown in Figures 12.10 and 12.11.

Gould and his team wanted to ensure that the OMS was successful. To achieve this goal a wide array of evaluation methods was used to collect feedback about its usability and whether users liked it. These included:

- Interviews with the Olympic committee and the Olympians themselves to get feedback about printed scenarios and screens.
- Tests in which Olympians, their families, and friends had to find information in the user guides.
- Tests in which users interacted with early simulations of the telephone keypad with a person speaking the commands back (a form of Wizard of Oz prototyping). These simulations tested how much a user needed to know about the system, what feedback was needed, and any incorrect assumptions about user behavior made by the designers.
- Early demonstrations with focus groups from outside of the USA to get their reactions.
- An Olympian joined the design team in order to provide informal feedback.

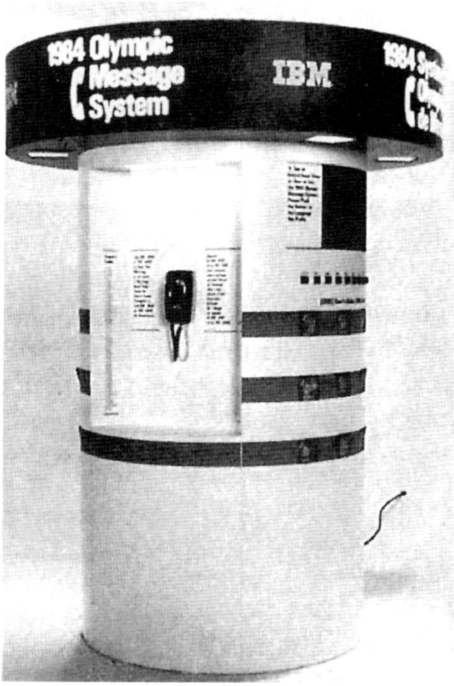

Figure 12.10 *An Olympic Message System kiosk*

Caller:	(Dials 213-888-8888.)
Operator:	Irish National Olympic Committee. Can I help you?
Caller:	I want to leave a message for my son, Michael.
Operator:	Is he from Ireland?
Caller:	Yes.
Operator:	How do you spell his name?
Caller:	*K-E-L-L-Y*.
Operator:	Thank you. Please hold for about 30 seconds while I connect you to the Olympic Message System.
Operator:	Are you ready?
Caller:	Yes.
OMS:	When you have completed your message, hang up and it will be automatically sent to Michael Kelly. Begin talking when you are ready.
Caller:	'Michael, your Mother and I will be hoping you win. Good luck.' (Caller hangs up.)

Figure 12.11 *The screen of the Olympic Message System*

- Interviews with Olympians to make sure that the system being developed was what they wanted.
- Tests with friends and family from overseas to check that cultural differences that might result in the interface being difficult to use had not been overlooked.
- Tests known as 'coffee and donut' tests in which 65 people tested the system in return for these treats.
- A 'try-to-destroy-it' test was conducted in which 24 computer science students were challenged to 'break' the system in any way they could. One of these tests involved all the students calling into the OMS at the same time. Needless to say, the students enjoyed the challenge and didn't need any other motivation!
- Two other tests examined the reliability of the system with heavy traffic generated by 2800 and 1000 users, respectively.
- Usability tests of a prototype involving 100 participants to check for problems before launching.
- The final test was a pre-Olympic field test of the interface at an international event with competitors from 65 countries. The outcome of this test was surprising because, despite all the other testing, 57 different usability problems were recorded by the end of the five-day test period. Many of these problems arose from strong cultural differences between users from different countries. Testers from Oman, Colombia, Pakistan, Japan, and Korea were unable to use the system. Gould and his colleagues were embarrassed by their own lack of sensitivity to cultural differences. They commented that "watching this . . . had a far greater impact than reading about it. It was embarrassing . . ." (Gould *et al.*, 1990, p. 274).

Activity 12.7

1. What is the most significant message you learn from this case study?

2. Why was it important for the evaluators to use a variety of methods?

Comment

1. The most significant lesson from this study is that the more evaluation with users, the better. While most design teams do not have the resources of this team, with ingenuity it is usually possible to test products extensively.

2. Different methods provide different kinds of data that enables evaluators to learn about different aspects of the users' experiences. This supports triangulation (discussed in Chapter 7).

12.4.6 Evaluating a new kind of interaction: an ambient system

Most systems are designed to replace or support tasks that we already do, but research in ubiquitous computing is producing completely new systems so that we can explore new ways of interacting with technology. In this situation there may be no alternative but to design a robust prototype, give it to users, and evaluate what they do with it, and what they like or don't like. This field study looks at a system in which software sensors are embedded in a wall-like structure which people interact with; such systems are known as ambient systems.

The ambient device being evaluated in this case study is known as the 'Hello.Wall' and it was developed by Norbet Streitz and his colleagues, as part of a project sponsored by the European Commission's Disappearing Computer Initiative (Streitz *et al.*, 2005). As the name suggests, this initiative supports projects that aim to break new ground by developing devices that blend in with the environment and do not look like a computer (Streitz *et al.*, 2005). When users interact with these devices they notice that their environment is changing according to their actions, rather than thinking: "*Oh! There's a computer over there on the table.*"

The Hello.Wall is a 1.8 meter-wide by 2-meter high artifact with integrated light cells and sensing technology (see Figure 12.12). It enhances awareness of their environment by 'notifying' people passing by or watching it. Different light patterns correspond to different types of information. Some of the patterns created by the light cells provide public information that everyone can know about, but some provide private information known only to those people allowed to know it, which enables users to communicate private information with people of their choice. In addition, the Hello.Wall has an aesthetic impact that helps to create the 'mood' of the space that it occupies and this can influence social gatherings.

There are three different zones of interaction created around the Hello.Wall: a close *interaction* zone which is close up to the wall, a *notification* zone which is further away, and an *ambient* zone which is still further away (see Figure 12.13).

People in the ambient zone contribute to the experience by generating continuously displayed ambient patterns. These patterns suggest general presence information. People in the notification zone are identified and the Hello.Wall reacts to and enriches their personal presence. People in the interaction zone can interact directly with the Hello.Wall environment. In each circumstance the wall generates interaction patterns that are appropriate.

Activity 12.8

1. **The Hello.Wall is an innovative device. It is designed to allow people to explore the possibilities offered by such devices and to see how their physical presence impacts the social environment that they inhabit. What evaluation methods would you use to evaluate the Hello.Wall?**
2. **Imagine that you are evaluating users' impressions of the Hello.Wall and write**

Figure 12.12 The Hello.Wall in which the ambient display combines unobtrusive, calm technology and a continual display of high-quality aesthetic patterns to convey the idea of turning everyday spaces into social places where people can meet and interact

a few interview questions that you would ask users.

Comment

1. Since the underlying concept of the Hello.Wall is to allow people to interact with it as they wish, any evaluation method that intruded upon this free-form exploratory environment would be counterproductive. One way of collecting data about these interactions would be to discretely position video cameras to record what people do when they are in the Wall's environment. This raises some privacy concerns that need to be considered and this is a topic for Chapter 13. Interviews and questionnaires could also be used to collect data from people who have moved out of the Wall's range.
2. There are several questions that you might have thought of. Here are our suggestions:
   (a) What were your initial reactions when the Hello.Wall reacted to your presence?
   (b) What did you actually do when you saw the Hello.Wall?
   (c) How did it respond?
   (d) How did that make you feel?

   Probing for more information would be useful depending on how users answer these questions.

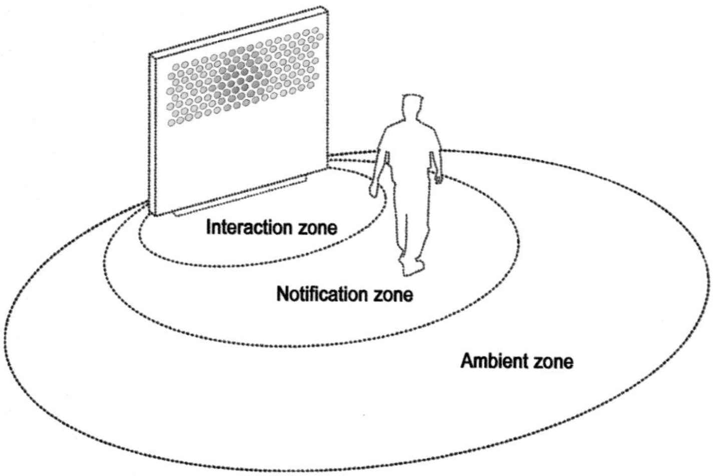

Figure 12.13 *Communication zones which depend on the distance from the display*

12.5 What did we learn from the case studies?

Together the case studies provide examples of how different evaluation approaches (i.e. usability testing, field studies, and analytical evaluation) and methods (i.e. observing users, asking users their opinions, asking experts their opinions, testing users' performance, and modeling users' task performance) are used, and the kinds of practical challenges that evaluators routinely face. These include:

- What to do when there are not many users, e.g. HutchWorld and the collaborative immersive game case studies.
- How to observe users in their natural location (i.e. field studies) without disturbing them, e.g. cell phone case study.
- Communicating with users who come from a different culture, and speak a different language, e.g. record-keeping system for the auxiliary nurse midwives in India.
- How best to respect different cultural norms, e.g. record-keeping system for the auxiliary nurse midwives in India.
- Triangulating data from different sources to gain an overview of the system's usability, e.g. Olympic Messaging System and HutchWorld.
- Working with users who are sick and may be emotionally fragile, e.g. HutchWorld.
- The need to cope with rapidly changing physical environments, e.g. cell phone study.
- Ensuring that users are safe and not in discomfort, e.g. collaborative immersive game).
- Avoiding any impact on users who are exploring a new kind of technology, e.g. Hello.Wall).

- Having to develop different data collection and analysis techniques to evaluate user experience goals such as challenge and engagement, e.g. collaborative immersive game.
- Creating 'on-the-fly' ways of testing usability that are quick and inexpensive, e.g. some of the methods used in the Olympic Messaging System case study.
- Respecting users and their privacy (all of the case studies, but particularly HutchWorld and the record-keeping system for the auxiliary nurse midwives in India because these studies involve medical information).

Assignment

In this assignment we want you to think about the case studies you read in this chapter and reflect on the evaluation methods used.

1. For each of the six case studies think about the role of evaluation in the design of the system and note the artifacts that were evaluated, *when* during the design they were evaluated, which methods were used, and *what* was learned from the evaluations? Note any issues of particular interest. You may find that constructing a table like the one that follows is a helpful approach.

Artifact evaluated	When evaluated	Method(s) used	What was learned	Notable issues

2. How was the design advanced after each evaluation?
3. What were the main constraints that influenced the evaluation?
4. How did the use of different approaches and methods build on and complement each other to give a broader picture of the evaluation?
5. Which parts of the evaluation were directed at usability goals and which at user experience goals?

Summary

The aim of this chapter was to introduce a range of evaluation methods and concepts that will be revisited in the next three chapters. We defined *evaluation* as a process for collecting information about users' or potential users' experiences when interacting with a prototype, computer system, a component of a computer system, or a design artifact, e.g. screen sketch, in order to improve its design. Evaluation is done throughout design. Typically early evaluations involve observing and interviewing users, whereas usability testing is particularly useful for refining designs that are well advanced.

In order to evaluate the wide range of products currently being developed, evaluators must be creative. This is particularly true when evaluating mobile and ubiquitous devices, such as cell phones which are used in different environments. Current methods work well for evaluating usability and questionnaires and interviews capture many aspects of user satisfaction. However, new methods are needed to evaluate the kinds of emotional reactions that can occur when interacting with online entertainment systems. Physiological measures may provide one solution but other solutions are also needed.

Key points

- Evaluation and design are very closely integrated in user-centered design.
- Some of the same data gathering techniques are used in evaluation as for establishing requirements and identifying users' needs, but they are used differently, e.g. observation, interviews and questionnaires, etc.
- Three main evaluation approaches are: usability testing, field studies and analytical evaluation.
- The main evaluation methods are: observing users, asking users, asking experts, user testing, inspection methods (i.e. heuristic evaluation and walkthroughs), and modelling users' task performance.
- Different evaluation approaches and evaluation methods are usually combined in any one evaluation study.
- Dealing with constraints, such as gaining access to users or accommodating users' routines, is an important skill for evaluators to develop.

Further Reading

BLOM, J., CHIPCHASE, J. and LEHIKOINEN, J. (2005) Contextual and cultural challenges for user mobility research. *CACM*, **48**(7), 37–41. This article provides a fascinating account of the challenges of evaluating mobile devices for use by different cultures.

CHENG, L., STONE, L., FARNHAM, S., CLARK, A.M. and ZANER-GODSEY, M. (2000) *Hutchworld: Lessons Learned. A Collaborative Project: Fred Hutchinson Cancer Research Center & Microsoft Research.* In the Proceedings of the Virtual Worlds Conference 2000, Paris, France. This paper describes the HutchWorld study and, as the title suggests, it discusses the design lessons that were learned. It also describes the evaluation studies in more detail.

GOULD, J.D., BOIES, S.J., LEVY, S., RICHARDS, J.T. and SCHOONARD, J. (1987). The 1984 Olympic Message System: a test of behavioral principles of systems design. *Communications of the ACM*, **30**(9), 758–769. This is the original, full version of the OMS paper.

GRISEDALE, S., GRAVES, M. and GRUNSTEIDL, A. (1997) Designing a graphical user interface for healthcare workers in rural India. *CHI 97 Conference Procs (Design Briefings)*, 471–478. This paper provides a very readable, amusing, and sensitive account of the challenges of developing a product for people from a different culture. It also highlights some of the constraints involved in designing for mobile devices with small displays.

MANDRYK, R.L. and INKPEN, K.M. (2004) Physiological indicators for the evaluation of co-located collaborative play. *Proceedings ACM Conference CSCW*, Chicago, IL, November 6–10, 102–111. This paper describes how the researchers set up an experiment to investigate the efficacy of a range of physiological measures for evaluating users' experience of challenge and engagement when playing a collaborative immersive ice-hockey game against a friend compared with playing the same game against the computer. The results indicate that these measures correspond well with the participants' subjective ratings. The paper provides a valuable alternative to standard usability testing, which is less well suited to evaluating this kind of user experience.

SHNEIDERMAN, B. and PLAISANT, C. (2005) *Designing the User Interface: Strategies for Effective Human–Computer Interaction*, 4th edn. Addison-Wesley. This text provides an alternative way of categorizing evaluation methods and offers a good overview.

WHITESIDE, J., BENNETT, J. and HOLTZBLATT, K. (1998) Usability engineering: our experience and evolution. In M. Helander (ed.), *Handbook of Human–Computer Interaction*. North Holland. Though written several years ago, this chapter provides a useful review of the strengths and weakness of usability engineering and explains why ethnographic techniques can provide a valuable alternative, or supplement, in some circumstances, 791–817.

13

13.1 Introduction

Designing useful and attractive products requires skill and creativity. As products evolve from initial ideas through conceptual design and prototypes, iterative cycles of design and evaluation help to ensure that they meet users' needs. Deciding when and how to evaluate a product requires careful consideration and may be different for different kinds of products.

The case studies in the previous chapter illustrate some of the approaches used.

The design process starts with the designers working to develop a product that meets users' requirements, but, as you have seen, understanding requirements tends to happen by a process of negotiation between designers and users. As designers understand users' needs better, their designs reflect this understanding. Similarly, as users see and experience design ideas, they are able to give better feedback that enables the designers to improve their designs further. The process is cyclical, with evaluation facilitating understanding between designers and users.

Evaluation is driven by questions about how well the design or particular aspects of it satisfy users' needs and offer appropriate user experiences. Some of these questions provide high-level goals to guide the evaluation. For example, does this product excite users so that they will buy and use it? Others are much more specific. Can users find a particular menu item? Do they interpret a particular graphic as the designers intended and do they find it attractive? Practical constraints play a big role in shaping how evaluation is done: tight schedules, low budgets, or little access to users constrain what evaluators can do. There are ethical considerations too: medical records must be private and so are certain areas of people's homes.

Experienced designers get to know what works and what doesn't. As you have seen in Chapter 12, there is a broad repertoire of evaluation methods that can be tailored for specific circumstances. Knowing and having the confidence to adapt methods is essential. The wide variety of mobile and ubiquitous systems coming onto the market challenges conventional evaluation practices, which must be adapted to provide useful feedback. Therefore, when planning evaluations, evaluators must consider the nature of each product, the kinds of users that will use it, and the contexts of use, as well as logistical issues, such as the budget, the schedule, the skills and equipment required for the evaluation. Planning evaluation studies involves asking questions about the process and anticipating potential problems. Within interaction design there are many books and websites that list different techniques and guidelines for conducting an evaluation, but there is very little overarching guidance for how to plan an evaluation. To help you, we propose the DECIDE framework, which provides a structure for planning evaluation studies.

The main aims of this chapter are to:

- **Discuss the conceptual, practical, and ethical issues involved in evaluation.**
- **Introduce and explain the DECIDE framework.**

13

An evaluation framework

13.2 DECIDE: A framework to guide evaluation

Well-planned evaluations are driven by *goals* which aim to seek answers to clear *questions*, which may be stated explicitly, upfront, as in usability testing, or may emerge as the evaluation progresses, as in ethnographic evaluation. The way questions are stated also varies depending on the stage in the design when the evaluation occurs. Questions help to determine the kind of *evaluation approach* that is adopted and the *methods* used. *Practical issues*, such as the amount of time available to carry out the evaluation, the availability of participants, and suitable equipment, also impact these decisions. *Ethical issues* must also be considered, particularly when working with users, and evaluators must have enough time and expertise to evaluate, analyze, interpret, and present the *data* that they collect. The *DECIDE* framework provides the following checklist to help you plan your evaluation studies and to remind you about the issues you need to think about. It has the following six items:

1. Determine the *goals*.
2. Explore the *questions*.
3. Choose the *evaluation approach* and *methods*.
4. Identify the *practical issues*.
5. Decide how to deal with the *ethical issues*.
6. Evaluate, analyze, interpret, and present the *data*.

A list has the tendency to suggest an order in which things should be done. However, when working with the DECIDE framework, it is common to think about and deal with items iteratively, moving backwards and forwards between them. Each item in the framework is related to the other items, so it would be unusual to work in any other way.

13.2.1 Determine the goals

What are the high-level goals of the evaluation? Who wants it and why? An evaluation to help clarify that user needs have been met in an early design sketch has different goals from an evaluation to select the best representation of a metaphor for a conceptual design, or an evaluation to finetune an interface, or to examine how mobile technology changes working practices, or to inform how the next version of a product should be changed, or to explore the impact of ambient technology in a social space; or to investigate what makes collaborative computer games engaging.

Goals guide the evaluation by helping to determine its scope, so identifying what these goals are is the first step in planning an evaluation. For example, we can restate the first general goal statement mentioned above more clearly as:

Check that the sketch indicates that designers have understood the users' needs.

Activity 13.1

Rewrite each of the general goal descriptions above as a goal statement and suggest which case study or part of a case study from Chapter 12 fits the goal statement.

Comment

- **Identify the best representation of the metaphor on which the design will be based, e.g. HutchWorld, record-keeping system for Indian auxiliary nurse midwives.**
- **Ensure that the interface is consistent, e.g. Olympic Messaging System, HutchWorld.**
- **Investigate the degree to which mobile technology influences working practices, e.g. record-keeping system for Indian auxiliary nurse midwives, perhaps also the Nokia cell phone study, though we are not told this explicitly in the case study.**
- **Identify how the interface of an existing product could be engineered to improve its usability for use by people from a different culture, e.g. the Nokia cell phone study.**
- **Investigate the impact of the technology on social interaction, e.g. the HelloWall.**
- **Determine the nature of collaborative computer games, e.g. the digital hockey game.**

In turn, these goals influence the approach chosen to guide the study and the selection of evaluation methods.

13.2.2 Explore the questions

In order to make goals operational, we must clearly articulate the questions to be answered by the evaluation study. For example, the goal of finding out why some customers prefer to purchase paper airline tickets over the counter rather than e-tickets can be broken down into a number of relevant questions for investigation. What are customers' attitudes to these e-tickets? Perhaps they don't trust the system and are not sure that they will actually get on the flight without a ticket in their hand. Do customers have adequate access to computers to make bookings? Are they concerned about security? Does the electronic system have a bad reputation? Is the user interface to the ticketing system so poor that they can't use it? Maybe some people can't managed to complete the transaction. Maybe some people like the social interaction with a ticketing agent?

Questions can be broken down into very specific subquestions to make the evaluation even more finegrained. For example, what does it mean to ask, "Is the user interface poor?" Is the system difficult to navigate? Is the terminology confusing because it is inconsistent? Is the response time too slow? Is the feedback confusing or maybe insufficient? Subquestions can, in turn, be further decomposed if even more specific issues need to be addressed.

Activity 13.2

Imagine you have been asked to evaluate the impact of the HelloWall on users' behavior. Based on what you know about the HelloWall from Chapter 12, write two or three questions that you could investigate.

Comment

You could ask a variety of questions. Here are some that we thought of:

1. **Do users notice the HelloWall?**
2. **For those who do notice it, how do they react to it?**
3. **Do they explore how it behaves when they are different distances from the wall?**
4. **Do they seem to enjoy interacting with it?**
5. **Do they tell others about it? If so, what do they say?**

13.2.3 Choose the approach and methods

Having identified the goals and some questions that you want to investigate, the next step is to choose the evaluation approach and methods that you will use. As mentioned in Chapter 12, the evaluation approach influences the kinds of methods that are used. For example, when performing an analytical evaluation, methods that directly involve users will not be used. During usability testing, ethnography will not be used. Often different approaches are used in this way, depending on the questions to be answered and the resources available for performing the study. Practical and ethical issues (discussed next) have to be considered and trade-offs made. For example, the methods that seem most appropriate may be too expensive, or may take too long, or may require equipment or expertise that is not available, so compromises are needed.

As you saw in several of the case studies discussed in Chapter 12, combinations of approaches and methods are often used to obtain different perspectives. For example, the methods used in field studies tend to involve observation, interviews, or informal discussions with participants. Questionnaires may also be used and so might diary studies in which participants record aspects of their technology usage. Usability testing also involves multiple methods and, as we have already said, is often supplemented with field studies. Each type of data tells the story from a different point of view. Together these perspectives give a broad picture of how well the design meets the usability and user experience goals that were identified during requirements gathering.

Activity 13.3

Which approaches and methods could be used in an evaluation to answer the questions that we provided for Activity 13.2? These were:

1. Do users notice the HelloWall?
2. For those who do notice it, how do they react to it?
3. Do they explore how it behaves when they are different distances from the wall?
4. Do they seem to enjoy interacting with it?
5. Do they tell others about it? If so, what do they say?

Comment

A field study is most appropriate because we want to investigate how people react to this new technology being placed in their natural environment. The methods that could be used are as follows. Observation could be used for answering both questions and subquestions. This could be done by video or by a person making notes. Questionnaires and interviews could also be designed to collect data to answer these questions.

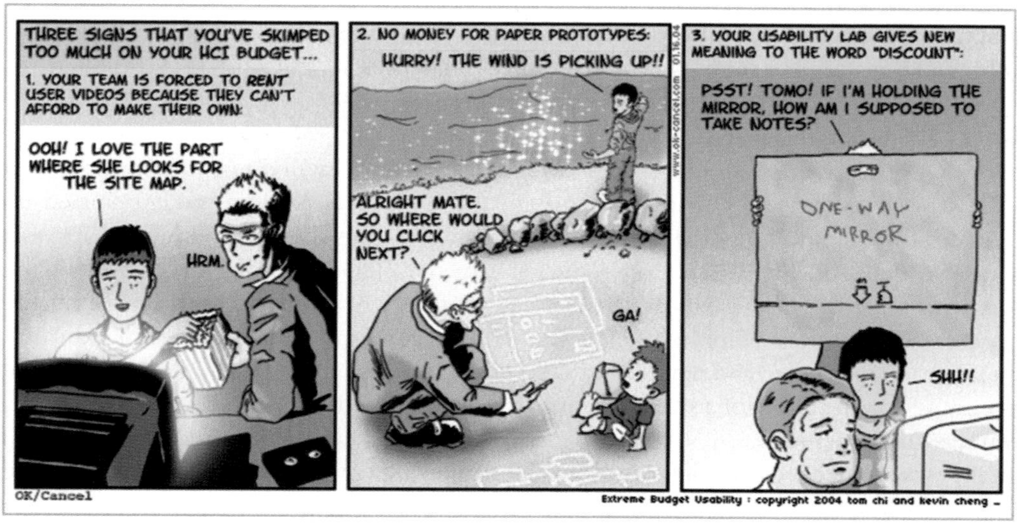

13.2.4 Identify the practical issues

There are many practical issues to consider when doing any kind of evaluation, and it is important to identify as many of them as possible *before* starting the study. However, even experienced evaluators encounter surprise events, which is why it is useful to do a pilot study (discussed in Chapter 7). Some issues that should be considered include access to appropriate users, facilities and equipment, whether schedules and budgets are realistic, and whether the evaluators have the appropriate expertise to conduct the study. Depending on the availability of resources, there may have to be compromises that involve adapting or substituting methods. For example, evaluators may wish to perform usability tests using 20 users and then to run a three-week-long field study, but the budget available for the study may only cover the cost of five testers and a shorter field study. Another example is provided by the Nokia cell phone, which involved evaluating cell phones in a country where the evaluators do not speak the language fluently and are only slightly aware of cultural norms. In this situation the evaluators had to work out how to collect the data that they needed to answer their evaluation questions. Furthermore, cell phone users are highly mobile so the evaluators knew that there would be places where the cell phones would be used that they could not go, e.g. in bathrooms, bedrooms. During the study the evaluators may also have experienced surprise events that required them to take decisions there and then. For example, it may not have been possible to ride in the taxi or car with the user because there was not enough room. Of course, no evaluation is going to be perfect, and a good field study can be done without the evaluator seeing how the product is used 100% of the time, but it is helpful to be aware of the kind of compromises that may be necessary. Thinking about the kind of users who will be involved and logistical issues, such as availability of equipment, the schedule and the budget, and the kind of expertise needed to perform the study, when planning a study will help to ensure its success.

Users

It goes without saying that a key aspect of an evaluation is involving appropriate users or, in the case of analytical evaluation, focusing on the characteristics of the anticipated user population. When doing usability testing, for example, users must be found who represent the user population for which the product is targeted. This generally involves identifying users with a particular level of experience, e.g. novices or experts, or users with a range of expertise. The number of males and females within a particular age range, cultural diversity, educational experience, and personality differences may also need to be taken into account, depending on the kind of product being evaluated. Questionnaire surveys require large numbers of participants, so ways of identifying and reaching a representative sample of participants are needed. For field studies to be successful, the evaluator needs access to users who will interact with the technology in their natural setting.

Another issue to consider is how the users will be involved. The tasks used in a usability laboratory study should be representative of those for which the product is designed. However, there are no written rules about the length of time that a user should be expected to spend on an evaluation task. Ten minutes is too short for most tasks and two hours is a long time, so what is reasonable? Task times will vary according to the type of evaluation, but when tasks go on for more than 20 minutes, consider offering breaks. It is accepted that people using desktop computers should stop, move around, and change their position regularly after every 20 minutes spent at the keyboard to avoid repetitive strain injury. Evaluators also need to put users at ease so they are not anxious and will perform normally; it is important to treat them courteously. Participants should not be made to feel uncomfortable when they make mistakes. Greeting users, explaining that it is the product that is being tested and not them, and planning an activity to familiarize them with it before starting the task all help to put users at ease in test situations.

In field studies the onus is on the evaluators to fit in with the users and to cause as little disturbance to participants and their activities as possible. This requires practice, and even anthropologists who are trained in ethnographic methods may cause unforeseen changes (see Dilemma box below).

Dilemma

Is it possible to study people's behavior without influencing it?

A newspaper article describes how an anthropology student traveling through northern Kenya happens by chance to come upon an unknown tribe. He studies their rituals and reports the study in his PhD dissertation and several published articles in acclaimed journals. The study draws considerable attention because finding an unknown tribe is unusual in this day and age. It is the dream of many anthropologists because it allows them to study the tribe's customs before they are changed by outside influences. Of course, having published his work, the inevitable happens; more anthropologists make their way to the village and soon members of the tribe are drinking coke and wearing tee-shirts from prestigious universities and well-known tourist destinations. The Western habits of these outsiders gradually changes the tribe's behavior.

Ethnographers face a dilemma: is it possible to study people's behavior without changing it in the process? ■

Facilities and equipment

There are many practical issues concerned with using equipment in an evaluation. For example, when using video you need to think about how you will do the recording: how many cameras and where do you put them? Some people are disturbed by having a camera pointed at them and will not perform normally, so how can you avoid making them feel uncomfortable? How will you record data about use of a mobile device when the users move rapidly from one environment to another? Several of the case studies in Chapter 12 addressed these issues. Think back, or reread the Nokia cell phone study, the Indian auxiliary midwife data collection study, and HutchWorld.

Activity 13.4

The evaluators of the Nokia cell phones described some of the logistics that they needed to consider; what were they?

Comment

The evaluators did not speak Japanese, the language of the users, and they knew that people using cell phones can be fast-moving as they go about their busy lives. Some of the things that the evaluators suggest may be necessary when conducting such a study include: spare batteries for recording devices; change and extra money for taxies or unforeseen expenses; additional clothes in case the weather suddenly changes, e.g. a rain jacket; medications; and snacks in case they don't have an opportunity to buy meals.

Schedule and budget constraints

Time and budget constraints are important considerations to keep in mind. It might seem ideal to have 20 users test your interface, but if you need to pay them, then it could get costly. Planning evaluations that can be completed on schedule is also important, particularly in commercial settings. However, as you have seen in the interview with Sara Bly, there is rarely enough time to do the kind of studies that you would ideally like, so you have to compromise and plan to do the best job possible with the resources and time available.

Expertise

Different evaluation methods require different expertise. For example, running user tests requires knowledge of experimental design and video recording. Does the evaluation team have the expertise needed to do the evaluation? If you need to analyze your results using statistical measures and you are unsure of how to use them, then consult a statistician before starting the evaluation and then again during data collection and analysis, if needed.

Activity 13.5

1. Direct observation in the field, user testing, and questionnaires were used in the HutchWorld case study. What practical issues are mentioned in the case study? What other issues do you think the developers had to take into account?
2. Direct observation in the field and interviews were the main methods used for evaluating early design ideas for the Indian auxiliary nurse midwives' record-keeping system. What practical issues had to be taken into account?
3. In the study to investigate the conditions that make a collaborative digital ice hockey game engaging, the evaluators had to consider several practical issues, what were they?

Comment

1. No particular practical issues are mentioned for the direct observation in the hospital, but there probably were restrictions on where and what the team could observe. For example, it is likely that access would be denied to very sick patients and during treatment times. Not surprisingly, user testing posed more problems, such as finding participants, putting equipment in place, managing the tests, and underestimation of the time needed to work in a hospital setting compared with the fast production times at Microsoft.
2. The team did not speak the language of the users and both the Indian culture and the local culture of the nurses was foreign to them. There were other practical issues too, but these were the main ones. The team needed to establish acceptable ways of behaving, observing, and asking questions that were respectful, yet timely, and provided the data that they needed.
3. The evaluators collected physiological data so they had to ensure that they did not cause physical or emotional harm to the participants. Expertise was needed to use the recording equipment which was strapped to the participants, so the study had to be done in a controlled environment. They also had to find participants whose ability to play the game was similar.

13.2.5 Decide how to deal with the ethical issues

The Association for Computing Machinery (ACM) and many other professional organizations provide ethical codes (Box 13.1) that they expect their members to uphold, particularly if their activities involve other human beings (ACM, 1992). All data gathering requires you to consider ethical issues (see Chapter 7), but this is particularly important for evaluation because the participants are often put into unfamiliar situations. People's privacy should be protected, which means that their name should not be associated with data collected about them or disclosed in written reports (unless they give explicit permission). Personal records containing details about health, employment, education, financial status, and where participants live should be confidential. Similarly, it should not be possible to identify individuals from comments written in reports. For example, if a focus group involves nine men and one woman, the pronoun 'she' should not be used in the report because it will be obvious to whom it refers.

Box 13.1
ACM code of ethics

The ACM code outlines many ethical issues that professionals are likely to face (ACM, 1992). Section 1 outlines fundamental ethical considerations, while section 2 addresses additional, more specific considerations of professional conduct. Statements in section 3 pertain more specifically to individuals who have a leadership role. Principles involving compliance with the code are given in section 4. Three principles of particular relevance to this discussion are:

- **Ensure that users and those who will be affected by a system have their needs clearly articulated during the assessment of requirements; later the system must be validated to meet requirements.**
- **Articulate and support policies that protect the dignity of users and others affected by a computing system.**
- **Honor confidentiality.**

For a broad discussion of the code, read Anderson *et al.* (1993). ■

Most professional societies, universities, government, and other research offices require researchers to provide information about activities in which human participants will be involved. This documentation is reviewed by a panel and the researchers are notified whether their plan of work, particularly the details about how human participants and data collected about them will be treated, is acceptable. Drawing up such an agreement is mandatory in most universities and major organizations. Indeed, special review boards generally prescribe the format required and many provide a detailed form which must be completed. Once the details are accepted the review board checks periodically in order to oversee compliance. In American universities they are known as Institutional Review Boards (IRB). Other countries use different names for similar processes. Over the years IRB forms have become increasingly detailed, particularly now that much research involves the Internet and people's interaction via communication technologies across the Internet. Several law suits at prominent universities have heightened attention to IRB compliance to the extent that it sometimes takes several months and multiple amendments to get IRB acceptance. IRB reviewers are not only interested in the more obvious issues of how participants will be treated and what they will be asked to do, they also want to know how the data will be analyzed and stored. For example, data about subjects must be coded and stored to prevent linking participants' names with that data. This means that names must be replaced by a code and that the code and the data must be stored separately, usually under lock and key. Figure 13.1 contains part of a completed IRB form to evaluate a Virtual Business Information Center (VBIC) at the University of Maryland.

Activity 13.6

Imagine you plan to conduct online interviews with 20 participants in a new chat environment (perhaps using AIM, AOL, or Yahoo! chat). What privacy issues would you need to consider when completing your IRB form?

Comment

You would need to discuss how you will perform the interview so that it is private; how you will collect the data; how the data will be stored, analyzed, and reported. For each, you will need to specify privacy and security considerations. For example, each participant will have a code. The codes and the names to which they relate will be stored separately from the data. At no time will real names be used, nor will there be reference to any markers that could enable identity of the participant, e.g. where the participant lives, works, gender, or ethnicity if these are distinguishing features among the pool of participants.

People give their time and their trust when they agree to participate in an evaluation study and both should be respected. But what does it mean to be respectful to participants? What should participants be told about the evaluation? What are participants' rights? Many institutions and project managers require participants to read and sign an informed consent form similar to the one in Box 13.2. This form explains the aim of the study and promises participants that their personal details and performance will not be made public and will be used only for the purpose stated. It is an agreement between the evaluator and the participants that helps to confirm the professional relationship that exists between them.

Abstract: *Provide an abstract (no more than 200 words) that describes the purpose of this research and summarizes the strategies used to protect human subjects.* (Not included in this excerpt)

Subject selection *Who will be the subjects? How will you recruit them? If you plan to advertise for subjects, please include a copy of the advertisement. Will the subjects be selected for any specific characteristics (e.g. age, sex, race, ethnic origin, religion, or any social or economic qualities?*
State why the selection will be made on the bases given above. How many subjects will you recruit?
Phase I: The electronic survey will be sent via e-mail to all members of the RHS Community. Phase II: Respondents to the survey in phase I will be asked to volunteer to participate in the usability study. The number of participants in the usability study will depend upon the number of volunteers.
The only characteristic for selection is the affiliation with the Smith School of Business.
The VBIC has been developed for the students, faculty and staff of the VBIC so their input is essential.

Procedures: *What precisely will be done to the subjects? Describe in detail your methods and procedures in terms of what will be done to subjects. How many subjects are being recruited? What is the total investment of time of the subjects? If subjects will complete surveys and/or other instruments on more than one occasion, state this in the procedures section. If you are using a questionnaire or handout, please include a copy within each set of application documents. If you are conducting a focus group, include a list of the questions for the focus group. If you plan to collect or study existing data, documents, records, pathological specimens or diagnostic specimens, state whether the sources are publicly available and if the information will be recorded in such a manner that subjects can be identified, directly or through identifiers linked to the subjects. If you are collecting or studying existing data, describe the dataset and the information that you will extract from the dataset.*
Phase I: An e-mail message will be sent to all students, faculty and staff. Attachment 1 contains a sample e-mail message. The e-mail message will contain the necessary explanation found in the consent form and recipients of the e-mail will be informed that response to the survey indicates their agreement with the conditions of the study that were stated in the e-mail message. Recipients of the e-mail message will be asked to click on a link to the survey which will ask questions about awareness, use and satisfaction with VBIC. Attachment 2 contains the survey instrument to be used. After submitting the survey, respondents will be sent to a webpage that contains an optional form for participation in the usability study. Attachment 3 contains the voluntary sign-up sheet for the usability study. Phase II: Volunteers for the usability study will be contacted and a date and time will be set for the usability study session. A researcher and a librarian will be on hand for the usability study session [Before beginning the process, participants will be asked to sign a consent form that is found in Attachment 4. Participants will be asked to identify a project or assignment for which they need business information. Then, they will talk aloud as they search for information using VBIC. The researcher will take notes during the session. After the session, the librarian will offer suggestions for additional resources to assist the participant with his/her research. This phase of the research will be iterative. If certain enhancements or modifications become evident after a few individual sessions, these enhancements will be incorporated into VBIC and then additional sessions will be held to obtain reactions to these enhancements.

Risks and Benefits: *Are there any risks to the subjects? If so, what are these risks including physical, psychological, social, legal and financial risks? Please do not describe the risk(s) as minimal. If there are known risks, please list them. What are the benefits? If there are known risks associated with the subject's participation in the research, what potential benefits will accrue to justify taking these risks?* (Not included in this excerpt)

Confidentiality: *Adequate provisions must be made to protect the privacy of subjects and to maintain the confidentiality of identifiable information. Explain how your procedures accomplish this objective, including such information as the means of data storage, data location and duration, description of persons with access to the data, and the method of destroying the data when completed. If the research involves audio taping, videotaping or digital recordings, state who will have access to the tapes or recordings, where the tapes or recordings will be kept, and state the final disposition of the tapes or recordings (i.e. Will the tapes or recordings be destroyed? If so, when will the tapes or recordings be destroyed?).* (Not included in this excerpt)

Figure 13.1 *Excerpt from an IRB to evaluate a Virtual Business Information Center (VBIC) at the University of Maryland*

Box 13.2
Informed consent form

I state that I am over 18 years of age and wish to participate in the evaluation study being conducted by Dr. Hoo and his colleagues at the College of Extraordinary Research, University of Highland, College Estate.

The purpose of the study is to assess the usability of HighFly, a website developed at the National Library to provide information to the general public.

The procedures involve the monitored use of HighFly. I will be asked to perform specific tasks using HighFly. I will also be asked open-ended questions about HighFly and my experience using it. In addition, the evaluators will observe my use of HighFly in my workplace and home using a handheld device and laptop or desktop computer.

All information collected in the study is confidential, and my name will not be identified at any time.

I understand that I am free to ask questions or to withdraw from participation at any time without penalty.

______________________ _____

Signature of Participant Date

(Adapted from Cogdill, 1999.)

The following summary provides guidelines that will help ensure evaluations are done ethically and that adequate steps to protect users' rights have been taken.

- Tell participants the goals of the study and exactly what they should expect if they participate. The information given to them should include outlining the process, the approximate amount of time the study will take, the kind of data that will be collected, and how that data will be analyzed. The form of the final report should be described and, if possible, a copy offered to them. Any payment offered should also be clearly stated.
- Be sure to explain that demographic, financial, health, or other sensitive information that users disclose or is discovered from the tests is confidential. A coding system should be used to record each user and, if a user must be identified for a follow-up interview, the code and the person's demographic details should be stored separately from the data. Anonymity should also be promised if audio and video are used.
- Make sure participants know that they are free to stop the evaluation at any time if they feel uncomfortable with the procedure.
- Consider your relationship with the participants and decide whether it is appropriate to provide incentives such as food, book tokens, or financial payment. For example, if it is your child taking part in a colleague's study, a gift token or a toy would be more appropriate than offering payment as an incentive.
- Avoid including quotes or descriptions that inadvertently reveal a person's identity by using numbers or fictitious names to record and identify individuals. Where quotes are reported to illustrate findings then it is convention to replace words that would reveal

the source with representative words, in square brackets. For example, if the study was evaluating a university's information system and one of the participants commented: "When I tried to send a message to Harry Jones about my meeting with Mary Ann Green the whole system suddenly froze," then the comment would be quoted as: "When I tried to send a message to [...] about my meeting with [...] the whole system suddenly froze."

- Ask users' permission in advance to quote them, promise them anonymity, and offer to show them a copy of the report before it is distributed.

Activity 13.7

Think back to the HutchWorld and Indian auxiliary nurse midwives case studies. What ethical issues did the developers have to consider?

Comment

The developers of HutchWorld considered all the issues just listed above. In addition, because the study involved patients, they had to be particularly careful that medical and other personal information was kept confidential. They were also sensitive to the fact that cancer patients may become too tired or sick to participate, so they reassured them that they could stop at any time if the task became onerous.

The team working with the Indian auxiliary nurse midwives were particularly careful to make sure that the nurses knew their rights and that they felt treated with respect. This was essential in order to build trust. Furthermore, it is likely that the participants may not have known about the usual evaluation ethics so the team was particularly careful to ensure that they were informed. Since this study also involved a medical system the team needed to ensure that personal medical information was treated confidentially. Privacy and security were major considerations.

The explosion in Internet and web usage has resulted in more research on how people use these technologies and their effects on everyday life (Jones, 1999). Consequently, there are many projects in which developers and researchers are logging users' interactions, analyzing blogs, recording web traffic, or examining conversations in chatrooms, bulletin boards, or on email. These studies can be done without users knowing that they are being studied. This raises ethical concerns, chief among which are issues of privacy, confidentiality, informed consent, and appropriation of others' personal stories (Sharf, 1999). People often say things online that they would not say face to face. Furthermore, many people are unaware that the personal information they share online can be read by someone with technical know-how years later, even after they have deleted it from their personal mailbox (Erickson *et al.*, 1999).

Activity 13.8

Studies of user behavior on the Internet may involve logging users' interactions and keeping a copy of their conversations with others. Should users be told that this is happening?

Comment

Yes, it is better to tell users in advance that they are being logged. Knowledge of being logged often ceases to be an issue as users become involved in what they are doing.

Dilemma

What would you do?

There is a famous and controversial story about a 1961–62 experiment by Yale social psychologist Stanley Milgram to investigate how people respond to orders given by people in authority. Much has been written about this experiment and details have been changed and embellished over the years, but the basic ethical issues it raises are still worth considering, even if the details of the actual study have been distorted.

The participants were ordinary residents of New Haven who were asked to administer increasingly high levels of electric shocks to victims when they made errors in the tasks they were given. As the electric shocks got more and more severe, so did the apparent pain of the victims receiving them, to the extent that some appeared to be on the verge of dying. Not surprisingly, those administering the shocks became increasingly disturbed by what they were being asked to do, but several continued, believing that they should do as their superiors told them. What they did not realize was that the so-called victims were, in fact, very convincing actors who were not being injured at all. Instead, the shock administrators were themselves the real subjects of the experiment. It was their responses to authority that were being studied in this deceptive experiment.

This story raises several important ethical issues. First, this experiment reveals how power relationships can be used to control others. Second and equally important, this experiment relied on deception. The experimenters were, in fact, the subjects and the fake subjects colluded with the real scientists to deceive them. Without this deception the experiment would not have worked.

Is it acceptable to deceive subjects to this extent for the sake of scientific discovery? What do you think?

13.2.6 Evaluate, interpret, and present the data

Decisions are must be made about what data is needed to answer the study questions, how the data will be analyzed, and how the findings will be presented (see Chapter 8). To a great extent the method used determines the type of data collected, but there are still some choices. For example, should the data be treated statistically? Some general questions also need to be asked. Is the method reliable? Will the method measure what is intended, i.e. what is its validity? Are biases creeping in that will distort the results? Will the results be generalizable, i.e. what is their scope? Will the evaluation study be ecologically valid or is the fundamental nature of the process being changed by studying it?

Reliability

The reliability or consistency of a method is how well it produces the same results on separate occasions under the same circumstances. Another evaluator or researcher who follows exactly the same procedure should get similar results. Different evaluation methods have different degrees of reliability. For example, a carefully controlled experiment will have high reliability, whereas observing users in their natural setting will be variable. An unstructured interview will have low reliability: it would be difficult if not impossible to repeat exactly the same discussion.

Validity

Validity is concerned with whether the evaluation method measures what it is intended to measure. This encompasses both the method itself and the way it is performed. If, for example, the goal of an evaluation study is to find out how users use a new product in their homes, then it is not appropriate to plan a laboratory experiment. An ethnographic study in users' homes would be more appropriate. If the goal is to find average performance times for completing a task, then a method that only recorded the number of user errors would be invalid.

Biases

Bias occurs when the results are distorted. For example, expert evaluators performing a heuristic evaluation may be more sensitive to certain kinds of design flaws than others, and this will be reflected in the results. Evaluators collecting observational data may consistently fail to notice certain types of behavior because they do not deem them important. Put another way, they may selectively gather data that they think is important. Interviewers may unconsciously influence responses from interviewees by their tone of voice, their facial expressions, or the way questions are phrased, so it is important to be sensitive to the possibility of biases.

Scope

The scope of an evaluation study refers to how much its findings can be generalized. For example, some modeling methods, like the keystroke model, have a narrow, precise scope.

The model predicts expert, error-free behavior so, for example, the results cannot be used to describe novices learning to use the system. The problems of overstating the results were discussed in more detail in Chapter 8.

Ecological validity

Ecological validity concerns how the environment in which an evaluation is conducted influences or even distorts the results. For example, laboratory experiments are controlled and are quite different from workplace, home, or leisure environments. Laboratory experiments therefore have low ecological validity because the results are unlikely to represent what happens in the real world. In contrast, ethnographic studies do not impact the environment as much, so they have high ecological validity.

Ecological validity is also affected when participants are aware of being studied. This is sometimes called the *Hawthorne effect* after a series of experiments at the Western Electric Company's Hawthorne factory in the USA in the 1920s and 1930s. The studies investigated changes in length of working day, heating, lighting, etc., but eventually it was discovered that the workers were reacting positively to being given special treatment rather than just to the experimental conditions. Similar findings sometimes occur in medical trials. Patients given the placebo dose (a false dose in which no drug is administered) show improvement that is due to receiving extra attention that makes them feel good.

Assignment

Find a journal or conference publication that describes an interesting evaluation study or select one from `www.hcibib.org` *or from a digital library such as the ACM Digital Library. Then use the DECIDE framework and your knowledge from Chapters 7 and 8 to analyze it. Some questions that you should seek to answer include:*

(a) What are the goals and the questions that provide the focus for the evaluation?
(b) Which evaluation approaches and methods are used?
(c) What data is collected and how is it analyzed?
(d) What practical and ethical issues have been considered?
(e) Comment on the reliability, validity, ecological validity, biases, and scope of the study.
(f) Is there evidence of one or more pilot studies?
(g) Is triangulation used?
(h) What are the strengths and weaknesses of the study report? Write a 50–100 word critique that would help the author(s) improve their paper.

Summary

In this chapter we introduced the DECIDE framework, which will help you to plan an evaluation. There are six steps in the framework:

1. Determine the goals.
2. Explore the questions.
3. Choose the approach and methods.
4. Identify the practical issues.
5. Decide how to deal with the ethical issues.
6. Evaluate, interpret, and present the data.

Key Points

- There are many issues to consider before conducting an evaluation study. These include the goals of the study, the approaches and methods to use, practical issues, ethical issues, and how the data will be gathered and analyzed.
- The DECIDE framework provides a useful checklist for planning an evaluation study.

Further Reading

DENZIN, N.K. and LINCOLN, Y.S. (2005) *The SageHandbook of Qualitative Research, 3rd Edition.* Sage Publications. This book is a collection of chapters by experts in qualitative research. It is an excellent resource.

HOLTZBLATT, K. (ed.) (2005) Designing for the mobile device: experiences, challenges and methods. *Communications of the ACM* **48**(7), 32–66. This collection of papers points out the challenges that evaluators face when studying mobile devices, particularly when the most appropriate study is a field study that may involve working in a different culture and changing physical environments regularly.

JONES, S. (ed.) (1999) *Doing Internet Research: Critical Issues and Methods for Examining the Net.* Sage Publications. As the title states, this book is concerned with research. However, several of the chapters provide information that will be useful for those evaluating software used on the Internet.

SHNEIDERMAN, B. and PLAISANT, C. (2005) *Designing the User Interface: Strategies for Effective Human–Computer Interaction*, 4th edn. Chapter 4: Evaluating interface designs, pp. 139–171. Addison-Wesley. This chapter provides a useful overview of evaluation and provides valuable references.

MALONEY-KRICHMAR, D. and PREECE, J. (2005) A Multilevel Analysis of Sociability, Usability and Community Dynamics in an Online Health Community, *ACM Transactions on Computer-Human Interaction, 12 (2),* 1–32. This paper describes how activity in an online community was evaluated using a combination of theoretical frameworks and evaluation methods.

14

14.1 Introduction

Imagine you have designed a new shared web space intended for advertising second-hand goods. How would you find out whether householders would be able to use it to find what they wanted and whether it was a reliable and effective service? What evaluation methods would you employ? In this chapter we describe two very different approaches—usability testing and field studies. The first you would use to evaluate its effectiveness, ease of use, and satisfaction, and the second you would use to assess how it would support householders finding desired items. The first, usability testing, takes place mainly in a controlled environment; the second, a field study, examines how a product is used in natural home environments.

Typically, the performance of users interacting with a product is measured for set tasks in a usability test. This allows the system's effectiveness to be assessed and usability problems to be identified, e.g. problems printing a document or finding information. Usability testing varies in terms of the amount of control over the study. At one end are experiments, typically carried out in laboratory settings, that test user performance (e.g. reading) on one or two variables (e.g. font size, resolution) on a number of participants. At the other end are more opportunistic studies, that investigate a subset of usability and user experience goals, e.g. satisfaction, fun, frustration, for a handful of users. Between these two extremes are controlled tasks that examine such things as the ease of searching for and locating information items.

Recently, it has become more common for field studies to be conducted in natural environments, such as homes, offices, and outdoors. This is especially so for the evaluation of new technologies, such as mobile devices. Observation, diaries, and interviews are commonly used methods. Importantly, they take place in the setting where the product is used.

The main aims of this chapter are to:

- **Explain how to do usability testing through examples.**
- **Outline the basics of experimental design.**
- **Discuss the methods used in usability testing.**
- **Discuss the role of field studies in evaluation.**

14

Usability testing and field studies

14.2 Usability testing

Usability testing is an approach that emphasizes the property of being usable, i.e. it is the product that is being tested rather than the user. It is conducted in a controlled environment. By this is meant placing the product to be tested in a usability laboratory, or similar controlled environment, where the performance of users on pre-planned tasks is repeatedly measured. The goal is to test whether the product being developed is usable by the intended user population to achieve the tasks for which it was designed (Dumas and Redish, 1999). It has been most commonly used to test desktop-based applications, such as websites, wordprocessors, and search tools.

Data is collected using a combination of methods. Key components are the user test and the user satisfaction questionnaire. The user test measures human performance on specific tasks, e.g. reaction time such as pressing a key when a light first appears. Examples of tasks include reading different typefaces (e.g. Helvetica and Times), navigating through different menu types (e.g. context versus cascade), and information searching. Software logging of keystrokes and mouse movements together with video recordings of the user's actions are used for recording user performance for the set tasks. The user satisfaction questionnaire is used to find out how users actually feel about using the product, through asking them to rate it along a number of scales, after interacting with it. The combined measures are analyzed to determine if the design is efficient and effective. Interviews, which are usually structured or semi-structured, may also be conducted with users.

Time and number are the two main measures used, in terms of the time it takes typical users to complete a task, such as finding a website, and the number of errors that participants make, such as wrong menu options selected when creating a spreadsheet. Quantitative performance measures are obtained during the tests that produce the following types of data (Wixon and Wilson, 1997):

- Time to complete a task.
- Time to complete a task after a specified time away from the product.
- Number and type of errors per task.
- Number of errors per unit of time.
- Number of navigations to online help or manuals.
- Number of users making a particular error.
- Number of users completing a task successfully.

In the early days of usability testing, user tests were conducted to investigate the efficacy of specific features of an interface. For example, a team of scientists from Xerox Corporation ran a series of user tests to determine what was the optimal number of buttons to put on a mouse, how many items to put in a menu, and how to design icons, as part of their Xerox Star office workstation system (Bewley *et al.*, 1990). In total, over 15 user tests were performed involving over 200 users and lasting over 400 hours. This averaged out at 10–15 users per test, taking 2 hours each. The results of

"Oh, the commute in to work was a breeze, but I've been stuck in internet traffic for four hours!"

the various tests were then fed back into the design of the interface; for example, three buttons on the mouse was found to be best for selecting from a set of options.

It is considered that 5–12 users is an acceptable number to test in a usability study (Dumas and Redish, 1999), but sometimes it is possible to use fewer when there are budget and schedule constraints. For instance, quick feedback about a design idea, such as the initial placement of a logo on a website, can be obtained from only two or three users.

Many companies, such as Microsoft and IBM, test their products in custom-built usability labs (Lund, 1994). These facilities comprise a main testing laboratory, with recording equipment and the product being tested, and an observation room where the evaluators sit and analyze the data. There may also be a reception area for testers, a storage area, and a viewing room for observers. The space may be arranged to superficially mimic features of the real world. For example, if the product is an office product or for use in a hotel reception area, the laboratory can be set up to look like that environment. But in other respects it is artificial. Soundproofing and lack of windows, telephones, fax machines, co-workers, and other workplace and social artifacts eliminate most of the normal sources of distraction so that the users can concentrate on the tasks set for them to perform.

Typically there are two to three wall-mounted video cameras that record the user's behavior, such as hand movements, facial expression, and general body language. Microphones are also placed near where the participants will be sitting to record their utterances. Video and other data is fed through to monitors in the observation room. The observation room is usually separated from the main laboratory or work-room by a one-way mirror so that evaluators can watch participants being tested but testers cannot see them. It can be a small auditorium with rows of seats at different levels or, more simply, a small backroom

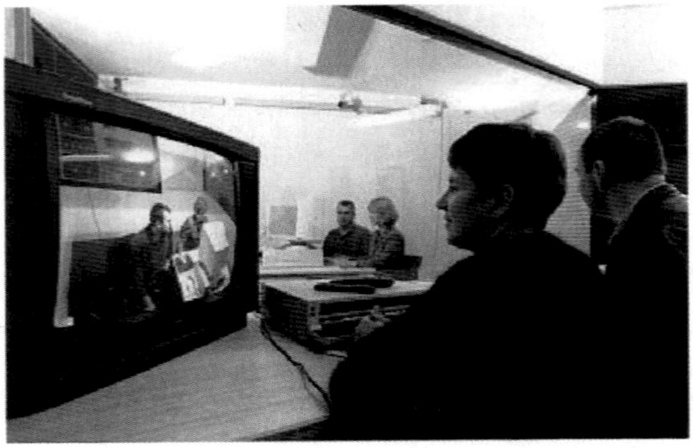

Figure 14.1 *A usability laboratory in which evaluators watch participants on a monitor and through a one-way mirror*

consisting of a row of chairs, facing the monitors. They are designed so that evaluators and others can watch the tests while ongoing, both on the monitors and through the mirror. Figure 14.1 shows a typical arrangement.

Sometimes, modifications may have to be made to the room set-up to test different types of applications. For example, Chris Nodder and his colleagues at Microsoft had to partition the space into two rooms when they were testing early versions of NetMeeting, a videoconferencing product, in the mid-1990s, as Figure 14.2 shows (Nodder *et al.*, 1999). This allowed users in both rooms to be observed when conducting a meeting via the videoconference system.

Figure 14.2 *The testing arrangement used for NetMeeting videoconferencing product*

Usability labs can be very expensive and labor-intensive to run and maintain. A less expensive alternative, that is becoming increasingly popular, is the use of mobile usability testing equipment. Video cameras, laptops, and other measuring equipment are temporarily set up in an office or other space, converting it into a makeshift usability laboratory. Another advantage is that equipment can be taken into work settings, enabling testing to be done on site, making it less artificial and more convenient for the participants.

As mentioned in Box 7.10, there is an increasing number of evaluation products coming onto the market that are specifically designed for mobile evaluation, and in particular, evaluating mobile devices. They are often referred to as 'lab-in-a-box' or 'lab-in-a-suitcase' because they pack away neatly into a convenient carrying case. One example is the Tracksys portable lab which costs around $5000 (Figure 14.3). It is composed of off-the-shelf components that plug into a PC and can record video direct to hard disk (Figure 14.4).

Another trend has been to conduct remote usability testing, where users perform a set of tasks with a product in their own setting and their interactions with the software are logged remotely. A popular example, is userzoom, which enables users to participate in usability tests from their home, illustrated in Figure 14.5. An advantage is that many users

***Figure 14.3** The Tracksys 'lab-in-a-box' system, which comprises components that pack into a heavy duty padded flight case plus a PC system*

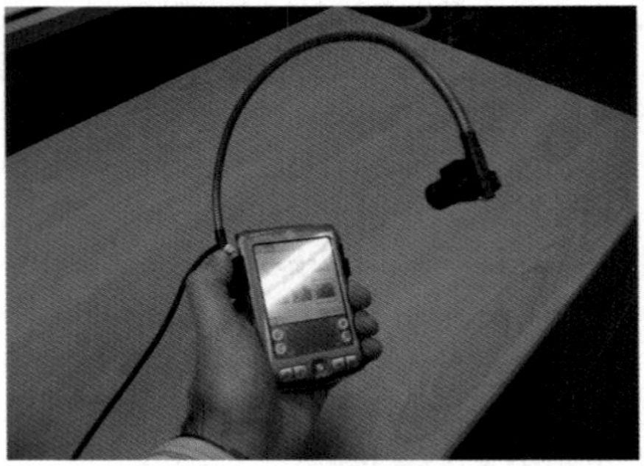

Figure 14.4 *The Tracksys system being used with a mobile device camera that attaches to a flexible arm, which mounts on a mobile device, and is tethered to the lab*

Figure 14.5 *Userzoom enables remote usability testing*

can be tested at the same time and the logged data automatically compiled into statistical packages for data analysis. For example, the number of clicks per page and the tracking of clicks when searching websites for specified tasks can be readily obtained.

To illustrate how usability testing takes place in practice we now look at the steps involved in testing a large website. This was for a medical information system called MedlinePlus.

14.2.1 Usability testing of a large website: MedlinePlus

MedlinePlus is a large website created by the National Library of Medicine (NLM) to provide health information for a wide range of the general public, doctors, and other medical professionals across the USA and the rest of the world. It was first developed in the 1990s and modified over the years, with a complete revision starting in 2002 (Marill *et al.*, 2006). The original homepage for this system is shown in Figures 14.6–14.8. In 1999, usability consultant Keith Cogdill was commissioned by NLM to evaluate MedlinePlus.

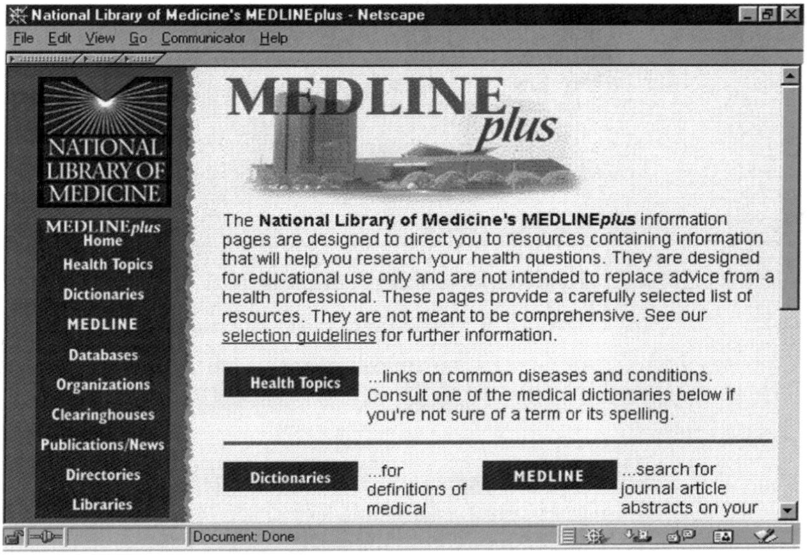

Figure 14.6 *Homepage of MedlinePlus*

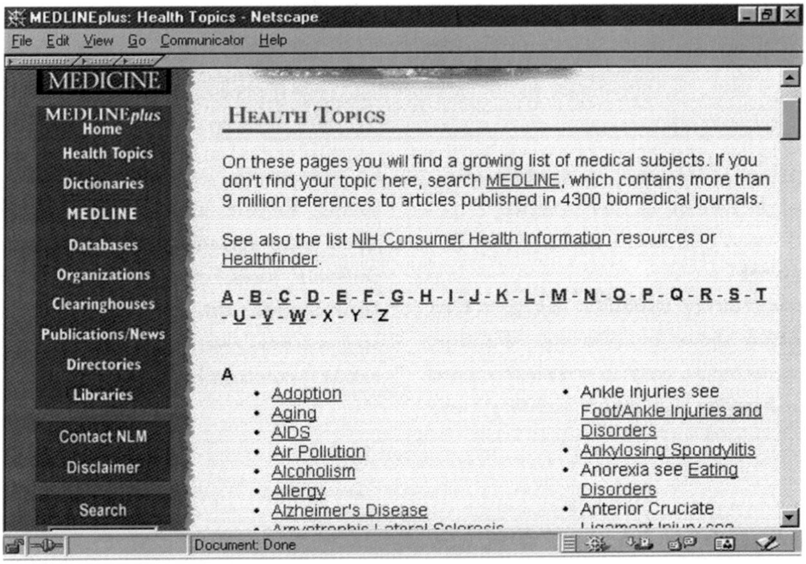

Figure 14.7 *Clicking 'Health Topics' on the homepage produced this page*

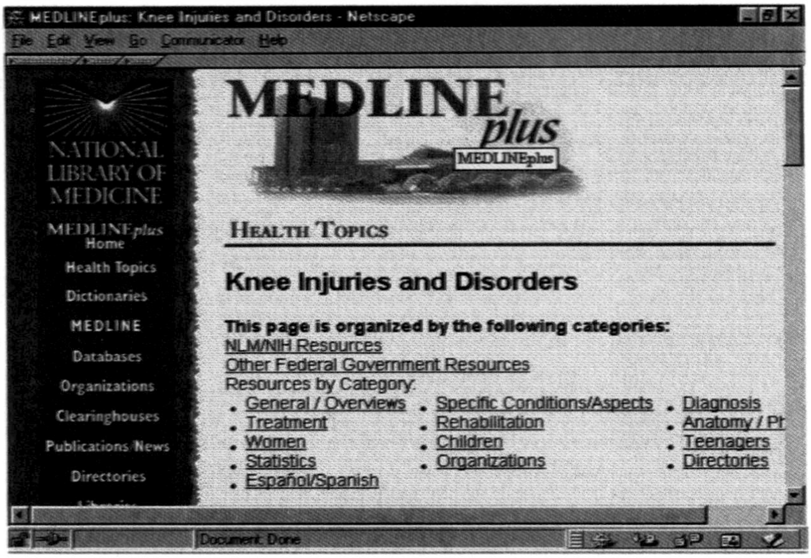

Figure 14.8 *Categories of links within Health Topics for knee injuries*

Activity 14.1

Data gathering requires a specific goal. What might this be in this context?

Comment

Our definition of usability suggests that MedlinePlus had to be: efficient, effective, safe, easy to learn, easy to remember, and have good utility (i.e. good usability); and be rewarding, support creativity, motivating, helpful, and satisfying to use (i.e. good user experience). There are many different kinds of users for this website, for example, the general public, doctors, and medical researchers, each with different information needs.

The evaluation of Medline was extensive, involving usability testing and heuristic evaluation. Here, we report on the various steps taken for the usability testing, including: what the goals of the evaluation were, how participants were selected, what kinds of tasks were set, how the testing was managed, what the ethical issues were, how the data was collected, analyzed, and interpreted.

Goals and questions

The goal of the evaluation study was to identify the range of usability problems. Cogdill (1999) wanted to know if the way the topics on the homepage were categorized was usable by the majority of users. His team also wanted to check how users navigated around a large website for a number of tasks.

Selection of participants

MedlinePlus was tested with nine participants selected from primary health care practices in the Washington, DC metropolitan area. This was accomplished by placing recruitment posters in the reception areas of two medical practices. People who wanted to participate were asked to complete a brief questionnaire, which asked about age, experience in using the web, and frequency of seeking health-related information. Cogdill then called all those who used the web more than twice a month. He explained that they would be involved in testing a product from the NLM, but did not mention MedlinePlus so that potential testers would not review the site before doing the tests. Seven of the nine participants were women, because balancing for gender was considered less important than web experience. It was considered important to find people in the Washington, DC region so that they could come to the test center and for the number of participants to fall within the range of 6–12 recommended by usability experts (Dumas and Redish, 1999).

Development of the tasks

The following five tasks were developed in collaboration with NLM staff to check the categorizing schemes and navigation support. The topics chosen for the tasks were identified from questions most frequently asked by website users.

- Task 1: Find information about whether a dark bump on your shoulder might be skin cancer.
- Task 2: Find information about whether it is safe to use Prozac during pregnancy.
- Task 3: Find information about whether there is a vaccine for hepatitis C.
- Task 4: Find recommendations about the treatment of breast cancer, specifically the use of mastectomies.
- Task 5: Find information about the dangers associated with drinking alcohol during pregnancy.

The efficacy of each task was reviewed by colleagues and a pilot test was conducted with potential users who would not be involved in the main testing procedure. Criteria for successfully completing each task were also decided. For example, participants had to find and access between three and nine web page URLs for each of the five tasks.

The test procedure

Five scripts were prepared in advance for the user test (see Figures 14.9–14.13). The purpose of each script was to ensure that all participants were given the same instructions

Thank you very much for participating in this study.

The goal of this project is to evaluate the interface of MedlinePlus. The results of our evaluation will be summarized and reported to the National Library of Medicine, the federal agency that has developed MedlinePlus. Have you ever used MedlinePlus before?

You will be asked to use MedlinePlus to resolve a series of specific, health-related information needs. You will be asked to ''think aloud'' as you search for information with MedlinePlus.

We will be videotaping only what appears on the computer screen. What you say as you search for information will also be recorded. Your face will not be videotaped, and your identity will remain confidential.

I'll need you to review and sign this statement of informed consent. Please let me know if you have any questions about it. (*He hands an informed consent form similar to the one in Box 11.3 to the participant.*)

Figure 14.9 *The script used to greet participants in the MedlinePlus study*

We'll start with a general overview of MedlinePlus. It's a web-based product developed by the National Library of Medicine. Its purpose is to link users with sources of authoritative health information on the web.

The purpose of our work today is to explore the MedlinePlus interface to identify features that could be improved. We're also interested in finding out about features that are particularly helpful.

In a few minutes I'll give you five tasks. For each task you'll use MedlinePlus to find health-related information.

As you use MedlinePlus to find the information for each task, please keep in mind that it is MedlinePlus that is the subject of this evaluation — not you.

You should feel free to work on each task at a pace that is normal and comfortable for you. We *will* be keeping track of how long it takes you to complete each task, but you should not feel rushed. Please work on each task at a pace that is normal and comfortable for you. If any task takes you longer than *twenty* minutes, we will ask you to move on to the next task. The Home button on the browser menu has been set to the MedlinePlus homepage. We'll ask you to return to this page before starting a new task.

As you work on each task, I'd like you to imagine that it's something you or someone close to you needs to know.

All answers can be found on MedlinePlus or on one of the sites it points to. But if you feel you are unable to complete a task and would like to stop, please say so and we'll move on to the next task.

Before we proceed, do you have any questions at this point?

Figure 14.10 *The script used to explain the procedure*

Before we begin the tasks, I'd like you to explore MedlinePlus independently for as long as ten minutes.

As you explore, please "think aloud." That is, please tell us your thoughts as you encounter the different features of MedlinePlus.

Feel free to explore any topics that are of interest to you.

If you complete your independent exploration before the ten minutes are up, please let me know and we'll proceed with the tasks. Again, please remember to tell us what you're thinking as you explore MedlinePlus.

Figure 14.11 *The script used to introduce and describe the initial exploration task*

Please read aloud this task before beginning your use of MedlinePlus to find the information.

After completing each task, please return to the MedlinePlus home page by clicking on the "home" button.

Prompts: "What are you thinking?"

"Are you stuck?"

"Please tell me what you're thinking."

[*If time exceeds 20 minutes*: "I need to ask you to stop working on this task and proceed to the next one."]

Figure 14.12 *The script used to direct participants' behavior*

How did you feel about your performance on the tasks overall?

Tell me about what happened when [cite problem/error/excessive time].

What would you say was the best thing about the MedlinePlus interface?

What would you say was the worst thing about the MedlinePlus interface?

Figure 14.13 *The debriefing script used in the MedlinePlus study*

and information. The scripts included an introduction to the study, reassurance, e.g. "It does not matter if you make a mistake, we are testing the website not you", a statement of the purpose of the test, a consent form, information on how to start the test with open-ended questions, the list of tasks, a description saying that the users can carry the tasks out in their own way, and finally what to say to the users once they have completed the task.

Testing was done in laboratory-like conditions. The participants were asked to sit down alone at a monitor, and the goals of the study and test procedure were explained. Before starting the main tasks the participants were invited to explore the website for up to 10 minutes to familiarize themselves with it. Each participant was then asked to work through the five tasks, thinking aloud. They were given up to 20 minutes for each task. If they did not finish a task in the allotted time they were asked to stop. If they forgot to think out loud or appeared to be stuck they were prompted. When all the tasks were completed, the participants were given a post-test questionnaire to fill in consisting of items derived from the QUIS user satisfaction questionnaire (first version, Chin *et al.*, 1988). Finally, when the questionnaire was completed, a debriefing session was held in which participants were asked for their opinions.

Data collection

Completion times for the tasks were automatically recorded and calculated from the video. The participants' actions were also logged using a software tool. The logged data revealed the pathways that the participants took for each task. For example, Table 14.1 shows the online resources that participant A visited while trying to complete the first task. The performance data contained the following:

- Start time and completion time.
- Page count (i.e. number of pages accessed during the search task).

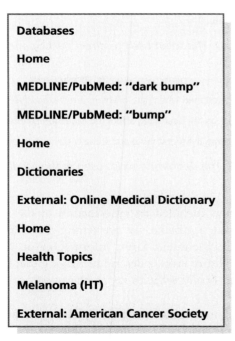

Databases
Home
MEDLINE/PubMed: "dark bump"
MEDLINE/PubMed: "bump"
Home
Dictionaries
External: Online Medical Dictionary
Home
Health Topics
Melanoma (HT)
External: American Cancer Society

Table 14.1 *The resources visited by participant A for the first task*

- External site count (i.e. number of external sites accessed during the search task).
- Termination of tasks.
- Medical publications accessed during the search task.
- The user's search path.
- Any negative comments observed during the search.
- Ratings from the user satisfaction questionnaire and comments from the debriefing interview.

Table 14.2 contains the performance data for the nine participants for task 1. It shows the time to complete the task and the different kinds of searches undertaken. Similar tables were produced for the other four tasks.

Activity 14.2

Examine Table 14.2.

1. **Why do you think letters are used to represent participants?**
2. **What do you notice about the completion times when compared with the reasons for terminating tasks (i.e. completion records)?**
3. **What does the rest of the data tell you?**

Comment

1. **Participants' names should be kept confidential in reports, so a coding scheme is used.**
2. **Completion times are not closely associated with successful completion of this task. For example, completion times range from 5–15 minutes for successful completion and from 9–13 minutes for those who asked to terminate the task.**
3. **From the data it appears that there may have been several ways to complete the task successfully. For example, participants A and C both completed the task successfully but their records of visiting the different resources differ considerably.**

Data analysis

The data was analyzed using a number of categories, including:

- Website organization in terms of the arrangement of topics, menu depth, and organization of links.
- Browsing efficiency including navigation menu location and text density.
- Use of the search features.

Participant	Time to nearest minute	Reason for task termination	MEDLINE-plus Pages	External sites accessed	MEDLINE-plus searches	MEDLINE publication searches
A	12	Successful completion	5	2	0	2
B	12	Participant requested termination	3	2	3	0
C	14	Successful completion	2	1	0	0
D	13	Participant requested termination	5	2	1	0
E	10	Successful completion	5	3	1	0
F	9	Participant requested termination	3	1	0	0
G	5	Successful completion	2	1	0	0
H	12	Successful completion	3	1	0	6
I	6	Successful completion	3	1	0	0
M	10		3	2	1	1
SD	3		1	1	1	2

***Table 14.2** Performance data for task 1: Find information about whether a dark bump on your shoulder might be skin cancer. Mean (M) and standard deviation (SD) for all subjects are also shown*

A main finding was that reaching external sites was often difficult. Furthermore, analysis of the search moves revealed that several participants experienced difficulty finding the health topics pages devoted to different types of cancer. The user satisfaction questionnaire showed that participants' opinions of MedlinePlus were fairly neutral. They rated it well for ease of learning but poorly for ease of use, because there were problems in going back to previous screens. The set of findings was then fed back to the developers in an oral presentation and in a written report.

Activity 14.3

1. **Was the way in which participants were selected appropriate? Justify your comments.**
2. **Why do you think participants were asked to read each new task aloud before starting it and to return to the homepage?**
3. **Was the briefing material adequate? Justify your comment.**

Comments

1. **The evaluator tried to get a representative number of users across the user age range from both genders. There were, however, more women participants than men participants because the evaluator was more concerned about getting experienced web users than getting an even gender balance.**
2. **This was to make it easy for the evaluator to detect the beginning of a new task on the video log. Sending the participants back to the homepage before starting each new task ensured that logging always started from the same place. It also helped to orient the participants.**
3. **The briefing material was full and carefully prepared. Participants were told what was expected of them and the scripts were pre-planned to ensure that each participant was treated in the same way. An informed consent form was also included.**

The second version of MedlinePlus is shown in Figures 14.14–14.15. It had much more content, with over 700 health topic pages, licensed material including drug information, a medical encyclopedia, a dictionary, news feeds, and tutorials. The new homepage (Figure 14.14) was designed to be simple, intuitive, and accessible to users whose web expertise varied. The pages were designed to have a uniform look and feel and the branding to be simple and distinctive. Other new features included a search engine and a bilingual site. The changes that were made were based upon more recent usability testing recommendations and user survey results, new technical requirements, web design trends, and the need to grow the site in an orderly way (Marill *et al.*, 2006, p. 30).

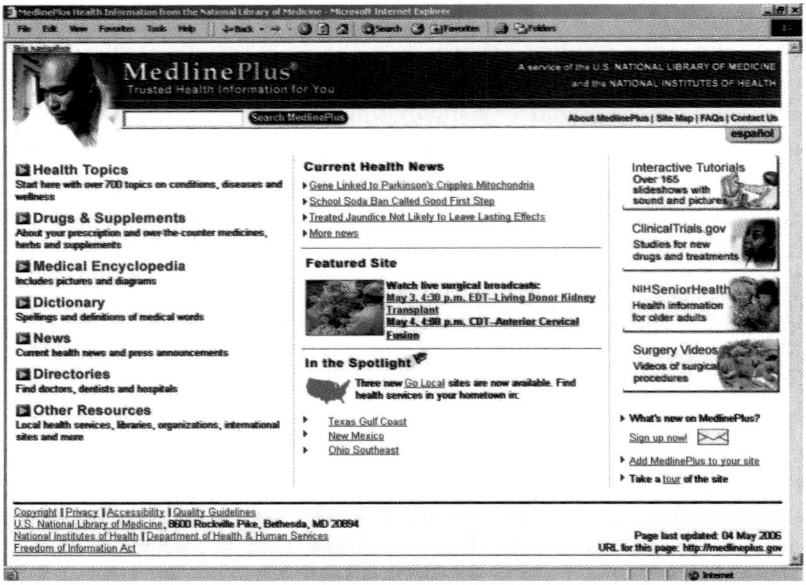

Figure 14.14 Homepage of revised version of MedlinePlus

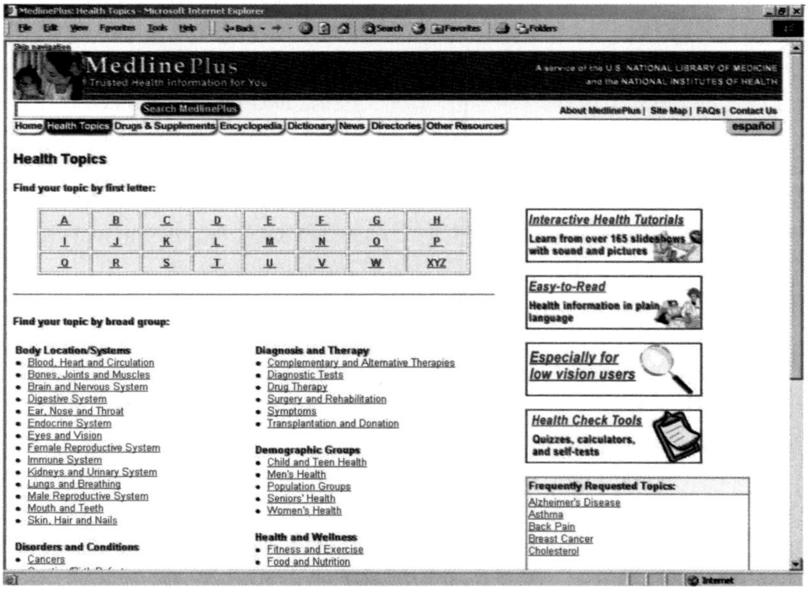

Figure 14.15 *Clicking 'Health Topics' on the homepage of the revised version produced this page*

14.2.2 Conducting experiments in usability testing

Sometimes, it is important to test a specific hypothesis that makes a prediction about the way users will perform with an interface. In this context, the user test is run more like a scientific experiment. An example of a hypothesis is: context menus are easier to select options from compared with cascading menus. Hypotheses are often based on a theory, such as Fitt's Law (see next chapter), or previous research findings. Specific measurements are decided upon as a way of testing the hypothesis. In the above example, the accuracy of selecting menu options would be compared by counting the number of errors each participant makes for each menu type.

Typically, a hypothesis involves examining a relationship between two things, called variables. In the above example the variables are menu types and error rate. Another example of a relationship that could be tested is between time and font, for the hypothesis "reading text displayed in 12-point Helvetica font is faster than reading text displayed in 12-point Times New Roman." Variables can be independent or dependent. An independent variable is what the investigator 'manipulates' (i.e. selects), and in the above example it is the different font types. The experimenter could have equally selected to compare another sans serif with a serif font, e.g. Geneva versus Times. The other variable is called the dependent variable, and in our example, this is the time taken to read the text. It is a measure of the user performance and if our hypothesis is correct, will vary depending on the different types of font used.

When setting up a hypothesis to test the effect of the independent variable(s) on the dependent variable it is usual to derive a 'null' and an 'alternative' one. The null hypothesis in our example would state that there is no difference between Helvetica and Times font on reading time. The alternative hypothesis would state that there was a difference between the two on reading time. When a difference is specified but not what it will be, it is called a two-tailed hypothesis. This is because it can be interpreted in two ways: either the Helvetica font or the Times font is faster to read. Alternatively, the hypothesis can be stated in terms of one effect. This is called a one-tailed hypothesis and would state that Helvetica is easier to read than Times, or *vice versa*. A one-tailed hypothesis would be made if there was a strong reason to believe it to be the case. For example, it could be based on the findings of previous experiments investigating paper-based text that have all shown that sans serif is easer to read because of the simple shape form of the letters. A two-tailed hypothesis would be chosen if there was no reason or theory that could be used to support the case that the predicted effect would go one way or the other.

You might ask why do you need a null hypothesis since it seems the reverse of what the experimenter believes. Counter-intuitively, it is put forward to allow the data to contradict it. If the experimental data shows a big difference between reading times for the two different fonts, then the null hypothesis that font type has no effect can be rejected. Conversely, if there is no difference between the two then the alternative hypothesis is rejected, i.e. the claim that Helvetica font is easier to read is not supported.

In order to test a hypothesis, the experimenter has to set up the conditions and find ways to keep other variables constant, to prevent them from influencing the findings. This is called the experimental design. Examples of other variables that need to be kept constant for both fonts include color of text and screen resolution. For example, if the text is blue in one condition and black in the other then it could be this which causes the effect (i.e. differences in reading rates). Often a control condition is set up as part of the experimental design. This is typically used when you want to determine if a new method (e.g. presenting learning material as dynamic multimedia software), enhances performance (e.g. learning) compared with an existing method (e.g. presenting the same material in a static paper-based form). More than one condition can be compared with the control, for example:

Control condition = Paper-based

Condition 1 = Multimedia

Condition 2 = Virtual reality

The independent variable in this example is the type of media, e.g. paper-based, multimedia, virtual reality. The dependent variable measures learning performance, and could include the number of questions that are answered successfully for each condition before and after the experiment.

Sometimes an experimenter might want to investigate the relationship between two independent variables, for example, age and educational background. A hypothesis might be that young people are faster at finding text on the web than older people and that those with a scientific background are more effective at selecting search terms. An experiment would be set up to measure the time it takes to complete the task and number of searches carried out. The analysis of the data would focus on both the effects of the main variables (age and background) and also look for any interactions among them.

Hypothesis testing can also be extended to include even more variables, but it makes the experimental design more complex. An example is testing the effects of age and educational background on user performance for two methods of web searching: one a search engine and the other a browser. Again, the goal is to test the effects of the main variables (age background, web searching method) and to look for any interactions among them. However, as the number of variables increases in an experimental design, it makes it more difficult to work out from the data what is causing the results.

Another concern in experimental design is to determine which participants to use for which conditions of an experiment. The experience of participating in one condition will affect the performance of those participants if asked to partake in another condition. For example, having learned about the way the heart works using a multimedia condition it would be unfair to expose the same participants to the same learning material via another medium, e.g. virtual reality. The reason being that they would have had more time to learn about the same topic and this would increase their chances of answering more questions correctly. In some experimental designs, however, it is possible to use the same participants for all conditions without letting such training effects bias the results.

The names given for the different designs are: different-participant design, same-participant design, and matched-pairs design. In different-participant design, a single group of participants is allocated randomly to each of the experimental conditions, so that different participants perform in different conditions. In experimental jargon this is called between-subjects. An advantage is that there are no ordering or training effects, caused by the influence of participants' experience of one set of tasks on performance in the next, as each participant only ever performs in one condition. A disadvantage is that large numbers of participants are needed so that the effect of any individual differences among participants, such as differences in experience and expertise, is minimalized. Randomly allocating the participants and pre-testing to identify any participants that differ strongly from the others can help.

In same-participant design, all participants perform in all conditions so only half the number of participants is needed; the main reason for this design is to lessen the impact of individual differences and to see how performance varies across conditions for each participant. In experimental jargon this is called within-subjects. It is important to ensure that the order in which participants perform tasks for this set-up does not bias the results. For example, if there are two tasks, A and B, half the participants should do task A followed by task B and the other half should do task B followed by task A. This is known as counterbalancing. Counterbalancing neutralizes possible unfair effects of learning from the first task, i.e. the order effect.

In matched-participant design, participants are matched in pairs based on certain user characteristics such as expertise and gender. Each pair is then randomly allocated to each experimental condition. A problem with this arrangement is that other important variables that have not been taken into account may influence the results. For example, experience in using the web could influence the results of tests to evaluate the navigability of a website. So web expertise would be a good criterion for matching participants.

The advantages and disadvantages of using different experimental designs are summarized in Table 14.3.

Similar to user tests, the data collected to measure user performance on the tasks set in an experiment usually includes response times for subtasks, total times to complete a task, and number of errors per task. Analyzing the data involves comparing the performance data obtained across the different conditions. The response times, errors, etc. are averaged across conditions to see if there are any marked differences. Statistical tests are then used, such as *t*-tests, that statistically compare the differences between the conditions, to reveal if these are significant. For example, a *t*-test could reveal whether Helvetica or Times font is faster to read on the screen.

t-Tests are the most widely used statistical test in HCI and other fields, such as psychology. They can be used to answer the question of whether two variables are related

Design	Advantages	Disadvantages
Different participants	**No order effects**	**Many participants needed. Individual differences among participants are a problem. Can be offset to some extent by randomly assigning to groups.**
Same participants	**Eliminates individual differences between experimental conditions.**	**Need to counterbalance to avoid ordering effects.**
Matched participants	**Same as different participants, but the effects of individual differences are reduced.**	**Can never be sure that subjects are matched across variables.**

***Table 14.3** The advantages and disadvantages of different allocation of participants to conditions*

or not. The scores, e.g. time taken to read a page of text, for each participant in each condition are used to compute the means (x) and standard deviations (SD). The standard deviation is a statistical measure of the spread or variability around the mean. The t-test uses a simple equation to test the significance of the difference between the means. If they are significantly different from each other we can reject the null hypothesis and in so doing infer that the alternative hypothesis holds. A typical t-test result that compared reading time for two groups with 9 and 12 participants each might be: $t = 4.53$, $p < 0.05$, $df = 19$. The t-value of 4.53 is the score derived from applying the t-test; df stands for degrees of freedom, which represents the number of values in the conditions that are free to vary. This is a complex concept that we will not explain here other than to mention how it is derived and that it is always written as part of the result of a t-test. The dfs are calculated by summing the number of participants in one condition minus one and the number of participants in the other condition minus one. It is calculated as $df = (N_a - 1) + (N_b - 1)$, where N_a is the number of participants in one condition and N_b is the number of participants in the other condition. In our example, $df = (9 - 1) + (12 - 1) = 19$. p is the probability that the effect found did not occur by chance. So, when $p < 0.05$, it means that the effect found is probably not due to chance and that there is only a 5% chance of that being the case. Typically, a value of $p < 0.05$ is considered good enough to reject the null hypothesis, although lower levels of p are more convincing, e.g. $p < 0.01$ where the effect found is even less likely to be due to chance, there being only a 1% chance of that being the case.

Box 14.1 describes an experiment to test whether broad, shallow menu design is preferable to deep menus on the web.

Box 14.1
An experiment to evaluate structure in web page design

A large body of research has been done on exploring the optimal number of items in a menu design, and most studies conclude that breadth is preferable to depth in organizing menu content. By this it is meant having a large number of top-level menu items with few levels rather than a small number of top-level items with many levels. Around 1997, when the web was still a relatively new phenomenon, there was an assumption that the number of links from a homepage to other items should be fewer than 10. The assumption was based on misapplying Miller's magic number, 7±2. This assumption fails to recognize, however, that users do not need to remember the items, they need only to be able to identify them, which is far easier. A contrary position was that because recognition is easier than recall, it would be better to have a much larger number of links on the homepage. This goes against a rule of thumb for information display on paper that advocates the use of white space to prevent confusion and an unpleasing, cluttered design. To solve this controversy Kevin Larson and Mary Czerwinski (1998) from Microsoft Research carried out an experiment. The following account outlines the main points of their study.

The goal of the experiment was to find the optimal depth versus breadth structure of hyperlinks for expertly categorized web content. Three conditions were tested using different link designs varying in depth/breadth for the same web content. Each design had 512 bottom-level nodes.

Condition 1: 8 × 8 × 8 **(8 top-level categories, each with 8 sublevels, with 8 content levels under each)**

Condition 2: 16 × 32 **(16 top-level categories, each with 32 content-level categories)**

Condition 3: 32 × 16 **(32 top-level categories, each with 16 content-level categories)**

These conditions were compared using a same-participant experimental design. 19 experienced web users each performed eight search tasks for each condition, making a total of 24 searches. The eight searches were selected for each participant at random from a bank of 128 possible target items that were categorized according to content and complexity. Participants were given the same number of items from each category and no one searched for the same item more than once (i.e. there was no duplication of items across conditions).

Reaction times (RT) to complete each search were recorded. The data was collated in terms of the averages (Avg.) and standard deviations (SD) for each condition. The averages showed that participants completed search tasks fastest in the 16 × 32 hierarchy (Avg. RT = 36 seconds, SD = 16), second fastest in the 32 × 16 hierarchy (Avg. RT = 46 seconds, SD = 26), and slowest in the 8 × 8 × 8 hierarchy (Avg. RT = 58 seconds, SD = 23). These results suggest that breadth is preferable to depth for searching web content. However, very large numbers of links on one page may be detrimental to searching performance. More experiments are needed to identify the ideal number at the top level. ■

Activity 14.4

1. What were the independent and dependent variables in the study described in Box 14.1?
2. Write two possible hypotheses.
3. The participants are all described as 'experts.' Is this adequate? What else do you want to know about them?
4. How do controlled experiments differ from typical usability testing (i.e. that done in most companies)?

Comment

1. The independent variable is menu link structure. The dependent variable is reaction time to complete a search successfully.
2. Web search performance is faster with broad, shallow link structures.

   There is no difference in search performance using different link structures.
3. 'Expert' could refer to a broad range of expertise. The evaluators could have used a screening questionnaire to make sure that all the participants had reached a basic level of expertise and there were no super-experts in the group. However, given that all the participants did all the conditions, differences in expertise had less impact than in other experimental designs.
4. Controlled experiments compare two or more conditions (i.e. treatments of the independent variable) based on quantitative measures of human performance. Therefore other evaluators can follow the same procedure and can apply the same statistical tests in order to check the results. Typically, usability testing is designed to find the problems that users encounter when carrying out a set of standardized tasks. ■

14.3 Field studies

Field studies are typically conducted to find out how a product or prototype is adopted and used by people in their working and everyday lives. Such settings are very different from the controlled environments used during usability testing, where tasks are set and completed in an orderly way. Instead, they are 'messy' in the sense that activities often overlap and are constantly interrupted. It follows that the way people interact with products in their everyday messy worlds is often different from how they perform on set tasks in a laboratory setting. Hence, by evaluating how people think about, interact, and integrate products within the settings they will ultimately be used in, we can get a better sense of how successful the products will be in the real world. The trade-off, however, is that we cannot test specific hypotheses about an interface nor account, with the same degree of certainty, for how people react to or use a product—as we can do in the laboratory setting. This makes it more difficult to determine what causes them to behave in a certain way or what is problematic about the usability of a product. Instead, qualitative accounts and descriptions of people's behavior and activities are obtained that reveal how they used the product and reacted to its design.

Field studies can range in time from just a few minutes to a period of several months or even years. Data is collected primarily by observing and interviewing people; collecting video, audio, and field notes to record what occurs in the chosen setting. In addition, participants may be asked to fill out paper-based or electronic diaries, that run on cell phones or other handheld devices, at particular points during the day, such as when they are interrupted during their ongoing activity or when they encounter a problem when interacting with a product or when they are in a particular location (see Figure 14.16). This technique is based on the experience sampling method (ESM) used in healthcare (Csikszentmihalyhi and Larson, 1987). Data on the frequency and patterning of certain daily activities, such as the monitoring of eating and drinking habits, or social interactions like phone and face-to-face conversations, are recorded. Software running on the PDAs or

Figure 14.16 *An example context-aware experience sampling tool running on a PDA*

cell phones triggers participants at certain intervals, requesting them to answer questions or fill out dynamic forms and checklists. These might include recording what they are doing, what they are feeling like at a particular time, where they are or how many conversations they have had in the last hour.

When conducting a field study, it is important to let the people being observed, or asked to record information, know how long the study or session will take. The investigators will need to work out and agree with the participants what part of the site is to be recorded and how. If setting up cameras they need to be situated in an unobtrusive place. For example, if a field study is being conducted on how families use a new messaging system, they will need to agree on if and where cameras can be placed in their house. The participants will need to be told how to switch them on and off. The investigators will also need to work out in advance what to do if the prototype or product breaks down while *in situ*. Can the participants reboot the system or will the investigators need to be called in? Security arrangements will also need to be made if expensive or precious equipment is being evaluated in a public place.

Examples of field studies were presented in Chapter 12. Two of these were the Nokia phone study and the HutchWorld portal; the Nokia phone study explored how users from a different cultural environment, Japan, used a cell phone designed for Europeans while the HutchWorld portal was evaluated with patients in a hospital setting to see how the practical constraints of that environment impacted its use by patients. A number of other field studies have explored how new technologies have been appropriated by people in their own cultures and settings. By appropriation is meant how the participants use, integrate, and adapt the technology to suit their needs, desires, and way of living. For example, the drift table, an innovative interactive map table described in Chapter 6, was placed in a number of homes in London for a period of weeks to see how the home owners appropriated it. The field study showed how the different home owners interacted with it in quite different ways, providing a range of different accounts for how they understood it and what they did with it. Another field study, mentioned in Chapter 4, was of the Opinionizer system that was designed as part of a social space where people could share their opinions visually and anonymously, via a public display. The system was intended to facilitate the initiation of conversations with strangers at a party or other social gathering. Observations of it being interacted with at a number of parties showed a 'honey-pot' effect: as the number of people in the immediate vicinity of the system increased, a sociable 'buzz' was created, where a variety of conversations were started between the strangers.

The findings from these and other field studies are typically written up in the form of vignettes, excerpts, critical incidents, patterns, and narratives to illustrate how the products are being adopted and integrated into their surroundings. Another approach is to use a particular conceptual framework to guide the analysis (see Chapter 8). This enables the data to be explained at a more general level in terms of cognitive processes, or social practices such as learning, or conversational or linguistic interactions. To show how this is done we present a field study that used a framework of learning artifacts, derived from Activity Theory, to analyze how people understand and learn how to use a new technology in their own home. The field study was carried out by Marianne Graves Petersen, Kim Holskov Madsen and Arne Kjaer (2002), who analyzed how two different families' behavior evolved as they learned to use their newly purchased Bang and Olufsen TV and integrated video system. The system was integrated in the sense that both the TV and video were operated by a single remote control. For example, after pressing the button for the TV, the same sequence of steps is followed to get channel 7 as to get track 7 on the video. The families each consisted of two parents and two children. One family, who had two small children, had not owned a Bang and Olufsen system before. The other family, with two adult children, had owned a Bang and Olufsen system and they bought the new one to be part of their home entertainment system with 'surround-sound.'

Only two families were chosen for the study because the investigators wanted to study how the learning and adoption process evolved in depth over a period of several months. The families were visited four times each at intervals of approximately a month during this time in their homes, in the evenings. The investigators restricted their use of video and the duration of their visits, conscious that they were visiting people during their leisure time in their homes. The families were asked a series of open-ended questions during the visits. For example: Why did they decide to buy it? Where did the idea come from? What were their expectations? Did the two families discuss their idea for the purchase with their families and friends? Did they visit and talk with the distributor before making the purchase? In addition, they were asked to fill in an incident diary form whenever they noted anything interesting or unusual happening.

Following the initial interviews, the investigators constructed scenario-based, hands-on activities to further develop their understanding of the families' expectations and use of the system.

Activity 14.5

Petersen *et al.* (2002) note that the incident diary method failed to be used by the families. Why do you think this was and how might it have been used differently?

Comment

The incident diary probably failed in this context because it was distracting from the relaxed atmosphere in which the families used the product. They were probably enjoying watching TV or videos on the family sofa, and did not wish to interrupt this experience to complete a diary entry. Alternatively, if they had been asked to fill in a simple form at the end of each day, reflecting on their experiences, it may have been used more.

Activity theory as an analytic framework

In Chapter 8 you were introduced to Activity Theory, where it was used to explain how artifacts mediate activity. A number of concepts were introduced. Following Engestrom's (1990) and Wartofsky's (1979) adaptation of the theory, Petersen *et al.* propose that artifacts can be conceptualized in terms of how people learn and understand how to use new technologies. The four types they describe are: (i) '*what* artifacts,' which describe the purpose of the design; (ii) '*how* artifacts,' which indicate how the 'what artifacts' are used; (iii) '*why* artifacts,' which suggest why a particular way of doing something is chosen; and (iv) '*where to* artifacts,' which indicate a motive to change a behavior or understanding of how a product works. Having this way of conceptualizing artifacts helps understand how design supports the development of a product's use as people learn more about how to use it within the context of their activities.

Collecting and analyzing data

Using this conceptual framework, the investigators analyzed their data (observations, interviews, video recordings), looking through it several times and noting themes. Other themes also developed from the interests of the families. They then described a series of episodes that were particularly successful, problematic, surprising, or difficult to tackle. These episodes included: the cinema experience, programming the video recording, and sticking to old procedures. Here we describe one of them for one family: the cinema experience.

The chosen episode shows how one mother, called Sarah, pursued the promise of the cinema experience. When the system was being installed Sarah explained, excitedly, how her family was looking forward to the large screen and surround-sound of the cinema experience, which was their prime motive for buying the new system. A demonstration in the shop and the marketing literature helped to create this expectation. The description that is presented illustrates how this expectation pervaded Sarah's learning of how to use the new system. It also shows how her knowledge of the family's previous system impeded her learning the new system and about how the integration of functions for operating the TV and CD player in the design of the remote control affected her. The story is told through the analysis of salient excerpts from the investigator's observations and interviews with Sarah and her husband, Paul.

where-to artifacts
  The cinema experience as it is formed in the shop, in sales brochures, and at Sarah's sister's house.

why artifacts
  —

how artifacts
  Something to do with the LIST button on the remote control.

what artifacts
  The electronic curtains rising and falling.

Figure 14.17 *Learning artifacts one month after delivery when trying to achieve the cinema experience*

After one month of the initial set-up of the new system, Sarah is still using the remote from the old system, which does not give her the cinema experience. One of the problems that Sarah faces is that the new remote is highly modal. The following excerpt illustrates that Sarah still has to learn how to use the function *LIST* on the new remote.

Sarah: "... what I can't do now and what I have not learned or asked about or read myself, that is to make the screen ... if I'm watching a video ... to make ... what is it called ... to enlarge or reduce the size of the picture ... I can't do that ... I mean it would take a long time for me to sit and experiment, it would be easier to read the manual, but it would be even easier to ask someone, if there was someone to ask."

[Some discussion about whether Sarah would use the manual or not]

Question: Are there any other things that you would like to do with the new remote control?

Sarah: "I can operate the video, but there is still the thing about making the picture bigger and smaller and then there is surround sound, too. I have not worked it out. I know it is [she studies the new remote control in her hand] ... no I don't know ... yes LIST ... I know it has something to do with LIST."

This initial experience was analyzed in terms of the various categories of artifacts, noting the important role of the LIST button as a 'how artifact' (see Figure 14.17).

The analysis then describes how she learns from her husband, Paul, while he is being interviewed by the investigators. The conversation informs Sarah about what she needs to do to learn to operate the remote to get surround-sound. The following excerpt illustrates how he does this:

Paul: "Now I would like to have the right size of the picture and the surround sound on. If we start with the size, we do ..."

[Paul does this without problems]

Paul: "Then when we want surround sound, we must connect all five loud speakers. Then we need to go over to what is called 'speaker' mode and you do this by pressing LIST ... there we have speaker mode [the text 'speaker' appears in the display of the remote control], *then we press number button 5 ..."*
Question: And you pressed 5 because you remember ...?
Paul: "Well there was some logic involved as I know that you have five speakers in surround sound, right?"
Sarah: "Oooohh, yes of course ... that is a strange kind of logic isn't it! It's so simple really!"

This excerpt also indicates that Sarah has learned that she must connect the speakers. By the time of the investigators' next visit, Sarah has connected the speakers and proudly announces that she has achieved the surround-sound. She did this by connecting the TV through the CD player that only required four speakers to be connected. It was only when Paul achieved the surround-sound with the TV—which required all five speakers to be connected—that Sarah realized her understanding was faulty.

Sarah: "Then I turned on the CD player. And then I wanted to connect the loudspeakers—all five of them."

Question: What did you do then?

Sarah: "Well, then I needed to start by turning up the volume [she turns up the volume] *... and then ... hmm ...* [Sarah studies the remote control] *... I put on ... I pressed twice on ... hmm ... on lift ... LIFT! ... and then I pressed number button 4 and now they are on"* [the surround sound is on].

Question: When you experimented with this yourself, do you remember how you found out that this is the way to do it?

Sarah: "Well I recalled that I needed to press ... that LIFT button ... that one I've always remembered ... a few times [actually twice], *and then there is nothing to it apart from pressing up to ... you see, I knew we have up to five loudspeakers, right !? ... and then I pressed number button 4 and the lights* [on the loudspeakers] *turned green"* [she points to the speakers].

The investigators observe that a breakdown occurred because Sarah needed to find the *LIST* button, which she then referred to as the *LIFT* button, probably because she didn't understand what it is for. However, she has now developed the principle of pressing the number to get the number of speakers that she wants. In terms of activity theory, this operation has become her '*why* artifact,' which she did not have before. Meanwhile, her previous '*how* artifact' that was "*something to do with LIST*" has been refined to "*press LIST or LIFT a few times.*" The learning artifacts in Figure 14.18 show how Sarah's efforts have evolved to successfully obtain the cinema experience in her living room.

The outcome from this detailed analysis is an explanation of the motivation for Sarah's behavior when operating the TV; a trace of where breakdowns in her understanding of the design of the TV occurred and how her understanding evolved as she learned to use it. It also accounted for why Sarah had problems accomplishing the task of turning on the loudspeakers in the surround-sound system to obtain the cinema experience, in terms of lacking some of the learning artifacts on the '*how* and *why* artifacts'—which she later discovered through listening to her husband explain how he did the same task. Highlighting

where-to artifacts
The cinema experience as it is formed in the shop, in sales brochures, and at Sarah's sister's house.

why artifacts
Press number button for number of loudspeakers to be connected.

how artifacts
Press LIFT [LIST] button a few times.

what artifacts
The electronic curtains rising and falling.

Figure 14.18 *Learning artifacts two months after delivery: finally establishing the cinema experience* the family's problems with the TV system also showed how they could be changed by, for example, modifying the design, improving the manual, and providing better help. It is unlikely that the same findings would have been revealed through usability testing.

The case study on communicability evaluation describes how another theory—semiotic engineering, which is based on a branch of linguistics known as semiotics—provides another theoretical perspective for analyzing data collected in field studies or from usability testing.

CASE STUDY 14.1
Communicability evaluation

Clarisse de Souza (2005) and her colleagues have developed a theory of HCI—*semiotic engineering*—that provides a series of tools for HCI design and evaluation. In semiotics the fundamental entity is the *sign*, which can take the form of a gesture, a symbol, or words, for example. One way or another all of our communication is through signs, even when we don't intend to produce signs, our mere existence conveys messages about us—how we dress, how old we are, our gender, the way we speak, etc., can all be interpreted as signs that carry information.

Semiotic engineering views human–computer interaction in terms of communication between the designers of the artifact and the user. In linguistic terms the designer and the user are thought of as interlocutors and the artifact is thought of as a message from the designer to users. You can read more about the theory of semiotic engineering on the website (`id-book.com`). Of main interest here is how the theory is applied in evaluation, which focuses on identifying breakdowns in communication between the user and the designer. These breakdowns occur when the user fails to understand the message (i.e. the design of the artifact) sent by the designer—in other words, the problems that the user has interacting with the artifact—i.e. the *communicability* of a design. The method used is *communicability evaluation*. Like usability testing and field studies, evaluating communicability is based on observing a user's experiences with an application either directly or, more usually, recorded on video or audio. Using a predefined set of tags the evaluator analyzes the user's behavior, focusing on breakdowns in which the user either could not understand the designer's intentions (as encoded in the interface) or could not make herself understood by the application. The first step in the communicability evaluation involves tagging the user's interaction with communicability utterances. In other words, it consists of "putting words into the user's mouth" in a kind of reverse protocol analysis (de Souza, 2005, p. 126). The evaluator looks for patterns of behavior that correspond to tags such as: "Oops!," "Where is it?," "I can do it this way," "I can do otherwise," "Looks fine to me." Figure 14.19 presents a schematic image of communicability utterances for a few frames of recorded video. Thirteen such tags have been identified and you can see how they are applied in the case study on the book website.

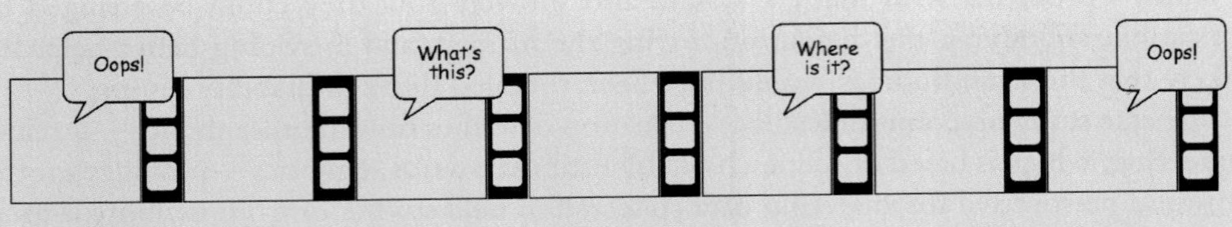

Figure 14.19 Schematic image of tagging communicative utterances

In sum, usability testing in a laboratory is most suitable for testing software upgrades, prototypes, and working systems. Although the goal of a usability study can be broad, such as determining how usable a product is, more specific questions are typically addressed, such as, "can users complete a certain task within a certain time, or find a particular item, or find the answer to a question" as in the MedlinePlus study. In contrast, field studies are useful when wanting to discover how products and prototypes will be used within their intended social and physical context of use. Routines and other types of activities are analyzed as they unfold in their natural settings, describing and conceptualizing the ways artifacts are used and adopted. There are no interventions on behalf of the investigator other than the placement of the prototype or product in the setting, and questions and/or probes to discover how they are learned, used, and adopted. Case study 14.2 about developing cross-cultural children's book communities provides another example of a field study. Here we see how a group of evaluators worked with teachers and school children to evaluate prototypes of online community spaces at various stages of development.

CASE STUDY 14.2
Developing cross-cultural children's book communities

The 'International Children's Digital Library' (ICDL) (`www.icdlbooks.org`) is an online library for the world's children developed by Allison Druin, Ben Bederson, Ann Weeks, and researchers from the University of Maryland. To support this mission, research is being conducted on how children access and use digital books to explore diverse cultures. With over 1000 books, from more than 200 countries in 35 languages, ICDL is the world's largest international library online for children, ages 3–13. Figure 14.20 below shows the introductory screen for the ICDL. This interface is available in 10 different languages.

The 'ICDL Communities' project explores the social context surrounding next generation learners and how they share books. This research focuses on how to support an online global community of children who don't speak the same languages but want to share the

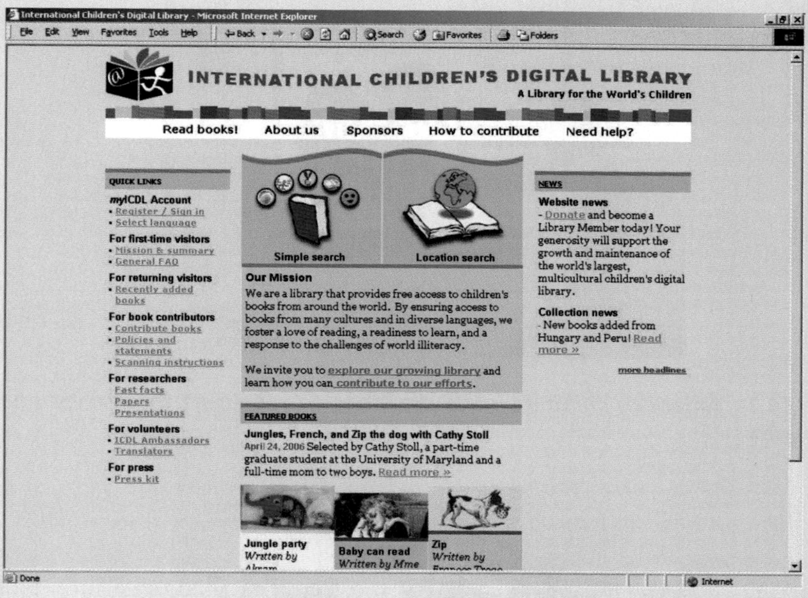

Figure 14.20 *The homepage of the International Children's Digital Library*

same digital resources and interact with each other socially, learn about each others' cultures, and make friends even if they do not speak the same language. Using specially developed tools, children communicate inter-culturally, create and share stories, and build cross-cultural understanding.

This case study reports the results of three rounds of evaluations during the iterative development of the ICDL Communities software with children in three pairs of countries: Hungary/USA; Argentina/USA; Mexico/USA (Komlodi *et al.*, 2007). In the early evaluations the researchers investigated how the children liked to represent themselves and their team using paper (Figure 14.21). In later prototypes the children worked online in pairs using tablet PCs (Figure 14.22).

The findings from each round of evaluation enabled the researchers to learn more about the children's needs, which enabled them to extend the functionality of the prototype and refine its usability and sociability. As the development proceeded it became clear that it was essential to support the entire context of use, including providing team-building activities for children and support for teachers before using the online tools.

Figure 14.21 *American children make drawings to represent themselves and their community*

Figure 14.22 *Mexican children working with an early prototype using a tablet PC*

From these evaluation studies researchers learned that: children enjoy interacting with other children form different countries and a remarkable amount of communication takes place even when the children do not share a common language; identity and representation are particularly important to children when communicating online; drawing and sharing stories is fun; providing support for children and teachers off-line as well as online is as essential as developing good software for the success of this kind of activity.

Dilemma
How many users should I include in my evaluation study?

A question students always ask is how many users do I need to include in my study? Deciding on how many to use for a usability study is partly a logistical issue that depends on schedules, budgets, representative users, and facilities available. As already mentioned, many professionals recommend that 5–12 testers is enough (Dumas and Redish, 1999), although a handful of users can provide useful feedback at early stages of a design. Others say that as soon as the same kinds of problems start being revealed and there is nothing new, it is time to stop. The more testers there are, the more representative the findings will be across the user population but the study will also be more expensive and time-consuming, so there is a trade-off to be made.

Field studies generally focus on one or two sites where a new prototype or product is being evaluated. The number of people being studied at these sites will vary, depending on what is of interest. It may be a family at home, a software team in an engineering firm, or a large group of students in a classroom setting. The problem with studying only one or two settings is that the findings from one group of people may not be representative of how other groups would act. However, the detailed findings gleaned for these one or two groups with respect to how they learn to use a technology and adopt it over time can be very revealing. ■

Assignment

This assignment continues work on the web-based ticket reservation system introduced at the end of Chapter 10 and continued in Chapter 11. Using either the paper or software prototype, or the HTML web pages developed to represent the basic structure of your website, follow the instructions below to evaluate your prototype.

(a) Based on your knowledge of the requirements for this system, develop a standard task, e.g. booking two seats for a particular performance.

(b) Consider the relationship between yourself and your participants. Do you need to use an informed consent form? If so, prepare a suitable informed consent form. Justify your decision.

(c) Select three typical users, who can be friends or colleagues, and ask them to do the task using your prototype.

(d) Note the problems that each user encounters. If you can, time their performance. (If you happen to have a video camera, you could film each participant.)

(e) Since the system is not actually implemented you cannot do a full field study of this system. However, imagine that you are planning a field study of this system. How would you do it? What kinds of things would you need to take into account? What sort of data would you collect and how would you analyze it?

(f) What are the main benefits and problems with usability testing and field studies?

Summary

This chapter described usability testing focusing on how to do user testing. MedlinePlus was introduced as an example where usability testing was conducted for a large web-based medical information system. Experimental design was then introduced as a more rigorous form of testing a hypothesis. These were contrasted with the evaluation approach of using field studies and included a field study of how families purchased and learnt how to use and understand an integrated entertainment system. Interview data from the study was analyzed using an adapted version of Activity Theory as a conceptual framework. Key differences between usability testing and field studies include the controlled nature of usability testing in which tests are performed under laboratory-like conditions verses the naturalistic approach adopted in field studies where the focus is on understanding how users interact with technology in their work or everyday environments.

Key Points

- User testing is a central component of usability testing; it also can include observation, user satisfaction questionnaires, and interviews.
- Field studies are carried out to discover how people interact with technology in the real world.
- Testing is commonly done in controlled laboratory-like conditions, in contrast to field studies that focus on how the product is used in a working or everyday context.
- 'Usability-in-a-box' and remote testing systems have been developed that are more affordable than usability labs and also more portable, making them suitable for field use and remote evaluations.
- Experiments aim to test a hypothesis by manipulating certain variables while keeping others constant.
- The experimenter controls independent variable(s) in order to measure dependent variable(s).

Further Reading

DUMAS, J.S. and REDISH, J.C. (1999) *A Practical Guide to Usability Testing.* Intellect. Many books have been written about usability testing, but this one is particularly useful because it describes the process in detail and provides many examples.

LARSON, K. and CZERWINSKI, M. (1998) *Web page design: Implications of memory, structure and scent for information retrieval.* In *Proceedings of CHI'98*, pp 25–32. This paper describes the breadth-versus-depth web study outlined in Box 14.1.

LAZAR, J. (2006) *Web Usability: A User-Centered Design Approach.* Addison-Wesley. This book covers the entire user-centered design process for websites, from determining the site mission and target user population, through requirements gathering, conceptual and physical design, usability testing, implementation, and evaluation. It contains useful case studies and pays special attention to universal usability issues.

PETERSEN, M.J., MADSEN, K.H. AND KJAER, A. (2002) The usability of everyday technology; Emerging and fading opportunities. *Transactions on Computer–Human Interaction (TOCHI)* **9**(2), 74–105. This paper describes a field study in which the evaluators traced the evolution of how two families used their entertainment system over a period of several months. The study demonstrates how activity theory can be used to frame the study and guide data analysis.

ROBSON, C. (1994) *Experimental Design and Statistics in Psychology.* Penguin Psychology. This book provides an introduction to experimental design and basic statistics.

RUBIN, J. (1994) *Handbook of Usability Testing: How to Plan, Design and Conduct Effective Tests.* John Wiley & Sons. This book also provides good practical advice about preparing and conducting user tests, analyzing and reporting the results.

DE SOUZA, S.C. (2005) *The Semiotic Engineering of Human–Computer Interaction.* MIT Press. This book discusses how semiotic engineering, a practical approach that is based on the theory and practice of semiotic analysis, provides an alternative approach to usability testing.

INTERVIEW with Ben Shneiderman

Ben Shneiderman is Professor of Computer Science at the University of Maryland, where he was founder and director of the Human–Computer Interaction Laboratory from 1983 to 2000. He is author of the highly acclaimed book *Designing the User Interface: Strategies for Effective Human–Computer Interaction*, now in its fourth edition with co-author Catherine Plaisant. He developed the concept of direct manipulation and created the user interface for the selectable text link that makes the web so easy to use. Now he works on universal usability, information visualization, and creativity support tools.

JP: Ben you've been a strong advocate of measuring user performance and user satisfaction. Why is just watching users not enough?
BS: Watching users is a great way to begin, but if we are to develop a scientific foundation for HCI that promotes theory and supports prediction, measurement will be important. The purpose of measurement is not statistics but insight.

JP: OK can you give me an example?
BS: Watching users traverse a menu tree may reveal problems, but when you measure the time and number of clicks you prove that broader and shallower trees are almost always the winning strategy. This conflict between broader and shallower trees emerged in a conference panel discussion with a leading researcher for a major corporation. She and her colleagues followed up by testing users' speed of performance on searching tasks with two-level and three-level trees.
(You can read about this experiment in Box 14.1).

JP: But is user performance speed always the important measure?
BS: Measuring user performance speed, error rates, and user satisfaction separately is important because sometimes users may be satisfied by an elaborate graphical interface even if it slows them down substantially. Finding the right balance among performance, error rates, and user satisfaction depends on whether you are building a repetitive data-entry system, a life-critical air-traffic control system, or an enjoyable game.

JP: Experiments are an important part of your undergraduate classes. Why?

BS: Most computer science and information systems students have had little exposure to experiments. I want to make sure that my students can form lucid and testable hypotheses that can be experimentally tested with groups of real users. They should understand about choosing a small number of independent variables to modify and dependent variables to measure. I believe that students benefit by understanding how to control for biases and perform statistical tests that confirm or refute the hypotheses. My students conduct experimental projects in teams and prepare their reports on the web. For example, one team did a project in which they varied the display size and demonstrated that web surfers found what they needed faster with larger screens. Another group found that bigger mouse pads do not speed task performance (`www.otal.umd.edu/SHORE2000`). Even if students never conduct an experiment professionally, the process of designing experiments helps them to become more effective analysts. I also want my students to be able to read scientific papers that report on experiments.

JP: What 'take-away messages' do you want your students to get from taking an HCI class?

BS: I want my students to know about rigorous and replicable scientific results that form the foundation for understanding human–computer interaction. Just as physics provides a scientific foundation for mechanical engineering, HCI provides a rigorous foundation for usability engineering.

JP: How do you distinguish between an experiment and usability testing?

BS: The best controlled experiments start with a hypothesis that has practical implications and theoretical results of broad importance. A controlled experiment has at least two conditions and applies statistical tests such as *t*-test and analysis of variance (ANOVA) to verify statistically significant differences. The results confirm or refute the hypothesis and the procedure is carefully described so that others can replicate it. I tell my students that experiments have two parents and three children. The parents are "a practical problem" and "a theoretical foundation" and the three children are "help in resolving the practical problem," "refinements to the theory," and "advice to future experimenters who work on the same problem."

By contrast, a usability test studies a small number of users who carry out required tasks. Statistical results are less important. The goal is to refine a product as quickly as possible. The outcome of a usability test is a report to developers that identifies frequent problems and possibly suggests improvements, maybe ranked from high to low priority and from low to high developer effort.

JP: What do you see as the important usability issues for the next five years?

BS: I see three directions for the next five years. The first is the shift from emphasizing the technology to focusing on user needs. I like to say "the old computing is about what computers can do, the new computing is about what users can do," which is the

Figure 14.23 PhotoFinder for personal photo libraries, includes drag-and-drop annotations for family member names

theme of my book *Leonardo's Laptop: Human Needs and the New Computing Technologies.*

JP: But hasn't HCI always been about what users can do?

BS: Yes, but HCI and usability engineering have been more evaluative than generative. To clarify, I believe that deeper theories about human needs will contribute to innovations in mobility, ubiquity, and community. Information and communication tools will become pervasive and enable higher levels of social interaction. For example, museum visitors to the Louvre, white-water rafters in Colorado, or family travelers to Hawaii's Haleakala volcano will be able to point at a sculpture, rock, or flower and find out about it. They'll be able to see photos at different seasons taken by previous visitors and send their own pictures back to friends and grandparents. One of our projects allows people to accumulate, organize, and retrieve the many photos that they will take and receive. Users of our PhotoFinder software tool can organize their photos and annotate them by dragging and dropping name labels. Then they can find photos of people and events to tell stories and reminisce (see Figure 14.23).

HCI researchers who understand human needs are likely to come up with innovations that help physicians to make better diagnoses, enable shoppers to find what they want at fair prices, and allow educators to create more compelling experiences for students.

JP: What are the other two directions?

BS: The second opportunity is to support universal usability, thereby bringing the benefits of information and communications technology to the widest possible set of users. Website designers will need to learn how to attract and retain a broad set of users with divergent needs and differing skills. They will have to understand how to accommodate users efficiently with slow and fast network connections, small and large displays, and various software platforms. System designers who invent strategies to accommodate young and old, novice and expert, and users with varying disabilities will earn the appreciation of users and the respect of their colleagues. Evidence is accumulating that designs that facilitate English, French, Chinese and other versions of a website also make it easy to accommodate end-user customization, convert to wireless applications, support disabled users and speed modifications. The good news is that satisfying these multiple requirements also produces interfaces that are better for all users. Diversity promotes quality.

The third direction is the development of tools to let more people be more creative more of the time. Word processors, painting tools and music-composition software are a good starting point, but creative people need more powerful tools so that they can explore alternative solutions rapidly. Creativity-support tools will speed search of existing solutions, facilitate consultations with peers and mentors, and record the users' history of activity so that they can review, revise, and share their work.

But remember that every positive development also has a potential dark side. One of the formidable challenges for HCI students is to think carefully about how to cope with the unexpected and unintended. Powerful tools can have dangerous consequences. I encourage students to embrace the opportunity and accept the responsibility.

15

15.1 Introduction

All the evaluation methods you have encountered so far in this book have involved interaction with, or direct observation of, users. In this chapter we introduce an approach, known as analytical evaluation, where users are not directly involved. This approach includes various inspection methods and predictive models. Inspection methods typically involve an expert role-playing the users for whom the product is designed, analyzing aspects of an interface, and identifying any potential usability problems by using a set of guidelines. The most well known are heuristic evaluation and walkthroughs. Predictive models involve analyzing the various physical and mental operations that are needed to perform particular tasks at the interface and operationalizing them in terms of quantitative measures. They predict the times it will take a user to carry out the same task using different interfaces, enabling different designs to be compared. For example, the optimal layout of the physical and soft keys for a cell phone can be predicted in this way. We cover two of the most commonly used in HCI: GOMS and Fitts' Law.

Inspections are often used to evaluate a fully working system such as a website, whereas predictive modeling techniques are used more for testing specific aspects of an interface, such as the layout of keys or menu options. One of the advantages of analytical methods is that they are relatively quick to perform and do not require involving users to take part in a usability test or field study. However, they are only ever 'guesses' of the time it will take for hypothetical users to carry out a given task, or the potential usability problems they might come across when interacting with a product. It requires the usability expert to put themselves in the shoes of another kind of user besides themselves. When reading this chapter imagine yourself as the expert trying to be the hypothetical user and consider how easy or difficult it is.

The main aims of this chapter are to:

- **Describe the important concepts associated with inspection methods.**
- **Show how heuristic evaluation can be adapted to evaluate different types of interactive products.**
- **Explain what is involved in doing heuristic evaluation and various kinds of walkthrough.**
- **Describe how to perform two types of predictive technique, GOMS and Fitts' Law, and when to use them.**
- **Discuss the advantages and disadvantages of using analytical evaluation.**

15

Analytical evaluation

15.2 Inspections: heuristic evaluation

Sometimes users are not easily accessible, or involving them is too expensive or takes too long. In such circumstances, experts or combinations of experts and users can provide feedback. By an expert is meant someone who is practiced in usability methods and has a background in HCI. Various inspection techniques began to be developed as alternatives to usability testing in the early 1990s, drawing on software engineering practice where code and other types of inspections are commonly used. These inspection techniques include expert evaluations called heuristic evaluations, and walkthroughs. In these, experts examine the interface of an interactive product, often role-playing typical users, and suggest problems users would have when interacting with it. One of their attractions is that they can be used at any stage of a design project, including early design before well-developed prototypes are available. They can also be used to complement user-testing.

15.2.1 Heuristic evaluation

Heuristic evaluation is a usability inspection technique first developed by Jakob Nielsen and his colleagues (Nielsen and Mohlich, 1990; Nielsen, 1994a), in which experts, guided by a set of usability principles known as *heuristics*, evaluate whether user-interface elements, such as dialog boxes, menus, navigation structure, online help, etc., conform to the principles. These heuristics closely resemble the high-level design principles and guidelines discussed in Chapters 1 and 3, e.g. making designs consistent, reducing memory load, and using terms that users understand. When used in evaluation they are called heuristics. The original set of heuristics identified by Jakob Nielsen and his colleagues was derived empirically from an analysis of 249 usability problems (Nielsen, 1994b); a revised version of these heuristics is listed below (`useit.com`, accessed February 2006):

- **Visibility of system status**
  The system should always keep users informed about what is going on, through appropriate feedback within reasonable time.

- **Match between system and the real world**
  The system should speak the users' language, with words, phrases, and concepts familiar to the user, rather than system-oriented terms. Follow real-world conventions, making information appear in a natural and logical order.

- **User control and freedom**
  Users often choose system functions by mistake and will need a clearly marked 'emergency exit' to leave the unwanted state without having to go through an extended dialog. Support undo and redo.

- **Consistency and standards**
  Users should not have to wonder whether different words, situations, or actions mean the same thing. Follow platform conventions.
- **Error prevention**
  Even better than good error messages is a careful design which prevents a problem from occurring in the first place. Either eliminate error-prone conditions or check for them and present users with a confirmation option before they commit to the action.
- **Recognition rather than recall**
  Minimize the user's memory load by making objects, actions, and options visible. The user should not have to remember information from one part of the dialog to another. Instructions for use of the system should be visible or easily retrievable whenever appropriate.
- **Flexibility and efficiency of use**
  Accelerators—unseen by the novice user—may often speed up the interaction for the expert user such that the system can cater to both inexperienced and experienced users. Allow users to tailor frequent actions.
- **Aesthetic and minimalist design**
  Dialogues should not contain information that is irrelevant or rarely needed. Every extra unit of information in a dialog competes with the relevant units of information and diminishes their relative visibility.
- **Help users recognize, diagnose, and recover from errors**
  Error messages should be expressed in plain language (no codes), precisely indicate the problem, and constructively suggest a solution.
- **Help and documentation**
  Even though it is better if the system can be used without documentation, it may be necessary to provide help and documentation. Any such information should be easy to search, focused on the user's task, list concrete steps to be carried out, and not be too large.

The way in which experts are intended to use these heuristics is by judging them against aspects of the interface. For example, if a new email system is being evaluated, the expert would use the last one by examining the kind of help and documentation it provides. For example, he might consider how a user would find out how to import an address book and see how quick it is to find this information from the help facility and whether the instructions for doing this are easy to follow. The evaluator is meant to go through the interface several times inspecting the various interface elements and comparing them with the list of usability principles (i.e. the heuristics), picking up on any missed out and revising others until they are satisfied they have identified the majority of the usability problems.

Some of the core heuristics are too general for evaluating products that have come onto the market since they were first developed, such as mobile devices, digital toys, online communities, and new web services. Nielsen suggests developing category-specific heuristics that apply to a specific class of products as a supplement to the general heuristics. Evaluators and researchers have typically developed their own heuristics by tailoring Nielsen's heuristics together with other design guidelines, market research, and requirements documents for the specific products. Exactly which heuristics are appropriate and how many are needed for different products is debatable and depends on the goals of the evaluation. Most sets of heuristics have between five and ten items, which provides a range of usability criteria by which to judge the various aspects of an interface. More than ten becomes difficult for evaluators to remember, fewer than five tends not to be sufficiently discriminating.

A key question that is frequently asked is how many evaluators are needed to carry out a thorough heuristic evaluation? While one evaluator can identify a large number of usability problems, she may not catch all of them. She may also have a tendency to concentrate more on one usability aspect at the expense of missing others. For example, in a study of heuristic evaluation where 19 evaluators were asked to find 16 usability problems in a voice response system allowing customers access to their bank accounts, Nielsen (1992) found a substantial amount of non-overlap between the sets of usability problems found by the different evaluators. He also notes that while some usability problems are very easy to find by all evaluators, there are some problems that are found by very few experts. Therefore, he argues that it is important to involve multiple evaluators in any heuristic evaluation and recommends between three and five evaluators. His findings suggest that they can typically identify around 75% of the total usability problems, as shown in Figure 15.1 (Nielsen, 1994a).

However, employing multiple experts can be too costly. Skillful experts can capture many of the usability problems by themselves and some consultancies now use this technique as the basis for critiquing interactive devices—a process that has become known as an 'expert crit' in some countries. But using only one or two experts to conduct a heuristic evaluation can be problematic since research has challenged Nielsen's findings and questioned whether even three to five evaluators are adequate (e.g. Cockton and Woolrych, 2001; Woolrych and Cockton, 2001). These authors point out that the number of experts needed to find this percentage of problems depends on the nature of the problems. Their analysis of problem frequency and severity suggests that highly misleading findings can result. The take-away message about the question of how many experts are needed is that 'more is more,' but more is expensive. However, because users and special facilities are not needed for heuristic evaluation and it is comparatively inexpensive and quick, it is popular with developers and it is known as discount evaluation. For a quick evaluation of an early design, one or two

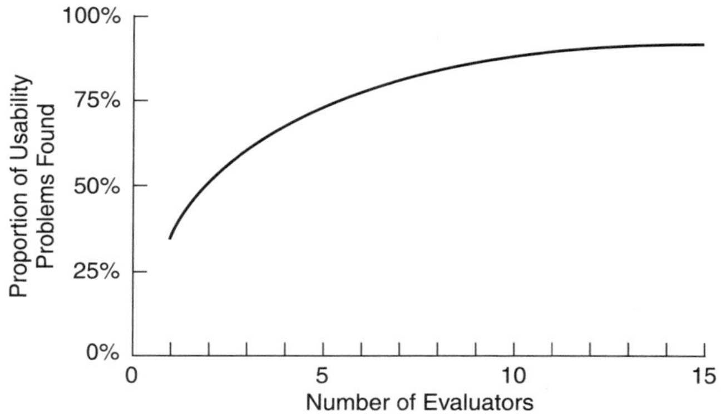

***Figure 15.1** Curve showing the proportion of usability problems in an interface found by heuristic evaluation using various numbers of evaluators. The curve represents the average of six case studies of heuristic evaluation (Nielsen 1994a)*

experts can probably identify most potential usability problems but if a thorough evaluation of a fully working prototype is needed then having a team of experts conducting the evaluation and comparing their findings would be advisable.

15.2.2 Heuristic evaluation for websites

In this section we examine heuristics for evaluating websites. We begin by discussing MedlinePlus, the medical information website created by the National Library of Medicine (NLM) that you read about in the previous chapter (Cogdill, 1999). The homepage and two other screens are shown in Figures 14.6–14.8. Prior to doing a usability evaluation, Keith Cogdill developed a set of heuristics customized for identifying usability problems of a large healthcare website, intended for the general public and medical professionals. The heuristics were based partly on Nielsen's core set and partly on Cogdill's own knowledge of the users' tasks, problems that had already been reported by users, and advice from documented sources (e.g. Shneiderman, 1998a; Nielsen, 1993; Dumas and Redish, 1999). The seven heuristics listed below were identified, some of which resemble Nielsen's original set:

- *Internal consistency*
  The user should not have to speculate about whether different phrases or actions carry the same meaning.
- *Simple dialog*
  The dialog with the user should not include information that is irrelevant, unnecessary, or rarely needed. The dialog should be presented in terms familiar to the user and not be system-oriented.

- *Shortcuts*
  The interface should accommodate both novice and experienced users.
- *Minimizing the user's memory load*
  The interface should not require the user to remember information from one part of the dialog to another.
- *Preventing errors*
  The interface should prevent errors from occurring.
- *Feedback*
  The system should keep the user informed about what is taking place.
- *Internal locus of control*
  Users who choose system functions by mistake should have an 'emergency exit' that lets them leave the unwanted state without having to engage in an extended dialog with the system.

These heuristics were given to three expert evaluators who independently evaluated MedlinePlus. Their comments were then compiled and a meeting was called to discuss their findings and suggest strategies for addressing problems. The following points were among their findings:

- *Layout*
  All pages within MedlinePlus have a relatively uncomplicated vertical design. The homepage is particularly compact, and all pages are well suited for printing. The use of graphics is conservative, minimizing the time needed to download pages.
- *Internal consistency*
  The formatting of pages and presentation of the logo are consistent across the website. Justification of text, fonts, font sizes, font colors, use of terms, and links labels are also consistent.

The experts also suggested improvements, including:

- *Arrangement of health topics*
  Topics should be arranged alphabetically as well as in categories. For example, health topics related to cardiovascular conditions could appear together.
- *Depth of navigation menu*
  Having a higher 'fan-out' in the navigation menu in the left margin would enhance usability. By this they mean that more topics should be listed at the top level, giving many short menus rather than a few deep ones. Remember the experiment on breadth versus depth discussed in Chapter 14, which provides evidence to justify this.

Activity 15.1

The heuristic evaluation discussed above was done during the creation of the first version of MedlinePlus.

1. **Using your Internet browser go to** `http://www.MedlinePlus.org` **and try out Cogdill's seven heuristics with the revised version. In your opinion, do these heuristics help you to identify important usability issues?**
2. **Does being aware of the heuristics influence how you interact with MedlinePlus in any way?**
3. **Are there other heuristics that you think should be included, or heuristics in the list that you think are not needed?**

Comment

1. **In our opinion the heuristics enabled us to focus on key usability criteria such as whether the interface dialog is meaningful and the consistency of the design.**
2. **Being aware of the heuristics caused us to focus more strongly on the design and to think about the interaction. We were more aware of what we were trying to do with the system and how the system was responding.**
3. **Internal locus of control was difficult to judge. The concept is useful but judging internal locus of control when role-playing users is difficult. All the heuristics focus on task-oriented design aspects, but the user will react to the aesthetic design as well. For example, I happen to like purple so the purple on the homepage was pleasing to me. I also reacted to the picture of a father and young boy holding a teddy bear. The heuristics do not address these user experience features, which are important to some users. For example, a colleague tells a story about how her teenage daughter selected a cell phone to purchase. The choice was determined by which were available with blue casing!**

Turning Design Guidelines into Heuristics for the Web

The example above shows how a set of guidelines was turned into heuristics for evaluating a website. This approach happens quite often because there are many books on web design and several of them offer design heuristics (e.g. Horton, 2005; Koyani *et al.*, 2004; Lazar, 2006); there are also numerous websites, e.g. `useit.com`, from which to select. So how do experts choose the most appropriate set for the product, service, or device they have to evaluate—given the ever-increasing body of knowledge from which to choose?

The approach that Cogdill adopted when evaluating MedlinePlus is quite common. He started by assessing Nielsen's original set of heuristics and then selected from other guidelines, other experts, and his own experience. He made his selection by considering what are the key interaction issues for the product in question. For example, one of the biggest problems for users of large websites is navigating around the site. The following six guidelines (adapted from Nielsen (1998) and others) are intended to encourage good navigation design. Typically, to develop heuristics, the guidelines would be turned into short statements or questions; these are shown following each guideline.

- Guideline (G): *Avoid orphan pages, i.e. pages that are not connected to the homepage, because they lead users into dead ends.*
  Heuristic (H): Are there any orphan pages? Where do they go to?
- G: *Avoid long pages with excessive white space that force scrolling.*
  H: Are there any long pages? Do they have lots of white space or are they full of texts or lists?
- G: *Provide navigation support, such as a strong site map that is always present* (Shneiderman and Plaisant, 2005).
  H: Is there any guidance, e.g. maps, navigation bar, menus, to help users find their way around the site?
- G: *Avoid narrow, deep, hierarchical menus that force users to burrow deep into the menu structure.*
  H: Are menus shallow or deep? Empirical evidence indicates that broad, shallow menus have better usability than a few deep menus (Larson and Czerwinski, 1998; Shneiderman and Plaisant, 2005).
- G: *Avoid non-standard link colors.*
  H: What color is used for links? Is it blue or another color? If it is another color, then is it obvious to the user that it is a hyperlink?
- G: *Provide consistent look and feel for navigation and information design.*
  H: Are menus used, named, and positioned consistently? Are links used consistently?

Activity 15.2

Consider the following design guidelines for information design and for each one suggest a question that could be used in heuristic evaluation:

- ***Outdated or incomplete information is to be avoided*** **(Nielsen, 1998). It creates a poor impression with users.**
- ***Good graphical design is important.*** **Reading long sentences, paragraphs, and documents is difficult on screen, so break material into discrete, meaningful chunks to give the website structure (Lynch and Horton, 1999; Horton, 2005).**

- *Avoid excessive use of color.* Color is useful for indicating different kinds of information, i.e. cueing (Koyani *et al.*, 2005).
- *Avoid gratuitous use of graphics and animation.* In addition to increasing download time, graphics and animation soon become boring and annoying.
- *Be consistent.* Consistency both within pages (e.g. use of fonts, numbering, terminology, etc.) and within the site (e.g. navigation, menu names, etc.) is important for usability and for aesthetically pleasing designs.

Comment

We suggest the following questions; you may have identified others:

- *Outdated or incomplete information*
  Do the pages have dates on them? How many pages are old and provide outdated information?
- *Good graphical design is important*
  Is the page layout structured meaningfully? Is there too much text on each page?
- *Avoid excessive use of color*
  How is color used? Is it used as a form of coding? Is it used to make the site bright and cheerful? Is it excessive and garish?
- *Avoid gratuitous use of graphics and animation*
  Are there any flashing banners? Are there complex introduction sequences? Can they be short-circuited? Do the graphics add to the site?
- *Be consistent*
  Are the same buttons, fonts, numbers, menu styles, etc., used across the site? Are they used in the same way?

Activity 15.3

Look at the heuristics for navigation above and consider how you would use them to evaluate a website for purchasing clothes, e.g. `http://www.REI.com`, which has a homepage similar to that in Figure 15.2). While you are doing this activity think about whether the heuristics are useful.

1. Do the heuristics help you focus on what is being evaluated?
2. Might fewer heuristics be better? Which might be combined and what are the trade-offs?

Comment

1. Most people find that the heuristics encourage them to focus more on the design.
2. Some heuristics can be combined and given a more general description. For example, *providing navigation support* and *avoiding narrow, deep, hierarchical menus* could be replaced with "help users to develop a good mental model," but this is a more abstract statement and some evaluators might not know

Figure 15.2 *Homepage of* `REI.com`

what is packed into it. Producing questions suitable for heuristic evaluation often results in more of them, so there is a trade-off. An argument for keeping the detail is that it reminds evaluators of the issues to consider.

Another important issue when designing and evaluating web pages is their accessibility to a broad range of users (see case studies 6.1 and 10.1). As much as possible, web pages need to be universally accessible. By this we mean that older users, users with disabilities, non-English speakers, and users with slow Internet connections should be able to access the basic content of the pages. In the USA, Section 508 of the U.S. Rehabilitation Act of 1973 was updated and refined in 1998 to make it more specific. This involved setting forth how the Act should be applied to technology so that it is universally accessible (See Lazar, 2006,

2007 for examples of the application of Section 508). In a comparative evaluation study of methods for assessing web page accessibility for the blind, Jen Mankoff and her colleagues found that multiple developers, using a screen reader, were most consistently successful at finding most types of problems (Mankoff *et al.*, 2005). Approximately 50% of known problems were identified which, surprisingly, was more successful than testing directly with blind users.

As the web diversifies, heuristics have been identified for evaluating a range of applications and services, such as web-based online communities.

Heuristics for web-based online communities

Here, a key concern for applications designed for web-based online communities, such as those that have been developed for social networks and support groups, is how to evaluate both usability and social interaction (i.e. sociability) aspects. The following nine sets of example questions are suggested as a starting point for developing heuristics to evaluate aspects of sociability and usability in web-based online communities (Preece, 2000).

- *Sociability:* Why should I join this community? (What are the benefits for me? Does the description of the group, its name, its location in the website, the graphics, etc., tell me about the purpose of the community and entice me to join it?)
- *Usability:* How do I join (or leave) the community? (What do I do? Do I have to register or can I just post, and is this a good thing?)
- *Sociability:* What are the rules? (Is there anything I shouldn't do? Are the expectations for communal behavior made clear? Is there someone who checks that people are behaving reasonably?)
- *Usability:* How do I get, read, and send messages? (Is there support for newcomers? Is it clear what I should do? Are templates provided? Can I send private messages?)
- *Usability:* Can I do what I want to do easily? (Can I navigate the site? Do I feel comfortable interacting with the software? Can I find the information and people I want?)
- *Sociability:* Is the community safe? (Are my comments treated with respect? Is my personal information secure? Do people make aggressive or unacceptable remarks to each other?)
- *Sociability:* Can I express myself as I wish? (Is there a way of expressing emotions, such as using emoticons? Can I show people what I look like or reveal aspects of my character? Can I see others? Can I determine who else is present—perhaps people are looking on but not sending messages?)
- *Sociability:* Do people reciprocate? (If I contribute will others contribute comments, support, and answer my questions?)
- *Sociability:* Why should I come back? (What makes the experience worthwhile? What's in it for me? Do I feel part of a thriving community? Are there interesting people with whom to communicate? Are there interesting events?)

Activity 15.4

Go to a discussion board that interests you or type 'Yahoo Groups' in your browser and find one. Social interaction was discussed in Chapter 4, and this activity involves picking up some of the concepts discussed there and developing heuristics to evaluate web-based online communities. Before starting you will find it useful to familiarize yourself with the group:

- Read some of the messages.
- Send a message.
- Reply to a message.
- Search for information.
- Count how many messages have been sent and how recently.
- Find out whether you can post to people privately using email.
- Can you see the physical relationship between messages easily?
- Do you get a sense of what the other people are like and the emotional content of their messages?
- Is a sense of community and of individuals present?

Then use the nine questions above as heuristics to evaluate the community site:

1. Did these questions support your evaluation of the web-based online community for both usability and sociability issues?
2. Could these questions be used to evaluate other online communities such as HutchWorld discussed in Chapter 12 or www.myspace.com, or another application?

Comment

1. You probably found that these questions helped focus your attention to specific issues. However, sociability and usability are two closely related topics and sometimes it is difficult or not useful to distinguish between them. Unlike the website evaluation it is important to pay attention to social interaction, but you may have found that your web-based community had very few visitors. A community without people is not a community no matter how good the software is that supports it.
2. HutchWorld is designed to support social interaction among cancer patients and their carers and the questions could therefore be used to evaluate these aspects. However, HutchWorld offers many additional features not found in most online communities. For example, it encourages a sense of social presence by allowing participants to show pictures of themselves, tell stories, etc., and HutchWorld has avatars, which are graphical representations of people. The nine questions above are useful but may need adapting to account for these extra features.

15.2.3 Heuristic evaluation for other interactive products

You have seen how heuristics can be tailored for evaluating websites and web-based applications. However, the diversity of new products that need to be evaluated are quite different from the software applications of the early 1990s that gave rise to Nielsen's original heuristics. For example, computerized toys are being developed that motivate, entice, and challenge, in innovative ways. Researchers are starting to identify design and evaluation heuristics for these and other products, and Activity 15.5 is intended to help you start thinking about them.

Activity 15.5

Allison Druin works with children to develop computerized toys, among other interactive products (Druin, 1999). From doing this research Allison and her team know that children like to:

- **be in control and not to be controlled**
- **create things**
- **express themselves**
- **be social**
- **collaborate with other children**

1. **What kind of tasks should be considered in evaluating a fluffy robot toy dog that can be programmed to move and to tell personalized stories about itself and children? The target age group for the toy is 7–9 years.**
2. **Suggest heuristics to evaluate the toy.**

Comment

1. **Tasks that you could consider: making the toy tell a story about the owner and two friends; making the toy move across the room, turn, and speak. You probably thought of others.**
2. **The heuristics could be written to cover: being in control, being flexible, supporting expression, being motivating, supporting collaboration, and being engaging. These are based on the issues raised by Druin, but the last one is aesthetic and tactile. Several of the heuristics needed would be more concerned with user experience, e.g. motivating, engaging, etc., than with usability. As developers pay more attention to user experience, particularly when developing applications for children and entertainment systems, we can expect to see heuristics that address these issues (e.g. Sutcliffe, 2002).**

Heuristic evaluation is suitable for devices that people use 'on-the-move' as it avoids some of the difficulties associated with field studies and usability evaluation in such circumstances (e.g. see Section 12.4.2 and Brewster and Dunlop, 2004 for a collection of papers on this topic). An interesting example is evaluating a mobile fax application, known

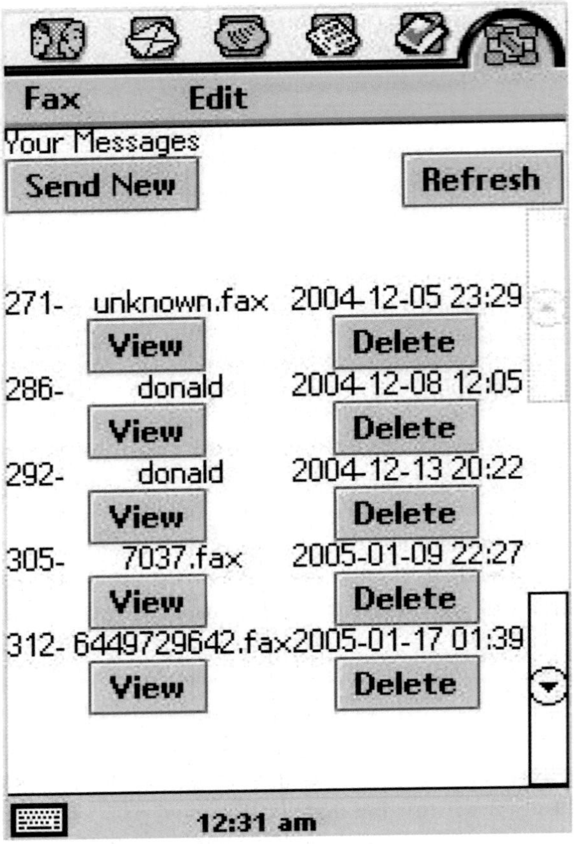

Figure 15.3 *A screen showing MoFax on a cell phone*

as MoFax (Wright *et al.*, 2005). MoFax users can send and receive faxes to conventional fax machines or to other MoFax users. This application was created to support groups working with construction industry representatives. This user group often sends faxes from place to place to show plans. Using MoFax enables team members to browse and send faxes on their cell phones while out in the field (see Figure 15.3). At the time of the usability evaluation, the developers knew there were some significant problems with the interface, so they carried out a heuristic evaluation using Nielsen's heuristics to learn more. Three expert evaluators performed the evaluation and together they identified 56 problems. Based on these results the developers redesigned MoFax.

Heuristic evaluation has also been used to evaluate ambient devices, which are abstract aesthetic peripheral displays that portray non-critical information at the periphery of the user's attention (Mankoff *et al.*, 2003). Since these devices are not designed for task performance, the researchers had to develop a set of heuristics that took this into account. They did this by developing two ambient displays: one indicated how close a bus is to the bus-stop by showing its number move upwards on a screen; the other indicated how light or dark it was outside by lightening or darkening a light display (see Figure 15.4). Then they selected a subset of Nielsen's heuristics that were applicable for this type of application and asked groups of experts to evaluate the devices using these heuristics.

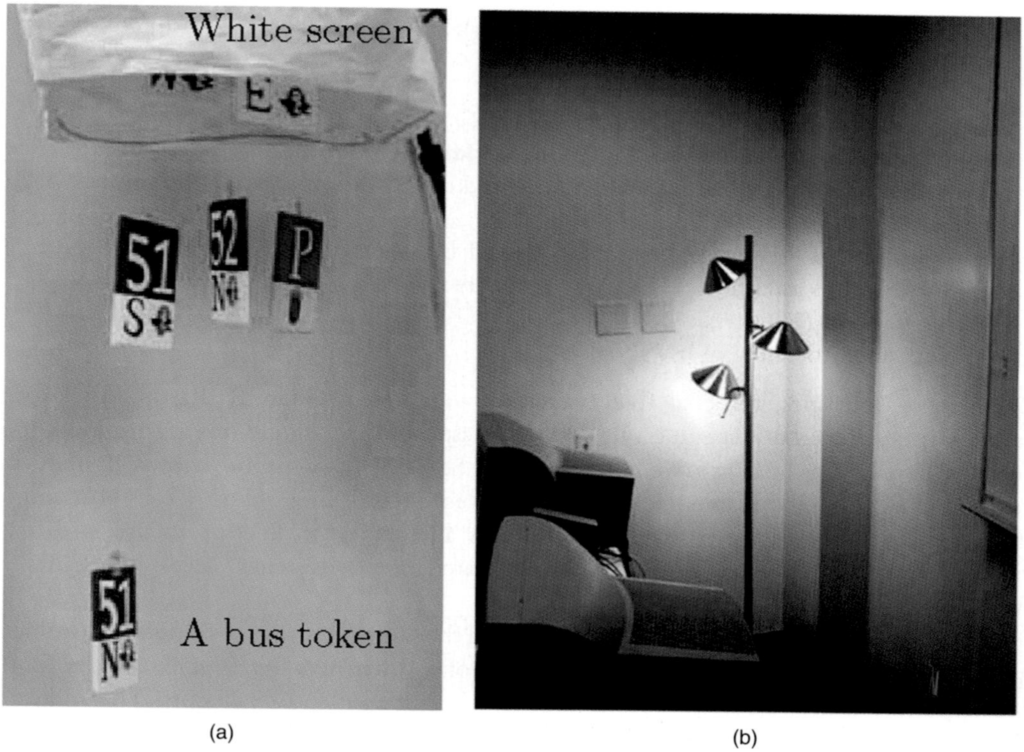

Figure 15.4 *Two ambient devices: (a) bus indicator, (b) lightness and darkness indicator*

The heuristics that were developed are listed below in the order of the number of issues that were identified using each. Those in bold were derived by the researchers, the others are Nielsen's heuristics.

- **Sufficient information design** The display should be designed to convey 'just enough' information. Too much information cramps the display, and too little makes the display less useful.

- **Consistent and intuitive mapping** Ambient displays should add minimal cognitive load. Cognitive load may be higher when users must remember what states or changes in the display mean. The display should be intuitive.
- Match between system and real world (Nielsen).
- **Visibility of state** An ambient display should be pleasing when it is placed in the intended setting.
- **Aesthetic and pleasing design** The display should be pleasing when it is placed in the intended setting.
- **Useful and relevant information** The information should be useful and relevant to the users in the intended setting.
- Visibility of system status (Nielsen).
- User control and freedom (Nielsen).
- **Easy transition to more in-depth information** If the display offers multi-leveled information, the display should make it easy and quick for users to find out more detailed information.
- **Peripherality of display** The display should be unobtrusive and remain so unless it requires the user's attention. User should be able to easily monitor the display.
- Error prevention (Nielsen).
- Flexibility and efficiency of use (Nielsen).

Using these heuristics, three to five evaluators were able to identify 40–60% of known usability issues. This study suggests two important aspects. First, different types of applications need to be evaluated using different heuristics. Second, the method by which they are derived needs to be reliable. The authors tested their set of heuristics by running a study in which they gave a survey to students and expert evaluators to use with two different systems. The results were then validated for consistency across the different evaluators.

In a follow-up study different researchers used the same heuristics with different ambient applications (Consolvo and Towle, 2005); 75% of known usability problems were found with eight evaluators and 35–55% were found with three to five evaluators. This indicates that the more evaluators you have, the more accurate the result will be.

15.2.4 Doing heuristic evaluation

Heuristic evaluation has three stages:

1. The *briefing session*, in which the experts are told what to do. A prepared script is useful as a guide and to ensure each person receives the same briefing.
2. The *evaluation period*, in which each expert typically spends 1–2 hours independently inspecting the product, using the heuristics for guidance. The experts need to take at least *two* passes through the interface. The first pass gives a feel for the flow of the

interaction and the product's scope. The second pass allows the evaluator to focus on specific interface elements in the context of the whole product, and to identify potential usability problems.
If the evaluation is for a functioning product, the evaluators need to have some specific user tasks in mind so that exploration is focused. Suggesting tasks may be helpful but many experts suggest their own tasks. However, this approach is less easy if the evaluation is done early in design when there are only screen mockups or a specification; the approach needs to be adapted to the evaluation circumstances. While working through the interface, specification, or mockups, a second person may record the problems identified, or the evaluator may think aloud. Alternatively, she may take notes herself. Experts should be encouraged to be as specific as possible and to record each problem clearly.
3. The *debriefing session*, in which the experts come together to discuss their findings and to prioritize the problems they found and suggest solutions.

The heuristics focus the experts' attention on particular issues, so selecting appropriate heuristics is critically important. Even so, there is sometimes less agreement among experts than is desirable, as discussed in the dilemma below.

There are fewer practical and ethical issues in heuristic evaluation than for other techniques because users are not involved. A week is often cited as the time needed to train experts to be evaluators (Nielsen and Mack, 1994), but this depends on the person's initial expertise. Typical users can be taught to do heuristic evaluation, although there have been claims that this approach is not very successful (Nielsen, 1994a). Some closely related methods take a team approach that involves users (Bias, 1994).

Dilemma
Problems or false alarms?

You might have the impression that heuristic evaluation is a panacea for designers, and that it can reveal all that is wrong with a design. However, it has problems. Shortly after heuristic evaluation was developed, several independent studies compared heuristic evaluation with other techniques, particularly user testing, indicating that the different approaches often identify different problems and that sometimes heuristic evaluation misses severe problems (Karat, 1994). This argues for using complementary techniques. Furthermore, heuristic evaluation should not be thought of as a replacement for user testing.

Another problem that Bill Bailey (2001) warns about is of experts reporting problems that don't exist. In other words, some of the experts' predictions

are wrong. Bailey cites analyses from three published sources showing that only around 33% of the problems reported were real usability problems, some of which were serious, others trivial. However, the heuristic evaluators missed about 21% of users' problems. Furthermore, about 43% of the problems identified by the experts were *not* problems at all; they were false alarms! Bailey points out that if we do the arithmetic and round up the numbers, what this comes down to is that only about half the problems identified are true problems. "More specifically, for every true usability problem identified, there will be a little over one false alarm (1.2) and about one half of one missed problem (0.6). If this a ... is true, heuristic evaluators tend t... more false alarms and miss m... lems than they have true hits."

How can the number of fal... or missed serious problems be... Checking that experts really ... expertise that they claim wou... but how can you do this? On... overcome these problems is to ... eral evaluators. This helps to re... impact of one person's experienc... performance. Using heuristic e... along with user testing and ot... niques is also a good idea. ■

15.3 Inspections: walkthroughs

Walkthroughs are an alternative approach to heuristic evaluation for pred... problems without doing user testing. As the name suggests, they involve walki... task with the system and noting problematic usability features. Most walkthroug... do not involve users. Others, such as pluralistic walkthroughs, involve a team t... users, developers, and usability specialists.

In this section we consider cognitive and pluralistic walkthroughs. Both we... developed for desktop systems but, similar to heuristic evaluation, can be ... web-based systems, handheld devices, and products such as VCRs.

15.3.1 Cognitive walkthroughs

"Cognitive walkthroughs involve simulating a user's problem-solving process a... in the human–computer dialog, checking to see if the user's goals and memory ... can be assumed to lead to the next correct action" (Nielsen and Mack, 1994, ... defining feature is that they focus on evaluating designs for ease of learning—a fo... motivated by observations that users learn by exploration (Wharton *et al.*, 1994). ... involved in cognitive walkthroughs are:

1. The characteristics of typical users are identified and documented and sample ... developed that focus on the aspects of the design to be evaluated. A descr...

prototype of the interface to be developed is also produced, along with a clear sequence of the actions needed for the users to complete the task.

2. A designer and one or more expert evaluators then come together to do the analysis.
3. The evaluators walk through the action sequences for each task, placing it within the context of a typical scenario, and as they do this they try to answer the following questions:
   - Will the correct action be sufficiently evident to the user? (Will the user know what to do to achieve the task?)
   - Will the user notice that the correct action is available? (Can users see the button or menu item that they should use for the next action? Is it apparent when it is needed?)
   - Will the user associate and interpret the response from the action correctly? (Will users know from the feedback that they have made a correct or incorrect choice of action?)

   In other words: will users know what to do, see how to do it, and understand from feedback whether the action was correct or not?
4. As the walkthrough is being done, a record of critical information is compiled in which:
   - The assumptions about what would cause problems and why are recorded. This involves explaining why users would face difficulties.
   - Notes about side issues and design changes are made.
   - A summary of the results is compiled.
5. The design is then revised to fix the problems presented.

It is important to document the cognitive walkthrough, keeping account of what works and what doesn't. A standardized feedback form can be used in which answers are recorded to the three bulleted questions in step 3 above. The form can also record the details outlined in points 1–4 as well as the date of the evaluation. Negative answers to any of the questions are carefully documented on a separate form, along with details of the system, its version number, the date of the evaluation, and the evaluators' names. It is also useful to document the severity of the problems, for example, how likely a problem is to occur and how serious it will be for users.

Compared with heuristic evaluation, this technique focuses more on identifying specific users' problems at a high level of detail. Hence, it has a narrow focus that is useful for certain types of systems but not others. In particular, it can be useful for applications involving complex operations to perform tasks. However, it is very time-consuming and laborious to do and needs a good understanding of the cognitive processes involved.

Example: find a book at `www.Amazon.com`

This example shows a cognitive walkthrough of buying this book at `www.Amazon.com`.

Task: to buy a copy of this book from `www.Amazon.com`

Typical users: students who use the web regularly

The steps to complete the task are given below. Note that the interface for `www.Amazon.com` may have changed since we did our evaluation.

Step 1. Selecting the correct category of goods on the homepage
Q: Will users know what to do?
Answer: Yes—they know that they must find 'books.'

Q: Will users see how to do it?
Answer: Yes—they have seen menus before and will know to select the appropriate item and click go.

Q: Will users understand from feedback whether the action was correct or not?
Answer: Yes—their action takes them to a form that they need to complete to search for the book.

Step 2. Completing the form

Q: Will users know what to do?
Answer: Yes—the online form is like a paper form so they know they have to complete it.
Answer: No—they may not realize that the form has defaults to prevent inappropriate answers because this is different from a paper form.

Q: Will users see how to do it?
Answer: Yes—it is clear where the information goes and there is a button to tell the system to search for the book.

Q: Will users understand from feedback whether the action was correct or not?
Answer: Yes—they are taken to a picture of the book, a description, and purchase details.

Activity 15.6

Activity 15.3 asked you to do a heuristic evaluation of `REI.com` or a similar e-commerce retail site. Now go back to that site and do a cognitive walkthrough to buy something, say a pair of skis. When you have completed the evaluation, compare your findings from the cognitive walkthrough technique with those from heuristic evaluation.

Comment

You probably found that the cognitive walkthrough took longer than the heuristic evaluation for evaluating the same part of the site because it examines each step of a task. Consequently, you probably did not see as much of the website. It is likely that you also got much more detailed findings from the

cognitive walkthrough. Cognitive walkthrough is a useful technique for examining a small part of a system in detail, whereas heuristic evaluation is useful for examining whole or parts of systems. As the name indicates, the cognitive walkthrough focuses on the cognitive aspects of interacting with the system. The technique was developed before there was much emphasis on aesthetic design and other user experience goals. The effort and motor skills for physical interaction are also not a focus.

Variation of the cognitive walkthrough

A useful variation on this theme is provided by Rick Spencer of Microsoft, who adapted the cognitive walkthrough technique to make it more effective with a team that was developing an interactive development environment (IDE) (Spencer, 2000). When used in its original state, there were two major problems. First, answering the three questions in step 3 and discussing the answers took too long. Second, designers tended to be defensive, often invoking long explanations of cognitive theory to justify their designs. This second problem was particularly difficult because it undermined the efficacy of the technique and the social relationships of team members. In order to cope with these problems, Rick Spencer adapted the technique by reducing the number of questions and curtailing discussion. This meant that the analysis was more coarse-grained but could be completed in much less time (about 2.5 hours). He also identified a leader, the usability specialist, and set strong ground rules for the session, including a ban on defending a design, debating cognitive theory, or doing designs on the fly.

These adaptations made the technique more usable, despite losing some of the detail from the analysis. Perhaps most important of all, Spencer directed the social interactions of the design team so that they achieved their goals.

15.3.2 Pluralistic walkthroughs

"Pluralistic walkthroughs are another type of walkthrough in which users, developers and usability experts work together to step through a [task] scenario, discussing usability issues associated with dialog elements involved in the scenario steps" (Nielsen and Mack, 1994, p. 5). Each group of experts is asked to assume the role of typical users. The walkthroughs are then done by following a sequence of steps (Bias, 1994):

1. Scenarios are developed in the form of a series of hardcopy screens representing a single path through the interface. Often just two or a few screens are developed.
2. The scenarios are presented to the panel of evaluators and the panelists are asked to write down the sequence of actions they would take to move from one screen to another. They do this individually without conferring with one another.

3. When everyone has written down their actions, the panelists discuss the actions that they suggested for that round of the review. Usually, the representative users go first so that they are not influenced by the other panel members and are not deterred from speaking. Next the usability experts present their findings, and finally the developers offer their comments.
4. Then the panel moves on to the next round of screens. This process continues until all the scenarios have been evaluated.

The benefits of pluralistic walkthroughs include a strong focus on users' tasks at a detailed level, i.e. looking at the steps taken. This level of analysis can be invaluable for certain kinds of systems, such as safety-critical ones, where a usability problem identified for a single step could be critical to its safety or efficiency. The approach lends itself well to participatory design practices by involving a multidisciplinary team in which users play a key role. Furthermore, the group brings a variety of expertise and opinions for interpreting each stage of an interaction. Limitations include having to get all the experts together at once and then proceed at the rate of the slowest. Furthermore, only a limited number of scenarios, and hence paths through the interface, can usually be explored because of time constraints.

15.4 Predictive models

Similar to inspection methods, predictive models evaluate a system without testing users, but rather than involving expert evaluators role-playing users it does so by involving experts using formulas to derive various measures of user performance. Predictive modeling techniques provide estimates of the efficiency of different systems for various kinds of tasks. For example, a cell phone designer might choose to use such a predictive method because it can enable her to determine accurately which is the optimal layout of keys on a cell phone for allowing common operations to be performed.

A well-known predictive modeling technique is GOMS. This is a generic term used to refer to a family of models that vary in their granularity concerning the aspects of a user's performance they model and make predictions about. These include the time it takes to perform tasks and the most effective strategies to use when performing tasks. The models have been used mainly to predict user performance when comparing different applications and devices. Below we describe two of the most well-known members of the GOMS family: the GOMS model and its 'daughter,' the keystroke level model.

15.4.1 The GOMS model

The GOMS model was developed in the early 1980s by Stu Card, Tom Moran, and Alan Newell (Card *et al.*, 1983). It was an attempt to model the knowledge and cognitive processes involved when users interact with systems. The term 'GOMS' is an acronym which stands for *goals, operators, methods, and selection rules:*

- *Goals* refer to a particular state the user wants to achieve, e.g. find a website on interaction design.
- *Operators* refer to the cognitive processes and physical actions that need to be performed in order to attain those goals, e.g. decide on which search engine to use, think up and then enter keywords in search engine. The difference between a goal and an operator is that a goal is obtained and an operator is executed.
- *Methods* are learned procedures for accomplishing the goals. They consist of the exact sequence of steps required, e.g. drag mouse over entry field, type in keywords, press the 'go' button.
- *Selection rules* are used to determine which method to select when there is more than one available for a given stage of a task. For example, once keywords have been entered into a search engine entry field, many search engines allow users to press the return key on the keyboard or click the 'go' button using the mouse to progress the search. A selection rule would determine which of these two methods to use in the particular instance. Below is a detailed example of a GOMS model for deleting a word in a sentence using Microsoft Word.

Goal: delete a word in a sentence
Method for accomplishing goal of deleting a word using menu option:

Step 1. Recall that word to be deleted has to be highlighted
Step 2. Recall that command is 'cut'
Step 3. Recall that command 'cut' is in edit menu
Step 4. Accomplish goal of selecting and executing the 'cut' command
Step 5. Return with goal accomplished

Method for accomplishing goal of deleting a word using delete key:

Step 1. Recall where to position cursor in relation to word to be deleted
Step 2. Recall which key is delete key
Step 3. Press 'delete' key to delete each letter
Step 4. Return with goal accomplished

Operators to use in the above methods:

Click mouse
Drag cursor over text
Select menu
Move cursor to command
Press keyboard key

Selection rules to decide which method to use:

1: Delete text using mouse and selecting from menu if large amount of text is to be deleted
2: Delete text using delete key if small number of letters are to be deleted

"Okay, well, I think we all get the gist of where Jerry was going with the site map."

15.4.2 The keystroke level model

The keystroke level model differs from the GOMS model in that it provides actual numerical predictions of user performance. Tasks can be compared in terms of the time it takes to perform them when using different strategies. The main benefit of making these kinds of quantitative predictions is that different features of systems and applications can be easily compared to see which might be the most effective for performing specific kinds of tasks.

When developing the keystroke level model, Card *et al.* (1983) analyzed the findings of many empirical studies of actual user performance in order to derive a standard set of approximate times for the main kinds of operators used during a task. In so doing, they were able to come up with the average time it takes to carry out common physical actions (e.g. press a key, click on a mouse button) together with other aspects of user–computer interaction (e.g. the time it takes to decide what to do, the system response rate). Below are the core times they proposed for these (note how much variability there is in the time it takes to press a key for users with different typing skills).

Operator name	Description	Time (sec)
K	Pressing a single key or button Skilled typist (55 wpm) Average typist (40 wpm) User unfamiliar with the keyboard Pressing shift or control key	0.35 (average) 0.22 0.28 1.20 0.08
P	Pointing with a mouse or other device to a target on a display	1.10
P_1	Clicking the mouse or similar device	0.20
H	Homing hands on the keyboard or other device	0.40
D	Draw a line using a mouse	Variable depending on the length of line
M	Mentally prepare to do something, e.g. make a decision	1.35
R(t)	System response time—counted only if it causes the user to wait when carrying out their task	*t*

The predicted time it takes to execute a given task is then calculated by describing the sequence of actions involved and then summing together the approximate times that each one will take:

$$T_{\text{execute}} = T_{\text{K}} + T_{\text{P}} + T_{\text{H}} + T_{\text{D}} + T_{\text{M}} + T_{\text{R}}$$

For example, consider how long it would take to insert the word *not* into the following sentence, using a wordprocessor like Microsoft Word:

Running through the streets naked is normal.

So that it becomes:

Running through the streets naked is not normal.

First we need to decide what the user will do. We are assuming that she will have read the sentences beforehand and so start our calculation at the point where she is about to carry out the requested task. To begin she will need to think what method to select. So we first note a mental event (M operator). Next she will need to move the cursor into the appropriate point of the sentence. So we note an H operator (i.e. reach for the mouse). The remaining sequence of operators are then: position the mouse before the word normal (P), click the mouse button (P_1), move hand from mouse over the keyboard ready to type (H), think about which letters to type (M), type the letters *n*, *o*, and *t* (3K), and finally press the spacebar (K).

The times for each of these operators can then be worked out:

Mentally prepare (M)	1.35
Reach for the mouse (H)	0.40
Position mouse before the word 'normal' (P)	1.10
Click mouse (P_1)	0.20
Move hands to home position on keys (H)	0.40
Mentally prepare (M)	1.35
Type '*n*' (good typist) (K)	0.22
Type '*o*' (K)	0.22
Type '*t*' (K)	0.22
Type 'space' (K)	0.22
Total predicted time:	5.68 seconds

When there are many components to add up, it is often easier to put together all the same kinds of operators. For example, the above can be rewritten as: $2(M) + 2(H) + 1(P) + 1(P_1) + 4\,(K) = 2.70 + 0.88 + 1.10 + 0.2 + 0.80 = 5.68$ seconds.

Over 5 seconds seems a long time to insert a word into a sentence, especially for a good typist. Having made our calculation it is useful to look back at the various decisions made. For example, we may want to think why we included a mental operator before typing the letters *n*, *o*, and *t* but not one before any of the other physical actions. Was this necessary? Perhaps we don't need to include it. The decision when to include a time for mentally preparing for a physical action is one of the main difficulties with using the keystroke level model. Sometimes it is obvious when to include one (especially if the task requires making a decision), but for other times it can seem quite arbitrary. Another problem is that, just as typing skills vary between individuals, so too do the mental preparation times people spend thinking about what to do. Mental preparation can vary from under 0.5 of a second to well over a minute. Practice at modeling similar kinds of tasks together with comparing them with actual times taken can help overcome these problems. Ensuring that decisions are applied consistently also helps. For example, if comparisons between two prototypes are made, apply the same decisions to each.

Activity 15.7

As described in the GOMS model above there are two main ways words can be deleted in a sentence when using a word-processor like Word. These are:

1. Deleting each letter of the word individually by using the delete key.
2. Highlighting the word using the mouse and then deleting the highlighted section in one go.

Which of the two methods is quickest for deleting the word 'not' from the following sentence?

I do not like using the keystroke level model.

Comment

1. Our analysis for method 1 is:

Mentally prepare	M	1.35
Reach for mouse	H	0.40
Move cursor one space after the word 'not'	P	1.10
Click mouse	P_1	0.20
Home in on delete key	H	0.40
Press delete key 4 times to remove word plus a space (using value for good typist)	4(K)	0.88

Total predicted time = 4.33 seconds

2. Our analysis for method 2 is:

Mentally prepare	M	1.35
Reach for mouse	H	0.40
Move cursor to just before the word 'not'	P	1.10
Click and hold mouse button down (half a P_1)	P_1	0.10
Drag the mouse across 'not' and one space	P	1.10
Release the mouse button (half a P_1)	P_1	0.10
Home in on delete key	H	0.40
Press delete key (using value for good typist)	K	0.22

Total predicted time = 4.77 seconds

The result seems counter-intuitive. Why do you think this is? The reason is that the amount of time required to select the letters to be deleted is longer for the second method than pressing the delete key three times in the first method. If the word had been any longer, for example, 'keystroke,' then the keystroke analysis would have predicted the opposite. There are also other ways of deleting words, such as double clicking on the word (to select it) and then either pressing the delete key or the combination of ctrl+X keys. What do you think the keystroke level model would predict for either of these two methods?

CASE STUDY 15.1
Using GOMS in the redesign of a phone-based response system

Usability consultant Bill Killam and his colleagues worked with the US Internal Revenue Services (IRS) to evaluate and redesign the telephone response information system (TRIS). The goal of TRIS is to provide the general public with advice about filling out a tax return—and those of you who have to do this know only too well how complex it is. Although this case study is situated in the USA, such phone-based information systems are widespread across the world.

Typically, telephone answering systems can be frustrating to use. Have you been annoyed by the long menus of options such systems provide when you are trying to buy a train ticket or when making an appointment for a technician to fix your phone line? What happens is that you work your way through several different menu systems, selecting an option from the first list of, say, seven choices, only to find that now you must choose from another list of five alternatives. Then, having spent several minutes doing this, you discover that you made the wrong choice back in the first menu, so you have to start again. Does this sound familiar? Other problems are that often there are too many options to remember, and none of them seems to be the right one for you.

The usability specialists used the GOMS keystroke level model to predict how well a redesigned user interface compared with the original TRIS interface for supporting users' tasks. In addition they also did usability testing.

15.4.3 Benefits and limitations of GOMS

One of the main attractions of the GOMS approach is that it allows comparative analyses to be performed for different interfaces, prototypes, or specifications relatively easily. Since its inception, a number of researchers have used the method, reporting on its success for comparing the efficacy of different computer-based systems. One of the most well known is Project Ernestine (Gray *et al.*, 1993). This study was carried out to determine if a proposed new workstation, that was ergonomically designed, would improve telephone call operators' performance. Empirical data collected for a range of operator tasks using the existing system was compared with hypothetical data deduced from doing a GOMS analysis for the same set of tasks for the proposed new system.

Similar to the activity above, the outcome of the study was counter-intuitive. When comparing the GOMS predictions for the proposed system with the empirical data collected for the existing system, the researchers discovered that several tasks would take longer to accomplish. Moreover, their analysis was able to show why this might be the case: certain keystrokes would need to be performed at critical times during a task rather than during slack periods (as was the case with the existing system). Thus, rather than carrying out these keystrokes in parallel when talking with a customer (as they did with the existing system) they would need to do them sequentially—hence the predicted increase in time spent on the overall task. This suggested to the researchers that, overall, the proposed system would actually slow down the operators rather than improve their performance. On the basis of this study, they were able to advise the phone company against purchasing the new workstations, saving them from investing in a potentially inefficient technology.

While this study has shown that GOMS can be useful in helping make decisions about the effectiveness of new products, it is not often used for evaluation purposes. Part of the problem is its highly limited scope: it can only really model computer-based tasks that involve a small set of highly routine data-entry type tasks. Furthermore, it is intended to be used only to predict expert performance, and does not allow for errors to be modeled. This makes it much more difficult (and sometimes impossible) to predict how an average user will carry out their tasks when using a range of systems, especially those that have been designed to be very flexible in the way they can be used. In most situations, it isn't possible to predict how users will perform. Many *unpredictable* factors come into play including individual differences among users, fatigue, mental workload, learning effects, and social and organizational factors. For example, most people do not carry out their tasks sequentially but will be constantly multi-tasking, dealing with interruptions and talking to others.

A dilemma with predictive models, therefore, is that they can only really make predictions about predictable behavior. Given that most people are unpredictable in the way they behave, it makes it difficult to use them as a way of evaluating how systems will be used in real-world contexts. They can, however, provide useful estimates for comparing the efficiency of different methods of completing tasks, particularly if the tasks are short and clearly defined.

15.4.4 Fitts' law

Fitts' Law (1954) predicts the time it takes to reach a target using a pointing device. It was originally used in human factors research to model the relationship between speed and accuracy when moving towards a target on a display. In interaction design it has been used to describe the time it takes to point at a target, based on the size of the object and the distance to the object. Specifically, it is used to model the time it takes to use a mouse and other input devices to click on objects on a screen. One of its main benefits is that it can help designers decide where to locate buttons, what size they should be, and how close together they should be on a screen display. The law states that:

$$T = k \log_2(D/S + 1.0)$$

where

T = time to move the pointer to a target

D = distance between the pointer and the target

S = size of the target

k is a constant of approximately 200 msec/bit

In a nutshell, the bigger the target the easier and quicker it is to reach it. This is why interfaces that have big buttons are easier to use than interfaces that present lots of tiny buttons crammed together. Fitts' Law also predicts that the most quickly accessed targets on any computer display are the four corners of the screen. This is because of their 'pinning' action, i.e. the sides of the display constrain the user from over-stepping the target. However, as pointed out by Tog on his AskTog website, corners seem strangely to be avoided at all costs by designers.

Fitts' Law, therefore, can be useful for evaluating systems where the time to physically locate an object is critical to the task at hand. In particular, it can help designers think about where to locate objects on the screen in relation to each other. This is especially useful for mobile devices, where there is limited space for placing icons and buttons on the screen. For example, in a study carried out by Nokia, Fitts' Law was used to predict expert text entry rates for several input methods on a 12-key cell phone keypad (Silfverberg *et al.*, 2000). The study helped the designers make decisions about the size of keys, their positioning, and the sequences of presses to perform common tasks for the mobile device. Trade-offs between the size of a device, and accuracy of using it, were made with the help of calculations from this model. Comparisons of speed and accuracy of text entry on cell phones have also been informed by the application of Fitts' Law (MacKenzie and Soukoreff, 2002).

Activity 15.8

Microsoft toolbars provide the user with the option of displaying a label below each tool. Give a reason why labeled tools may be accessed faster. (Assume that the user knows the tool and does not need the label to identify it.)

Comment

The label becomes part of the target and hence the target gets bigger. As we mentioned earlier, bigger targets can be accessed more quickly.

Furthermore, tool icons that don't have labels are likely to be placed closer together so they are more crowded. Spreading the icons further apart creates buffer zones of space around the icons so that if users accidentally go past the target

they will be less likely to select the wrong icon. When the icons are crowded together the user is at greater risk of accidentally overshooting and selecting the wrong icon. The same is true of menus, where the items are closely bunched together.

Assignment

This assignment continues the work you did on the web-based ticketing system at the end of Chapters 10, 11, and 14. The aim of this assignment is to evaluate the prototypes produced in the assignment of Chapter 11 using heuristic evaluation.

(a) Decide on an appropriate set of heuristics and perform a heuristic evaluation of one of the prototypes you designed in Chapter 11.

(b) Based on this evaluation, redesign the prototype to overcome the problems you encountered.

(c) Compare the findings from this evaluation with those from the usability testing in the previous chapter. What differences do you observe? Which evaluation approach do you prefer and why?

(d) Now you have applied methods from each evaluation approach: usability testing, field studies, and analytical evaluation. Draw up a table that summarizes the findings, benefits, costs, and limitations of each.

Summary

This chapter presented analytical evaluations, focusing on heuristic evaluation and walkthroughs which are done by experts who role-play users' interactions with designs, prototypes, and specifications and then offer their opinions. Heuristic evaluation and walkthroughs offer the evaluator a structure to guide the evaluation process.

The GOMS and keystroke level models, and Fitts' Law can be used to predict user performance. These techniques can be useful for determining whether a proposed interface, system, or keypad layout will be optimal. Typically they are used to compare different designs for a small sequence of tasks. These methods are labor-intensive so do not scale well for large systems.

Key points

- Inspections can be used for evaluating requirements, mockups, functional prototypes, or systems.
- User testing and heuristic evaluation often reveal different usability problems.
- Other types of inspections used in interaction design include pluralistic and cognitive walkthroughs.
- Walkthroughs are very focused and so are suitable for evaluating small parts of systems.
- The GOMS and keystroke level models and Fitts' Law can be used to predict expert, error-free performance for certain kinds of tasks.

- Predictive models require neither users nor experts, but the evaluators must be skilled in applying the models.
- Predictive models are used to evaluate systems with limited, clearly defined functionality such as data entry applications, and key-press sequences for cell phones and other hand-held devices.

Further Reading

CARD, S.K., MORAN, T.P. and NEWELL, A. (1983) *The Psychology of Human Computer Interaction*. Lawrence Erlbaum Associates. This seminal book describes GOMS and the keystroke level model.

COCKTON, G. and WOOLRYCH, A. (2001) Understanding inspection methods: lessons from an assessment of heuristic evaluation. In A. Blandford and J. Vanderdonckt (eds), *People & Computers XV*. Springer-Verlag, pp. 171–191. This paper evaluates the efficacy of heuristic evaluation, and questions whether it lives up to the claims made about it.

HORTON, S. (2005) *Access by Design: A Guide to Universal Usability for Web Designers*. New Riders Press. This book challenges the belief that designing for universal access is a burden for designers. It demonstrates again and again that everyone benefits from universal usability and provides important guidelines for designers.

KOYANI, S.J., BAILEY, R.W. and NALL, J.R. (2004) *Research-Based Web Design and Usability Heuristics*. National Cancer Institute. This book contains a thorough review of usability guidelines derived from empirical research. The collection is impressive but each guideline needs to be evaluated and used thoughtfully.

MACKENZIE, I.S. (1992) Fitts' law as a research and design tool in human–computer interaction. *Human–Computer Interaction*, **7**, 91–139. This early paper by Scott Mackenzie, an expert in the use of Fitts' Law, provides a detailed discussion of how it can be used in HCI.

MACKENZIE, I.S. and SOUKOREFF, R.W. (2002) Text entry for mobile computing: models and methods, theory and practice. *Human–Computer Interaction*, **17**, 147–198. This later paper provides a useful survey of mobile text-entry techniques and discusses how Fitts' Law can inform their design.

MANKOFF, J., DEY, A.K., HSICH, G., KIENTZ, J. and LEDERER, M.A. (2003) Heuristic evaluation of ambient devices. *Proceedings of CHI 2003, ACM*, **5**(1), 169–176. This paper will be useful for those wishing to derive rigorous heuristics for new kinds of applications. It illustrates how different heuristics are needed for different applications.

NIELSEN, J. and MACK, R.L. (eds) (1994) *Usability Inspection Methods*. John Wiley & Sons. This book contains an edited collection of chapters on a variety of usability inspection methods. There is a detailed description of heuristic evaluation and walkthroughs and comparisons of these techniques with other evaluation techniques, particularly user testing. Jakob Nielsen's website `useit.com` provides additional information and advice on website design. See particularly `http://www.useit.com/papers/heuristic/` (accessed February 2006) for more recent work.

PREECE, J. (2000) *Online Communities: Designing Usability, Supporting Sociability*. John Wiley & Sons. This book is about the usability and sociability design of online communities. It suggests guidelines that can be used as a basis for heuristics.

INTERVIEW with Jakob Nielsen

Jakob Nielsen is a pioneer of heuristic evaluation. He is currently principal of the Nielsen Norman Consultancy Group and the author of numerous articles and books, including his recent book, *Designing Web Usability* (New Riders Publishing). He is well known for his regular sound bites on usability which for many years have appeared at `useit.com`. In this interview Jakob talks about heuristic evaluation, why he developed the technique, and how it can be applied to the web.

JP: Jakob, why did you create heuristic evaluation?

JN: It is part of a larger mission I was on in the mid-'80s, which was to simplify usability engineering, to get more people using what I call 'discount usability engineering.' The idea was to come up with several simplified methods that would be very easy and fast to use. Heuristic evaluation can be used for any design project or any stage in the design process, without budgetary constraints. To succeed it had to be fast, cheap, and useful.

JP: How can it be adapted for the web?

JN: I think it applies just as much to the web, actually if anything more, because a typical website will have tens of thousands of pages. A big one may have hundreds of thousands of pages, much too much to be assessed using traditional usability evaluation methods such as user testing. User testing is good for testing the homepage or the main navigation system. But if you look at the individual pages, there is no way that you can really test them. Even with the discount approach, which would involve five users, it would still be hard to test all the pages. So all you are left with is the notion of doing a heuristic evaluation, where you just have a few people look at the majority of pages and judge them according to the heuristics. Now the heuristics are somewhat different, because people behave differently on the web. They are more ruthless about getting a very quick glance at what is on a page and if they don't understand it then leaving it. Typically application users work a little harder at learning an application. The basic heuristics that I developed a long time ago are universal, so they apply to the web as well. But as well as these global heuristics that are always true, for example 'consistency,' there can be specialized heuristics that apply to particular systems. But most evaluators use the general heuristics because the web is still evolving and we are still in the process of determining what the web-specific heuristics should be.

JP: So how do you advise designers to go about evaluating a really large website?

JN: Well, you cannot actually test every page. Also, there is another problem: developing a large website is incredibly collaborative and involves a lot of different people. There may be a central team in charge of things like the homepage, the overall appearance, and the overall navigation system. But when it comes to making a product page, it is the product-marketing manager of, say, Kentucky who is in charge of that. The division in Kentucky knows about the product line and the people back at headquarters have no clue about the details. That's why they have to do their own evaluations in that department. The big thing right now is that this is not being done, developers are not evaluating enough. That's one of the reasons I want to push the heuristic evaluation method even further to get it out to all the website contributors. The uptake of usability methods has dramatically improved from five years ago, when many companies didn't have a clue, but the need today is still great because of the phenomenal development of the web.

JP: When should you start doing heuristic evaluation?

JN: You should start quite early, maybe not quite as early as testing a very rough mockup, but as soon as there is a slightly more substantial prototype. For example, if you are building a website that might eventually have ten thousand pages, it would be appropriate to do a heuristic evaluation of, say, the first ten to twenty pages. By doing this you would catch quite a lot of usability problems.

JP: How do you combine user testing and heuristic evaluation?

JN: I suggest a sandwich model where you layer them on top of each other. Do some early user testing of two or three drawings. Develop the ideas somewhat, then do a heuristic evaluation. Then evolve the design further, do some user tests, evolve it and do heuristic evaluation, and so on. When the design is nearing completion, heuristic evaluation is very useful particularly for a very large design.

JP: So, do you have a story to tell us about your consulting experiences, something that opened your eyes or amused you?

JN: Well, my most interesting project started when I received an email from a co-founder of a large company who wanted my opinion on a new idea. We met and he explained his idea and because I know a lot about usability, including research studies, I could warn him that it wouldn't work—it was doomed. This was very satisfying and seems like the true role for a usability consultant. I think usability consultants should have this level of insight. It is not enough to just clean up after somebody makes the mistake of starting the wrong project or produces a poor design. We really should help define which projects should be done in the first place. Our role is to help identify options for really improving people's lives, for developing products that are considerably more efficient, easier or faster to learn, or whatever the criteria are. That is the ultimate goal of our entire field.

JP: Have there been any changes in the way heuristic evaluation and discount usability methods are used or perceived?

JN: I have changed my preferred approach to heuristic evaluation from emphasizing a small set of general heuristics to emphasizing a large set of highly specific usability guidelines. I did this because there are now millions of people who perform user interface design without knowing anything about general HCI principles, and it's difficult for these people to apply general heuristics correctly. One of my earliest research results for heuristic evaluation is that the method works best with experienced evaluators who have a deep understanding of usability. All very well, but when a team doesn't have experienced usability professionals on staff, what should it do? That's where the specific guidelines come into play. When you tell people, for example, that search should be represented on a website by a type-in box on every page and that the box should be at least 27 characters wide, then you are giving them evaluation criteria that anybody can apply without knowing the theory. For example, my group developed a set of 75 usability guidelines for the design of the public relations area of a corporate website. There are guidelines for everything from the way to present press releases online to how to show the PR department's contact information. These guidelines are based on our own user testing of a broad range of journalists working in newspapers, magazines, and broadcast media in several different countries, so we know that the guidelines represent the needs and wants of the target audience. In real life, PR information is placed on a website by the PR department, and they don't have time to conduct their own user testing with journalists. Neither does the typical PR professional have any educational background in HCI. Thus, I don't think that the broad list of general heuristics would do them much good, but we know from several examples that a company's PR pages get much better when the PR group has evaluated it with the 75 detailed guidelines.

JP: What about changes regarding usability in general?

JN: The general trend has been toward hugely increased investment in usability around the world. I don't think anybody has the real numbers, but I would not be surprised if the amount of resources allocated to usability increased by a thousand percent or more from 1995 to 2005. Of course, this is not nearly enough, because during the same ten years, the number of websites increased by 87,372%. In other words, we are falling behind by a factor of about 87. This is why discount usability engineering is more important than ever.

JP: And how do you think the web will develop? What will we see next, what do you expect the future to bring?

JN: I hope we will abandon the page metaphor and reach back to the earlier days of hypertext. There are other ideas that would help people navigate the web better. The web is really an 'article-reading' interface. My website `useit.com`, for example, is mainly articles, but for many other things people need a different interface, the current interface just does not work. I hope we will evolve a more interesting, useful interface that I'll call the 'Internet desktop,' which would have a control panel for your own environment, or another metaphor would be 'your personal secretary.' Instead of the old goal where the computer spits out more information, the goal would be for the computer to protect you from too much information. You shouldn't have to actually go and read all those webpages. You should have something that would help you prioritize your time so you would get the most out of the web. But, pragmatically speaking, these are not going to come any time soon. My prediction has been that Explorer Version 8 will be the first good web browser and that is still my prediction. The more short-term prediction is really that designers will take much more responsibility for content and usability of the web. We need to write webpages so that people can read them. For instance, we need headlines that make sense. Even something as simple as a headline is a user interface, because it's now being used interactively, not as in a magazine where you just look at it. So writing the headline, writing the content, designing the navigation are jobs for the individual website designers. In combination, such decisions are really defining the user experience of the network economy. That's why we really have an obligation, every one of us, because we are building the new world and if the new world turns out to be miserable, we have only ourselves to blame, not Bill Gates. We've got to design the web for the way users behave.

JP: Finally, can heuristic evaluation be used to evaluate mobile systems and games?

JN: I only have direct experience from mobile devices, and heuristic evaluation certainly works very well in this domain. You can identify a lot of issues with a phone or other mobile user experience by using exactly the same heuristics as you would for any other platform. However, you have to interpret the heuristics in the context of the smaller screen, which changes their relative importance. For example, say that a user selects a headline from a list of news stories on a mobile device, the next screen will usually be the full text of the story. You might expect that the standard heuristic "visibility of system status" should imply that the system should provide feedback by repeating the selected headline on top of the story. And that's indeed what I would recommend for a Web page. But on a small screen, it's better to devote more of the space to new information and assume that the user can remember the headline from the previous screen. This doesn't violate the heuristic "recognition rather than recall" because you don't need to use the exact wording of the headline for anything while reading the typical news story. If the headline were in fact used on the next screen, then it should be repeated, in order to minimize the user's memory load.

Games are a different matter. I haven't done such a project, so I don't know for a fact, but I suspect that traditional heuristic evaluation might help on the limited question of evaluating the controls of a game. Games are no fun if you can't figure out how to play them, For example, the heuristic for "consistency and standards", would indicate that if there's a certain way to pick up guns, it should be the same for all forms of guns. Similarly if there's a certain button on the controller that's used to shoot the gun in all other games then our game should use the same button. However, I don't think that the standard heuristics would be very helpful in evaluating the gameplay quality of a game. It's hard to say, for example, whether a game like Civilization should have fewer raging barbarians, or how much more food should be grown on a tile if you irrigate it. It's possible that one could discover a different set of heuristics to help make such decisions, maybe by studying how successful games designers make their trade-offs. ■

References

Abowd, G. and Mynatt, E. (2000) Charting past, present, and future research in ubiquitous computing. *ACM Transactions on Computer–Human Interaction* **7**(1), 29–58.

Abowd, G.D., Atkeson, C.G., Bobick, A.F., Essa, I.A., MacIntyre, B., Mynatt, E.D. and Starner, T.E. (2000) Living laboratories: the future computing environments group at the Georgia Institute of Technology. In CHI '00 Extended Abstracts on Human Factors in Computing Systems (The Hague, The Netherlands, April 1–6, 2000). *CHI '00*. ACM Press, New York, pp. 215–216.

Ackermann, M.S. and Halverson, C.A. (2000) Re-examining organizational memory. *Communications of the ACM* **43**(1), 58–64.

Adams, A. and Blandford, A. (2005) Social empowerment and exclusion: a case study on digital libraries. *ACM Transactions on Computer–Human Interaction* **12**(2), 174–200.

Alexander, I.F. and Maiden, N. (2004) *Scenarios, Stories and Use Cases*. John Wiley & Sons, New York.

Allison, D., Wills, B., Bowman, D., Wineman, J. and Hodges, L. (1997) The virtual reality gorilla exhibit. *IEEE Computer Graphics and Applications*, 30–38.

Alty, J.L. (1991) Multimedia—what is it and how do we exploit it? In D. Diaper and N. Hammond (eds), *People and Computers IV*. Cambridge University Press, Cambridge.

Andrews, D., Preece, J. and Turoff, M. (2001) A conceptual framework for demographic groups resistant to online community interaction. In *Proceedings of IEEE Hawaiian International Conference on System Science (HICSS)*.

Andrews, D., Nonnecke, B. and Preece, J. (2003) Electronic survey methodology: a case study in reaching hard-to-involve internet users. *International Journal of Human–Computer Interaction* **16**(2), 185–210.

Annett, J. and Duncan, K.D. (1967) Task analysis and training design. *Occupational Psychology* **41**, 211–221.

Apple Computer Inc. (1987) *Human Interface Guidelines*. Addison-Wesley, Harlow, Essex.

Armitage, J. (2004) Are agile methods good for design? *ACM Interactions* **Jan/Feb**, 14–23.

Armitage, U. (2004) Navigation and learning in electronic texts. PhD thesis, Centre for HCI Design, City University London.

Arroyo, E., Bonnanni, L. and Selker, T. (2005) WaterBot: exploring feedback and persuasive techniques at the sink. In *CHI Proceedings*. ACM Press, New York, pp. 631–639.

Atkinson, P. and Hammersley, M. (1994) Ethnography and participant observation. In N.K. Denzin and Y.S. Lincoln (eds), *Handbook of Qualitative Research*. Sage, London.

Austin, J.L. (1962) *How to Do Things with Words*. Harvard University Press, Cambridge, MA.

Bailey, B. (2000) How to improve design decisions by reducing reliance on superstition. Let's start with Miller's Magic 72. Human Factors International, Inc. www.humanfactors.com

Bajura, M., Fuchs, H. and Ohbuchi, R. (1992) Merging virtual objects with the real world: seeing ultrasound imagery within the patient. In *Proceedings of SIGGRAPH '92. Computer Graphics* **26**(2), 203–210.

Baker, M., Casey, R., Keyes, B. and Yanco, H.A. (2004) Improved interfaces for human–robot interaction in urban search and rescue. In *Proceedings of the IEEE Conference on Systems, Man and Cybernetics*, October.

Barnard, P.J., Hammond, N., Maclean, A. and Morten, J. (1982) Learning and remembering interactive commands in a text editing task. *Behavior and Information Technology* **1**, 347–358.

Bates, J. (1994) The role of emotion in believable characters. *Communications of the ACM* **37**(7), 122–125.

Baudel, T. and Beaudouin-Lafon, M. (1993) CHARADE: remote control of objects using free-hand gestures. *Communications of the ACM* **36**, 28–35.

Baum, F.L. and Denslow, W. (1900) *The Wizard of Oz*. Random House, New York.

Baym, N. (1997) Interpreting soap operas and creating community: inside an electronic fan culture. In S. Kiesler (ed.), *Culture of the Internet*. Lawrence Erlbaum Associates, Hillsdale, NJ, pp. 103–119.

Beck, K. (2000) *eXtreme Programming Explained: Embrace Change*. Addison-Wesley, Harlow, Essex.

Bederson, B.B. and Shneiderman, B. (eds) (2003) *The Craft of Information Visualization: Readings and Reflections*. Morgan Kaufmann, San Francisco, CA.

Bekker, M., Olson, J. and Olso, G. (1995) Analysis of gestures in face-to-face design teams provides guidance for how to use groupware in design. In *Proceedings of DIS'95*. ACM Press, New York, pp. 157–166

Bell, G. (2001) Looking across the Atlantic. *Intel Technical Journal* **5**(3): August.

Bell, G. (2003) Other homes: alternate visions of culturally situated technologies for the home. In *Proceedings of CHI'03*.

Bell, G., Blythe, M. and Sengers, P. (2005) Making by making strange: defamiliarisation and the design of domestic technologies. *ACM Transactions on Computer–Human Interaction* **12**(2), 149–173.

Bellotti, V. and Rogers, Y. (1997) From web press to web pressure: multimedia representations and multimedia publishing. In *Proceedings of CSCW'97*, pp. 279–286.

Bellotti, V., Back, M.J., Edwards, W.K., Grinter, R.E., Lopes, C.V. and Henderson, A. (2002) Making sense of sensing systems: five questions for designers and researchers. In *Proceedings of CHI'02*. ACM Press, New York, pp. 415–422.

Ben Achour, C. (1999) Extracting requirements by analyzing text scenarios. Thèse de Doctorat de Université Paris-6.

Benford, S., Schnädelbach, H., Koleva, B., Anastasi, R., Greenhalgh, C., Rodden, T., Green, J., Ghali, A., Pridmore, T., Gaver, B., Boucher, A., Walker, B., Pennington, S., Schmidt, A., Gellersen, H. and Steed, A. (2005) Expected, sensed, and desired: a framework for designing sensing-based interaction. *TOCHI* **12**(1), 3–30.

Bergman, E. and Haitani, R. (2000) Designing the PalmPilot: a conversation with Rob Haitani. In *Information Appliances*. Morgan Kaufmann, San Francisco.

Bernsen, N.O. (1993) Matching information and interface modalities: an example study. WPCS-92-1, Roskilde University.

Bewley, W.L., Roberts, T.L., Schroit, D. and Verplank, W. (1990) Human factors testing in the design of Xerox's 8010 'Star' office workstation. In J. Preece and L. Keller (eds), *Human–Computer Interaction: A Reader*. Prentice Hall, Hemel Hempstead, pp. 368–382.

Beyer, H. and Holtzblatt, K. (1998) *Contextual Design: Defining Customer-Centered Systems*. Morgan Kauffman, San Francisco.

Bittner, K. and Spence, I. (2002) *Use Case Modelling*. Addison-Wesley, Harlow, Essex.

Blom, J., Chipchase, J. and Lehikoinen, J. (2005) Contextual and cultural challenges for user mobility research. *CACM* **48**(7), 37–41.

Blumberg, B. (1996) Old tricks, new dogs: ethology and interactive creatures. PhD Dissertation, MIT Media Lab.

Bly, S. (1997) Field work: is it product work? *ACM Interactions Magazine* **Jan/Feb**, 25–30.

Blythe, M.A., Overbeeke, A.F. and Monk, A. (eds) (2003) *Funology: From Usability to Enjoyment*. Kluwer Publishers, Amsterdam.

Bødker, S. (2000) Scenarios in user-centered design—setting the stage for reflection and action. *Interacting with Computers* **13**(1), 61–76.

Bødker, S., Greenbaum, J. and Kyng, M. (1991) Setting the stage for design as action. In J. Greenbaum and M. Kyng (eds), *Design at Work: Cooperative Design of Computer Systems*. Lawrence Erlbaum Associates, Hillsdale, NJ, pp. 139–154.

Boehm, B.W. (1988) A spiral model of software development and enhancement. *IEEE Computer* **21**(5), 61–72.

Boehm, B. and Basili, V.R. (2001) Software Defect Reduction Top 10 List. *IEEE Computer* **34**(1), 135–137.

Boehm, B., Egyed, A., Kwan, J., Port, D., Shah, A. and Madachy, R. (1998) Using the WinWin spiral model: a case study. *IEEE Computer* **31**(7), 33–44.

Borchers, J. (2001) *A Pattern Approach to Interaction Design*. John Wiley & Sons, Chichester, UK.

Borovoy, R., Martin, F., Vemuri, S., Resnick, M., Silverman, B. and Hancock, C. (1998) Meme tags and community mirrors: moving from conferences to collaboration. In *Proceedings of CSCW'98*. ACM Press, New York, pp. 159–168.

Bouchet, J. and Nigay, L. (2004) ICARE: a component-based approach for the design and development of multimodal interfaces. In *Proceedings of CHI'04*, pp. 1325–1328.

Braiterman, J., Verhage, S. and Choo, R. (2000) Designing with users in internet time. *ACM Interactions Magazine* **VII.5**, 23–27.

Breazeal, C. (1999) Kismet: a robot for social interactions with humans. `www.ai.mit.edu/projects/kismet/`

Breazeal, C. (2005) Socially intelligent robots. *Interactions* **12**, 19–21.

Brewster, S. and Dunlop, M. (eds) (2004) *Heuristic Evaluation and Mobile Usability: Bridging the Realism Gap*. Lecture Notes in Computer Science, Vol. 3160. Springer-Verlag, Berlin.

Brignull, H. and Rogers, Y. (2003) Enticing people to interact with large public displays in public spaces. In *Proceedings of INTERACT'03*, Zurich, pp. 17–24.

Brignull, H., Izadi, S., Fitzpatrick, G., Rogers, Y. and Rodden, T. (2004) The introduction of a shared interactive surface into a communal space. In Proceedings of the 2004 Conference on Computer Supported Cooperative Work, CSCW '04. ACM Press, New York, pp. 49–58.

Brown, B.A., Sellen, A.J. and O'Hara, K.P. (2000) A diary study of information capture in working life. In *Proceedings of CHI 2000*, The Hague, Holland, pp. 438–445.

BS EN ISO13407 (1999) Human-centred design processes for interactive systems, CEN.

Buchenau, M. and Suri, J.F. (2000) Experience prototyping. In *Proceedings of DIS 2000 Design Interactive Systems: Processes, Practices, Methods, Techniques*, pp. 17–19.

Burak, A. and Sharon, T. (2004) Usage patterns of FriendZone—mobile location-based community services. In *Proceedings of 3rd International Conference on Mobile and Ubiquitous Computing*. ACM Press, New York, pp. 93–100.

Callahan, E. (2005) Interface design and culture. *Annual Review of Information Science and Technology* **39**, 257–310.

Caplin, S. (2001) *Icon Design: Graphic Icons in Computer Interface*. Watson-Guptill Publications.

Card, S.K., Moran, T.P. and Newell, A. (1983) *The Psychology of Human–Computer Interaction*. Lawrence Erlbaum Associates, Hillsdale, NJ.

Card, S.K., Mackinley, J.D. and Shneiderman, B. (eds) (1999) *Readings in Information Visualization: Using Vision to Think*. Morgan Kaufmann, San Francisco.

Carroll, J.M. (1990) *The Nurnberg Funnel*. MIT Press, Cambridge, MA.

Carroll, J. (ed.) (2003) *HCI Models, Theories and Frameworks: Towards a Multidisciplinary Science*. Morgan Kaufmann, San Francisco.

Carroll, J.M. (2004) Beyond fun. *Interactions* **11**(5), 38–40.

Carter, S. and Mankoff, J. (2005) When participants do the capturing: the role of media in diary studies. *CHI2005*, pp. 899–908.

Cassell, J. (2000) Embodied conversational interface agents. *Communications of the ACM* **43**(3), 70–79.

Chang, T. (2004) The results of student ratings: paper vs online. *Journal of Taiwan Normal University: Education* **49**(1), 171–186.

Chapman, N. and Chapman, J. (2004) *Digital Multimedia*, 2nd edn. John Wiley & Sons, New York.

Chen, C. (2004) *Information Visualization: Beyond the Horizon*, 2nd edn. Springer-Verlag, Berlin.

Cheng, L., Stone, L., Farnham, S., Clark, A.M. and Zaner-Godsey, M. (2000) HutchWorld: Lessons Learned. A Collaborative Project: Fred Hutchinson Cancer Research Center & Microsoft Research. In *Proceedings of the Virtual Worlds Conference 2000*, Paris, France.

Cheverst, K., Davies, N., Mitchell, K. and Friday, A. (2000) Experiences of developing and deploying a context-aware tourist guide: the GUIDE project. In *Proceedings of the 6th Annual International Conference on Mobile Computing and Networking*. ACM Press, New York, pp. 20–31.

CHI Panel (2000) Scaling for the Masses: Usability Practices for the Web's Most Popular Sites.

Chin, J.P., Diehl, V.A. and Norman, K.L. (1988) Development of an instrument measuring user satisfaction of the human–computer interface. In *Proceedings of CHI'88*.

Chisnell, D. and Brown, M. (2004) Matching user and business goals. In *Proceedings of CHI2004*, April 24–29, Vienna, Austria, pp. 943–958.

Christiansen, E. (1996) Tamed by a rose: computers as tools in human activity. In B.A. Nardi (ed.), *Context and Consciousness*. MIT Press, Cambridge, MA, pp. 175–198.

Churchill, E.F., Nelson, L. and Denoue, L. (2003) Multimedia fliers: informal information sharing with digital community bulletin boards. In *Proceedings of Communities and Technologies*, Amsterdam.

Cobb, S., Beardon, L., Eastgate, R., Glover, T., Kerr, S., Neale, H., Parsons, S., Benford, S., Hopkins, E., Mitchell, P., Reynard, G. and Wilson, J. (2002) Applied virtual environments to support learning of social interaction skills in users with Asperger's Syndrome. *Digital Creativity* **13**(1), N-22.

Cockburn, A. (2000) *Writing Effective Use Cases*. Addison-Wesley, Harlow, Essex.

Cockburn, A. (2005) *Crystal Clear: A Human-Powered Methodology for Small Teams*. Addison-Wesley, Harlow, Essex.

Cockton, G. and Woolrych, A. (2001) Understanding inspection methods: lessons from an assessment of heuristic evaluation. In A. Blandford and J. Vanderdonckt (eds), *People & Computers XV*. Springer-Verlag, Berlin, pp. 171–191.

Cogdill, K. (1999) MEDLINEplus Interface Evaluation: Final Report. College of Information Studies, University of Maryland, College Park, MD.

Cohen, M., Giangola, J.P. and Balogh, J. (2004) *Voice User Interface Design*. Addison-Wesley, Harlow, Essex.

Collins, P., Shukla, S. and Redmiles, D. (2002) Activity theory and system design: a view from the trenches. *Computer-Supported Cooperative Work* **11**(1&2), 55–80.

Comer, E.R. (1997) Alternative lifecycle models. In M. Dorfman and R.H. Thayer (eds), *Software Engineering*. IEEE Computer Society Press, Piscataway, NJ.

Consolvo, S. and Towle, J. (2005) Evaluating an ambient display for the home. In *CHI 2005*, Late Breaking Results: Posters, pp. 1304–1307.

Constantine, L.L. and Lockwood, L.A.D. (1999) *Software for Use*. Addison-Wesley, Harlow, Essex.

Cooper, A. (1999) *The Inmates are Running the Asylum*. SAMS, Indianapolis.

Cooper, A. and Reiman, R. (2003) *About Face 2.0: The essentials of interaction design*. John Wiley & Sons, New York.

Couch, C.J. (1996) In D.R. Maines and S. Chen (eds), *Information Technologies and Social Orders*. Aldine de Gruyter, New York.

Coyle, A. (1995) Discourse analysis. In G.M. Breakwell, S. Hammond and C. Fife-Schaw (eds), *Research Methods in Psychology*. Sage, London.

Crabtree, A. (2003) *Designing Collaborative Systems: A Practical Guide to Ethnography*. Springer-Verlag, Berlin.

Crabtree, F. and Miller, W.L. (eds) (1992) *Doing Qualitative Research*. Sage, Newbury Park, CA.

Craik, K.J.W. (1943) *The Nature of Explanation*. Cambridge University Press, Cambridge.

Crampton Smith, G. (1995) The hand that rocks the cradle. *ID Magazine* **May/Jun**, 60–65.

Csikszentmihalyi, M. (1996) *Wired* interview. Go with the flow. `http://www.wired.com/wired/archive/4.09/czik.html` (retrieved 06/05/05).

Csikszentmihalyi, M. (1997) *Finding Flow: The Psychology of Engagement with Everyday Life*. Basic Books, New York.

Csikszentmihalyhi, M. and Larson, R. (1987) Validity and reliability of the experience-sampling method. *Journal of Nervous and Mental Disease* **175**, 526–536.

Curtis, P. (1992) Mudding: social phenomena in text-based virtual realities. In *Proceedings of the 1992 Conference on Directions and Implications of Advanced Computing*, Berkeley, CA, May.

Curzon, P., Blandford, A., Butterworth, R. and Bhogal, R. (2002) Interaction design issues for car navigation systems. In *Proceedings of HCI 2002*, Vol. 2.

Cusumano, M.A. and Selby, R.W. (1995) *Microsoft Secrets*. Harper-Collins Business, London.

Danis, C. and Boies, S. (2000) Using a technique from graphic designers to develop innovative systems design. In *Proceedings of DIS 2000*, pp. 20–26.

Davis, A.M. (1995) *201 Principles of Software Development*. McGraw-Hill, New York.

De Angeli, A., Athavankar, U., Joshi, A., Coventry, L. and Johnson, G.I. (2004) Introducing ATMs in India: a contextual inquiry. *Interacting with Computers* **16**(1), 29–44.

De Angeli, A., Coventry, L., Johnson, G. and Renaud, K. (2005) Is a picture worth a thousand words? Exploring the feasibility of graphical authentication systems. *International Journal of Human Computer Studies* **63**, 128–152.

De Souza, S.C. (2005) *The Semiotic Engineering of Human–Computer Interaction*. MIT Press, Cambridge, MA.

Deng, L. and Huang, X. (2004) Challenges in adopting speech recognition. *Communications of the ACM* **47**(1), 69–75.

Dietz, P.H. and Leigh, D.L. (2001) DiamondTouch: a multi-user touch technology. In *Symposium on User Interface Software and Technology (UIST)*. ACM Press, New York, pp. 219–226.

Dix, A., Finlay, J., Abowd, G. and Beale, R. (2004) *Human–Computer Interaction*, 3rd edn. Pearson Education, Harlow, Essex.

Dourish, P. and Bly, S. (1992) Portholes: supporting awareness in a distributed work group. In *Proceedings of CHI'92*, pp. 541–547.

Dourish, P., Grinter, R.E., Delgado de la Flor, J. and Joseph, M. (2004) Security in the wild: user strategies for managing security as an everyday, practical problem. *Personal and Ubiquitous Computing* **8**, 391–401.

Drascic, D. and Milgram, P. (1996) Perceptual issues in augmented reality. In M.T. Bolas, S.S. Fisher and J.O. Merritt (eds), *SPIE Volume 2653: Stereoscopic Displays and Virtual Reality Systems III*. SPIE, San Jose, CA, pp. 123–134.

Dray, S.M. and Mrazek, D. (1996) A day in the life of a family: an international ethnographic study. In D. Wixon and J. Ramey (eds), *Field Methods Casebook for Software Design*. John Wiley & Sons, New York, pp. 145–156.

Druin, A. (2002) The role of children in the design of new technology. *Behaviour and Information Technology* **21**(1), 1–25.

Ducheneaut, N. and Moore, R.J. (2004) The social side of gaming: a study of interaction patterns in a massively multiplayer online game. In *Proceedings of CSCW 04*, November 6–10, Chicago.

Dumas, J.S. and Redish, J.C. (1999) *A Practical Guide to Usability Testing* (Revised Edition). Intellect, Exeter.

Eason, K. (1987) *Information Technology and Organizational Change*. Taylor and Francis, London.

Ebling, M.R. and John, B.E. (2000) On the contributions of different empirical data in usability testing. In *Proceedings of ACM DIS 2001*, pp. 289–296.

Edwards, A.D.N. (1992) Graphical user interfaces and blind people. In *Proceedings of ICCHP'92*, Austrian Computer Society, Vienna, pp. 114–119.

Ehn, P. (1989) *Word-Oriented Design of Computer Artifacts*, 2nd edn. Lawrence Erlbaum Associates, Hillsdale, NJ.

Ehn, P. and Kyng, M. (1991) Cardboard computers: mocking-it-up or hands-on the future. In J. Greenbaum and M. Kyng (eds), *Design at Work*. Lawrence Erlbaum Associates, Hillsdale, NJ.

Eliot, C. and Woolf, B. (1994) Reasoning about the user within a simulation-based real-time training system. In *Proceedings of 4th International Conference on User Modeling*, Mitre Corp., Bedford, MA.

Elrod, S., Bruce, R., Gold, R., Goldberg, D., Halasz, F., Janssen, W., Lee, D., McCall, K., Pedersen, E., Pier, K., Tang, J. and Welch, B. (1992) Liveboard: a large interactive display supporting group meetings, presentations and remote collaboration. In *Proceedings of CHI'92*. ACM Press, New York, pp. 599–607.

Engeström, Y. (1999) *Perspectives on Activity Theory*. Cambridge University Press, Cambridge.

Erickson, T.D. (1990) Working with interface metaphors. In B. Laurel (ed.), *The Art of Human–Computer Interface Design*. Addison-Wesley, Boston.

Erickson, T.D. and Simon, H.A. (1985) *Protocol Analysis: Verbal Reports as Data*. MIT Press, Cambridge, MA.

Erickson, T., Smith, D.N., Kellogg, W.A., Laff, M., Richards, J.T. and Bradner, E. (1999) Socially translucent systems: social proxies, persistent conversation and the design of 'Babble.' In *Proceedings of CHI'99*, pp. 72–79.

Esselink, B. (2000) *A Practical Guide to Localisation*. John Benjamins, Amsterdam.

Evers, V. and Hillen, H. (2007) Online redesign of a website's information architecture to offer audio navigation to blind users. In J. Lazar (ed.), *Universal Usability: Designing Information Systems for Diverse User Populations*. John Wiley & Sons, Chichester, UK.

Faraday, P.F. and Sutcliffe, A.G. (1997) Designing effective multimedia presentations. In *Proceedings of CHI'97*. ACM Press, New York, pp. 272–279.

Fekete, J.-D. and Plaisant, C. (2002) Interactive information visualization of a million items. In *Proceedings of IEEE Symposium on Information Visualization 2002 (InfoVis 2002)*, Boston.

Fish, R.S. (1989) Cruiser: a multimedia system for social browsing. *SIGGRAPH Video Review* (video cassette), Issue 45, Item 6.

Fishkin, K.P. (2004) A taxonomy for and analysis of tangible interfaces. *Personal and Ubiquitous Computing* **8**, 347–358.

Fiske, J. (1994) Audiencing: cultural practice and cultural studies. In N.K. Denzin and Y.S. Lincoln (eds), *Handbook of Qualitative Research*. Sage, Thousand Oaks, CA, pp. 189–198.

Flanagan, J.C. (1954) The critical incident technique. *Psychological Bulletin* **51**, 327–358.

Fogg, B.J. (2003) *Persuasive Technology: Using Computers to Change What we Think and Do*. Morgan Kaufmann, San Francisco.

Fontana, A. and Frey, J.H. (1994) *Interviewing: The Art of Science*. In N. Denzin and Y. Lincoln (eds), *Handbook of Qualitative Research*. Sage, London, pp. 361–376.

Frohlich, D. and Murphy, R. (1999) Getting physical: what is fun computing in tangible form? In *Computers and Fun 2, Workshop*, 20 December, York.

Gabrielli, S., Rogers, Y. and Scaife, M. (2000) Young children's spatial representations developed through exploration of a desktop virtual reality scene. *Education and Information Technologies* **5**(4), 251–262.

Galitz, W.O. (1997) *The Essential Guide to User Interface Design*. John Wiley & Sons, New York.

Garrett, J.J. (2003) *The Elements of User Experience: User centered design for the web*. Easy Riders, London.

Gaver, B., Dunne, T. and Pacenti, E. (1999) Cultural probes. *ACM Interactions Magazine* **Jan/Feb**, 21–29.

Gaver, W., Boucher, A., Pennington, S., Walker, B., Bowers, J., Gellerson, H., Schmidt, A., Villars, N. and Steed, A. (2004) The Drift Table: designing for Ludic Engagement. *Extended Abstracts of the 2004 Conference on Human Factors and Computing Systems*. ACM Press, New York, pp. 885–900.

Gentner, D. and Nielsen, J. (1996) The anti-Mac interface. *Communications of the ACM* **39**(8), 70–82.

Giddens, A. (1984) *The Constitution of Society: Outline of the Theory of Structure.* University of California Press.

Gigante, M.A. (1993) Virtual reality: enabling technologies. In R.A. Earnshaw, M.A. Gigante and H. Jones (eds), *Virtual Reality Systems.* Academic Press, London, pp. 15–25.

Gill, J. and Shipley, T. (1999) *Telephones— What Features do Disabled People Need?* RNIB.

Glaser, B.G. (1992) *Basics of Grounded Theory: Emergence vs Forcing.* Sociology Press.

Glaser, B.G. and Strauss, A. (1967) *Discovery of Grounded Theory.* Aldine, London.

Glossary (2005) `www.lib.berkeley.edu/TeachingLib/Guides/Internet/Glossary.html` (retrieved 10/03/05).

Goetz, J.P. and Lecompte, M.D. (1984) *Ethnography and Qualitative Design in Educational Research.* Academic Press, Orlando, FL.

Gottesdiener, E. (2002) *Requirements by Collaboration: workshops for defining needs.* Addison-Wesley, Harlow, Essex.

Gould, J.D. and Lewis, C.H. (1985) Designing for usability: key principles and what designers think. *Communications of the ACM* **28**(3), 300–311.

Gould, J.D., Boies, S.J., Levy, S., Richards, J.T. and Schoonard, J. (1987) The 1984 Olympic Message System: a test of behavioral principles of system design. *Communications of the ACM* **30**(9), 758–769 (full paper).

Gould, J.D., Boies, S.J., Levy, S., Richards, J.T. and Schoonard, J. (1990) The 1984 Olympic Message System: a test of behavioral principles of system design. In J. Preece and L. Keller (eds), *Human–Computer Interaction (Readings).* Prentice Hall International Ltd., Hemel Hempstead, pp. 260–283.

Greenberg, S. and Rounding, M. (2001) The notification collage: posting information to public and personal displays. *CHI Letters* **3**(1), 515–521.

Greif, I. (1988) *Computer Supported Cooperative Work: A book of readings.* Morgan Kaufmann, San Francisco.

Grisedale, S., Graves, M. and Grunsteidl, A. (1997) Designing a graphical user interface for healthcare workers in rural India. In *CHI'97 Conference Proceedings (Design Briefings)*, pp. 471–478.

Grudin, J. (1989) The case against user interface consistency. *Communications of the ACM* **32**(10), 1164–1173.

Guha, M.L., Druin, A., Chipman, G., Fails, J.A., Simms, S. and Farber, A. (2005) Working with young children as technology design partners. *CACM* **48**(1), 39–42.

Guimbretiere, F., Stone, M. and Winograd, T. (2001) Fluid interaction with high-resolution wall-size displays. In *Proceedings of CHI'01.* ACM Press, New York, pp. 1–10.

Guindon, R. (1990) Designing the design process: exploiting opportunistic thoughts. *Human–Computer Interaction* **5**(2&3), 305–344.

Gunn, H. (2002) Web-based surveys: changing the survey process. *First Monday* **7**(12) (retrieved from firstmonday.org/issues/issue7_12/index.html).

Gunther, V.A., Burns, D.J. and Payne, D.J. (1986) Text editing performance as a function of training with command terms of differing lengths and frequencies. *SIGCHI Bulletin* **18**, 57–59.

Gutwin, C. and Penner, R. (2002) Visual information and collaboration: improving interpretation of remote gestures with telepointer tracers. In *Proceedings CSCW'02.* ACM Press, New York, pp. 49–57.

Hafner, K. (2005) You there, at the computer: pay attention. *New York Times.*

Halverson, C.A. (2002) Activity theory and distributed cognition: or what does CSCW need to DO with theories? *Computer Supported Cooperative Work* **11**, 243–267.

Halverson, C.A., Erickson, T. and Sussman, J. (2003) What counts as success? Punctuated patterns of use in a persistent chat environment. In *Proceedings of GROUP 2003*. ACM Press, New York, pp. 180–189.

Harper, R. (ed.) (2003) *Inside the Smart Home*. Springer-Verlag, Berlin.

Harrison, S., Bly, S., Anderson, S. and Minneman (1997) The media space. In K.E. Finn, A. Sellen and S.B. Wilbur (eds), *Video-Mediated Communication*. Lawrence Erlbaum Associates, Mahwah, NJ, pp. 273–300.

Hartfield, B. and Winograd, T. (1996) Profile: IDEO. In T. Winograd (ed.), *Bringing Design to Software*. ACM Press, New York.

Hartson, H.R. and Hix, D. (1989) Toward empirically derived methodologies and tools for human–computer interface development. *International Journal of Man–Machine Studies* **31**, 477–494.

Haumer, P., Jarke, M., Pohl, K. and Weiden-Haupt, K. (2000) Improving reviews of conceptual models by extended traceability to captured system usage. *Interacting with Computers* **13**(1), 77–95.

Heath, C. and Luff, P. (1992) Collaboration and control: crisis management and multimedia technology in London Underground line control rooms. In *Proceedings of CSCW'92* **1**(1&2), 69–94.

Heath, C.C. and Luff, P.K. (1994) Work, interaction and technology: the naturalistic analysis of human conduct and requirements analysis. In M. Jirotka and J. Goguen (eds), *Requirements Engineering*. Academic Press, New York, pp. 255–284.

Heinbokel, T., Sonnentag, S., Frese, M., Stolte, W. and Brodbeck, F.C. (1996) Don't underestimate the problems of user centredness in software development projects—there are many! *Behaviour & Information Technology* **15**(4), 226–236.

Highsmith, J. (2002) *Adaptive Software Development: a collaborative approach to managing complex systems*. Dorset House.

Hines, M. (2005) Spyware industry worth billions (retrieved from `http://news.com.com/Research+Spyware+industry+worth+billions/2100-1029_3-5693730.html` on 9/06/2005).

Hix, D. and Gabbard, J.L. (2002) Usability engineering of virtual environments. In K. Stanney (ed.), *Handbook of Virtual Environments: Design implementation and applications*. Lawrence Erlbaum Associates, Hillsdale, NJ, pp. 681–699.

Hochheiser, H. and Shneiderman, B. (2001) Using interactive visualization of WWW log data to characterize access patterns and inform site design. *Journal of the American Society for Information Science* **52**(4), 331–343.

Hofstede, G. (1994) *Cultures and Organisations, Intercultural Cooperation and its Importance for Survival*. Harper-Collins, London.

Hofstede, G. and Hofstede, G.J. (2005) *Cultures and Organizations Software of the Mind*. McGraw Hill, New York.

Holmquist, L.E. (2005) Prototyping: generating ideas or cargo cult designs? *Interactions* **Mar/Apr**, 48–54.

Holtzblatt, K. and Jones, S. (1993) Contextual inquiry: a participatory technique for systems design. In D. Schuler and A. Namioka (eds), *Participatory Design: Principles and Practice*. Lawrence Erlbaum Associates, Hillsdale, NJ, pp. 177–210.

Hornecker, E. (2005) A design theme for tangible interaction: embodied facilitation. In Proceedings of the 9th European Conference on Computer Supported Cooperative Work (*ECSCW'05*). Kluwer/Springer, pp. 23–43.

Horton, S. (2005) *Access by Design: A Guide to Universal Usability for Web Designers*. New Riders Press, Indianapolis, IN.

Horton, W. (1994) *The Icon Book. Visual Symbols for Computer Systems and Documentation.* John Wiley & Sons, New York.

Hutchings, D., Smith, G., Meyers, B., Czerwinski, M. and Robertson, G. (2004) Display space usage and window management operation comparisons between single monitor and multiple monitor users. In *Proceedings of the Working Conference on Advanced Visual Interfaces, AVI 2004*, pp. 32–39.

Hutchins, E. (1995) *Cognition in the Wild.* MIT Press, Cambridge, MA.

Hutchins, E., Holan, J.D. and Norman, D. (1986) Direct manipulation interfaces. In D. Norman and S.W. Draper (eds), *User Centered System Design.* LEA, Hillsdale, NJ, pp. 87–124.

Isensee, S., Kalinoski, K. and Vochatzer, K. (2000) Designing Internet appliances at Netpliance. In E. Bergman (ed.), *Information Appliances and Beyond.* Morgan Kaufmann, San Francisco.

Ishii, H. and Ullmer, B. (1997) Tangible bits: towards seamless interfaces between people, bits and atoms. In *Proceedings CHI 1997.* ACM Press, New York, pp. 234–241.

Ishii, H., Kobayashi, M. and Grudin, J. (1993) Integration of interpersonal space and shared work-space: clearboard design and experiments. *ACM Transactions on Information Systems* **11**(4), 349–375.

Izadi, S., Brignull, H., Rodden, T., Rogers, Y. and Underwood, M. (2003) Dynamo: a public interactive surface supporting the cooperative sharing and exchange of media. In *Proceedings of UIST 2003, Symposium on User Interface Software and Technology*, November 2–5, Vancouver. ACM Press, New York, pp. 159–168.

Jacob, R.J.K. (1996) A visual language for non-WIMP user interfaces. In *Proceedings IEEE Symposium on Visual Languages.* IEEE Computer Society Press, pp. 231–238.

Jacobson, I., Christerson, M., Jonsson, P. and Overgaard, G. (1992) *Object-Oriented Software Engineering—A Use Case Driven Approach.* Addison-Wesley, Harlow, Essex.

Johnson, J. and Henderson, A. (2002) Conceptual models: begin by designing what to design. *Interactions* **Jan/Feb**, 25–32.

Johnson-Laird, P.N. (1983) *Mental Models.* Cambridge University Press, Cambridge.

Jones, S. (ed.) (1999) *Doing Internet Research: Critical Issues and Methods99*

for Examining the Net. Sage Publications, Thousand Oaks, CA.

Jones, C. (2000) *Software Assessments, Benchmarks and Best Practices.* Addison-Wesley, Harlow, Essex.

Jones, Q., Grandhi, S.A., Whittaker, S., Chivakula, K. and Terveen, L. (2004) Putting systems into place: a qualitative study of design requirements for location-aware community systems. In *Proceedings of CSCW'04*, Chicago, IL, pp. 202–211.

Jordan, B. and Henderson, A. (1995) Interaction analysis: foundations and practice. *The Journal of the Learning Sciences* **4**(1), 39–103.

Jordan, P.W. (2000) *Designing Pleasurable Products.* Taylor & Francis/Morgan Kaufmann, San Francisco.

Jouppi, N.P. (2002) First steps towards mutually-immersive mobile telepresence. In *Proceedings of the 2002 ACM Conference on Computer Supported Cooperative Work, CSCW'02.* ACM Press, New York, pp. 354–363.

Kahn, R. and Cannell, C. (1957) *The Dynamics of Interviewing.* John Wiley & Sons, New York.

Kalawsky, R.S. (1993) *The Science of Virtual Reality and Virtual Environments.* Addison-Wesley, New York.

Kangas, E. and Kinnunen, T. (2005) Applying user-centred design to mobile application development. *Communications of the ACM* **48**(7), 55–59.

Karat, J. (1995) Scenario use in the design of a speech recognition system. In J.M. Carroll (ed.), *Scenario-based Design.* John Wiley & Sons, New York, pp. 109–134.

Kay, A. (1969) The reactive engine. PhD Dissertation, Electrical Engineering and Computer Science, University of Utah.

Ke, W., Börner, K. and Viswanath, L. (2004) Analysis and visualization of the IV 2004 contest dataset. *Poster Compendium, IEEE Information Visualization Conference*, pp. 49–50.

Keil, M. and Carmel, E. (1995) Customer–developer links in software development. *Communications of the ACM* **38**(5), 33–44.

Kelley, T. (2001) *The Art of Innovation.* Profile Books, Croydon, Surrey.

Kempton, W. (1986) Two theories of home heat control. *Cognitive Science* **10**, 75–90.

Kim, S. (1990) Interdisciplinary cooperation. In B. Laurel (ed.), *The Art of Human–Computer Interface Design.* Addison-Wesley, Reading, MA.

Kindberg, T., Spasojevic, M., Fleck, R. and Sellen, A. (2005) The ubiquitous camera: an in-depth study of camera phone use. *IEEE Pervasive Computing* **4**(2), 42–50.

Kirijian, A., Myers, M. and Charland, S. (2007) Web Fun Central: online learning tools for individuals with Down syndrome. In J. Lazar (ed.), *Universal Usability: Designing Information Systems for Diverse User Populations.* John Wiley & Sons, Chichester, UK.

Klemmer, S.R., Newman, M.W., Farrell, R., Bilezikjian, M. and Landay, J.A. (2001) The designer's outpost: a tangible interface for collaborative website design. In *Symposium on User Interface Software and Technology.* ACM Press, New York, pp. 1–10.

Knight, J.F., Schwirtz, A., Psomadelis, F., Baber, C., Bristow, H. and Arvanitis, T. (2005) The design of the SensVest. *Personal Ubiquitous Computing* **9**, 6–19.

Koenemann-Belliveau, J., Carroll, J.M., Rosson, M.B. and Singley, M.K. (1994) Comparative usability evaluation: critical incidents and critical threads. In *Proceedings of CHI'94.*

Komlodi, A., Alburo, J., Preece, J., Druin, A., Hou, A., Liao, S., Elkiss, A. and Resnik, P. (2007) Lessons learned for developing an international children's online community: evaluating sociability and usability for cross-cultural exchange. *The Interdisciplinary Journal, Interacting with Computers.* In press.

Kotonya, G. and Sommerville, I. (1998) *Requirements Engineering: processes and techniques.* John Wiley & Sons, Chichester, UK.

Koyani, S.J., Bailey, R.W. and Nall, J.R. (2004) *Research-Based Web Design and Usability Heuristics.* GSA.

Kraut, R., Fish, R., Root, R. and Chalfonte, B. (1990) Informal communications in organizations: form, function and technology. In S. Oskamp and S. Krug (eds), *Don't Make Me Think.* `Circle.com` library.

Kuhn, T.S. (1972/1962) *The Structure of Scientific Revolutions*, 2nd edn. The University of Chicago Press, Chicago.

Kujala, S. and Mäntylä, M. (2000) Is user involvement harmful or useful in the early stages of product development? In *CHI 2000 Extended Abstracts.* ACM Press, New York, pp. 285–286.

Kurosu, M. and Kashimura, K. (1995) Apparent usability vs. inherent usability. In *CHI'95 Conference Companion.* ACM Press, New York, pp. 292–293.

Kuutti, K. (1996) Activity theory as a potential framework for human–computer interaction. In B.A. Nardi (ed.), *Context and Consciousness.* MIT Press, Cambridge, MA, pp. 17–44.

Lakoff, G. and Johnson, M. (1980) *Metaphors we Live By.* The University of Chicago Press, Chicago.

Lambourne, R., Feiz, K. and Rigot, B. (1997) Social trends and product opportunities: Philips' Vision of the Future Project. In *Proceedings of CHI'97*, pp. 494–501.

Landay, J. (2005) Interview. `http://www.intel.com/research/network/j_landay.htm` (retrieved 05/05/05).

Lansdale, M. and Edmonds, E. (1992) Using memory for events in the design of personal filing systems. *International Journal of Human–Computer Studies* **26**, 97–126.

Larson, K. and Czerwinski, M. (1998) Web page design: implications of memory, structure and scent for information retrieval. In *Proceedings of CHI'98*, pp. 25–32.

Lazar, J. (2006) *Web Usability: A user-centered design approach*. Addison-Wesley, Boston.

Lazar, J. (ed.) (2007) *Universal Usability:Designing Information Systems for Diverse User Populations*. John Wiley & Sons, Chichester, UK.

Ledgard, H., Singer, A. and Whiteside, J. (1981) Directions in human factors for interactive systems. In G. Goos and J. Hartmanis (eds), *Lecture Notes in Computer Science*, 103. Springer-Verlag, Berlin.

Lee, J., Kim, J. and Moon, J.-Y. (2000) What makes Internet users visit cyber stores again? Key design factors for customer loyalty. In *Proceedings of CHI 2000*, pp. 305–312.

Leontiev, A.N. (1978) *Activity, Consciousness and Personality*. Prentice Hall, Englewood Cliffs, NJ.

Leontiev, A.N. (1981) *Problems of the Development of Mind*. Progress, Moscow.

Leontiev, A.N. (1989) The problem of activity in the history of Soviet psychology. *Soviet Psychology* **27**(1), 22–39.

Lester, J.C. and Stone, B.A. (1997) Increasing believability in animated pedagogical agent. In *Proceedings of Autonomous Agents'97*, pp. 16–21.

Liddle, D. (1996) Design of the conceptual model. In T. Winograd (ed.), *Bringing Design to Software*. Addison-Wesley, Reading, MA, pp. 17–31.

Lieberman, H. and Fry, C. (1995) Bridging the gap between code and behavior in programming. *Proc. CHI'95*. ACM Press, New York, pp. 480–486.

Liu, Z., Coventry, L., White, R., Wu, H. and Johnson, G. (2005) Self-service technology in China: exploring usability and consumer issues. In *Proceedings of HCI2005*, Vol. 2, pp. 173–178.

Lopuck, L. (1996) *Designing Multimedia*. Peachpit Press, Berkeley, CA.

Lowgren, J. and Stolterman, E. (2004) *Thoughtful Interaction Design: A design perspective on information technology*. MIT Press, Cambridge, MA.

Luce, K.H., Winzelberg, A.J., Das, S., Osborn, M.I., Bryson, S.W. and Taylor, C.B. (2003) Reliability of self-report: paper versus online administration. *Computers in Human Behavior* (accessed online 20/1/2005).

Lund, A.M. (1994) Ameritech's usability laboratory: from prototype to final design. *Behaviour & Information Technology* **13**(1&2), 67–80.

M880 (2000) OSS CD part of *M880 Software Engineering*. The Open University, Milton Keynes, UK.

MacCarthy, J. and Wright, P. (2004) *Technology as Experience*. MIT Press, Cambridge, MA.

Mackay, W. (1999) Media spaces: environments for informal multimedia interaction. In C. Beaudouin-Lafon (ed.), *Computer Supported Cooperative Work*. John Wiley & Sons, New York.

MacKay, W.E., Ratzer, A.V. and Janecek, P. (2000) Video artifacts for design: bridging the gap between abstraction and detail. In *Proceedings of DIS 2000*, pp. 72–82.

Maglio, P.P., Matlock, T., Raphaely, D., Chernicky, B. and Kirsh, D. (1999) Interactive skill in Scrabble. In *Proceedings of Twenty-first Annual Conference of the Cognitive Science Society*. Lawrence Erlbaum Associates, Mahwah, NJ.

Maher, M.L. and Pu, P. (1997) *Issues and Applications of Case-Based Reasoning in Design*. Lawrence Erlbaum Associates, Hillsdale, NJ.

Maiden, N., Robertson, S. and Gizikis, A. (2004) Provoking creativity: imagine what your requirements could look like. *IEEE Software* **21**(5), 68–75.

Mandryk, R. and Inkpen, K. (2004) Physiological indicators for the evaluation of co-located collaborative play. In *CSCW'2004*. ACM Press, New York, pp. 102–111.

Mankoff, J., Dey, A.K., Hsich, G., Kientz, J. and Lederer, M.A. (2003) Heuristic evaluation of ambient devices. *Proceedings of CHI 2003*. ACM Press, New York, pp. 169–176.

Mankoff, J., Fait, H. and Tran, T. (2005) Is your web page accessible? A comparative study of methods for assessing web page accessibility for the blind. In *Proceedings of CHI 2003*. ACM Press, New York, pp. 41–50.

Mann, S. (1997) An historical account of the 'WearComp' and 'WearCam' inventions developed for applications in personal imaging. In *The First International Symposium on Wearable Computers: Digest of Papers*. IEEE Computer Society, pp. 66–73.

Mao, J.-Y., Vredenburg, K., Smith, P.W. and Carey, T. (2005) The state of user-centered design practice. *Communications of the ACM* **48**(3), 105–109.

Marcus, A. (2002) The cult of cute: the challenge of user experience design. *Interactions* **9**(6), 29–34.

Marcus, A. and Gould, W.E. (2000) Crosscurrents: cultural dimensions and global Web user-interface design. *Interactions* **7**(4), 32–46.

Marill, J.L., Miller, N. and Kitendaugh, P. (2006) The MedlinePlus public user interface: studies of design challenges and opportunities. *Journal of the Medical Library Association* **94**(1), 30–40.

Mark, G., Fuchs, L. and Sohlenkamp, M. (1997) Supporting groupware conventions through contextual awareness. In *Proceedings of the Fifth European Conference on Computer-Supported Co-operative Work*. Kluwer, Dordrecht, pp. 253–268.

Markoff, J. (2005) Web content for the masses. *New York Times*, 6/29/05.

Marmasse, N. and Schmandt, C. (2000) Location-aware information delivery with ComMotion. In *Proceedings of Handheld and Ubiquitous Computing, Second International Symposium, HUC 2000*. Springer-Verlag, Berlin, pp. 157–171.

Marshall, P., Price, S. and Rogers, Y. (2003) Conceptualising tangibles to support learning. In *Proceedings of Interaction Design and Children*. ACM Press, New York, p. 101-N0.

Marti, S. and Schmandt, C. (2005) Physical embodiments for mobile communication agents. In *Proceedings of UIST'2005*, Seattle, Washington, October, pp. 23–26.

Martin, H. and Gaver, B. (2000) Beyond the snapshot: from speculation to prototypes in audiophotography. In *Proceedings of DIS 2000*, pp. 55–65.

Mateas, M., Salvador, T., Scholtz, J. and Sorensen, D. (1996) Engineering ethnography in the home. *Companion for CHI'96*. ACM Press, New York, pp. 283–284.

Mayhew, D.J. (1999) *The Usability Engineering Lifecycle*. Morgan Kaufmann, San Francisco.

McCarthy, J. (2002) Using public displays to create conversation opportunities. *Workshop on Public, Community and Situated Displays. CSCW 2002.*

McCarthy, J. and Wright, P. (2004) *Technology as Experience*. MIT Press, Cambridge, MA.

McCullough, M. (2004) *Digital Ground: Architecture, Pervasive Computing and Environmental Knowing*. MIT Press, Cambridge, MA.

McLaughlin, M., Goldberg, S.B., Ellison, N. and Lucas, J. (1999) Measuring Internet audiences: patrons of an online art museum. In S. Jones (ed.), *Doing Internet Research: Critical Issues and Methods for Examining the Net*. Sage, Thousand Oaks, CA, pp. 163–178.

Miller, G. (1956) The magical number seven, plus or minus two: some limits on our capacity for processing information. *Psychological Review* **63**, 81–97.

Miller, L.H. and Johnson, J. (1996) The Xerox Star: an influential user interface design. In M. Rudisill, C. Lewis, P.G. Polson and T.D. McKay (eds), *Human–Computer Interface Design*. Morgan Kaufmann, San Francisco.

Millington, D. and Stapleton, J. (1995) Special report: developing a RAD standard. *IEEE Software* **12**(5), 54–56.

Molin, L. (2004) Wizard-of-Oz prototyping for cooperative interaction design of graphical user interfaces. In *Proceedings of NordiCHI'04*, October 23–27, Tampere, Finland, pp. 425–428.

Morikawa, O. and Maesako, T. (1998) HyperMirror: towards pleasant-to-use video mediated communication system. In *Proceedings of CSCW'98*, pp. 149–158.

Morrison, J.B., Pirolli, P. and Card, S.K. (2001) A taxonomic analysis of what World Wide Web activities significantly impact people's decisions and actions. Interactive poster, presented at the *Association for Computing Machinery's Conference on Human Factors in Computing Systems*, Seattle, March 31–April 5.

Mullet, K. and Sano, D. (1995) *Designing Visual Interfaces*. Prentice Hall, Mountain View, CA.

Myers, B. (1988) Window interfaces: a taxonomy of window manager user interfaces. *IEEE Computer Graphics and Applications* **8**(5), 65–84.

Myers, B., Hudson, S.E. and Pausch, R. (2002) Past, present and future of user interface software tools. In J.M. Carroll (ed.), *Human–Computer Interaction in the New Millennium*. Addison-Wesley, Harlow, Essex.

Nardi, B.A. and O'Day, V.L. (1999) *Information Ecologies: Using Technology with a Heart*. MIT Press, Cambridge, MA.

Nardi, B.A. (ed.) (1996) *Context and Consciousness*. MIT Press, Cambridge, MA.

Nelson, T. (1980) Interactive systems and the design of virtuality. *Creative Computing* **Nov/Dec**.

Newell, A. (2003) Design for all: an inclusive approach to digital TV. *Consumer Policy Review* **13**(1), 2–6.

Newman, M.W., Lin, J., Hong, J.I. and Landay, J.A. (2003) DENIM: an informal web site design tool inspired by observations of practice. *Human–Computer Interaction* **18**(3), 259–324.

Nie, N.H. and Ebring, L. (2000) *Internet and Society. Preliminary Report*. The Stanford Institute for the Quantitative Study of Society, Stanford, CA.

Nielsen, J. (1992) Finding usability problems through heuristic evaluation. In *Proceedings of CHI'92*, pp. 373–800.

Nielsen, J. (1993) *Usability Engineering*. Morgan Kaufmann, San Francisco.

Nielsen, J. (1994a) Heuristic evaluation. In J. Nielsen and R.L. Mack (eds), *Usability Inspection Methods*. John Wiley & Sons, New York.

Nielsen, J. (1994b) Enhancing the explanatory power of usability heuristics. In *Proceedings of ACM CHI'94*, pp. 152–158.

Nielsen, J. (2000) *Designing Web Usability*. New Riders Press, Indianapolis, IN.

Nielsen, J. (2006) Ten usability heuristics. `www.useit.com/papers/heuristic_list.html` (accessed February 2006).

Nielsen, J. and Mack, R.L. (1994) *Usability Inspection Methods*. John Wiley & Sons, New York.

Nielsen, J. and Mohlich, R. (1990) Heuristic evaluation of user interfaces. In *Proceedings of ACM CHI '90 Conference*.

Nodder, C., Williams, G. and Dubrow, D. (1999) Evaluating the usability of an evolving collaborative product—changes in user type, tasks and evaluation methods over time. In *Proceedings of GROUP'99*, pp. 150–159.

Noldus (2000) *The Observer Video-Pro*. `www.noldus.com/products/observer/obs_spvta30.html`

Nonnecke, B. and Preece, J. (2000) Lurker demographics: counting the silent. In *Proceedings of CHI 2000*, pp. 73–80.

Norman, D. (1983) Some observations on mental models. In D. Gentner and A.L. Stevens (eds), *Mental Models*. Lawrence Erlbaum Associates, Hillsdale, NJ.

Norman, D. (1986) Cognitive engineering. In D. Norman and S.W. Draper (eds), *User Centered System Design*. LEA, Hillsdale, NJ, pp. 31–62.

Norman, D. (1988) *The Design of Everyday Things*. Basic Books, New York.

Norman, D. (1990) Four (more) issues for cognitive science. *Cognitive Science Technical Report No. 9001*, Department of Cognitive Science, UCSD, USA.

Norman, D. (1993) *Things That Make Us Smart*. Addison-Wesley, Reading, MA.

Norman, D. (1999) Affordances, conventions and design. *ACM Interactions Magazine* **May/Jun**, 38–42.

Norman, D. (2004) *Emotional Design: Why we Love (or Hate) Everyday Things*. Basic Books, New York.

Nygaard, K. (1990) The origins of the Scandinavian school, why and how? *Participatory Design Conference 1990 Transcript*. Computer Professionals for Social Responsibility.

O'Hara, K., Perry, M., Churchill, E. and Russell, D. (eds) (2003) *Public and Situated Displays*. Kluwer Publishers, Dordrecht.

O'Malley, C. and Stanton Fraser, D. (2005) Literature review on learning with tangible technologies. *NestaFutureLab Report 11*. Downloadable from `http://www.nestafuturelab.org/research/reviews/reviews_11_and12/12_18.htm`

O'Connaill, B., Whittaker, S. and Wilbur, S. (1993) Conversations over video conferences: an evaluation of the spoken aspects of video-mediated communication. *Human–Computer Interaction* **8**, 389–428.

Olson, J.S. and Moran, T.P. (1996) Mapping the method muddle: guidance in using methods for user interface design. In M. Rudisill, C. Lewis, P.B. Polson and T.D. McKay (eds), *Human–Computer Interface Design: Success Stories, Emerging Methods, Real-World Context*. Morgan Kaufmann, San Francisco, pp. 269–300.

Oostveen, A.-M. and van den Besselaar, P. (2003) From small scale to large scale user participation: a case study of participatory design in e-government systems. In *Proceedings of the Participatory Design Conference 2004*, Toronto, Canada, pp. 173–182.

Oviatt, S. (2002) Multimodal interfaces. In J. Jacko and A. Sears (eds), *Handbook of Human–Computer Interaction*. LEA, New Jersey.

Oviatt, S., Darrell, T. and Flicker, M. (2004) Multimodal interfaces that flex, adapt, and persist. *Communications of the ACM* **47**, 30–33.

Oyserman, D., Coon, H.M. and Kemmelmeier, M. (2002) Rethinking individualism and collectivism: evaluation of theoretical assumptions and meta-analyses. *Psychological Bulletin* **128**, 3–72.

Payne, S. (1991) A descriptive study of mental models. *Behaviour and Information Technology* **10**, 3–21.

Petersen, M.J., Madsen, K.H. and Kjaer, A. (2002) The usability of everyday technology; emerging and fading opportunities. *Transactions on Computer–Human Interaction (TOCHI)* **9**(2), 74–105.

Petrie, H., Schlieder, C., Blenkhorn, P., Evans, G., King, A., O'Neill, A.-M., Ioannidis, G.T., Gallagher, B., Crombie, D., Mager, R. and Alafaci, M. (2002) TeDUB: a system for presenting and exploring technical drawings for blind people. In K. Miesenberger, J. Klaus and W. Zagler (eds), *Lecture Notes in Computer Science 239: Computers Helping People with Special Needs*. Springer-Verlag, Berlin.

Picard, R.W. (1998) *Affective Computing*. MIT Press, Cambridge, MA.

Pressman, R. (1992) *Software Engineering: A Practitioner's Approach*. McGraw-Hill, New York.

Quintana, C., Krajcik, J. and Solloway, E. (2000) Exploring a structured definition for learner-centered design. In B. Fishman and S. O'Connor-Divelbiss (eds), *Fourth International Conference of the Learning Sciences*. Lawrence Erlbaum Associates, Hillsdale, NJ, pp. 256–263.

Quintana, C., Carra, A., Krajcik, J. and Soloway, E. (2002) Learner-centered design: reflections and new directions. In J.M. Carroll (ed.), *Human–Computer Interaction in the New Millennium*. Addison-Wesley, Harlow, Essex, pp. 605–626.

Quintanar, L.R., Crowell, C.R. and Pryor, J.B. (1982) Human–computer interaction: a preliminary social psychological analysis. *Behavior Research: Methods and Instrumentation* **13**(2), 210–220.

Raskin, J. (2000) *The Humane Interface*. Addison-Wesley, Harlow, Essex.

Read, J., Macfarlane, S. and Casey, C. (2002) Endurability, engagement and expectations: measuring children's fun. In *Interaction Design and Children*. Eindhoven, Amsterdam, pp. 189–198.

Reeves, B. and Nass, C. (1996) *The Media Equation: How People Treat Computers, Television, and New Media like Real People and Places*. Cambridge University Press, Cambridge.

Reeves, L., Lai, J.C., Larson, J.A., Oviatt, S.L., Balaji, T.S., Buisine, S., Collings, P., Cohen, P.R., Kraal, B., Martin, J.-C., McTear, M.F., Raman, T.V., Stanney, K.M., Su, H. and Wang, Q.Y. (2004) Guidelines for multimodal user interface design. *Communications of the ACM* **47**(1), 57–59.

Reitmayr, G., Eade, E. and Drummond, T. (2005) Localisation and interaction for augmented maps. In *Proceedings IEEE ISMAR'05*, October 5–8, Vienna, Austria.

Rekimoto, J. (2002) SmartSkin: an infrastructure for freehand manipulation on interactive surfaces. In *Proceedings of CHI'02*. ACM Press, New York, p. N3-120.

Resnick, M., Martin, F., Berg, R., Borovoy, R., Colella, V., Kramer, K. and Silverman, B. (1998) Digital manipulatives. In *Proceedings of the CHI '98 Conference*, Los Angeles, April.

Rettig, M. (1994) Prototyping for tiny fingers. *Communications of the ACM* **37**(4), 21–27.

Rhodes, B., Minar, N. and Weaver, J. (1999) Wearable computing meets ubiquitous computing: reaping the best of both worlds. In *Proceedings of the Third International Symposium on Wearable Computers (ISWC'99)*, San Francisco, pp. 141–149.

RIBA (1988) *Architect's Job Book: Volume 1, Job Administration* (5th edn). RIBA Publications, London.

Robertson, D.W., Johnston, W.E. and Nip, W. (1994) Virtual frog dissection: interactive 3D graphics via the web. In *Proceedings, The Second International WWW Conference '94: Mosaic and the Web*, Chicago, IL.

Robertson, S. and Robertson, J. (2006) *Mastering the Requirements Process*, 2nd edn. Addison-Wesley, Boston.

Robinson, J.P. and Godbey, G. (1997) *Time for Life: The Surprising Ways that Americans Use Their Time*. The Pennsylvania State University Press, University Park, PA.

Rogers, Y. (1989) Icons at the interface: their usefulness. *Interacting with Computers* **1**(1), 105-N7.

Rogers, Y. (1993) Coordinating computer-mediated work. *Computer-Supported Cooperative Work* **1**, 295–315.

Rogers, Y. (1994) Exploring obstacles: integrating CSCW in evolving organisations. In *CSCW'94 Proceedings*. ACM Press, New York, pp. 67–78.

Rogers, Y. and Aldrich, F. (1996) In search of clickable Dons: learning about HCI through interacting with Norman's CD-ROM. *SIGCHI Bulletin* **28**(3).

Rogers, Y. and Bellotti, V. (1997) Grounding Blue Sky Research: how can ethnography help? *Interactions* **May/Jun**, 58–63.

Rogers, Y. and Lindley, S. (2004) Collaborating around vertical and horizontal displays: which way is best? *Interacting With Computers* **16**, N33-N52.

Rogers, Y. and Muller, H. (2006) A framework for designing sensor-based interactions to promote exploration and reflection. *International Journal of Human–Computer Studies* **64**(1), 1–14.

Rogers, Y. and Scaife, M. (1998) How can interactive multimedia facilitate learning? In J. Lee (ed.), *Intelligence and Multimodality in Multimedia Interfaces: Research and Applications*. AAAI Press, Menlo Park, CA.

Rogers, Y., Scaife, M., Harris, E., Phelps, T., Price, S., Smith, H., Muller, H., Randall, C., Moss, A., Taylor, I., Stanton, D., O'Malley, C., Corke, G. and Gabrielli, S. (2002) Things aren't what they seem to be: innovation through technology inspiration. In *DIS2002 Designing Interactive Systems Conference*, June, London. ACM Press, New York, pp. 373–379.

Rogers, Y., Scaife, M., Gabrielli, S., Harris, E. and Smith, H. (2002a) A conceptual framework for mixed reality environments: designing novel learning activities for young children. *Presence* **Dec**.

Rogers, Y., Scaife, M., Aldrich, F. and Price, S. (2003) Improving children's understanding of formalisms through interacting with multimedia. *CSRP Technical Report*, School of Informatics, University of Sussex, No. 559.

Rogers, Y., Hazlewood, W., Blevis, E. and Lim, Y. (2004) Finger talk: collaborative decision-making using talk and fingertip interaction around a tabletop display. In *Proceedings CHI'2004*. ACM Press, New York, pp. 1271–1274.

Rogers, Y., Price, S., Randell, C., Fraser, D.S., Weal, M. and Fitzpatrick, G. (2005) Ubi-learning integrates indoor and outdoor experiences. *CACM* **48**(1), 55–59.

Rogers, Y., Lim, Y. and Hazlewood, W. (2006) Extending tabletops to support flexible collaborative interactions. In *Proceedings of Tabletop 2006*, Adelaide, Australia, January 5–7. IEEE, pp. 71–78.

Rønby-Pedersen, E., McCall, K., Moran, T.P. and Halasz, F.G. (1993) Tivoli: an electronic whiteboard for informal workgroup meetings. In *Proceedings of CHI'93*. ACM Press, New York, pp. 391–398.

Rose, A., Shneiderman, B. and Plaisant, C. (1995) An applied ethnographic method for re-designing user interfaces. In *Proceedings of DIS 95*, pp. 115–122.

Rosson, M.B. and Carroll, J.M. (2002) *Usability Engineering: scenario-based development of human–computer interaction*. Morgan Kaufmann, San Francisco.

Roth, I. (1986) An introduction to object perception. In I. Roth and J.B. Frisby (eds), *Perception and Representation: A Cognitive Approach*. The Open University Press, Milton Keynes, UK.

Ryall, K., Forlines, C., Shen, C. and Ringel-Morris, M. (2004) Exploring the effects of group size and table size on interactions with tabletop shared-display groupware. In *Proceedings of Conference on Computer Supported Cooperative Work (CSCW)*. ACM Press, New York.

Sacks, H., Schegloff, E. and Jefferson, G. (1978) A simplest systematics for the organization of turn-taking for conversation. *Language* **50**, 696–735.

Sagawa, H., Takeuchi, M. and Ohki, M. (1997) Description and recognition methods for sign language based on gesture components. In *Proceedings of the 2nd International Conference on Intelligent User Interfaces*. ACM Press, New York, pp. 97–104.

Sarker, S. and Sahay, S. (2003) Understanding virtual team development: an interpretive study. *Journal of the Association for Information Systems* **4**, 1–38.

Sarker, S., Lau, F. and Sahay, S. (2001) Using an adapted grounded theory approach for inductive theory building about virtual team development. *The Data Base for Advances in Information Systems* **32**(1), 38–56.

Scaife, M. and Rogers, Y. (1996) External cognition: how do graphical representations work? *International Journal of Human–Computer Studies* **45**, 185–213.

Scaife, M. and Rogers, Y. (2001) Informing the design of virtual environments. *International Journal of Human–Computer Systems* **55**(2), 115–143.

Scaife, M., Rogers, Y., Aldrich, F. and Davies, M. (1997) Designing for or designing with? Informant design for interactive learning environments. In *Proceedings of CHI'97*, pp. 343–350.

Scapin, D.L. (1981) Computer commands in restricted natural language: some aspects of memory of experience. *Human Factors* **23**, 365–375.

Schank, R.C. (1982) *Dynamic Memory: A Theory of Learning in Computers and People*. Cambridge University Press, Cambridge.

Schegloff, E. (1981) Discourse as an interactional achievement: some uses of 'uh-huh' and other things that come between sentences. In D. Tannen (ed.), *Analyzing Discourse: Text and Talk*. University Press, Georgetown.

Schegloff, E.A. and Sacks, H. (1973) Opening up closings. *Semiotica* **7**, 289–327.

Schilit, B., Adams, N., Gold, R., Tso, M. and Want, R. (1993) The PARCTAB mobile computing system. In *Proceedings of Fourth Workshop on Workstation Operating Systems (WWOS-IV)*. IEEE, pp. 34–39.

Schön, D. (1983) *The Reflective Practitioner: How Professionals Think in Action*. Basic Books, New York.

Schrage, M. (1996) Cultures of prototyping. In T. Winograd (ed.), *Bringing Design to Software*. Addison-Wesley, Boston.

Schwaber, K. and Beedle, M. (2002) *Agile Software Development with Scrum*. Prentice Hall, Englewood Cliffs, NJ.

Scott, S.D., Grant, K.D. and Mandryk, R.L. (2003) System guidelines for co-located, collaborative work on a tabletop display. In *Proceedings of European Conference Computer-Supported Cooperative Work (ECSCW) 2003*, September, Helsinki, Finland, pp. 159–178.

Searle, J. (1969) *Speech Acts*. Cambridge University Press, Cambridge.

Segall, B. and Arnold, D. (1997) Elvin has left the building: a publish/subscribe notification service with quenching. In *Proceedings of AUUG Summer Technical Conference*, Brisbane, Australia.

Sellen, A., Buxton, W. and Arnott, J. (1992) Using spatial cues to improve videoconferencing. In *Proceedings of CHI'92*, pp. 651–652.

Sharf, B.F. (1999) Beyond netiquette: the ethics of doing naturalistic discourse research on the Internet. In S. Jones (ed.), *Doing Internet Research: Critical issues and methods for examining the net*. Sage Publications, Thousand Oaks, CA, pp. 243–256.

Sharp, H., Hovenden, F. and Woodman, M. (2005) Using metaphor to analyse qualitative data: Vulcans and Humans in software development. *Empirical Software Engineering* **10**(3), 343–365.

Sharp, H., Biddle, R, Gray, P.G., Miller, L. and Patton, J. (2006) Agile development: opportunity or fad? Addendum to *Proceedings of CHI2006*, Montreal.

Shen, C., Lesh, N.B., Vernier, F., Forlines, C. and Frost, J. (2002) Building and sharing digital group histories. In *Proceedings CSCW 2002*. ACM Press, New York, pp. 324–333.

Shneiderman, B. (1983) Direct manipulation: a step beyond programming languages. *IEEE Computer* **16**(8), 57–69.

Shneiderman, B. (1998) *Designing the User Interface: Strategies for Effective Human–Computer Interaction*, 3rd edn. Addison-Wesley, Reading, MA.

Shneiderman, B. (1998a) Relate–Create–Donate: a teaching philosophy for the cyber-generation. *Computers in Education* **31**(1), 25–39.

Shneiderman, B. and Plaisant, C. (2005) *Designing the User Interface: Strategies for effective human–computer interaction*. Addison-Wesley, Reading, MA.

Sidner, C. and Lee, C. (2005) Robots as laboratory hosts. *Interactions* **12**, 24–26.

Siek, K.A., Rogers, Y. and Connelly, K.H. (2005) Fat finger worries: how older and younger users physically interact with PDAs. In *Proceedings of INTERACT'05*, Rome.

Simon, H.A. (1981) *The Sciences of the Artificial*. MIT Press, Cambridge, MA.

Singer, J., Lethbridge, T., Vinson, N. and Anquetil, N. (1997) An examination of software engineering work practices. Paper presented at Centre for Advanced Studies Conference (CASCON), Toronto, Ontario.

Slater, M. and Wilbur, S. (1997) A framework for immersive virtual environments (FIVE): speculations on the role of presence in virtual environments. *Presence: Teleoperators and Virtual Environments* **6**, 603–616.

Slater, M., Pertaub, D. and Steed, A. (1999) Public speaking in virtual reality: facing an audience of avatars. *IEEE Computer Graphics and* Applications **19**(2), 6–9.

Smith, D., Irby, C., Kimball, R., Verplank, B. and Harslem, E. (1982) Designing the Star user interface. *Byte* **7**(4), 242–282.

Smyth, J.D., Dillman, D.A., Christian, L.M. and Stern, M.J. (2004) How visual grouping influences answers to Internet surveys. Technical Report #04-023. Washington State University Social and Economic Sciences Research Center, Pullman, 32 pp.

Smyth, J.D., Dillman, D.A., Christian, L.M. and Stern, M.J. (2005) Comparing check-all and forced-choice question formats in web surveys: the role of satisficing, depth of processing, and acquiescence in explaining differences. Technical Report #05-029. Washington State University Social and Economic Sciences Research Center, Pullman, 30 pp.

Snyder, C. (2003) *Paper Prototyping*. Morgan Kaufmann, San Francisco.

Sommerville, I. (2001) *Software Engineering*, 6th edn. Addison-Wesley, Boston.

Spacapan, S. (ed.) *People's Reactions to Technology in Factories, Offices and Aerospace*. The Claremont Symposium on Applied Social Psychology. Sage Publications, Thousand Oaks, CA.

Spool, J.M., Scanlon, T., Schroeder, W., Snyder, C. and DeAngelo, T. (1997) *Web Site Usability: A Designer's Guide*. User Interface Engineering, North Andover, MA.

Spreenberg, P., Salomon, G. and Joe, P. (1995) Interaction design at IDEO product development. In *Proceedings of ACM CHI'95 Conference Companion*, pp. 164–165.

Sproull, L., Subramani, M.M., Kiesler, S., Walker, J.H. and Waters, K. (1996) When the interface is a face. *Human–Computer Interaction* **11**, 97–124.

Stevens, M.M., Abowd, G.A., Truong, K.N. and Vollmer, F. (2003) Getting into the Living Memory Box: family archives and holistic design. *Personal Ubiquitous Computing* **7**, 210–216.

Strauss, A. and Corbin, J. (1998) *Basics of Qualitative Research: Techniques and Procedures for Developing Grounded Theory*, 2nd edn. Sage, London.

Streitz, N.A., Rocker, C., Prante, T., van Alphen, D., Stenzel, R. and Magerkurth, C. (2005) Designing smart artifacts for smart environments. *IEEE Computer* **38**(3), 41–49.

Strøm (2006) The reader creates a personal meaning: a comparative study of scenarios and human-centred stories. In *People and Computers XIX—The Bigger Picture*, Proceedings of HCI2005. Springer-Verlag, Berlin, pp. 53–68.

Strommen, E. (1998) When the interface is a talking dinosaur: learning across media with ActiMates Barney. In *Proceedings of CHI'98*, pp. 288–295.

Suchman, L.A. (1987) *Plans and Situated Actions*. Cambridge University Press, Cambridge.

Sullivan, K. (1996) Windows 95 user interface: a case study in usability engineering. In *Proceedings of CHI'96*, pp. 473–480.

Sutcliffe, A. (2002) Assessing the reliability of heuristic evaluation for Web site attractiveness and usability. *System Sciences. HICSS. Proceedings of the 35th Annual Hawaii International Conference*, pp. 1838–1847.

Sutcliffe, A. (2003) *Multimedia and Virtual Reality: Designing Multisensory User Interfaces*. LEA, Hillsdale, NJ.

Taylor, A. (2000) IT projects: sink or swim. *The Computer Bulletin* **Jan**, 24–26.

Teasley, B., Leventhal, L., Blumenthal, B., Inkstone, K. and Stone, D. (1994) Cultural diversity in user interface design. *SIGCHI Bulletin* **26**(1), 36–40.

TechstyleNews (2005) `Thinkingmaterials.com` (retrieved 04/04/05).

Thackara, J. (2001) The design challenge of pervasive computing. In *Interactions* **May/Jun**, 47–52.

Thimbleby, H. (1990) *User Interface Design*. Addison-Wesley, Harlow, Essex.

Thompson, B. (2004) My online password jumble. `http://news.bbc.co.uk/1/hi/technology/3747688.stm` (retrieved 25/05/05).

Tiger, L. (1992) *The Pursuit of Pleasure.* Little Brown & Co., London.

Tractinsky, N. (1997) Aesthetics and apparent usability: empirically assessing cultural and methodological issues. *CHI'97 Electronic Publications:Papers* (`http://www.acm.org/sigchi/chi97/proceedings/paper/nt.htm`).

Tractinsky, N., Shoval-Katz, A. and Ikar, D. (2000) What is beautiful is usable. *Interacting with Computers* **13**(2), 127–145.

Tran, Q., Calcaterra, G. and Mynatt, E. (2005) How an older and a younger adult adopted a cooking memory aid. In *Proceedings of HCII 2005*, York, April 13–15.

Trimble, J., Wales, R. and Gossweiler, R. (2002) NASA position paper for the CSCW 2002 workshop on Public, Community and Situated Displays: MERBoard.

Tsukada, K. and Yasumura, M. (2002) Ubi-Finger: gesture input device for mobile use. In *Proceedings of APCHI 2002*, Vol. 1, pp. 388–400.

Tufte, E. (1991) *Envisioning Information.* Graphics Press, Cheshire, CT.

Tullis, T.S. (1997) Screen design. In M. Helander, T.K. Landauer and P. Trabhu (eds), *Handbook of Human–Computer Interaction*, 2nd edn. Elsevier, New York, pp. 377–411.

Ullmar, B., Ishii, H. and Jacob, R.J.K. (2005) Token+Constraint Systems for tangible interaction with digital information. *TOCHI* **12**(1), 81-N8.

Underkoffler, J. and Ishii, H. (1998) Illuminating light: an optical design tool with a luminous–tangible interface. In *Conference Proceedings on Human Factors in Computing Systems.* ACM Press/Addison-Wesley, pp. 542–549.

van den Bergh, J. and Coninx, K. (2005) Towards modelling context-sensitive interactive applications: the context-sensitive user interface profile (CUP). In *Proceedings of the 2005 ACM Symposium on Software Visualization*, St Louis.

Van Rens, L.S. (1997) Usability problem classifier. Unpublished Master's Thesis, Virginia Polytechnic Institute and State University, Blacksburg, VA.

Vavoula, G. and Sharples, M. (2003) SpyCam and RoboCam: an application of the Future Technology Workshop method to the design of new technology for children. In *Proceedings of HCI'03 Conference*, Crete, June 22–27. Lawrence Erlbaum Associates, Hillsdale, NJ, pp. 1071–1075.

Vavoula, G.N., Sharples, M. and Rudman, P.D. (2002) Developing the 'Future Technology Workshop' method. In M.M. Bekker, P. Markopoulos and M. Kersten-Tsikalkina (eds), *Proceedings of the International Workshop on Interaction Design and Children (IDC2002)*, August 28–29, Eindhoven, The Netherlands. Shaker Publishing, The Netherlands, pp. 65–72.

Veen, J. (2001) *The Art and Science of Web Design.* New Riders Press, Indianapolis, IN.

Verplank, B. (1989) Tutorial notes. In *Proceedings of CHI'89 Conference.*

Verplank, B. (1994) Interview with Bill Verplank. In J. Preece, Y. Rogers, H. Sharp, D. Benyon, S. Holland and T. Carey (eds), *Human–Computer Interaction.* Addison-Wesley, Wokingham, UK, pp. 467–468.

Vinson, N. (1999) Design guidelines for landmarks to support navigation in virtual environments. In *Proceedings of CHI'99.* ACM Press, New York, pp. 287–285.

Vygotsky, L.S. (1926/1962) *Thought and Language.* MIT Press, Cambridge, MA.

Walker, J., Sproull, L. and Subramani, R. (1994) Using a human face in an interface. In *Proceedings of CHI'94*, pp. 85–91.

Ward, M. (2004) Mobile multimedia slow to catch on. BBC News (http://news.bbc.co.uk/1/hi/technology/4073849.stm)

Web Content Accessibility Guidelines Version 1.0. http://www.w3.org/TR/WAI-WEBCONTENT/ (retrieved 1/9/06).

Webb, B.R. (1996) The role of users in interactive systems design: when computers are theatre, do we want the audience to write the script? *Behaviour and Information Technology* **15**(2), 76–83.

Weinberg, G.M. (1997) *Quality Software Management, Volume 4: Anticipating change.* Dorset House.

Weiser, M. (1991) The computer for the 21st century. *Scientific American*, 94–104.

Weiss, S. (2002) *Handheld Usability*. John Wiley & Sons, New York.

Weller, D. (2004) The effects of contrast and density on visual web search. *Usability News* **6**(2). http://psychology.wichita.edu/surl/usabilitynews/62/density.htm (retrieved 11/7/2005).

Wellner, P. (1993) Interacting with paper on the DigitalDesk. *Communications of the ACM* **36**(7), 86–96.

Whiteside, J., Bennett, J. and Holtzblatt, K. (1988/1998) Usability engineering: our experience and evolution. In H. Helander (ed.), *Handbook of Human–Computer Interaction*. Elsevier Science Publishers, Amsterdam, pp. 791–817.

Whittaker, S. and Schwartz, H. (1995) Back to the future: pen and paper technology supports complex group coordination. In *Proceedings of CHI'95*, pp. 495–502.

Wikipedia: en.wikipedia.org/wiki/RFI (retrieved 13/04/05).

Williams, F., Rice, R.E. and Rogers, E.M. (1988) *Research Methods and the New Media*. The Free Press/Macmillan Inc., New York.

Wilson, C. (2005) Usability and user experience design: the next decade. *Intercom* **Jan**, 6–9. www.stc.org/intercom/pdfs/2005/200501_6.pdf (retrieved 28/06/05).

Winograd, T. (1994) Categories, disciplines, and social coordination. *Computer Supported Cooperative Work* **2**, 191–197.

Winograd, T. (ed.) (1996) *Bringing Design to Software*. Addison-Wesley, Reading, MA.

Winograd, T. (1997) From computing machinery to interaction design. In P. Denning and R. Metcalfe (eds), *Beyond Calculation: The Next Fifty Years of Computing*. Springer-Verlag, Amsterdam, pp. 149–162.

Winograd, T. and Flores, W. (1986) *Understanding Computers and Cognition*. Addison-Wesley, Norwood, NJ.

Wixon, D. and Wilson, C. (1997) The usability engineering framework for product design and evaluation. In M.G. Helander, T.K. Landauer and P.V. Prabju (eds), *Handbook of Human–Computer Interaction*. Elsevier, Amsterdam, pp. 653–688.

Wood, J. and Silver, D. (1995) *Joint Applications Development*, 2nd edn. John Wiley & Sons, New York.

Woolf, B.P. and Hall, W. (1994) Multimedia pedagogues: interactive systems for teaching and learning. *Computer* **May**, 74–80.

Woolrych, A. and Cockton, G. (2001) Why and when five test users aren't enough. In *Proceedings of IHM-HCI 2001 Conference*, Vol. 2. Cépadèus Éditions, Toulouse, pp. 105–108.

Wright, T., Yoong, P., Nable, J., Cliffe, R., Hoda, R., Gordon, D. and Andreae, C. (2005) Usability methods and mobile devices: an evaluation of MoFax. *Proceedings of HCI International*. Available from the conference CD-ROM.

`www.tracksys.co.uk` (downloaded January 21, 2005).

`www.userzoom.com` (downloaded October 4, 2005).

Yahoo! (2004) What's the most popular password? `http://ask.yahoo.com/ask/20041022.html` (retrieved 21/05/05).

Yamazaki, T. (2005) Ubiquitous home: real-life testbed for home context-aware service. In *Proceedings of the First International Conference on Testbeds and Research Infrastructures for the DEvelopment of NeTworks and COMmunities (TRIDENTCOM'05)*, Trento, Italy. IEEE, pp. 54–59.

Zeiliger, R., Reggers, T., Baldewyns, L. and Jans, V. (1997) Facilitating web navigation: integrated tools for active and cooperative learners. In *Proceedings of the 5th International Conference on Computers in Education, ICCE'97*, December, Kuching, Sarawak, Malaysia.

Zuckerman, O. and Resnick, M. (2005) Extending tangible interfaces for education: digital Montessori-inspired manipulatives. In *Proceedings of Conference on Human Factors in Computing Systems.* ACM Press, New York, pp. 859–868.

Credits

Preface

Photograph of Jenny Preece courtesy of Ben Schniederman.

Chapter 1

Fig. 1.1 The marble answering machine. Adapted from Gillian Crampton Smith: "The Hand that Rocks the Cradle" *ID Magazine*, May/June 1995, pp. 60–65 **Fig. 1.2(a)** The TiVo remote. TiVo Inc. **Fig. 1.3(a)** Beatbug interactive music toy. Reproduced by permission of MIT Media Lab. **Fig. 1.3(b)** Interactive mirror. Photo courtesy of Philips. **Fig. 1.3(c)** "Illum" Commuting Jacket. Photo courtesy of PDD, www.pdd.co.uk **Fig. 1.5** Four different team members. Based on figure under section heading 32.1 Interdisciplinary Cooperation, Chapter by S. Kim in *The Art of Human Interface Design*, edited by B. Laurel (1990), Addison Wesley. **Fig. 1.6** Wireless cell phones for Telespree. IDEO, http://www.ideo.com/portfolio/re.asp?x=50088 **Fig. 1.7** iPod advertisement. Apple Computer Inc., http://www.apple.com/ipod/ipod.html **Fig. 1.8** Anna the online sales agent. IKEA, http://www.ikea.com/ms/en_GB/ and http://www.ikea.com/ms/en_US/ **Fig. 1.9(a)** A safe and unsafe menu. Screenshots from QUALCOMM Eudora Products www.qualcomm.com/eudora **Fig. 1.9(b)** A warning dialog box for MacOSX. Apple Computer Inc. **Fig. 1.10** Are attractive interfaces more or less usable? Figures 1(a), 1(b), 2(a) & 2(b) Tractinsky, N. (1997) "Aesthetics and Apparent Usability: Empirically Assessing Cultural and Methodological Issues". *CHI 97 Electronic Publications: Papers*. http://www.acm.org/sigchi/chi97/proceedings/paper/nt.htm **Fig. 1.11** A sign at the restrooms in Cincinnati. http://www.baddesigns.com/ **Fig. 1.12** Menu showing restricted availability of options. Adobe product box shot reprinted with permission from Adobe Systems Incorporated. **Fig. 1.13** Where do you plug the mouse and keyboard? http://www.baddesigns.com/

Chapter 2

Fig. 2.1(a) Overlaying X-rays on a patient. Reproduced by permission of Michael E. Leventon **Fig. 2.1(b)** Interactive windshield. Hewlett-Packard, reproduced from http://www.ibiblio.org/jlillie/cooltown/lillie.htm **Fig. 2.2** Visicalc

screenshot. Reproduced from http://www.bricklin.com/firstspread-sheetquestion.htm **Fig. 2.3** Microsoft Excel. Microsoft product screen shot reproduced with permission from Microsoft Corporation. **Fig. 2.4(a)(b)** The Xerox star and GUI. Reproduced from http://www.thocp.net/hard-ware/3
Fig. 2.5(a)(b) Two virtual calculators. Mullet, K. and Sano, D. *Designing Visual Interfaces*, Prentice Hall, 1995. **Fig. 2.7(a)** An online agent, Anna. http://www.ikea.com **Fig.** Ask for kids. http://www.askforkids.com/ **Fig. 2.9** Cricket components. Reproduced from http://llk.media.mit.edu/projects.php?id=1942
Fig. 2.10(a) Original Mac desktop interface. Screenshot of Macintosh desktop interface © Apple Computer Inc. **Fig. 2.10(b)** Recent Mac desktop interface. Screenshot of Apple MacOSX © Apple Computer Inc. **Fig. 2.11** Example of a 3D virtual city. The Equator Interdisciplinary Research challenge. http://www.cs.ucl.ac.uk/research/equator/gallery/images/all_city2_med.jpg **Fig. 2.12(a)** CAVE insect. Reproduced from http://www.ento.vt.edu/%7Esharov/3d/cave.html
Fig. 2.12(b) A life-like simulation of a newly designed train station. Reproduced from http://www.answers.com/topic/cave **Fig. 2.13** NCSA's CAVE. Reproduced from http://cave.ncsa.uiuc.edu/ **Fig. 2.15** A game using a text-based instruction mode of interaction. Screenshot from Zork © Infocom. **Fig. 2.16** A 3D virtual game (Voodoo Island. Reproduced from http://www.3dgamers.com/screenshots/games/voodooislands/387479/ **Fig. 2.17** Conceptual models. Fig. 1.10, p. 16, Norman, D *The Psychology of Everyday Things*, Perseus Books, 1988

Chapter 3

Fig. 3.2 Two different ways of structuring the same information at the interface. Reproduced by permission of Dr T. S. Tullis, from his Ph.D. Dissertation "Predicting the Usability of Alphanumeric Displays", Rice University, Houston, Texas, USA. **Fig. 3.3** The Google search engine. Reproduced by permission of Google Inc. **Fig. 3.4** Two ways of structuring information on a webpage. Figures 3 & 4, D. Weller: "The Effects of Contrast and Density on Visual Web Search" from *Usability News*, 2004. **Fig. 3.5** Apple Computer's Spotlight search tool. Screenshot from Mac OS X Searchlight © Apple Computer Inc. **Fig. 3.6** Cook's College screenshots. Reproduced from http://www-static.cc.gatech.edu/fce/ecl/projects/dejaVu/cc/ **Fig. 3.8** The Google help center. Reproduced by permission of Google Inc. **Fig. 3.9** Bridging the gulfs of execution and evaluation. Adapted from p. 40, D. Norman (1986): "Cognitive Engineering" in D. Norman and S.W. Draper *User Centered System Design*, LEA pp. 31–62. **Fig. 3.10** Zstep 94: An early debugging tool. H. Lieberman and C. Fry (1995): "Bridging the Gap Between Code and Behaviour in Programming", *Proc. CHI'95 ACM*, pp. 480–486. **Fig. 3.11** Human information processing model. Redrawn and adapted from Barber, P. (1988) *Applied Cognitive Psychology*, Figure 3.1 (page 63) published by Routledge and reproduced by permission of ITPS Ltd. **Fig. 3.12** The human processor model. Card, S.,

Moran, T. and Newell, A. (1983) *The Psychology of HCI*, Figure 2.1, page 26, reproduced by permission of Lawrence Erlbaum Associates, Inc. **Fig. 3.13** ComMotion. Reproduced from `http://alumni.media.mit.edu/~nmarmas/comMotion.html` **Fig. 3.15** Preece, J. and Keller, L. (1994) *Human-Computer Interaction*, Figure 3.5 (page 70) Addison Wesley, 1994.

Chapter 4

Fig. 4.1(a) Text-based conversation from an early MUD. Reproduced from `http://www.nwe.ufl.edu/%7Eltaylor/temp/muds.html` **Fig. 4.1(b)** A conversation held at the virtual 'the U'. Reproduced from `http://www.digitalspace.com/avatars/book/chus/chus1.htm` **Fig. 4.2** The Hydra System. A. Sellen, W. Buxton and J. Arnott (1992): "Using Spacial Cues to Improve Videoconferencing". *Proc. Of CHI'92* pp. 651–652 **Fig. 4.3** The VideoWindow system. Reproduced by permission of Promethean Ltd. **Fig. 4.4** The Dynamo system. H. Brignull, S. Izadi, G. Fitzpatrick, Y. Rogers and T. Rodden (2004): The Introduction of a shared interface surface into a communal space". In *Proc. Of the 2004 Conference on Computer Supported Cooperative Work CSCW '04.* **Fig. 4.6** Group system layout. Reprinted from D *ecision Support Systems*, 5(2) Nunamaker *et al*: *Experiences at IBM with Group Support Systems* 183–196 (1989), with permission from Elsevier Science. **Fig. 4.7** ACTIVBoard whiteboard. Reproduced from `http://www.caedmon.n-yorks.sch.uk/pages/subjects/english2/pages/activboard.htm` **Fig. 4.8(a)** One of BT's early videophones. © British Telecommunications Plc. Reproduced with permission. **Fig. 4.8(b)** Recent mobile "visualphone" developed in Japan. **Fig. 4.9** Hypermirror. Reproduced from `http://staff.aist.go.jp/morikawa.osamu/soft/int01.htm` **Fig. 4.10** BiReality. N.P. Jouppie (2002) "First steps towards mutually-immersive mobile telepresence". In *Proceedings of the 2002 ACM Conference on Computer Supported Cooperative Work, CSCW '02*, pp. 354–363 **Fig. 4.11** Fill-in record table. Figure 3, Y. Rogers (1993): "Coordinating Computer-Mediated Work" in "Computer Supported Cooperative Work" 1(4) pp.295–315, Kluwer **Fig. 4.13** Screen dump of Portholes. Reproduced by permission of the Xerox Research Centre Europe. **Fig. 4.14** Sticker tickertape interface. Reproduced from `http://www.tickertape.org:8080/projects/sticker/index.html` **Fig. 4.15** The Babble interface. Reproduced from `http://researchweb.watson.ibm.com/SocialComputing/babble.htm`

Chapter 5

Fig. 5.1 Kismet. © Peter Menzel, reproduced with permission. **Fig. 5.2(a)(b)** Smiling and sad Apple Mac icons. Mullet, K. and Sano, D. *Designing Visual Interfaces*, Prentice Hall, 1995. **Fig. 5.2(c)** Sad iPod icon. Reproduced from `http://docs.info.apple.com/article.html?artnum=61771` © Apple Computer Inc. **Fig. 5.3** A collection of graphical smiley icons used in MSN Messenger. Icons from MSN Messenger, © Microsoft.

Fig. 5.4(a)(b) Round and square dialog boxes. Marcus, A. (1993) "Human communication in advanced UIs", Figures 2 and 4 (pages 106 and 107) in *Communications of the ACM*, 36(4), 101–109. **Fig. 5.5** "At Home with Bob" software screenshot. Microsoft product screen shot reproduced with permission from Microsoft Corporation. **Fig. 5.6** Microsoft's agent Clippy. Microsoft product screen shot reproduced with permission from Microsoft Corporation. **Fig. 5.8** Error message. Reproduced from `http://www.nsf.gov/` **Fig. 5.9** Pokemon Pikachu virtual pet. Reproduced from `http://www.pokemon.com` **Fig. 5.10** Waterbot monitoring system. Ernesto Arroyo, Leonardo Bonanni, Ted Selker (2005): "Waterbot: Exploring Feedback and Persuasive Techniques at the Sink" in *CHI 2005*. **Fig. 5.11** Cigarette counter. Reproduced from `http://www.cgets.com/item-Cigarette-Counter-:-Quit-Smoking-Aid-cigarette_counter` **Fig. 5.12** Playmates interactive doll Amanda. Reproduced from `http://www.playmatestoys.com/html/amazing_amanda/` **Fig. 5.13(a)** Early virtual popstar, E-cyas. Reproduced by permission of I-D Media. **Fig. 5.13(b)** Virtual newscaster, Ananova. Reproduced by permission of Ananova Ltd. **Fig. 5.14** The Woggles. Figure 1, J. Bates (1994), "The role of emotion in believable characters", in *Communications of the ACM* 37(7) **Fig. 5.15(a)(b)** Silas the virtual dog. Reproduced by permission of Prof. Bruce Blumberg. **Fig. 5.16(a)(b)** Cellular squirrel and rabbit. S. Marti and C. Schmandt (2005) "Physical Embodiments for Mobile Communications Agents" in *Proceedings of UIST'05* **Fig. 5.17(a)(b)** Rea, the life-like realtor. Reproduced by permission of Professor Justine Cassell. **Fig. 5.18** Norman's model of emotional design. Reproduced from `http://www.mprove.de/script/04/nng/expectationdesign.html`

Chapter 6

Fig. 6.1(a) Rich Gold Xerox PARC. Reproduced by permission of Rich Gold **Fig. 6.1(b)** Typical HCI—tangible UI. Reproduced by permission of Hiroshi Ishii. **Fig. 6.1(c)** BlueEyes. Reproduced from `http://www.almaden.ibm.com/cs/BlueEyes/` **Fig. 6.2(a)(b)** AutoCAD LT Screenshot. Microsoft product screen shot reproduced with permission from Microsoft Corporation. **Fig. 6.3** First generation of GUIs. Mullet, K. and Sano, D. *Designing Visual Interfaces*, Prentice Hall, 1995. **Fig. 6.4** Window management technique. Screenshot of Mac OS © Apple Computer Inc. **Fig. 6.5** A scrolling menu. Screenhot of Camino browser, © The Camino Project. **Fig. 6.6** Two different ways of classifying menus designed for different cultures. Reproduced from `http://www.cheeseburgerinparadise.com/pdf/Menu.pdf` and `http://ccms.ntu.edu.tw/~fss/coconet/mos/menu.JPG` **Fig. 6.7** A cascadingmenu. Reproduced by permission of the British Standards Institute. **Fig. 6.8** Standard design for a menu. Exert from BS-EN-ISO 9241, © The British Standards Institute. **Fig. 6.9** Poor icon set. Mullet, K. and Sano, D. *Designing Visual Interfaces*, Prentice Hall, 1995. **Fig. 6.10** Mac icon designs for the TextEdit application. Icons from TextEdit © Apple Computer Inc. **Fig. 6.11** Contrasting genres of Aqua icons used for the Mac. Icons

from Apple Mac © Apple Computer Inc. **Fig. 6.12** Logo-based icons for Microsoft and Macromedia applications. Icons from Microsoft applications © Microsoft Corporation. Reprinted with permission from Adobe Systems Incorporated. **Fig. 6.13** Examples of simple and distinguishable icons used in Windows XP toolbar. Icons from Windows XP, © Microsoft Corporation. **Fig. 6.14** Icons used by Toshiba for three of its digital camera operations. Reproduced from `http://www.toshiba.com/taisisd/isd_svc/svcdsc/_pdf/t20/t20_icons_erase.gif` **Fig. 6.15** Screen dump from the multimedia environment BioBlast. Screenshot from BioBlast, © Wheeling Jesuit University. **Fig. 6.16** The Virtual Gorilla Project. Reproduced from `http://gtresearchnews.gatech.edu/reshor/rh-sf96/gorillas.htm` **Fig. 6.17** Magic Cap's 3D desktop interface. Reprinted by permission of General Magic Inc. **Fig. 6.19** Two types of visualizations. Reproduced from `http://www.cs.umd.edu/hcil/millionvis/million-treemap.gif` **Fig. 6.20** The front page of the Aftonbladet newspaper. Reproduced from `http://www.aftonbladet.se/` **Fig. 6.21** Three main areas of a web page. Reprinted by permission of New Riders Publishing/Jeff Veen. **Fig. 6.22** Sony's EyeToy. Reproduced from `http://www.firingsquad.com/media/gallery_image.asp/170/12` **Fig. 6.23** Microsoft's Digital Ink in action. Reproduced by permission of Dennis Groth. **Fig. 6.24** Ubi-Finger. Reproduced from `http://mobiquitous.com/ubi-finger-e.html` **Fig. 6.26** The Blackberry 7780 wireless device. Reproduced from `http://www.blackberry.com/products/blackberry7700/blackberry7780.shtml` **Fig. 6.27** The AVLA MPO model 550. Reproduced from `http://www.afb.org/afbpress/pub.asp?DocID=aw050305` **Fig. 6.28(a)** Treo 65. Reproduced from `http://www.the-register.co.uk/2005/05/17/review_palmone_treo650/` **Fig. 6.28(b)** VodafoneSimple Sagem VS1. Reproduced from `http://www.theregister.co.uk/2005/05/23/vodafone_phone_phobe/` **Fig. 6.29** BlueEyes. Reproduced from `http://www-06.ibm.com/jp/ibm/ibmtopics/year2000.html` **Fig. 6.30(a)** Smartboard. ©2006 SMART Technologies Inc. Used with permission. **Fig. 6.30(b)** Mitsubishi's interactive tabletop. Reproduced from `http://www.merl.com/projects/?proj_area=Off+the+Desktop+Inter-action+and+Display`
Fig. 6.31 Drift table. Reproduced from `http://www.interaction.rca.ac.uk/equator/weight_furniture.html` **Fig. 6.32** Roomware furniture. By permission of AMBIENTE. **Fig. 6.33(a)** Tangible flow blocks. Figure 5, Zuckerman *et al* (2005): Extending Tangible Interfaces for Education: Digital Montessori-inspired Manipulatives. In *Proceedings of Conference on Human Factors in Computing Systems*. ACM Press, 2005 **Fig. 6.33(b)** Urp. Figure 1, B. Ullmer and H. Ishii: Emerging Frameworks for Tangible User Interfaces (`http://www.research.ibm.com/journal/sj/393/part3/ullmer.html`). **Fig. 6.34(a)** A scanned womb. Reproduced from `http://www.cs.unc.edu/%7Eazuma/azuma_AR.html` **Fig. 6.34(b)** Head up display. Reproduced from `http://avmag.com.ar/n3/evs.html` **Fig. 6.35** Augmented map and PDA

device. http://mi.eng.cam.ac.uk/%7Egr281/augmentedmaps.html **Fig. 6.36** The Giant Heart. Reproduced from http://www2.fi.edu/exhibits/permanent/giant-heart.php **Fig. 6.38** The evolution of wearable computing. Reproduced from http://wearcam.org/steve5.jpg **Fig. 6.39** The SensVest prototype. Reproduced from http://www.eee.bham.ac.uk/wear%2Dit/LOT/ **Fig. 6.40(a)** Mel, the penguin robot. Reproduced from http://www.merl.com/projects/hosting/ **Fig. 6.40(b)** Paro, an interactive seal. Reproduced from http://paro.jp/english/

Chapter 7

Fig. 7.1 Smileyometer. Figure 2, Janet Read, Stuart MacFarlane, Chris Casey: "Endurability, Engagement and Expectations: Measuring Children's Fun" Department of Computing, University of Central Lancashire. **Fig. 7.2** The cut up and remixed big idea. Figure 2, M.L. Guha, A. Druin, G. Chipman, J.A. Fails, S. Simms and A. Farber (2005): "Working with young children as technology design partners", *CACM* 48(1), 39–42. **Fig. 7.3** The probing tool in the ambient wood project. Figure 3, Y. Rogers, S. Price, C. Randell, D.S. Fraser, M. Weal and G. Fitzpatrick (2005): "Ubi-learning integrates indoor and outdoor experiences", *CACM* 48(1), 55–59. **Fig. 7.4** Cybelle the intelligent agent. Reproduced from http://www.agentland.com/ **Fig. 7.10** Mars Exploration Rover. Reproduced by permission of NASA Jet Propulsion Laboratory (NASA-JPL). **Fig. 7.11** MERboard. Figure 2 & 8, J. Trimble, R. Wales and R. Gossweiler (2002): "NASA position paper for the CSCW 2002 workshop on Public, Community and Situated Displays: Merboard." **Fig. 7.12** Homepage of Lycos search engine. Reproduced from http://www.lycos.com **Fig. 7.13** Lycos people screen. Reproduced from http://www.lycos.com **Fig. 7.14** Tangible objects collected by participants involved in a study about a jazz festival. S. Carter and J. Mankoff (2005): "When participants do the capturing: the role of media in diary studies" *CHI 2005* pp. 899–908. **Fig. 7.15** A display from WebLog. Reproduced by permission of University of Maryland, Human-Computer Interaction Lab.

Chapter 8

Fig. 8.4 The cantina in SWG's Coronet City. Reproduced from N. Ducheneaut and RJ Morris (2004): "The social side of gaming: a study of interaction patterns in a massively multiplayer online game" in *Proceedings of CSCW 04.* **Fig. 8.5** Summary of the activity in the cantina over the course of a day. Reproduced from N. Ducheneaut and RJ Morris (2004): "The social side of gaming: a study of interaction patterns in a massively multiplayer online game" in *Proceedings of CSCW 04.* **Fig. 8.6** Interaction profiles of players in the cantina. Reproduced from N. Ducheneaut and RJ Morris (2004): "The social side of gaming: a study of interaction patterns in a massively multiplayer online game" in *Proceedings of CSCW 04.* **Fig. 8.7** Interaction profile of players in the starport. Reproduced from N. Ducheneaut and RJ Morris (2004): "The social side of gaming: a study of interaction patterns in a massively multiplayer online game" in *Proceedings of CSCW 04*. **Fig. 8.8** Bell interviewing a German family. Reproduced from `http://www.intel.com/technology/techresearch/people/bios/bell_g.htm#publications` **Fig. 8.9** The structure of an affinity diagram. Figure 9.1, p. 155, Hugh Beyer and Karen Holtzblatt: *Contextual Design* 1998, Morgan Kaufman. **Fig. 8.10** Building the affinity diagram of Indian ATM usage. Figure 1, A. DeAngeli, U. Athavamker, A. Joshi, L. Coventry and GI Johnson (2004): "Introducing ATMs in India: a contextual inquiry" in *Interacting with Computers* 16(1) pp. 29–44. **Fig. 8.11** Excerpt from a transcript of a think aloud protocol when using an online educational environment. Reproduced from Armitage, U. (2004) "Navigation and learning in electronic texts". PhD thesis, Centre for HCI Design, City University London. **Fig. 8.12** Criteria for identifying usability problems from verbal protocol transcriptions. Reproduced from Armitage, U. (2004) "Navigation and learning in electronic texts". PhD thesis, Centre for HCI Design, City University London. **Fig. 8.13** The excerpt in Figure 8.11 using the categorisation scheme in Figure 8.12. Reproduced from Armitage, U. (2004) "Navigation and learning in electronic texts". PhD thesis, Centre for HCI Design, City University London. **Fig. 8.14** Axial coding for the Technology category. Reproduced from Figure 1, S. Sarker, F. Lau and S. Sahay (2001): "Using an adapted grounded theory approach for inductive theory building about virtual team development". *The Data Base for Advances in Information Systems*, 32(1), pp. 38–56. **Fig. 8.15** An excerpt from an early draft of an integrative memo for the technology category. Excerpt from S. Sarker, F. Lau and S. Sahay (2001): "Using an adapted grounded theory approach for inductive theory building about virtual team development". *The Data Base for Advances in Information Systems*, 32(1), pp. 38–56. **Fig. 8.16** Joan's workplace and shared resources used by the operators. Reproduced from Ackerman, M.S., and C.A. Halverson (2000) "Re-examining organizational memory". *Communications of the ACM*, 43(1), 58–64. **Fig. 8.17** A diagram showing the propagation of representational states for the employee verification process. Reproduced from Ackerman, M.S., and C.A. Halverson (2000) "Re-examining organizational memory". *Communications of the ACM*, 43(1), 58–64. **Fig. 8.19** Engeström's activity system model. Reproduced from Y. Engeström *Perspectives on Activity Theory* CUP, 1999. **Fig. 8.20** Examples of activities, actions and operations. Reproduced from K. Kutti (1996) "Activity Theory as a potential framework for Human-Computer Interaction". In B.A. Nardi (ed.) *Context and Consciousness*. MIT Press. 17–44.

Chapter 9

Fig. 9.2 The Tech Box at IDEO. Reproduced by permission of IDEO. **Fig. 9.3** The web page for metal injection moulding. Reproduced by permission of IDEO. **Fig. 9.4** Items from the Techbox used in the design of a medical product. Reproduced by permission of IDEO, photographs by Jorge Davies. **Fig. 9.5** Overview of the synch-and-stabilise approach. Reproduced from Figure 2, p. 57, Michael A. Cusumano and Richard W. Selby (1997): "How Microsoft Builds Software" in *CACM*, 40(6). **Fig. 9.6** Milestones in the synch-and-stabilise approach. Reproduced from Figure 3, p. 57, Michael A. Cusumano and Richard W. Selby (1997): "How Microsoft Builds Software" in *CACM*, 40(6). **Fig. 9.9** Netpliance's spiral development circle. ©1988 IEEE. **Fig. 9.11** The DSDM lifecycle model. Reproduced from `http://www.dsdm.org/en/about/lifecycle.asp` **Fig. 9.12(a)(b)** Sample Image produced from SketchBookPro v2.0. Reproduced from `http://www.alias.com/glb/eng/community/image_gallery_details.jsp?itemId=6900001&start=4` **Fig. 9.13** Cycle 0 and its relationship to later cycles. Based on L. Miller (2005): "Case Study of Customer Input for a Successful Product" in *Proceedings of Agile 2005* IEEE. **Fig. 9.14** The parallel interaction design and implementation tracks. Based on L. Miller (2005): "Case Study of Customer Input for a Successful Product" in *Proceedings of Agile 2005* IEEE. **Fig. 9.15** The Star lifecycle model. Reproduced by permission of Academic Press Ltd. London, UK. **Fig. 9.16** The Usability Engineering Lifecycle. Reproduced by permission of Academic Press, Orlando, Florida. **Fig. 9.17** The ISO 13407 human-centered design lifecycle. The ISO 13407 human-centered design lifecycle © British Standards Institute.

Chapter 10

Fig. 10.1 An example requirement using the Volere shell. Reproduced from Figure 10.3, p. 184, Robertson and Robertson, *Mastering the Requirements Process*, Addison Wesley, 1999. **Fig. 10.2** Every pixel counts. Reproduced from Fig. 4, p. 86, Eric Bergman and Rob Haitani: "Designing the PalmPilot: a conversation with Rob Haitani" from *Information Appliances and Beyond* ed. Eric Bergman, Morgan Kaufmann, 2000. **Fig. 10.3(a)** The KordGrip interface. Reproduced by permission of Wet PC. **Fig. 10.3(b)** The KordGrip in use under water. Reproduced by permission of the Australian Institute of Marine Science. **Fig. 10.4** A cultural probe package. Reproduced from Figure 1, p. 22B. Gaver, T. Dunne and E. Pacenti (1999): "Cultural Probes" from *Interactions* 6(1) pp.21–29. **Fig. 10.7** The living memory box. Design and Copyright Florian Vollmer, Interaction and Product Design, `mail@florian-vollmer.de` **Fig. 10.8** The Volere shell for requirements. Reproduced from `http://www.volere.co.uk/template.htm` **Fig. 10.10** A scenario showing how two technologies, a Smartphone and wCommerce (wireless commerce) might be used. Reproduced by permission of Symbian Ltd.

Chapter 11

Fig. 11.1 An example storyboard. Reproduced from Figure 8.2, p. 169, B. Hartfield and T. Winograd : "Profile: IDEO" in *Bringing Design to Software* ed. by Terry Winograd, Addison Wesley, 1996. **Fig. 11.5** The patient kit for experience prototyping. Reproduced from Figure 1, Boyarski and Kellogg: DIS 2000—Design Interactive Systems, Processes, Practices, Methods, Techniques, Conference Proceedings, ACM. **Fig. 11.6(a)(b)** The third age suit: riding a bike & mobile phone. Photographs reproduced by permission of ICE Ergonomics Ltd., Loughborough, UK. **Fig. 11.7** An example of a process-oriented conceptual model. From pp.212–214, *The Usability Engineering Lifecycle* by Deborah Mayhew, Morgan Kaufman, 1999. **Fig. 11.8** Example plus and minus scenarios. Reproduced from "Scenarios in user-centered design—setting the stage for reflection and action" by Bodker, in *Interacting with Computers* Vol 13, Issue 1, 2000 Elsevier Science. With permission from Elsevier. **Fig. 11.15** The "computer" highlights a term the user has just clicked on. Reprinted from "Paper Prototyping: Fast and Simple Techniques for Designing and Refining the User Interface" Caroline Snyder, 2003, with permission of Elsevier. **Fig. 11.16** A newspaper cutting showing a parcel sorting machine mock up. Reproduced from P. Ehn and M. Kyng (1991): "Cardboard computers: mocking-it-up or hands-on the future" in *Design at Work: Cooperative Design of Computer Systems*, ed by J. Greenbaum and M. Kyng. **Fig. 11.18** DENIM. Reproduced by permission of Prof. James Landay.

Chapter 12

Fig. 12.2 Mockup of a household overview. Reproduced from S. Grisedale, M. Graves and A. Grunsteidl (1997): "Designing a graphical user interface for healthcare workers in rural India" in *Proceedings CHI'97* pp. 471–478. **Fig. 12.3(a)** Icons drawn by ANWs in Punjab. Reproduced from S. Grisedale, M. Graves and A. Grunsteidl (1997): "Designing a graphical user interface for healthcare workers in rural India" in *Proceedings CHI'97* pp. 471–478. **Fig. 12.3(b)** Representing people by gender and age. Reproduced from S. Grisedale, M. Graves and A. Grunsteidl (1997): "Designing a graphical user interface for healthcare workers in rural India" in *Proceedings CHI'97* pp. 471–478. **Fig. 12.3(c)** Modal icons reflect state of patient. Reproduced from S. Grisedale, M. Graves and A. Grunsteidl (1997): "Designing a graphical user interface for healthcare workers in rural India" in *Proceedings CHI'97* pp. 471–478. **Fig. 12.4(a)** The display shows the physiological data, two participants and a screen of a game they played. Reproduced from Mandryk and Inkpen (2004) "Physiological Indicators for the Evaluation of Co-located Collaborative Play", *CSCW 2004*, pp. 102–111. **Fig. 12.5(a)** A participant's skin response when scoring a goal against a friend versus against the computer. Reproduced from Mandryk and Inkpen (2004) "Physiological Indicators for the Evaluation of Co-located Collaborative Play", *CSCW 2004*, pp. 102–111. **Fig. 12.5(b)** Another participant's response when engaging in a hockey fight against a friend versus against the computer. **Fig. 12.6** The preliminary design showing a view of the entrance into HutchWorld. Reproduced by permission of Springer-Verlag. **Fig. 12.7** The Hutch V-Chat prototype. Reproduced by permission of Springer-Verlag. **Fig. 12.8** A sample of the structured tasks used in the HutchWorld evaluation. Reproduced by permission of Springer-Verlag. **Fig. 12.9** A fragment of the analysis of participant's ratings of ease of use of features encountered in the structured tasks. Reproduced by permission of Springer-Verlag. **Fig. 12.10** The Olympic Message System kiosk. Reproduced from figure 12.4, p. 265, J. Gould, S.J. Boies, S. Levy, J.T. Richards and

J. Schoonard (1990): "The 1984 Olympic message system: A test of behavioral principles of system design". In J. Preece and L. Keller (Eds.) *Human Computer Interaction (Readings)* pp. 260–283. Prentice Hall. **Fig. 12.11** Parent leaving a voice message for an Olympian. Reproduced from figure 12.4, p. 265, J. Gould, S.J. Boies, S. Levy, J.T. Richards and J. Schoonard (1990): "The 1984 Olympic message system: A test of behavioral principles of system design". In J. Preece and L. Keller (Eds.) Human *Computer Interaction (Readings)* pp. 260–283. Prentice Hall. **Fig. 12.12** The Hello.Wall. Reproduced from Figure 1, p. 45, Streitz *et al.* (2005) Designing smart artifacts for smart environments. *IEEE Computer* 38(3), pp.41–49. **Fig. 12.13** Communication zones which depend on the distance from the display. Reproduced from Figure 2, p. 45, Streitz *et al.* (2005) "Designing smart artifacts for smart environments". *IEEE Computer* 38(3), pp.41–49.

Chapter 14

Fig. 14.3 The Tracksys "lab-in-a-box system". Reproduced by permission of Dr. Harry Brignull. **Fig. 14.4** The Tracksys system being used with a mobile device camera. Reproduced by permission of Dr. Harry Brignull. **Fig. 14.5** The sequence of activities involved in remote usability testing using Userzoom. Reproduced from `http://www.userzoom.com/` **Fig. 14.6** Homepage of MedlinePlus. Reproduced by permission of Prof. Keith Cogdill. **Fig. 14.7** Clicking Health Topics on the home page produced this page. Reproduced by permission of Prof. Keith Cogdill. **Fig. 14.8** Categories of links within Health Topics for knee injuries. Reproduced by permission of Prof. Keith Cogdill. **Fig. 14.9** The script used to greet participants in the MedlinePlus study. Reproduced by permission of Taylor & Francis Ltd. `http://www.tandf.co.uk/journals` **Fig. 14.10** The script used to explain the procedure. Reproduced by permission of Taylor & Francis Ltd. `http://www.tandf.co.uk/journals` **Fig. 14.11** The script used to introduce and describe the initial exploration task. Reproduced by permission of Taylor & Francis Ltd. `http://www.tandf.co.uk/journals` **Fig. 14.12** The script used to direct the participant's behaviour. Reproduced by permission of Taylor & Francis Ltd. `http://www.tandf.co.uk/journals` **Fig. 14.13** The debriefing script used in the MedlinePlus study. Reproduced by permission of Taylor & Francis Ltd. `http://www.tandf.co.uk/journals` **Fig. 14.14** Homepage of revised version of MedlinePlus. Reproduced from `http://medlineplus.gov/` **Fig. 14.15** Clicking Health Topics on the home page of the revised version produced this page. Reproduced from `http://medlineplus.gov/` **Fig. 14.16** An example context-aware experience sampling tool running on PDA. Reproduced by permission of Stephen Intille. **Fig. 14.17** Learning artifacts one month after delivery when trying to achieve the cinema experience. Reproduced from Figure 5, p. 85, M.J. Peterson, K.H. Madsen and A. Kjaer (2002): "The usability of everyday technology: Emerging and fading opportunities" in *Transactions on Computer-Human Interaction (TOCHI)* 9(2) pp.74–105. **Fig. 14.18** Learning artifacts two months after delivery: finally establishing the cinema experience. Reproduced from Figure 6, p. 86, M.J. Peterson, K.H. Madsen and A. Kjaer (2002): "The usability of everyday technology: Emerging and fading opportunities" in *Transactions on Computer-Human Interaction (TOCHI)* 9(2) pp.74–105. **Fig. 14.19** Schematic image of tagging communicative utterances. Reproduced from S.C. De Souza *The Semiotic Engineering of Human-Computer Interaction*, MIT Press, 2005. **Fig. 14.20** The homepage of the International Children's Digital Library. Reproduced from `http://www.icdlbooks.org/` **Fig. 14.21** American children make drawings to represent themselves and their community. Reproduced by permission of Anita Komlodi. **Fig. 14.22** Mexican children working with an early prototype using a tablet PC. Reproduced by permission of Anita Komlodi.

Chapter 15

Fig. 15.1 Curve showing the proportion of usability problems. Usability Inspection Methods, J. Nielson & R.L. Mack ©1994. Reproduced with permission of John Wiley & Sons Inc. **Fig. 15.2** Homepage of REI.com. Reproduced from `http://www.rei.com` **Fig. 15.3** A screen showing MoFax on a cell phone. Reproduced from T. Wright, P. Yoong, J. Nable, R. Cliffe, R. Hoda, D. Gordon and C. Andrease (2005): "Usability methods and mobile devices: A evaluation of MoFax" in *Proceedings of HCI International* LEA. **Fig. 15.4(a)** A bus indicator. Reproduced from Figure 1, p. 170, J. Mankoff, A. K. Dey, G. Hsich, J. Kientz, S. Lederer and A. Morgan (2003): "Heuristic evaluation of ambient devices". In *Proceedings of CHI 2003*, ACM. **Fig. 15.4(b)** Lightness and darkness indicator. Reproduced from Figure 1, p. 170, J. Mankoff, A. K. Dey, G. Hsich, J. Kientz, S. Lederer and A. Morgan (2003): "Heuristic evaluation of ambient devices". In *Proceedings of CHI 2003*, ACM.

Tables

Table 8.5 An illustration of open coding. Adapted from Table 4, S. Sarker and S. Sahay (2003) "Understanding Virtual Team Development: an interpretive study", *Journal of the Association for Information Systems* 4, 1–38. **Table 11.1** Relative effectiveness of low- vs. high-fidelity prototypes. Reproduced from J. Rudd, K.R. Stein and S. Insensee (1996): "Low vs. High-fidelity Prototyping Debate" in *ACM Interactions Magazine*, January 1996 pp.76–85. **Table 11.2** Design guidelines for tabletop displays. Reproduced from S.D. Scott, K.D. Grant, & R.L. Mandryk (2003). "System Guidelines for Co-located, Collaborative Work on a Tabletop Display". In *Proceedings of European Conference Computer-Supported Cooperative Work (ECSCW)* 2003 pp. 159–178 Kluwer Academic Publishers. **Table 12.3** Mean subjective ratings given on a user satisfaction questionnaire. Reproduced from R.L. Mandryk and K.M. Inkpen (2004) "Physiological indicators for the evaluation of co-located collaborative play". In *Proceedings ACM Conference CSCW*, pp.102–111. **Table 12.4** Usability issues ranked according to importance. Reproduced by permission of Springer-Verlag. **Table 14.1** The resources visited by participant A for the first task. Reproduced by permission of Taylor & Francis Ltd.

http://www.tandf.co.uk/journals **Table 14.2** Performance data for task 1. Reproduced by permission of Taylor & Francis Ltd. http://www.tandf.co.uk/journals

Cartoons

Chapter 1 © Randy Glasbergen. **Chapter 2** © Randy Glasbergen. **Chapter 3** © CartoonStock http://www.cartoonstock.com/ **Chapter 4** © CartoonStock http://www.cartoonstock.com/ **Chapter 6** A Guide to Usability, Jenny Preece, ©1993 Pearson Education Limited. Reproduced with permission. **Chapter 6** DOONESBURY ©1993 G. B. Trudeau. Reprinted with permission of UNIVERSAL PRESS SYNDICATE. All rights reserved. **Chapter 9** © CartoonStock http://www.cartoonstock.com/ **Chapter 11** © Roger Penwill. **Chapter 12** © Randy Glasbergen. **Chapter 13** © CartoonStock http://www.cartoon-stock.com/ **Chapter 15** © The 5th Wave, www.the5thwave.com

Index